My Tongue Is My Own

A Life of Gwen Harwood

Ann-Marie Priest

LA TROBE
UNIVERSITY PRESS

IN CONJUNCTION WITH BLACK INC.

Published by La Trobe University Press in conjunction with Black Inc.
Wurundjeri Country
22–24 Northumberland Street
Collingwood VIC 3066, Australia
enquiries@blackincbooks.com
www.blackincbooks.com
www.latrobeuniversitypress.com.au

La Trobe University plays an integral role in Australia's public intellectual life, and is recognised globally for its research excellence and commitment to ideas and debate. La Trobe University Press publishes books of high intellectual quality, aimed at general readers. Titles range across the humanities and sciences, and are written by distinguished and innovative scholars. La Trobe University Press books are produced in conjunction with Black Inc., an independent Australian publishing house. The members of the LTUP Editorial Board are Vice-Chancellor's Fellows Emeritus Professor Robert Manne and Dr Elizabeth Finkel, and Morry Schwartz and Chris Feik of Black Inc.

9781760642341 (paperback)
9781743822319 (ebook)

A catalogue record for this book is available from the National Library of Australia

Cover design by Akiko Chan
Text design and typesetting by Typography Studio

PRAISE FOR *MY TONGUE IS MY OWN*

'Gwen Harwood, that excellent poet and critic, deserves a
sympathetic and lively biography. Ann-Marie Priest, to her credit,
has just written that book.'
—Ann Blainey, winner of the 2009 National Biography Award

'Absolutely splendid'
—Alison Hoddinott, author of *Gwen Harwood: The Real and the Imagined
World* and co-editor of *Gwen Harwood's Collected Poems, 1943–1995*

'Essential reading for anyone interested in Australian poetry
and/or the situation endured by creative women before our
allegedly more enlightened times'
—*The Canberra Times*

'Admirably lucid … written with sensitivity'
—Gregory Kratzmann, editor of *Gwen Harwood: Selected Poems* and
co-editor of *Gwen Harwood's Collected Poems, 1943–1995*

'Gwen Harwood's life story shows the familiar tension felt by
a gifted poet who is also a dedicated wife and mother, but it is
more complex than that division suggests. This self-styled "Hobart
housewife" was passionate in love and friendship, a trickster
who waged war on literary editors, a shapeshifter with half a dozen
identities as poet, a brilliant letter writer. Why and how Harwood used
her formidable creative powers in unexpected ways is explored by
Ann-Marie Priest in this fine biography.'
—Brenda Niall, author of *True North: The Story of Mary and Elizabeth Durack*
and the multi-award-winning *Mannix*

'A compelling biography. Priest puts Harwood's voice – or rather,
her many voices – at the heart of this volume.'
—Stephanie Trigg, *Australian Book Review*

'Ann-Marie Priest's biography is an invaluable addition to the
literature on this writer.'
—Susan Sheridan, *Sydney Review of Books*

'Priest's spirited biography does provide the occasion to
hope we can be clear-sighted about the love stories and the
ghost stories in the work of a poet.'
—*ArtsHub*

'[An] accessible recounting of Gwen Harwood's crowded
and emotionally vertiginous life, strengthened by many quotes
from her witty correspondence. It should return readers to
what matters: her poetry.'
—Gig Ryan, award-winning poet and former poetry editor of *The Age*

'Fearless, fascinating accounts of rule breakers, rule makers
and rule enforcers. Happy summer reading.'
—Clare Wright

To Greg Kratzmann and Alison Hoddinott,
who made this book possible

and

to John Fitzsimmons, who makes everything possible

Contents

Introduction

GWEN HARWOOD TOOK GREAT INTEREST IN THE WRITING OF her biography. In general, she was wary of literary scholars; having people pontificate about her in print made her feel like 'peaches being put in a tin & the lid soldered on'.[1] But when it seemed, in the early 1990s, that more than one biographer had taken on the task of writing her life story, she was pleased. With two different versions of her life in circulation, she might slip out between them. There would be room to manoeuvre, an elusive in-between space for her to occupy. For a time, she encouraged both would-be biographers to believe that he or she alone was her 'official' choice, sending them off to hunt down her letters and speak to old friends. In her mind, the book to be written by her long-time friend and Harwood scholar Alison Hoddinott would be a 'sensitive' literary biography, while the one by young medievalist Gregory Kratzmann would 'dish the dirt'.[2] The would-be biographers found the situation less than ideal, however. When Hoddinott discovered that Harwood had made the same promises to them both, she withdrew, leaving Kratzmann in possession of the field.

Over the following months, as the friendship between Kratzmann and Harwood grew, the poet became less and less guarded, giving him access to restricted papers held in various library collections and telling him things she had never told anyone else. She wanted to be known, to share her secrets. She was very curious about how he would tell her life story, and even suggested some possible opening paragraphs for his use.[3] In one, she impersonated her biographer coming upon his subject unawares:

Before I opened the door of All Saints I heard the swelling harmonies of a Bach prelude, brilliantly played; inside, as my eyes adjusted to the darkness, I became aware of the diminutive, surprisingly youthful figure of the organist, engrossed in her playing. Could this be the author of 'Burning Sappho' and 'Carnal Knowledge'? I asked myself . . .

Another made shameless use of the opening line of David Marr's biography of Patrick White, which she had recently read: 'The bride was a pretty woman who did not wear a big hat. A big hat would have obscured her face . . .'

Yet another introduced a sinister twist: 'Long ago a titian-haired girl child was born in a nursing home at Taringa to a couple called Joe and Agnes. They called her Gwendoline Nessie, "Gwendoline" for a friend of her mother, "Nessie" for her mother. Nessie, of course, is also the name of a monster . . .'

Needless to say, none of these openings was ever used. Harwood died before Kratzmann was far into his book, and with her husband and other key people still alive, the project became too difficult to navigate. Kratzmann decided to publish a volume of her letters instead – the story of her life, as he thought of it, in her own, genuinely inimitable words.

This compromise would have pleased her. In place of a biographer's authoritative tones, her many voices would be on display. She was the trickster-poet, after all, an enigmatic figure of wigs and masks. Even as a young woman, she hated being confined to a single identity, a single narrative, a single voice. At twenty-two, working as a clerk in the public service in Brisbane and playing the organ at weddings on weekends, she liked to channel a range of personas. 'I have three characters – with variations – which I play at weddings,' she told a friend: 'the Young Genius, the Soulful Maiden and the Embittered and Disillusioned Musician. Circumstances and singers determine which I am to be.'[4] These characters were mocking parodies, but they were also dimensions of herself that were highly satisfying to perform. A little less than two decades later came the first of the pseudonyms with which she would launch guerrilla raids on the Australian literary establishment. The earnest Walter Lehmann was the author of a pair of acrostic sonnets smuggled into *The Bulletin* – one of which read 'Fuck all Editors' – that brought the Vice Squad down on that august journal. Even as all hell broke loose, the anguished Francis Geyer, a supposed migrant-musician from Hungary, continued to sing to his lost love on *The Bulletin*'s famous Red Page. Most daring of all was the 'lovely lady poet' Miriam Stone,[5] who wrote a series of furious, brilliant poems about domestic life. In this guise ('Nobody will be expecting me to be a lady poet'), Harwood was able to say things about women's experiences that nobody else was – until she was outed by eagle-eyed readers and had to shut Mrs Stone down. The Australian poetry community was in a frenzy. 'It was not simply that a new and unsuspected poet of virtuoso technical accomplishment, wit and insight had appeared,' wrote poet Andrew Taylor. 'Rather, there seemed to be two of them, or possibly more. Guessing which poems, over different names, in *The Bulletin* were actually written by Gwen Harwood became a regular game.'[6]

In her private life, Harwood was always alert for moments of crossover between the everyday and the storied realm. As a 1950s housewife, she was 'the stately flower of female fortitude', endlessly capable and good-humoured. As an aspiring poet, she was Burning Sappho, a woman of incandescent gifts, cruelly caged in Hobart suburbia and fighting for her life.[7] Neither role contained her. 'I wish I had several lives,' she once sighed, 'one for songs, one for poetry, one for being an abandoned alcoholic, one for being a cored and peeled hausfrau, one for beachcombing, one for being an Italian . . .'[8] In her seventies, she told an audience at a poetry reading that she had been born in the back streets of Naples and left on a doorstep in a wicker basket with 'a bag of sweet biscuits and a packet of dry spaghetti'.[9] Fortunately, she had been adopted by an Australian couple who were touring Italy – which was why her maiden name was Foster. (Her friend Chris Wallace-Crabbe, who shared the stage with her that day, said it took a few moments for the audience to realise that this story was entirely untrue. He wondered if it might have been inspired by Peter Sarstedt's 'Where Do You Go To, My Lovely' – a song Harwood certainly knew.)[10]

Harwood's great imaginative fecundity when it came to the stories of her life was partly sheer exuberance; her inventiveness bubbled up like a spring, set off by anything at all. But it was also a form of resistance to being corralled into fixed roles and identities. When I began, tentatively, to follow in Hoddinott's and Kratzmann's footsteps, trekking around the country to the various repositories of Harwood's letters and papers, I was dazzled by the playful brilliance of her personal writings. Her letters – of which there are several thousand, many still unpublished – made me laugh aloud. But for all her merriment, it was evident that she often felt painfully trapped. Her letters to her closest friends – Ann Jennings, Edwin Tanner and, later, Alison Hoddinott – speak of her restlessness, her impatience, her resentment of a confinement from which she could never quite break free. Long before second-wave feminism hit Australia in the early 1970s, she was aware of the ways in which women's lives and potential were constrained by social ideals of womanliness. Yet as a young woman, she herself had succumbed to the ideal of 'Holy Motherhood', making earnest efforts to mould herself into the shape she believed she should take, one that would please her husband, her society and her own demanding self.

She would later date this torturous period precisely: it began with her marriage and continued for twelve years. This was also, not coincidentally, the period of her poetry apprenticeship, when she was reading widely and trying on different voices, approaches, techniques and subjects. Yet in all this time, she rarely wrote of herself, *from* herself. It was only when she began to realise the warping effects of her efforts 'to please others who were indifferent'[11] that she began to give attention to what she would later call 'the self that made my tongue my own'.[12] This was the self – not single, not simple – whose contradictory and multiplicitous impulses, fed by music and literature and sex and friendship and her own fierce intellect, created all the characters and roles, all the loves and hates, all the interweaving voices of her poems. 'No-one may like the shape I take,' she growled in the 1970s, 'but no-one is going to espalier me again.'[13] When she claimed the right to find her own shape, she became that rare poet who forges her own style. With her fierce 'independence of spirit',[14] she discovered the gift of communicating her inner life to her readers – thus making her way into theirs. She went on to become, in Peter Porter's words, a 'true master', the most accomplished Australian poet of her century.[15]

◆ ◆ ◆

This is not to say that Harwood moved effortlessly from silence to a confident, assured poetic voice. To read her letters, memoirs, stories and poems together is to understand the assertion she once made that she was 'full of old selves, half-devils inhabiting the body'.[16] There was no clean break, no simple rebirth. Indeed, her determination to achieve some 'independence of spirit' caused her pain and trouble, and often deep unhappiness. It brought her into conflict with those she loved, and with herself. More than once, after vowing never again to allow herself to be deformed, she would catch herself busily pruning her new growth into the old shapes. Yet, however imperfectly it was realised, her determination persisted.

While she was still young, she found a story that resonated with her efforts at self-liberation. In its earliest incarnation, 'Thomas the Rhymer' was a seventeenth-century English ballad, but Harwood also knew it as a German poem set to music by Carl Loewe. True Thomas is a wandering poet who is taking his ease by the river one day when a fair-haired woman rides up – the most beautiful woman he's ever seen. She tells him she is Queen of Elfland, and warns him that if he once kisses her, he will belong to her for seven years. Dazzled, slain, Tom takes her in his arms. Seven years of servitude, he tells her, is a small price to pay for such a prize. So she takes him up on her milk-white steed and rides with him to Elfland. 'How happy the Rhymer was,' carols Loewe's lied.

The German song ends there, but the English ballad continues for many more stanzas. When the queen and the Rhymer come at last to the border of Elfland, she reveals a detail she had not mentioned before: while he is in her kingdom, he must not speak. If he says a single word, he will never return to his own land. As she tells him this, she plucks an apple from a tree and gives it to him as his reward. It is a magic apple, and when he returns to his own country it will give him a 'tongue that can never lie'. Far from being grateful, Thomas is indignant. A true tongue is hardly a reward, he points out. How is he to ply his trade if he can't stretch the truth now and then? 'My tongue is my ain,' he declares. But the elven queen is inexorable: 'For as I say, so must it be.'[17]

Harwood identified with Tom the Rhymer – particularly his spirited assertion that his tongue was his own. She believed that when she married, she willingly surrendered her voice for love, disappearing into Elfland. Unlike Tom, though, when her years of servitude were over, she was determined to 'keep my tongue my own'. Owning her tongue was about claiming the right not only to speak but also to be silent – even to lie. It was about using her voice as she chose: to hide or to reveal herself, to try out different characters, different truths and possibilities, and to speak – as she put it in another poem, 'Chance Meeting' – the love she felt compelled to own. It was about claiming her sexual freedom, too. Above all, it was about claiming her freedom as a poet. This she did – and Australian poetry would never be the same.

Part I:
1920–1945

1

Once I Lived Like the Gods

Gwen Harwood, Postcard to A.D. Hope, 1963

WHEN GWEN HARWOOD WAS IN HER MID-FIFTIES, SHE sent some childhood photos to a younger poet who had recently become her lover. In one, a jubilant three-year-old sits astride a beautifully carved and painted rocking horse in the dusty yard of her family's war-service cottage in country Mitchelton, just north of Brisbane. Barelegged and barefoot, in a short gingham dress, head an unruly mass of curls, she beams at the camera, utterly at home, radiating joyful self-satisfaction. Out of focus behind her is a large, leafy tree, perhaps an orange or lemon tree, alongside some distant, grainy structures that may be a barn and some chook sheds.

On the back of the photo, the adult Gwen scrawled a three-stanza ditty in which she described her childhood self, with characteristic glee, as about to 'take a ride' up 'the gullies of Parnassus' – legendary Grecian home of the Muses, and thus of poetry, music, literature and learning. But for now, she is 'secure among the shining / orange trees', happy and free. It is a vision of sheer effortless being: 'artless, thoughtless, unrepining / Gwendoline goes rocking on.'[1]

This was how she liked to think of her early childhood: as a time of untrammelled joy, when she had as yet nothing to long for and nothing to regret. Even so, she was aware that this was only one way of looking at it.[2] From the perspective of her later exile from Queensland, her time at Mitchelton was a rural idyll: little Gwendoline among the chookies, doted upon by mother, father and maternal grandmother, poor but happy in the 'land wherein the citrons bloom'.[3] But with only a slight twist of the lens, Mitchelton becomes a sinister place, 'half Gothic, half biblical',[4] where poverty dragged at war-blighted families, kind Granny slaughtered the ducks and chickens for the pot, and the boys next door threatened little Gwendoline with a knife.

Both versions were true. Gwen's childhood was safe, happy and full of small joys: the doves in the barn, so tame she could hold them; her parents singing spirited duets at the piano after tea; the creek lined with 'yellow and blue flowering trees' that ran through the flat fields of the rural settlement. It was also full of terrors. An intensely imaginative child, Gwen was capable not only of great delight but also of great dread. She was haunted by the 'small horrors' pictured in *Little Buttercup's Picture Book*, a Victorian children's annual that belonged to her grandmother, and terrified by the 'gorilla-like monsters' in Norman Lindsay's World War I recruitment posters, secreted in a trunk under the house, who 'threatened women and children in kitchens like ours'.[5] Such images were delightfully thrilling by day, but she was their helpless prey at night when they took on flesh and came 'step by evil step through the shadows' to her bed.[6] Tormented by nightmares, she 'could not bear / to see the sun go down'.[7]

In interviews and essays, the adult Gwen preferred to focus on the idyllic aspects of her childhood. 'At my public readings I always paint my childhood as radiant & unclouded,' she told a friend when she was in her early fifties, 'as in extreme old age I shall probably paint this [troubled] period of my life.'[8] This was partly strategic; by depicting her childhood as unproblematic, she could stymie any critics who might seek to draw dark inferences about her from her poems.[9] But she also took profound pleasure in revisiting, recreating, the happiness of her childhood. She drew sustenance from savouring and celebrating past joys. In old age, she would mildly satirise her own tendency to see the past through a golden veil, joking that she suffered from 'chronic morbid nostalgia' and telling one interviewer that she was 'nostalgic even for five minutes ago'.[10] But her attachment to the past was more than nostalgia. All her life, she would believe that moments of beauty, pleasure and human connection, no matter how fleeting, had a life-transforming power. Not only could they lift her for an instant from the drudgery of daily life, but they could also become a talisman against future darkness.

This belief had its roots in her earliest experiences. Her first memories were of her beloved Grandmother Maud adjuring her to remember things.[11] 'She would show me "a phenomenon" – an odd-shaped cloud, a root growing through a bracelet she had lost in the garden and found again – and say "Now remember this, you won't see such a thing again".[12] The most impressive of all the things young Gwennie was urged to store in her memory was a total eclipse of the sun, an occasion she was later able to date precisely to a Thursday afternoon in September 1922, when she was two years old: 'I can remember my Granny holding me up and saying now look, look, you must remember this, it may not happen again in your lifetime. And I did remember it, I can remember the apocalyptic light and the glimpse of the corona through smoked glass, and the birds all going to rest.'[13]

Gwen Foster with grandmother Maud Jaggard (left) and
glamorous 'aunts', her namesake Gwendoline Stenlake (right)
and Clarice Stenlake, in Mitchelton, 1921

Grandmother Maud found joy and wonder in the everyday – 'a carrot constricted by a curtain ring it had grown through, a piece of firewood with worm-holes spelling MUM'[14] – and she passed that capacity on to Gwen. This was the quality her friend Tony would describe as an 'intense and special power of delight'. All her life she found myriad sources of enchantment in daily life – particularly in time spent with those she loved. After her death, one friend would describe, with some bemusement, her ability to take a simple experience, 'a day, an afternoon, an hour' they had spent together, and bathe it in 'so radiant an aura of fond recollection that you stood astonished at the transfiguration of the scene and your part in it'.[15] To Gwen, such heightened experiences were the truth of life, 'those moments when we wake / alive from the sleep of time'.[16] The memory of them was necessary sustenance when life fell disastrously short of glorious. As she put it in 'The Double Image', 'heart remembers, lives / on nothing, if need be, until it wakes again / tasting joy it cannot name'. The last two lines of 'An die Parzen', by the German Romantic Friedrich Hölderlin, would become her mantra, referred to often in her letters: 'Einmal / lebt' ich wie Götter, und mehr bedarfs nicht ('Once I lived like the gods, and nothing more is needed'). She would recite this to herself in times of misery as in times of rapture[17] and even put the lines in an early poem: 'Once in a shadowless time we lived / as gods might live . . .'[18] Her purest delight, and the most sustaining – in retrospect, at least – belonged to the 'unrepining' days of earliest childhood.

◆ ◆ ◆

Gwen's father was English and her mother Australian, a distinction that led to a continuous, teasing rivalry between them as to which culture was superior. 'England had Shakespeare, the Empire, the King James Bible, snow', Gwen would write, while 'Australia had a decent climate and equality'.[19] Gwen herself was in no doubt that she was Australian, the latest in 'a line of independent, energetic Australian women'. Before her mother, Agnes, came Agnes's mother, Maud Jaggard, and grandmother, Matilda Markwell, both of whom Gwen knew well. They were 'marvellous models':

> These women weren't all like each other, they were totally different in their beliefs, and their abilities, and their gifts. And their inclinations. The thing they had in common was their independence, and their feeling that . . . there was a great deal of simple happiness in the world, and people shouldn't keep you from it.[20]

Of the three, Grandmother Maud was the most significant in Gwen's mind. A few months after Gwen was born, Maud moved in with her daughter and son-in-law, and to Gwen, it was Maud, not Agnes, who brought her up. 'My mother, beautiful & selfish, always seemed to be out playing tennis or visiting or bossing committees or arranging parties,' she told a friend. 'Granny had endless time for me.'[21] In her fifties, Gwen wrote four stories about her childhood – attempts at an autobiography she never completed.[22] In each, Maud is the central figure: brisk, calm, efficient, taking charge in every situation, sought after throughout the fledgling community for practical aid as much as for tea and gossip. She is strict with her granddaughter and does not hesitate to smack her if she is naughty. But she is also kind and humorous, and takes evident pleasure in the little girl's company. After Maud's death, Gwen would tell a friend that she and her grandmother had 'a deep understanding that the difference in our ages did not diminish at all'.[23] It was Granny who understood her night terrors and did what she could to help her feel safe.[24] Granny was also the one who recited poetry to her before she was old enough to read.[25] The sentimental Victorian verse Maud favoured, along with the thunderous rhythms of the King James Bible, was the music that first 'tuned' Little Gwendoline's ear 'to metre'.[26]

Maud Jaggard was only forty-one when her granddaughter was born. She had lost her husband, William Jaggard, some six years earlier, when they were living in the small city of Rockhampton in central Queensland. Eighteen years older than his wife, Willy was headmaster at Crescent Lagoon School when he died suddenly of heart failure at fifty-two, just before World War I. Agnes, their only child, was then sixteen, a scholarship student at Rockhampton Girls Grammar School. While Agnes completed her Senior Certificate and went on to take up a teaching post at the newly established Mount Morgan High School, some forty kilometres south-west of Rockhampton, Maud threw herself into the war effort. She helped to establish the Soldiers' Rest and Recreation Rooms on Bolsover Street, providing meals and wholesome entertainment to servicemen passing through Rockhampton, and was soon running the place.

She was a very capable woman. The eldest of eleven children, Maud grew up on a property outside Alpha in Central West Queensland. Her father, Richard Markwell ('a splendid horseman over timber'), bred and trained racehorses, and the family were comfortably off.[27] Maud could turn her hand to anything, from tending farm animals and managing a household to setting up a charity.[28] Forthright and assured, excelling in 'sharp repartee',[29] she could also be fierce. One evening, Gwen was out with Maud in the sulky when they came across a man 'bothering' a woman on the side of the ride. Maud struck him with the horsewhip. She was 'never . . . afraid of anything'.[30]

Agnes was as redoubtable as her mother. According to family folklore, she once shot a crocodile in Rockhampton's Fitzroy River and claimed its skin as a trophy.[31] She was a clever student, a champion tennis player and a talented pianist with a 'vibrant personality'.[32] During the war, she helped her mother at the Rest and Recreation Rooms when she could, playing at informal concerts, making sandwiches and raising funds. When the Rooms became the headquarters of the local recruiting office, she got to know the newly arrived recruitment sergeant, twenty-eight-year-old Joseph Foster.

Agnes Jaggard and Joseph Foster, Rockhampton, 1918

Joe had emigrated to Melbourne with his younger brother, Bill, in 1913. Some two years later, he joined the Australian Army and went to the Middle East as an orderly on a hospital ship. By mid-1916, he was back in Melbourne with a medical discharge,[33] and as Bill had also been invalided out of the army, he and Joe decided to go north to work as recruiters on the show circuit. The 'notable Foster brothers' quickly gained a reputation for talking reluctant men into doing their duty for king and country. Joe then took on a succession of recruiting jobs in Townsville, Maryborough and – in April 1918 – Rockhampton, where he met Maud and her spirited daughter.

Twenty-year-old Agnes was very much attracted to the lively, garrulous Joe.[34] According to Gwen, he was irresistible: 'handsome, with curly hair, sparkling green eyes, beautiful teeth' and the gift of the gab.[35] He played fiddle and piano by ear, was a master of the billiard cue and could improvise high-spirited entertainments at a moment's notice. He was equally drawn to the vivacious Agnes, with her 'wonderful waist-length chestnut hair' and inexhaustible energy.[36] In late 1918, they established the Rockhampton Loyalty League to support returned servicemen,[37] but it was barely off the ground when the war ended. This meant Joe was out of a job. He soon left Rockhampton in search of work, but returned the following June to marry Agnes at St Paul's Anglican Cathedral. Maud walked her daughter down the aisle. The newlyweds honeymooned in Yeppoon before going south and settling in a war service cottage at Mitchelton. A year later, on 8 June 1920, Gwendoline Nessie Foster was born.

◆ ◆ ◆

Gwen quickly allied herself with her grandmother. 'Never once in my childhood did it occur to me that she was in the world for any other purpose than to *be there for me*,'[38] she would declare. Agnes she had to share with a legion of friends and causes; Maud belonged to Gwen. Yet Maud was at least as active in the community as her daughter. Both women were closely involved with the newly formed Returned Soldiers and Sailors Imperial League of Australia (the forerunner of the RSL) – for which Joe worked as the state organiser in the early 1920s – and took on numerous other causes. Gwen would joke that as a child, she could 'recite by heart like a litany' the committees her mother served on, including the Soldiers' and Sailors' Widows and Orphans Committee, the Japanese Earthquake Relief Fund, the Brisbane Centenary Committee, the Queensland Bush Children's Committee, the Limbless Soldiers' Association and the Government House Fete Committee.[39]

For Maud and Agnes, this voluntary work was their civic duty – a phrase which, to Gwennie, meant travelling into town on the train and 'having lunch in a genteel café where the cups and saucers were rimmed with gold and my milk came in an alabaster goblet'.[40] Though the women of the household did all the domestic chores, they were not confined to the home, nor defined by their roles as wives and mothers. It seemed to Gwen that none of the women of her family 'felt at all constrained by being housewives'; they were 'free, active, energetic women' who would not dream of leaving an important meeting 'to boil potatoes'.[41] This perception would shape Gwen's expectations of her own life as a wife and mother. In the 1950s, immured in domesticity, she would ruefully reflect that something had changed for women since the 1930s – they were no longer free in the way her mother and grandmother had been.[42] 'There was no question of equality in our household,' she would write. 'The women knew themselves to be stronger, wiser, longer-lived.'[43]

Their confidence gave Gwen a sense of 'security' from a young age, a conviction that she had a place in the wider world, not just in the domestic sphere.[44] From her earliest years, young Gwennie was 'part of the plan to close liquor bars early; to catch and imprison deserting husbands; to give preference to British goods; to house disabled soldiers and sailors; to give a thousand poor orphans a massive treat at the exhibition grounds once a year'.[45] She often played a role at her mother's 'functions', presenting bouquets, giving recitations, and – once she began ballet classes – performing dances, as well as 'doing humble work with trays & cups'.[46] She was never nervous. She loved the sense of pleasurable anticipation, of people in high spirits, dressed in their best, coming together solely to enjoy themselves.

Her father, a very sociable man, was an important part of these events. 'Theatrically inclined', he was always up for a lark and had an endless store of jokes, anecdotes, limericks and songs.[47] He and Agnes once held a function for 150 people that featured a bridal party in drag, complete with speeches and mock hymns.[48] He was known to put on impromptu one-man shows 'with a number of characters', and to perform popular songs with his own 'ludicrous' lyrics – particularly when he was 'not quite sober'. When she was in her early twenties, Gwen gave a description of him in full flow one evening that conveys something of his sheer inventiveness. Sitting down at the piano, he 'drew out of his waist-coat pocket an advertisement for TAUFIK RAAD'S STANDARD WHITE OIL OF LEBANON' and put it on the music rest.[49] He then proceeded to 'set the whole thing to music in the style of Grand Opera'. Beginning with 'a sort of recitative with the appropriate chords', he sang: 'This oil is invaluable for the following complaints.' He then 'became dramatic and sang the list of complaints staccato, punctuated with heavy chords: Gout! Cramp! Bruises! Lumbago!

Neuritis! After that he sang (falsetto) a beautiful aria: "For weeks I suffered severely with pains in my right knee." His audience – Gwen and her younger brother, Joey – was left 'helpless with laughter and admiration'.[50]

Mock wedding party, with Gwen and her brother, Joey, in drag, c. 1928

In the early 1920s, Joe made good use of his 'fluency',[51] earning his living in a variety of fundraising and speechifying roles: among other things, he sold government bonds, ran a buy-Australian campaign and raised money for the construction of Brisbane's City Hall. Gwen often saw him in front of an audience, perfectly at home, telling tall tales and keeping everyone entertained, and she honed her own wit to impress him.[52] As an adult, she would always feel that a speaker's primary obligation was to be amusing, entertaining. Like her father, she loved to make people laugh.

As a child, Gwen felt that 'the household came to life' when her father was home.[53] He introduced his children to the joys of parody – 'if there was anything to parody, we parodied it'[54] – and loved to terrify them on winter nights with 'blood-chilling' Victorian true-crime stories.[55] But he was also kind. When the red-headed Gwen bemoaned her freckled skin, he would tell her that freckles were a mark of distinction: 'people without freckles are very ordinary, I never take any notice of them.'[56] And he shared with his daughter his love of music, sitting with her on the back verandah on Sunday afternoons, playing Beethoven on the wind-up gramophone. All her life, she would associate Beethoven's first symphony with the backyard at Mitchelton, 'the path leading between our modest crops of peas and corn to the orchard and fowlyard', the orange trees in the distance framing her 'happy childhood'.[57]

◆ ◆ ◆

Her happiness suffered a serious blow when she went to school. 'O the misery of those classrooms,' she would lament, some forty years later, 'the uncomfortable seats, the smell when children opened their fibre suitcases (always called PORTS in Queensland) to get their lunch (jam or corned beef sandwiches, an orange), the fearful colour of the school buildings (like infantile diarrhoea), the prison-air of the corridors.'[58] In 1926, there were 259 students crammed into the five rooms of Mitchelton Primary School, a high-set weatherboard Queenslander catering for all the local children.[59] Gwen would remember with a shudder the gravel playground, 'with no living blade of grass', and the 'wooden forms set round the stumps under the school' where the children ate their lunch. [60] Worse were the children themselves. A 'real Lord of the Flies atmosphere' prevailed, with the pupils tormenting one another 'with hair-tweak, nib-prick, Chinese burns'.[61]

Gwen was small and skinny for her age – 'I was like a collection of loosely-assembled dowels, or broomsticks, topped with red hair' – and felt painfully vulnerable.[62] On her way to school, she was tormented by a 'tribe of bullies', the Bowman boys, who 'lived three houses up and had sworn to throw my bag in the creek and drown me'.[63] She was terrified. 'It wasn't the drowning that worried me so much as the loss of my schoolbag,' she would later confess. In one of her autobiographical stories, she describes walking past the Bowman house one afternoon and seeing the boys out on their front verandah, busily skinning frogs. 'Two frogs waiting their turn were impaled on wooden meat skewers, still moving feebly.' One of the boys 'lifted his knife towards [her] and said quietly, "We'll get you".'[64]

She was as appalled by their treatment of small, helpless creatures as by their threats against her. She loved animals, and was particularly devoted to the 'fattish, plumpish, green frogs' that lived among the violets under the tank stand at her house and would 'just about fit into your hand comfortably'.[65] Yet some of her schoolmates took pleasure in torturing them. One of their special tricks was to blow up a frog with a straw, like a balloon, and then puncture it with a stick. In her fifties, Gwen would vividly remember her 'feeling of helpless misery . . . I felt the frogs at home knew about it & could not understand why I allowed it'.[66] She was haunted as much by her own powerlessness as by the senseless cruelty. In several poems, she would equate these small acts of brutality with the atrocities of war, the after-effects of which were very much evident among the returned soldiers – some with missing limbs – who visited her home.

Even as a young child, she was troubled and distressed by death in all its guises. Her poems of childhood are haunted by reproachful creatures: the trusting eyes of a slaughtered calf in 'The Spelling Prize', the vengeful malice of a murdered crab in 'Night and Dreams', the obscenity of a slain bird in 'Barn Owl'. Young Gwennie grieved over 'fallen finches, drowned frogs' and ducklings that 'did not live to be eaten'.[67] She was distraught when her father told her that the elephant they had seen at the circus at Enoggera had been shot after it attacked its keeper. 'My father said that the other elephants were used to dig the grave and I still have the picture I had then in childhood of the elephants with garden spades in their trunks slowly digging the grave for their brother.'[68]

The revelation that people also died filled her with horror. She did not understand at first that they died 'one by one, and not all together with their families': 'An old man whose wife had died came to ask for my grandmother's advice about his garden; I hid in the ferns because I was sure he was dead if his wife had died; Granny coaxed me out to speak to him and I was unable to voice my fear.'[69] This fear persisted all her life. Its essence was 'that we shall die alone, I mean that I shall die alone'. She would struggle against this seeming inevitability in all kinds of ways, including by stockpiling those transcendent moments when it seemed the human spirit was immortal. It would become one of her deepest motivations as a poet: to counteract the power of death with her own creative abundance. In her darker moments, however, she feared this was delusion, that no accomplishments, no self-transformation, not even the rapturous heights of love and poetry could save her from death. 'Even if the rest of my life is occupied with ceaseless creation,' she mused, despairingly, at forty-two, 'that moment will come.'[70]

As a child, darkness and death were linked in her mind. Her first prayers were 'that darkness would not come again, and that I would never die'.

It seemed to her that if only the sun would stay in the sky, death itself could be vanquished. An early poem, 'The Glass Jar', dramatises the terror and desperation of her fear of the dark. A young boy – an avatar of herself[71] – conceives the idea of gathering some sunlight in a jar to unleash against the darkness. He soaks the jar in sunbeams, wraps it in a scarf and stashes it under his bed. That night, when he wakes, distraught, from a nightmare, he snatches up the jar and pulls off the scarf, only to find that the sunlight has gone. No beam of daylight shines out to chase away the monsters. He leaps out of bed and runs to his parents' room, but his mother and father are engrossed in each other and oblivious to him. There is no rescue, no safety. Returning to bed, he falls again into nightmare-riddled sleep. Nothing but the coming of day will restore peace to the world.

Gwen's childhood nightmares were full of 'violence & terror'.[72] In later life, she would reflect that many of her 'nightmare pursuers' came from *Little Buttercup's Picture Book*, the precious children's annual that Grandmother Maud would allow her to pore over as a reward for good behaviour. This substantial blue-and-gold volume, first published around 1880, features pious stories and sentimental poems about good, brave children, as well as a scattering of illustrated jokes and puns. (A boy with his pants falling down is captioned, 'A boy of loose habits'; a female centaur is captioned, 'The centaur of attraction'.) Also spread through its pages, barely registering on an adult eye, are various 'tiny wood-engraved horrors': 'a man in a frock-coat whose wooden legs have caught alight as he warms them at the fireside; a quartet of sinister cats, two foxes tearing a living goose apart by its wings, a horrible Mr Punch'.[73] For Gwen, these images had a terrible fascination, slipping into her all-too-receptive imagination to re-emerge in her dreams.

Other sources of horror included the tales from Homer's *Iliad* that she and her friends re-enacted in their games under the house and the Old Testament stories that Maud read her. Both featured largely inexplicable violence, a 'world without abstraction, / where spears pushed eyeballs out and went clean through the socket'.[74] Maud loved a rousing sermon, and would take Gwen with her to churches all over Brisbane to hear visiting preachers of the fire-and-brimstone variety. Gwen drank in 'great performances on the spoiling of Samaria, the iniquity of Israel, the lament over Tyre, the judgment of Ammon and Edom, the destruction of the worshippers of Baal'.[75] The sermons had an impact on her, but not the sanctifying one Maud must have hoped for. To Gwen, the God of the Old Testament was disturbingly irascible, and she worried that she was not virtuous enough to win his favour. She knew she was naughty – self-willed, disobedient, full of unseemly passion. Even her beloved grandmother sometimes declared that 'Satan' had got into her.[76] So she decided to hedge her bets and pray to whomever might be listening – including God's ancient rivals, Baal and Moloch, and the fairies from her storybooks.[77]

She felt very much in need of some kind of magical intervention when her brother, Joe, was born in August 1925. His appearance at her mother's breast marked 'really the first memory I have of my own rage and envy'.[78] The adults found her jealousy amusing, but Gwen's feelings were desperate. She prayed earnestly to Jesus (a gentler version of God she had recently encountered at Sunday School) to 'take my troublesome little brother to his eternal bosom – I thought I could fool Jesus by pretending my brother would be happier with him than with me'.[79] Her poem 'The Wasps', which she wrote in her early fifties, depicts a childhood incident (with details slightly altered) that she had interpreted as God's punishment for her evil thoughts. 'It was just about sunset,' she told a friend. 'I had been told never to play on a stack of boards because they were full of wasps, but I thought the wasps would have gone to sleep for the night. I jumped on the boards and danced around for a moment only, but the wasps were quicker and stung me & my brother.'[80] The pain was ferocious, and she was convinced her suffering was divine retribution. The incident signalled the beginning of a lifelong tug-of-war between her defiant spirit and her fear of the consequences of giving free rein to her inner rebel.

◆ ◆ ◆

As a child, Gwen did not think of herself as a poet-in-waiting. To her, poetry was either light entertainment, intended to make people laugh, like her father's improvised ditties, or it was a dull school exercise. She had a good ear for poetic form, falling easily into the rhythms of poetry. Throughout her youth she happily made up comic verses to amuse her schoolmates;[81] friends from her teenage years would be able to recite snatches of her comedic verse some fifty years later.[82] She was also good with a limerick, and once won a limerick contest run by a local radio station.[83] But this was play, not art.

In the classroom, poetry was presented not as 'an object of enjoyment' but as 'something to exercise your powers of grammatical analysis on':

'Thou shalt not enjoy it, thou shalt parse, analyse and underline in red.'[84] She enjoyed the technical analysis – she was always good at grammar. But for the time being, it got in the way. She did not 'feel' poetry, and it did not occur to her that it had anything to do with her own life. Her far greater passion, in childhood and for many years after, was music.

2

Affetuoso

Kröte plays for a tenor bleating
Schubert songs at an Afternoon.
Some idiot biscuit-nibbler beating
time on a saucer with a spoon
makes him accelerate his pace.
Annoyance clouds the tenor's face.

Gwen Harwood, 'Matinee'

ACCORDING TO FAMILY LEGEND, AGNES 'LONGED FOR A PIANO' when she was expecting Gwen, and her longing mystically communicated itself to her unborn child.[1] Some such story seemed necessary to account for the fervour of Gwen's feeling for music, which for her would always be – in the words she would give her musician character, Kröte – 'my joy, my full-scale God'.[2]

But a passion for music was not unusual in Gwen's world. She grew up around musicians; in the 1920s, as she once explained, 'if you wanted music, you had to make it.'[3] Agnes and Joe played and sang together, and often hosted musical 'evenings', while scales floated from the house of Mrs Lebanon, a Mitchelton neighbour who had 'a baby grand in a real music room'.[4] At neighbourhood supper parties, anyone who could play was invited to take their turn at the piano, and the evening would usually end in a singalong. Gwen heard sea chanties, ballads, operettas and German art songs at the homes of neighbours. Agnes's own musical 'functions' increasingly aspired to the professional. She kept an eagle eye on the Brisbane musical scene, and begged or cajoled up-and-coming musicians to perform at her fundraisers. She was triumphant when she was able to snaffle a local celebrity – or, better yet, one visiting from interstate – for one of her entertainments.

Gwen was enchanted by it all: the music, the glamorous beings who made it, the high-spirited sociability. The autobiographical poems she would write, many years later, about her mother's musical afternoons tend to emphasise the human drama swirling through these seemingly innocuous gatherings: the jostling among performers for pride of place, the arrows of lust and rage shot from limpid eyes, the sweetly cutting remarks.[5]

To the child, the singers and musicians were impossibly beautiful and accomplished, yet had intriguingly clay-like feet. She watched and learned, noting and, later, laughing at their vanities and foibles. Even in private, Joe and Agnes made music seem like a competitive sport. When they sang duets, their daughter felt 'it was a kind of game or competition, like playing draughts or ludo'.[6] Joe loved to tease Agnes, telling her, 'Nessie, you're out of tune again.' 'She often was, slightly,' her disloyal daughter admitted.

PASTORALE

Gwen Foster performing at the Queensland Eisteddfod,
Brisbane Telegraph, *March 1934*

While Agnes delighted in performing, Joe was less keen, except in his cups. But as secretary of the Queensland Band Association – a position he assumed in 1926 and held on and off for forty years (though he 'couldn't blow a toot') – he organised plenty of musical events of his own, including street parades and massed band concerts.[7] He also received complimentary tickets to every noteworthy musical performance in Brisbane – tickets his daughter made good use of in her teens and early twenties.

Unlike poetry, music to the young Gwen was 'a delight, a joy, something that enriched you'.[8] It was beauty and majesty and drama and tears, and it was also great fun, drawing everyone together. As a child, she would go to the piano 'now and then' in the eager hope that 'this was the day when I could play it, as the day had come when I could reach the biscuit barrel on its shelf, and the wax matches and the scissors'. Alas, she did not have her father's gift of playing by ear anything he heard, 'with correct harmonies'.[9] Her first music lessons, at the age of ten, with the 'stern' Miss Mabel were a disappointment; she had not been prepared for all the 'boring work' involved in learning an instrument and found the scales and exercises daunting.[10] Only when she was skilled enough to play 'the Mozart sonatas, and some of the easier [Bach] preludes and fugues' did she begin to enjoy herself.[11] She was soon good enough to perform at Agnes's musical afternoons, playing duets with her mother as well as performing solo. In secret, she began to design the 'glorious dresses' she would wear when she finally took her place on the concert platform.[12]

◆ ◆ ◆

By this time, the Fosters had left Mitchelton. In the early 1920s, the family had struggled to make ends meet as Joe went from job to job. As Gwen remembered it, they sometimes 'had to eat only what actually was there': the vegetables they grew, the ducks from their fowl house, milk and cream from their cow.[13] There was no money for luxuries like shop-bought bread – though Gwen, unlike many children at her school, always had shoes and hair ribbons.[14] But things changed around 1925 when, with the help of family friends, Joe opened a haberdashery in central Brisbane. His business was to sell shirts and ties, but he was increasingly fascinated by the new 'wireless' technology and began to sell radios on the side. Joining the newly formed Queensland Institute of Radio Engineers, he taught himself all there was to know about the medium, and was soon in demand for parts, repairs and advice. His sideline was so successful that he abandoned haberdashery altogether to become a 'pioneer' of radio retail.[15]

The year Gwen turned seven, the family was ready to move closer to the city. Joe bought a big house at Auchenflower for a thousand pounds, and they travelled down to the riverside suburb by train. When they arrived at the new house, Agnes swept into the kitchen and declared she was 'not having that stove'. Before Gwen's amazed eyes, she dismantled the offending wood cooker and 'threw the pieces over the veranda in triumph'. The next day, a brand new, state-of-the-art gas stove was installed.[16] Their new life was to be mod cons all the way.

Gwen loved the house at 14 Grimes Street. Large and gracious, with a double staircase leading up to the wraparound verandah, it was 'one of the true Queenslanders'.[17] At its heart was a forty-foot lounge room with a fireplace at one end and the piano at the other. There was a dining room with enchanting 'panes of pink and green bubble glass', and more than enough bedrooms for them all.[18] Gwen and Joey (as her brother was then known) slept on the verandah, in sleepouts loosely enclosed by venetian blinds; Gwen loved to lie in bed and look out at the shadowy trees and the fruit bats lumbering past.[19] Her grandmother's room opened onto hers, which gave her a sense of safety in the dark. At bedtime, Grandmother Maud would 'make excuses to sit in her room . . . and let me know she was there'.[20] The big yard was lush with ferns, camphor laurels and mango trees, and there was plenty of room to play under the house. When Gwen wanted solitude, as she sometimes did as she grew older, she could climb onto the flat roof of one of the garden sheds with a supply of bread and dripping, and settle herself in a shady spot to think 'deep impenetrable thoughts'.[21]

Auchenflower was a leafy suburb known for its parks and gardens.[22] Toowong Park, with its 'wealth of old bush trees', was only ten minutes' walk from the Fosters' new home, and there was a football field, a croquet club and a bowling green nearby. At one end of Grimes Street was a train station, and at the other a tram stop, and though bread was still delivered by horse and cart, there was a small shop, selling cigarettes and ice cream, and a post office.[23] Gwen and Joey soon made the suburb their own, playing outside with the neighbourhood children and wandering far and wide with their Pomeranian, Flossie. There were rules – they could not 'wander until after dark' or 'play in the road' – but within those limits, they had a great deal of freedom.[24] They often took the tram all the way down Milton Road to the Toowong Cemetery, whose stone mausoleums and crumbling funerary statues delighted Gwen, or up to the slopes of Mount Coot-tha for a bush picnic.[25] Or they took the train into town and spent the day at the Botanic Gardens or the museum.

The only blight on Gwen's new life was having to return to school. She had a reprieve for a couple of months, going along with two-year-old Joey to a local 'dame school' run by a former Rockhampton woman, Bride O'Shea. But early in 1928, her parents enrolled her in Grade 3 at Toowong

State School. With some nine hundred students,[26] Toowong was much bigger than Mitchelton, and Gwen found it 'perilous'. As at Mitchelton, she felt 'really frightened by some of the big boys,'[27] and was once again the victim of bullies: three older boys who liked to chase her and her new friend Gracie on their way home from school. 'Pringle's got a womb, Foster's got a womb', they would shout. '"We haven't," we'd shout back, almost in tears.'[28] When the boys were caned one day, the girls listened to their 'howls and choking sobs' with 'remorseless pleasure'.

All her life, Gwen would be sceptical of sentimental views of children. She was particularly dismissive of what she called the 'tender lambs of Jesus' style of parenting: the belief that children were angelic creatures, incapable of cruelty or malice.[29] She had first-hand experience not only of other children's malice but also of her own capacity to rejoice at the suffering of her enemies.

◆ ◆ ◆

With so much more room at the Auchenflower house, Joe and Agnes scaled up their social activities. Their evening events began to include roulette (not, strictly speaking, legal at the time) and dancing, followed by wonderful suppers: 'O the passionfruit sponges and the flaky sausage rolls and the fresh crustless egg & lettuce sandwiches!'[30] The house and verandah would be transformed with flowers, bunting and even strings of electric lights. Gwen was an avid observer on these occasions, keeping out of the way but missing very little – including the odd 'dalliance under the camphor laurels'.[31] Her father – considered 'a one' and 'a bit of a devil' – was in his element, 'squeezing and teasing the more presentable ladies, especially two sisters (Florrie & Dagmar Lund) who always came and always expected to be squeezed'.[32] To Gwen, there was nothing sinister about such behaviour; it was all part of the fun. All her life she would have a soft spot for 'heroic drinkers' (as she would later designate her father) and jocular men with what used to be called 'an eye for the ladies'.

As Agnes's musical 'afternoons' grew in scope and stature, she began to look about her for a new piano teacher for her daughter, someone worthy of Gwen's gifts. The pianist who caught her eye was a young man from Ipswich named Hardy Humphreys, whom she often requisitioned for her functions. Recently returned from London, he had set himself up in a Brisbane studio as Hardy Gerhardy. A 'marvellous pianist with a passion for showing off',[33] Gerhardy would become one of the prototypes for Kröte, the self-dramatising musician Gwen would invent in her early forties. His party trick was a performance of Weber's virtuosic 'Perpetuum Mobile': 'He would start off fairly fast, to the metronome, then get somebody to advance the speed of the metronome as the piece progressed, until he ended in a breathtaking cascade of notes.'[34] Agnes hastened to enrol both her children at his studio.

But Gerhardy was 'a terrible teacher' who Gwen would later complain may well have ruined her as a pianist. He made his students 'practise with pennies balanced on the backs of our hands, always to the metronome',[35] and focused on technique rather than understanding, driving them 'mercilessly' through 'the standard pianoforte repertoire'.[36] Gwen was 'forced & bullied into learning works quite incomprehensible to my Lolita-like brain'. Nevertheless, she quickly became an impressive young pianist. Within a couple of years, she was playing on the same bill as Gerhardy himself at various musical events, a minor celebrity in her own right, 'fed on bourgeois praise, stuffed with delicacies'. Working steadily, she passed all her Australian Music Examinations Board exams before she finished school. At sixteen, she performed in a student recital at City Hall, and her rendition of Bach's *Chromatic Fantasia and Fugue* was singled out by *The Courier Mail* for its 'impressive accomplishment'. 'Still in her middle teens, this pianist already has brilliance in her technical handling of exacting passages,' the reviewer declared. Even more importantly, she had 'an innate music-consciousness': 'She has a future at the piano, with executive development in keeping with developing musical thought.'[37]

A couple of years later, another review would echo these sentiments, declaring that the young pianist had 'an artist's sense of the piano', allying 'polished technique to warmth in interpretation'.[38] She received her associate diploma of music a few weeks after her sixteenth birthday. The next step for her was the licentiate diploma, which would certify that she was at concert standard.

Over this time, her admiration for musicians and composers began to verge on adoration. One year, she won a copy of *Lives of the Great Composers* as a prize in her music exams and spent hours poring over the book, studying the word-portraits of Bach and Beethoven and drinking in the stories of their eccentric but incandescent lives.[39] As well as her mother's 'evenings', she went to as many concerts as she could, and was transported by the auras cast by legendary performers: pianists such as Josef Hofmann and Artur Rubinstein, singers such as Ukrainian bass Alexander Kipnis and German soprano Lotte Lehmann. 'I remember shaking Kipnis's hand, and I thought, "This great singer, and I've actually touched his hand."'[40] She also venerated homegrown stars, musicians and singers visiting from other states. These were the people whose world she hoped one day to join.

◆ ◆ ◆

Gwen's musical period coincided with what she would later dub her 'rebellious' adolescence.[41] Exactly how she rebelled – what forms her rebellion took – she never really made clear. Though the adult Gwen dwelt lovingly on her childhood in both poetry and prose, she wrote surprisingly little about her teenage years. Even when she deliberately set out to tackle the subject, she would find herself reverting to 'the usual barefoot in the chicken-yard piece'.[42] This was partly because it was simply not a happy time. 'I did not enjoy adolescence,' she once noted crisply.[43] But it was also because there were things about her teenage self she did not want to reveal. As she put it to a friend, 'I'm not going to tell every son-of-a-bitch about my adolescence.'[44] More than one poem suggests that she experienced much inner turmoil. In 'Past and Present', she describes her adolescent self, 'neither woman nor child', as a 'nest of self-torturing demons'.[45] The eager enthusiasm of her early childhood seems to have been replaced by a corrosive cynicism, at least for a time, and she had little respect for 'authority of any kind' – with her parents, and perhaps even her beloved Maud, at the top of the list.[46]

Around the time Gwen reached her teens, Maud left the household, opening a café in the city. Gwen later hinted that Maud's departure was the result of a falling-out with Agnes; she would never live with the Fosters again, and some twenty-five years later, Gwen would tell a friend that 'Granny & Agnes can't stand one another'.[47] Gwen was not getting on too well with Agnes herself – nor with Joe. 'I don't think I believed anything my parents told me,' she would later reflect.[48] When she herself had teenage children, she would muse that 'adolescents & middle-aged parents are a fearful strain on one another'.[49] She would also remember how secretive she had been, and 'how little my parents knew about me & my friends at 14'.[50] Elsewhere, she hinted darkly at torrid sexual passions in her teenage years, saying she was 'always in love with something or somebody' and gave most of her time to 'poetry and desperate love affairs'.[51] 'No need to tell what you know well / about adolescent sex,' she would write, coyly, in 1993.[52] Discussing D.H. Lawrence's *Lady Chatterley's Lover* with a friend in the early 1960s (Gwen 'loved it but thought it funny'), she wondered whether Lawrence 'had a passion for men; he writes about women like a woman'. Without segue, she added: 'I'd love to write a novel about my sixth form year, but nobody would believe it, except the other sixth-formers.'[53]

When she finished primary school, she went on to Brisbane Girls Grammar School. She found it very different from the state schools she had attended. In place of bullying boys, she was surrounded by 'lovely, kind girls'.[54] The school day began with a Bible reading and a hymn, and there were regular assemblies at which the head mistress, the 'formidable' Miss Lilley, lectured the students 'on such topics as behaviour, recognition of outstanding achievements, hard work and community responsibility'.[55] One girl in Gwen's cohort, Joyce Dempsey, also from Toowong, would reflect some seventy-five years later that what she learned at the school was 'very strict obedience' and society 'manners'.[56]

Brisbane Girls Grammar School prefects, 1937
(Gwen Foster second row, first left)

Gwen had no interest in such lessons – nor in much else the school had to teach her. Years later, she would say that she 'resisted formal education': 'I am easily bored. When bored I am extremely mischievous. I was bored for 12 years at school & mischievous all the time.'[57] On her 1935 school report, her form mistress remarked: 'Is working at her favourite subjects only. This will not do.'[58] These subjects included art, French and English. She did not like maths. 'I had to take comfort in mathematical exams from "he that is low need fear no fall,"' she once wrote. 'It has no *content*; I always felt as if I were moving on a spider's web over an abyss.'[59] She also had no interest in sport ('I *hate* team games')[60] and took little part in the school's musical program, pursuing her piano studies privately. In letters written after her school days, she was derisive about Miss Lilley and contemptuous of some of her school fellows, who considered themselves to be of a different social class to the Fosters and did not deign to recognise Gwen outside of school. Yet she did have good friends among her classmates, and was certainly not wholly on the outer scholastically, winning several prizes and even becoming a prefect.

She had great respect for at least two of her teachers: Miss Macmillan, her English teacher, and Miss Cottew, who taught art. Lexie Macmillan was an old school chum of Agnes's who had earned a BA from the University of Queensland and gone on to become Second Mistress at Gwen's school.[61] Gwen admired her calm astringency. Many years later, she wrote a poem in her English teacher's honour for her old school's magazine in which she declared that it was in Miss Macmillan's classes that she 'first learned / to know myself, my fears, hopes and new being.'[62] The poem gives a rare insight into Gwen's school years, depicting her sitting alone during the lunch hour one day, reading Keats under a mango tree. She was 'sighing over/ "All is cold beauty, pain is never done"' when Miss Macmillan appeared. Far from praising her dedication, her teacher mocked her for scoring thick lines under all the heart-rending passages and chided her for spending her time with her nose in a book. Gwen's life lacked 'balance', she pronounced. She should put on her sandshoes and 'get some exercise'.

In later life, Gwen would applaud this deflation of her Romantic sensibilities; she was inclined to laugh at her teenage self for her moody obsession with the Romantics. At the time, though, she thrilled to the works of Keats and Shelley, revelling in their ecstatic highs and lows. She had discovered that it was possible to 'feel' poetry. 'In childhood you enjoy [poetry] simply for its rhythms and its stories,' she once told an interviewer. 'But once it begins to strike you to the heart it's different.'[63] In her teenage years, poetry struck her heart with a vengeance. She feasted on the works of the great English writers of earlier centuries collected in standard texts such as Palgrave's *Golden Treasury* (there was nothing contemporary on the curriculum, and certainly nothing Australian). The influence of their metrical forms, if not their subject matter, was evident in an essay she wrote in fifth form. Addressing the pious theme that 'the path of duty was the way to glory', the essay was written entirely in blank verse, and won her that year's Betty Woolcock Challenge Cup, a school prize aimed at encouraging students 'to be creative and innovative in the writing of English'. As a pastiche of the classic nineteenth-century narrative poem, Gwen's piece is astonishingly accomplished: 130 lines of flawless iambic pentameter, a tour-de-force for a sixteen-year-old. The content is less impressive: a hotchpotch of idealised English history, Christian piety and nineteenth-century colonial sentiment that shows her mastery of the dominant discourses of the day but gives no hint of her later wicked subversion of them. Her impressive ability to assimilate and reproduce the style and rhythms of other writers – a gift that would underlie her later brilliant parodies – is very much on display.

But for all her skill at composition, Gwen's favourite subject was not English but art. She fell in love with the visual arts at the same time and in somewhat the same way that she fell in love with her art teacher, Vera Cottew. She was twelve when she met Miss Cottew, and felt at once – or so she would later say – a 'very deep affinity' with her.[64] Vera was a brisk, merry, bright-eyed thirty-year-old artist with a birdlike air, a no-nonsense manner and a quick, satirical sense of humour.[65] Gwen's classes with her were a revelation: 'From the day I walked into her studio . . . my way of looking at the natural world was re-formed.'[66] 'She took infinite pleasure in the small details of the world,' Gwen would remember, decades later. 'Nothing was ever dull to her; we could be standing waiting a long time for our tram on some boring ill-lit stop on a cloudy night, and she'd find subtleties in the monotone darkness and half-seen shapes.'[67] Vera's ability to see the familiar in fresh ways transformed Gwen's perceptions; what she saw through Vera's eyes was the texture of art in the ordinary world. Her later poems are full of moments when Vera – echoing Maud – commands her to 'look'. 'See how these eggs / marry colours of earth and stone,' Vera says of a plover's nest in 'Driving Home'. 'See how / light speaks always of *now*,' she urges in 'Nightfall', drawing her pupil's attention to the fruit and flowers she has arranged for a still life.[68]

The relationship defied categorisation. Gwen idolised her teacher, bringing her flowers every day, 'like a mad secretary bringing in a flower to the boss'.[69] Vera seems to have welcomed both the flowers and the 'crazy love' that prompted them.[70] Outside of the classroom, she offered Gwen her friendship, and they spent a lot of time together, sometimes alone, sometimes with their respective families or Vera's many other friends. Vera lived at Milton, adjacent to Auchenflower, in a house she had built next door to her parents' home. She and her mother were quickly adopted by Agnes and the rest of the Fosters, and the two families went to movies and concerts together and, later, on seaside holidays to Redcliffe or Yeppoon. Agnes, Gwen and Vera even went to Sydney together. In Brisbane, Gwen attended Vera's lectures on art for the Brisbane Women's Club and her exhibitions with other Queensland artists, including Vida Lahey. She would later say that Vera was 'the most delightful companion I've ever known'.[71]

Vera Cottew in 1943

It is difficult to know how Vera regarded Gwen; their voluminous correspondence has not survived.[72] It was certainly not unusual for Vera to befriend her students,[73] and no one seemed to see anything untoward in this relationship between a young teenager and a woman in her thirties. In letters and poems, Gwen made no secret of the glimmer of the erotic in her passion for Vera. 'Past and Present' tells of an evening they spent fishing together on the Redcliff pier. When Gwen jagged her finger on a fishhook, Vera seized her hand and sucked the wound. The two women then sat hand in hand on the pier 'until darkness fell', consecrating the moment. 'I've been thinking lately about the nature of love,' Gwen wrote to a friend apropos of another Cottew poem, 'Dust to Dust'. 'As I grow older I find it more mysterious than ever; I dream a good deal about a teacher (Vera Cottew) who did more than anyone to find what was stable in my adolescent flux & help me preserve it.' 'Dust to Dust' was based on a dream in which Gwen waited 'near the fire station in Brisbane on a hot night for Vera . . . I saw her face (which I find hard to remember now) as it was when I was a schoolgirl'. The poem reworks phrases from John Donne's most erotic of love poems to depict their meeting: 'So, so, resume our last / rejoicing kiss. Your eyes / flecked with my image stare / in wonder through my own.' In the dream, a steam train emerged from the underground station as they talked, 'puffing out sparks which ignited the whole sky'. This became, in the poem, an ecstatic rain of fire.[74]

◆ ◆ ◆

Not even Vera's presence, however, could make Gwen want to stay at school. At the end of sixth form, she was awarded her senior certificate, but her exam results were uneven. She received As for English and ancient history, Bs for French, modern history and art, and a C for Latin. Maths, she failed.[75] This meant that she did not qualify for university, for which passes in both English and maths were required. She could have returned to school to get the requisite grades, but she had no desire to pursue further study. She knew exactly what she wanted to do with her life, and it did not require a university education: she was going to be a musician.[76]

3

Girl Genius

Once she played for Rubinstein, who yawned.

Gwen Harwood, 'Suburban Sonnet'

TOWARDS THE END OF 1937, AS GWEN WAS PREPARING FOR her senior exams, her piano teacher pulled off a marvellous coup. The great Polish pianist Artur Rubinstein was visiting Brisbane as part of his world tour, and Hardy Gerhardy had managed to arrange for his prize pupil to play for the legendary artist. It was a potentially career-making opportunity for Gwen: if she could win Rubinstein's approval, doors would open – or so she hoped. On an October afternoon after school, she met Gerhardy in the city and they went together to the celebrated Bellevue Hotel on George Street, where the visiting pianist was staying. According to Gwen's later account, Gerhardy cornered Rubinstein in the hotel lounge and presented his pupil as 'a girl genius'.[1] Rubinstein, himself a former child prodigy, was not enthusiastic. '[He] looked with distaste at my school uniform and said in foreign tones "I haff only a few minutes before dinner,"' Gwen wrote. Undaunted, she sat down at the grand piano and began to play the Bach *Chromatic Fantasia and Fugue* that had garnered so much praise at her student recital the year before. Once she was well launched, she risked a quick glance over her shoulder to see how he was taking it. To her dismay, he was less than enthralled. 'Out of the corner of my right eye [I] saw Artur yawning repeatedly through the recitatives. As I started the fugue he gave a gigantic yawn & looked at his watch. Before the last chord had died away he was making for the dining room saying over his shoulder, "Thank you very much, lovely, beautiful, nice."'

Gwen was disconcerted. Until then, her playing had been almost universally praised. It was her first real intimation that, in her own words, she 'wasn't as good as [she] thought'.[2] Twenty years later, she would write a poem in which a woman's descent into dull familial servitude begins when Rubinstein yawns.[3]

Gerhardy, however, insisted that the 'audition' had been a triumph, and the following day, *The Courier Mail* ran a story under the headline 'Promising Young Pianist: Mr Rubinstein Impressed'. 'Mr. Rubinstein told Miss

Foster he was impressed by her technique and her artistic sensibilities,' the paper reported, 'and considered it would be well worth her while to study abroad.'[4] In Gwen's view, this was all spin from her press-savvy teacher, who reported Rubinstein's comments as 'lavish praise all-round'. In any case, she was already planning, in a vague way, to go to Europe at some point to further her studies – a necessary rite of passage for Australian musicians. For now, she was more than happy to keep studying and performing in Brisbane while she saved her pennies.[5] She was finished with Gerhardy, however. She was coming to understand that there was more to musicianship than agile fingers, and set her sights on a quite different style of teacher. Her choice fell on Dr Robert Dalley-Scarlett, 'a sensible [man] of gentle character (he used to cry)' who was also a distinguished composer, conductor and scholar – and a whirlwind of musical energy.

Dalley-Scarlett had moved to Brisbane from Grafton in 1919, at the age of thirty-two, to work as organist and choirmaster at St Andrew's Presbyterian Church in Creek Street. Over the next decade, he set about transforming Brisbane's musical life, staging Queensland's first performance of Bach's *St Matthew's Passion* and launching what was billed as the first Bach festival in the southern hemisphere.[6] In the early 1930s, having moved to All Saints' Anglican Church on Wickham Terrace, he founded the Brisbane Handel Society and embarked on the mammoth task of broadcasting Handel's complete works on ABC Radio.[7] He taught both piano and organ, performed his own music, worked indefatigably as a conductor and director, and took an active role in the Brisbane social scene. As well as his musical gifts, he was well versed in literature and poetry, spoke several languages and had 'a genius for attracting people'.[8] Though he was reported to be 'easygoing and humorous', in front of an orchestra he was irascible and exacting – just like the great composers in Gwen's childhood book. In fact, with his passions, his tears and his temperament, he was very much Gwen's idea of a musical genius.

In appearance, however, he did not at all resemble her hero, the wild-haired, beetle-browed Beethoven. Tubby and bald, his bare pate surrounded by 'a long fringe which curl[ed] behind his ears and just above his coat collar', he wore horn-rimmed spectacles and his mouth was 'faintly ringed with nicotine' from the 'pungent cigarettes' he unceasingly smoked. Gwen's brother, Joe, likened him to Mr Magoo.[9]

For Gwen, his eccentricity was a sign of his genius; she adored him at once. She first went to his studio on Wharf Street in early 1938, eager to begin the next phase of her music training now that school was behind her for good. The studio consisted of two rooms over a chemist directly opposite the fire station, from whence the fire trucks would issue day and night with a great clanging of bells. In old age, Gwen would remember with infinite fondness the 'dusty palms, an old veranda stacked with lovebirds in cages & myself waiting there for my piano lesson while a bass sang "Those are Grecian ghosts, that in battle were slain, and unburied remain . . ."'[10] Ever after, the sound of a bass voice singing Handel would take her back to that time and place, and to her own feeling of 'intense happiness' when she knew that she was 'going to play well and please [Bob]'.[11] In this studio, soon after she became his student, the seventeen-year-old Gwen and her fifty-year-old teacher became lovers.

According to Gwen, she seduced Bob. Yet Dalley-Scarlett had a reputation for preying on young women. One Dalley-Scarlett scholar recalled that local musicians had remarked on his 'wandering eyes and hands'. It was rumoured that 'if you were a younger female and had a reason to visit him in his city teaching studio, you had to have your wits about you so as not to get caught in a compromising situation'.[12] By today's standards, this would be considered sexual harassment, or even assault. But in the 1930s, it was seen as very much in the nature of things for highly respectable men to grope or proposition young women. Gwen's attitude to such behaviour, for much of her life, ranged from good-humoured tolerance to high-spirited encouragement.[13]

Though Gwen did not know it, Dalley-Scarlett had form when it came to affairs with his students. His first marriage had ended when his wife, Gertrude, discovered that he was involved with a local teacher who taught him Latin and Greek in return for music lessons. When Gertrude confronted him, he apparently told her that he needed 'someone younger to inspire me'. He expected his wife to accept the affair, and when she left him, he refused to pay maintenance to her and their two boys on the grounds that he was perfectly willing to support them, provided they returned to live with him. In the subsequent court hearing, a cache of Bob's letters to his paramour were produced, written in Latin and full of extravagant endearments and sexual innuendo.[14] To a reader of a more liberal age, they suggest a man of deeply romantic temperament carried away by his own thrilling rhetoric. To the Grafton magistrate, however, they were evidence that Dalley-Scarlett was 'either a libertine or a person suffering from a diseased mind'.

Gwen was friendly with Bob's second wife, Joyce Dalley-Scarlett, a well-known Brisbane soprano who had once been Bob's singing student. Joyce was one of Agnes's musical friends, and Gwen had often been to her house as a child.[15] Gwen occasionally went to concerts with Joyce,[16] and the two women kept in touch all their lives. Whether Joyce knew about Gwen's affair with her husband is not clear. A friend of Bob's once told Joyce that he knew 'things [had] not always been easy' in their marriage, but that she had triumphed by learning 'to cope with genius'.[17] The idea that a woman could find her life's purpose in ministering to a great artist was not unusual at the time. Elaine Simpson, who married the American poet John Berryman in 1942, summed up such attitudes: 'To be the "helpmate" (wasn't that the word we undergraduates used in the student cafeteria, talking of such things?) . . . would be the most interesting and useful way for a woman to spend her life.'[18] Joyce may well have felt that being 'helpmate' to Bob required a willingness to look the other way.[19]

For her part, Gwen seems to have felt that she was doing Joyce no wrong by sleeping with her husband. Gwen would always hold that extramarital affairs, no matter how strongly felt, were nothing to end a marriage over.[20] She had already had some experience of the sexual predations of married men. Mixing with musicians at various functions, as she did throughout her teens, as well as seeking out musical celebrities for their imprimatur, she often found herself fending off unwanted sexual advances.[21] She was resigned to this, and even, on occasion, amused and gratified by it, regaling friends with stories of being leered at by lecherous celebrities.[22] It upset her only when she felt that she was being seen solely as a nubile young thing, rather than as a fellow musician.[23]

She seems to have told no one about her relationship with Dalley-Scarlett until some thirty years after Bob's death, when she was in her seventies. In letters to Greg Kratzmann, putative biographer and good friend,[24] she described the affair as 'one of the most joyful experiences of my life', dwelling fondly on 'the sheer pleasure of those years'.[25] It seems clear that she was not in love with Bob; she had no secret dreams of running off with him or becoming his third wife. She was simply revelling in the pleasures of a sexual relationship with a man she greatly admired. The affair was largely carried on in Bob's 'pleasant studio', which conveniently included a private room 'with shower!!' Contraception was supplied by the obliging chemist downstairs, a friend of Dalley-Scarlett's.[26] As teacher and student, they had 'every reason' to be immured there. 'Sometimes we'd just sit and listen to records (78s of course) eating sandwiches and fruit,' she remembered. 'Sometimes we'd go in at night and do a bit of work on the ABC scores, then go for a walk and talk idly about books, music, painting, language.' She imagined it going on happily forever.

Bob's view of the relationship is difficult to gauge. No correspondence between them survives, though according to Gwen, she wrote Bob 'long extravagant letters' when she was away on family holidays in Rockhampton, Yeppoon or Redcliffe.[27] Ever cautious, Bob insisted they encrypt their communications, and they devised a 'musical code in which chords represented letters – it looked like a harmonic exercise'. It was almost certainly less decodable than the Latin that Bob had used with his Grafton mistress. It seems reasonable to assume that he was as romantic in his letters to Gwen as he had been in those earlier epistles, in which he wrote that his heart 'sang for joy' to hear from his lover and that he had 'kissed all over what you had written'.[28] Gwen certainly felt that he was besotted with her. He composed an *Andante & Fughetta* for her eighteenth birthday,[29] and gave her gifts of books and music. In her seventies, she still had a copy of Thomas Aquinas's writings that Bob had inscribed to her on 2 March 1940. 'We had already been lovers for two years,' she wrote to Kratzmann, 'and he was still trying to please me.'[30]

◆ ◆ ◆

By 1940, however, her romantic interest in Bob was waning. In retrospect, she felt that he had found this hard. 'I suppose Bob knew he would have to surrender me sooner or later, but it must have been terrible for him,' she wrote. 'Her eyes now see him *old* . . .' The phrase is an allusion to one of her poems, 'The Silver Swan', which features the irascible Professor Kröte, a middle-aged pianist who struggles to make a living teaching music to children and playing at suburban soirees. In this poem, Kröte runs into a former student of his in a museum, a 'brilliant girl' now transformed into a 'shabby housewife'. She had been in love with him in her youth: 'I'd often get my fingering wrong / just to get you to hold my hand,' she confesses.[31] But now she is over her 'schoolgirl crush', as Kröte realises with some dismay: 'Those eyes, astonished blue, / now find him old.'

Robert Dalley-Scarlett was certainly one of the models for Kröte, along with Hardy Gerhardy. But he was also an influence on another of Gwen's fictional characters, Professor Eisenbart, the nuclear physicist who features in a series of poems she wrote in the 1950s. Eisenbart is not a musician, but he is a distinguished figure in his local community, and he does have an affair with a much younger woman, a redheaded pianist he meets at a school speech day.[32] In the poem that depicts their meeting, 'Prize-Giving', he is the guest of honour, seated on the stage during proceedings and charged with giving out the awards. As he assumes a pose of dignified gravitas, he sees a girl grinning up at him from the auditorium, 'her hand bent / under her chin in mockery of his own'. This cheeky young woman turns out to be the winner of the music prize, a 'cup / of silver chased with curious harps', not entirely unlike the Woolcock Challenge Cup Gwen once received. When the girl comes up to collect her prize, Eisenbart is thrown off balance by the sexual charge between them; as he takes her hand, its 'voltage' flings him 'from his calm age and power'. He is undone by her, while she – transformed from 'casual schoolgirl' to musical 'master' when she sits at the piano – remains entirely composed. Throughout the Eisenbart poems, the professor's young 'mistress' seems to have the upper hand, keeping her cool when he rants and poses and tries to bully her, and making gentle fun of his pretensions. However accomplished he is as a scientist, he is no master of love or sex.[33]

Both of Gwen's fictional professors, the musician and the physicist, are stern, prickly, egotistical and, at times, comic. She seems to regard them tenderly as well as satirically, identifying with them as well as chiding them, challenging them, holding them up to ridicule. The tenderness seems to have its origins in her relationship with Bob, whom she loved even as she cast a disconcertingly sharp eye on his pomposities and self-regard.

◆ ◆ ◆

Professionally, Dalley-Scarlett was a poor mentor to Gwen. He convinced her that she did not have what it took to be a concert pianist, telling her 'firmly' that she 'would never make it'.[34] Nevertheless, she studied with him for her Associate Diploma Trinity College London (ATCL), a recital diploma which would certify her both to teach and to perform. She also talked him into teaching her composition. In stories of her youthful musical ambitions, Gwen never mentions a desire to be a composer, but in her late teens and early twenties it seems to have been an identity she coveted; when her very first poem was published in 1944, she described herself in her author bio as a 'pianist, organist and composer'.[35] In letters from her early twenties, she makes casual mention of setting to music some poems written by a friend, and of being asked by a singer friend to compose a song for him.[36]

The autobiographical 'A Simple Story' features a young composer who takes a composition of hers to a visiting conductor in his hotel room. Instead of engaging with her work, however, he makes a grab for her, putting 'one hand on the manuscript / and the other down my dress'. When he does consent to read through her 'crude sonata', he dismisses it with a patronising 'That's *lovely*, dear', putting the score down 'in a way that made it clear / that I was no composer.'

To friends, she identified the visiting celebrity as trombonist Percy Code, conductor of the Sydney Symphony Orchestra, who made frequent visits to Brisbane in the 1930s as guest conductor of the Brisbane Symphony.[37] Groping aside, the story is a rerun of her earlier encounter with Rubinstein: once again, a visiting celebrity becomes the ultimate authority on her musical ability, and thus the arbiter of her fate, and once again, his ruling is not in her favour. She does not seem to have suspected that an ingrained sexism may have been at play in these dismissals of her work. Some years later, though, she would question – and sometimes vigorously reject – similarly negative judgements of her poetry that seemed to turn on her gender.

As well as studying piano, organ and composition with Bob, Gwen also acted as his assistant and general factotum, roughing out piano accompaniments for his compositions, writing out orchestral parts and copying music by hand. Indeed, she 'got very good at writing fast legible music', and was able to earn some income performing this service for other musicians. She also took on a handful of piano students of her own – 'a few children who came for lessons after school'.[38] At the same time, she was learning to sing. Bewitched by the 'magnificent bass' who sang Handel in Bob's studio in the hour before her own lesson, she 'nagged a score & a promise of singing in the Handel Society out of Dr D-S'.[39] As part of the Society choir (she was an alto), she performed under Bob's direction at numerous concerts and broadcast performances. Her lifelong passion for Handel, and particularly the oratorio *Israel in Egypt* ('the greatest choral work ever written'),[40] which the Society performed in the Brisbane City Hall in 1939,[41] dates from this time.

She loved being part of a choir, and found Dalley-Scarlett a delightfully cantankerous musical director. She remembered being 'called trembling from the altos' to fill in when the pianist was away, with 'Dr Dalley-Scarlett whacking the lid of the piano with the rolled-up *Women's Weekly* he used

for conducting, growling out various parts as the choristers faltered –
"There WAS not ONE, not ONE, there WAS not ONE, not one of them
LEFT, count you fool . . ."[42] It was not just Dalley-Scarlett who delighted
her. The choir itself was a mini-community she found absurdly, hilariously
'quarrelsome': jealous and competitive, rippling with in-jokes, arcing with
sexual tension. A guest tenor would ambush her in the corridors of the
ABC to kiss her, 'importuning me with his blue, most innocent blue eyes'.[43]
And she would always remember 'little Leo Callaghan, bespectacled & very
earnest, singing "My lust shall be satisfied upon them", while Reg Best, a
Rabelaisian bass, grinned at the women's ranks'.[44]

◆ ◆ ◆

Gwen completed her ACTL in May 1940, just a month before her twentieth birthday, winning a silver medal for her outstanding results.[45] A week
later she performed solo at City Hall, playing the Sonatina in C Major by a
new Russian composer, Kabalevsky, and 'The King's Hunting Jig' by John
Bull. *The Courier Mail* reported admiringly that the nineteen-year-old Miss
Foster had 'an artist's sense of the piano', able to ally 'polished technique to
warmth in interpretation'.[46] The following week, she played at the Trinity
College prize ceremony. The Trinity examiner, Adolph Mann, was effusive
in his praise. 'Seldom have we the opportunity of listening to a performance
so consistently well rendered – of so high a level of proficiency – as that just
given by the prize winners,'[47] he assured concertgoers. It was a wonderful
evening for Gwen. 'I remember my father standing at the back of the hall
smiling and clapping (he had come in late, just in time to hear me) and
looking radiantly around telling the people near him I was his daughter,'
she would write years later.[48]

Soon afterwards, she climbed the stairs to Bob's studio one afternoon
to find her own name on the door beside his: 'only painted metal, true (his
was brass), but MINE: Gwendoline N. Foster A.Mus.A, A.T.C.L., Piano
and Theory.'[49] No longer mere student, she had been promoted to assistant
teacher. It was a thrill, but she was already seeking broader horizons.

4

Always in Love

. . . not how, but that I love
beyond thought or knowledge, turning to your face
with profound instinct as earth's creatures move
from night's cold shadow into sunlit space.
Gwen Harwood, 'Late Autumn, Sydney'

ALL SAINTS' ANGLICAN CHURCH ON WICKHAM TERRACE IS A small, Gothic construction made of Queensland porphyry and sandstone, with a gabled roof, a carved bellcote and lancet windows featuring some of the oldest stained glass in Brisbane. It stands on a tiny wedge of land in the inner city, a fairytale of the past amid a jumble of mismatched high-rise. When it was built in 1869, it was surrounded by dense scrub; the first parishioners had to trek through the bush to attend services.[1] But in the 1930s, when Gwen first encountered it, it sat sedately behind a row of palm trees at the junction of three broad streets lined with shops and offices. Beside it was the rectory, a substantial two-storey building housing the vicar and his curates, as well as a church hall of rendered brick where Girl Guides and Boy Scouts met, plays were mounted and dances were held. The whole precinct was a hub of activity, a bustling community where idealistic young people congregated, charitable causes were championed, families worshipped and music was made. The church itself was the highest of High Anglican, with all the ritual and pomp Gwen had yearned for as a child, when she was cruelly – in her view – forced to make do with the 'cold-blooded' Presbyterians.[2] Here, among the incense and candles and plainchant, the eighteen-year-old Gwen found God.

She would later downplay her religious 'phase'. 'I really had a Great Affair with [Jesus]!' she confessed to a friend. 'But I am as ashamed of it as if it were an illegitimate child.'[3] To another friend, she admitted that she 'once joined the C of E of my own accord,' but insisted that it was due to her 'mad passion for a clergyman.'[4] The clergyman in question was a twenty-three-year-old curate, Peter Bennie, who arrived from Melbourne in 1939 with master's degrees in theology and literature, and a brilliant wit that dazzled the young Gwen. She fell in love with Peter, she would say, 'in the way one can do perhaps only once in a lifetime, since one is utterly changed by the experience itself'. For the next five years, he occupied 'all her thought, affection, hope and longing'.[5] Indeed, she would later insist that her 'grand passion' for him never really faded, remaining 'untouched by time, distance, age, decay'.[6] Her belief in this great love – 'I have never felt separate from him'[7] – would become one of the central mythologies of her life.

Gwen Foster, 1940

Under the influence of not only Peter Bennie but also the All Saints rector, the charismatic Reverend Bates, she began to take instruction to enter the church. She did not scruple to take her theological learning home, making mealtimes 'hideous' with her attempts to convert her cynical parents.[8] In the first flush of her fervour, she took every opportunity to prove the existence of God to hapless interlocutors 'by St Thomas Aquinas's approved methods'.[9] She even tried to turn her bedroom into a monastic cell, 'with icons and other paraphernalia'.[10] In short, she was as smitten with Christianity as she was with Peter. In October 1939, a few months after her nineteenth birthday, she was baptised and confirmed in the Anglican faith.

Her new-found religiosity did not, at first, interfere with her relation-ship with Bob Dalley-Scarlett, which had been going on for more than a year by this time. Nevertheless, he was somewhat dismayed by this development. He had himself introduced Gwen to All Saints, which was just across the road from his studio, giving her organ lessons there in the hope of making her his assistant organist when she was good enough. But Bob's delight at the chance to have the occasional Sunday off was tempered when he realised that in the new curate he had a serious rival for Gwen's affections. Soon after Peter arrived, Gwen began to take every opportunity to walk over to All Saints to 'practise the organ (hoping for a chance meeting with Peter) or call at the rectory for Sunday's hymns (hoping Peter would answer the door) or walk through the churchyard on my way to town (hoping to meet Peter)'.[11] Bob watched his protégé's growing intimacy with the curate with deep misgiving, though he was unable to intervene. As Gwen would later reflect, he must have known he would lose her eventually – that she would one day meet someone she would want to marry. Even so, he was far from reconciled to the prospect.

At first, it seemed that Bob had little to fear from Peter in regard to marriage. Though the young cleric was attracted to Gwen, he made it abundantly clear that he had no intention of marrying anyone. He was enthusiastically committed to the Anglo-Catholic doctrine of the celibate priesthood, and liked to give impassioned disquisitions from the pulpit on the moral and ethical imperative of clerical celibacy. So confident was he in his resolve that he felt no need to hold himself aloof from his female parishioners. Indeed, Gwen would later say that all her friends had been in love with him – and that he flirted with them all, making each one feel she was the object of his special regard.[12] Peter was not handsome; years later, students at the university college where he was rector would nickname him 'The Toad'. But he was an excellent public speaker, an accomplished footballer and a talented scholar[13] who exuded confidence. His sermons, Gwen would remember, were 'very wild and heroic and poetical',[14] and there was virtually nothing he could not discuss with energy and conviction. To Gwen, he seemed to stream with 'sexual radiance'.[15] While he did not share her anarchic sense of humour – his jokes, she would later say, were 'almost always scatological'[16] – he knew how to laugh. He also knew how to drink, a quality Gwen appreciated in a man. Even his amphibian look enchanted her; ever after, she would have a soft spot for men who looked like frogs.

While Peter's vocation was the church, his passion was literature. Gwen would later say that for her, he was like a 'one-man literature course'.[17] Before she met him, her literary knowledge was largely limited to the English classics: the likes of Shakespeare, Milton, Keats and Tennyson. Peter, however, was interested in contemporary writers, particularly those in the avant-garde, who were changing the shape of literature: Dostoevsky, T.S. Eliot, the scandalous James Joyce. It was another kind of conversion for Gwen: 'At one go I suddenly realised the great change that had come into English,' she would say. All at once, literature seemed the most exciting thing in the world, surpassing even music in its attractions. New poetry, plays and novels from Britain and Europe were challenging the old, dull conventions of writing and thinking, and Gwen was quick to respond to the whiff of rebellion and anarchy. She read G.M. Hopkins, along with Eliot and Joyce, and turned to Peter for an explanation of 'some of the difficulties that I found in it'. Delighted to have an acolyte, he gave her 'a detailed commentary' on *The Waste Land* and a 'series of lectures' on *Ulysses* during long sessions in his red-curtained study and leisurely walks home to Grimes Street.[18] She drank it all in.

Ulysses particularly attracted Gwen because it had been banned in Australia on the grounds of obscenity. She was thrilled to be able to buy a copy (in a brief period when the ban was temporarily lifted), considering the book a kind of talisman against the staid values of 1940s Australian society. She took to reading it – a mute provocation – in the All Saints churchyard between services, and was almost triumphant when one day an old parishioner noticed what she was reading and pounced: 'He wrenched the book from my hands and flung it on the ground: "Filth, filth!" Peter Bennie came to my rescue. A work of art, he said . . . It was an almost biblical scene: the philistine, the young prophet, the woman taken in pornography.'[19]

Peter saw himself as a writer, and was busily producing not only sermons and essays but also poems. It was Gwen's first exposure to a contemporary poet other than the sentimental or humorous kind, and it made her realise that great poets need not belong solely to past centuries and distant continents but could be working here and now, in Brisbane. She began to think of writing poems herself, along with plays and stories, to win Peter's admiration. She soon put pen to paper, and took the results – her 'first derivative efforts' – to him for his judgement.[20] He was not complimentary, but she took it on the chin. His critiques 'hurt', she would later confess, but 'did me inestimable good'. Even then, she preferred a strenuous attack to the 'That's lovely, dear' style of criticism; it meant she was at least being taken seriously.

But though she was on the side of the rebels when it came to literature, she was happily allying herself with a very traditional form of Christianity. The All Saints community practised all the Catholic sacraments, including penance (also known as confession), and fasted before receiving Holy Communion. Modern music was eschewed in favour of plain chant. Reverend Bates insisted his parishioners attend both morning mass and Evensong on Sundays, as well as at least one mass during the week.[21] Gwen often rose before dawn to go to weekday mass, and attended both high mass and evening benediction on Sundays, even if she wasn't required to play. She found these services moving and powerful, and especially loved to participate in the church's many feast days. In one letter, she spoke of her elation when singing the Athanasian Creed in procession: 'It filled me with joy to see the priests walking round solemnly vested in white, and the servers with lights and incense going before.'[22] The liturgical music was irresistible; years after she had lost her faith, she would say that 'as a musician' she was 'totally given over to the splendours of the mass.'[23]

Her attraction to All Saints was also about the sense of community she found there. She met many young people, 'theological students, university students, teachers, public servants, secretaries', all of whom were seekers in some sense. Many became good friends.[24] 'We were drawn together not by religion but by affinities of temperament,' she would later say. 'After Benediction we would go down to Basil's coffee shop where you could get a cup of excellent coffee for fourpence and endless subsequent cups for twopence.' There they would canvass such fascinating subjects as 'the Great Russians, modern poetry, the late quartets, Bartók, and philosophy'. They were earnest and idealistic, full of schemes for the establishment of 'an ideal society', and argued 'endlessly about the nature of the world'. They pored over the works of theologians such as Maritain and Gilson, philosophers such as Kant and novelists such as Dostoevsky, whose mystical Father Zosima in *The Brothers Karamazov* inspired them to try monasticism. As the evening grew late, they would often repair to Gwen's home in Auchenflower, where they would be welcomed by the ever-hospitable Agnes, make themselves a late supper and listen to gramophone records. Ever after, this would be Gwen's ideal of social life: a group of like-minded friends arguing about literature, art and philosophy in an easy, relaxed environment, buoyed by good food, music and laughter.

◆ ◆ ◆

Even as she was drawn ever more strongly to All Saints, Gwen continued her musical activities. By this time, however, she knew that she would not be able to go to Europe to study music – or for any other reason. In September 1939, Australia had once again followed Mother England into a world war, and Gwen, like everyone else, had to put her plans on hold for an indefinite – and seemingly interminable – period.

For the first year or so, the war seemed a far-distant thing, and Australians accepted their prime minister's assurance that on the home front, life would continue to be 'business as usual'.[25] Certainly Gwen's life went on very much as before. Her father was too old to enlist and her brother too young, and those of her friends who had signed up had not yet seen conflict. Her mother and grandmother, however, sprang instantly into action. 'My Granny was in her element again, organizing entertainments for the gallant boys, and my mother dashed from committee to committee,'[26] Gwen wrote. Agnes was a kind of charitable whirlwind, devoting herself to the Queensland branch of the Australian Comforts Fund while opening her home to friends, relations, stray acquaintances and friends of friends with unhesitating generosity. Gwen would remember coming home many an evening to find she had been turfed out of her room – a woman on her way to farewell her soldier-husband needed a night's accommodation in Brisbane, or a sailor on leave had no one to take him in. Often she woke in the morning to find random servicemen sleeping on mattresses on the lounge room floor.[27]

She continued to study and teach music, and, increasingly, to work as a wedding organist in churches around Brisbane. Here, her slight stature told against her; formidable mothers of the bride, confronted with a slip of a girl, would demand to see the real organist.[28] Gwen was more than capable of standing her ground, however, adopting her haughtiest 'Young Genius' mien or her angriest 'Disillusioned Musician' scowl.[29] She enjoyed playing at weddings; it gave her the chance to observe different social scenes, and the money was good.

Gwen also attended art exhibitions and concerts with Vera Cottew, as well as accompanying her on walks and drives. Just as Peter was introducing Gwen to modern literature, Vera was introducing her to modern art. Even before the war, refugees from Europe had begun arriving in Brisbane, and Vera had many friends among them. In her company, Gwen 'began to hear the languages I didn't know, and to hear about people's childhoods utterly different from mine'.[30] Through Austrian friends of Vera's, she discovered contemporary artworks by Munch, Redon and Heckel, utterly strange to her eyes. They changed her sense of the world. 'The haunting prints from Redon's dreams took hold of my imagination and led me towards intense and radical new feelings,' she wrote. 'I lost my old certainties.'[31] The Austrians themselves seemed to possess an enigmatic wisdom that made her feel like an unschooled child. They 'treated me kindly but distantly', she would write, 'as though trying to explain civilization to a tent-dweller. They spoke English well, but in short oracular sentences, with much thoughtful nodding: "But my dear, we know that space and time are not *facts*." "My dear, the most essential colour is *black*."'[32] These hints of entirely new ways of looking at things exhilarated her.

Though her professional life continued to revolve around Bob's studio, Gwen was spending more and more time with Peter. The curate had become a regular visitor at the Foster home, spending many evenings with Gwen 'listening to music and having supper with the family'.[33] Bob was 'furious' about this, but powerless to intervene: 'He couldn't tell my mother not to invite Peter nor stop me from being at home.' Moreover, Gwen's interest in writing was beginning to outstrip her interest in music. She was working on stories and plays, and sharing all she wrote with Peter. When he went back to Melbourne to see his family over Christmas in 1940, Gwen followed him, taking a room in a guesthouse near Fitzroy Gardens in January 1941.[34] She spent her days visiting Peter, walking in the gardens, attending mass at St Patrick's and writing. 'I was writing a play called *The Sparks Fly Upwards*, full of men with bears and suicidal photographers, and very Dostoevskian,' she would recall. Being with Peter gave the whole experience a golden glow. 'In the evenings I used to sit in the Fitzroy gardens until it was quite late. . . . How lovely it was!'[35] More than fifty years later, Peter's sister would recall the 'redheaded girl who came to see you': 'You both talked to each other incessantly about poetry. I have never forgotten her vividness.'[36]

Shortly after her return to Brisbane, Gwen ended her relationship with Bob. Because their professional lives were so entwined, the split caused serious disruption for them both. Bob decided to leave teaching altogether, giving up his studio for a full-time job with the ABC as a presenter, arranger and conductor,[37] which meant that Gwen lost not only her teacher but also her teaching work. Bob also left his job at All Saints, moving to St Benedict's Catholic Church. This was a happier change for Gwen, as she was able to step into his shoes at All Saints, becoming one of only a hand-ful of female church organists at the time.[38] Her long-term future, however, remained shrouded in uncertainty. The desire of her heart was to marry Peter, but that was out of the question. Given his praise of the celibate life as the purest and best vocation, she began to wonder whether she, too, should embrace celibacy. In the full flush of her new-found faith, it seemed entirely possible she was being called to the consecrated life.

5

Blessed Gwendolina

While studying for my music teacher's diploma I got myself accepted
as deputy organist at a very high Church of England (about 20 ft
above street level on the built-up side) and began wondering whether
I shouldn't make a great success as Mother Superior of the Franciscan
Convent in our parish.
Gwen Harwood, Letter to Edwin Tanner, 26 May 1958

GWENDOLINE, B[lesse]d. Patron of telephonists. Mart. 1943 . . .
Gwendolina.
Gwen Harwood, Letter to Tony Riddell, *Blessed City*, p. 34

WHEN GWEN ANNOUNCED TO HER PARENTS THAT SHE wanted to enter the local Anglican convent, they were appalled. Despite their daughter's best efforts, Agnes and Joe had remained 'violently anti-clerical', with a Protestant suspicion of religious orders.[1] But in any case, they simply could not see their lively, rebellious daughter as a nun. She must have seemed to them to be possessed by a kind of madness.

As she was under twenty-one, she needed parental permission, and they refused to give it. Instead, they showered her with gifts, hoping she would abandon the scheme. 'Books, clothes, records, pictures, tickets for concerts – everything they could think of, they gave me to try to "make me happy"', Gwen wrote, 'and drive away my thoughts of leaving.'[2] Far from being tempted, Gwen was outraged that her parents would attempt to stand in her way. How could they not see that testing her vocation was 'a necessary thing' for her to do?[3] The atmosphere turned poisonous, incessant arguments leaving the family home 'simply strewn with wreckage'. 'Peace departed from us,' Gwen recalled gloomily.[4] But she would not back down. This was a matter of principle; it would be morally wrong, she insisted, for her to abandon 'an essential experience' simply to keep her parents happy.[5] The ongoing conflict took its toll, however.

A couple of years later, she would write a story about a young man who wants nothing more than to travel to Germany, which he feels is his spiritual home.[6] His mother, however, cannot bear to lose him and uses all her powers of emotional manipulation to get him to stay. Unable to withstand her tears, the young man gives in, resigning himself to an empty life. It is a fictionalised version of Gwen's own situation[7] in which her avatar's sacrifice of his dearest desire is depicted as little short of tragedy. For Gwen, there was no question of capitulating. In mid-1941 she turned twenty-one, and two months later, on a bright Saturday in mid-August, she packed her things and took herself off to St Clare's convent in neighbouring Toowong.

The Daughters of St Clare had been founded eleven years earlier by Reverend Bates, who was eager to establish Anglican religious communities for both women and men in Brisbane.[8] He had spent time in a monastery in England testing his own vocation, but had determined that his calling was properly to the priesthood. Nevertheless, he was adept at fostering vocations among his youthful parishioners. Gwen knew several young men studying theology with a view to a church career and a number of women giving earnest thought to joining a religious order.[9] Gwen would later joke that ambition led her to the convent: she had seen herself as a church reformer, leading a community of women as their all-powerful Mother Abbess. But there is no doubt that at the time, she sincerely believed she may have been meant for religious life. She had found in Christianity a sense of peace and healing, a 'release from my stormy adolescent troubles'.[10]

Exactly why she needed peace – the precise nature of those 'stormy adolescent troubles' – is not entirely clear. For all her later nostalgia about this time, it seems that her years of freedom and exploration after leaving school were not entirely blissful. She had entered adulthood confident that she knew who she was – a musician – and what she wanted – a career as a performer. But doubt had crept in. Forced to accept that she would not have a musical career, she had set her heart on poetry and Peter Bennie, but here, too, she had met with discomfiting checks. Happy though he was to flirt with her, Peter was not much interested in her as a sexual being. Her gleeful performance of the 'sex kitten' role lost something of its glamour when she found herself unable to captivate the one man she desired above all others.[11] Religious life may well have seemed a welcome new beginning after a series of bewildering failures.

The purpose of the Daughters of St Clare was to perform charitable work in the community, beginning with the care of indigent elderly women. In 1941, the congregation consisted of three professed sisters and a shifting population of postulants, of which Gwen would become one. Postulants were 'trying out' religious life to see whether they had a genuine calling; those who did would then enter the order as novices. The postulants did not take vows, but agreed to abide by the community's rule while they lived within it. They were required to eschew not only sexual contact with men but almost any contact with them at all.[12] The 'Handmaids' (as they were known) were not to 'walk in the streets with a man', eat with them or even 'acknowledge them when out of doors'. They were not to attend social events except by permission. Close friendships with other women were also frowned upon, and there was to be no hugging, kissing or, indeed, touching of any kind: 'No one shall indulge familiarities, caresses or acts of affection.' In their cells, the Handmaids were to be alone in order that they might commune with their 'Divine Spouse'.

Everything was regulated, including the women's posture (they should not be 'slothful in bodily attitude, always sitting upright and standing upon both feet') and their laughter ('Loud laughter and cries are never to be permitted'). Though it was not a silent order, 'The ordinary custom of the House shall be to keep silence, exceptions being made for times and places'. Yet Gwen did not find the rule at all draconian. For her, St Clare's was a loving community focused on the things that mattered: the inner life, contemplation, music, worship. Choosing a new name – she would be Sister Cecilia, after the Patron Saint of Music – she threw herself into the daily cycle of work and prayer.

The community repaired to the little chapel at set times each day to pray the daily office together (matins, terce, sext, none and vespers – they omitted lauds and compline for logistical reasons). Gwen loved to take her seat in the chapel, with its view of a young silvery gum through the window, and join in prayer and song. Her only complaint was that they did not sing the entire office, only the hymns.[13] She also loved celebrating daily mass; she would have liked to belong to 'an order that devoted itself entirely to the singing of the Liturgy'.

She enjoyed spending time in her peaceful cell, whose doors 'opened out so that I could see the trees outside', reading the Psalms and the Book of Common Prayer. The daily recitations of prayer and scripture helped to embed the rhythms of the Authorised Version deep in her being, from whence they would later become part of the rhythms of her poetry.

She got into the habit of reciting the Anima Christi, a medieval prayer invoking the saving power of Christ – 'Soul of Christ, save me, body of Christ, sanctify me' – which she would silently repeat throughout the day.[14]

This formulation she would later secularise, following Cyril Connolly, to invoke not Christ but the material world: 'Bougainvillea of Brisbane, pray for me, parking meters of Brisbane, intercede for me.'[15]

◆ ◆ ◆

Gwen spent her days working with the sisters at St Clare's House of Rest for Women. 'I learned to love the silences and the old ladies in the home under the sisters' care,' she would later write.[16] She also participated in the sisters' parish work, which included 'Sunday Schools, Religious Instruction in State Schools, various clubs and Mothers' Meetings, a tea for destitute men at St Francis Mission every Sunday night . . ., house-to-house visiting', and making altar bread for distribution throughout the state.[17]

At the same time, she continued with her work as organist and choir-master at All Saints – which meant that she wasn't 'ever properly sequestered from the world'. 'I continually saw my old friends and lovers (lovers in the innocent 1940s sense when "made love to" just meant "chat up lovingly")', she would muse many years later. 'The convent life wasn't all that different.'[18] She would later tell of a visit from one 'fellow-devil', Manfred Ritter, who, in order to gain admittance, brought with him 'a squat ferocious-looking redheaded boxer' he'd met in the pub, intending to claim he was Gwen's brother. Summoned to the parlour, Gwen burst out with: '"*That's* not my brother!" "But my dear," said the sister who had admitted the bruiser, "he *looks so like you.*"'[19]

Partial though it was, Gwen's encounter with silence was transformative. 'I found that when I was in the convent . . . a lot of things that seemed to be important dissolved and vanished and didn't matter at all,' she told a friend.[20] 'Six months of silence and having literally nothing, not even a piece of soap, of one's own, showed me that the whole meaning of life is lost to most people who go rushing about madly trying all the time to *do* something or other instead of to *be* something.' Time itself, she went on, came to have a different meaning: 'I think John Donne said something like this: "Days, weeks, hours, these are the rags of time."' It was a quote she would return to again and again in the following years in both letters and poems, an encapsulation of her theory that everything that really mattered happened in a time outside of time.

Meanwhile, she brushed up on her housekeeping skills: 'Anything I didn't know about sweeping, polishing, etc. (and that was plenty) I learned at the Convent, where the Mother Superior "took me in hand" the first morning. I can remember her gentle eyes as she told me about polishing the bake-house floor for the glory of God.'[21] She also learned to grow vegetables, calling the veggie patch 'one of my greatest delights'.[22] She enjoyed the physical labour. 'Sometimes I would hoe out the weeds near the path, or pick them from the wet soil in the beds with my hands,' she would write a year later, the glow of nostalgia already infusing her memories. 'How happy I was! I made a cupboard out of old fruit boxes for the bake-house, and mended a fence, and sawed wood.'[23] The starkness of convent life helped her to live in the present, 'doing simple things not for the purpose of getting them over and done with as quickly as possible but because they are really part of one's life'.[24]

There were things she disliked, however. Chief among these was the food, which was awful on principle (the rule specified that the sisters should 'take such food as may be left when the House has been served' and that their food should 'always be plain'). Gwen, whose appreciation of good food was ardent, would later describe with contempt breakfasts consisting of 'some form of chicken-feed', and puddings 'of a sponge-like texture' with 'cold fat on the edges'.[25] She also struggled with the rough soap the sisters were mandated to use. A friend gave her something gentler, and when she carelessly left some in the convent bathroom she was summoned to explain herself to the mother superior: 'Did I not understand the true nature of the Vow of Poverty?' When she explained that the convent soap gave her a rash, the mother superior ('a gentle and reasonable woman') told her that 'of course I could use a milder soap, but I should have explained why before accepting gifts'.[26]

She did not see her parents while she was at the convent, though in her first few weeks there, Agnes would call her 'in tears, and tell me how I was "breaking father's heart" etc.'[27] She was touched to discover, many years later, that the friend who had smuggled in the soap used to go and see Joe in his shop after each visit to report on his daughter's wellbeing.[28]

When in January 1942 Gwen decided that she did not have a vocation to religious life after all, both Joe and Agnes welcomed her home with open arms. Agnes, indeed, was triumphant, Gwen remembered wryly, taking Gwen's decision to leave as a personal victory.[29]

Gwen was never very forthcoming about her defection from the convent less than six months after she had joined it. Spiritual discernment aside, it seems likely that it had something to do with Peter Bennie. Sometime either in late 1941 or early 1942, Gwen was at her regular Thursday-night choir practice when one of the singers dropped a bombshell: Reverend Peter was engaged to be married. For Gwen, this was a body blow. Later that night, out for a walk with Manfred, she climbed a high parapet and thought of throwing herself off.[30] Until that moment, she had felt fairly sure that if Peter had been free to marry, he would have married her; it was only his commitment to celibacy that was keeping them apart. Now she was forced to realise he was quite capable of rearranging his faith commitments for the right woman. She simply was not that woman. To add insult to injury, his fiancée, Joyce Sweetman, was not even one of his parishioners, but a nurse he met during a brief hospitalisation.[31]

Gwen would later say that this news marked the end of her Christian belief: 'With Peter's departure into Holy Matrimony my faith evaporated like the rainbow's lovely form.'[32] This was not true, however – or not immediately. She did not leave the church when she left the convent, but continued to attend mass faithfully and to work as organist and choirmaster at All Saints. Her letters in the following years show that she was still very much engaged with Christian spirituality and theology, and would energetically defend the Anglican Church if it was attacked (unless, as sometimes happened, she herself was doing the attacking). But it does seem as though she took Peter's decision to marry – like his earlier decision to remain single – as a model for her own life. As passionately as he had championed celibacy in the past he now championed marriage, preaching the surpassing virtue of the married state. Celibacy was an obstacle, not an aid, to the priesthood, he argued; sex was 'the great humanising factor'.[33] Gwen was easily convinced. Though she could not marry Peter, she could and would follow his example by adopting for herself the vocation of marriage.

Not everyone in the All Saints community was so amenable to persuasion. One church historian would later write that Peter's parishioners strenuously disapproved of his decision to abandon the Anglo-Catholic ideal of the celibate priesthood, noting that for some years, Peter was 'universally hated' at All Saints.[34] Fortunately, in May 1942, he was appointed as parish priest at Imbil, just north of Brisbane, where he could make a new start. He returned to Brisbane briefly in August to marry Joyce at St John's Anglican Cathedral, with the Reverend Bates as his best man, and went back to Imbil a husband, ready to take the next steps in what would be an illustrious clerical career. Gwen, meanwhile, picked herself up and began to cast around for a new start of her own.

6

Gwendolina's Flying Circus

I was a Monty Python before them.
Gwen Harwood, Letter to Alison Hoddinott, 28 February 1990

THE WORLD GWEN RETURNED TO WAS NOT THE ONE SHE HAD left when she entered the convent. While she was taking care of her tomato plants at St Clare's, Japan had attacked Pearl Harbour and the United States had entered the war. In early 1942, as Japanese fighter planes bombed Darwin and other northern cities, the new prime minister, John Curtin, began to recall Australia's troops from the Middle East. For the first time, it began to seem not only possible but likely that the war would come to Australian soil, and the absence of Australia's fighting forces, who were currently on the other side of the world defending Europe, was alarming. In Queensland, everything north of Rockhampton was declared a war zone, and Brisbane prepared for the worst.[1] Concrete bunkers lined the streets, the peaceful slopes of Mount Coot-tha were surrendered to the military, and ever-growing numbers of troops set up camp on ovals and racecourses around the city.

At the Foster home, there was now an air-raid shelter in the backyard, and Gwen's father, rejoicing in the title of air-raid warden, directed regular drills adorned with hard hat, armband and whistle.[2] Agnes spent all her free time at the opportunity shop she managed in Queen Street for the Australian Comforts Fund, a charity dedicated to providing home comforts to Australians serving overseas. As well as coordinating donations of food and goods, chivvying the other volunteers and serving behind the counter, Agnes gave numerous talks and radio broadcasts promoting the fund.[3] Gwen's brother, Joey, had become obsessed with planes – and, much to Gwen's amusement, with building up his physique for when he would finally be old enough to join the air force. There were other changes, too. Gwen's friend Manfred, who had been born in Germany, though he had lived in Australia since the age of eight, was classified as an 'enemy alien' and sent to an internment camp at Tatura in Victoria. Other friends had enlisted and been shipped off for training or deployment. Things were beginning to get serious.

At the prompting of the All Saints rector, Reverend Bates, Gwen decided to apply for the position of music teacher at St Christopher's Lodge, an Anglican boys' school at Brookfield, just west of Brisbane. Reverend Bates had established the lodge in 1934 as a boys' home and set up a cattle stud there to breed Ayrshires. The idea was that the boys would work on the farm outside of school hours, thus ensuring they learned not only the three Rs but also 'the rudiments of farming'. Those not suited to farming were to be taught other 'skilled crafts' that would equip them to earn a living once they left school.[4] Gwen seems not to have understood the somewhat precarious status of St Christopher's when she applied. She told a friend that the school 'sounded very grand in its prospectus' and that she had 'got some of [her] father's friends to write [her] superb references'.[5] Her illusions did not survive the job interview. Arriving dressed 'in my best clothes, bearing my flawless character (on paper), wearing my silver medal (for music)', she trudged up a 'long gravel drive bordered with burrs & cow droppings' towards 'some imposing buildings which stank, as one approached, of manure'.[6] These turned out to house the rector's Ayrshires. The schoolhouse was the unassuming cottage she had passed on her way in and taken to belong to the gardener.

It was all downhill from there. The only teachers were the headmistress, 'a crazy iron-grey spinster', and the maths master, an eighteen-year-old boy named Robin Wolter, a former student at the lodge whom Gwen would later conclude was 'definitely unhinged mentally'.[7] Then there were the cook and the nurse, both of whom appeared entirely incompetent, and the chaplain, who was never there.

Also resident at St Christopher's was a 'filthy and malicious' sow, whose name appeared to be Gwen; only later did she learn that it bore 'the name of whatever female teacher . . . could be persuaded to stay in the school for more than a month'.[8] There was great joy among the students when 'Gwen' was farrowing.

Gwen soon found that in addition to music, she was expected to teach 'geography, scripture-at-an-elementary-level, mental arithmetic, physiology, drawing, clay modelling, copybook writing, blackboard cleaning, nose-wiping and agriculture'.[9] She was required to live in, but travelled home on the weekends to fulfil her duties as church organist and fill up on her mother's cooking.[10]

In after years, Gwen would treat her time at St Christopher's solely as a source of humorous stories, but she did take her work there seriously.

Determined not to replicate the deadening teaching methods of her own school days, she did what she could to make her lessons interesting, priding herself on never teaching 'from the beastly Grade books' and 'taking the little boys out in the sun when we got tired of being inside'.[11]

Despite the awful food and lack of mental stimulus, she stayed at the school for five months before retreating to Grimes Street in mid-1942, bringing with her the young maths master. Robin had enlisted, and as he had no family, Gwen had invited him to stay while he waited to be called up.[12] She soon regretted her hospitality. 'Although Robin started off by being a jolly schoolboy who was rather fun, he and [Agnes] together make a combination that I cannot bear,'[13] she told a friend.

The problem was that Robin was Agnes's ally against Gwen. Mother and daughter were not getting on, and Gwen felt that Robin took her mother's side. By far the biggest source of tension between them was Agnes's tree-cutting. Full of schemes for backyard improvement, Agnes would prune, fell or root out trees without warning, and Gwen would arrive home from work to find a bare patch of earth where a beloved plant had stood.[14] She could not get used to her mother's acts of ruthless annihilation and veered between fury and despair. Agnes's inability to understand Gwen's feelings on the matter was, to Gwen, evidence of their fundamental incompatibility. '[Agnes] has never been able to help me in the ways that I most need help,' she wrote in 1943. 'In material things her generosity exceeds anything one could imagine or deserve. Outwardly I have all I could wish for, [but] it means almost nothing to me.'[15] Her struggles were inward, and it was here, she felt, that her mother failed her.

Agnes may well have been bewildered by the change in her daughter. The pair had been united in their dream of a concert career for Gwen, and for years, Gwen had been an enthusiastic participant in her mother's musical 'functions', with all their attendant dramas. But Agnes did not enter into Gwen's literary interests. She lived in fear of appearing in Gwen's literary productions, knowing all too well that whatever she said or did, there was always the chance Gwen would 'write it down and tell all her friends'.[16] (Gwen did nothing to mitigate this fear, telling her mother serenely that 'Any incident at all is legitimate food for a writer'.)

Now Gwen was distancing herself from her mother's values and interests. She saw Agnes as worldly, all action and no contemplation, a disposition that led Gwen to start referring to her (thanks to a typo in a letter) as 'Agens', the Latin word for 'active' or 'efficient'. In Gwen's newly spiritualised view, her mother was one of those people on whom 'the whole meaning of life' is lost because they focus on doing rather than being.

When friends commented on the likeness between them, Gwen was 'furious' – and incredulous.[17] It seemed to her that she and her mother were utterly different, not only physically but also in temperament. In particular, her mother was not 'motherly', and Gwen was beginning to take on the Christian ideal of the self-sacrificing wife and mother as a holy calling. In 1942, Gwen was devouring not only the works of Christian theologians and philosophers but also the heady writings of mystics such as Julian of Norwich and Thérèse of Lisieux.[18] They fed an exalted romanticism in her, as well as an increasingly indignant sense that all that was truly important was missing from the kind of lives most people were encouraged to lead. She had no intention of following the masses into a life of dull, unreflecting materialism. She would resist mindless complacency wherever she found it.

◆ ◆ ◆

Gwen's feeling of dissonance became acute as the war spread its tentacles ever further into Brisbane. In mid-1942, the American general in charge of operations in the South-West Pacific, General Douglas MacArthur, moved his headquarters from Melbourne to Brisbane, and the city was soon bursting at the seams. Thousands of American troops were quartered at various sites around Brisbane, notably Doomben Racecourse, Wacol and Enoggera. To add to the congestion, the Australian Army also moved its headquarters to Brisbane, with Australian troops camping on the unfinished St Lucia campus of the University of Queensland.[19] With the troops came a 'whole substructure of camp-followers [and] black marketeers', and 'supplies of goods and services legitimate and illegitimate' flourished.[20] From a modest population of around 350,000, Brisbane became home to more than half a million people; by the end of 1944, some two million Allied troops had passed through the city.[21] As Judith Wright observed when she moved to Brisbane in 1943, the very character of the city was changed by this influx: it grew 'shabby and rakish'. Soldiers brawled in the streets, and skirmishes occasionally escalated into full-blown riots.[22] Rationing was introduced, and there were shortages – from which the 'sleek' American troops seemed to be somewhat protected, much to the annoyance of their comparatively 'sloppy' Australian counterparts. Nevertheless, 'Brisbane, if corrupt was cheerful, if dirty was warm'. It was also, in Wright's words, 'disposed to enjoy life'.[23]

By this time, Gwen was in the thick of the action. Having taken a course in shorthand and typing at a business college in the city,[24] she found a job as a clerk in the War Damage Commission, whose offices were in Adelaide Street, on the top floor of the building that housed the American Postal Exchange. Australian soldiers were not allowed to frequent the PX, which supplied all kinds of luxury goods, including duty-free cigarettes, to American troops. This was a source of simmering tension, and in November 1942, after a day of provocations and counter-provocations, a riot erupted. Some two thousand Australian soldiers tried to raid the canteen, while the American Military Police tried to beat them back.[25] Gwen was on her way to choir practice on the evening the battle broke out. 'I could see ahead of my tram a couple of trams derailed and a solid bloody fight going on beyond,' she wrote. 'I slipped off the tram and doubled round to Wickham Terrace by another way, and went home later by train.' When she arrived for work the next morning, 'the Post Exchange was a mass of wreckage'.[26] An Australian soldier was killed that night, and many other servicemen, both Australian and American, were injured.

The War Damage Commission, however, had no official interest in such matters. It had been established to provide insurance for Queensland homes and businesses against possible damage caused by the war, but to Gwen, its painstaking and cumbersome procedures seemed grimly ludicrous.[27] It was her first encounter with the public service, and she was appalled, and darkly fascinated, by the amount of busywork that went on. Despite all the activity in the WDC offices, it seemed to her that nobody was actually doing anything. Her boss, Robert Reed (whom Gwen always referred to by his patriotic middle name, Mafeking), spent his days piling up correspondence, trying to light his pipe and barking at his secretary, as far as Gwen could see.[28] Yet he happily declared to anyone who would listen that he was 'in love with [his] work!' 'Work!' Gwen sputtered. 'The work he does could not be taken seriously by any person whose brain was normally developed.'

Mafeking's secretary, Melva Harvey, was similarly devoted to the cause. 'Her forehead is permanently creased with worry and she mutters to herself continually,' Gwen wrote scornfully. 'She told me that if her work goes badly during the day she "has a bad night". Her favourite remark to those who say she is looking tired is "But I live so *intensely* every moment that it wears me out."'[29] To Gwen, this was at best self-delusion, at worst egregious pretention. The idea that this kind of activity was meaningful verged on the heretical. Immersed as she was in philosophical debates about the meaning of life, Gwen saw the WDC as the epitome of purposeless action. She felt the place was actively malevolent, robbing people – including herself – 'of life and spirit'.[30] To be there every day was to be exposed to 'scenes calculated to deaden everything original, spare, strange, peculiar and curious'.[31] Rather than succumb, she determined to retaliate with the most powerful weapons she knew: ridicule and satire. In this, she was abetted by a new friend, a young naval lieutenant named Thomas Riddell.

Lieutenant Riddell, known as Tony, was a friend of Peter Bennie's from his University of Melbourne days. In mid-1942, he had been transferred from Australian naval intelligence in Melbourne to the new Combined Operational Intelligence Centre in Brisbane, where he had looked up his old friend. Tony was a singer, and mentioned to Peter that he was looking for a pianist to rehearse with. Naturally, Peter introduced him to Gwen, who invited him round to Grimes Street. In the large central family room, with the piano at one end and the billiard table at the other, she played Schubert and he sang. Tony's lovely baritone shaping the beautiful German words of yearning, joy and anguish went straight to her heart. 'Schubert speaks to me so directly, as a god might speak,' she would one day tell him, 'that I am truly enraptured.'[32] She would forever associate these songs, and the German Romanticism behind them, with Tony. In them she would find the confirmation of her own apprehension that love always entails suffering – and that suffering is redeemed when it gives rise to art. The lieder she would explore in her rehearsals with Tony over the next several months would become a shared language between them, and a framework for their inner lives.

Gwen was as dazzled by Tony as she had been by Peter. A year older than his friend, Tony had the same wit and intelligence, but more reserve. At twenty-eight, he was handsome and accomplished, with all the confidence an elite education can bestow. As a schoolboy at Melbourne's Scotch College he had excelled at drama and athletics, and at university, where he studied classics, he was one of the stars of student theatre and competed in the Australian Athletics Championships.[33]

Tony wanted to be an actor and a singer, but the war put his plans on hold, and he began to write poetry and plays instead. Because he had a master's degree, he was in demand for intelligence roles, but he found working for 'Our Glorious Navy' stultifying. Like Gwen, he could not understand how the people around him could devote themselves so unquestioningly to work that seemed to him entirely meaningless.[34] While Gwen's sense of disjuncture came from her belief in spiritual values, Tony's came from his belief in art. He brought to what he thought of as high art – ancient Greek theatre, Shakespeare, opera and lieder, poetry in its most traditional forms – the same kind of faith and fervour Peter brought to religion. He could be arrogant, contemptuous of those who adulterated or fell short of his high standards, but Gwen loved this about him, as she loved almost everything else.

As well as sharing his favourite music and poetry with her, Tony introduced Gwen to the surreal humour of Beachcomber, the pseudonym of English newspaper columnist J.B. Morton. The Beachcomber columns had recently begun appearing in Australian newspapers, syndicated from the UK *Daily Express*, and Tony and Gwen seized on them with joy. Morton specialised in satirical sketches featuring a cast of ludicrous characters that sent up authority and pomposity – a style of humour that would be taken up in the next generation by the Goons and Monty Python.[35] Gwen and Tony were particularly delighted by the hapless Mr Justice Cocklecarrot, whose attempts to impose order were continually overset by twelve anarchic, red-bearded dwarfs, whom the red-headed Gwen immediately adopted as a kind of collective alter ego. She was soon inventing capers of her own for the dwarfs (dubbed 'rufo-nanine' by Tony, a pseudo-Latin translation of 'red dwarf'), developing extended skits in which they were let loose at the WDC to wreak havoc on the most self-important of her colleagues.

She and Tony began to encourage one another to commit small, Beachcomber-inspired acts of sabotage in their respective places of work, on which they would gleefully report back. These ranged from the obstructive – one of Gwen's early sorties was to reorganise her boss's files along idiosyncratic lines, making it impossible for anyone else to find the all-important client 'correspondence' – to the merely irritating (such as her determination to 'mutter to myself in German or French all day').[36] One of her favourite ploys was to answer only 'yes' or 'no' to any question asked of her, rendering conversation increasingly absurd ('The monosyllabic method is most effective', she reported to Tony).[37] She also took great pleasure in violating workplace etiquette, nabbing the iced buns reserved for dignitaries or sitting on the floor to sort through files.[38] Once, when Tony came to visit her at work, he walked straight through to her desk, rather than waiting at the front counter to be admitted. This breach of protocol caused outraged mutterings throughout the WDC. One of Gwen's colleagues declared that she would 'die' if a young man called to see her at the office,[39] but Gwen took pride in being pointed out as the girl who received 'gentlemen callers'.

When in January 1943 Tony was transferred to Darwin, they began to document their antics in a voluminous correspondence.[40] Gwen's letters to Tony regularly included three- or four-page scripts of court proceedings under Justices Tickleturnip, Rotbat and Pickleparsnip, in which the red-bearded dwarves were prosecuted for invading the WDC.[41] She also retailed the misadventures of eccentric characters such as Fred Hackle-skinner, peanut diviner, and Miss Mehitabel Pankhurst, headmistress of St Fotheringill's Seminary for Young Ladies, demonstrating the skill with a comic tale that would enliven all her later correspondence. Tony found Gwen's letters so entertaining that he read them aloud to his messmates and threatened to publish them in a volume entitled 'Dear Tony'.[42]

Rereading her WDC letters many years later, Gwen was amazed that she hadn't been fired.[43] 'Mafeking really did like me in spite of my atrocious behaviour,' she reflected. At the time, she had been disgusted to learn that he prided himself on getting on 'very well' with the difficult Miss Foster.[44] His secretary, Miss Harvey, was made of sterner stuff. One day, fed up with Gwen's refusal to take her work seriously, she lost her temper, telling her she had 'NEVER NEVER NEVER seen ANYONE carry on like you do'.[45] 'Everyone here knows you're not normal,' she went on, warming to her theme. Then she began to get personal:

> I'll tell you something I heard outside, too: I heard someone outside say, 'Mr and Mrs Foster are nice people, *thoroughly nice* people, but they can't do a thing with her. The minute she gets inside that house, she rules the roost . . . They're charming people, but she's out of all control.' And do you know, when I heard that I can't tell you how relieved I felt to know that at least your parents are decent. I thought you came from a *family* of lunatics, the way you go on.

Gwen claimed she found this 'funny, and laughed a great deal'. That night, when she repeated Miss Harvey's words to her parents, they also 'exploded with laughter'. But the jibes did sting. The surviving letter in which she told Tony about Harvey's diatribe has a crucial page missing: at first she thought it 'funny', she wrote, 'but it's terrible' – and then the letter cuts off. Exactly what she found terrible has been lost to history, but it is clear that the episode contributed to Gwen's growing feeling of depression. At times, she told Tony, she felt she was 'cracking up'.[46] She was eager to get on with some work of her own: she had found a new piano teacher, a talented pianist named Ernest Watson, and was working hard at her music again; she was teaching herself German, inspired by the poems and ballads on which the lieder were based; and she was reading theology, philosophy and modern literature. But her day job was sapping her strength. At the end of each work day, she was tired 'not so much physically as in spirit . . . I have to spend the evenings regaining my balance instead of going on to something new'.[47]

Whatever Gwen did at the WDC, it was always a performance. She took her cue from her co-workers, improvising scenes like a practised thespian – which was how she felt. 'It always seems a little unreal to me [in the WDC office],' she wrote to Tony, 'as if the people here were just playing parts, pretending to be examining officers, state controllers and so on. Sometimes it is hard to believe that they are not acting what they are.'[48] Even outside the WDC, she always felt at a certain remove from what was going on around her: 'I watch myself performing on different levels.'[49] She was by nature an observer, trapped in 'an endless state of watching, observing, seeing without being able to take part in things'. Though it kept her at an ironic distance, playing a role was one way of taking part.

◆ ◆ ◆

Gwen missed Tony greatly when he left for Darwin, not just as a comrade who helped her dream up ever more outrageous pranks but as a fellow traveller who understood her desire for meaningful work. 'I know quite clearly that what I am doing now is not what I should be doing,' she wrote to him late in 1943. 'I am unsettled and restless because I haven't really found what I should be doing with my life. I feel that I am corked up in a bottle . . . However the answer to my own question: What should I be doing? escapes and eludes me.'[50] Tony was entirely serious about his own vocation as an artist. Working on poems and plays he hoped would one day qualify as literature, he encouraged Gwen to claim a similar calling. They read one another's work, and Tony – unlike Peter – was encouraging, finding promise in Gwen's stories and poems, and urging her to publish them. Yet in her letters, Gwen was uncharacteristically diffident about her literary efforts, attributing her stories to her 'rufo-nanine' alter egos. 'Fred Hackleskinner tried his hand at a story called *The Crazy Mistress*, which was supposed to be related by an insufferable young person, but the person was so insufferable that Fred couldn't finish the story,' she wrote in one letter.[51] 'I'm glad you liked Theophilus Panbury's "Rose-tree",' she wrote in another. 'Theophilus enjoys writing, but thinks you exaggerate his powers.'[52]

It is telling that her pseudonyms were male. While there were women writers publishing at the time, and some were even regarded as having a certain facility, the category of literary genius was reserved for men. A woman properly derived creative satisfaction from motherhood, and attempts to veer into literature were met with suspicion, pity or ridicule. Those female writers whose novels or poems found popular success were largely derided by critics. Gwen and Tony loved to make fun of two such poets, Felicia Hemans and Eliza Cook, beloved of generations of readers but – in the view of critics, at least – utterly unworthy of the title 'artist'. Their writing was sentimental, small in scope, inherently minor. Gwen was determined not to be lumped in with the much-scorned 'authoresses'. She wanted to be a writer, not a 'lady writer'.

The three early stories of hers that survive were not only written under male names but also have male protagonists. In one of these, 'The Gorgon's Head', the central characters are themselves aspiring writers. Paul and Harry both dream of a writing career but approach their goal in very different ways. Paul lives a solitary existence, struggling to support himself by teaching while writing stories alone in his cold boarding-house room at night. Harry has recently married and lives a lively, happy life in a cottage by the sea with his wife, Elsa. While Paul is struggling with writer's block, Harry is writing 'most of the day and night', and one of his plays is soon to be produced. Elsa was an actress before her marriage, but now devotes herself entirely to supporting Harry. She has created the loving environment in which Harry is able to be so productive, while Paul, wifeless, is paralysed by loneliness. The moral seems to be that marriage is more conducive to the creative life than solitude – for a man, that is. The secondary moral is that a woman will find her happiness not in creative work of her own but in nurturing the creative work of her husband. Indeed, bright, bantering Elsa seems delighted by her husband's refusal to let her work. 'Harry won't let me act in his plays,' she tells Paul lovingly. 'He won't even let me be a servant in the background.' 'I wouldn't even let you be "thunder off-stage,"' Harry confirms. This, in the world of the story, is how it should be. The irony that the author of this story is an unmarried woman does not seem to have occurred to Gwen. Officially, properly, men were writers and women were helpmeets, even when a woman was wielding the pen.

Something of this perception may have been behind Gwen's reluctance to openly claim a desire to be a writer. The 'drive to create' was seen as a masculine urge, incompatible with the ideal of womanliness.[53] When Gwen told Tony in a letter that she was 'quite empty of ambition', she was performing her womanliness with a vengeance. In a similar vein, she once told him, half-jokingly, that she'd quite like 'to retire and study philosophy for seven years, but as von Hugel says, "What can one do with a learned woman – except drown her?" I agree with him. I shall devote the time to cooking.'[54] She was parodying society's view of women, as Tony knew. But even so, such views had a persistent, malignant effect. 'I have spent most of my life pretending to be less intelligent than I am,' she would reflect when she was in her seventies. 'Why? Perhaps I didn't want to get beaten up.'[55] This fear of a beating – metaphorical or literal – was very real for women who sought to move beyond the social roles prescribed for them.

◆ ◆ ◆

Though she downplayed her own artistic ambitions, Gwen was extremely supportive of Tony's. 'You are born to be an actor and a singer,' she told him fervently. 'You have a power to move people, to stir them up and pierce the armour they wear over all deep feeling because they are afraid; that power is given to so few that you *must* use it.'[56] Whether as a singer, actor or writer, he would make his mark, she was sure. As for herself, though she would have liked to make people 'hear, and be afraid', as the words of Scripture had it, she was not confident that she had Tony's power.[57] She did not seek out other aspiring writers, though there were many in Brisbane at the time, nor look for possible avenues of publication. Thea Astley, who was then studying at the University of Queensland, joined the Catholic Writers Movement as well as the young writers' group Barjai, while Judith Wright spent her spare time in Brisbane helping Clem and Nina Christesen get the fledgling *Meanjin Papers* off the ground.[58] Gwen met no writers other than those in Tony's and Peter's circles, and sought no other writing mentors.

Peter's opinion still mattered enormously to her. In mid-1943, she sent him her story 'Another Country', and was dismayed when he told her frankly that it wasn't very good. He felt that it lacked all the elements of an effective story – 'plot, dialogue and dramatic cause and effect' – and that the central character was 'quite infantile'. The central character, of course, was an avatar for Gwen herself; this was her deeply felt story about a young man who had set his heart on going to Germany, a place he had romanticised and idealised since childhood, but who was cudgelled into giving up his dream by his mother, who couldn't bear to let him go. Gwen had felt that the reader would identify and sympathise with the young man, and feel the injustice of his mother's behaviour, which was based on her own experience with Agnes. Besides, she had given her central character her own childhood longing for forests full of fir trees and the snowy world of the Brothers Grimm; Peter's dismissal of him as infantile was a dismissal of herself. He did, however, praise her technical skills, assuring her that 'the word grouping and rhythm' are 'excellent', and that she conveyed her 'information quite effortlessly without distortion – and this is high compliment'.[59] He ended his critique with some generic encouragement: 'the main thing – capable writing – sentence construction, diction – choice of words – is all there, so keep going and send me some more.'

Gwen's initial response to his appraisal was rather subdued. Peter's criticism 'seems to be very sound,' she told Tony dolefully, forwarding on the critique. '[The story] really was rather infantile.'[60] But a few days later, she sent Tony a review of the work of 'Mrs Herodias Smith' by critic 'Subidir Hooser': 'The first line is rather good, I think. The character of Claude Sluce, while showing a lack of philosophical speculation, is presented without effort. The verbs are in the right places, and this is high compliment ... However the main thing, the spelling, is there.'[61]

It was a powerful rally, poking fun at both Peter and herself. Nevertheless, she admitted that 'Theophilus Panbury' had 'been in a terrible mood for days', 'unable to laugh, sing, play the zimbummer or write'. Still, she did not hold Peter's judgements against him. She trusted him to tell her the truth. Kindliness in criticism was the province of the drawing room; the artist needed, and deserved, honest and unflinching critique.

Already she was focusing on poetry. She was reading widely – one of her cherished books was an anthology of world poetry in English with selections from Chinese, Japanese and Persian poets alongside French, German and Scandinavian ones[62] – and developing a mature sense of what contemporary poetry could do. Her early poems drew on her reading, not her own experiences or feelings. The two that have survived from this time, 'Lazarus' and 'The Rite of Spring', are formal works, stiff and obscure. Both allude to the literature of ancient Greece (one of Tony's specialisms) and the Bible

(Peter's area of expertise), weaving the two mythologies together in ways that are more confusing than illuminating. There are some nice phrases in both (deep in earth, the dead Lazarus hears 'the lilies being born'), and they are formally impressive, but they read like technical exercises written by someone who cannot imagine a 'great' poem that does not allude to Homer. Tony, whose own poems were similarly formal, liked what she was doing and encouraged her, though he did suggest, tentatively, that 'Lazarus' needed a more 'obvious' climax: in his view, it rather petered out.[63] Gwen did not accept his criticism, referring him back to the story of Lazarus in St John's Gospel to show how biblically sound her ending was. In general, though, she and Tony agreed on what a good poem looked like, and Gwen's ambition was quietly forming itself. She soon confided in Tony her hope of writing real poetry one day, and 'promised him then that if ever I did have a book published he should have the dedication'.[64]

Tony and his naval friend Frank Kellaway were urging her to send out her poems and stories for publication. Both men had had poems accepted for an anthology entitled *Poets at War*, and Frank, at least, was sending his work out as widely as possible. Gwen disapproved, telling Tony that Frank had been 'bitten by the publication bug' and that this was 'a bad thing'.[65] Her view was that artists should labour away in silence and secrecy to perfect their work. Frank was not yet ready to publish, she told Tony loftily; 'I don't think he should publish anything for (say) five years'. She herself had no intention of seeking such premature glory – until, that is, Frank had a poem accepted by the newly established Brisbane journal *Meanjin Papers*. Gwen was taken aback that Frank's as-yet-immature work should have received the imprimatur of a serious publisher. When the issue came out at the end of 1943, she got hold of a copy and stood in the street jealously scanning Frank's poem, which was entitled 'Sonnet'. 'It certainly had 14 lines,' she told Tony waspishly. 'I don't know what policy dictated the rhyme-scheme (except necessity).' The last two lines, in which Frank rhymed 'paraphernalia' with 'proud Australia', caused her to 'burst into helpless laughter'.[66] The poem, she concluded, was 'trash'. Yet not only had it been accepted for publication, but Frank had been paid good money for it: ten shillings and sixpence.[67] She found this 'intensely annoy[ing]'. With no apparent concern about her inconsistency, she immediately decided to send off one of her own poems, 'The Rite of Spring', to the same publication. 'If they don't give me 10/6 I shall be enraged but not at all surprised, and will send them things until they wear out,' she told Tony. Luckily, her stamina was not tested – not yet, at least. *Meanjin* took her poem, and it appeared at the end of 1944. At twenty-four, she was a published poet – and, to her delight, a minor celebrity at the WDC.

Among the poems in this issue of *Meanjin*, Gwen's work stands out for its high finish. The issue also contains a poem by Judith Wright, as well as verse by R.G. Howarth, Ian Mudie, American poet Harry Roskolenko (then in Australia with the US Army) and seventeen-year-old Barrie Reid, of the Barjai group. There are articles by Nettie Palmer and Miles Franklin and an essay on G.M. Hopkins, a poet Gwen greatly admired. The back cover advertised forthcoming work from Arthur Koestler, A.D. Hope and Peter Bennie – in the case of the latter, an essay on Kierkegaard. It was not bad company for a first-time poet to be in. Many years later, Gwen would tell an interviewer that the ease with which this poem was 'accepted and published' gave her 'a confidence which has never left [her]'.[68] Unfortunately, it would be well over a decade before she would find publishing this easy again.

◆ ◆ ◆

For all her flirtation with an artist's vocation, Gwen was still inclined to accept Peter's newly formulated view that holy matrimony was the greatest vocation of all. If she could not devote herself to the Divine Spouse, she could nevertheless commit herself in love and service to a human one. Though Peter was unavailable, there were other men she felt she could love. One was Manfred Ritter, still locked up in the internment camp in Victoria.[69] Another was Tony.

Gwen loved Tony from the beginning. Her letters sparkle with the joy of it. 'When I write to you,' she told him, early in their correspondence, 'I feel as happy as a croquet player whose ball has just gone through five hoops without stopping.'[70] Writing to him about her daily life, turning it into a story that would elicit laughter, was a huge liberation for her. 'It is so good to be able to write to you that Theophilus feels better just by writing,' she declared.[71] He was the perfect audience, stimulating both her humour and her outrage, able to match her in insight and playfulness. In their correspondence, they exchanged spoofs and parodies not only of sentimental poets but of great ones, and vied with one another in writing ludicrous verse commemorating each other's deaths in the style of the 'In Memoriam' columns of the newspapers.[72] He could take the full force of her intelligence and energy – no small thing for a woman like Gwen who, in full flight, could overwhelm lesser beings.

It was not just writing to Tony that made Gwen happy. When he was in Brisbane on leave, the time they spent together, making music, walking and talking, was blissful. 'You have made me so happy that I am still full of joy,' she wrote after a brief visit from him in April 1943. 'How lovely it has been to hear you sing and to walk and sit with you in the bright sunshine.'[73]

'It must be about a year now since I first met you,' she wrote in August. 'How quickly the year has gone, and yet it seems to me to be a much longer time in some ways. You have made me very happy.'[74]

It was not Gwen's way to hold back in matters of the heart. If she loved, she would speak her love. But despite his own professions of joy in Gwen's companionship and the delight he took in their correspondence, Tony showed no signs of wanting to take the relationship further. Theirs, it seemed, was to be a fiercely loving but platonic friendship. It was not until some years had passed that Gwen understood that Tony was gay. Peter Bennie, who did know, had tried to steer her clear of the shoals, writing to explain 'firmly (though not too clearly, remember this was [1943]) that Tony loved me as a friend but was not interested in young women'.[75] Many years later, Peter told her that he and his friends had been 'terrified you'd prevail on Tony to marry you and find out something you couldn't have known'.[76] 'How cruel,' she comments. 'But I suppose in those days one couldn't speak. Certainly I didn't understand. Peter only said vague things like "You're barking up the wrong tree."' Later, the knowledge would help her to make sense of Tony's confession that love, for him, was 'the bitterest experience of all'.[77] But his sexual orientation made no difference to her: she would love Tony all her life.

Early in September 1943, Tony again returned to Brisbane on leave – a cause of much joyful anticipation for Gwen. This time, when he came out to Grimes Street he brought with him a fellow naval officer, a tall, shy, brilliant man named Frank William Harwood. Once again, Gwen fell head over heels in love.

7

———

'*I Am* Bill'

Love cannot endure discretion and I know no way of keeping anything;
my own nature says "give", though in a sense I have nothing to give: the
sun doesn't give its light, it just shines.
Gwen Harwood, Letter to Tony Riddell, 16 March 1944

GWEN WOULD ALWAYS SAY THAT SHE FELL IN LOVE WITH Bill 'at first sight'. 'He was wonderfully handsome, he was tall, blond, marvellously intelligent – I was besotted.'[1] Physically, he was her 'type': fair and slender, with intensely blue eyes.

He was twenty-five when they met, a quiet young officer in a blue naval uniform and white peaked cap who had worked in naval intelligence with Tony, first in Melbourne and then in Darwin, and who had just been transferred to Brisbane. He had heard scraps of Gwen's letters, which Tony shared with all his naval friends, and knew of both Tony's and Frank's admiration for her, though if he was excited to meet her, he did not betray it. When he came with Tony to Grimes Street in the evenings, he sat quietly while Tony and Gwen rehearsed Schubert, or played billiards with Gwen's father, keeping himself to himself.

On weekends, Gwen would take long walks with both men 'around Auchenflower & Toowong and along the river bank, to Toowong Cemetery & up Mt Coot-tha'.[2] It seems likely that Gwen and Tony had the lion's share of the conversation on these outings; Bill, as Gwen would plaintively remark in a letter, did not say much. Besides, she and Bill at first seemed to have little in common. Bill was not a musician and was not really keen on music. Nor was he religious; he had no time for the Christian church or for scholastic philosophy. He was entirely without writing aspirations, though he knew his Romantic poets: his master's thesis was on Coleridge's theory of the imagination. Gwen would later say that this was 'like a crate of orchids, how could I resist?'[3] She did not know then that Bill was in the process of turning completely and permanently against the Romantics and their ilk. As Peter would one day say, Bill, having been brought up on Romantic poetry, 'seems to have reacted to it, much as I did at the age of 7 to watermelon, when I ate a whole one, with a total revulsion that lasted 30 years'.[4]

Lieutenant F. W. (Bill) Harwood, c. 1945

Bill was interested in logic, in the formal, philosophical sense – particularly in demonstrating, à la Wittgenstein, the absurdity of metaphysical assertions about such fantasies as truth, beauty and the soul. He was intrigued by computing, then in its infancy, and the question of whether machines could think. He also had a deep fascination with boats, and was making plans to build one after the war. Gwen was more than willing to expand her mental furniture to accommodate these interests. She loved talking to Bill, whose intelligence she found both daunting and dazzling – though she did find that he tended to underrate her knowledge. 'He thinks I don't know about a lot of things I understand quite clearly and explains them to me,' she remarked fondly to Tony. It was a trait she found adorable.[5] Besides, she did have much to learn from him. She had encountered no twentieth-century philosophy except that of Catholic theologians, and Bill introduced her to positivist thinkers like Bertrand Russell and Gilbert Ryle; under his tutelage, she began to think for the first time about 'logical atomism, truth tables &c'.[6] He loaned her his books, which she teasingly dubbed the 'Master Works', including 'Symbolic Logic, which makes me Feel Terrible every time I look at it'.[7]

Bill seemed to her extraordinarily unconventional in his thinking.[8] She told Tony that she was sometimes 'astonished at the thought of his great intellectual power not bound or harnessed in any way by ordinary considerations'. This power was directed towards not only unpacking abstruse philosophical theorising but also practical ends. One evening, Gwen reported, Bill gave her 'a talk on How to Make People Do What You Want': 'I listened to him carefully. He *is* ruthless.' Frank Kellaway, who had worked with Bill in Darwin, agreed, telling Gwen several years later that he knew 'few people better qualified than Bill for the struggle of manipulating people to produce results'.[9] He saw Bill as having a quiet, patient determination that enabled him to turn an unfavourable situation around.

In the navy, Lieutenant Harwood was highly regarded. He had recently been transferred to the Brisbane headquarters of the operation codenamed 'Ferdinand' – otherwise known as the Coastwatchers – whose job was to run the secret network of local spies spread throughout New Guinea and the Pacific.[10] As signals officer, Bill's role was to develop codes to be used by the Coastwatchers in sending and receiving information. If a team on the ground was captured, it was assumed they would crack under torture, and Bill would be called upon to rapidly generate a new set of codes. This he did extremely well. Years later, the US colonel Allison Ind would note that 'scholarly William Harwood' was 'a wizard at creating cipher systems to keep the enemy in ignorance'.[11] A young WRANS (Women's Royal Australian Naval Service) colleague of Bill's remembered that his codes 'were so good that they were sent to . . . the Director of Naval Intelligence in Melbourne, and were going to be put in safe keeping in case they were ever to be used again'.[12] One of their distinctive features was that they were based on nursery rhymes; his colleague would always remember one that used the story of 'The Three Little Pigs'. She did, however, consider him a 'strange man': 'Kept to himself very much, I find that these very clever people don't communicate very well with you. He lived in a world of his own . . . You could be talking to him sometimes and you didn't get an answer.'

Gwen found this delightful. She saw not only his arrogance but also his cool, sardonic humour, as well as a hidden vulnerability that would have astonished his navy colleagues. As they grew closer, Bill confided details of his past that he had told no one else, and which roused her protective instincts. Bill's father, Harold Harwood, an auctioneer who dabbled in real estate, had killed himself at fifty, when Bill, the eldest child, was just seventeen. According to the testimony of his wife, Beatrice, the suicide was a surprise to the family. She told the coroner that as far as she knew, Harold had no reason to want to kill himself. He had seemed perfectly normal on the morning that he dropped his daughter at school as usual, drove to Mentone Pier and shot himself with his own revolver. She added, however, that he was 'a highly strung man, and for the last fortnight he looked very tired, and complained of feeling cold'.[13] She insisted that he had no financial troubles, but it seems likely that he had got in over his head with a real estate company and could not see any way out. Certainly, in later life, Gwen would link Bill's extremely cautious approach to money to his father's financial ruin and death.[14]

In early December 1943, some two months after his return to Brisbane with Bill in tow, Tony left for Melbourne. Bill continued to visit Grimes Street on his own for a couple more weeks before he also departed, headed for what he dubbed the 'revolting regions' up north. He was to be part of a small mission charged with taking supplies to the Coastwatchers and gathering what intelligence they could. They were to travel by submarine to the New Guinea coast, from where they would make their way ashore by rubber dinghy, carrying all their supplies, including their disassembled radio equipment. It was a perilous operation: if their equipment was damaged or lost, they would be stranded, unable to signal for a pick-up; if they were captured, they would be tortured.[15] Gwen was allowed to know none of these details; all she knew was that Bill was going into danger, and her fear for him brought an added intensity to her feelings. No sooner had he left than she wrote to tell Tony that she and Bill were in love. 'I feel that I couldn't live with anyone else, or without him,' she wrote. Though Bill had not said much, she continued, she knew he felt the same.[16] Given that Tony had introduced them, and that her friendship with him had preceded this new relationship, she was anxious that he should not feel excluded. Even as she professed her love for Bill, she spoke as warmly as ever of the happiness she had found with Tony and the importance of his friendship. When she was with Bill, she wrote, she felt that Tony was there too, their 'invisible companion'.[17]

Tony responded graciously, telling Gwen that he was delighted by this turn of events; when he had brought his two dear friends together, he had 'hoped' this would happen.[18] Many years later, after she had come to understand Tony's sexuality, Gwen would wonder whether he had been in love with Bill himself – hopelessly and self-sacrificingly so.[19] At the time, she felt only that this new love involved all three of them, and that they would go forward together in deep, abiding friendship. One of her favourite fantasies was of a day when Tony would be 'travelling through many lands to sing', and she and Bill would 'turn up in our small boat and come to your concert weatherbeaten and crusted with salt!'[20] She was a little surprised that Bill had not confided in Tony himself, but she was coming to understand how intensely private he was. At his behest, she agreed to keep their new relationship a secret from everyone but Tony, and urged Tony to keep their secret too,[21] explaining that for Bill, the idea that he and Gwen should become 'objects of interest to the "reading public"' through her letters to Tony was abhorrent.[22]

By the end of February, Bill was safely back in Brisbane, thin and shaky after his time in the field and subject to attacks of fever.[23] While he was recovering, he moved in with the hospitable Fosters. Gwen spent her nights in his room, though 'officially' she slept in her usual bed on the verandah.[24] It was a kind of blissful honeymoon. 'I feel that I am growing like a tree, putting forth new leaves and branches, that sealed fountains are bursting open, that enclosed gardens are blossoming,'[25] she told Tony, drawing freely on the language of the biblical Song of Songs. The happiness she and Bill were tasting was 'immortal', she assured him. They were to each other 'a paradise of delights'.[26] Everything she had ever read about what love could be she was now experiencing. She and Bill were Cathy and Heathcliff from *Wuthering Heights* ('I know what Catherine meant when she said "I *am* Heathcliff"'),[27] John Donne and his beloved (we are 'made of one another'),[28] the incarnation of all of Schubert's most ravishing love songs. 'Late at night I was lying in Bill's arms and they played "Du Bist die Ruh"' arranged for strings,' she wrote to Tony. 'The house was still, only the trees were rustling outside softly, and the music moved me almost to tears.' The words of the song she had rehearsed with Tony 'sang themselves in the quietness of my mind as I lay there looking at Bill', she went on, 'and I knew that without him everything else in the world would be nothing to me – as my friend Donne says: "compared to this / all honour's mimic, all wealth alchemy."'[29]

Donne's love poems and the passionate language of Christian mysticism came together for Gwen in a kind of frenzy of self-surrender. 'If I am to be Bill's, I can keep nothing,' she wrote earnestly. 'I will make myself his: the treaty will be drawn up and signed, and the whole country will be taken.'[30] 'We have grown into one another in an impossible way,' she wrote in another letter. 'There is no language to tell you of this, Donne's words "we are made of one another" are the nearest . . . It is something more than all the unbelievable speech of hands and eyes – something that makes the words "I" and "you" unnecessary'.[31] In light of the social mores of today, her ecstatic words have a faintly sinister ring. 'This girl belongs to H[arwood],' Gwen wrote happily in one letter.[32] In others, she referred to Bill as her 'lord and master'. This was not hyperbole. She believed, in keeping with the conventions of her time, that the husband was the head of the household, and expected that after their marriage, Bill would lay down the rules. The prospect did not frighten her. 'Bill loves me so much that I have no fear at all of giving him not only what I am now but what I shall be,' she assured Tony. 'My love for him is measureless . . . There are no limits, no bounds at all'.[33]

◆ ◆ ◆

The degree of her self-surrender would be tested sooner than she could have imagined. Before long, Bill began to express displeasure at her ongoing correspondence with Tony. He did not like to see her writing to him, he told her, and her obvious pleasure in the friendship gave him pain. In fact, Bill had a tendency, she confessed to Tony, to resent not only present friendships but past ones. He was distressed when former beaus called to see Gwen. The thought that she might ever have loved someone else as much as she now loved him was 'unbearable to him'.[34] Gwen was dismayed by this. She saw it as a failure on her part to show Bill how completely she belonged to him. If he could just understand that, she felt, his jealousy would melt away. Tony urged Gwen to stand up to her beloved. 'Don't let Bill mould you to his shape,' he begged. 'He must accept your life, not possess it.'[35] Gwen agreed. 'If H. tries to possess me instead of loving me he will find himself with nothing,' she wrote grimly. 'I will give myself to him utterly and keep nothing; I would die gladly for him or suffer most bitter pain, but if the element of possession enters in he will taste bitterness instead of the fair fruit. I am his, and he knows I am, but if I am not free I am nothing.'

Around this time, Gwen had a dream she would come to think was significant. She dreamed that her father brought home 'a young lion and a baboon for pets'.[36] The baboon sat in Tony's place at the dining table, the lion in Bill's: 'The lion was snapping its jaws together in a menacing fashion. The baboon had little trousers on, and smiled at me.' Gwen was 'suddenly overcome with fear' and fled to her room. The baboon outpaced her, reaching the door first, and 'the lion came up the passage after him'. She found herself on the tank stand, 'looking down at [Agnes], who said "Don't be frightened, they only want to play." I thought to myself, the lion could easily snap my hand off, and how could I play the piano.' She told Agnes that the 'pets' had to go. When she recounted the dream to Tony, he was 'very impressed' and told Gwen that she had 'assessed the situation unconsciously; the handsome Bill would bite off my hands and remodel my soul'.[37] Certainly the threat from the lion is the most immediate, but the baboon is frightening, too, pursuing Gwen up the passageway and cutting off her escape. Between the two urgent and demanding young men, Gwen was feeling increasingly trapped.

Bill soon returned to the attack, telling Gwen that he loved her so much that he could not share her with anyone. He wanted her to break off all correspondence with Tony and end their friendship. It was, he insisted, the only kind thing to do, given that once he and Gwen were married, he intended to cut Tony out of their lives. Better for all of them to make a clean break now. He asked her to consider how she would feel if the situation were reversed. How would she like it if he 'had someone like that and wrote her long delightful letters'?[38] In this, however, he misjudged his future bride. Gwen was not possessive. 'I shouldn't care if he wrote long delightful letters to all the young ladies in Australia, if it made him happy,' she retorted – though only to Tony. She was not exaggerating. She believed that love was an infinite resource. As she would say many years later, 'Two people in the sun [do not] make the sun less warm.'[39] She did not take what she called a 'capitalistic' view of relationships, in which people's passions and desires were bought and paid for. 'Bill seems to think that my deep love for you will rob him, but how can it when it enriches me, and I am his?' she wrote to Tony. 'I hope Bill gets over it soon; a company of red-beards should be sent to deal with him!'[40]

Although she thought Bill's attitude 'unreasonable', even 'silly', she could not bring herself to openly defy him. She understood that his pain was real, and she was even a little in awe of the strength of his feelings. 'He cannot bear me to give a look or a word or a thought to anyone else,' she told Tony. What's more, he was so overwrought that she couldn't even tease him about it.[41] He wanted her 'entirely for himself': 'If he could make me invisible to everyone but himself he would do so gladly.' Deeply in love, and confident that she understood Bill better than he did himself, she felt sure he would soon realise the error of his ways. In the meantime, she tried to placate him by keeping her letters to Tony out of sight. As she told Tony, she would be 'worthless rubbish' if she 'closed [her] heart' to him after all he had done for her, and all they had shared. 'I just couldn't, anyway!'[42]

But it was not enough to keep her correspondence with Tony to herself: Bill wanted her promise that she would not write to him again. She tried a form of passive resistance, sympathising with Bill's feelings but evading his demands, but this did not satisfy him either. Finally, when he told her that her ongoing contact with Tony was destroying him, she capitulated. She would stop writing to Tony for good. Bill dictated the letter – signed by her alone – in which she told him she would no longer write, and that he should henceforth write only to her and Bill together. Far away in Melbourne, trying to extract himself from the navy and struggling 'with lethargy & morose depression',[43] Tony reacted furiously. Though he had had some idea that it was coming, Gwen's letter felt like an unwarranted betrayal. His angry response, which implied that cutting off contact was as much her desire as Bill's, struck Gwen to the heart, but though it cost her a great deal, she kept her promise and did not reply.

A few weeks later, however, when Bill was sent north on another mission, Gwen seized the opportunity to write Tony a 'MOST SECRET' letter. In it, she assured him of her love, and tried to make excuses for Bill. 'Bill has suffered bitterness that would have broken me,' she wrote. 'I am sure you would think differently if you knew what I do.' He was neither tyrannical nor cruel, she insisted. 'He just loves me without measure and what you see as tyranny is only the immeasurable demands of love.'[44] These 'immeasurable demands' included that she not talk about Tony or even think of him.[45] 'I have not played the piano since you went away . . . Bill is jealous even of that,' she confessed. Yet she was willing to make the sacrifice. 'I love Bill without any measure or restraint,' she declared. 'What he wrote is quite true – in some ways I *am* Bill.'

She still believed Bill's possessiveness would prove to be temporary. In the meantime, though, she proposed a compromise: why not continue to write in secret? *She* had promised not to write, certainly, but 'what is to stop Theophilus Panbury writing to you? Or Fred Hackleskinner?' Tony could send his letters to her at the WDC, and Bill need never know. Tony, however, was affronted by the suggestion that he engage in a 'surreptitious correspondence'. He wrote one last time, to declare that he would never forgive Bill, and Gwen replied, begging Tony to 'hold no bitterness' against him, 'for that wounds me more deeply than anything else could'.[46] With that, the correspondence ceased.

There was a brief interregnum in mid-July 1944, when Tony wrote to say that his sister, Ruby, also a singer, was visiting Brisbane with the Gilbert and Sullivan company. The Fosters immediately invited Ruby to stay with them, and Gwen took the opportunity to write Tony a joyful, rambunctious letter, in her old style, about how she had met up with Ruby at her hotel and brought her home to Grimes Street. She even enclosed two lengthy Justice Tickleturnip skits. But Tony's wounds had not healed, and he refused to engage in further communication. The following June, however, he sent her a birthday gift – a couple of moralising Victorian-era books he knew she would love – care of the WDC. Gwen had been transferred to a different branch of the public service by then, but went back to collect the parcel. When she saw who it was from, she 'stood in War Damages little kitchen overcome with joy, and all the long and terrible silence was over'.

Over the next two days, she wrote Tony a flurry of rapturous letters. 'At the last day, it is said, the secrets of all hearts shall be revealed. Until then, perhaps, you will never know how dearly I love you, and how much it has cost me to keep my promise to Bill never to write to you again,' she told him. 'If you think that I wrote a word of that ridiculous letter you are MAD.' She dreamed of him night after night, she went on, and woke up 'longing for a word between us that would break the bitter silence'.[47] A second letter on the same day begins: 'This morning after I had written to you I walked to my dentist's rooms on Wickham Terrace, and the joy of breaking the leaden silence was almost unbearable . . . As I look at your dear familiar writing I can feel something reviving within me that I thought was dead.' She was more convinced than ever that Bill's interdiction on their friendship was wrong. Even so, in practical terms, nothing had changed: 'If Bill knows that I have written to you, hearts as well as promises will be broken, and who will mend them?'

The question of broken promises was preying on her mind. 'I have not told [Bill] I have written to you, it would hurt him terribly,' she wrote the following day. 'Today I feel myself all the grief it would cause him.'[48] Yet she was determined to continue the correspondence: 'Now that the silence is broken I don't think I can live without your letters again.' After her various harrowing confessions were out of the way, she made a concerted effort to get their friendship back onto its old footing, catching him up on family news and telling him amusing tales of her new place of work. Agnes had denuded Grimes Lodge of its last trees, she told him sorrowfully. 'Oh, it was an evil day. I felt as if they were tearing my heart out.'[49] With the letter she enclosed an account of 'A Strange Dream', just as she used to. In this dream, she wandered at night through a snowy landscape until she came to a Cistercian abbey, where she saw a monk who was looking for someone. In a house with 'seven stairways', she found the missing man 'in a small lighted room'. The man 'was the image of Bill, and yet he was not Bill. Bill was lying on a small bed somewhere else – I knew this, but could not see him.' She discovered that the stranger was 'destined to be one of the contemplatives of the church', and allowed him to lead her to a bookcase filled with 'well-known books on mystical theology'. 'Then the young man said "I want you to love Bill and take care of him. You are always his, and he is yours."' Whether or not she intended it, in recounting this dream she was giving Tony a very clear message about where her loyalties lay. He did not write to her again.

◆ ◆ ◆

Throughout 1944 and into 1945, Bill came and went from Brisbane, staying with the Fosters when he could. Gwen spent her time thinking and dreaming of her future as his wife. The restless energy she had poured into destabilising the WDC seemed now to be in abeyance. In her new place of work, the Queensland Prices Branch of the federal Department of Trade, the red-bearded dwarfs did not visit. She still went out with Vera to concerts and lectures, and performed her duties as organist and choir master at All Saints, but her heart was not in it. She gave up her piano lessons on the grounds that she did not have the time to put in the work. She was focused on preparing for the new life she would embark upon with Bill when the war was over. They would be poor, she knew; neither had money behind them, and Bill was not yet sure what kind of work he would find when he came out of the navy. Gwen was saving her pennies and dreaming of the home she would make and the children she would have.

Though she missed Tony, she did not resent Bill's determination to ban the correspondence. Like the wife in 'The Gorgon's Head', she was more than willing to devote her life to supporting and caring for her husband, serving what she laughingly called the 'Great Intellect'. Not even Peter's disapproval of Bill could disturb her. Peter had met Bill late in 1943, when Tony took them both out to dinner, and Gwen had eagerly sought his verdict.[50] Peter was not impressed. Bill was 'intellectually unscrupulous', he told her, and had no interest in the arts. He would end up, Peter opined, as 'an unimaginative dentist or doctor'. Gwen was disconcerted, but not put off. In this instance, she was sure, her infallible guru was wrong; his objectivity was compromised by his disapproval, as an Anglo-Catholic, of Bill's 'non-scholastic attitude in philosophical matters'. Besides, the dislike was mutual: Bill had dismissed Peter as 'the usual muddled clergyman'.[51] When it came to religion, Gwen herself was growing ever closer to Bill's point of view. In the light of Bill's steady rationalism, faith seemed increasingly absurd.[52] Her new idol was replacing the old one.

◆ ◆ ◆

The war ended on 15 August 1945, and little more than a fortnight later, on Tuesday, 4 September, Bill and Gwen were married at All Saints church. There was a transport strike that day, so they walked the two and a half miles into the city from Auchenflower along the river, 'with the jacarandas flowering'.[53] Years later, Gwen would speak of the 'inexpressible peace and joy that filled us'.[54] They were married by the Reverend Bates, who had baptised and confirmed Gwen back in 1939, as well as seeing her into (and out of) the Franciscan convent, and into (and out of) her teaching job at St Christopher's Lodge. Gwen's only friend from the WDC, Diana Gill, was one of their witnesses, her father the other.

After the ceremony, the newlyweds went to lodgings in New Farm while Bill waited to be discharged from the navy. It was the first time they had been alone together for more than a few days, and they revelled in it. Not even an eavesdropping landlady could dampen the joy of their first weeks as a married couple.[55] By this time, Bill had secured a job as a lecturer in the tiny English department at the University of Tasmania. Before he left for Hobart – a couple of weeks earlier than Gwen, as he had yet to be officially demobbed – they had a bonfire. All Gwen's letters from Tony, as well as from Manfred Ritter and other male friends, went up in smoke.[56] Though she made the sacrifice willingly, these lost letters would haunt her.

While she waited for a flight to Tasmania, Gwen read W. Somerset Maugham's *The Razor's Edge*, the soulful tale of a young American man, Larry, whose life is utterly changed by his experiences of war.[57] Rejecting the trappings of conventional success, he devotes himself to the quest for meaning, travelling to India, among other places, and discovering meditation and mysticism. Gwen loved the book: Larry reminded her of Tony.

Finally, she got her passage and boarded a plane for the south. She would never live in Brisbane again.

Part II:
1946 - 1969

8

The Days of Whine and Noses

Nineteen forty-five. I have been sick
all the way from Brisbane; first time in the air.
My husband's waiting in civilian clothes.
Another name now. All those burning glances
cancelled, all those raging letters burned.

Gwen Harwood, '1945'

Sometimes I think my hatred of Tasmania sprang not from the place
but from the sheer blood loss of leaving friends and idle talk. How could
I have imagined I would have all that and holy matrimony too?

Gwen Harwood, Letter to Greg Kratzmann, 20 July 1994

GWEN ARRIVED AT THE TINY AIRPORT AT CAMBRIDGE, JUST outside of Hobart, on a chilly Saturday afternoon in late October 1945. She had flown from Brisbane via Melbourne, where she stayed briefly with Bill's mother at the family home in Mont Albert. It was her first meeting with Bill's family, and she was somewhat overawed. Bill was his mother's darling, and the pride and joy of his three 'formidable aunts', who told Gwen repeatedly 'what a clever man I had married'.[1] Proudly, they described his life as a student before the war: 'He had a study upstairs to which he retired after breakfast. At ten his mother took up his morning tea; at 12.30 he had lunch, then studied away until afternoon tea. Of course he had lectures to go to and sometimes he went for a walk.' It was a life the lively, sociable Gwen could barely imagine. For perhaps the first time, she began to have a sense of how very different she was from her beloved. 'He sounded like a lottery I shouldn't have won or even thought of having a ticket in.'

When she finally arrived in Tasmania, she was overjoyed to find Bill waiting for her at the airport in his civvies. They melted into each other's arms 'with good old-fashioned happiness'. By the time they had made their way by bus and ferry into the small city, it was well past lunch time and they were hungry. They found a café and asked for the menu, only to be told by a snippy waitress, 'Lunch is off and afternoon tea's/ not on!'[2] It was, in retrospect, an ominous warning of the lack of sustenance Gwen would find in her new Tasmanian life.

Gwen immediately felt uneasy in her new surroundings. Though Hobart's Georgian buildings and English country gardens were charming, 'something about the place [spelt] *death* to me', she wrote to a friend. 'This was my first feeling when I landed here in 1945: not, "how beautiful" but "Get me out of here."'[3] The dark bulk of Mount Wellington looming over the town seemed to hem her in. This chill island was most definitely not the sunny, relaxed lotus land of her childhood. If Brisbane was a sprawling, brawling, open-air city, Hobart was a stone fortress against the bitter weather. To a child of the tropical north, it was inexpressibly gloomy.[4] Gwen and Bill spent their first night together at the Astor Hotel on Macquarie Street, where they lay in bed listening to the rain drumming on the roof. Gwen would later say that the sound filled her 'with a kind of existential terror'.[5] She could not shake the sense that there was 'something ominous in some parts of Hobart', an element of 'terror and regret'. The evil that had been done there in the colonial era – the attacks on Indigenous people, the dreadful convict prison – had left an intangible trace.

More prosaically, Tasmania seemed depressingly backwards to Gwen. Peter Bennie used to complain that Brisbane was 'twenty years behind the times', but Hobart, in Gwen's opinion, was 'at least fifty'.[6] It was small – its population about one-fifth of Brisbane's[7] – and much more staid. Even so, it had most of the facilities of a major city. If bread and milk were still home-delivered by horse and cart, Hobart did have department stores and cinemas, a museum and library, a symphony orchestra and a well-established theatre scene. The poet Vivian Smith, who grew up there in the 1940s, remembered the city as 'a pleasant mingling of the urban and the pastoral, the cultivated and the wild'.[8]

Gwen and Bill lived at the Astor for three weeks while they looked for a house to rent.[9] Like all Australian cities in the immediate aftermath of the war, Hobart was teeming with ex-servicemen. The housing shortage was so acute that the government decreed that those who owned holiday homes must make them available for rent, and this was how Gwen and Bill finally found a cottage in Fern Tree, a scattered village halfway up Mount Wellington. Hobart had a reputation for snobbish conservatism, but there were pockets of bohemianism, and Fern Tree was one of them; it was a haven for those who eschewed city living on principle. Hal Porter, who lived there briefly in the early 1950s, felt there was far too much 'nature' on the mountainside for civilised living. The weatherboard houses were 'cabin-like' and of 'singular unsightliness', he wrote, set 'in what much resemble the crude clearings of early settlers'.[10] They came with 'built-in snowstorms, visiting bushfires, and resident soggy clouds'. They did, however, have marvellous views.

The Harwoods' cottage sat in a sheltered hollow on a curve of Pillinger Drive between Bracken Lane, above, and the Fern Tree Hotel, below. It was a beautiful spot, and Gwen and Bill spent weekends exploring the walking paths that wound through densely growing snow gums, Australian oaks and mountain ash to icy waterfalls or craggy outcrops with vistas of the foothills, the city, the Derwent River and the ocean. Conditions in the cottage were primitive, especially when compared with the luxuries of Grimes Street. For cooking and heating, they had 'a monstrous old fuel stove with holes in the fire-box that let cinders through onto anything in the oven'.[11] Gwen did the laundry in an outside copper washer, a strenuous chore that was particularly trying in the freezing winters. Their furniture was mostly made by Bill out of packing cases and old wireless cabinets. They didn't have a car or telephone, or even, in their first months, a radio. Hobart was thirty minutes away by bus. By night, possums made a 'ghastly racket in the roof' and 'bush rats [ran] round [their] bedroom'. By day, the birds descended upon their newly planted vegetable garden.[12]

But the newlyweds were happy. Gwen threw herself into domesticity with zeal, baking her own bread, tending the struggling garden and preparing the regulation hot meal each day for her husband. She was still glowing with idealism about her new role as wife and helpmeet, and determined to be the embodiment of the perfect housewife. In the evenings, she and Bill sat by the fire reading and talking 'endlessly',[13] and on weekends, they worked in the garden, picnicked in the bush and argued happily about philosophy, poetry and linguistics.

When Bill was at work, however, Gwen felt her isolation keenly. He took the bus each day to the university, which then occupied the old Hobart High School in the Domain in central Hobart – a grand but impractical building that was already cramped and would soon be stretched to breaking point by the postwar expansion in student numbers. Bill had been warmly welcomed by his colleagues in the English Department, which at that point comprised one professor, Bert Taylor, and one part-time lecturer, Joyce Eyre (staff numbers would soon be swelled by the addition of another lecturer, Ted Stokes, who, with his wife, Margaret, would become lifelong friends of the Harwoods). But while Bill had a ready-made community through work, Gwen knew no one. She missed her parents and friends, her church community and the busy, sociable world of which the Fosters' Auchenflower home had been the centre. She missed her piano. More than ever, she missed being able to write to Tony. 'I just can't remember those [early] years [in Tasmania] without remembering how I longed above all just to write to him and tell him about my life,' she would later confess.[14] Lonely and homesick, she would 'walk to a spot on the hill where a cluster of red roofs reminded [her] of a corner near the river at home, and stare at these until the desolate landscape faded and the winter was of little account'.[15]

◆ ◆ ◆

Gwen was delighted to find, early in 1946, that she was pregnant. Bill was full of idealistic schemes for raising their child as a 'genius', following the John Stuart Mill model,[16] while Gwen surrendered to happy daydreams of motherhood, taking long, solitary walks in the bush with her head full of fantasies of life with her child.[17] On the night she went into labour, it was snowing – at last she had fulfilled her childhood dream of seeing snow – and the snow was piled so high that the taxi Bill called to take her to hospital could not get up the drive. She had to make her way on foot through the dark and the cold to where it had come to a standstill some half a mile down the road.[18]

All went well with the birth, though she would later say that she was 'unprepared for the pain, and howled like a Wagnerian soprano'. When she brought baby John Francis home a fortnight later, she was overcome with happiness. 'I took him onto the balcony; snow started to fall. I stood with my child in a state of inexpressible joy.'[19] She and Bill had just bought their first radio and Beethoven's *Pastoral* Symphony began to play. 'It was too much: that marvellous Movement . . . the snow falling, the great tall gum trees and to hold my own child. Every time I hear that great flowing theme, I am back there with the child, in the snow.'

She loved being a mother, revelling in the 'absolute unquestioning love' of a young baby and the 'ravishing close physical contact'.[20] Breastfeeding she found 'a very great pleasure'. She also enjoyed the company of other mothers her age. Scattered among the trees, out of sight of one another, were other holiday homes occupied by other young couples starting their lives anew after the war. The women began to run into one another at the

Fern Tree general store or on the bus to the city, and friendships soon sprang up. They supported one another with emergency childminding or loans of household supplies, and got together regularly for afternoon tea. One of these women, Betty Pybus, remembered young Mrs Harwood as 'quiet and shy, with long straight hair hanging down her back'.[21] Another, Ann Jennings, who would later become one of Gwen's closest friends, found the new arrival dauntingly perfect.[22] 'Gwen was a Franciscan novice for several years apparently before she married, and in reaction now adores the married state and her child,' she wrote in her diary in 1947. '[She] wears her red hair long to the waist with a chaste band round her head.'[23] Gwen seemed to Ann to be serenely self-sufficient in her devotion to her husband and son. She had no inkling that Gwen was lonely until a mutual friend suggested it, and then she found the idea rather comforting, since Gwen seemed 'otherwise to have no human weakness or inadequacy'. Even then, she did not really believe that Gwen and her handsome husband, who were so 'very much in love – almost moist in their mutual solicitude', could really be lacking in anything, writing two years later that the young couple were 'contented hermits'.[24]

Gwen and baby John at Fern Tree, c. 1947

This quiet, composed and 'chaste' young wife and mother seems to bear no resemblance to the wild girl of the WDC – or the tempestuous teenager who preceded her. It seems that Gwen had put away that 'neurotic child' in order to don the socially sanctioned persona of 'a reasonable woman': one who accepted that her role in life was to marry and have children.[25] She had eagerly embraced Peter Bennie's view that marriage was 'a wonderful institution'[26] and felt sure she had made the right decision in adopting it as her own vocation. Nevertheless, as she and Bill settled in to their new lives, she began to become aware of the gap between her idealised vision of love and the reality of marriage. This was becoming evident in all kinds of small ways. She had assumed she would have 'a household like my hospitable mother's',[27] but she was gradually coming to understand that Bill had no desire to replicate the merry sociability of life at Grimes Street. He did not enjoy 'frolicsome company', and was 'indifferent' to 'art and music'.[28] Less sociable than she, he was also more private. He was happiest immured with his books, his work and his wife.

A couple of incidents brought this home to Gwen. The first was a visit from her friend Diana Gill's family, their first Brisbane visitors since they had moved to Hobart. 'It was a fine warm day and we took rugs out and sat under a tree. B, after an introduction during which he did not display any enthusiasm, declined to join us and took his tools to a remote corner to hack at blackberries. He would not join us in the house for arvo but had his tea in the blackberries, where he stayed.'[29]

The other incident involved Bill's colleague Joyce Eyre, whom Gwen invited to Fern Tree for lunch. In preparation for their guest's arrival, she put some fruit on the table. 'There were two bananas among other fruit. B said "Don't put the bananas on, Joyce might eat one."' Gwen was shocked. She had come from 'a household where of course the guest ate the banana and the fruit after its kind, and the household saved up for or did without a banana'. It was a revelation of their fundamentally different perspectives. For the first time, she began to feel her lack of independence. Bill paid for the household, so he could order it as he chose. 'I wished I had listened to my mother – her last words as I left Brisbane were, "Keep your own bankbook." I stupidly didn't and passed my savings into the common fund.'[30]

Having no money of her own was increasingly burdensome. She had been accustomed to buying things for herself: music, books, hats. Now she had to account for whatever she spent from the household budget, and felt she could no longer buy things purely for her own pleasure.[31] She very much wanted Bill's approval, and was alert to any subtle signs that she had disappointed him. She had learned that he conveyed his displeasure with looks and silences – what she dubbed 'Bill's coldness'.[32] This was not the way upsets had been regulated in her childhood home, and she found it difficult to deal with. She was a rager and could cope with storms and outbursts, but she quickly became depressed when the emotional temperature was cool. Bill's silences inflamed her fear that if she did not live up to his expectations, he would cease to love her.[33] She was determined not to risk that. If that meant being aloof with others instead of warm and lively, she was prepared to do it. If it meant keeping art and music in the background, she would do that, too. Later, she would say that she lost her 'natural shape': 'When I look back on the early years of our marriage I cannot imagine myself.'[34] At the time, though, it seemed only natural that she should adapt to accommodate her husband. And there was so much that was good in their marriage – in their intellectual companionship, their sex life, their 'mutual solicitude' – that such sacrifices seemed a small price to pay.

Gwen did not, however, give up poetry. When she left Queensland, she was still in the frame of mind that Tony had designated her 'Brisbane indifference to publication'.[35] Though she had published one poem, she was in no hurry to publish another, determined to allow her gift – assuming she had one – to develop in its own way and in its own time, as she had advised Frank Kellaway to do, rather than vulgarly seeking to force it through early acclaim. But in Hobart, writing and publishing assumed a new urgency for her. In leaving Brisbane, she had left behind her identity as a 'practising musician'[36] – without a piano, she could not even play for her own pleasure – and she was unprepared for the anguish this caused her. 'The absence of music from my fingertips is sometimes unbearable,' she wrote. 'Nothing can equal it in depth of pain.'[37] After all her years of playing, music was so layered into her 'nerves and muscles' that her fingers would literally ache when she heard a piece of music she used to be able to play.[38] The loss was so intolerable, she would later say, that she turned to poetry to assuage it: 'I was driven to seek wholeness and forced to develop in another way, as a blind man in his eternal night must sharpen his other senses.'[39] She had given up the piano, but she could not give up her identity as an artist.

She would later see these early years in Tasmania as her poetry apprenticeship. With no mentors available, she became her own teacher, reading all the contemporary poetry she could get her hands on. 'When you are learning music you do the best you can with your technique; and then, listening to others, you hear that is not what you are doing,' she once explained to an interviewer.[40] She did the same thing with poetry, doing the best she could and then comparing her attempts with the work that was being published. The comparison was not, at first, in her favour: 'Reading others I thought: that is not the kind of thing I am doing.' She read not only the Australian literary periodicals, of which there were few, but also the English and American ones, which she was able to access through the library at the University of Tasmania. Soon, she was familiar with the work of all the poets of her generation. She did not have much time for her Australian contemporaries,[41] but she was excited by the new American voices appearing in magazines like *Poetry* and *The Kenyon Review*. 'Anthony Hecht, Robert Lowell, Richard Wilbur & Stanley Kunitz are my masters,' she would write in the 1950s. 'I've learnt more from them than from the English poets.'[42] Later, she would add to the list Theodore Roethke ('the best lyric poet in the world at present') and Robert Penn Warren ('Of all the writers I've ever read I feel closest to [Warren]').[43] She preferred poets who used traditional forms to those experimenting with free verse; she would always find it easier to write when she had a specific rhythmical structure to bounce off. But she was also very much interested in the new freedom, especially evident in American poetry, to talk about personal and even domestic experiences. The old idea that only classical and/or mythological themes were fit subjects for poetry was crumbling, and Gwen was excited by the possibilities – though not yet confident enough to try them out herself.

She was not entirely on her own in her pursuit of a poetry career. Her friend Ann Jennings was also toying with becoming a writer, and her interest, like Gwen's, had become more urgent with marriage and motherhood, and the concomitant fear that her independent selfhood would be lost. As she confided to her diary, she had an overwhelming need to 'do something creative with my mind': 'I must feel in some way necessary, successful, capable. I must justify my existence beyond housework.'[44]

Ann was studying for an arts degree, with the idea of one day going on to do medicine. As a married woman, and soon a pregnant one, she attracted awed admiration from younger undergraduates, who considered her not only beautiful and sophisticated but also liberated.[45] Nevertheless, Ann had doubts about her own abilities. Her early encounters with Gwen came through Bill, who was Ann's English lecturer, and the seeming brilliance of the two of them together brought out Ann's insecurities. She first went to their house in December 1946, when she was just twenty-one, to discuss an essay of hers with Mr Harwood, and there she met Gwen. Bill she found 'very young and dewy with an astounding brain', but Gwen was just 'too abnormally intelligent and articulate'.[46] The usually confident and outgoing Ann had 'the most terrifying inhibitions before such intellect and fluency of conversation'.[47] It seemed to her that Gwen was 'able to do without effort all the things I long to do'.[48] In the couple's presence she found herself 'subnormally tongue-tied'. 'I can hardly put a sentence together sensibly when the Harwoods are in the full flush of their intellectual moods,' she grumbled. Spending time with them gave her 'an intolerable inferiority complex'.

Where Ann shone, she felt, was in her relationships with others, but Gwen, she felt, did not think other people 'important enough to concern herself with them'. It would be several more years before Ann would know Gwen well enough to understand that her seeming aloofness was all show; Gwen had the same kind of passion for friendship as Ann. She had simply parked this side of herself, temporarily, in order to emulate her new husband's tastes and inclinations. One of the people Gwen was most passionate about, ironically, was Ann herself, whose beauty and life deeply stirred her. She had been drawn to Ann before she even knew who she was, catching sight of her on the bus into town: 'masses of glorious hair, eyes blazing with experience – nineteen? thirty? I couldn't tell.'[49] But though the two women saw one another often, Ann had no idea how much Gwen liked and admired her – nor how wistfully Gwen regarded the bohemian circles in which Ann and her husband, Roger, moved.

Despite her wariness, Ann took to dropping in on Gwen on her way home from the bus in the afternoon for a cup of tea and a cigarette.[50] They had a lot in common. Ann's attitudes were liberal; she was unencumbered by traditional Christian views of sex as sinful, and keen to expand her sexual experience.[51] She was also ambivalent about motherhood, loving the intimate bond she had with her babies but chafing at the need to sacrifice so much of her own identity to care for them. 'The most frustrating and even agonising aspect of leading this undergraduate domestic life is that one returns home [from university] keen to work, and the precious mood must be thrust down to be replaced by house work and baby minding,' she wrote in 1949. 'And then when night comes and I can indulge the mood, it has gone and I am tired. It hurts me intensely to have to do this three times a week.'[52] Gwen felt similarly stifled – a feeling that would appear some ten years later in a series of powerful poems.

Fern Tree friends (L to R) Shirley Jennings, Ann Jennings (front),
Roger Jennings, Hal Porter, 1947

The two women shared their draft poems with one another. In one diary
entry, Ann records Gwen's announcement that 'one of her recent poems'
had been accepted by *Meanjin*, and a few weeks later, she notes that 'Gwen
has re-written a couple of my poems. They sound marvellous, and I shall
consider publishing them.'[53] When Ann got to know Hal Porter, another
aspiring writer whose stories and poems were beginning to appear regularly
in *The Bulletin*, she took him to meet Gwen. In after years, Gwen often told
the story of that meeting: 'When I opened the door he said, in a perfect sort
of Arthur Askey voice, "Ah, look, it's a dear little woman." And I said, "What
did you expect, Mr Porter?", to which he replied: "A bead-hung vampire."'[54]
Hal, then in his mid-thirties, was already a flamboyant, even outrageous,
character, and Gwen was amused. She understood that men were wary of
women with aspirations to write – 'Lady Poets', as Hal called them, with
mock reverence – and all too ready to dismiss them. It was a victory for her,
of sorts, to be able to pass herself off as a 'dear little woman'.

Gwen was grateful to Hal for accepting her as a fellow poet. When
she first met him, she had published only one poem, while Hal was well
launched on his writing career. Yet he treated her as a peer.[55] He shared his
work with her and was 'ruthlessly critical of what [she] wrote', which she

took as a mark of respect. Forty years later, she would remember how he 'lit my mind up in the days of whine and noses'.[56] She was, like Ann, greatly impressed with what Hal was writing; he was so different from 'the boring high-minded pleasant-enough crowd of poets who were on the stage at the time'. His witty, sophisticated and tantalisingly obscure verse expanded her idea of what was possible for an Australian poet, giving her 'a picture of Australian poetry that was quite different from the one that I had had'.[57] His poetry was urban, rather than rural – one of his characteristic declarations was that he hated 'scenery' – and he had no interest in establishing a distinctively Australian literature. As Ann put it in her diary, 'He refuses to rave about gum trees, billabongs, nulla nullas, brolgas etc.'[58]

Gwen's own poetry in the late 1940s did owe something to gum trees and billabongs. Only three poems have survived from this time – 'The Dead Gums', 'The Fire-Scarred Hillside' and 'Water-Music' – and all three were published in 1949. It is likely there were others, perhaps many more, which she jettisoned or which were rejected by the literary magazines to which she sent them.[59] The first two are meditations on her new landscape, which she depicts as speaking to her of her own mortality. The third, 'Water-Music', tells the story, in the first person, of Eve in the Garden of Eden, and is both livelier and more subversive than the other two. Harwood's Eve is not the foolish dupe of the evil snake, as in the biblical story, but its willing collaborator. She is a mischief-maker who does not so much unleash the world's darkness as reveal it: its 'sweet corrosive core / and the sorrows at its heart'.

This poem was accepted by *Meanjin* in May 1949, while two others (not identified by name, but sent in October 1948 and January 1949 respectively) were rejected.[60] The *Meanjin* archives show that the magazine's poetry reader, Elizabeth Vassilieff, was not impressed by any of Mrs Harwood's poetry. Writing to the editor, Clem Christesen, about 'Water-Music', she noted that this new poem was 'much better than the other two I saw before – not so wholly derivative'. Yet even 'Water-Music' was barely satisfactory: it was 'too neat, too tidy, too flat and correct', its 'rigidly metrical' rhythm 'dull'. To Vassilieff, it was evident that 'the writer is clearly a predominantly intellectual type rather than an emotive one, and this is a philosophical poem rather than a lyric'. This is perhaps a fair assessment of Harwood's poetry, but is wildly wrong about Gwen as a person, devotee of *Wuthering Heights* and quintessential Romantic that she was. 'Technically [the poem] is quite deft but not brilliant,' Vassilieff concluded. 'Her best characteristic here is the selection of very good verbs.' The echo of Peter Bennie's criticism of her short story 'Another Country' several years earlier is striking.

When Christesen wrote to accept 'Water-Music', he reproduced Vassil-ieff's criticism almost word for word, claiming it as his own.[61] For Gwen, the sting was no doubt alleviated by the fact that he had decided to pub-lish the poem; for some years, she would consider 'Water-Music' to be her 'masterpiece'.[62] Her other two surviving poems were published in *The Bul-letin* and *Southerly*: a nice haul for a poet who was only just beginning to discover what she could do. But she had other things to distract her. By late 1949, she was pregnant again, and she and Bill were looking for a house of their own.

◆ ◆ ◆

Gwen had become pregnant with her second child towards the end of 1947, about a year after the birth of John, but the baby – a much-wanted girl – was stillborn on 4 April 1948. When Ann Jennings stopped at the Harwoods' on her way home that afternoon, the door was opened not by Gwen but by a forlorn-looking Bill. He told her that Gwen was in hospital. At her monthly check-up, her doctor had been unable to find the baby's heartbeat and had admitted her at once. 'I could only say "I'm so sorry" and turn off the electric jug which was boiling over,' Ann wrote in her diary that night. 'Bill looked so distracted and young, and the child had scattered the room with so many toys, that all my irritation with his untouchableness vanished, and I just felt sorry and inadequate.'[63] Ann herself knew what it was like to lose a child; her first baby, Mark, had been born around the same time as Gwen's, in August 1946, but had lived only a few hours. Ann never even saw him; he was whisked away as soon as he was born, according to the custom of the day. She was 'conscious of a tremendous sense of loss, deprivation', but fought to 'rise above' the pain, or to 'shut it out or quell it'.[64] Her sec-ond, healthy, child, Karen, was born a little more than a year later. 'It must be hell to go through labour with a dead child and know it,' she reflected. Wryly, she noted that she would 'no longer be able to accuse [Gwen] of never having suffered'.

Gwen herself said little about this loss. She had told Peter Bennie, now living with his family on Thursday Island (where he was archdeacon of Carpentaria), that she was expecting a second child, so she had to let him know that the baby had died. Her letter has not survived, but his expression of sympathy has. He wrote that he could 'imagine the desolate sense of frustration and waste that you must have after it all. I am so sorry.'[65] She probably took comfort from this, and from his invitation – which she could not afford to accept – to come and stay with them, promising that the blazing tropical heat would 'cure' her of her 'sun worship'.

At the time, medical opinion held that it was best not to talk about a miscarriage or stillbirth but simply to forget about it as soon as possible. Gwen probably adopted this approach. Some thirty years later, however, she saw a photograph of an unborn foetus that brought back to her the child she had lost. The image enabled her 'to approach something I had never been able to touch in poetry'.[66] Her poem 'Dialogue' addressed her stillborn daughter:

> . . . I saw you lying
> still folded   one moment   forever
> your head bent down to your heart
> eyes closed on unspeakable wisdom
> your delicate frog-pale fingers
> > spread
> apart as if you were playing
> a woodwind instrument.

The child was never named, and Gwen was not told the fate of the tiny body: 'I suppose / the hospital burnt you.' But the image of the baby's delicate, frog-like fingers would haunt her. In tribute to those fingers, she chose to write her poem in dactyls, a metre named for the Greek word for 'finger' that is supposedly an aural echo of a finger's shape: one stressed syllable followed by two unstressed syllables.

◆ ◆ ◆

By 1949, the Harwoods were thinking of leaving Tasmania. Gwen wanted to go back to Queensland, having had more than enough of Hobart's gloomy weather and longing for what she saw as the ease and freedom of northern life. But there were no opportunities for academics at that time in Brisbane. Besides, Bill had never really taken to Queensland and had no desire to return there. He would have liked to leave the University of Tasmania, though, where conditions were far from ideal for both staff and students.

When the position of chair of English at the University of Adelaide was advertised, he put in an application, but he did not get the job. So instead of moving to Adelaide, they moved down the road to Taroona, a seaside town some ten kilometres from Hobart, where they bought their first home, a newly built weatherboard house by the sea.[67]

They were both excited at the prospect of living so close to the ocean; for Bill, it was his chance to try his hand at building boats, while for Gwen, the new locale offered not only space but light. Fern Tree had been cold and dark, with the sun disappearing behind a rocky outcrop at around 2.30 p.m. in winter,[68] and Gwen had never been able to adapt to the lack of daylight. She was sorry to leave Ann, but regretted little else about her life on the mountainside.

The young family settled in quickly at Taroona. Gwen and Bill soon established a vegetable garden and bought their first chickens – 'magnificent Black Orpingtons'.[69] Bill set up a home workshop and built his first dinghy out of plywood, with Gwen acting as builder's mate. The venture was a success – they sold their first boat to one of Bill's colleagues and set about making more.[70] It was the beginning of Gwen's lifelong love of boating and fishing. As a teenager, she had been afraid of the sea; now she found it an 'utter delight'.[71] Tasmanian shorelines were very different from the gleaming subtropical beaches of Queensland, but she loved their wildness: the great waves crashing on the ocean beaches, the oysters and mussels clinging to the rocks, the sculpted stone cliffs and ledges, the teeming microcosms of the rock pools. 'I don't think there is anything I love more than poking about on the margin of the sea,' she would declare a couple of years later.[72] She loved beach picnics, too, with her own children and other people's in tow: 'buckets & spades, egg sandwiches, lemonade, currant cake, bathers-in-towels, public transport, the gritty return. I embrace them all.'[73] On sunny days, she was thrilled to see the Derwent shining blue, with 'the mountain against a sky of feathery cirrus . . . like some scarcely credible backdrop – the sort of mountain one might *imagine* perfect in line and fold and colour'.[74]

More often, though, the river, like the sky, was grey, and despite its handiness to the sea, Taroona was really too far away from Hobart to be practical for a young family – especially without a car. In her first year at Taroona, while Gwen was happily pregnant again, she was also lonely and dealing with a new grief. Early in 1950, she learned that her old teacher and beloved friend, Vera Cottew, now forty-eight, was dying of cancer.

Gwen was desperate to see her again, but the family could not afford air travel, and, in any case, she was too pregnant to make the trip.[75]

In late March, Bill's mother, Beatrice, came down from Melbourne to help out when the baby was born. The whole family were taking a Sunday stroll on the shore when Gwen's labour began. She made it to the hospital and welcomed her second son, Christopher Eric, with joy. It was Palm Sunday, which seemed to Gwen auspicious: '*benedictus qui venit in nomine Domini, hosanna in excelsis* [blessed is he who comes in the name of the lord, hosanna in the highest]'.

$$9$$

The Sappho of Lenah Valley

*Our English housewife must be of chaste thought, stout courage,
patient, untired, watchful, diligent, witty, pleasant, constant in friendship, full of good neighbourhood, wise in discourse, but not frequent
therein, sharp and quick of speech, but not bitter or talkative, secret in
her affairs, comfortable in her counsels, and generally skilful in all the
worthy knowledges which do belong to her vocation.*

Gervase Markham, *The English Hus-Wife*, 1615

*Change 'English' to 'Australian' – and could a more perfect exemplar be
imagined than G.H.?*

Gwen Harwood[1]

WITH A CHILD AGED THREE AND A NEW BABY, GWEN'S life was hectic. Vera's death in October was a hard blow in the midst of the chaos and sleepless nights. It was the first time Gwen had lost a friend to death, and she would mourn the other woman for the rest of her life. Vera haunted her dreams: they would meet as they used to in Brisbane, and Gwen would be seized with joy at the realisation that she was not dead after all, that it had all been a terrible mistake – only to awaken to the painful reality that she was gone. More than once, her waking was attended by a powerful feeling of Vera's presence – something she would explore in many poems.[2]

Meanwhile, her babies were catching every childhood illness that went around. In late 1951, she told Peter despairingly that the whole family was suffering from 'constant sickness'.[3] His letters refer sympathetically to her 'stream of psychotic woes' and 'succession of misfortunes', culminating early in 1952 in troubles of 'almost apocalyptic proportions'. But the details of these woes have been lost.

After less than two years at Taroona, with Gwen pregnant once again, the Harwoods began to look for a house in Hobart. Early in 1952, they moved into a large, well-established family home on Augusta Road in Lenah Valley. From here, it was only a short tram ride to the Queen's Domain, where Bill worked, and there were regular buses into town. If it was not always easy for Gwen to leave the house with her children in tow, she was no longer quite so cut off from the world.

She loved the house itself, with its bay windows, leadlight panels and generous front verandah. Like Mitchelton, Lenah Valley had once been dedicated to orchards, and she was thrilled to have fourteen fruit trees in her garden. They were plums and apricots rather than the oranges and pawpaws of Osborne Road, but they made her feel at home. Soon, they would have grapevines and espaliered almonds, too, as well as an ever-expanding vegetable garden. They could walk down Augusta Road to the Lenah Valley Creek to take the children tadpoling, and have family picnics in the foothills of Mount Wellington. The children's pre-school was close by. If it was not quite the open, relaxed, Brisbane-style home for which Gwen still longed, it was large enough for their growing family, with plenty of outdoor spaces for games and hobbies. Soon after they moved in, they planted a cypress hedge around the property. It would eventually grow into a twenty-foot barricade, breached only by a square-cut hole for the gate.

One of their early visitors was a former student of Bill's, Alison Wright (later Hoddinott), a brilliant twenty-one-year-old who had topped all her subjects to graduate with first-class honours in arts and a string of prizes. Early in 1952, she embarked on a master's program under Bill's supervision and became his research assistant, and Bill announced that it was time she met his wife.[4] Alison would vividly remember her first visit to the Harwood house. At that stage, all she knew about her lecturer's wife was 'student gossip': that she had red hair and 'wrote poetry that was sometimes published in *Meanjin*'. She was expecting someone of the same formidable intelligence as quiet, intense Mr Harwood, and with the same touch of aloofness. But when she presented herself at 89 Augusta Road, the door was opened by 'a small (my height), friendly, red-haired, very pregnant woman in fur-lined boots'. Far from being dauntingly intellectual, Gwen was warm and approachable, 'darting from domestic tasks . . . to animated conversation about teaching herself German in order to read German poetry'. When Alison, who had also studied German, ventured an opinion on the superiority of German love poetry to the English kind, the two forged an instant bond.[5] What followed was 'an evening of lively and stimulating fireside conversation and laughter, culminating in tea and hot buttered toast and an invitation to come again'.[6] There was little trace in Gwen's cheerful sociability of the shy newlywed whom Betty Pybus met in Fern Tree, or the aloof new mother Ann Jennings had once taken her to be. She was beginning to reclaim those aspects of herself she had tried – for love – to suppress.

Gwen was expecting twins, and in July, her doctor ordered her to bed. Agnes was sent for from Brisbane to help with the children. She arrived, Gwen wrote, 'looking like a duchess, shedding bags of shortbread, home-grown tomatoes and toys for the children and an incredible array of baby wear over the room where I lay helpless'.[7] In her inimitable fashion, Agnes immediately took charge, giving advice to Gwen's doctor on her treatment even as she spread across Gwen's mountainous stomach 'the new variety of tomatoes, pawpaws, magazines, a veiled & jewelled hat, and paper bags at which John & Chris were snatching'.[8]

When Gwen went into Calvary Hospital in early August to give birth, she found that she was slated to provide a teaching moment for the medical staff. '[It was] really a drama of the first order because all the nurses were brought into the delivery room to see the delivery of twins,' she told an interviewer.[9] 'It was to be a natural birth and all the doctors and nurses who were present came and stood around like a great audience in a semi-circle, and I felt that I really ought to try and do well and not scream terribly much, as I had let go a bit with the other children.' To her relief, 'the twins, being twins, were small and neat', and the births, on 3 August, were relatively easy. 'The first one was born, another boy, and then, one of the sisters . . . came up with a little bundle and said: "Look at this, it's your daughter." Joy, joy.' They named the babies Peter Richard and Mary Beatrice, and Gwen asked Peter Bennie to be their godfather, though he was unable to attend the baptism, or to meet them for many years.[10]

◆ ◆ ◆

With the arrival of the twins, Gwen's family responsibilities doubled overnight. She had been busy before, but now she was completely submerged in household labour.[11] Some time later, she would reel off a list of the kinds of domestic woes that stymied her during these years: 'the measles, boils, wet beds, fevers, tonsils and their endless endless endless proliferations', not to mention the babies howling 'night after night until I was half-schizo from lack of sleep'.[12] Confined to the house, she often felt 'disoriented': 'one seems to have no frame of reference.'[13] Home sometimes felt like a prison as 'spirit beat at flesh as in a grave / from which it could not rise'.[14]

Despite her lack of time, writing became ever more important to her, a way to hold on to some part of her old, non-domestic identity in the midst of the daily deluge. But it was impossible to make poetry her priority. She 'kept all that out of the way; a secret vice, like drinking with bottles in the wardrobe', she would later say. 'I had my poems in odd places. Late at night, I'd take them out, or early in the morning, just in my head.'[15] She wrote 'while the household slept', so that neither the children nor Bill could feel that her poetry was taking time and energy that rightly belonged to them. The very desire to write was a kind of betrayal of the full-hearted presence she felt she owed them. And yet ignoring that desire was, she increasingly saw, a betrayal of herself. The inner conflict took its toll: divided as she was, she felt unable to do justice either to her family or her art. Why could she not simply be happy, she would wail a few years later, as a loving and much-loved wife and mother? Why must she be continually tempted by her dark alter ego, the 'savage, nasty part' of her that would sacrifice everything – love, children, home – for a few hours of solitude?[16] Yet she pressed on, working on her poems when she could and sending them out, receiving nothing but rejections.

Bill had little interest in her poetic endeavours. Indeed, it was becoming increasingly evident to Gwen that not only did she and Bill have different attitudes to poetry, they also had fundamentally different world views. When they first met, she had assumed that Bill, a student of Coleridge, was a lover of poetry and sympathetic to the Romantics. It took time for her to realise that he was in fact largely indifferent to poetry and actively hostile to the Romantics. One of his intellectual goals as both scholar and teacher was to debunk the 'nonsense' that surrounded concepts such as 'imagination' and 'creativity'.[17] If the Romantics believed that a poem was an expression of the soul, a mysterious alchemical fusion of matter and spirit that could ennoble humankind, Bill was set on proving that it was nothing of the kind. A poem was merely words on a page, arranged according to certain identifiable rules; abstractions such as 'Truth' and 'Beauty' were meaningless, and critics who propounded them little more than frauds. The only things an intellectually honest critic could definitively establish about a literary text were the mechanics of its construction: specifically, the linguistic rules that brought it into being. Increasingly, linguistics became his focus.[18]

Bill followed the lead of American scholar Leonard Bloomfield, whose book *Language* was one of the textbooks he prescribed for his students.[19] As Alison Hoddinott explains, Bloomfield 'stressed the impropriety of using meaning in linguistic analysis because meaning was perceived by intuition and was therefore the weakest link in an attempt to make a properly scientific study of language'. Bill sought to 'dispense completely with questions of meaning and to base descriptions of language on purely formal criteria'. By the early 1950s, he was working on ways to demonstrate the purely material basis of poetry (and other linguistic forms) using machines. If he could only be precise enough in his analysis of literary language, he believed, he would be able to program a machine to write poetry that would be indistinguishable from poetry written by humans. This would prove once and for all that there was nothing more to the poet than a set of synapses and a knowledge of the rules of language: in Gilbert Ryle's famous formulation, there was no 'ghost in the machine'. Using his formidable technical skills, Bill began to build 'analysers' – early versions of computers – that he was convinced would one day both speak and write.

For Gwen, as both poet and devoted poetry lover, this was a species of madness. What she loved about poetry was precisely its capacity to speak of the human spirit; it was a form of connection, 'a unique way of reaching from one mind to another'.[20] The idea that poetry was merely the end product of a set of linguistic processes bearing no necessary relationship to a living, breathing, feeling person was absurd. The 'imaginative powers' could 'never be explained by showing the nervous system offered as a machine'.[21] It seemed obvious to her that linguistic rules were no more than the skeleton that the living poet clothed with flesh. The poet's very being was a 'crucible' in which half-apprehended poems slowly formed themselves until they were able to be grasped and lifted into the world; a poem was not merely a form of words but a 'form of light'.[22]

The differences in the ways Gwen and Bill approached poetry reflected deep disparities in their temperaments and perspectives on the world. Their conflicting readings of philosopher Ludwig Wittgenstein were a further example. Back in Brisbane, Bill had been eager to introduce Gwen to Wittgenstein, who through his Cambridge-trained disciples had revolutionised academic thought at the University of Melbourne.[23] To Bill, Wittgenstein's *Tractatus Logico-Philosophicus* had single-handedly put an end to 'metaphysical nonsense'[24] and the woolly logic and muddled thinking that attended it, in both literature and philosophy. But Gwen, who read Wittgenstein's masterwork in the chilly afternoons in Fern Tree before the birth of her first child, responded to him very differently. By her reading, the *Tractatus* did not scuttle metaphysics but elevated it to a new plane. Wittgenstein had shown, through assiduous attention to language, that metaphysical concepts could not be spoken about in any logical way – but that did not mean they did not exist. Gwen's interpretation of the book's famous closing aphorism, 'Whereof one cannot speak, thereof one must be silent', was that Wittgenstein was affirming the value of the unsayable. While positivists like Bill understood Wittgenstein to mean that 'what we can speak about is all that matters in life', Gwen's view was the opposite: for the philosopher, 'all that really matters in human life is precisely what, in his view, we must be silent about'.[25] To Gwen, this was the realm of the artist. As a poet, she was 'aiming for . . . something that cannot be *said* but only *shown*'.[26] For her, Wittgenstein was not the rationalist champion of a new age of reason but 'a poet trying to convey the otherness of the world'.[27] She cited one of his most dazzling propositions as a case in point: 'Not *how* the world is, is the mystical, but *that* it is.' For her, there was 'pure poetry' in Wittgenstein's works.[28]

Never one to wear her enthusiasms lightly, Gwen became passionately devoted to the philosopher, just as she had once been to the great musicians and composers, seeing him as a kind of wisdom figure, a secular mystic. For many years, she would devour everything she could about his life, imagining him as a person of transcendent insight and having vivid dreams of meeting him, or even just catching a glimpse of him in the street. She felt that if she could meet him just once, look into his eyes, touch his hand, her life would be transformed.[29] When he died in 1951, she was devastated by the loss of this possibility, however remote it had been. 'If I could go backwards in my life,' she once told an interviewer, 'the one thing I would like to do, though it wouldn't be possible, is just to go and see Wittgenstein. He wouldn't have liked me, I don't think he liked women . . . but I just wish I could have seen that man once.' During her first winter in Tasmania, she had absorbed his mysterious words just as she had those of Donne and Heine in her Brisbane days: 'the splendid beginning, "The world is everything that is the case" . . . And curious sentences thrown in among all the logic: . . . "Our life is endless in the way that our visual field is without limit," "Death is not an experience that is lived through." That is the poet speaking.'[30] These phrases would become part of her mental furniture, and appear in many a poem.

Gwen's reading of Wittgenstein bordered on the heretical to Bill. He persevered with his innovative work in linguistics and his efforts at building a functional computer, while Gwen persisted with her attempts to write a masterpiece – a writer's only task, according to another of her idols, Cyril Connolly.[31] Bill challenged her in debate and argument, and she pushed back in poems such as 'Hesperian', in which a lab full of smug scientists accidentally destroys the world.[32] During her visits to Augusta Road in the early 1950s, Alison Wright often found herself caught in the middle of skirmishes on these subjects. As a lover of poetry, she had a foot in both camps and would alternate between talking linguistics with Bill and talking poetry with Gwen. Earnest discussions of 'the function of English prefixes and suffixes' would be interrupted by Gwen 'dropping a draft poem in my lap and asking my opinion of it'.[33] When Alison asked Bill whether it was really possible to construct 'a machine that would talk, and even write poetry', he replied: 'It will talk as well as Gwen!'[34] In response, Gwen rose from her seat, went to the piano (which Ann Jennings had temporarily loaned her) and played 'a sequence of thunderous chords'. The battlelines were drawn.

◆ ◆ ◆

Though husband and wife increasingly took opposite points of view on subjects that mattered deeply to them both, the arguments were stimulating rather than destructive. They admired each other's intellect and – crucially – laughed at one another's jokes.[35] As parents, they were united, running 'a tight ship'. Visitors found them the 'image of a devoted couple with a young family'.[36] To Alison, theirs was the ideal marriage. She had grown up in a household where husband and wife kept to their separate spheres and talked to one another only about domestic matters; the lively sparring between Gwen and Bill was a revelation to her of what a modern marriage could be. 'The Harwood home in Augusta Road drew me like a magnet to evenings of laughter, of discussion and argument,' she would write.[37] The conversation 'ranged widely – from Shakespeare to Wittgenstein, from Heine's lyrics to machine translation'[38] – and the arguments were exhilarating. A couple of years later, when she went to Oxford to do a doctorate, she was disappointed to find that 'nothing in the academic programme I was offered could compare with the intellectual excitement of those evenings with the Harwoods'.

Meanwhile, Gwen was beginning to question some of the assumptions she had made about how her marriage would work. Though she still considered matrimony 'a wonderful institution', she chafed at some of the constraints imposed by her 'lord and master'. Eager to pursue her own friendships, she felt hampered by Bill's disapproval. He did not like her to socialise on her own or spend too much time with friends, and he had an 'irrational and incurable' dislike of 'seeing me deep in conversation with *anyone*'.[39] Years later, she would tell Ann angrily that Bill had wanted nothing less than 'an immured wife of dowdy aspect who spoke and wrote to nobody without his permission'.[40] At the time, she felt only that his possessiveness was suffocating. 'It is close to the feeling one has in nightmares, of being unable to escape or to bear an impending terror,' she confessed.[41]

When Hal Porter returned to Hobart in 1951 to live at Fern Tree with the Jenningses as a paying guest, Bill made it clear to Gwen that he did not like her new, disturbingly louche friend. Less willing than she had been to give up friendships at Bill's behest, Gwen continued to see Hal, whom she found 'endlessly fascinating'.[42] She did not, however, invite him to the house. Instead, she saw him at Ann's, whom she often visited, bundling the children onto the bus to spend the day at Fern Tree. Because Hal spent much of his time producing or performing in plays for the Hobart Repertory Company (of which Ann and Roger were leading lights), he was often at home in the afternoons, working on radio plays (which he never managed to sell), stories and poems. Gwen was particularly impressed by his ability to work amid domestic chaos. While she and Ann rushed around mediating squabbles, hushing tears, providing food and toys, Hal would sit serenely, 'children crawling on and off his lap', and write.[43] He was 'quite indifferent to noise & distraction, and would read out bits of his work among the mashed vegetables & general confusion'.

Both Gwen and Ann deeply admired his poems. Gwen was impressed not only by the 'brilliance' of his language but also by the 'total cutting-through of convention in every way'.[44] When his first book of poems, *The Hexagon,* came out in 1956, she was 'knocked flat with envy',[45] and for some years it was among her favourite volumes. He admired her poems, too, telling a mutual friend that she was 'in many ways a brilliant and disturbing creature with a rather wonderful mind'.[46] In the early 1950s, Gwen was working on the first of her poems about Professor Eisenbart, her fictional nuclear scientist, and his youthful, red-headed, piano-playing mistress, and Hal was intrigued. He made detailed comments on her drafts, identifying words and phrases that worked, as well as those that were not quite right: 'All this done, you know, with infinite love'.[47] In relation to his own drafts, he told her to be 'utterly ruthless': 'a brutality from you is better at this stage than a disappointed look later on'.[48] They even talked about writing some poems together – 'a great series of sonnets' – but Bill intervened. 'My husband absolutely LOATHES Hal, and let him know it,' Gwen told a friend.[49]

Hal took his revenge by writing a poem about the Harwoods' marriage called 'Brute's Wife', supposedly 'a portrait of GH'.[50] The 'wife' of the title is a prisoner in her suburban home, and entertains elaborate fantasises of killing her husband/jailor – with his own knife, with 'the scarf he gave her', by drowning him in the bath or by decking him with a 'heavy statuette'. At the same time, 'sweet' but 'false', she pretends to love him, and in the marital bed, 'mimes to sate him, / stroking the ramrod jolts that mar and burn'.

Hal left Hobart in early 1953, after an unhappy love affair with a much younger man. For several years, he and Gwen wrote to one another, sharing their works in progress and gleefully demolishing the contemporary poetry scene. Whenever Hal was back in Hobart – he visited at least annually during that decade, usually staying with the Jenningses – he would summon Gwen, who looked forward to stimulating hours of 'shop talk'. Increasingly, though, he was too drunk for the kind of conversation she craved. One night at Ann's, he became weepy and embarked on a drunken lament of all the things he'd never done with Gwen: 'I've never taken you for a walk through Battery Point; I've never taken you to the talkies (I said "THE WHAT?") . . . and bought you a 3/6d box of chocolates tied with green ribbon, and thought I should really have bought you the big 15/6d box, but you'd understand, I've never walked with you anywhere, not on grass, or cement, or asphalt, or gravel, or sand, or terrazzo, or boards, or clods, or rock . . .'[51] At this point, he began 'drunkenly kissing the back of [her] neck', so Gwen removed herself from his immediate vicinity. 'Why have you moved away from me?' Hal wailed. 'Do I *smell*?'

When she finally excused herself – she had promised Bill she would be home before midnight – he insisted on going with her in the taxi, bringing the brandy bottle with him. As they trundled through the streets, 'he alternately drank & sobbed that he loved Bill Harwood, who had thrown a spanner in his works . . . and he feared he would never see him again, and patronised the taxi-driver horribly, offering him drinks & smokes & mocking him loudly to me (I loathe this aspect of Hal) when he declined'. When Gwen got out of the cab and said goodnight, Hal climbed into the front seat with the driver, and Gwen grimly suspected that he was 'preparing to offer the driver something more advanced than drink & cigarettes – he was a fairly personable driver'.

Gwen gave Bill 'a more sober account of the evening' and asked those friends to whom she told the story not to speak of it in front of him – 'unless you want to see me in Bill's disfavour'.[52] But she was fast becoming disillusioned with Hal. A master at belittling others, he was too often 'stinkingly drunk' when they met and unpleasantly abrasive, even abusive. Gwen soon ceased to find his wit amusing – especially when his barbed words were directed at people she loved, such as Ann. 'He has never offered me anything but praise & kindness, but I know what he said about someone who had fed him, comforted him, housed him & trusted him for years, to get a laugh among louts in a bar,' she wrote to a friend in 1959. She understood that Hal carried his own wounds; she agreed with a mutual friend who said that Hal lived 'in a mediaeval castle defended by his army of mercenary wits'. But she was no longer willing to make the effort to scale those walls. 'I have met that kind of character before (in musicians),' she confessed, and found, 'at terrible cost', that even highly gifted artists could be horrible human beings.[53]

Hal's departure from Hobart in early 1953 may have left a bigger hole had Gwen not found a way to rekindle her friendship with Tony Riddell later that year. Since leaving Brisbane, she had kept up with his doings through Peter, who joked that every time he heard from Tony, his old friend was in the process of rejecting yet another 'avocation'. Then in August 1950, she saw in the Hobart *Mercury* that Tony – who was working as a stage manager in Stratford-on-Avon – had won a travelling scholarship from the Italian government to study opera production. She immediately wrote to him at the Shakespeare Memorial Theatre, and followed up with a second breezy missive a fortnight later. He did not reply.

Two years later, when she read that his theatre company was planning an Australian tour, she wrote again to beg him to stay with them when he came to Hobart, assuring him that the invitation came from both her and Bill. Again, Tony did not reply. Nevertheless, Gwen was determined to ensure he did not slip in and out of Hobart without making contact. When the company arrived in August 1953, she managed either to speak to him on the phone or to leave him a note he felt compelled to answer.[54] His response was friendly enough for Gwen to follow up, after his departure, with a high-spirited, irresistibly comic missive referring to 'ludicrous notices' and other shared jokes. She was in the middle of a second letter to him when she received a reply to her first that was seemingly as light-hearted as her own, filled with newspaper cuttings and his own selection of weird and wonderful 'notices'. Yet there was a touch of reserve in his tone. They could not simply resume their friendship as though nothing had happened, he told her; there were things they needed to discuss. Gwen was unwilling to have that conversation. 'I am sure there is not and could not be any need of explanation between us,' she wrote back. She wrote again two days later, noting that it was her eighth wedding anniversary and launching into more humorous anecdotes, including one about 'our professor', Bill. She finished by asking if she could send him some of her poems.[55] To this, Tony responded coolly, telling her he had little time for correspondence. Gwen was hurt, but insisted that she would continue to write 'until I receive a clearly worded notice of dismissal.'[56] Despite the bravado, she was losing some of her confidence; this letter was a single page, and riffed only on the weather.

Tony wrote back at once to tell her that, despite the passage of time, he could not forgive her for her rejection of him at Bill's command. Gwen was 'wounded . . . to the heart' by this. The old denials came pouring forth as she hastened to defend herself. 'I had no part in what Bill wrote and I could not have spared you the mortal blow he dealt you even if I had dismissed him instead of accepting his cruel terms,' she wrote.[57] His determination to turn his back on her had thrown her into such despair that she felt she might as well kill herself. It was a heartfelt cry. Tony was the person who knew her most intimately as she had been before her marriage – a 'zany gamin girl', bursting with vitality, destined to be an artist.[58] If he shunned her, that girl and her potential might disappear forever.

His first response was not promising: he wrote with stern disapproval of her threat of suicide. Abashed, she quickly reneged: 'I will revoke what I said on Monday – I would never copy the cowardly & useless act of Judas. You were right to despise my weakness.'[59] She insisted, however, that there was no barrier between them but 'your own bitterness, and will you nourish that forever . . .?' What had been done could not be undone, but things had changed since those days. Even Bill had changed, offering Tony 'his welcome and his home'. Surely it was possible to forgive and move on? She finished with an affirmation of her feelings for him: 'Even if I am nothing at all to you now, I want you to know that you are, and will always be, an inexhaustible source of joy to me. The love I have for you will bridge any gulf of time, and the radiance of your mind will always transfigure human deeds & sufferings for me.' Gwen at her most despairing was also Gwen at her most exalted.

Tony had already softened. Even as she was pouring out her love for him, he was writing to tell her that he still loved her too. In his heart, he had never abandoned their friendship – its seeds had only been 'lying dormant in the winter soil'. Gwen received this letter rapturously. To know that she could write to him once more, pouring out the details of her daily life in the heightened language they shared, filled her with joy. His warmth and approval, his ability to enter into her sorrows and delights, was necessary ballast in the alien environment she had found herself in after her marriage. She immediately began to send him her poems and he responded as of old, sending her his finely judged appreciation along with drafts of his own poems and plays. Almost at once, their relationship was back on its old footing. They were two aspiring artists, determined to resist the idiocies of a world that did not understand the true nature of life or art. Ridicule and satire were again their best recourse.

She would later say that Tony's friendship saved her. 'Without you my individuality would never have survived the stresses of my life and there would have been no poems,' she wrote some twelve years later. 'If it had not been for you I'd have written nothing at all that might matter.'[60] His love was 'a source of cold & sober courage in . . . moments of despair',[61] a courage she needed as she struggled to disentangle herself from the domestic roles threatening to subsume her and to recreate herself as a poet.

◆ ◆ ◆

The only obstacle to the resumption of her epistolary friendship with Tony was her lack of time. 'I am so tired at night I can't remember all the brilliant expositions of the contemporary scene I haven't time to set down during the day,' she wrote grimly.[62] 'The endless preparation of food & clothes seems to melt time into nothing, though the days have enough hours in [them] theoretically,'[63] she reflected in another letter. Once, she did manage to send him a Beachcomber-style skit featuring Professor Edeledel Edel, dean of feleology at the Rufo-Nanine University, who was being tried by Mr Justice Cocklecarrot for the crime of eating a cat and making an academic gown out of its fur. It was the kind of thing she could write only for Tony.

Yet she was gradually making other friends who shared her love of poetry and art. One was Charlotte Wilmot, a specialist in modern languages and lecturer in education, one of only a handful of female academics at the University of Tasmania. Lotte had been married to Norman Wilmot (eldest son of Melbourne writer and poet Frank Wilmot) not quite three years when he was diagnosed with terminal brain cancer in 1952. She took time off to nurse him, and he died in May 1953. She and Gwen became friends the following year, when Lotte was living with her two-year-old daughter, Claire, in a top-floor flat in an old house in Battery Point. Gwen was very aware of how much Lotte had suffered. 'I think that after the hideous agony of Padie's long illness, decay & death, Lot had no feeling left for anyone in the world & it was only having Claire, then a very small baby, that anchored her to the world at all,' she told Tony.[64] She worried that Lotte could still 'retreat into her despair', and did all she could to help her. Her new friend reminded Gwen of her old love, Vera Cottew – she had that same bird-like air – and for Gwen, the friendship had a similar glow about it. It seemed to her that Lotte was exceptional in every way: 'strong, witty, astringent, generous'[65] and endlessly capable. She excelled at languages, athletics, music and acting. As was her wont, Gwen surrendered herself wholeheartedly to love.

Lotte Wilmot and Gwen Harwood with their children at
Augusta Road, c. 1955

One of her great delights was to accompany Lotte on the piano while she sang Schubert, just as she had once done with Tony – though 'we never get more than 10 minutes before some child needs attention or Bill comes scowling on the scene to say that x or y must be done at once with our help'.[66] The two women made plans to study German together, and Lotte would often drop in to Augusta Road for a morning coffee while Gwen pottered in the kitchen. Lotte and Claire came to lunch on Saturdays – the weekly roast dinner was a treat for Claire – and the two families went on outings together, picnicking at the beach or hiking in the bush.[67] Lotte was happy to ferry Gwen and her children around in her tiny green Austin A30, and Gwen would happily take Claire if an emergency sitter was needed. Though Gwen sometimes found Lotte's style somewhat 'militant' – she had a tendency to subject Gwen to 'a Socratic harangue' over coffee, '& I find myself mentally reaching for the hemlock' – she remained besotted. 'I think I love her more than any of the women I do love,' she told Tony in 1956.[68]

By this time, Tony had met Lotte. He had returned to Australia in mid-1955 to take up a job with the ABC, and to Gwen's joy, was soon transferred to the broadcaster's Hobart office. After more than ten years, they were living in the same city again. Gwen lost no time in welcoming him into her social circles – and into her family. Things were somewhat awkward with Bill: he and Tony did not discuss the events of 1944, then or ever, and Tony felt that the three of them – he, Bill and Gwen – made an 'uneasy trio'.[69] But this did not stop Tony from spending many weekends with the Harwood family, joining in their social routines and getting to know the children. He and Lotte got on well. Several years later, Gwen would still glow with delight to remember the evenings she had spent at Lotte's flat 'with my two favourite human beings listening to Mozart: what more could anyone want?'[70]

Thomas (Tony) Riddell, Hobart, 1955

But Tony could not settle. He was still burning to write, and dreamed of establishing himself in London as a playwright. By March 1956, he had decided to give up his job and return to Europe. Gwen did not try to hold him, telling their mutual friend Frank Kellaway that Tony was 'full of pride and power; I am sure he is going towards fulfilment at last'.[71]

After his departure, however, Gwen found herself once again struggling under the weight of a 'barren spell of domestic troubles'. Her second son was having his tonsils out, the twins were 'sick & crabby', and she was 'playing the stately flower of female fortitude' when 'Burning Sappho seems a more desirable role'.[72] The 'Stately Flower', a phrase borrowed from Tennyson, was Gwen's term for the domestic saint she felt she was supposed to embody. She was only too aware that the ideal wife was – in the words of Edward Lear – a combination of '15 angels, several hundreds of ordinary women, many philosophers, a heap of truly wise and kind mothers, 3 or 4 minor prophets, and a lot of doctors and schoolmistresses'.[73] 'Burning Sappho' was her incendiary alter ego,[74] her poet-self who seethed with frustration and flared with rage. The phrase came from Byron's *Don Juan,* which Gwen loved; Byron's satirical style had long since eclipsed for her the works of her old Romantic favourites, 'those nongs Sheets & Kelly'.[75] As for Sappho, she was 'beyond all question and comparison the very greatest poet that ever lived' – according to Gwen's *Anthology of World Poetry,* at least[76] – and Gwen was eager to claim this literary lineage. She often scrawled 'The Sappho of Lenah Valley' on envelopes as her return address, and was given to exclaiming 'O Burning Sappho!' when she found herself chopping cucumbers in the kitchen instead of joining the literary conversation in the lounge.

Burning Sappho took particular exception to the constrictions of domestic life. She resented having to snatch her 'private life' in 'ten minute stretches among the endless preparation of clothes and food and the recitation of what Jolly Joking Jumbo said to Jovial Jacko at Tiger Tim's tea party'.[77] While the Stately Flower presided with imperturbable calm over all kinds of household disasters, Burning Sappho seethed. 'I have just spilt the contents of my "private drawer" in hunting for the OHMS envelope & the twins have descended like vultures on my private life,' Gwen wrote to Tony one evening. 'I'll fling pepper in their faces.'[78]

In the early 1960s, she would turn this simmering inner conflict into a series of powerful poems. 'Lip Service' depicts a woman determined to embrace her role as domestic goddess by banishing her inconvenient longing to write. 'No more I'll walk at a late hour / restless about the house,' she resolves. 'I'll not / Wrestle with words, nor show one sour / Look in my neat domestic plot.' She will be content, she vows, with the life she has, and she will achieve this by the simple stratagem of cutting out her own 'core' – removing 'the seeds / Of discontent' as she would de-seed an apple. Purged of her bitterness, she will become sweet nourishment for her family, serving herself up to 'fill the needs / Of husband and importuning child'. But in the poem's last stanza, she rebels. Such an act of self-mutilation would be little less than a lobotomy, leaving her unrecognisable to herself, a stranger in the mirror 'with an idiot grin'.

'Burning Sappho' takes the opposite tack, depicting a woman who refuses to give up her deepest ambition no matter how impossible it is. Owing something to Hal Porter's 'Brute's Wife',[79] this poem is full of murderous fantasies. The speaker struggles throughout the day to find a few private moments in which to write, but is thwarted at every turn. 'The clothes are washed, the house is clean,' she begins. 'I find my pen and start to write.' At once her child 'kicks her good / new well-selected toys with spite / around the room, and whines for food'. The woman leaves her work to tend to the toddler, but behind her smile is a 'monster' who 'sticks her [child's] image through with pins'. With the child down for her nap, the dishes washed, the clothes 'ironed and aired', she takes up her pen once more. But no sooner has she grasped it than a 'kind friend' appears at the door, wishing 'to gossip while she darns her socks'. While they are talking, 'The child wakes, and the Rector knocks'. Behind the woman's smile, 'a fiend pours prussic acid'. At last the day is over, and all her tasks are done. She has persevered, and won 'this hour' of time for herself. But just as she starts to write, her husband calls her 'to bed': 'Now deathless verse, good night. / In my warm thighs a fleshless devil / chops him to bits with hell-cold evil.'

It is now too late to do anything for herself. She surrenders to sleep until 'Some air of morning stirs afresh / my shaping element'. In the pre-dawn, she seeks her pen: 'I'll find / my truth, my poem, and grasp it yet.'

10

Some Combat Worthy of My Sword

My children grew. Like wine I poured
knowledge and skill, fought love's long war
with trivial cares. My spirit gave
a cry of hunger: 'Grant me more
than this bare sustenance, I crave
some combat worthy of my sword.'

Gwen Harwood, 'The Old Wife's Tale'

THE MORE DEMANDING GWEN'S DOMESTIC LIFE BECAME, THE more determined she was to establish herself as a poet. Bill told her – 'quite without malice' – that she couldn't 'hope to be much good – it's simply a matter of statistics'.[1] But she did hope. In her 'irresponsible' moments, she was sure she was doing good work. Tony, Ann, Frank, Hal and Alison all told her that her poems were good. Yet she had not had a new poem accepted for publication since 1949. Back in 1944, when she sent off her first poem to *Meanjin*, she had told Tony that if they rejected it, she would 'send them things until they wear out'. This policy she now adopted. When a poem was rejected, she immediately sent it out again, and if an editor did not like one poem, she sent them another. With Tony's encouragement, she nurtured her outrage. Tony condemned incompetence wherever he found it: newspaper typos, poor restaurant service and inept poems all incited his wrath. When the postal service returned a letter he had mis-addressed, he was furious: 'What incompetent & lazy & irresponsible fools there must be in Hobart G.P.O!'[2] Gwen delighted in his 'arrogance'.[3] Together, they fumed over the ineptitude of the various editors of literary magazines (in Gwen's case) and producers of plays (in Tony's). Gwen, who still read all the Australian literary journals and knew what was being published, was convinced that some of it was rubbish. Her letters to Tony often included quotations from hopelessly bad or embarrassingly banal poems that had appeared in the very literary magazines that persisted in rejecting her work. Surely the editors were incompetent?

She had had a small reprieve in 1955 when 'Windy Night, Fern Tree' was published in *Southerly*, but this was an old poem. Her newer material was very different in both subject and style, but no one outside of her own circle seemed to see its power. Then in late 1956, *Meanjin* published one of these newer poems, 'Death of a Painter' ('directly inspired by [Vincent Van Gogh's] terrible self-portrait [of] 1888, where the face seems to be full of daemonic power'). Her pleasure was marred, however, by the lack of communication from the editor, Clem Christesen. He had not notified her of the poem's acceptance before it appeared, and had still not published an Eisenbart poem, 'Daybreak', that he had accepted a year earlier. 'I am sick of editorial delays,' she complained to Tony. 'You never know where you are.'[4]

At the same time, an anthology of Australian verse entitled *Australian Signpost* appeared featuring her poem 'The Old Wife's Tale', which she had sent to the editors, along with several others, back in 1954. But though she was happy to see this poem in print, she was annoyed that the editors had included only one poem when they had accepted two. By holding on to 'Joseph', they had done her an ill turn. If they had simply rejected it, she could have sent it to another anthology, 'where it would almost certainly have been accepted'. 'I suppose anything is good enough for a poor bloody poet in this country,' she raged to Tony. 'I hope whoever bungled this gets indecently assaulted by a bunyip, and wish I could attack somebody personally.'[5]

She was in good company in *Australian Signpost*, which included, among others, poems by Rosemary Dobson, Judith Wright, A.D. Hope, James McAuley and Francis Webb – the cream of that generation of poets. But she had little admiration even for them. 'Current reputations *are* beyond understanding,' she told Tony in 1958.[6] 'One of the things I'd like to do, & it is a project on which your help would be needed, is to publish an "Australian anthology" with all the famous names appended to competent parodies of their worst style – a sort of Ern Malley in reverse':

One could have a heavy-handed 'metaphysical' Judith Wright, an attenuated Rosemary Dobson, some Max Harris muck-tuck, a super-hawky David Campbell, a waspish over-hyphenated Hal Porter, and, to distract attention, an impossibly obscure tribute by myself to a non-existent painter. One could get it reviewed seriously, I'm sure. Imagine the howls!

It would take another five years, but her 'anthology' did appear in *Westerly* in 1963, entitled 'Variations on a Theme': seven brief, brilliant versions of the children's rhyme 'Pop Goes the Weasel' in the style of seven poets, including herself.

Gwen loved the idea of orchestrating a literary hoax. She was a fan of the Ern Malley affair, which had broken in 1944, when she was just beginning to publish. A youthful James McAuley and his friend Harold Stewart, both then cooling their heels in the army, had spent an idle Saturday afternoon at the Victoria Barracks concocting the life works of an unknown – and tragically deceased – modernist poet.[7] Their aim was to take down a new-ish, avant-garde literary magazine, *Angry Penguins*, which they considered intolerably pretentious. They cobbled together Malley's literary output from the books they happened to have on their desks that day, including Shake-speare's plays, a dictionary of quotations and a US Army report on mosquito control, which they padded out with mangled excerpts from their own seri-ous poems. Inventing a plausible backstory for their imaginary poet, they sent the Malley oeuvre to Max Harris, the twenty-two-year-old enfant terri-ble of Australian poetry and co-editor of *Angry Penguins*. When Harris took the bait, proclaiming that he had discovered a gifted new Australian mod-ernist, the conspirators chortled with glee. As far as they were concerned, they had definitively proven that the modernist poetry Harris championed was drivel, since even those who praised it couldn't tell the real thing from a fake. It was just the kind of mischief Gwen relished.

For now, though, she was focused on getting her work into print. She had been working on the Eisenbart poems throughout the early 1950s, but 'Daybreak' was the only one that had got so much as a nibble. She felt that these poems were better than anything she had previously writ-ten, and it was frustrating to have them so comprehensively dismissed. They were certainly very different from most Australian poetry; serious poems featuring made-up characters with their own storylines were all but unknown, and poems that were urban and sardonic were equally unusual. Gwen's imaginary professor, a nuclear physicist wrestling with the weight of responsibility for newly discovered weapons of mass destruction, was an unlikely verse protagonist. Yet in this persona, Gwen could impersonate the intellectual confidence of positivists such as Bill and the sexual arrogance of high-status males such as Robert Dalley-Scarlett, while at the same time lampooning them in the persona of Eisenbart's 'affectionate' but 'astringent' mistress.[8] These poems were also her way of reframing her ongoing con-flict with Bill over the so-called 'scientific point of view'. For all Eisenbart's brilliance, and his pleasurable fantasies of his own power, he is morally and emotionally impoverished: empty, lonely and blind to the sources of his own anguish.

Gwen had great fun with Eisenbart. His name, which translates loosely as Iron Beard, came from a German drinking song she used to perform during the war and signals his comedic status, though the poems themselves mostly have a tone of high seriousness. Her drafts are much longer than the published versions and give the character of the mistress a bigger role; she had 'immense quantities of material' and kept 'boiling it down'.[9] She shared the poems with all her friends, featured 'portraits' of Eisenbart in her homemade postcards and spoke about him so much that he began to develop a life of his own. Ann confessed that she 'hated' Professor Eisenbart: 'He's wonderfully done, but I *loathe* that man.'[10] Several people suspected that he was based on a real person. 'I need to know who is Prof Eisenbart?' Peter Bennie wrote. 'A masculine protest? Bill?'[11] Her friend Lotte became offended when she heard rumours that Gwen had told other people the true identity of Eisenbart while keeping Lotte in the dark.[12] Even Bill 'occasionally tried to identify himself with the Professor,' Gwen told Tony, 'but I assure him I haven't "put him in a poem"'.[13]

In her letters, she mocks the idea that Eisenbart was anything other than an invention. A new young poet friend, Vivian Smith, came closest when he speculated that Eisenbart was 'a mask, a *personae*, through which you voice your own private despair impersonally'.[14] A couple of years later, she would tell another friend, in a fit of gloom, that 'Eisenbart split off from my personality to become an anti-self'.[15] Certainly, it is not difficult to recognise in Eisenbart Gwen's own explosive anger. In early 1957, she told Tony that she sometimes felt 'so mischievous I could burst, like a pressure cooker with the safety valve soldered down'.[16] In a later letter, she would describe herself as a human bomb: her head was so 'crammed with terrible ideas' for which she could not find expression that she felt she was likely to 'explode & blow up Tasmania'.[17]

At the same time, she saw parallels between Bill's 'terrifying electric machinery'[18] and the kind of destructive power that had been so recently unleashed on the world in the form of nuclear weapons. In 1957, she reported to Tony that Bill had been 'invited to give a paper on programming computing machinery to learn a natural language at Weapons Research Establishment', the defence department's arm in Woomera, South Australia.[19] 'Isn't it amazing how we are all drawn into the last, most terrifying war?'[20] A couple of months later, she noted that Bill had 'built a second logical analyser (electronic computer thing) and is closeted with it day & night: he is unbelievably brilliant & *inhuman*'.[21] When Bill travelled to Armidale in the early 1960s to give some lectures, she noted that he took with him 'in his suitcase a small, home-built analyser which looks extremely like a bomb, wires and all. The children think he'll be arrested.'[22] Bill was not a nuclear scientist, but his efforts to replace human consciousness with machine-generated language were associated, in Gwen's mind, with destruction.

◆ ◆ ◆

Hal Porter was an early champion of Professor Eisenbart, and in 1957 he found himself in a position to help Gwen's character into print. Since 1941, Angus & Robertson had been publishing an annual anthology entitled *Australian Poetry*, appointing a different poet each year to edit it and giving him or her carte blanche. Hal's reputation was growing – his first novel had just been accepted by Angus & Robertson's star editor Beatrice Davis – and he was invited to edit the 1957 anthology. He was delighted to have the chance to correct what he saw as the poor judgement of other editors by championing some of the poets he felt had been neglected – with Gwen top of the list. By convention, poets were represented by a single work, two at the most, but he selected three of Gwen's poems for his anthology, and three by another virtually unknown poet, Peter Hopegood. Gwen, who had never yet had anything accepted for *Australian Poetry*, was thrilled. To be included at all was high honour, but to be represented by three poems, including one of her knottiest Eisenbart works, 'Panther and Peacock', was a huge fillip to her career. She would later say that in publishing her in this anthology, Hal 'gave me my poetic start on the stage'.[23]

There were consequences, however. Established poets such as Jim McAuley (represented by only one poem) and Vincent Buckley (not included at all) struck back at Hal and his 'idiosyncratic' choices in their reviews. Both poets, Gwen would later say, went for her 'with hatchets'.[24] McAuley pronounced the anthology 'a shocking mess which one would hate to see placed in the hands of an overseas visitor as a mirror of Australian poetry to-day'. He cited Gwen's work as an instance of 'those poems where the attempt at a sophisticated mannerism breaks down into pathetic ineptitude'.[25] To have her first major outing in print savaged by a writer of McAuley's standing was devastating. She was 'appalled' at McAuley's 'nasty tone', which she felt was motivated by personal malice.[26] 'When I first appeared in print [McAuley] chopped off the fingers I'd set on the poetic ladder,' she would tell a friend many years later. 'I didn't take insult well or plan to do good to him.'[27]

Buckley's critique in *The Age* was less vitriolic but more targeted. He declared Porter's anthology 'far from an exciting collection', and picked out 'Panther and Peacock' for special notice. The poem 'has moments of strength and passion,' he wrote, 'but is muddled and, in places, derivate'.[28] Again, Gwen was deeply affronted. More than thirty years later, she would still remember his exact words, telling an interviewer, '[He] said of me that I was "muddled and derivate" and I thought you'll eat that, you are going to.'[29] From that moment, she would never lose an opportunity to deride Buckley. Hal was happy to feed her outrage. He had no time for either McAuley or Buckley, but was particularly scathing about 'the scapular-bedecked Buckley (a conceited cipher to boot)'.[30] (Buckley, like McAuley, was a Roman Catholic.)

It was hardly a warm welcome from a poetry community that could be highly combative, as well as reflexively masculine. But it made Gwen only the more determined to fight her way in. And she was beginning to find allies. Not only did she have Hal on her side, but her new friend Vivian Smith was also making a name for himself on the poetry scene. Vivian published his first book of poems, *The Other Meaning*, in 1956, when he was only twenty-three. Gwen was impressed by his work, considering him 'a very fine poet'.[31] After completing a master's in French, he began teaching at the University of Tasmania, and Gwen invited him around to Augusta Road. Vivian liked both the Harwoods, whom he found 'very friendly, Bill calm and quiet, Gwen, busy and ebullient'.[32] He admired Gwen's 'robust energy' and 'intensity'. Gwen also befriended Vivian's fiancée, Sybille Gottwald, who taught German at the university and whose loveliness, Gwen told Vivian, she found 'quite unnerving'[33] – though she was 'so warm and sympathetic [it] makes her beauty doubly compelling'.

Gwen had also made friends with a painter and aspiring poet she met in 1955, Edwin Tanner. A couple of months younger than she, Eddie was an engineer by profession who had moved to Hobart with his wife, Shirley, and their two young children late in 1949 to work at the Hydro-Electric Commission. For some years he studied art at the Hobart Technical College at night, and in the mid-1950s he started an arts degree at the University of Tasmania, where he became a student of Bill's. Gwen saw Eddie's work before she met him: his painting *Engineers* was exhibited among the winning entries in the Tasmanian Sesquicentenary Art Competition in 1954. All flat planes and geometrical shapes, the work depicts two tall, narrow figures hunched on either side of a desk at the back of an almost bare room. It looks like a scene from a Kafka novel: a spare, slightly surreal interior made up almost entirely of straight lines and angles, alleviated only by the curves of a cluster of milk bottles on the ground. It reminded Gwen of the reproductions of European paintings she had seen during the war – 'Klee and Feininger', as well as 'the serene metaphysical charm of Morandi's commonplace objects'.[34] Yet it was the work not of an artist from the Old World but of a young man who had grown up in Port Kembla, just south of Wollongong. It resonated deeply with Gwen. 'The elements of the painting were not in themselves poetical, but the work spoke to me directly with the force and clarity of a poem.'[35]

Eddie was as passionate about poetry as he was about painting. On his first visit to Augusta Road, he announced with innocent pride that he had recently met a poet, and Gwen, guessing at once that this was Clive Sansom, an English writer who had settled in Tasmania, gave him a sceptical look. Sansom's poems, though very popular, were earnest and conventional, and Gwen considered him a mere journeyman. 'That pink and blue Jesus poet up the hill?' she demanded scornfully. Eddie was embarrassed to admit that it was. 'I felt humiliated,' he later confessed, 'though honest to God I'd never seen his work. You then went on to announce that you were a poet (of the proper kind). You produced a poem which in my embarrassment I read . . . It was a poem.'[36]

From that time on, they were friends. Eddie came to believe that Gwen was a genius. She had 'a very strange intensity', he once told her, as if she had 'the depth & intelligence of two'.[37] They spent hours in 'endless quicksilver talk' at his house, looking out over the Derwent as night fell. 'I always used to wish that time could be suspended on those evenings when we sat and talked,' she would say.[38]

Their conversation ranged over logic, philosophy, music, poetry, engineering and of course painting. His great loves were Cézanne and Morandi. 'Look at that,' he would say, staring at a print. 'You can't explain it, you just have to eat it.'[39] This was her territory: the realm of things that could not be rationalised, only felt in the gut, in the blood. He was an explorer just as she was, and similarly fascinated by Wittgenstein – who had also trained as an engineer. 'Wittgenstein is like Prussian Blue,' he once wrote to her. 'If you touch Prussian Blue it goes everywhere – its covering capacity is enormous – you can't wash it off completely.'[40] He also did a number of paintings of Gwen's Professor Eisenbart, the first of which Gwen professed to find 'terrifying': 'so towering, & that phallic umbrella – utterly marvellous'.[41]

Eddie and Gwen sometimes joked about running away together to live in a lighthouse and devote themselves to the muse, but this was never more than a beguiling fantasy. Gwen did think she could have been happy with Eddie,[42] but he was devoted to his wife and would not have dreamed of leaving her.[43] Besides, much as they enjoyed their times together, they did not see each other often.[44] Both were busy, Gwen with her young family and her poetry, and Eddie with his job, his painting and his studies, as well as ongoing work on the house he was building. Then, in the late 1950s, he got caught up in the Orr affair, a university scandal that threw all Hobart into an uproar, divided the community and turned common rooms around the country into battle grounds.

Eddie's involvement was almost accidental; he knew little about the politics raging around the philosophy professor Sydney Orr when he made a complaint about him to the university. All he knew was that Orr was a terrible lecturer, and that he had tried to bribe Eddie to paint a mural in his house with the promise of a scholarship. 'It seems unreasonable that an undergraduate, even a mature one, should feel that his academic success depends on his ability to satisfy the private requests of a professor,' he said in his complaint.[45]

Unbeknown to him, his accusation preceded an even more serious one from the father of another of Orr's students, Suzanne Kemp, who claimed that Orr had 'seduced' his daughter. After an internal investigation, the university found that the allegations were true and summarily dismissed Orr. Outraged, Orr sought support from the staff association and sued the university for wrongful dismissal. Pro- and anti-Orr camps formed, and the debate quickly become vitriolic. Cassandra Pybus, who was a child in Fern Tree at the time and later wrote a book about the affair, recalled that Orr's name was everywhere. 'Hobart society fed on it,' she wrote. 'Everyone had taken sides.'[46] As staunch supporters of Eddie, the Harwoods were in the anti-Orr camp. They watched in helpless dismay as Orr's supporters did all they could to discredit their friend, vilifying his character and causing him and his family great distress. By early 1957, the Tanners had had enough and moved to Melbourne. Gwen was very sad to see them go. Years later, she would tell Eddie that she remembered 'as clearly as if it were yesterday the evening when we said goodbye in 1957 – your children laughed (as children always do) when I put my arms around you; for me that night was the end of a time of comfort & reassurance. God's curse on separations!'[47]

◆ ◆ ◆

Gwen's loss of 'comfort and reassurance' was not solely the result of Eddie's departure. She was already feeling the absence of some of her closest friends. In mid-1956, Lotte had gone to France with her four-year-old daughter for a period of study leave. Bill's former research assistant, Alison Wright, was also overseas, having taken up a scholarship at Oxford in early 1955. Tony was back in London. Everyone seemed to be going somewhere, while she was stuck at home with four children and a husband who showed increasing signs of wanting to become a hermit. Worse, towards the end of 1956, she was scheduled to have a hysterectomy. She had been putting it off; she had known she needed the procedure for two years,[48] but was afraid of going under the knife.

Two years after the twins were born, she had had minor surgery, which entailed having a general anaesthetic for the first time. The experience had brought home to her 'what Peter [Bennie] calls "the extreme natural probability of total annihilation". This seems to me conceivable & quite unbearable.'[49] It was one thing to let go of her religious faith on an intellectual level, but quite another to sense in her own breathing flesh that death was final. Since then, her dreams had been haunted by the feeling 'that I alone know how fearful the true nature of the world is'. Now, she was 'in a state of mortal terror about that operation I can't even spell'.[50] She was afraid not only that she might die under anaesthetic, but also that the loss of her uterus might change her in unpredictable yet disastrous ways. What if there turned out to be some occult connection between her physical fertility and her creativity? What if she should find, after the operation, that she could no longer write? 'What I'm afraid of is that I shall never lay hold of The Poem,' she told Ann, 'that the tight hard masculine core of the mind will atrophy; that middle-age will shake me till my teeth rattle.'[51] She felt that she had not yet done the creative work that would prove – à la Friedrich Hölderlin – that her life had not been wasted. The idea that she might lose the capacity ever to do such work terrified her.

In mid-December, Agnes came down from Brisbane to look after the children while Gwen was in hospital. She was calmer by this time. At the last moment, she had written to Peter Bennie expressing her panic, and he had told her that 'the spirit makes use of the body if it can; if it cannot, of something else'.[52] She found this deeply comforting. It would soon become an article of faith for her that no physical wound could destroy the essential self.

In recovery, Gwen was a difficult patient. The first night, delirious with fever, it seemed the world had 'contracted to a single dimension of pain'.[53] 'I kept falling into a state where I saw a jungle growing from my bed – twisting vines and creepers with tendrils like steel springs crept towards me; huge coloured flowers burst open and showed menacing human faces.' She called for pain relief, but the nurses told her sternly she couldn't have any more and began to ignore her cries. 'So without any change of pitch I began calling "JESUS! JESUS!" Immediately feet clattered at both ends of the corridor and *two* sisters were at my side.'[54] She got her pain relief.

When the pain subsided, she began almost to enjoy her time in hospital: the enforced rest, with no one else's needs to tend to, was very welcome. As soon as she could hold a pen, she began to work on a poem.[55] 'It really was a resurrection,' she told Tony. The poem, 'A Postcard', was a continuation of one she had begun several months earlier on the back of a postcard of a sixteenth-century Bruegel painting, *The Hunters in the Snow*. Written in the persona of an elderly woman who remembered the painting from her childhood, it is a meditation on the 'blind, beaked hunger, crying to be filled', that has haunted her life.[56] When it was finished, Gwen dedicated it to Tony and sent it off to *Meanjin*, which, to her delight, accepted it immediately and published it almost at once; it appeared in their second issue for 1957. Tony wrote from England to pour out his admiration and gratitude, speaking of the 'strange feeling of *importance* it gives me to know that you dedicate such a lovely thing to me'.[57] He felt 'fulfilled', he went on, 'to know that I am linked to you by such exquisite art'. Later, she would write another poem, 'The Wound', that would address directly both her fear of the surgery and her new confidence that physical mutilation could not constrain her creativity: 'Spirit can build, make shift / with what is there.' Pain became the crucible from which new poems were made.

11

My Tongue Is My Own

Ah, wordless leap of mind to mind!
We had no need of speech, who gazed
while love and luck, our double star,
in unforeseen concurrence blazed.

Gwen Harwood, 'Frontier Guards'

I N 1956, GWEN'S YOUNGEST CHILDREN, THE TWINS, PETER AND Mary, started kindergarten. In April, she reported to Tony that the twins' teacher, Mrs Skomorowska, had said to her, 'Zose twins, I don't know how you *bear* zem.' She responded sympathetically, 'Yes they are fiendish, aren't they, *very* trying.' Mrs Skomorowska replied, 'No, I mean I don't know how you *bear* them, you are so leetle, you'd think zere wouldn't be room for two bebbies.'[1] After four children and two surgeries, she was still slight and youthful, easily mistaken in the right light for 'a young girl'.[2] With her red hair cut short, her beaming smile and her seemingly boundless physical energy, she looked, as she liked to say, like a choir boy, if an ageing one.

With something of her mother's weakness for a good committee, Gwen agreed to join the Augusta Road Pre-School Association and soon became its secretary, an honorary role in which she carried on 'incessant correspondence with the Education Department'.[3] Early in 1957, the association elected a new president, 'a Hungarian Ph.D. of great charm' named Thomas Pick. He was a psychologist in his early thirties who had come to Australia with his Dutch wife, Louisli, in 1950. The child of an Austrian Catholic mother and a Hungarian Jewish father, Tom grew up speaking German, Hungarian and English. During World War II, he was forced into a labour battalion, along with all able-bodied Hungarian men of Jewish descent, but managed to desert en route to Nazi Germany, fleeing to Switzerland.[4] After the war, he and Louisli migrated to Australia as part of the United Nations' Displaced Persons scheme.[5] They lived for a time in Melbourne, then moved to Tasmania, where he was appointed to the role of child psychologist with the education department. When he and Gwen met in 1957, he was thirty-two, five years younger than her, with two children at the

Augusta Road Pre-School and a new baby at home – an object of envy to Gwen's twins, who begged her to 'get them one just like it'.[6] Five-foot-nine, dark-haired, slender and earnest, Dr Pick was described in a newspaper article as 'a quiet and scholarly New Australian'.[7]

Dr Thomas Pick, 1950

Gwen was delighted by this cultured European. One evening, he came to see her at home on association business – to Bill's displeasure – and they spent several hours poring over one of Gwen's modern art books together.[8] A couple of days later, she went to a fundraiser for the preschool, held at Friends' Senior School. She was in the reception hall looking at a print of the Bruegel painting that featured in 'A Postcard' when Dr Pick appeared. 'He didn't know where to go either, so we stood changing eyes in front of a tapestry of Venice; it turned out he had known Venice from childhood, and he was speaking of it with the passion it calls up in every breast when a glorious Senior Girl approached and directed us to the assembly hall, which was utterly grim.'[9] The evening, a slideshow night, went downhill from there. Gwen was alternately amused and appalled by the inevitable technological failures and the idiosyncrasies of the presenters. She hoped to salvage the evening, she told Tony, by talking Dr Pick into walking home with her, but was thwarted when she was offered a lift by friends.[10]

Sometime over the next few weeks, she would discover that she was in love – not simply conducting a highly public flirtation for comedic effect, as she had indicated in playful letters to Tony, but deeply, truly, tragically in love. At last she had met someone 'who loved me & did not wish to change me' – and the feeling was 'mutual'.[11] She would later tell Alison she believed this love was predestined. She had dreamed of Tom before she ever met him and had told Ann about the dream, saying 'He was *dark*, and I don't fancy dark men, but we had an instant, total understanding.' In the dream, he said to her: 'I know you, I will make you so happy you will never forget me.'[12] When she met him in the flesh, it seemed 'only a recognition'.

It was an idea she had first encountered in Donne's 'Aire and Angels', which begins: 'Twice or thrice had I loved thee, / Before I knew thy face or name.' She would borrow these lines for a poem of her own that described her first meeting with Tom:

> Mystery grows lifesize as I'm brought to meet you.
> (Loved, as Donne says, before your face or name . . .)
> A day like any other, with the same
> things to be done, and soon after I greet you
> I have to take my leave. Others demand
> your presence, and I walk, away from you,
> on the fine edge of *now*, as we all do,
> with an eternity at either hand.[13]

She had stepped out of time, and her world had been transformed 'by / the simple rightness of a human face'. Trying to describe to Tony their mutual attraction, she drew on Bertrand Russell's account of meeting the novelist Joseph Conrad:

> At our very first meeting, we talked with continually increasing intimacy. We seemed to sink through layer after layer of what was superficial, till gradually both reached the central fire . . . We looked into each other's eyes, half appalled and half intoxicated to find our-selves together in such a region . . . I came away bewildered, and hardly able to find my way among ordinary affairs.

'That's how it was with me & *ce que j'aime*,' Gwen wrote.[14]

Exactly how they came to consummate their love, between school drop-offs and Pre-School Association meetings, she never explained, though there are hints in certain poems.[15] One of these, 'Carpe Diem' – published in 1961 under a male pseudonym – dramatises the moment of decision. The would-be lovers find themselves alone – '*at last*' – and he embraces her, urging her to seize the day. She hesitates, trying to think – in the moment 'between kiss and eyelid fall' – of consequences, reasons to demur. But her mind 'conjures away tomorrow', refusing to acknowledge any possible sorrow. Her decision is already clear. She will not deny her passion; her 'true tongue' has 'not learned / lying, and will not learn to lie'. And so she throws caution to the winds: '*Carpe diem*, my dear one', she tells him. 'Lie / light in my arms and on my life.'

Several poems suggest that the lovers snatched moments outside: on an empty beach in the dawn, on a mountainside in the afternoon. Given that it was early winter in a place that could be bitingly cold, it is more likely that they made use of a rented room, or even a car. Gwen does not seem to have enlisted Ann's aid – she did not tell her about Tom until several years later. The only other friend who might have helped, Lotte, was still overseas. It is possible they met at Gwen's house during the day. One of her bolder poems about the affair, 'The Supplicant', suggests this. It speaks of a lovers tryst in a bedroom with a framed print of a 'samurai whose servant held a sword' – the very print that hung above the bed in Gwen and Bill's room at Augusta Road.[16]

The sex itself was rapturous – for Gwen, at least. Her lover 'rocked [her] to ecstasy', being 'so schooled in love'.[17] But the spiritual dimension of their sexual encounters was even more shattering. In poem after poem, Gwen would write of how in the act of sex, the spirit is set free, the fragmentary self made whole. In that moment of 'blinding rapture', the spirit comes into its own, swept up – as Zeus sweeps up Ganymede in the Greek myth – into paradise. Yet no mortal can live in paradise, and all too soon, spirit falls back into flesh, leaving the lovers to flounder in the banality of the everyday.[18]

The 'ordinary' sense of let-down after sex – the sadness known as *post coitum triste* – was magnified a thousandfold for Gwen by the knowledge that each tryst with her lover might be the last. From the beginning, the relationship took place in the shadow of its end: Gwen could not contemplate leaving her family for her lover. There was 'no choice', she told Tony. 'I have young children, I am bound to Bill by twelve years of loyalty; I am a tree of life to them.' No matter how she and Tom felt about one another, leaving Bill was never an option. 'What a paradox', she lamented. 'The love which can only be fulfilled with the sacrifice of others, and denied with the sacrifice of oneself.'[19] Though she made the sacrifice willingly, it was agonising to live through. Having been touched by the gods, she was now to be thrown back into her old life, her old self – a mere 'urn of unproliferating bones'.[20]

The lovers' parting was precipitated by Tom's decision to take a job with the Department of Public Health in Sydney.[21] They had been lovers only a few weeks,[22] and the news that he was leaving plunged Gwen into a state of anguish. One Saturday morning a few days before he left, she was in town when she found herself 'nearly mad with despair, and on the point of dissolving in tears'. Determined not to break down in public, she ducked into the post office and 'pretended to be writing a telegram'. As she stood at the writing stand, she felt suddenly that she could not go through with the parting. '[I] thought "I *cannot* bear this, and after all I do not *have* to bear it, I will kill myself."' As relief flooded through her, she glanced up to see a man in postal uniform approaching 'with a huge stack of blotting paper borne across his forearms as an altar-boy might bear the altar-cloths'. Going up to one of the stands, he 'put down his blotting-paper & bowed his head'. 'I thought: "He has gone mad; he imagines himself to be an acolyte in some divine office", then realised he was inspecting the inkwell. He came slowly round with enough blotting-paper to mop up any tears of mine, and of course I started to laugh.'[23] The sudden shift of perspective saved her. How absurd life was, and how full of unimaginable possibilities. A line from a fifteenth-century balled floated into her mind: 'Men are fools that wish to die.'

Even so, Tom's departure hit her hard. She felt she had been stranded in a nightmare. Though she was consumed by heartbreak, she had to behave as if everything was normal. 'I feel that I am acting in a dream from which I cannot wake,' she wrote. 'Only sleep restores to me the face I shall not see again.'[24] 'If only I could have some time alone!' she wailed in November. 'A day even, to gather myself together.' But it was impossible. Even when she was 'nearly wild with grief and despair'[25] she had to conduct her everyday tasks with her accustomed smile. She found it hard to believe she was fooling anyone – and yet she fooled everyone.[26] 'Look at Gwen,' one of her friends declared admiringly one evening, 'I've *never* seen her cast down.'[27] Gwen would come to think that such pretence was 'natural' to women. 'Since they are (or seem to be) the pursued they learn early all the arts of the hunted: speed, camouflage, lightning change, merging into the background, leaping like a hare in one direction and then another in one breath,' she mused. 'To me now it seems impossible to see beneath the surface of women if they don't show their interior life of their own accord.'[28] From this time on, her poems would be full of images of masks, disguise and duality.

Her children may have been more sensitive to her suffering than she allowed. One day her six-year-old daughter, coming across her in a state of anguished reverie, began to stroke her knee, saying: 'You seem so sad I think you are crying without tears.'[29] But in general, the children were absorbed in their own affairs – to Gwen's relief. 'The great joy of having children is that they are always full of prospects, hope, going forward, and one is carried with them,' she wrote.[30]

Tony was her 'greatest source of strength'. But she also found comfort in Lotte, newly returned from Europe and 'showing her delight in being home'.[31] Gwen hastened to tell her friend the whole story. Alison Wright had also returned, accompanied by her new husband, Bill Hoddinott, whom she had met at Oxford, and their first child, baby Anne. Gwen did not confide in Alison, but she was very glad to see her. In retrospect, Alison would feel that both the Harwoods fell upon her and Bill with rather more alacrity than was strictly warranted, as though they were very much in need of some circuit-breaking company.[32] Alison had always been a favourite of Bill Harwood's, and he and Gwen both liked her husband.[33] When Bill Hoddinott found work in the university's English department, he would often give Bill Harwood a lift home from work in the afternoons (the Harwoods still did not have a car) and come in for a pre-dinner drink. The two families were soon firm friends.

And so, to the outside view, life went on very much as usual for Gwen. Internally, though, she felt fatally riven. For many months, she could neither sleep nor write. Even Schubert gave her no comfort. 'I can't bear to listen to the *Winterreise*,' she told Tony in January 1958. 'It echoes my inmost despair, the pain "enthroned on the darkest altar of our heartbreak".'[34] She had 'some terrifying nights' in which she felt she was being shown 'pictures of great intricacy', 'terrifying, nightmarish Gothic things', and was unable to look away.[35] She also found herself receiving 'verse after verse of bad poetry' from some misbegotten angel: 'not spoken, but presented quite clearly'.[36] To her disgust, her 'nocturnal daemons' – unlike those of William Blake – could not even scan.[37] She did write one of these poems down, entitling it 'In Articulo Mortis' (At the point of death). It is addressed to 'Christ the Falcon' and harks back to her earliest poems, with their framework of biblical and theological imagery. She sent it not to a literary journal but to Peter Bennie, who had recently become editor of the *Australian Church Quarterly*, and who promptly published it. Publication, she remarked to Ann, seemed to satisfy the 'Blake-like voices, who have been silent since then'.[38]

Difficult though this time was, Gwen clung to her belief that if she could just endure, her anguish would pass. By March 1958, she was noting signs of 'recovery' in her letters to Tony. 'Somehow, somehow,' she told him, 'I have lived through the pain of parting and find I can bear it without bitterness.'[39] The 'bitterness' she had managed to evade was not 'towards human beings' ('I never feel that: as if we weren't all hanging over the bottomless black silence!') but the bitterness of futile longing and regret. She could even spare a thought for her banished lover, 'who has the heaviness of life . . . to bear without me'. She had not heard a word from him, and the silence was crushing. 'The spirit lives by words,' she would declare in 'The Supplicant', and 'cries for a thought to hold, a word to keep'. Even so, she could now affirm to Tony that 'our lives were enriched, simply by our meeting and recognition: it all sounds tragic, but what I have never conveyed was the absolute joy that sprang from the knowledge that the other existed'.

She felt that her marriage was stronger for her secret affair. 'Things are much better with Bill now,' she told Tony early in 1958. 'I have overcome my old fear of his threat, spoken or implied, with which he always whipped me to heel: if you so & so, perhaps I shan't love you.'[40] The affair with Tom felt like a liberation. She had dared to claim her own shape,[41] and not only were she and Bill now getting on well, but the 'overwhelming physical attraction which has always cancelled out the temperamental differences between Bill & me . . . is unchanged after nearly thirteen years'.[42] She was even moved to contemplate her own failures in the relationship, her 'selfishness & weakness', and plan to do better.

Best of all, she was writing again, poems 'new and most exciting',[43] and for the first time in her fledgling poetry career, it was her 'own heartsblood on the page'.[44]

◆ ◆ ◆

Gwen's post-1957 poems have a new urgency. Her decision to sleep with Tom Pick marked the definitive end of her attempt to be the perfect 1950s wife and mother. Her tongue was her own again, and she was determined to write what mattered most to her. At the same time, she had no intention of revealing her affair to the world. She knew that would only invite judgement. Her new poems would be not personal outpourings but carefully crafted works of art designed to thwart the prying eye. As she would admit many years later, she behaved in these poems 'like a mother duck feigning a broken wing to draw enemies away from her secret nest'.[45]

One of her first poems about the love affair exemplifies this. It was an Eisenbart poem, 'Group from Tartarus', the last she would write of her prickly professor for another thirty years. At first glance, the poem seems several removes from the experiences of a suburban housewife. It is based on a Schubert song of the same title, which is itself based on a poem by Friedrich Schiller about an episode in Virgil's *The Aeneid*. In Virgil's epic, Aeneas visits the underworld in search of his father and is taken by his guide past the gates of hell, where he hears the shrieks of souls in torment and glimpses their eternal suffering. In Gwen's poem, Professor Eisenbart is a modern-day Aeneas, walking past a scene of eternal torment disguised as an everyday interaction in an ordinary suburban street. The hellish scene he witnesses is that of a woman exchanging a casual greeting with a man and his two children. It would be an utterly banal interaction were it not that the married woman and the father have been lovers, and love one another still. They exchange a single glance, charged with the utter joy of this chance meeting and the utter despair of their necessary parting. The misanthropic Eisenbart reads, in this look, 'their fugue of love and loss', and is himself stricken by 'a hard beak of anguish'; their hopeless situation seems to contain all the sorrow of the world.

Gwen was delighted with this poem, and sent it straight off to *Meanjin* – always her first choice of publisher. 'Christesen sent it back by return mail,' she reported darkly to Tony.[46] The rejection was particularly galling because the poem was so personal, a snapshot of the feelings she had been so relentlessly suppressing. She sent it off again – to *Southerly*, *The Bulletin*, *Quadrant*, *Australian Letters*. No one wanted it. Gwen ground her teeth. To Eddie, she speculated that it was the poem's immorality that was putting editors off. They were not comfortable with a poem that took a sympathetic view of adultery. 'I must get to work on my pink & blue epic, "The Parish Church",' she growled. 'It will tell, in unrhymed eccentric pentameter, how the choir made paper chains out of their hymn books.'[47]

At the same time, she was working on a series of poems that would tell the story of the affair more explicitly – while shrouding the details in myth. Again, she went to her favourite German lieder for her framework, selecting Loewe's setting of 'Thomas the Rhymer'.[48] The story seemed to Gwen to encapsulate her own experience with Tom Pick – who, despite his name, is not the Rhymer but the glamorous elf queen, mysterious seducer from a distant land. Gwen herself is the Rhymer. The gender inversion was all to the good – readers would be less likely to guess that the story was about her if the poet-protagonist was male. The long, intricately rhymed poem begins with a tryst between the Rhymer and his married lover on the mountain-side. She criticises his verse – it is 'too cerebral', she scolds – and suggests he 'release [his] lyric spring' (a suggestion it is conceivable Tom Pick made of Gwen's early poetry). They go on to speak of how they fell in love:

> . . . swifter than their speech
> eyes looked and locked with eyes, to pierce
> through layer on layer of self and reach
> love's central fire.

The pair make love on the hillside, finding 'love's right / true end in bodies' (Gwen's adaptation of Donne), their physical union setting their 'fierce spirits' free to walk 'a floor of light, / singing beyond their mortal stuff'.

The naked Tom is enraptured, telling his lover that 'A lifetime will not be enough' for their love. But the woman will not offer him a lifetime. What they have experienced is only an 'island of unreality' in the tide of the every-day. Their 'daily bread' is their mundane lives – hers with her children, his with his wife and young son. Besides, she is leaving that very night, on the ship they can see far below in the harbour. Yet in this moment, they are 'free / from grief and time', and they make love once more before their idyll ends. The woman leaves for ports unknown, and Tom returns home to find his wife at the gate. He 'kissed her, and kept / his tongue his own'. Through all the years that follow, he labours to turn his 'torment and despair' into verse. Only when he is dying does his lover come to him again. Together, 'they [walk] light's flood'.

Gwen began work on this poem in late 1958, labouring at it 'with all my skill'.[49] For her, it was the vessel that would contain the truth of all she had been through: the sexual ecstasy she had found with Tom, her agonised renunciation of him and the consolation she found in the idea that their shared moments were outside of time. When it was done, she was satisfied; she felt she had written one of her best poems to date. It was a bitter dis-appointment when, early in 1959, *Meanjin* rejected it, along with another of her poems. There was no covering letter, just a hand-written scrawl on the manuscript from an unknown reader: 'Tom the Rhymer – a romantic narrative, reasonably well done: but really the whole thing is a cliché. No.'

The anonymous reviewer finished with a final insult: 'From these it would seem Mrs Harwood is becoming just a little casual – smooth, and ever so, but in danger of losing the harsh texture of truth?'[50]

Gwen was disgusted. That her most deeply felt poem, based on the truest experiences of her heart, could be rejected as a 'cliché' was intolerable. 'Well, there it is, unsigned, with not a word from the cowardly stinking shittard cackard filthard Christesen,' she seethed in a letter to Tony. 'What shall I do? I fear I am powerless . . . What would you do?' The letter is typed, but the words 'What shall I do?' are scrawled again in her own hand on the bottom of the page.[51] She felt that Christesen had struck at her. Over the coming months and years, 'Tom the Rhymer' was rejected by the editor of every literary magazine in Australia. As rejection piled upon rejection, Gwen ground her teeth and cursed the execrable judgement of Australia's literati. One day, when she collected the typescript yet again from the mailbox, Alison Hoddinott happened to be there. To Gwen's muttered animadversions on the poem, Alison protested that it was a good piece of work. It was, in fact, one of her favourites of Gwen's poems at the time. 'You like it? Here!' Gwen said, thrusting it at her. Alison put it in her handbag, where it remained for many years, getting more and more crumpled and creased.[52] In the meantime, Gwen herself began to 'turn against' the poem, declaring it 'too wet – perhaps I should wring it out once or twice and dry it off'.[53] She had come to realise that intensity of feeling was no guarantee of good writing.

Other early poems about the relationship were more successful. *Meanjin* accepted both 'Anniversary' – which grew out of Gwen's despairing sense that she was reliving her heartbreak each winter – and 'Frontier Guards', about two star-crossed lovers from different continents.[54] The latter poem contains perhaps the most direct allusion she would make in any poem to Tom Pick, in that it identifies one of the lovers as Hungarian by referring to Alföld (otherwise known as the Great Hungarian Plain). Gwen told Tony that 'the content of Frontier Guards was so charged emotionally I feared it might crack at the seams, but it held'.[55] Both poems appeared in *Meanjin* in 1959, along with another, 'Caro Autem Infirma', that was 'quite unlike anything I've written so far'.[56] It was the first of the series – including 'Triste, Triste', 'The Wine Is Drunk' and 'In Zurich by the Tideless Lake' – that would explore her new apprehension of the relationship between sex and spirit.[57] Other poems focused on her sense of having lost control of her many selves, as in the ironically titled 'I Am the Captain of My Soul'. The title is from the last line of William Ernest Henley's poem 'Invictus', which declares that no matter what life may throw at one, the self retains its mastery. Gwen's poem expresses the opposite, the sense that the 'ship' of the self is careening around wildly, directionless and in imminent danger of foundering; the captain is drunk, the crew terrified, and all the different parts of the self 'keel to the void' in 'a wilderness of water'.[58]

These poems seemed to Gwen to be in a different league to those she had written up until now, and her judgement was confirmed by Christesen. In December 1958, he wrote to say that he would try 'to run two or more of your poems together in the autumn issue'. 'You are certainly doing some nice work, and I'm becoming more and more interested,' he went on. 'Could you let me have a biographical note one of these days? Tell me something about yourself, and of your plans for book publication; and could you let me have a photograph for my "rogues" gallery?'[59] It was the kind of personal interest Gwen had longed for ten years earlier, but now, jaded by all the rejections, she was wary. She responded with a potted biography in the form of a parody of her favourite 'Lines to Ralph Hodgson Esqre' by T.S. Eliot:

> How delightful to meet Mrs Harwood!
>> (Everyone wants to know *her*)
> With her polished floor
> And her children (four)
> She types out her poetry neatly
> and attunes her attention sweetly
> as domestic crises occur.
>
>> . . .
>
> How delightful to meet Mrs Harwood!
>> (Everyone wants to know *her*).
> She writes 999 verses
> which her family greet with curses
> as she scrawls them without demur.
> How delightful to meet Mrs Harwood!
>> (Everyone wants to meet *her*).

She did not send a photograph, but Christesen sent her one of himself, looking rather jaunty in a Panama hat.

What Christesen made of her biographical 'note' is not recorded, but Gwen's playful tone changed when 'Caro Autem Infirma' was published early in 1959 with a misprint in the title. 'When you see the fucking mess they have made of the Latin you will share my helpless rage,' she spluttered to Tony.[60] Christesen agreed to publish a correction, but did not do so expeditiously, which further annoyed her. She was only partly mollified when, in November, she received word that she had won that year's *Meanjin* poetry prize for the poem. 'Bill brought the letter into the bathroom where I was washing my hair and I couldn't believe it,' she told Vivian.[61] 'I am still terrified they have made a mistake, but I have banked their cheque.' The cheque was for ten pounds, a goodly amount in 1959, but Gwen did not fail to note that the prize had been advertised as being worth ten guineas, a slightly larger sum. Bill, who was generally underwhelmed by Gwen's poetry, studied the cheque to see if it was 'genuine', then read the prize-winning poem carefully. He concluded that 'it had the same qualities as Keats's great odes'. Gwen was satisfied.[62]

◆ ◆ ◆

While Gwen was squabbling with Christesen in mid-1959, Hobart was gripped by scandal when, in the midst of the contentious Hursey industrial case, Ann Jennings left her lawyer husband for a communist waterside worker named Tas Bull. Gwen, who counted Ann among her closest friends, was shocked. She had had no idea this was brewing.[63] Now, she realised that she and Ann had been going through the same experience – a secret affair – but while she had decided to stay in her marriage, Ann had decided to leave. Her heart ached for her friend – and for herself. Soon after Ann and Tas went to Melbourne, temporarily leaving Ann's children behind, Gwen dreamed that she and Ann 'were standing together on a desolate shore which curved for miles on each side of us'. 'You were in great distress,' she told Ann, recounting the dream, 'saying you were very close to death; and I said "You have choked up your tears for too long"; and to comfort you I said "Let me show you what it is like to take the *other* decision" and showed you the desolate beach stretching away to nothing.'[64] The desolate beach was Gwen's life after she decided to stay with her husband. The choked-up tears were hers, too. Much as she deprecated divorce, she understood and even admired Ann's decision to leave her marriage.

She had not told Ann about Tom, but now she dropped hints in her letters. Ann was 'drinking . . . from a cup I put aside, and acting out a passion that I could not enter into,' she wrote, promising to tell her why 'when I talk to you again'.[65] She even sent her a copy of the still unpublished 'Tom the Rhymer'.[66] The judgement that rained down on Ann in her absence from 'feeble sentimental snivelling "child-lovers"' incensed Gwen.[67] She assured Ann that she well knew how her friend loved her children, and what sacrifices she had made for them over the years. To Gwen, Ann had had as little choice about leaving her marriage as Gwen had had about staying in hers. Ann had to be true to herself, and that meant, in the biblical phrase, giving up her life 'in order to save it'. While most women were 'essentially dead', Ann had chosen life, instinctively understanding that 'truth can only live in living tissue'.

As well as defending her friend fiercely from the gossips, Gwen sent a stream of loving cards and letters to her at the small, rented flat she and Tas shared in Melbourne. 'A word of affirmation,' she scrawled on a postcard in August: 'my love for you is absolute . . . All that matters is hope, going forward, and I wish you joy.'[68] Ann was beginning a career as a high-school teacher, and Gwen respected, even envied, her new-found independence. But she still hoped Ann might return to Hobart. She reached out to Roger, too, but her letter seemed designed chiefly to let him know what a jewel he had lost. 'I think you know how I love Ann – if I were a man I should do *anything* to have her,' she wrote. 'It is irrational, but I cannot choose not to love her.' It was an odd thing for her to tell Ann's husband – unless she was trying to urge him to fight for his wife. She repeated her words in a letter to Ann, and went on to tell her of a dream in which 'I had you in my arms . . . and I was shaking you with anguish saying "If only I were a man, then how I should love you."'[69]

Ann's departure from Hobart left her feeling painfully isolated. 'I am very much alone now,' she told Ann in January 1960. 'But it is bearable; I don't mean physical solitude, I hardly ever am alone in that sense – I could do with a year in a remote cave; [but] I felt such ease and freedom with you that most other relationships seem stiff and formal by comparison.'[70]

◆ ◆ ◆

Gwen felt Ann's departure the more keenly because she had also, over the course of a tumultuous year, lost her friend Lotte Wilmot. Since Lotte's return from Europe in late 1957, they had not settled back into the close friendship they had shared before Lotte's sabbatical.

For a time, all seemed well. Lotte and Claire resumed their weekend lunches with the Harwoods, and Lotte her morning visits to Gwen for coffee and conversation. Along with another friend, Eve Masterman, they began to study German again, and often went to social functions together. But the children were not getting along as well as they used to, and when there was 'friction' between them, Gwen upset Lotte by taking her own children's part. Too late, Gwen realised that 'it was silly of me to try to discipline the other tigress' cub'.[71] At the same time, Lotte was increasingly offended by Bill's continual teasing. He once referred to a falling out between the women as 'The War of the Bluestockings', which incensed Lotte, who was already fed up with having to fight for respect in the male-dominated university environment.[72] Gwen's sympathies were with Lotte. She understood that it was 'hard for her to be between Bill's arctic indifference & my passionate involvement'.[73]

Gwen had fallen hard for Lotte: her grace, her wit, her sharp intelligence. 'I love the woman,' she told Vivian in 1959.[74] 'I might say I am in love with her, if such ambivalence of nature were not suspect in British lands.' Increasingly, she did not distinguish between the passionate feelings she had for men and those she had for women. She had discovered with Ann that she could desire to 'possess' a woman sexually just as she did a man, and now she found that the phrase 'in love' could be as pertinent to a relationship with a female friend as a male one – though far less socially acceptable.

As her friendship with Lotte began to sour, Gwen's feelings became more intense. She agonised over every little interaction, hovered around the children's school at drop-off and pick-up time in the hope of running into Lotte, and obsessively analysed the other woman's tone and looks and smiles. The needier she became, the cooler Lotte grew, until Gwen found herself blurting out her love for Lotte at random moments ('somewhat theatrically I fear'),[75] only to be met with ironic impatience. Finally, Gwen learned caution. 'If I were not afraid of being lashed by Lotte herself I should importune her,' she told Tony, her confidante in all of this, 'but I recall too vividly her answer to my last affirmation of love: "Let us leave love out of this."'[76]

By now, Gwen sorely regretted having told Lotte about her affair with Tom: 'she tends to preach the virtues of holy matrimony . . . and domestic life, and declines to comfort me,' she had told Tony sadly in mid-1958.[77] Almost a year later, during a long conversation in Melbourne (where Tony was once again living), Lotte told Tony that Gwen's confidences had put her, as Bill's colleague, in an untenable position. Gwen was distraught when Tony relayed this to her. 'Lotte herself, early in our friendship, confided to me at great length about being involved with a married man,' she protested. 'I comforted her, listened to her for hours, and offered her love and consolation. It never occurred to me for a moment not to tell her of my own heart-breaking experience.' She was particularly upset that Lotte had characterised Gwen's decision to reveal her secret as a 'calculated risk'. 'My confidence in her was simply a measure of my love & trust – she could destroy my life tomorrow if she chose to,' wrote Gwen. 'I do not calculate in love and friendship; if I had "calculated" for a moment I should not have given Lotte knowledge that could rip this household apart for ever; my trust in her was ABSOLUTE.'[78]

Still her love for Lotte survived. 'I have never loved any woman more than I love her,' she wrote to both Vivian and Tony on the same day. 'It is heart-breaking for me even to see her in the distance; sharp despair when I think of a future without her.' As always with love and heartbreak, she drew on German lieder to express her feelings, citing Schubert's 'Gute Nacht' and 'Im Frühling' in letters to Vivian: 'Vorüber flieht der Liebe glück, und nur die leiber bleibt zurück, die Lieb' und ach! das Leid!' ('The happiness of love flies past, and only the love remains: the love, and ah! the sorrow!').[79] She reached for Rainer Maria Rilke, too, telling Tony: 'Die grosse Einsamkeit beginnt' ('the immense loneliness begins').[80]

In time, Gwen came to feel that Lotte's talk of being caught between her loyalty to her friend and to her colleague was an excuse. It seemed to her that the real cause of Lotte's anger was that Gwen had developed a passion for someone else – Tom Pick – in her absence. Lotte was Gwen's god, and would tolerate no other gods before her. 'She must have thought it was love taken from her,' Gwen mused to Tony.[81] But no matter what she told herself, nor how many times she repeated to Tony and Vivian that she was done with Lotte, she only had to see her to forget all her resolutions. 'I want to clasp her and cry, "I love you and you are killing me."'[82]

In July 1959, Lotte told Gwen that she had analysed their relationship in detail and was prepared to share her insights if Gwen 'promised not to lose [her] temper'.[83] She presented Gwen with a sixty-page document – a detailed accounting of Gwen's 'real & imaginary shortcomings, misdeeds, deficiencies and bad qualities'.[84] It seemed to have a cathartic effect on Lotte. Soon after Gwen read it (and destroyed it, at Lotte's insistence), she found that she and Lotte were 'getting on all right again'.[85] After several friendly interactions, she even began to hope for a return to their old intimacy. Then one day, in the car park before school, Lotte told Gwen that she had news of Tom Pick. She would not reveal it at once, but made her tearful friend beg, prefacing the 'scrap' of information with 'a sermon' on Gwen's wickedness. The experience, Gwen told Tony, had the same effect on her that 'Bill's cruel letter' had had on Tony all those years ago: it severed the friendship. 'I don't wish her ill; I still think she is brilliant, witty, beautiful and graceful; and I shall continue to meet her, and talk to her. But she cut me free of her, finally, in that moment.'[86]

In late 1959 or early 1960, Gwen gave vent to her mingled anger and contempt in a poem that played the passionate artist off against the cool intellectual. 'Clair de Lune: Poet to Bluestocking' characterises the artist as a 'towering spirit' and the intellectual as a vicious parasite. When it was published in *Meanjin* in late 1960, she remarked, somewhat disingenuously, that Lotte would probably take the poem as 'a personal insult, if she sees it when it appears'.[87]

If Lotte did see the poem, she did not confront Gwen about it. A couple of years later, however, Gwen wrote a poem, 'Chance Meeting', that referred directly to their relationship, and this poem Lotte did see – and took great exception to. For Gwen, the poem was a kind of elegy for the friendship. She had 'loved being Lotte's favourite', she explained to another friend while she was working on it, and their falling out made her feel like Archibald Douglas in the eponymous Scottish ballad, who has fallen from the king's favour. Douglas waylays his liege when he is out hunting, taking hold of his horse's reins and running alongside him in his chain mail, breathlessly pleading for reinstatement.[88] In her poem, Gwen similarly makes one last bid for Lotte's friendship after bumping into her by chance – but unlike Douglas, she fails to melt her sovereign's heart. Though she wrote the poem in 1963, Gwen did not publish it until 1965, and then under a pseudonym. Gwen had hoped the nom de plume would fool Lotte, but Lotte recognised Gwen's authorship at once. She considered it a huge betrayal. The poem seemed to put all the blame for the friendship's rupture on her, giving no space to Lotte's own perspective. She would never forgive Gwen.

Over the years, this poem was reprinted many times, in Gwen's own collections and in various anthologies. Every new printing was a fresh wound for Lotte. In the early 1970s, she determined to take revenge.[89] In her lounge room in the late evening, she began work on a series of parodies of Gwen's poems, framed by a dialogue between 'Watson' and 'Holmes'. The parodies, which show a close familiarity with Gwen's work, are nasty, accusing Gwen, among other things, of being afraid 'of an open fight' and dreading 'a fair one', and declaring that she had 'sponged' on their friendship. Lotte also complains that Gwen manipulated the facts in her poems to prove 'that black is white'. Lotte went to the trouble of getting her manuscript typed up and mailed it to Gwen anonymously. Gwen at first thought it was a joke from one of her friends, but gradually came to realise it was 'a great big shit sandwich wrapped in pseudo-literary cellophane'.[90] She recognised Lotte's hand at work: 'nobody else hates me so much – or, so far as I know, hates me at all'.

It is not clear whether Lotte tried to publish her parodies, or whether her 'concentrated malice' was meant for Gwen's eyes alone. But her bitterness remained undiluted. In later years, Gwen would receive a number of poison-pen letters she was sure were from Lotte. She always ignored them, but they bothered her. She hated to lose a friend under any circumstances, and Lotte had been among the inner circle of those she considered friends for life. Yet she did not regret publishing 'Chance Meeting'. Once the poem was on the page, it was no longer a true story but a work of art, with its own life: 'facts' could be changed to suit the rhyme scheme, details tweaked to fit the line. In any case, 'Chance Meeting' was not an attack on Lotte: 'if such a poem were addressed to me, it would soften my heart, not harden it,' she told Tony earnestly.[91] She never could understand why anyone might object to featuring in one of her poems.

Wily Walter and Fluent Frank

*I have been sowing confusion in the magazines – will tell you under
separate cover. Am entering middle age full of fight.*
Gwen Harwood, Letter to Edwin Tanner, 3 February 1961

TOWARDS THE END OF 1960, GWEN SENT A SAPPHO CARD TO
Vivian Smith featuring a Victorian woodcut of a young lady in a
many-flounced gown surrounded by languid gentlemen in frock
coats. She had begun making these cards in 1958, cutting illustrations from
old volumes of Victorian-era publications such as *Cassell's Weekly* and the
Sunday Magazine and gluing them onto cardboard, often adding speech
bubbles.[1] She laboured over them with care, joking to friends that when
she died, she would be made the patron saint of postcards ('an incurable
sufferer from advanced cartomania, Blessed Gwendolina bore her afflic-
tion with fortitude').[2]

A Gwen Harwood Sappho card, sent to Vivian Smith, 1 December 1960

On the card she sent Vivian, the young lady is clasping the hands of a gentleman who is bending eagerly towards her, while behind her a second gentleman with a drooping moustache looks on. A pallid face looms weirdly in the background, while a soberly dressed female figure presses her pince-nez to her eyes, the better to observe the scene. 'This was taken at the 5th year Epic Writers' party,' Gwen wrote on the back. 'L to R: Walter Lehmann, Lady Sappho, Fluent Francis; in the background, James McAuley; extreme right, The Epic Muse (A.D. [Hope] in disguise . . .).'[3]

Walter Lehmann, Lady Sappho and Fluent Francis were all Gwen, Lehmann and Francis Geyer being two of her pseudonyms, and Lady Sappho her poet-incarnation. The poets McAuley and Hope she saw as her main competitors. Both had authored 'epic' poems in recent months, which they had inflicted – Gwen's term – on their hapless publics. The card presented the first verses of Lady Sappho's own epic: 'Wily Walter & Fluent Frank / Were walking down the street / Walter was going to the bank / and Frank to buy the meat.' Here Gwen interjects some pertinent literary criticism – 'Notice the wonderful alliteration and the greatness of the theme' – before the epic continues: 'I love the town,' said Frank, / 'I halt at all the intersections, / and gaze about me, darling Walt, / at fabulous erections.'

By this stage, Walter ('Wally') Lehmann and Francis ('Frankie') Geyer were fully formed characters in Gwen's mind, but they had begun their existence as far more tenuous beings. Towards the end of October 1959, soon after *Meanjin* rejected her most recent batch of poems,[4] she had decided to start sending out work under a pseudonym. She was beginning to suspect that the rejections she was receiving were personal, that editors were knocking her back because of their preconceived ideas about her as a housewife from Tasmania. Half-jokingly, she speculated to Tony that she might be the victim of an editorial conspiracy: 'are they all in league against me? They won't answer my letters.'[5] With Bill's help, she came up with a gender-neutral name, W.W. Hagendoor (an anagram of Gwen Harwood), and early in November, she sent the poems that *Meanjin* had knocked back to Jim McAuley at *Quadrant* under this pseudonym, 'to see if he rejects them all or if he might think about the works of HAGENDOOR more kindly than about those of HARWOOD'.[6] McAuley did not: the poems were returned. Undaunted, Gwen sent them to Douglas Stewart at *The Bulletin*, but again, the poems were rejected.[7]

At the same time, she sent 'Critic's Nightwatch', another new poem, to *Meanjin* under her own name. This, too, was rejected, with an anonymous note that seemed deliberately insulting. 'Keats spoke of "the space of life" between boyishness & manhood when the "soul is in a ferment", the note read. 'It seems that for a woman this can happen in middle age . . . No.'[8] Her guess was that the comments came from David Moody, one of Christesen's poetry readers and an English lecturer at the University of Melbourne.

Gwen had already had a run-in with Moody. A few months earlier, Tony had heard from a friend that a sheaf of poems she had sent to *Meanjin* had been circulating in Melbourne University's English department.[9] Gwen was horrified. 'I have always imagined that [Christesen] was harassed and careless and incompetent but RELIABLE, I mean genuinely concerned about the normal privacy such mss have,' she sputtered. 'How DARE he hawk around my poems WHEN HE HASN'T EVEN LET ME KNOW HIS DECISION. You can't imagine what a rage I am in.'[10] How could she trust that her work was safe with him? 'Sometimes he keeps things for *years*,' she told Vivian. 'Where are they when they are away from me? I feel like someone whose children, believed to be safe, are reported playing on a cliff edge.'[11] She longed to storm into Christesen's office and tell him what she thought of him, but she had to settle for writing him a 'furious letter'. 'I am SICK of the way you treat me,' she began. After explaining what she had heard about her poems being 'shown round', she added a stinging PS: 'You are not running a Parish Gazette. I really am very angry.'[12]

A week later, she received an apology, not from Christesen but from David Moody, who took full responsibility. He tried his best to mollify her, assuring her that though he had taken some of her poems into the staff common room with him one afternoon, he hadn't shown them around. The only thing he had shared was the envelope in which the poems arrived, on which she had cast herself as 'Gwen Harwood, Dolcissima Cantatrice' – a variation on another of her favoured self-designations, 'The Sweet Singer of Lenah Valley'. 'The phrase on your envelope caught my eyes,' Moody explained. 'I asked of the staff in a general way, thinking someone might know you, whether it would be a title or a house name or what.' He assured her that 'No-one looked at your poems', and apologised that 'a distorted version' of this had been passed on to her. 'I sympathise with your distress at what you thought had been going on,' he finished. 'I hope you'll continue to send your poems to *Meanjin*. They are among the few I look for in hope.'[13]

Gwen wasn't sure she could believe him. Besides, even if he was telling the truth, she still felt let down. As she told Tony, she and Christesen had been 'exchanging notes' for a decade; a joke on an envelope made sense in that context, and he should have known it was not intended for a stranger's eyes.[14] 'I'd like NEVER again to have ANYTHING to do with CBC,' she told Tony, 'but *Meanjin* is really the only magazine here of international standard, and I'd rather appear there than anywhere.'[15]

The most recent comment from *Meanjin*'s anonymous reader, referring to her age, only compounded the offence. 'I wonder what is behind these personal insults?' she brooded. 'Is CBC so indifferent that he will allow these "editorial assistants" to do this? . . . Who told the writer that I was "middle-aged", I wonder?' She felt deeply disheartened. 'This . . . makes me wonder if I shall have the heart to try again. I know I shall, but today I feel beshitted and bemerded.'[16]

She had another grievance against Christesen. She was convinced that he had purloined a phrase of hers – 'the freckled shade' – from a poem he had rejected (her first version of 'Daphne Restored', then titled 'Transformation') for a poem of his own. 'I am utterly weary of all this,' she told Tony. 'In the end I'm going to write a sonnet the initial letters of each line spelling FUCKALLEDITORS. But I'd have to strike just the right texture of woolly nonsense.'[17] She then improvised such a sonnet on the spot, and concluded: 'The horrible ease with which one can write this crap makes it hardly worthwhile, but suppose CBC actually printed a tidied-up version! Sweet Jesus!' She went on to fantasise about writing a sequence of acrostic sonnets targeting editors who had rejected her work or messed her around: 'ClotChristesen', 'O!MadJimMcauley', 'O!StupidSlessor' – ending smugly with 'CleverGHarwood'.

Her mood was not improved when she received the December 1959 issue of *Meanjin* and discovered a review of that year's *Australian Poetry* anthology that savaged her poem 'A Postcard'. The review did not mention the poem by name, but quoted three lines from the first stanza, picking them apart to show that her carefully polished phrases were merely empty flourishes. The critic, Arthur Phillips, went on to praise, by comparison, the work of those 'established poets' who 'do not thus load every rift with new-chum gold'. Gwen was shaken by this 'frightful attack'. It was 'so fantastic that I must send it on – you will be amazed at his crudeness,' she told Tony.[18] 'Fuck all the critics and editors too, as they used to sing in the war (F all the corporals and WO1s, f all the sergeants and their f ing sons) – do you remember the tune?' She blamed Christesen for printing such a review in *Meanjin* – the publication in which the poem had originally appeared.

She suspected he was taking his revenge for her intemperate letters. 'I am sure CBC is out for blood,' she wrote darkly.

Bill found the whole thing grimly amusing. In his view, her protests were 'useless'. 'Bill thinks that they see me getting better at writing, and better known, and are determined to chop my hands off before I get a firm grip,'[19] she told Tony. She feared her husband was right. She had come to believe that there was no one with integrity in the Australian literary world. Tony's plays, which Gwen considered excellent, were being met with the same disdain meted out to her poems: equivocal responses from producers or no response at all, promises made and not kept, and, worst of all, manifestly inferior work being elevated, praised and performed. She responded to Tony's news of rejections and cold-shoulderings with furious empathy: 'What is there to do in this country but to ignore utterly the continual insults from people who have power?'[20]

Tales of editorial corruption were pouring in from all sides.[21] Rumour had it that Christesen had published 'lousy poems' by one particular poet because he was sleeping with her (when passing on this rumour, Gwen did have the grace to wonder 'if similar explanations of my current pre-eminence in *Meanjin* were being given').[22] Fellow Tasmanian Christopher Koch told her that he only appeared in *Southerly* because of his personal connection with the poetry editor, Kenneth Slessor. His success rate was much better than hers, he said, simply because 'when I was in Sydney I handed [my poems] personally to Slessor over a beer; that's the *only* way'.[23] She was appalled to hear that *Quadrant*'s James McAuley had published a 'frightful' poem by Clive Sansom because 'Sansom had gone to the trouble of getting something published for him, McAuley, and he felt he had to do something in return'. Though McAuley had rejected almost every one of her poems, including those Christesen had taken, she had felt that his decisions at least reflected his honest assessment of her work.[24] Now she knew that he could be bought and sold like all the others. It was all the more disappointing because of her admiration for McAuley's own work. As she confessed to Eddie around this time, 'I would rather be praised by McAuley than by anyone in Australia – I think he's on his own as a poet.'[25] He had been her last faint hope. Evidence of his corruption left 'NOBODY on the scene, not one decent editor'.[26]

It seemed to her that she was irrevocably outside the citadel of Australian poetry. As a housewife who lived far from the glittering east-coast hubs of the literary world, she was a nonentity. She had no favours to bestow, and would never have the capacity to 'buy Slessor a beer or do McAuley a good turn or offer Christesen anything but poetry which he allows editorial assistants to spit on'.[27] Nor was she, anymore, 'young & promising', able to attract the interest of more established poets on those grounds.[28] She was beginning to understand that Australia's literary world was a club, and membership was not, as she had naively assumed, based solely on merit.

She particularly resented Melbourne academic Vincent Buckley because he seemed to have had a meteoric rise. Five years younger than her, he had published his first book of poetry in 1954, when she was still struggling to get individual poems into print. While she had been busy bearing and raising her children, he had been forging connections that would prove invaluable to his careers in both poetry and academia. He had been a student of A.D. Hope's, who had become his patron and mentor and introduced him to Jim McAuley. The three of them formed a private poetry community, reading and commenting on one another's work.

It was all very blokey. In a letter from the early 1950s, Hope waxed lyrical about the trio's poetic virility, praising their ability to get the Muses 'up the spout'. The goddesses of the arts might well complain that 'The Aust. Lit. Prickle / Don't even tickle!', but all was not lost while Hope and his well-endowed friends were around. 'If it weren't for yourself', the Muses told Hope,

> We'd be quite on the shelf,
> And James P. McAuley
> – There's a lad that f – s brawly! –
> But last, and most luckily,
> We found Vincent Buckeley.
> Now there was a feast!
> What a Bard! What a Beast![29]

The three poet-professors did not scruple to review, publish and lecture on one another – 'poetical washerwomen starching one another's smalls', as Gwen contemptuously put it.[30] Indeed, when Buckley published a book of essays on Australian poetry in 1957 – the same year he attacked Gwen's first outing in *Australian Poetry* – he lauded Hope and McAuley (along with Slessor and Judith Wright) as the most significant poets in Australia, thus helping to situate his friends in the Australian literary canon.[31]

It was Gwen's dearest ambition to publish a book of poetry. All the up-and-coming young men already had their first slim volumes under their arms, yet here she was, approaching forty, with still no prospect of a book. For that she needed a champion. But even if she somehow 'licked the correct boots & got a book published', she told Tony gloomily, it would certainly be butchered by reviewers. It seemed to her that she was 'now in the position Hope was in ten years ago: a few people like what I write, some loathe it, most ignore it'. But how was she to get to Hope's current status with no university career to give her credibility and no network of contacts in the literary world? In terms of her output, she could do no more. 'I have not the physical energy to write more than I write and still write well,' she confessed. She longed for 'silence, solitude, complete freedom for even a short time' – but that was impossible. Nevertheless, she assured Tony, 'You may be sure that I shall not give up.'[32]

◆ ◆ ◆

Shortly after her unsuccessful outing as W.W. Hagendoor, Gwen embarked on another experiment. She asked Tony to send some of her poems to *Meanjin* under a made-up name ('any name you please') from his own address ('Bill says he thinks a Hobart postmark would be too obvious, since probably only 2 or 3 people ever send poems from Hobart anyway').[33] Among the poems was one she called 'the fuck-all sonnet' – the acrostic poem 'Abelard to Eloise', which spells out 'Fuck all editors'. She did not specify a gender for the new pseudonym, but did say that if Tony chose a male name, he would need to change the pronouns in one of the poems, 'Last Night', to make the speaker male. Tony chose the name Walter Lehmann. Gwen was pleased. 'A modestly endearing name,' she opined. 'I'm sure he'll become well known. Let's try *The Bulletin* next, if CBC rejects him.'[34]

Tony set up a Victorian post office box for Walter, and Gwen, excited, determined to 'write some more Lehmann'. There is no doubt that the poems Tony first sent out under Lehmann's name, including 'Triste, Triste' and 'Alter Ego', were written in Gwen's own persona. They were among the deeply felt, carefully constructed, philosophical poems she wrote about the aftermath of the Tom Pick affair. But the sudden appearance of Walter Lehmann, like a genie from a bottle, inflamed her imagination. Almost at once, she began to work on compositions she might never have attempted from outside the shelter of his masculinity. These included poems conceived from a male point of view, such as 'A Poem for My Wife' and 'A Kitchen Poem: The Farmer to His Wife', as well as poems that were not specifically gendered but may have seemed improper or unsuitable for a woman to write, such as 'In the Park' and 'Carpe Diem'. (When 'In the Park' appeared under her Lehmann pseudonym early in 1961, Gwen was delighted to be privy to a conversation in which one person opined to another that 'a woman couldn't have written' that poem: it 'takes a man to look at it like that'.)[35] It was liberating to shed her own name and write whatever she liked. She no longer had to worry about troubled past relationships with editors: she had a clean slate. And she need not be concerned that she might be judged harshly for writing about things that were not considered 'womanly'.

Alas, Lehmann had no more success with *Meanjin* than had Hagendoor. Having heard nothing from Christesen for several months, Gwen grew impatient.[36] Without telling Tony, she sent 'Alter Ego' to *Quadrant* under her own name, and five Walter Lehmann poems to *The Bulletin*, including some of those Walter had already sent to *Meanjin*. To her delight, McAuley accepted 'Alter Ego', and Douglas Stewart at *The Bulletin* accepted all five of the Lehmanns. 'They took the lot!' she crowed to Tony in June.[37] It was the first time *The Bulletin* had published her since 1949. She at once determined to 'send my new stuff to *The Bulletin* as Lehmann until [Douglas] Stewart finds out, then I shall change my name again'.

The appearance of 'Alter Ego' under her own name in *Quadrant* might have put a spanner in the works, as Christesen had seen the poem under the Walter Lehmann pseudonym. She apologised to Tony for the 'mix-up', but though Tony was annoyed – he told her that he and Frank Kellaway thought it was a 'silly game' – she was not repentant. Silly it might be, but it was so much fun. She was already planning to send Tony two more Lehmanns to forward for her: 'We can still Lehmannize *Aust Letters* and McAuley himself, possibly *Southerly*.'[38]

In June, she was delighted to see two poems under her own name in *Meanjin*: 'The Glass Jar' and 'My Tongue Is My Own' (the latter another account of the aftermath of her affair with Pick). When she leafed through the issue, however, she discovered a free verse poem called 'Goods Train' by Griffith Watkins that she thought so poor she copied it out for Tony in its entirety.[39] 'This is what CBC makes room for by rejecting Tom the Rhymer,' she sniffed. 'O Jesus! I am going to Ern Malley CBC sooner or later.' She loved the idea of orchestrating a Malley-style 'sting' for Christesen, something that would reveal, once and for all, the poverty of his literary judgements. Her favourite scheme was still an acrostic poem in which the first letter of each line would spell out a message entirely at odds with the poem's ostensible subject – preferably something insulting. A few weeks later, she sent Tony a manifesto in the form of a sonnet containing the acrostic message: 'Wreck that train.'[40] The sight of 'the rubbish spread / Carelessly through *Meanjin*', the poem declares, arouses all the 'spite', 'Knavishness, nastiness, readiness to fight / That mar my lovely nature'. She vows to go 'A-whoring':

> There'll be no peace for Editors who take
> Things like Goods Train. I'll prostitute my art
> . . .
> I'll tout myself all round, a lyric tart.
> No-one will know who is or isn't
> G.

All bets were off. If editors wouldn't take her seriously, then she would return the favour.

◆ ◆ ◆

Gwen invented her next pseudonym herself: Francis Geyer, a name intended to be 'mittel-Europa'. Later, she would specify that he was a Hungarian musician. This hoax was aimed specifically at Jim McAuley: 'I am out to get at *Quadrant*,' she told Tony.[41] It baffled and infuriated her that she could not seem to win McAuley over with even her very best poems. His rejection slips always stung. Back in 1958, he had told her that her poetry was 'over-worked & forced verbally',[42] and of her latest poems, he had written: 'These show promise but are not satisfactory.'[43] In late July, she sent him a handful of poems by Francis Geyer and held her breath when he asked if he could hang onto one 'for further consideration', a poem entitled 'Sunday'.[44] While she was waiting to hear his final judgement, she dreamed she was 'a man and had become a Roman Catholic' – like McAuley, who had converted to Catholicism as an adult.[45] But, alas, he rejected 'Sunday' a fortnight later, in terms she would describe as 'obscene'. 'O the bugger! O the bastard! (Excuse me, Reverend.)'[46]

As was her way, she sent the poem straight out again – to *Meanjin*, where again it was 'promptly rejected'. Hurt and frustrated, she did an Ern

Malley, concocting some 'oddments' under Geyer's name and sending them to *Meanjin*. To her mingled horror and delight, 'CBC went for the tongue-in-cheek "ex-patriate Hungarian" like a baby for a jellybean', accepting both 'Landfall' and 'Mid-Ocean'.[47] These 'cryptic utterances', she told Tony, were 'a mixture of oddments from my notebooks grafted on Wallace Stevens' rhythms in "The Man with the Blue Guitar". It *looks* like poetry at first glance. But what does it mean???' To Ann, she described the poems as 'very pretty but quite meaningless' and Christesen as a 'poor clot'.[48] She was almost abashed by the ease with which she had been able to fool him. It was oddly disheartening to be proved right. 'Do you know how I feel, having Geyer accepted and "Tom the Rhymer" rejected?' she asked Tony. 'I'm sure you do. I can't express my bitterness over *Meanjin*'s treatment of me.' She swore she would 'NEVER send them another poem in my name' – a promise she did not keep.

Geyer's success with *Meanjin* spurred her to try the same trick with McAuley. She threw together a pseudo-religious poem entitled 'All Souls' and submitted it to him as a Geyer poem. He took it. 'No wonder I'm becoming a raving paranoiac,' she told Tony, reporting her success and enclosing 'the innocuous "All Souls"'. 'WHY WHY WHY does McA reject the intricate fusion of "Sunday" and take this undistinguished piece?'[49] Still, she could not resist gloating when she told Eddie the news. 'All Souls' was a mere 'mishmash religious poem purporting to be by a new Australian', and McAuley had fallen for its cheap blandishments, even writing her 'a little note saying I was "an interesting poet"; really his brilliance is about 15 watts'.[50]

Unlike McAuley himself after he had pulled off the Ern Malley hoax, Gwen did not gloat publicly about her success. There was no attempt at public shaming. She had 'no real hope of dislodging the editors,' she told Tony. And besides, she reasoned, 'I think the Ern Malley affair shows how hopeless such attempts are, as there are no objective criteria for artistic excellence, and our generation will not judge its own masterpieces.'[51] It was her firm belief that work of true excellence would survive, while the dross, no matter how lauded, would fade into obscurity. Her Geyer hoaxes were purely for her own satisfaction – to prove her point to herself and those of her intimates (Bill, Tony, Ann, Alison, Vivian) who were in on the joke.

Geyer's first public appearance was in neither *Meanjin* nor *Quadrant* but *The Bulletin*, where he debuted with a poem on the Day of the Dead, 'All Souls', Janitzio'. This poem Gwen described to Tony as 'competent but uninspiring', thrown together from 'a travel page in an old *Manchester Guardian*'.[52]

To her delight, Douglas Stewart seemed as keen on Geyer as he was on Walter Lehmann. When she sent him a second batch of Geyer poems, he took three ('which is about as many as we can cope with at the moment') and expressed a personal interest in the poet: 'I should rather like to know who you are. Perhaps you could drop me a note or call in some time – any day about 12.30.'[53] Gwen had been sending her Geyer poems via Ann Jennings, who was then living in Sydney, so Stewart assumed Geyer lived in the vicinity. She responded as Francis, using Tony's Melbourne address, to explain that he could not pop in because he was currently on holiday in Victoria. Geyer was happy to give Stewart a potted biography, however. 'There is little to say about myself,' he wrote modestly. 'I am a musician, particularly interested in Bartók, and have spoken English fluently from about the age of seven.'

By now, Geyer had taken hold of Gwen's imagination. He was no longer writing only nonsense poems; over the next two years, he would seize her pen and write about Hungarian music and art, as well as the experience of being a refugee.[54] He would even write about Gwen's doomed love affair from his own point of view – that of the man who had left his lover behind and longs, above all, for a word from her. Geyer's poem 'The Supplicant' was 'written back to front', Gwen once explained, 'i.e. addressed to me'.[55] In this poem, the speaker yearns for his lost love, who lives 'a hemisphere away' on 'that freezing island' and walks to school every afternoon to pick up her children 'along the road that led, / Once, past my house'. 'Ebb-Tide' is written from the same perspective: it features Gwen, unnamed, as the lost love of the poem's male speaker, and describes an actual photograph of Gwen which Alison had taken at a Hoddinott–Harwood picnic. When this poem appeared in *The Bulletin* in May 1961, Gwen sent Alison a copy with a scrawled note beside the fourth stanza: 'Seen any coloured photographs recently?'[56] Geyer even published a sonnet entitled 'The Farewell' in which a man says a final goodbye to his lover in a public place and thus is unable to make love to her, to his eternal regret. 'What's virtue without grace?' he muses. 'A useless trinket.'[57]

Geyer also wrote movingly about the deaths of his mother and father in separate poems – at a time when both of Gwen's parents were happily alive. But Geyer's most lasting contribution to her oeuvre was the 'Bitter and Disillusioned Musician', Professor Dietrich Kröte (the German word for 'toad', pronounced to rhyme with Goethe). Professor Kröte grew up in central Europe, where he seemed set for a glittering career as a pianist on the world stage. Somehow, he ended up in suburban Australia instead, performing in 'cultured drawing rooms' and teaching music to legions of untalented, uninterested children. He cultivated a Beethoven-esque manner, his 'disarrayed / Person' taken by music lovers as 'a sign of genius', and sang for his supper.[58] He drank, scowled, stamped and sighed, tormented his benefactors by playing on when they wanted him to stop, or playing fine music when they wanted pap, and in his moments of despair sighed: '*Ach! Himmel!* Was I born for this?'

Through Kröte, Gwen was able to recreate the musical soirees of her youth and transpose onto them her own experiences in the 'cultured drawing rooms' of Hobart in the 1950s and 1960s (her pithy assessment of the Arts Club in Hobart was: 'has nothing to do with art, ought to be clubbed').[59] With his furious sense that he was living only half a life, forced to cast the magnificent pearls of his musical gift before swine, Professor Kröte was more truly her doppelganger than Professor Eisenbart. Gwen was finished with Eisenbart by 1959, but Kröte outlasted Geyer by many years, as Gwen took him over and made him her creature. Through him, she told versions of her own story: as a young student in love with her grizzled and grandiose music teacher, as a music teacher in her own right and as a pianist performing at social functions. She mourned her lost musical career and explored her sense of being an artist transformed into the unwieldy shape of a suburban housewife.

Tony had understood and encouraged her desire to get her own back on editors, but he was perplexed when she began to use pseudonyms for her own serious work. 'Perhaps I don't know myself what drives me to adopt this disguise,' she admitted, in response to his questioning. 'Silence, exile, cunning, as the master said . . . What other weapons are there in this country where Doris Fitton and CBC treat us as they do?'[60] (Doris Fitton was the head of Sydney's Independent Theatre, and had declined to produce one of Tony's plays.) 'The master' she cites here is James Joyce, whose character Stephen Dedalus, in *A Portrait of the Artist as a Young Man*, declares:

> I will not serve that in which I no longer believe, whether it calls itself
> my home, my fatherland, or my church: and I will try to express myself
> in some mode of life or art as freely as I can and as wholly as I can,
> using for my defence the only arms I allow myself to use – silence,
> exile, and cunning.

They were the weapons of the oppressed: of the misfit, the rebel, the outcast.

A week later, Gwen returned to the subject in a letter to Tony: 'Why not Harwood? I don't know, I just know that I want to *hide* for a time.'[61] This feeling would only intensify. 'I find I cannot at present bear to write under my own name,' she told him in February 1961.[62] 'I have done some mordant sonnets and am working at odd poems, but I cannot bring myself to send them out as G.H.' She felt too vulnerable to submit herself to the literary world in her own person. The risk of being 'beaten up' was too high, and the freedom of anonymity too seductive.

13

The Poet-Professors

And the monkey, does he wear the socks you made him?
Does he, like me, from sheer exhaustion stop
to pull them up? And does the weasel follow
his hopeless path or, like my heart, go POP.

Francis Geyer, 'Bestial Morning'
(From Gwen Harwood's 'Variations' on
the theme of 'Pop Goes the Weasel')

ONCE GWEN STARTED SENDING OUT WORK AS WALTER Lehmann and Francis Geyer, her publication rate exploded. From 1957 to 1959, she published four new poems a year. In 1960, she published fifteen: ten under her own name, two as Lehmann and three as Geyer. The following year, she published some twenty-eight new poems, as well as achieving the extraordinary feat of appearing three times in the 1961 *Australian Poetry* anthology under three different names.[1] It was not so much that she was writing more, though her pseudonyms did have the unexpected effect of unleashing her creativity, but that she was publishing almost everything she wrote. The use of pseudonyms sped up her publication rate, since distributing her work among three different names meant she was able to get more poems into a single journal than an editor might have been willing to publish by any one author. She was also becoming less fussy about where she published, submitting work to a new magazine aimed at women entitled *Salient*, as well as to Max Harris's *Australian Letters* and a Melbourne University publication edited by Vincent Buckley, *Prospect*. She was embarrassed to have her brilliant 'Group from Tartarus' appear in *Salient* – 'like Melba appearing at the Mechanics' Institute' – but felt she had no choice: 'nobody else would print it. Utterly depressing!'[2]

At the end of 1960, Tony decided to return to London to work for the BBC and offered to take some of her poems and submit them on her behalf to the English quarterlies. Gwen had already attempted to publish in the United Kingdom, sending poems to John Lehmann at *The London Magazine* in 1958 and 1959, but had had no luck.[3] As postal services from Australia were slow and expensive, she was delighted by the prospect of having an 'agent' on the ground. She told Tony she would leave the choice of journals to him, saying only that Walter Lehmann 'has his mercenary eye on *Country Life*', a magazine reputed to pay well. But English editors showed even less interest in her poems than Australian ones, and Gwen's fantasy of being able to bypass the Australian literary scene faded.

Now that her children were older, she had a little more time for writing. It was utter luxury, she told Tony, to see the children off to school in the morning and sit down at the kitchen table with a cup of coffee to write to him.[4] She was playing the piano again – she and Bill had finally found the money for a second-hand instrument[5] – and it was beginning to seem possible to her that women could have 'a kind of second flowering in their forties: when the children are no longer eating them alive'. Some of her friends were discovering new joys and talents as they emerged from the child-rearing years; one was studying art and 'doing fine paintings with real style & vigour', another learning to work with silver, a third breeding 'fabulous birds'. Perhaps there really was life after children. She wrote this reflection on the eve of her fortieth birthday, which felt like 'crossing the equator – there's nothing to show, but one is in another hemisphere; and of course one can't cross back again'.[6]

But life with four children between eight and fourteen was still hectic. Gwen prepared a cooked breakfast for the family every day, a hot lunch for Bill and the older children, who came home for the noon meal, and dinner each evening. She also made cakes and biscuits and put on lavish afternoon teas for visitors, including the children's friends, who 'treat our large yard and pond like a clubhouse'. They had only a semiautomatic washing machine, in which Gwen did all the family's washing, and she mended their clothes herself. If the children were sick, she tended them and took them to the doctor on the bus. In August 1961, she told Tony that she had been mistaken in thinking that her workload was easing: 'Day after day passes when I have no time to myself at all; I used to think it would be easier when the children went to school, but they eat more, wear out more clothes, stay up later and take more of my energy. (The change of course is in *me*; it's called middle age, and I don't like it.)'[7]

She took an active role in the mothers' group at her children's school, as well as being responsible for the usual mother-craft activities of making costumes for her children to wear in school plays or ballet recitals, churning out piles of patty cakes for school fetes, cheering her children on at carnivals and taking the sports-minded among them to the football oval on weekends. She didn't begrudge the time she spent with her children. She played with them, took them on outings, read with them, taught them to play the piano, took them to the library and, occasionally, the cinema, and showed an interest in their comics, their music and their passions. In her letters to Tony, she refers to playing shuttlecock and hide-and-seek with the children, sailing model boats in the pond with them, taking them down to the creek at the end of Augusta Road to catch tadpoles and going fishing with them. She and Bill played Scrabble and chess with the children, too, and took them on long hikes and beach picnics. Gwen loved listening to the 'hit parade', and was delighted by Elvis Presley and bebop and the new rock'n'roll. Snatches of lyrics from popular songs of the 1950s and '60s would make their way into her letters and poems for many years to come.

Though she sometimes fumed at just how much of her vital self her children demanded, she did not feel she could give less. As she told Tony, 'their claims are TOTAL; if they are sick, or hurt, or in trouble, one is helpless with concern'.[8] It 'cut her to the heart' to realise 'how little one can spare one's children'.[9] Her sense of connection to them was one of the reasons she could not contemplate leaving her marriage. It was a feeling Bill shared. Around the time that Ann Jennings left her husband, another of Gwen's old friends, Frank Kellaway, left his wife and children for another woman. Gwen reported to Tony that 'Bill remarked, apropos of Frank & Ann, "No matter whom I loved, I could not imagine for a moment putting myself in a position where I could not get [my son] out of any trouble he might be in."' 'In a way I envy those who can "put down the weight of years" so lightly,' she added.[10] For her it was simply not possible.

This was impressed on her again when her ten-year-old, Chris, was hit by a car. He was on his way back to school after lunch at home, and was crossing the road at a pedestrian crossing when a car knocked him down. To Gwen and Bill's disgust, the driver had accelerated past a bus that had stopped to allow the child to cross. By coincidence, Bill and fourteen-year-old John were on the bus – they were heading home for lunch, John having a later lunch time than the younger children. Bill went to the hospital with Chris, while John ran home to let Gwen know what had happened. Terror in her heart, Gwen took a taxi to the hospital, where she found her son conscious and uninjured. 'Until I saw him, and saw that he was whole, I felt pain that made my ordinary troubles seem trivial,' she told Tony.[11] A little later, she would reflect that Chris's accident 'showed clearly how impossible it is to consider oneself – I thought as I went in to his room in the casualty ward, What if I had not been here?'[12] What if, in other words, she had left Tasmania with Tom Pick, ending both their marriages? How could she have lived with herself? It was confirmation of her agonising decision to stay.

She did sometimes think that she would like to return to work, as her grandmother had in mid-life. Maud, in her late seventies, was still earning her own living as a housekeeper at the University of Queensland's Union College, and she often spent her annual holiday in Tasmania with her granddaughter. She got along well with Bill (unlike Agnes, who clashed with her son-in-law), engaging him in 'terrific arguments on absurd subjects' – which Granny 'obviously' won.[13] She enjoyed the children too. They 'swarm over her and ask her what Halley's Comet really looked like, how long she is likely to live, whether Granny Foster (my mother) was truly always a good little girl, [and] whether her hundred boys [at Union College] always remember to clean their teeth,' Gwen told Vivian, when Maud was visiting in early 1959. As Maud grew older, Bill and Gwen invited her to come and live with them, but the old lady declined: 'she was too independent to stay and hated Tasmania.'[14]

Gwen toyed with the idea of finding work as a typist, or even as a babysitter. She longed to have some money of her own – money she didn't 'have to account for.'[15] But she made no serious attempts to enter the paid workforce. As she told Tony, it simply wasn't economically viable for her to work: 'I could never afford to pay anyone to do what I do at home.' Besides, it would cause friction with Bill, and that was not worth the few pounds she could earn: 'Our attitudes (Bill's & mine) would not change except into worse resentment if I had some [money] of my own.'[16]

She followed Ann's teaching career with interest. Though she knew her friend was struggling financially, she envied her these first steps towards independence. Fittingly, it was Ann's lover, Tas Bull, who first spoke to Gwen about the importance of economic freedom for women. He was the only man she had ever met, Gwen told Ann, 'who understood what economic equality means for women.'[17]

In letters to Ann, Gwen spoke openly about women's oppression in a way she never did to Tony, or even to Alison. She often waxed sardonic to Ann about her housewifely experiences. Reminiscing with her about their years of home servitude, she remarked: 'Anyway, what more are we supposed to want? A nice stove, a nice bed, there we are, happy as Eve in paradise.'[18] When Bill was away for a couple of weeks in mid-1960, attending conferences and giving seminars, she told Ann that he was missing her very much: 'And wouldn't I miss a creature who put 3 lovely meals in front of me . . . and cups of coffee and clean clothes and bathed and cared for my children and kept my house in order while I did the work I love doing!'[19]

Gwen, meanwhile, rejoiced 'in a kind of holiday' in Bill's absence.[20] 'When he works at home I have to keep things quiet,' she explained to Tony, 'and [now] I am able to give the piano a good bashing, sing, bang, listen to the Hit Parade . . . and eat in bed if I feel like it (I can quite understand one's bedfellow disliking such a habit, especially if a favourite snack is bread with Danish blue cheese and celery.)' She was relishing her period of 'disorderly freedom'. To Ann, she was even more exuberant. 'It is heavenly to have the place to myself during the day, to open the piano & beat hell out of it, to leave the work and eat oranges & throw the peel under the table, to rattle and scuffle and sing and cry O Jesus! Jesus! Jesus! when I lose my pencil, to bawl the kids out or bribe them with cake. I feel as if I had slid into a different gear.'[21] This environment seemed much more conducive to writing than her everyday ordered existence: 'Given time I could easily write 2 epics in ottava rima.'

She told Ann that it was 'Nature' that had given her 'the dirty end of the stick', but a year later she would muse about the possibility of a world in which women were not required to sacrifice their own lives for their children. The women's magazines, she told Ann, were 'currently [fixated] on the theme of Holy Motherhood v. Secular Career [and] the editorial line seems to be Go right ahead Sister & have a career, but we're telling you, you won't be happy.'[22] She was somewhat chagrined that as a young woman she had bought into the ideology at work in this 'line' and wondered 'what I'd have had to show if I'd devoted myself to the Muse . . . I suspect, a couple of sensitivissima novels & a few more poems.' She did not regret the choice she had made: marriage and children over a life as an artist. But she did regret that she had been forced to make it. 'I dream of a world in which there is no insoluble choice for women,' she told Ann. 'Not in our lifetime, I fear, but it will come if enough of us refuse (as you are now heroically refusing) the male interpretation.'[23]

What 'balance' Gwen had been able to achieve – being both a parent and an artist – was possible, she believed, only because she had had a hysterectomy. The contraceptive pill was not yet in use, and surgery was the only way a woman could confidently 'dissociate sex from childbirth'. If she had gone on having children until menopause, she feared she would no longer have had the 'strength to wrestle with the world'.

The fantasy of a life devoted to writing did sometimes beguile her. She would have liked to have written a novel, and several times in the late 1950s she considered the possibility, especially when various competitions advertised lavish prize money. 'But I know what I would write, and it would distress my parents & probably involve me in several libel suits, not to mention poisoned chocolates through the post,' she joked to Vivian.[24] More to the point, she knew she simply didn't have the time for a sustained work like a novel. It was hard enough to write poetry, which she could at least work on in her head at odd moments. To insist on having larger stretches of time to write would be 'monstrously selfish' – and she was not prepared to weather that.[25]

Yet she worried about neglecting her gifts. Perhaps it was the artist's duty to be selfish? No true genius, male or female, would let their talents go begging, she was sure. Did her decision to have children prove that she was no genius? Reading about the life of Rilke, whose work she deeply admired, she was much impressed by his single-minded pursuit of his art. 'Rilke certainly fed his genius at the expense of everything else; he would have scorned utterly my attempts to combine domesticity with poetry,' she reflected. 'I think that real genius brings with it the necessary hardness; I haven't got the final streak of hardness, and lack the corresponding stratum of talent.' But in any case, if she was to devote herself to her art, someone would have to pay the bills. 'I'd like to play Rilke for a few years, and write whether anyone cared about what I wrote or not,' she told Tony. 'But where shall I find a Princess (I suppose it would have to be a prince) Hohenlohe von Turm & Taxis.'[26] Gwen was, as she knew only too well, in the wrong century and of the wrong sex to attract a literary patron.

Financially, Gwen and Bill's fortunes were about to improve. Throughout the 1950s, they had enough money to meet the family's daily needs, but none for extras such as holidays or trips to the mainland. An unexpected doctor's bill could derail plans for some long-deferred purchase, and at times Gwen borrowed money from her mother to make ends meet. She worried about the cost of postage for submitting her poems, of sending letters by airmail and even of paper to write her poems on. She scavenged writing paper wherever she went, purloining random sheets from government departments and doctors' offices, which she delighted in sending to her many correspondents. She begged travelling friends for samples of notepaper from cruise ships and hotel rooms, and tore empty pages from her children's exercise books and from Bill's students' exam booklets.

Poems and letters were written on the backs of Bill's notes for his linguistics research and other people's correspondence. One year, in response to her complaints about her chronic paper shortage, Tony sent her a ream of paper for her birthday.[27] But in October 1960, Bill was promoted to Reader in English, which meant a pay rise, in addition to the welcome recognition of his work. The extra money would ease some of the pressures of daily life.

◆ ◆ ◆

Around the time Bill was promoted, the youthful professor of English, Murray Todd, decided to appoint a Reader in Poetry, and gave the job to Gwen's old adversary, Jim McAuley.

Gwen had met Jim in person earlier that year when he had come to Tasmania to lecture on Australian poetry. To her amazement, he was a riveting speaker. 'McAuley is terrific: burning, burning – he seems to be consumed with his own inner fire,' she reported to Tony.[28] When she spoke to McAuley afterwards at a gathering at Vivian's flat, she was doubly impressed because he seemed to know who she was – something she had not dared to assume. He said 'with real sincerity that he'd been looking forward to seeing Vivian & me, and talked shop to us. (I forgive him the Clive Sansom episode as you can see.)'

The next evening, she went to a dinner in McAuley's honour at the Imperial Hotel, where she was pleased to be seated in glory at the poet's right hand. But multiple courses of his endless pontificating changed her mind about him. 'My first impression of McAuley's brilliance has been confirmed, strengthened indeed. But his arrogance is so great that I am repelled by him personally.'[29] To Ann, she reported that he was 'burnt out, haggard, lined, consumed from within, arrogant beyond belief with the arrogance of intellectual RC's. As I listened to his political talk I could hardly reconcile his what-we-should-do-to-the-commos with [his poem beginning] "Now Ixion's wheel is stilled / By that pure rejoicing tone"[30]

The more she heard of his conservative views – 'real Vatican politics', 'arrogant Mannix-type pronouncements' – the more she disliked him. One example was his comments on New Guinea, where he had spent time during and immediately after the war. '"And I said to the Governor," McAuley said, "If they did give the natives their freedom, what should we have – a bloody coconut republic!" This remark was repeated with enjoyment later as the crown of wit.'[31]

Gwen was equally unimpressed by his 'rubbishy judgements of the contemporary [poetry] scene'.[32] He condemned everyone, even 'people like the American Richard Wilbur', and referred to Dame Mary Gilmore as 'the old bitch'.[33] Gwen was contemptuous of the way the members of the English department crowded round him adoringly, hanging on his words and 'trimming their opinions to his'. Venturing to disagree with his view of Harold Stewart's poetry, she earned herself 'an envenomed glance'. She was not invited to the next post-lecture soiree.

If her future as a poet really did depend, as she feared, on astute networking, this did not bode well. Gwen told Alison and Bill Hoddinott that she felt Jim's 'second-rate polemics & politics' should not have been rewarded with a readership.[34] One of Bill's colleagues 'suggested that McA. is really a Commo infiltrating & insinuating under the guise of Catholicism', but this delightful possibility seemed pretty improbable to Gwen: instead, 'it seems all too horribly like what it appears to be'. She urged Bill to find a job elsewhere; for most of Bill's time at the University of Tasmania, she had been hopefully mentioning to him positions at various other Australian universities. Bill was adamant, however, that they could not afford to move for less than a professor's salary, and a professorial position was not forthcoming. For the time being, it seemed, they were stuck with McAuley.

Gwen had also met A.D. Hope by this time. In August 1959, he too had come to Tasmania to lecture on Australian literature. She had been disappointed with Hope as a speaker (he 'doesn't present his material with any *force*,' she reported to Vivian),[35] and chastened to discover, when she spoke to him, that he didn't know her work. Hope was fifty-two when he met Gwen, thirteen years older than her, and she thought of him as something of a poetry elder. His standing as Australia's leading poetry critic was unquestioned, so she was bemused to realise that he knew few Australian poets and even fewer American ones. It was bad enough that he had not read her, even though her poems had appeared alongside his in two volumes of *Australian Poetry* and several issues of *Meanjin*; it was unforgivable that he had never heard of Anthony Hecht or Richard Wilbur, or any of the Americans who, in Gwen's view, 'run the English off the field'.[36] 'He seems to have read only Buckley and McAuley in recent years,' she told Tony incredulously.[37] But later, chatting with him at an English department soiree, she found herself warming to him. Grasping an opportunity to speak to him alone, she 'told him in ravishing tones how [she] loved his poetry',[38] and was charmed when he replied 'rather shyly that he was 50 when he published his first book of poems and felt very strange at submitting himself to the people he had criticized for so long'. She forgave him his ignorance, and promised to send him her volume of Hecht, to 'bring him up to date a little'. 'I'm sure he was worn out – he'd been getting the works every night from Hobart's leading intellectuals,' she told Tony. 'Bill thought he might snap under my assault. Still, I had hoped for so much, and had to be content with crumbs.'

The meeting did make an impression on Hope. Soon after he left Hobart, he wrote to tell her that he had looked up her poem 'A Postcard' and liked it very much. He then went on a quest for more of her work and wrote again to express his admiration. It was time she thought of 'publishing a volume', he told her.[39] 'So many formidable poems or rather so few over five years [suggests you have] others unpublished – or do you write as slowly as I do?' he asked. 'And particularly I suspect that Professor Eisenbart has a fuller biography – I hope so – than the two poems in which he appears publicly. I was particularly delighted with "Ganymede" – realised I had missed this number of *Meanjin* altogether, by being away last year.'

Gwen was thrilled by this letter. 'I said to myself, I'm not a bit excited, really, but I'll write & tell Tony – AND FOUND MYSELF TRYING TO INSERT A SHEET OF PAPER IN THE SEWING MACHINE.'[40] Hope had got some of the details wrong – Gwen's poems had appeared over three years, not five, and Professor Eisenbart featured in three of them, not two – but his praise of 'Ganymede', one of her own favourites, meant a lot. 'It is something to have this letter,' she wrote to Tony, 'after years of feeling that I might as well have dropped the poems in bottles off the Hobart Bridge.'[41] Soon after this, she told Tony that she was becoming more confident in her work: 'I didn't think I ever should, with such a long history of rejections and editorial insults; but I see that I shall improve if I can stand the delays of publishing.'[42]

When she heard that Hope was to be the editor of the 1960 edition of *Australian Poetry*, she made a point of submitting two previously published poems to him, only too aware that he was likely to have missed them. She braced herself for 'arrogance or indifference', and was pleasantly surprised when he accepted 'Prize-Giving', one of her Eisenbart poems.[43] Then, early in 1961, she heard from friends that Hope had praised her on TV. The Harwoods did not have a television – they couldn't afford it – but Gwen was told that the program he appeared on was a celebration of *Meanjin*'s twentieth anniversary. '*Meanjin* was to be praised for publishing the works of Gwen Harwood, regarded as a fine poet in Australia,' Hope had opined.

'So the old boy must have been reading a bit!' she reported to Tony, with satisfaction.[44]

A couple of months later, Hope wrote to tell her that he was planning to write an essay about her for *Meanjin* and asked for some biographical details.[45] This was yet further acknowledgement of her growing success as a poet, and she responded eagerly with 'a rapid panoramic survey of my uneventful life', the promise of more poems and effusive praise of his own work.[46] She also assured him – presumably with fingers crossed – that she was looking forward to McAuley's arrival at the University of Tasmania: 'I'm sure he'll liven everything up'.

This exchange led to a small flurry of playful letters in which she and Hope saluted one another in German – Gwen called him 'Glücklicher Dichter' (Fortunate Poet), while he called her 'Wahlverwandt gesellschafterin' (Chosen Companion) – and shared their mutual passion for bizarre names, satirical characters and each other's poetry. Hope confessed to a strong affinity with Professor Eisenbart, that 'powerful personality'. After he had read all the extant Eisenbart poems, he told her, her professor had 'got hold of me in a most uncanny way. He was in my dreams all last night playing a horrible Doppelgänger game with me.' He was delighted with Gwen's satirical bent and felt that Eisenbart was a true innovation in Australian poetry: no other poet had invented such a character. He also sent her a copy of a book by a friend of his, the Canadian writer George Johnston, entitled *The Cruising Auk,* telling her that 'the creator of Eisenbart should be acquainted with the creator of [satirical character] Mr Murfle'.[47] In June 1961, Gwen wrote exuberantly to Alison and Bill Hoddinott that 'A.D. Hope is coming down next month & is coming to dinner; my passion for him is absolute'.[48]

◆ ◆ ◆

By this time, Jim McAuley had settled in Hobart with his wife, Norma, and their five young children. Soon after he was appointed, the professor of English, Murray Todd, was diagnosed with leukemia, and to the dismay of all, he died in December 1960. This meant that the position of professor and head of department was vacant. Bill, who stepped into the role temporarily, was put off by all the 'tedious administrative work' and decided not to apply, but McAuley threw his hat into the ring.[49] The interview panel – which included McAuley's friend Hope – was convened in October 1961, and McAuley became the new professor.

Far from being outraged by the appointment, Gwen accepted it with equanimity. Soon after Jim's arrival in Hobart, she and Bill had had him and his family over to lunch, and Gwen found that Jim *en famille* was very different from Jim in professional mode: 'reasonably human & very much more subdued than he was on his own'.[50] At work, Jim and Bill got along 'very well',[51] and Jim soon got into the habit of having a drink with Bill at the end of the work day, as well as dropping around with his children for afternoon tea on weekends. On these occasions, Gwen found herself, as usual, caught between her two roles: hospitable housewife attending to her guests and fellow poet eager to be part of the conversation.

The first time Jim appeared on a Sunday afternoon, she alternated between whipping up a meal for the nine children and five adults present, and joining in the conversation at the tea table. 'Bill & Jim had a fierce though not heated argument about human problems and mathematical logic', and she herself took Jim to task for publishing in *Quadrant* a young Queensland poet whose work she felt was substandard. She wrung an admission from Jim that the work was 'n.b.g.' – no bloody good – but he defended himself by saying that he 'thought one little sonnet on the bottom of a page wouldn't cause any pain'. Gwen riposted, 'It caused pain to me.' 'It was all surprisingly pleasant', she reported to Alison and Bill Hoddinott.[52]

Gwen still found Jim's politics execrable, particularly his later support for the Vietnam War. And for all his religiosity, she felt he was 'a bit weak on Christian charity', as she told Ann in 1962. 'At English Dept. evenings (we can't always refuse, you know how it is in Hobart) he roars on like [American evangelist] Billy Graham against homosexuality, adultery & fornication.'[53] Gwen had political, as well as personal, objections to the church's attitude to adultery. 'Why I loathe the Christian view of adultery is that it makes marriage a purely sexual contract', she explained to Ann. 'Until (I think) 1937, adultery was the *only* ground for divorce in England: the idea that one should be tied to a mean, mad, drunken sadist (and there are plenty) for life as long as the bastard didn't commit adultery, or alternatively that one could lose children, home, everything for one evening's delight is so monstrous & so degrading to women that it's a wonder there wasn't mass murder.'[54]

Jim was incapable of appreciating such arguments, going 'on & on like a heaven-sent preacher; anyone would think he was 2nd in command to Jesus', Gwen complained. He was also a hypocrite. A big drinker, he was widely rumoured to have indulged in more than one adulterous affair.[55] But for Gwen, neither his politics nor his morals were any bar to their friendship. 'You don't want to judge things that enrich you, you just want to be grateful that there are things beyond yourself you can love without calculated choice,' she would one day write. She quickly came to feel that she and Jim were kindred spirits. 'There are a few people in your life who reach the heart's innermost recesses & all you can do is rejoice that you've met them,' she would say. For her, Jim McAuley was one such person.[56] She could not reconcile his contradictions, so instead chose to find him 'a fascinating mixture of opposing qualities'. More than fifteen years after they met, she would write that she doubted anybody knew 'the "real" Jim – he has more sides to his personality than anyone I know'.[57]

One of his less palatable qualities was his prejudice against women poets. Before he arrived in Hobart, she read his recent book of essays, *The End of Modernity*, and was bemused to find him complaining about the demands of domesticity on fathers. 'McAuley has some pages in his new book of essays on dishwashing & household chores,' she remarked to Tony, noting that he saw himself as oppressed by his children: they were 'dragging the fiery artist down'.[58]

She took special note of his book's claim that it was 'very rare indeed for women poets to rise beyond the upper reaches of mediocrity'.[59] The idea required some digesting. In 1961, she would endorse his view, writing to one of McAuley's friends that she agreed it was 'terribly hard' for women to achieve literary excellence.[60] But less than two years later, she would revise her opinion. In a letter to Tony, she reflected that McAuley had 'a "thing" about women poets', referring to his 'savage outburst over Mary Gilmore' and his publishing in *Quadrant* of an uncharacteristically mediocre poem by Judith Wright, potentially exposing her to criticism. She did not refer to his repeated rejection of her own work, but she must have wondered whether there was an element of gender bias in his dismissals. Certainly others on the literary scene noticed that for a long time, McAuley was not very interested in Gwen's poems. As Vincent Buckley would later write, 'It took him years to appreciate her poetry fully'.[61] But whether or not she felt she had personally suffered from it, Gwen did believe that Jim had 'a real deformation if he thinks poetry is by a woman'. In a 1964 letter to Tony, again quoting Jim's view that 'it was very rare for women writers "to rise above mediocrity"', she added tartly: 'Someone should tell him it's rare for men, too, and ask him why he's so sure he's in a position to adjudicate.'[62]

14

Bless All Editors

GREAT POEM HOAX: EXPERTS FOOLED
BY NAUGHTY SONNETS

Truth (Melbourne), August 1961

THOUGH GWEN AND JIM MCAULEY HAD BECOME FRIENDS, she still longed to show him up as an editor. Walter Lehmann and Francis Geyer had given her a new lease of poetic life. She could shuck off the shell of good, serious, respectable Mrs Harwood and dance around naked if she liked. She was no longer at the mercy of editors; instead, they were at her mercy, though they didn't know it. It was exhilarating.

In June 1961, when the opportunity arose for her to hoax Leonie Kramer, an academic at the University of New South Wales, she jumped at it. The opportunity came, ironically, through Vincent Buckley, the fledgling poet-professor she had heartily loathed for years. Like McAuley and Hope before him, Buckley was recruited to deliver some lectures in Hobart. Before he arrived, he wrote to Gwen to ask if he could meet her while he was there. His letter was complimentary, declaring that she was 'a fine poet of a sort Australia has needed for a long time'. He was disarmingly self-deprecatory, admitting that he tended to 'talk all the time' and warning her to prepare to be bored.[1] Gwen replied coolly. 'Yes of course I am looking forward to meeting you when you come to Hobart. We've been planning to have you for dinner.'[2] Did he not realise, she asked Tony, that she was the wife of Bill Harwood who, as acting head of the English department, had been the point of contact for his visit?

Buckley's first lecture was an afternoon session. 'Vin looked like a poetic spiv: black Italian-style hair, greenish eyes, cupid's bow mouth, aquiline nose; small, about Vivian's size; old black sweater, spongy shoes,' she reported to the Hoddinotts.[3] But his lecture, to her surprise, was 'excellent'.[4] She could not linger for afternoon tea, as she had to get dinner ready for the family so that she could attend the evening lecture, but his second performance she found equally impressive: 'He minced up established Australian reputations and put the literary scene in its proper perspective.' Afterwards she was invited, along with Jim McAuley and Vivian and Sybille Smith, to a supper party at the home of Ted and Margaret Stokes. As the small group of academics and poets gathered around the fire in the Stokes's sitting room, the conversation shifted from the ubiquitous Orr case to literary topics. All at once, Vin, who had been smoking 'incessantly' and scowling at the ceiling, 'woke up and began to sparkle and Jim began to bark the opposite and it all got pretty good'.[5] A young poet named Evan Jones, a friend of Vincent's and colleague of Hope's at the Australian National University, had just published his first book, *Inside the Whale*, and Leonie Kramer had savaged it in a recent review in *The Bulletin*.[6] Gwen, who was no fan of Jones, thought that Kramer's review was fair, and said so.[7] But Vincent was offended on behalf of his friend, and suggested to the group that, as Kramer was editing *Australian Poetry* that year, 'Someone should send her some fake poems'. Jim immediately ruled himself out: 'Well I've done my share of that; no more for me after Ern Malley.' Vincent turned to Gwen: 'How about you, Gwen?' He could not have known, then, that he had settled on precisely the right poet for the task. She leapt at the idea, and they agreed to submit fake poems under each other's names.[8]

It was after midnight when Gwen left the Stokes's house, but the next morning at breakfast, she whipped up a sonnet entitled 'Eloisa to Abelard' that parodied Vin's poetic style, and – so there would be no doubt that it was a fake – contained the acrostic 'Vincent Buckley'. Not coincidentally, it was a companion piece to the acrostic sonnet 'Abelard to Eloisa' that she and Tony had sent to *Meanjin* some two years earlier in the vain hope of snaring Clem Christesen. When the same group gathered after Vin's lecture that evening, Vincent turned to Gwen: 'Well, have you got that poem ready yet Gwen?'[9] To his bemusement, she opened her bag and pulled out the sonnet. As she handed it to him, she asked briskly: 'Well, where's mine?' 'Vincent said humbly "I misjudged you, didn't I? I didn't think you'd do it."' He read the poem through several times, but did not notice the acrostic.

The following day – which happened to be Gwen's birthday – was the day the Harwoods had fixed to have Vincent over for dinner. She spent the afternoon cooking – 'roast duck & jellied pears', with 'stacks of chokky bikkies' for dessert – and Bill brought Vincent home with him from the university by taxi.[10] After dinner, Vin was 'swarmed over [by the children] and covered in model aeroplanes, dolls, models of Stonehenge, beetles, fossils and comic books'.[11] Escaping from the scrum, he produced a poem, 'The Sentry', which he had written as a parody of Gwen's style: 'lists, bits of Latin, double-entendres'.[12] Gwen was delighted. She was keen to go ahead with the hoax:

she would send 'The Sentry' to Kramer as her own work and Buckley would send 'Eloisa to Abelard' as his. He still had not twigged that her poem was an acrostic, but, as she was 'by now exceedingly fond of him', she pointed it out.[13] He was taken aback, but quickly rallied. He had promised to send it to Kramer, he said stoutly, and so he would. Gwen took pity on him, however, and took the poem back. They spent the rest of the evening 'drinking endless pots of tea & tearing the literary field to rags' – exactly the kind of conversation Gwen thrived on. The next day, she sent 'The Sentry' to Kramer under her own name, apologising for its lateness (she had already submitted others for Kramer's consideration). Not wanting to waste her own hoax poem, she reworked it so that the acrostic read 'So long Bulletin' and sent it – together with 'Abelard to Eloisa', the sonnet that spelt out 'Fuck all editors' – to *The Bulletin* as Walter Lehmann poems.[14] She had heard a rumour that *The Bulletin*'s erstwhile poetry editor, Douglas Stewart, knew Lehmann's real identity, so she thought of this as Walter's last hurrah. 'If they print them they'll be classics & I'll buy you a shillingsworth,' she told the Hoddinotts.[15]

Buckley went back to Melbourne and life went on as usual for Gwen, apart from the addition of a lively exchange of letters and cards with Vin, her new darling. Bill was preparing for a four-month sabbatical in North America, and the prospect of being a 'widow' for such a length of time was casting 'a neurotic gloom' over her 'lovely nature' – or so, at least, she told the Hoddinotts.[16] Early in August, she told Tony that her spirits were 'so low that I hardly write anything to anyone at all'.

Then on Saturday, 5 August, she opened the latest issue of *The Bulletin* to discover Walter's two sonnets, 'Eloisa to Abelard' and 'Abelard to Eloisa', one above the other, on page thirty-three. They had been published, with no notice, beside an innocuous review of a couple of new Irish novels. Gwen was elated. Finally, someone had taken *the* sonnet!

She dashed off a Sappho card to the Hoddinotts telling them not to miss this issue, which 'contains Walter's farewell to his benefactors'.[17] Then she waited for the sky to fall. Nothing happened. 'So far nobody has noticed a thing,' Gwen wrote amazedly to Tony a few days later.[18] She could not believe she was going to get away with it. Surely someone would twig? But she had no time to obsess. Second term was about to begin, and she was caught up in the usual rush of getting the children ready to go back to school.

On Tuesday, she got a frantic phone call from Vivian, who was in on the hoax. A friend of his at *The Bulletin*, Desmond O'Grady, who was currently acting as literary editor, had sent him a telegram urgently requesting information on Walter Lehmann. Vivian did not know what to do. Should he divulge her secret? Gwen urged him to ignore O'Grady's telegram, but Vivian could not. He told Desmond that he couldn't disclose Walter Lehmann's identity, but suggested that Desmond get in touch with Walter at the address supplied with his poems. Walter's address was, of course, Gwen's, and Vivian soon had a second telegram from Desmond asking for Gwen's phone number.[19]

That day, Gwen had to take one of her sons to a doctor's appointment, so she missed *The Bulletin*'s first two calls. When she finally got home, she found herself on the phone with *The Bulletin*'s acting literary editor.[20] In a letter to the Hoddinotts, she wrote out the dialogue like a play, as she used to do in her WDC days. As in those days, her statements were replete with the rufonanine tactics of stonewalling, nonsensical replies and pretended ignorance.

HARWOOD: How do you do?

O'GRADY: Very well thank you. I want to speak to you about the two sonnets in last week's *Bulletin*.

HARWOOD: (real cool) Yes?

O'GRADY: (gibbering) Why did you write them? Why? Why?

HARWOOD: Because I'm a poet. I have had poetry published in *Meanjin, Quadrant, Southerly, Aust* . . .

O'GRADY: But I mean the acrostics – you know – So Long Bulletin . . . and . . . er . . . the rest.

HARWOOD: What do you mean, what acrostics?

O'GRADY: I mean when you read downwards.

HARWOOD: Oh, I'll have to go and get the text.

I wandered off (15/- for three minutes) and stayed away a while from the phone then returned with the text.

HARWOOD: Hello? I see what you mean. Fancy that now. Fancy that.

O'GRADY: Why did you write them?

HARWOOD: They're beautiful sonnets, if you read them horizontally.

O'GRADY: Well people do usually read poetry horizontally, but these read vertically as well.

HARWOOD: Purely fortuitous.

O'GRADY: (At bursting point) I'll have to believe you.[21]

O'Grady would later say that he had no recollection of making this phone call. What he did remember was that *The Bulletin* was in chaos in the wake of its takeover in 1960 by Frank Packer's Consolidated Press. The new editor, Donald Horne, had made significant changes to the magazine, and these had not gone down well with staff. Douglas Stewart, who had been the poetry editor for some twenty years, had resigned in protest, moving to Angus & Robertson as poetry reader. Many of the poets he had nurtured in *The Bulletin*'s famous Red Page literary section decided to boycott *The Bulletin* in solidarity.[22] O'Grady, who was then the foreign editor, took on the roles of both literary and arts editors at Horne's behest.[23] Dismayed by the backlog of poems to be read, he suggested to Horne that *The Bulletin* employ a poetry editor. He recommended his former English tutor at Melbourne University, Vincent Buckley, who had become a friend. In the meantime, O'Grady began to make his way through the slush pile, dividing 'possibles from the hopeless'. According to O'Grady, the decision to publish the Lehmann sonnets was almost random. The issue was going to press when the compositors found there was a gap to fill on one of the literary pages. O'Grady rushed upstairs to his office and grabbed a couple of poems from the basket containing the 'possibles'. They were the right length, so they were slotted in and the issue went to press.

It's not clear who first noticed the acrostics. Vincent Buckley told Gwen that some of his students had spotted them, and she assumed that he had tipped them off. She also heard a rumour that 'some cryptogrammic fiend' found them and contacted the editor.[24] As word spread, *The Bulletin* was besieged by 'hundreds of letters and phone calls complaining of the obscenity' – or so it later claimed.[25] At once, the 5 August edition of *The Bulletin* sold out, and a black market for illicit copies sprang up. Libraries around the country discovered that their copy of the issue had disappeared. Everywhere, the poems were copied and distributed, gasped and gloated over. Wild theories sprang up about Walter Lehmann's motivation – and identity. Were the poems part of 'a gigantic plot to discredit *The Bulletin*' orchestrated by Douglas Stewart 'in revenge' against Horne? Was it a counterattack by radicals over a recent 'Communist exposé'? Had *The Bulletin* orchestrated the hoax itself to boost circulation?[26]

After the irate phone call from O'Grady, things went quiet again for Gwen, until, on Saturday, a reporter from the Sydney *Telegraph* appeared at her door asking for an interview. Realising that the secret of her identity was out, Gwen decided to make a statement – not her preference, but better than letting 'sniggering journalists write it up', she told Eddie, who was following the story from Melbourne with interest. She typed up a short screed declaring that her purpose in staging the hoax was to show up editors who 'did not know the difference between poetry and contrived writing' and gave it to the *Telegraph*. The sonnets were 'incredibly bad poetry', she declared. 'One glance through them should have made any competent reader suspicious.'[27]

Somehow, this point was lost in the ensuing media coverage. For journalists, the salient facts were that a four-letter word had been published in a respectable magazine and that the person responsible for this outrage was a housewife. The Sydney *Telegraph*'s headline read 'Tasmanian Housewife Hoaxes *The Bulletin*', and the paper described the sonnets as in 'offensively bad taste'. The Melbourne *Truth* led with 'Great Poem Hoax: Housewife Fools the Experts with Her Naughty Sonnets'. In Brisbane, *Truth* went with 'Experts Fooled by Naughty Sonnets' – and pointed out that the notorious 'poet-housewife' was 'Queensland-born'. Tasmania's *Mercury* was somewhat milder, opening with: 'A Hobart authoress who wrote two "poems" for a joke and had them published last week in the "Sydney *Bulletin*" has caused a sensation in literary circles.' The use of the f-word – even vertically – was genuinely shocking. As the poet Thomas Shapcott wrote some years later, 'The scandal of a four-letter word appearing in public print broke all the rigid conventions, conventions that had been set in concrete in our culture.'[28] *The Bulletin* declared it a 'very sad jest indeed': 'What is achieved by using [the literary] section of THE BULLETIN as a place in which to scrawl a coarse word is hard to imagine.'[29]

Gwen was unpleasantly surprised by the collective intake of breath at her use of 'the Word'. She found it hypocritical. 'I thought hysteria had long ago been drained from the workman's word for a splintery pick handle, but there you are,' she told Eddie.[30] To many in Hobart society, it was an article of faith that, as a friend of Gwen's put it, 'No WOMAN would ever write such a word': 'I had a mental picture, as I heard her pronunciation of "WOMAN", of little bluebirds with daisies in their beaks.'[31] Even in more exalted literary circles, this view was common. Gwen learned from Vivian and Sybille that at a Sydney party, the poet Nancy Keesing asked them what 'this Tasmanian Gwen Harwood' was like 'as a woman': 'Sybille said I was OK. Nancy Keesing said, "Then why did she write THAT WORD?"'[32]

For a time, Gwen found herself stranded in a 'desert of disapproval', enduring the sideways looks of friends and neighbours, and the 'cold eye

& pursed lip in the grocer's'.[33] Even Bill, who despised the literary world, reproached her. 'He doesn't give a damn for bourgeois affectations,' she explained to Tony, 'but thinks I was foolish to expose the children to this monstrous publicity.'[34] To her dismay, 'the whole thing' had become 'incredibly nasty'. 'What with Bill's fury and snickering reporters who wouldn't know a poem from a bunyip's shit I have been too worried to eat & sleep.'[35] A reporter from *Truth* had been 'snooping round the local shops', and she was fully expecting a headline along the lines of 'Mother of 4 writes obscene poems'.

Ann was firmly in support of Gwen, writing from Sydney to affirm 'that she thought it a brilliant exposure of pretentious literary journalists whose only real concern is money'. Bill was supportive, too, after his initial exasperation. Once the media began to hound her, 'he forgot his annoyance at the publicity' and assured her that the frenzy would soon die down.[36] On one of the days 'when things were looking nastiest', he went out with her for 'a long walk in the bush'.[37] Tony poured out his support by airmail across the ocean, and urged Frank Kellaway to let Gwen know that he supported her too. Frank was 'not entirely in sympathy' with her hoax, however. Her use of bad language did not bother him: 'I am *delighted* for *The Bulletin* to be publicly fucked, farted, rooted and generally shat on. The cream of the jest for me was the prissy old maidish way the Editor clutched up his skirt and talked about the use of dirty words in public.'[38] The problem for him was that he could not agree that the sonnets were incompetent rubbish. 'I thought they were good poems,' he confessed. '*I* certainly would have published them as an editor, even if I'd spotted the acrostic.'

◆ ◆ ◆

Gwen was incredulous at any suggestion that the poems had genuine literary merit. To write a good acrostic sonnet, she told Tony, would require 'supernatural powers of composition': 'hard enough to write a good sonnet, God knows; to write a good acrostic sonnet must be astronomically harder; to write a good acrostic sonnet that can be altered from Vincent Buckley to So Long Bulletin and still have a good sonnet . . . well, it could happen, I suppose, but I wouldn't like to maintain it'.[39] This was the line *The Bulletin* would take, however. After the poems appeared, Vin rang her from *The Bulletin*'s Sydney office, where he was in the process of being installed as poetry editor (at a princely salary, as Gwen later discovered), and told her that he and journalist Peter Coleman were collaborating on an article about the hoax. As Vin knew all about the hoax's origins, and was presumably very much on her side, Gwen was more than happy to leave it in his hands. She was completely blindsided when *The Bulletin* published a piece entitled 'The Hoax That Misfired' that was little more than a 'stinking mess of lies'.[40] The article asserted that Gwen had shown the poems to Vin while the hoax was still in the planning stage, and he 'immediately saw that, despite Mrs Harwood's best efforts, they had two defects which made them unsuitable for their hoax: they made real sense and they had a limited but definite literary merit'. Gwen supposedly 'accepted these criticisms', and 'the plan for the hoax was abandoned'. Later, to satisfy her own 'special humour', she submitted the poems anyway. She had apparently 'imagined that the acrostic would remain her private secret for ever', the article finished. 'Such are the fantasies of lady poets.'

When Gwen read this, her 'fury boiled all the water in Bass Strait'.[41] The mangled account – 'a packet of lies and half-truths' – made her 'look a fool'.[42] She was immediately convinced that, with his lucrative poetry editorship in the balance, 'the shit-hawk Vincent Buckley sold me out'.[43] The most infuriating part of the article for her was the assertion that Vin had told her the poems had merit. This was utter perfidy; Vin had said no such thing, and in any case, she sputtered to the Hoddinotts, 'I wouldn't accept Vin's criticisms on the shape of a peanut'. The assertion had the power to render her hoax meaningless. Where was the shame, for a literary editor, in publishing good poems, even if they did include 'feelthy acrostics'? She responded by giving an interview to the Tasmanian *Truth* with her own version of events, which appeared in a front-page story headed 'Tas. Housewife in Hoax of the Year'. 'I must make it clear that I did not accept any criticism of the sonnets and did not send them because they had literary merits,' she finished. 'On the contrary, I think they are poetical rubbish, and show up the incompetence of anyone who publishes them.'[44]

It seemed that no one in the poetry community agreed – or was prepared to say so publicly, at least. Gwen was deeply hurt that people who had privately supported her, such as Vivian Smith and Jim McAuley, did not stand up for her. When the Ern Malley hoax broke in the 1940s, McAuley and Stewart were lauded as heroes in both the literary and the general press, brave young soldiers fighting the good fight on behalf of serious poets everywhere. But no one wanted to throw in their lot with the 'Tasmanian housewife'.[45] 'I do feel pretty much on my own and pretty much abandoned by the poets,' Gwen wrote to Tony. 'Nobody has written to thank me for drawing attention to the need for editorial competence . . . *Nobody* has come publicly to my side and said what should be said: that people who don't know poetry from rubbish shouldn't publish the stuff'.[46] Jim and Alec Hope did offer private support. Jim, who found the whole thing 'mildly amusing', promised to write to Donald Horne, who was a friend of his, and 'do what he could'. His line, however, was not that Gwen's hoax was 'a serious literary experiment' – the claim he had made for Ern Malley all those years ago – but that it was a mere 'harmless jeu d'esprit'.[47] Alec, meanwhile, wrote her 'a noble & generous letter . . . full of good counsel & encouragement' in which he tried to walk the difficult line of propitiating Gwen while defending Vin. Gwen had written to him soon after *The Bulletin* article appeared, giving him the full story; she 'couldn't bear that lovely man to think me malicious & stupid'.[48] Alec replied kindly: 'I have heard twenty different stories, all unsatisfactory and all insofar as they brought you into it suggesting that you were either malicious or silly or both. As I was not disposed to think either of you I was pleased and relieved to hear the whole story from you.'[49] He did not offer to make any kind of public defence of her, but did ask if he could 'pass [your explanation] on discreetly to people who will be glad to know it for your sake'. Alec assured Gwen that Vin would not have deliberately sac-rificed her to secure his editorship at *The Bulletin*. In his view, the offending article was either 'written or rewritten by Donald Horne who is the person most affected and most in need of saving face'. Horne's boss, Frank Packer, 'is said to hate being made a fool of, and his methods are said to be arbitrary and summary'. Indeed, he went on, she had 'probably made two enemies who would like to have their revenge and probably have the means to do so'. Gwen was almost incredulous. It had not occurred to her that her poetry colleagues might be afraid of the 'big boys', Packer and Horne; but it seemed they had 'scared everyone into submission'.[50]

Several friends warned her that she might find herself in court. Under the obscenity laws, *The Bulletin* could be prosecuted for publishing an 'obscene' word – defined, vaguely, as something with the 'tendency to deprave and corrupt' – and could prosecute her in their turn. Soon after the presence of the acrostic was revealed, *The Bulletin*'s Sydney offices were visited by the vice squad, who grilled Packer and Horne 'for hours'.[51] Des-mond O'Grady was called into Horne's office, 'where, in [Horne's] silent presence', he was interrogated by a police officer. 'He had a series of ques-tions which he repeated in the vain hope that I would give differing replies.

It was hugely boring.'[52] Gwen worried that she might be similarly investigated. She asked Ann, who had connections in Sydney legal circles through her lawyer ex-husband, to keep an ear out for any hint of legal proceedings against her. She also asked Alison whether her father, a barrister, would 'act for [her] if any cases arise.'[53] She was particularly anxious about having to deal with a prosecution while Bill was on study leave in America. 'I said to Bill "What shall I do if I'm prosecuted for obscenity while you're away?"', she told Tony. Bill's reply made her laugh: "'Enter the fine under 'Miscellaneous' in the account book; be sure not to enter it under the wrong heading." Thank God for his sanity.'[54] But though her friends joked, uneasily, that her next work would be 'the equivalent of The Ballad of Reading Gaol',[55] the general consensus was that *The Bulletin* was unlikely to take her to court; such proceedings would only create more publicity of a kind Packer would not relish.

Horne himself was greatly upset by the 'jest'. He was struggling with depression, which he would later say 'turned to obsessive and paranoid anger' at Gwen's 'private joke'. Since he had taken over at *The Bulletin*, he had been under attack on all sides, and felt that 'F-U-C-K A-L-L E-D-I-T-O-R-S meant, in particular, me'.[56] Given that he had fought hard to keep some kind of literary presence in Packer's magazine, this seemed 'strange thanks'. Gwen, of course, knew nothing of the various ructions behind the scenes at *The Bulletin*. The original focus of her wrath had been *Meanjin*, then *Quadrant*; *The Bulletin* was only ever an incidental target. At this point, she really was attacking *all* editors. Horne took no revenge beyond insisting that *The Bulletin* publish no more poetry by Gwen Harwood or her alter ego, Walter Lehmann. Gwen could not help but grin when she heard this, as they had published a poem by Francis Geyer in their latest, post-hoax issue. Lehmann's identity had been definitively blown, but Geyer was still safe, it seemed.

She did hear from Alec that Clem Christesen was angry.[57] He had recognised one of Walter's sonnets and realised that Gwen had submitted it to him first. He had been wary of her ever since she sent him that angry letter in 1959 accusing him of running *Meanjin* like the Parish Gazette, and he had stopped writing to her personally, directing all correspondence through his secretary. Now he was muttering to his friends about banning her from *Meanjin* altogether. Alec assured her that he had told Clem that 'you were not really a bad girl at heart and that he'd better count up to ten million before he made up his mind to cut you out of his life and magazine'.[58] Clem did not follow through on his threat, but he did pull the article on her that

he had commissioned from Alec. Gwen was disappointed but unrepent-
ant. She would 'certainly do [Christesen] over if I feel like it with acrostics
up down and diagonally', she told Alec defiantly.[59] 'Who cares about CBC
anyway? If my stuff is any good at all it will survive without contemporary
help and if it isn't then I hope it will die mercifully and quickly.'

Other whispers to reach her in the aftermath of the hoax were more
congenial: Douglas Stewart, who had no reason to love *The Bulletin* under
Horne, had been heard to say that she was 'brilliant',[60] and others were
reported to have followed his lead, speaking admiringly of how she had
put one over on *The Bulletin*. She was not entirely softened by the change
of tone. 'Of course now I'm not in gaol & not fined heavily there'll be talk
of my brilliance & jeu d'esprit', she remarked sardonically. 'But *I* remember who was with me in the wilderness.' There was no denying, however,
that her profile had undergone a dramatic elevation. A new generation of
poets, including Thomas Shapcott and Rodney Hall in Brisbane and Chris
Wallace-Crabbe and Andrew Taylor in Melbourne, had been alerted to the
presence of an elder who was as anarchic as they could ever aspire to be.
If older poets were scandalised, younger poets wanted to meet her. Many
shared her resentment of 'all editors'; one, Noel Macainsh, even proclaimed
Walter Lehmann to be 'the patron saint of poets'.[61]

◆ ◆ ◆

For a while, Vin's friendship with Gwen seemed doomed. She reviled him
in every letter she sent about the hoax, impugning his religion, morals and
manners, bewailing her own trusting nature and vowing swift and bloody
vengeance. 'Buckley is now poetry editor of *The Bulletin*, a sitting target', she
told Tony. 'I am waiting in quietness for a few months, then I shall start again.'
To Eddie, she swore that 'Sooner or later he's going to publish something
that will turn his arse bright cadmium red.'[62] Vin, meanwhile, continued to
write to her as though nothing had happened. When he was in Hobart, he
had encouraged her to put a book manuscript together, and even offered to
compile it for her. She was pleased by the offer, though she had no intention
of deputing this task to anyone, let alone Vin. Instead, she 'pulled [herself]
together' and 'did [her] own assembling', sending the manuscript to Angus
& Robertson in June 1961.[63] She also sent it to Vin, who now responded with
a detailed critique, just as though they were still good friends. He must have
been uneasy, though, as he ended his cover note with: '*Are* you still speaking

to me?'[64] A few days later, he wrote again: 'You are annoyed with me, aren't you? . . . If you feel I have in any way sold you down (up?) the river, I can assure you that that was the precise antithesis of my situation.'[65]

Gwen was in a quandary. Angry as she was about the *Bulletin* article, she still liked Vin, and did not really want to consign him to the ranks of her enemies. She wanted to be able to talk shop with him, to enlist his help with her book and to continue to publish with him in both *The Bulletin* and *Prospect*. As the fuss over the hoax began to die down, both Alec and Jim again assured her that Vin had meant her no harm. This, coupled with his very complimentary comments on her manuscript, decided her. 'Your last letter conveyed a sadness beyond its words,' she wrote. 'That *was* what I thought [i.e. that he had sold her down the river], but your assurance (in curiously sibilant prose: "precise antithesis"!) is enough for me. You are one of the people in the world to whom I can talk with freedom and I am sorry if my silence has caused you the least distress.'[66]

It was quite an about-face for her friends to swallow, and she had to work hard to explain it. 'Perhaps I was too hard on Vin Buckley,' she told Eddie. 'People from Sydney assure me that he thought he was acting on my behalf whatever in fact he did, & that he showed genuine concern that my next poem shouldn't be The Ballad of Darlinghurst Gaol.'[67] Though she was prepared to cancel out her 'worst words against him', she assured Eddie that she would never 'trust him': 'The littery world is too awful; I shall never join in their gangs & clubs, NEVER.' To the Hoddinotts, she said that she was 'inclined to believe Vin's story that he did what he thought best in my interests', and that she liked him 'so much that I don't really care what he did or didn't do and anyway can get my own back at any time if I feel inclined. Editors are vulnerable.'[68] Tony was more difficult to convince, since he had taken her side so strenuously. She knew he was going to be annoyed that she had decided to let Vin off the hook, but defended her decision as 'based on intuition rather than reason'. 'I do think now that Vin was shifty & weak rather than malicious,' she explained. 'I don't propose to bitch the neurotic dear up any further . . . Life's too short for recriminations; after all he is a poet & I did like him & it's not his fault he was offered the pieces of silver.'[69]

Only a week later, however, she was complaining that in a recent *Bulletin* article, Vin gave a list of the 'best poets now writing apart from Hope, Wright, and McAuley' and did not mention her; yet he had recently told her that he thought her the only poet in Australia on a level with Hope, and that she was 'better than Judith Wright'.[70] 'I don't get a look-in or a mention or a footnote,' she grumbled. 'Perhaps he *is* afraid of Horne and Packer.' Nevertheless, she was 'determined not to manoeuvre on [her] own behalf'. She held to her belief that if her work was good, it would 'somehow or other make its way without effort of mine'.

◆ ◆ ◆

Vin really did think well of Gwen's work, though he could not say so in *The Bulletin*. In October, he ran a two-page feature on her in *Prospect*, with an editorial comment declaring that she was 'widely accepted' as 'one of Australia's most important poets'.[71] She wrote to thank him, declaring that he was 'the first Editor to say in black & white (or any other colour) that I am a good Lady Poet and publicly bless my green assertions'.[72] He also tried to enlist her as a reviewer, asking her to review six new volumes of poetry for *Prospect*, including his own – a move he had the grace to call a 'piece of editorial promotion'.[73] Gwen courteously declined. She told him she didn't like to be in the judging seat: 'Ever since I was an assistant adjudicator at a Brisbane eisteddfod and a clergyman's wife (C of E) attacked me because her little boy didn't win, I have kept my hi-fi sensibilities a secret'.[74] In any case, she had so little time for her own writing that she was loath to use it on anything other than poetry, as she told Jim McAuley a few months later, when he, too, asked her to do some reviewing.[75] Even so, it was nice to be asked. Somehow, after all this time as an outsider, she was passing almost imperceptibly into the enchanted circle.

Vin's comments on Gwen's manuscript had been overwhelmingly positive. 'The collection as a whole is a very fine and almost daunting achievement,' he told her, at the start of four pages of notes, and went on to use words like 'brilliance' and 'dazzling', declaring that at her best she was 'fiercely original'. He was especially enthusiastic about the Lehmann poems, which he felt were more 'objective' than the poems that bore her own name, singling out for particular praise 'In the Park', of which the last six lines were 'almost terrifying in their precision and fierceness of feeling'. If Gwen thought that his 'terror' sprang from the knowledge that these lines about the burden of maternity had been written by a woman, and a mother, rather than by a coolly detached man, she did not say so.

He also made suggestions for excisions and revisions, some of which Gwen accepted. But she was ready to move on. For some time now, she had felt that she needed to reinvent herself as a poet. 'I must begin again and again in poetry,' she told Tony shortly after her fortieth birthday. 'Sometimes I feel that everything I have attempted is poor – I can see why painters slash up canvases. I must explore myself more deeply, be humbler, quieter, less demanding of the world: "Myself I must remake," as Yeats wrote in his old age.'[76] More than a year later, she would say the same thing to Vin Buckley.[77] She was anxious not to repeat herself. But more than that, she was groping her way towards a new clarity and simplicity. She wanted to 'weld content and form into a closer unity, so that in the end it will appear that one is looking straight at the spiritual content of the poem without mediation: at what is, not at what is said.'[78] This was her new benchmark, encapsulated for her in Wallace Stevens' line that 'The tongue is an eye'.

Once Bill left at the end of August for his four-month sabbatical in the United States, she was too busy to write. She had been ambivalent about his departure. Before he left, she told Ann that she would 'probably enjoy being husbandless, turn on the hits when I feel like it, bash the works out of the piano & write me epic in the evenings'.[79] But to Alison she groaned: 'I hate widowhood & shall be permanently embittered I'm sure.'[80] She worried about how she was going to manage house and children alone, and was grateful when Agnes offered to come down in November to help out. Yet when Bill actually left, she rejoiced. 'Once I am away from Bill the Old Adam (or Eve I suppose) begins to range through creation touching, poking, examining, tasting, singing, leaping, playing Bach, making silly jokes (he doesn't really think Sappho cards are funny) & tearing off masks,' she confessed to Tony.[81] Outside the range of her husband's disapproval, she felt free to run amok. She took over his study while he was gone, turning it into 'a poetic boudoir', which gave her intense pleasure: 'I force the boys to knock before entering and feel tremendously refreshed by this small privacy.' Nevertheless, she and Bill wrote to one another every day.

If she had little time to write poems in Bill's absence, she did have a new freedom for correspondence, and cards and letters to Vin began to pour from her pen, sometimes at the rate of three or four a week. She wrote not only about her own poems but about his. He had sent her a copy of his new book in late July, and she responded with a letter of lavish praise. She was only partly sincere. 'There are three or four good poems,' she told Alison and Bill Hoddinott around the same time, listing the ones she liked. 'I'd be prepared to sign any of these (my current test of goodness, Would I Sign This?)'[82] Her cool tone is very different from the buoyant enthusiasm of her letters to Vin himself. Yet she did send him criticism – carefully phrased not to give offence – as well as praise, ruminating deeply on his work and posing question after question about exactly what he meant by the use of particular phrases, line lengths and metres. It was the kind of shop talk she longed for, isolated from other poets as she was.

Vin took it all in good part. 'Ah, but my dear,' he wrote in one letter, 'you have a constancy of poetic passion that I lack, and a brilliantly shifting texture that makes my texture look dull to me. Your problems now are, in my opinion, sophisticated textual ones.'[83] When she worried that she wasn't writing anything new, he told her to embrace the emptiness: 'There is a time for patient silence, not for "learning" but for listening. You are lucky if it has descended on you. I am in a quiet frenzy of ineptitude.'

Though Gwen did not know it, he was going through an extremely difficult time in his personal life. While Gwen was pouring out gleeful, hilarious letters to Vin at an astonishing rate, his marriage was breaking down, his wife and daughters moving temporarily to Sydney.[84] All Gwen knew was that Vin was unhappy; the world 'presses in intolerably', he told her.[85] She speculated that he was suffering from 'post-natal depression' following the 'birth' of his book. It seemed to her that he had described 'exactly what I felt after the birth of a child, "something is staring into nothingness"'. 'Sometimes I feel my mind clouding over, like a day that started bright, & cannot shake this irrational sadness off,' she wrote. 'The middle of life is hard, much harder than adolescence.' When it became evident that he could not keep up with her exuberant flow of words, she assured him that he need not feel any obligation to reply: 'quid pro quo hardly applies to belles-lettres.'[86]

In the meantime, she had no intention of letting him off the hook in his editorial capacity. In late September, only a little more than a month after the *Bulletin* scandal, she sent him another acrostic under Francis Geyer's name, 'The Prophet in the City'. Vin did not notice the vertical message, which, pointedly, read 'Hypocrite Lecteur' (hypocritical reader), a phrase from Baudelaire which T.S. Eliot had made famous in *The Waste Land*. He accepted the poem, but the acrostic was picked up by the typesetters before the issue went to print. Francis Geyer received an acerbic note from Donald Horne promising to 'make this poem available to the nearest kindergarten where there may be some market for it'.[87] Gwen sent Vin a chortling letter:

Dear Vin,
    An acrostic was showing,
But the editors pulled up your slip.

What readers would say there's no knowing –
('Vin's had it, Vin's losing his grip').

Wally Lehmann intoned his approval,
Gwen Harwood responded "Amen";
Frank, furious at his removal,
Assured them he'd try it again.[88]

Vin took it well, telling her ruefully that 'There's always *some* distinction in your bloody poems'.[89] Meanwhile, his parody of her style, 'The Sentry', was published in the September issue of *Meanjin* under Gwen's name. She was delighted. 'It looks terribly like a Harwood, you devil,' she wrote to him.[90] 'I shall receive congratulations like a cat getting at the cream.' This time, though, there was no revelation, no publicity, not even an attempt to spread the story any wider than Gwen's immediate circle. Meanwhile, she was delighted to learn from one of her 'spies' in Sydney that Leonie Kramer had accepted 'The Sentry' for *Australian Poetry 1961* – though she withdrew this acceptance when she heard (from Alec Hope, who had heard it from Gwen) of the poem's true authorship. When it was selected by Geoffrey Dutton for *Australian Poetry 1962*, Gwen's joy knew no bounds.[91]

Despite his personal preoccupations, Vin proved that he was more than capable of matching wits with Gwen when it came to hoaxes. When Gwen got her copy of the December edition of *Meanjin*, she was electrified to find a poem by Francis Geyer that she had not written. Entitled 'Dead Guitars', it was 'neither better nor worse' than other Geyer poems.[92] Nevertheless, when she saw it in *Meanjin*, she 'felt like a sniper who'd got one in the bum'.[93] Her first thought was that Christesen had written it, as a means of 'trying to get his own back on Geyer'.[94] But she quickly came to the conclusion that the 'faked Geyer (how far can this go? Copies of fakes of copies of fakes?)' had been written by Vin 'as a private joke'.[95] Again, no public statement was ever made. She managed to trip Vincent up again towards the end of 1962, when he accepted a new Kröte poem, 'Soiree', by Geyer, which included another acrostic – this one, deviously, in French. It read 'Mon Semblable, Mon Frere' (My Fellow, My Brother), the second part of the 'Hypocrite Lecteur' quote Gwen had used in her earlier acrostic. When the poem appeared in *The Bulletin* on 6 October 1962, she was jubilant, sending him a cheerful little ditty of unalloyed gloating.

◆ ◆ ◆

Geyer's days were numbered, however. Two young Brisbane poets, Tom Shapcott and Rodney Hall, both in their late twenties, had been watching Francis with interest.[96] They suspected that he might bear some relationship to the Hobart 'authoress', but if so, no one was telling. Because of the peregrinations of both Tony and Ann, Geyer had recently moved to Brisbane, where he inhabited Gwen's parents' letterbox. Late in 1962, Tom and Rod decided to drop in on the Hungarian-born poet to ask him to join the Queensland branch of the Fellowship of Australian Writers.[97] One Saturday afternoon, they set off for Geyer's Camp Hill address, arriving, to their bemusement, at a 'scene of deepest suburbia', 'riddled with little wooden or fibro erections on stilts, with tiny tidy and trimmed lawns and minute beds of anonymous flowers'.[98] They were greeted at the door by a 'grey haired mum-type (had been peering at us through the venetians)', and were dimly aware that 'Dad' was 'doddering in the garden somewhere . . . but very interested'. The grey-haired woman explained that Francis was their lodger, but he was unfortunately away in North Queensland at the moment. Tom asked her straight out whether 'anyone by name of Harwood lives here', but Agnes, loyal to the end, feigned ignorance. Indeed, she 'never actually admitted identity, even at the last'. Nevertheless, she was more than happy to tell them all about her 'clever daughter'. 'From the many photos she is a most charming and youthful woman, 4 children, animated face,' Tom wrote. 'Mum was delightful; dad a bit of a north-country rambler.'

Tom went straight home to write to Gwen. By the time his letter arrived, she had heard the story from her mother and knew that the game was up.[99] It must have been galling for her to have been smoked out by Tom Shapcott. She had watched his growing prominence in the poetry scene over the last couple of years with a jaundiced eye, often citing his poems as examples of the 'mucktuck' that was chosen by editors over her own carefully crafted masterpieces. Though he was fifteen years younger than her, he was soon to publish his second book, and Gwen found it 'maddening to see that Tennysonian babbler framed and distributed'.[100] She was particularly irritated by the title of 'Queensland's outstanding lyric poet' that had somehow been bestowed on him, a phrase that never failed to make her bristle.[101] Nevertheless, she responded graciously to his letter, sending him a beautiful Sappho card featuring a bewigged Victorian gentleman, labelled A.D. Hope, with two graceful children, a girl and a boy, identified respectively as Gwen Harwood and Francis Geyer, and a sad young man in knickerbockers, identified as Walter Lehmann. Tom's 'fantastic letter' made her 'utterly homesick', she told him gaily. 'My mother was charmed by you & R.H. and is hoping you'll call again – please do; but beware of her reminiscences: she has replaced my real childhood with an imaginary one in which I am always good, beautiful, talented, popular, sought in marriage by ½ Brisbane . . .'

It was the beginning of a long and lively correspondence in which, to her surprise, Tom showed himself eager to match her in playful invention. He was 'fascinated by her antics', reporting gleefully to Chris Wallace-Crabbe early in 1963 that she had sent him 'a priceless "Ode to Vin Buckley".'[102] Spurred to emulation, he began to create his own homemade postcards and invent ditties and joke poems. Early in 1963, in an act of open homage to Gwen, he even sent an acrostic poem to *The Bulletin*. This poem, 'Return Is Not Again', contained a phrase from Dylan Thomas's very popular radio play *Under Milkwood*, 'Kiss Gwennie where She Says'. Gwen, whose epistolary gaiety with Tom had been a touch forced until then, was delighted. Shapcott 'slapped a beaut acrostic on Vin in *The Bulletin* of 20 April 1963,' she told Tony gleefully. 'Various people think *I* wrote it & forged Shapcott's signature, but it was his own unaided work.'[103] Tony, no fan of Shapcott's poetry, was not amused, but Gwen shrugged this off, telling him she thought it very funny and had written to tell Tom so. She added that the issue had sold out in Tasmania, and that when people questioned her about it, she refused to answer: 'I just smirk like Agnes.'[104] Tom was disappointed that outside of Tasmania, nobody seemed even to have noticed his coup.

Francis Geyer survived long enough for his own last hurrah with *The Bulletin*. When Buckley resigned as poetry editor in 1964, to be replaced by Ron Simpson, Gwen sent in yet another acrostic, 'The Last Evening', a truly ingenious work in which the acrostic reads from the bottom up and spells out: 'Oh hello Ronald, goodbye Vin, heaven help The Bulletin'. It was published on 21 March, and no articles about it ever appeared in *Truth*.

◆ ◆ ◆

In late 1961, after the furore over the hoax had finally died down, Gwen's biggest concern was whether Angus & Robertson would accept her book manuscript. She knew that there were two hurdles to overcome: first, Angus & Robertson had to decide it was worth publishing, and, second, the Commonwealth Literary Fund had to decide it was worth subsidising, as A&R relied on subsidies for poetry titles.

She was anxious about the manuscript's fate from the moment she submitted it, and decided she wouldn't tell people 'so that when it was rejected I wouldn't have to pretend I didn't mind'.[105] She did tell Alec Hope and Jim McAuley, though, as well as Vin Buckley. In Bill's absence, Jim had taken to dropping in 'to borrow the mower or the wedge or a book & sits for hours having teas & sherries & tells me all about Norma's breast-feeding difficulties & how editors are vulnerable & about his children's peculiarities'.[106] Heading to Sydney 'on mysterious business', he promised Gwen that he would put in a good word for her with Beatrice Davis at Angus & Robertson. 'I said, real cool & offhand, "Thanks, Jim." But it should help.'

At last, at the end of October, she heard a rumour of good news. 'Jim told me that Beatrice Davis told him that A&R will publish The Good Book,' she reported joyfully to Vin. 'I hope they will tell ME someday.'[107]

She got the official letter a few weeks later, with the promise of a contract and an assurance that the book would appear at the end of 1962. Passing on the news to Tony, she told him that she would dedicate the volume to him. 'I have wished ever since I met you (nearly twenty years!) to give you some substantial acknowledgement of a debt that can't be paid in any human terms,' she told him.[108] In her mind, the dedication would link them forever. 'Never mind if the critics rip [the poems] to bits (as they will); I am firmly confident that a few of them will live when the spiders are crawling over the critics.'

15

With the Musicians

Sometimes I have flashes of unbearable insight as I listen to Beethoven's late music; I see what I could have made of my life & the shabby affair it is, with loose ends everywhere, half-finished plans, pockets of black despair and rags of unused gifts flapping in time's wind.
Gwen Harwood, Letter to Tony Riddell, 8 November 1962

EVEN BEFORE FRANCIS GEYER MET HIS UNTIMELY DEMISE, Gwen had launched a new alter ego. In January 1962, she wrote to Alison and Bill Hoddinott asking for suggestions for a name for 'this year's genius', saying that she wanted 'to teach Jim & that know-all Irishman Vin a few lessons about their own critical theories'.[1] A week later, she wrote again to say that she had decided to create 'a lovely lady poet, married (of course, how else would she have any grasp of the world's sorrows?) with child'. Choosing to masquerade as a woman was inspired: 'Nobody will be expecting me to be a lady poet.'

As Miriam Stone, Gwen was able to say things from a woman's perspective that she felt she could not say as herself. By the time she settled on Miriam's name and identity, she already had a sheaf of poems ready to go. One of these was the incendiary 'Burning Sappho'. Writing as Stone meant she could send this poem out with impunity, since all of Burning Sappho's rage was safely projected on to Frau Stein (as Gwen sometimes called her). Mrs Stone need not fear ostracism within her social circle for violating the tenets of Holy Motherhood, nor the lofty disapproval of those for whom the word 'woman' was always surrounded by cartoon bluebirds.

Gwen sent 'Burning Sappho' to Vin Buckley at *The Bulletin* from the Hoddinotts' Armidale address as part of a group of poems that included the equally dark 'Lip Service', in which the housewife narrator speaks of her desire to cut out her own 'core', removing 'the seeds of discontent'. It was a sentiment she had expressed directly to Vin a few months earlier in relation to her compulsion to write, telling him that she wished she 'could be cored like an apple'.[2] She was trying to explain that she felt hounded by her sense of vocation. 'It is to me a hateful talent,' she wrote. 'I cannot bury it. *I would rather have been happy.*' She saw her desire to write in biblical terms as a 'gift' she had a duty to nurture.[3] It made her life difficult, hauling her out of the daily round, bringing her into conflict with her family who felt – as she did – that they should have first claim on her time.[4] Yet she could not ignore it. Her gift had a mind of its own, a power 'indifferent / to any lost or ill / motion of mind or will', as she put it in 'Alter Ego'.[5] It cared nothing for her domestic life, her happiness or any other of her desires. It 'tears me apart', as she put it to Eddie Tanner, yet compelled her obedience.

Vin did not want 'Lip Service', explaining that while he liked it 'very much in bits', he felt that it did not work 'as a whole'.[6] Overall, though, he was very impressed with Mrs Stone. He accepted 'Burning Sappho' and another of her poems, 'The Blind Lovers', and was at pains to assure this emerging poet that her work was good. Her poems were 'highly individual, with a powerful jet of feeling and a willingness to probe the life-centre in a way that would frighten most contemporary poets under their beds in pork-pie hats'. Her work was uneven, however, with 'the diction wavering at times from one kind to another'. He did not immediately make the connection between this new Armidale poet and his Tasmanian trickster friend, though there were plenty of clues in 'Lip Service' to its true authorship. Not only was the poem a recapitulation of a conversation he and Gwen had had by letter, but its reference to a mother being eaten alive by her family also evokes 'In the Park'. And then there was the description of the woman's heart as a 'winged stone', a clear signal that the author's name was symbolic. Vin, evidently, was not yet paying attention.

Even with her pseudonym firmly in place, Gwen was ambivalent about the appearance of 'Burning Sappho' in *The Bulletin* in June. When Geoffrey Dutton subsequently chose this poem for the *Australian Poetry 1962* anthology, she wrote to withdraw it. 'I hate M. Stone for writing Burning Sappho,' she told Vivian. 'Please never refer to it.'[7] She did not want Bill to learn of the poem's existence. 'Please don't show it to Bill, it might hurt his feelings,' she begged Eddie when she sent him a copy a few months later. 'I did publish it in the Bully, but will leave it out of my collection. Too nasty.'[8]

There may have been other 'nasty' poems that never saw the light of day. Writing to Eddie in August 1962, she explained that she sometimes censored her own work. 'One of my troubles is recurrent respectability,' she wrote. 'I have fits of it (unpredictable) and wish I had never written a line but had stayed making pies in the kitchen. A lot of good savage work gets destroyed in these moods.'[9] Some of this lost work may well have been in the mode of 'Burning Sappho'.

One reviewer referred to Stone's work as 'the tough version of "housewife poems"',[10] including 'Suburban Sonnet' and 'Suburban Sonnet: Boxing Day' under this umbrella, poems that also drew on aspects of Gwen's domestic experience. The first dramatised her ongoing battle to regain her skill as a pianist, beginning: 'She practices a fugue, though it can matter / to no one now if she plays well or not.' 'Boxing Day' features a mother who is 'too tired to move'.

Miriam was not prolific. Gwen published only seven poems under this pseudonym, five of which appeared in *The Bulletin* in 1962 and 1963; the other two were not published until 1965, when Vivian Smith included them in a Tasmanian edition of the new journal *Poetry Australia*. Gwen reclaimed a further two before they were due to appear and published them as Harwoods.[11] Part of the problem was that Miriam's cover was blown very early. Before she was six months old, Vin began to suspect she was one of Gwen's alter egos and wrote to tax her with the new masquerade. She confessed all, and Vin was delighted by his own perspicacity. 'Miriam Stone was one of your more disconcerting personae, particularly for a man in my state of health to meet,' he wrote. 'Yet imagine opening *The Bulletin* mail and, among the gumnuts, the sheep-droppings, the drops of saliva and fallen tears, coming on *those* fiercely accurate, tough, intelligent, rugged poems. I could see no alternative to supposing that she was you; but her poetry doesn't really have the surface polish which makes your best poems glitter out from whatever company they are in.'[12] He was very willing to keep her secret, but Gwen herself could not resist telling various friends, and Miriam's identity leaked out. By September, Gwen was writing to the Hoddinotts that 'Everybody (but everybody) seemed to know who we were so we withdraw all mss'.[13]

Among the retracted manuscripts was a short story she had sent to an annual anthology, *Coast to Coast*. That year's editor was Hal Porter, and Gwen thought it would be 'great fun to send him a parody of his own style'.[14] He accepted the story with alacrity, but Miriam withdrew it at the last moment, having realised 'it was not her place to write PROSE'.[15] Angus & Robertson wrote to beg her to reconsider, but she was inexorable. The story has not survived.

◆ ◆ ◆

After the demise of Miriam Stone, Gwen no longer felt so driven to write under other names, and the poems she began in 1962 would all subsequently be published as Harwoods. These poems were stimulated by Beethoven. Early in 1962, a young pianist, Rex Hobcroft, embarked on a series of lunchtime concerts at the university's Domain campus. His ambition was to perform all thirty-two of Beethoven's piano sonatas over the period of a year or so. In April, Gwen attended one of these recitals and was utterly ravished. Rex's playing was superb, and the music took her irresistibly back to her Brisbane days.[16] To her eyes, Rex looked 'astonishingly' like Tony as he was in the early 1940s: handsome, commanding, an artist to his fingertips. The likeness, she told Tony, was 'enough to disturb me profoundly'.[17] Rex had been appointed in 1961 to head the university's newly established music department; he came from the fledgling Queensland Conservatorium in Brisbane, where he had set up their piano department. In Hobart, he was given an office on the overcrowded and chronically dilapidated Domain campus 'in a converted leaky garage'.[18]

For Gwen, the chance to hear Beethoven performed live was too good to miss, but she found the music as disturbing as Rex himself. Beethoven had long been a vivid figure in Gwen's imagination – ever since she was a child and sat on the shed roof at Auchenflower poring over the 'saccharine lives of the composers'. In her early thirties, she had dreamed of him repeatedly, as her occasional dream diary shows.[19] In one dream, he was her husband and the father of her four children, and his 'extremely bad temper made our lives a misery'.[20] A few weeks later, she managed to revise this dismal scenario by dreaming that Beethoven asked her to marry him and she turned him down, telling him that he was 'too ill-tempered'.[21] With his stomping and scowling and rudeness, Beethoven was the epitome of not only the great musician but also the great man. Her scientist, Eisenbart, bears his stamp, as does her musician, Kröte, who models his wild hair and demeanour on those of the great composer. Now, through Rex's concerts, she was meeting Beethoven again in his music. This time, he spoke to her not of the artistic temperament but of the uses of pain.

In Rex's first recitals, Gwen was simply conscious of the loveliness of the early Beethoven sonatas. As the sequence went on, however, and the music became both more complex and more glorious, she began to realise that the composer's musical development was intimately related to his personal sorrows. Beethoven had been slowly losing his hearing, and she suddenly saw that his growing misery was the creative force behind his greatest works. He 'pressed from deafness and despair / this heavenly wine for men to share'.[22] The revelation filled her with hope. It seemed to her that Beethoven's suffering almost two centuries ago had led directly to this moment in Hobart in which, listening to his music, her own spirit was set free.[23] She felt sure that her own suffering would serve a similar purpose; her passion of pain would turn out to be the refiner's fire from which she would emerge with a new song on her lips. In Beethoven's late sonatas she heard a difficult but liberating command: 'Suffer and love, burn, shine and sing.'[24]

This newfound faith she poured out in a series of poems that more or less kept pace with the recitals, extending throughout 1962 and into the first months of 1963. The poems were written specifically for Rex. She sent many directly to him without keeping a copy, seeing the words on the page as a gift in themselves, 'the original' in the same way as a painter's canvas.[25] She felt these poems were being drawn out of her by his playing and thus in a profound way belonged to him. In one poem, she compared her attendance at these recitals with her very first piano lesson: both opened up a new world.[26]

She was experimenting with free verse forms, using loose or even no rhymes, eschewing regular stanzas, playing with line lengths and rhythms. As Beethoven moved, over the course of the piano sonatas, from the classical mode of the eighteenth century to the Romantic of the early nineteenth, so she moved from strict adherence to classical poetic forms to experiments in which feeling created form. She had felt stuck, as though she was simply repeating herself in her poems. Now, she was finding a way forward – and she was eager to give Rex the credit. When Jim McAuley accepted 'Beethoven, 1798' for *Quadrant*, saying that it 'marked a change in [her] poetry', she told Rex that if Jim was right, the change had sprung from 'the refreshment (inexpressible but real) I've had from the Beethoven series'.[27]

With this letter, Gwen enclosed two further poems, 'impromptus' she was offering him 'by way of thanks'. One was another meditation on the composer, 'Beethoven in a Shabby Room'. It was prompted by a dream: 'you & I were talking about the late sonatas & you said "They were not made for use: they transcend all human needs. Remember that they were written by a deaf man in a shabby room and yet they are the shape through which the spirit appears."'[28] (This poem she would later drop from the 'Four Impromptus', which were published the following year in *Quadrant*, on the grounds that 'it only repeats what is said more forcefully elsewhere'.)[29] The second impromptu was a paean to their friendship, beginning:

> All who are lucky find a few:
> in the heart's innermost recesses
> their words and looks and gestures fall
> like light; and this is mutual.[30]

For her, he was such a friend.

Rex responded eagerly to Gwen's poems, and to her passion for his music-making. Many years later, he would say that he was aware of the pull of sexual attraction between them, but with a wife and young family and the demands of a new and exciting job to engross him, he did not consider an affair.[31] Gwen was happy to let the friendship take what form it would. She continued to write poems for Rex and send them to him, telling him that she would welcome any criticisms he cared to make. He replied thoughtfully, and she often revised her poems in line with his suggestions. At times, she even asked him to decide whether she should publish a particular poem or not. Late in 1962, he began to reciprocate in an unexpected way, sending her poems of his own for comment. She was delighted by this further evidence that they were kindred spirits, and gave him detailed feedback.

Between April 1962 and September 1963, Gwen sent Rex more than a dozen poems, some of which were not published in her lifetime. Many were inspired by the Beethoven recitals, but others sprang from experiences she shared with him outside of the recital room. The Hobcroft and the Harwood families had become friends, and they spent time together on weekends at beach picnics and on bushwalks. Several of the poems Gwen dedicated to Rex reflect such settings, including two poems she did not try to publish: 'The Double Image', which she sent him in February 1963 (increasing the value of the gift by explaining that she had 'destroyed the notes' and had no copy),[32] and 'The Speed of Light', which she sent him in September 1963.[33] 'To Another Poet' describes an evening they spent together talking while their children played cards. Though this poem does not carry a dedication, its title is an endorsement of Rex's aspirations as a poet. With his copy, she added a note explaining that she had changed the children's game from cards to toy soldiers to suit her poetic purpose. 'I wanted a small-scale image of meaningless violence, a "paraphrase of the world", to set against the dimensions of private grace,' she wrote.[34] The 'private grace' to which she referred was the release she experienced, in Rex's presence and through his music, from what she called her 'old tyrannic grief' – the loss of Tom Pick. Through Rex's friendship, she felt that those wounds were finally healing.

Yet the healing process was not easy. Gwen felt as though she was being forced to take stock of herself and her life, and the accounting was far from pleasant. To Tony, she wrote of having 'flashes of unbearable insight as I listen to Beethoven's late music'. She was seeing her life from a new perspective, and it seemed a 'shabby affair'.[35] Such revelations were 'so painful that one can only bear them for the brief time they last' – yet to ignore them would be to consign oneself to 'the grave of self-complacency'. She gave poetic form to this experience in 'The Waldstein', a sonnet named for Beethoven's Sonata No. 21 in C major, Op. 53, and modelled on its three movements. In this poem, she asks: 'Must I come to this painful self-knowledge now?' But music 'uncovers all', and she cannot look away. Another poem, 'Littoral', expresses something of the fall-out of this intense self-scrutiny. In it, the poet speaks with a new simplicity and directness, accepting her past, with all its miseries and mistakes, and affirming simply *what is*.

As well as mourning her affair with Tom Pick, Gwen was also reflecting on the failure of her friendship with Lotte, a source of ongoing pain. Lotte was also attending Rex's concerts when she could, and Gwen reported dismally that on one occasion, Lotte 'cut me dead'.[36] On another, she ran into Lotte at the university as she was leaving one of Rex's concerts. 'It was raining & she opened her car door – but when I got in she attacked me venomously and said she "warned" me never to approach her in public again,' Gwen told Tony. 'I said "Don't be silly, you can't stop me greeting you in public," whereupon she launched into an attack on my character & life so vicious that I felt shame for her and a fleeting doubt of her complete sanity.'[37] Gwen's response was rather subdued – not because she was 'a patient Griselda', but because she was 'almost in tears': 'I cannot root out the absolute love I feel for the woman deep down. I cannot forget what she was & how she loved me equally, once.' She felt as she imagined she would feel if someone she loved had gone mad: 'the heart responds as of old to the loved features and the terrible alien *otherness* tears one apart'.[38]

More than a year later, Gwen would draw on this encounter to write 'Chance Meeting'.[39] Even then, the roller-coaster of the break-up was not entirely over: she still veered from fury to despair to contempt to thwarted love when she saw Lotte or heard news of her. 'I dream of her quite often and would forget in a moment the sad years if she were kind to me,' she told Tony early in 1964. 'She's just had too much to bear, and my good luck must be a torment to her.'[40] Yet she also worried that she had been damaged by the way the friendship had ended, warped by the rejection. Because of her experience with Lotte, she could no longer give herself unstintingly, pour out her love 'without any thought of reserve or concealment'.[41] But this, too, she hoped would heal with time.

Gwen was dreaming often of Vera Cottew, coming to understand that she had subconsciously linked her and Lotte. It was Agnes who first pointed out that the two looked alike, and Gwen had begun to wonder whether this physical resemblance had caused her to 'load' Lotte with 'some of the attributes of the dead Vera'.[42] Was it possible her intense love for Lotte had been merely a kind of refraction of her love for Vera? The poems provoked by the Beethoven recitals focused almost as much on Vera as on Rex.[43] 'Past and Present' brings the two figures together, with the 'Past' section recreating a moment with Vera from Gwen's adolescence and the 'Present' section depicting a moment with Rex. The implied narrative is clear: Vera initiated her into the 'labour' of artistic creation through the medium of painting, and Rex carried on her artist's education through the medium of music, teaching her art's 'miracle': 'that hard-worked artifice / should sound innate and be music still'. This dazzling poem, a kind of self-portrait, is in some ways the culmination of the poetic outpouring stimulated by Rex and the Beethoven sonatas, though she did not complete it until late in 1965.[44] By then, she was well into a dry spell, which began towards the end of 1963 and led her, early in 1964, to change her life.

16

The Good Book

Freedom is power to choose. Each day

I choose my life, choose to be woven
in other lives, and weave my own
threads.

Gwen Harwood, 'Littoral'

GWEN FINALLY RECEIVED A CONTRACT FROM ANGUS & ROBertson in August 1962, nine months after they had formally accepted her manuscript. The long period of waiting was frustrating. She expressed her alternating fury and despair in letters to Tony, berating 'Anguish & Robbery, Arthritic & Rhematic, Astute & Roguish, Arbitrary & Repulsive, Archaic & Rotten, Apocryphal & Revolting, Apish & Ratlike, Archfiends & Rotters'.[1] Tony urged her to withdraw her manuscript in protest, but much as she would have liked to take such a stand, it was not an option. Her only alternative publisher, Cheshires, was 'reported to be worse' than Angus & Robertson: 'Poetry is despised & rejected and its disciples suffer.' When she finally received the contract, she was in no mood to celebrate. Nevertheless, she was glad to have this official assurance that her book would actually be published. She assumed it would soon go into production and planned to send out copies as Christmas presents.

But though Angus & Robertson had announced the book for 1962, they decided to defer publication until 1963. 'Fuck all editors, publishers and politicians,' Gwen groaned when she discovered this.[2] She toyed with the possibility that someone was plotting against her – perhaps Hal Porter had used his influence with Beatrice Davis against her? – but the experiences of other poets convinced her that such delays were simply par for the course in Australian publishing. When the new year came, there was still no sign of her volume. 'I've been in a state of suspended animation over The Book for so long that I fear I'll wither away,' she told Tony in February 1963. 'I shan't of course, I'll recover the moment it appears, but I can't go forward in this heavy, endlessly pregnant state.' A month later, she would describe it as 'a Kafka-like nightmare'.[3]

There was a lot at stake for her. She felt that once she had a book out she would be a Real Poet. She would no longer need to snatch at opportunities for publication, or feel herself to be on a lower rung than the young male poets springing up around her who all seemed to have at least one book in print. She could even stop sending work to the literary magazines if she wanted to and simply publish her new poems in book form. She loved the idea of abandoning *Meanjin* and *Quadrant* and the humiliations of submission forever. With a book behind her, she would have some standing in her own community, too, and would be treated as an 'author' at Book Week celebrations, to which she had never yet been invited.[4] In university circles, she already had some fame, largely as a result of the *Bulletin* hoax. She was somewhat bemused, in May, to find herself parodied in the 1963 university revue as '"Nancy Horzbush", a literary housewife', who 'recited a wild parody of me at my worst, and told a frightful dream of eagles ripping and tearing small birds'.[5]

In fact, her standing as a poet was growing, even without a book to her name. In mid-1963, Vincent Buckley lectured on her poetry in Brisbane for the Commonwealth Literary Fund, and told his audience that Gwen 'was one of the outstanding poets in Australia'.[6] Gwen's mother attended, with the Lady Mayoress in tow, '& was transported with pride'.[7] Her old friend Peter Bennie – who had moved back to All Saints as rector in 1953 – was also there, and wrote to tell Gwen that Vin had done her proud.[8] She was subsequently invited to appear on the ABC's *Writing Today* program, and to talk to students at Claremont High School, where she was gratified to see the headmaster listening 'with real or counterfeited glee'. 'I felt very much the 43-year-old public smiling woman,' she told Tony.[9] Later in the year, the Australian Society of Authors invited her to join their organisation – an honour she declined, without regret, on the grounds that she could not afford the five-guinea fee.[10]

Her own attitude toward her poems was increasingly ambivalent. At times she was confident that her early verse was good, but as 1963 wore on, she felt increasingly that she had outgrown it. 'I've been separated from the poems in my book for long enough now to see them afresh, and some of them are pretty bad,' she told Tony towards the end of March.[11] She was displeased by what she was coming to see as a stiff, artificial quality in her early work. Much of it had come to seem 'contrived, needle-workish'. She wanted to break through to a new style, to 'advance', with Beethoven's self-transformation as her inspiration. But she did not know how to do it.

'Sometimes I really think poetry has come to an end, or rather I cannot imagine what form it must take to renew itself,' she told Tony.[12] She was questioning her adherence to traditional verse styles. 'I can't go on forever with the old forms,' she wrote. 'Sometimes I work out sonnets in my head while doing the housework, but my very fluency deters me.'[13] She distrusted what was easy; she was convinced she could not win through to 'the heart's true voice' without struggle and suffering.

Her desire for something new was fanned when she attended the first conference of Australian composers in late April 1963, organised by the enterprising Rex and hosted by the University of Tasmania. Two 'electrifying concerts' of music by contemporary composers left her in a tumult and made her long for an equally radical reinvention of contemporary poetry. 'One could feel the ferment, the excitement, the exulting power of the new works,' she told Tony. 'I just don't know any equivalent in poetry.'[14] To Vin she wrote that she 'kissed the ground [the composers] walked on', thrilling to the sound of music 'still dripping ink (or blood?); new sonatas from the uttermost parts of the mind. *How* is one to revive poetry? Mouth to mouth? Compressed air? Heart massage?'[15] She was particularly struck by the music of Brisbane composer and pianist Larry Sitsky, which she found 'disturbing and quite new . . . totally strange.'[16] In one piece he had 'played on the strings of the grand piano with a nail punch, knocking the while on the sounding board with the other hand.'[17] To some, it was 'ugliness in the extreme' and the composer was hissed,[18] but Gwen was thrilled by his originality.[19]

Sitsky's compositions inspired her to write 'New Music', a poem she copied out by hand, signed and sent to him as a gift. In this poem, traditional musical forms are equated with traditional ways of doing, being and thinking, while Sitsky's radical compositions 'beckon the mind to move / out of the smiling context / of what's known'. While we allow ourselves to be soothed by the lovely and the familiar, the injustices of our world go unchallenged: 'The beggars' stumps / bang on the stones. Nothing will change.' Music such as Sitsky's compels us to wake up, Gwen believed, and she wanted to create poetry that would do the same.

◆ ◆ ◆

The world was entering upon a time of ferment, and Gwen was urgently aware of the need for change. As the Cold War arms race gathered speed, nuclear annihilation seemed not merely possible but probable. The pollution of the natural world was also beginning to seem dangerous and even irreversible. It was conceivable to Gwen that her children would be 'the last generation of men'.[20] At the same time, media coverage of the Vietnam War was 'casting a cloud over everything'.[21] Gwen knew that if the war went on, her sons would be at risk of being called up to fight, and felt 'the terrible sadness that must have struck women at the beginning of the 1914 war; it seems so much the same: one is so helpless, trapped in a waking nightmare'.[22] When she heard the news of the 'senseless murder of Kennedy' at the end of 1963, it seemed the whole world was 'clouded now'.[23] It was impossible, insane, to go on doing the same things in the same ways, and yet she could not see how to write poems that would have the world-rending force of music like Sitsky's.

Even if she had known how to proceed, she was struggling to find the time. 'I have needs I cannot express: for solitude, TOTAL concentration with no responsibility about domestic matters and yet certainty that all is well with the family,' she told Tony.[24] She toyed with the idea of simply neglecting her household work and leaving her family to pick up the slack, but could not bring herself to do it. 'No use letting everyone live in disorder; I know families where the mother pursues her own ends while the kids make do, and they don't appeal to me,' she wrote. Yet 'I feel that I MUST write some of the half-apprehended poems beating in my brain – poems that really try to grapple with my fear of physical annihilation.' Her consolation was the hope that this very tension – between her need to write and her need to take care of her family – was the thing that would make her poems 'better than those of the word-cooks who have all day to write in'.[25]

She was very aware that this was a gendered issue. All around she saw women struggling with the same problem: a lack of 'time, solitude, quiet . . . to serve the wandering spirit that may never come again'.[26] It was a topic Gwen had discussed with her husband, who took a detached view. 'Bill says mildly that we are in an intermediate stage – not yet enjoying the full freedom that women will have, and still striving against old prejudices,' she reported to Tony. Her own sense was that women's difficult domestic situation had been exacerbated by social and technological change. 'Two decades ago we'd have had servants or at least a "country girl" to help,' she wrote. 'Now we have electric gadgets & no sympathy at all.'[27]

Bill was ever more preoccupied with his work – which continued to attract interest from other linguists, particularly in the United States – and as unwilling as ever to socialise beyond his immediate circle of long-established friends and colleagues. 'Bill lives among his cards and indexes (indices?) and despises poetry,' Gwen wrote to Ann in August 1963. This did not overly bother her. 'Who wants one of those ghastly households where both partners are doctors or syntactic analysts or analytic syntacticians; cross-fertilization seems better, the crosser the better.' There was friction between them, but as she insouciantly remarked, 'apart from incompatibility' they got on 'very well'. She did feel that he had a lot to put up with: 'it must be terrible to be married to a Lady Poet. I'm glad I'm not.'[28]

As she moved into her mid-forties, she worried about menopause, reviving her old fear that a woman's reproductive cycle was 'bound up with creative energy in a real way, not just metaphorically'.[29] It was all very well to tell herself she would be able to settle to her writing once the children were grown, but what if she should find that her creative impetus disappeared with her youth? One day, she had a long talk to Jim McAuley about these worries.[30] Far from reassuring her, he told her that it wouldn't matter if she stopped writing, since her real work was to bear and raise children. It was 'surely better to bring persons to maturity than poems', he told her. It was cold comfort for someone who fervently hoped to be able to do both. Her poetry gurus were all men, and they could not tell her what she really wanted to hear: that her fears were groundless. The lack of older female poets in the literary pantheon meant that she had few role models and had to feel her way.

Despite the success of her pseudonyms, she was still getting rejected: the three poems she submitted for *Australian Poetry 1963* were all knocked back. 'I am not to be represented. Jesus!' she fumed. 'Most editors, I suppose, down-grade the lady poets.'[31] As 1963 wore on and her book failed to appear, she was increasingly unhappy. 'Sometimes I'm too sad to write even to you, and that is sad indeed,' she told Tony.[32] 'Hobart is slowly killing me with its snot-grey skies and eternal chill.'[33] There was also her physical exhaustion from housework, her lack of solitude and a plague of 'terrible dreams' of death.

As well, she was increasingly in pain from a benign tumour in her rectum – an annoyingly humorous locus for suffering, which she could not resist exploiting. When she consulted the doctor, she told Eddie, he 'shoved an electric light up my bum and said: "I've heard you're a poet, Mrs Harwood." O the things that happen to lady poets!'[34] She was scheduled to go into hospital in late July to have the tumour removed. To Eddie and Ann, she was determinedly lighthearted about the impending surgery. 'I'm going to sing obscene songs just before they give me the anaesthetic; make the most of any situation, that's my motto,' she told Eddie, signing herself 'Lady Directress, the Sorebum School of Poetry'.[35] But to Tony, she spoke openly of her fear of surgery and of the days 'of pain and worry' as she prepared to go into hospital. She could not leave the family even briefly without extensive preparation, and she was frantically readying 'piles of food & clean clothes' to tide them over in her absence.[36]

The surgery went well, but the aftermath was 'painful beyond belief'.[37] As with her last surgery, she amused her friends with stories of her bad behaviour after the anaesthetic:

> When I woke [after the surgery] I was in an absolute furnace of pain. I just couldn't believe it. Somebody had inserted a red hot nail studded club right up my behind. I began to bellow "Jesus, my bum's sore", "O Jesus my bum's on fire", "Christ my bum!"[38]

To Tony she spoke earnestly of her suffering, both bodily and mental. Once she was home again, she confessed to a deeply unsettling dream in which she was in a 'bower of green ferns' and began to shout for God to show himself. God did not appear, but the ferns replied: 'We are always here, the gentle presences,' they said, and began to recite Rilke. Leaving the bower, she walked into 'a dry street where feathery plumes of grass lay flat on bare ground'. Here, she experienced the agonising return of her 'old tyrannic grief' over Tom Pick: 'I saw clearly that the price of that love was too high, and that I was a fool.'[39] It was the first time she had allowed herself to consider this deflating possibility. She had always held to her romantic conviction that the short love affair had been sublime and glorious, destined in some way, and that the suffering it had caused had made her a better artist. Now, her subconscious betrayed her: she found herself forced to confront what she feared to be 'the truth'. 'Well,' she concluded, gamely, 'it is something to be stripped of illusion, even by a dream.'

Though her doctor assured her she was 'mending nicely' after the surgery and would soon be 'as good as new or better', she felt that her spiritual wounds would take much longer to heal. 'I can't seem to recover and turn outwards to the world,' she told Tony despondently. 'Perhaps, like a sick animal, I need to be alone.'[40] She finished the letter with: 'I dream of Queensland, of warmth, ease, and (I suppose) irresponsibility; once you have children you have no real privacy: the spirit cannot claim what it ought to have. Still, I must sit in my cage & sing.'

◆ ◆ ◆

Finally, there were hopeful signs for the book. Late in April 1963, Beatrice Davis contacted her to say that they would bring the book out in August and invited her to add some new work if she wanted to. Gwen took the opportunity to replace some early poems with others written in the two years since she had submitted the manuscript, including some she had composed for Rex, as well as what she considered to be the best of her new poems, 'The Wine is Drunk' and 'Alter Ego'. Among those she cut were two Tom Pick poems, 'Frontier Guards' and 'Tom the Rhymer'. She corrected the page proofs in early August, but the book still did not go to print. She was deeply disheartened when it failed to appear in September, as announced. It was already 'too late for overseas posting for Christmas', and 'too late for my inclusion in the Penguin Guide [to Australian Literature] (which closes at 1962)'. 'I feel very depressed about this,' she confessed. Finally, in early December, her publisher wrote to tell her that the book would come out early in 1964, 'when it will get the attention it deserves'.[41] Gwen felt defeated by this 'bastardry': 'What utter contempt they must hold me in!'

Gwen Harwood, Augusta Road, 1963

She was somewhat cheered, however, when a very favourable review from her old enemy David Moody appeared in the December issue of *Meanjin*. Moody found in her best poems – 'about half in the book' – an 'impressively strong and challenging originality'. He was particularly taken by the way her work 'challenges received emotions'. Oddly, he found her poetry peculiarly 'feminine' in its 'instinctive rejections of egotism'. In this, he felt, her poems were 'assuredly alien to the male temper'. He concluded by declaring the volume 'the most exciting book of poems by an Australian poet since A.D. Hope's *The Wandering Islands*'.[42] To Tony, Gwen would not admit to taking pleasure in the review,[43] but to the Hoddinotts, she allowed herself to show some excitement, noting that Moody had done her proud, and asking a few weeks later whether they had seen 'the beaut review in *Meanjin* by David Moody? That should set me up with all the poetry lovers.'[44] She had always said that her book would 'either make its way in the world or seenck [*sic*] down and die', and this seemed to be a sign that it would make its way. Even so, as publication neared, she felt 'particularly vulnerable', bracing herself for a rain of 'poison darts' from the critics.[45]

She was beginning to plan her next book, which would include 'all the good Geyer & Stone poems, and the new Harwoods'.[46] Because of the long delay in publishing her first volume, she already had enough new poems for a second, and this gave her confidence. She need not write anything else in the next little while, unless the spirit moved her. This was a relief because, for the moment, at least, she did not *want* to write. This feeling only intensified when, on New Year's Eve, her grandmother died. Maud was eighty-four, and had been in a Queensland nursing home for two years after suffering a series of strokes early in 1962. Nevertheless, her death was a profound shock for Gwen. She was seized with regret that she had not gone to visit Maud in her Brisbane nursing home, just to see her one last time.[47] 'I cannot remember a time when she was not *there* in the world,' she wrote to Tony a few days later. 'Half my life is gone with her.'[48]

Maud's death had a powerful catalysing effect. All at once, Gwen felt that her life was intolerable. She could no longer bear to spend her days shut up in the house at Augusta Road, with nothing to distract her from either her grief or the agonisingly slow progress of her book towards publication. She had been thinking for some time about returning to work. Now, with her grandmother gone, it suddenly seemed absolutely imperative that she get a job.[49] She set about convincing Bill and the children that she should rejoin the workforce, making 'knotty arguments' to 'tie the family to the idea.'[50] These arguments centred on the financial contribution she could make, and the assurance that she would keep everything running smoothly on the domestic front. Early in January, she wrote to ask Tony for a reference that would assert that she had been doing his typing for years with impressive speed and accuracy.[51] Two weeks later, she was employed. She was to work for an eye specialist in central Hobart as a stenographer, and would also do the accounts and give a hand at reception.

To the Hoddinotts, she announced that she was giving up poetry for 'commerce': 'I'm seeck [*sic*] of being poor and having one lipstick.'[52] She added that she had 'completely lost interest' in her book and was looking forward only to 'earning money & buying things (knives and forks, chairs, a good piano, rare birds, lipsticks).' To Tony, she explained her 'sudden decision to go & work' as 'an attempt at escape.'[53] To Vin, she said that she felt 'that the poetry I loved has left me, and I may as well waste my life in one way as in another.'[54] To Eddie she gave her most succinct and yet most comprehensive explanation. Her number-one reason for going to work, she told him, was the death of her grandmother, who 'understood me completely & encompassed my whole life'. Her second reason was that she was 'completely written out: when this happens you either repeat your successes or concoct rubbish that is no more alive for being well written'. Her third reason was cash. 'I'm saving enough money to get outa this turdy island.'[55]

Beneath the burst of activity was an agonising depth of sorrow over Maud's death. She felt she was 'on the very edge of physical breakdown': 'my head felt as if it would *literally* burst (and what would fly out, I wonder?) and my whole body seemed a torment to me; I have come out in a crop of intolerably itchy hives; I'd like to stand in the garden and howl at the heavens.'[56] She was plagued, once again, with nightmares about death.

In one such dream, she was happily preparing a meal when she 'remembered that my grandmother was dead':

> I fell into a heap of knotted string. While I was trying to unwind it from my feet, I fell through the space where my grandmother had been in time and found myself in another dimension of time where things were what they would be forever. In a small garden were cages of animals and birds, and I found myself looking at a cage made of a soap box in which a mother duck and one duckling were tightly curled; the ducks' feathers were of dazzling whiteness, and I touched them through the wire expecting to feel softness, but they were dry and

rough. Then I saw that the bottom of the cage was covered with salt instead of straw, and that the ducks, looking for food, had swallowed some of the salt and were dying of thirst.[57]

It was as though the world she had trusted to provide for her had turned hostile. Instead of bread, she would be given a stone, as the biblical phrase had it. The death of her grandmother was the death of her illusions of safety.

A few weeks later, she dreamed that she herself had died and was buried 'in an obscure corner of a railway yard behind a fowlhouse'. Trying to dress herself, she found that she had no body; trying to embrace her daughter, Mary, she found she had no arms. She was seized with terror that the hens would scratch up her hair 'and the children would see my remains'.[58] The chooks and ducks associated with her earliest childhood had become entangled in her unconscious with her Granny's death; the fowl yard was no longer a place of happy sanctuary but a nightmare.

When her job began, her mood started to shift. The joy of her liberation from home outweighed even the joy of finally seeing her book in print after more than two years of delays. She received her author's copies in the mail on 4 February 1964,[59] the day before she was due to begin work. 'You wouldn't know me: cool, crisp, HAPPY,' she crowed to the Hoddinotts.[60] 'I love the job & can hardly wait to crack out in the morning. I rise at 6.30, do some of the endless washing, cut 5 lunches, cook the breakfast, wash up, go to work (hooray! beaut!) come home & serve the meat & veg which B[ill] has put on, wash up, do some cooking towards the next day, do any vital ironing or mending, & drop dead till 6.30 am. I love it. No human power could get me to stay home all day again.' A month after beginning work, her greatest fear was of being 'confined to barracks' once more, 'instead of setting off to work in the real world'.[61] She had been having more health problems – in the wake of her hysterectomy, she needed 'extensive pelvic repair'[62] – but she was not prepared to take time off work for surgery and recovery if it meant risking her job.

Doing the double shift was taking a toll: she was 'nearly asleep on my feet' on weekdays, and spent her weekends frantically catching up on the housework.[63] But she was proud of herself. She had never liked being classified on official forms as 'housewife', and was much happier being able to describe herself as '"Dr Waterworth's Secretary" or "Medical Stenographer"'.[64] In this, she was unconventional. As the Tasmanian writer Margaret Scott notes, the phenomenon of 'married women going out to work' was considered a 'threat' in Hobart in the early 1960s – along with 'the miniskirt, modern art, eating in restaurants, . . . *Lolita* and *Lady Chatterley's Lover*'.[65] Gwen had always seen 'bourgeois' values as the enemy,[66] though she was cautious about how she presented herself, afraid of public shaming. In this case, however, she was happy to ally herself with the radicals.

Apart from the change in her status, she also enjoyed the job itself. Unlike the War Damage Commission, Dr Waterworth's clinic gave her 'lots of real work' to do.[67] She did fantasise about the kinds of disruptions that could be wrought by red-bearded dwarfs in such an environment – 'I have unlimited power: I could, by sending out the right cards, arrange for 1000 people to descend on the surgery at 11 a.m. . . . [or] leave old Waterworks without a lunch hour on any day this month'[68] – but she managed to limit her anarchic impulses to listening to *The Goon Show*, which made her 'shiver with rapture'.[69] She took a lively interest in the 'streams of patients' and their stories, and relished the social interaction.[70] 'I see there are others like myself in the world, and am comforted,' she wrote to Tony.[71] She also admired her 'curt and forbidding' boss, who had once been a serious student of the piano, and set herself to win his friendship; the other employee, Sister Warren, was eccentric enough to keep Gwen well supplied with comic anecdotes. Having money of her own transformed her sense of herself. As she told Ann, it was amazing 'the confidence that 10/- an hour buys . . . It still gives me a feeling of absolute joy to walk into (say) Fuller's and buy (say) a Penguin.'[72] She had no time in her new life for writing, but this didn't bother her. She had been only half-joking when she told the Hoddinotts she was giving up poetry. 'I might not publish any more,' she told Tony, in response to his questions about what she was writing. 'I can only repeat myself at the moment: better to get out into the cutthroat world for a few years.'[73]

◆ ◆ ◆

When Gwen received the advance copies of her book, the first thing she did was bundle one off to Tony. 'It's a beautiful production,' she assured him. 'The cover itself is printed with the design of the dust-jacket. The type is beaut. I couldn't be more delighted. All the years of waiting faded away when I held it in my hands at last.'[74] The book's cover featured a clean, contemporary, abstract design in cream, soft green and grey, with the simple title *Poems*. The jacket flap declared that 'here is a new and significant voice in Australian literature'. 'You'll be amazed at its beauty,' she told the Hoddinotts. 'A&R have done a super job.'[75]

Letters of praise and congratulation arrived from Alec Hope, Vin Buckley, Vivian Smith, Tom Shapcott and other friends, old and new. Vin's lavish words made her smile, remembering 'his original whack at me in the early days'. But 'he was right, then', she told Tony. 'I have been slowly growing away from the old encrusted ornate adjective-hung style. God knows when I'll write again, but when I do I hope to keep the old ache & anger but match the calm energy of the natural world'.[76]

Early in May, the ABC ran a program on her poetry by Wilson Blackman, a student of Vin's, who praised the 'unmistakable quality' of her work, 'so personally felt, so strong, so free of milk-and-watery sentimentalism'. He gave her book a rave, calling it 'one of the most important volumes of poetry to appear in Australia for many years'. He also blew the lid on Francis Geyer and Miriam Stone, definitively outing Gwen as their progenitor, and recounting other instances of her 'pranksterish behaviour'. 'Not since the golden age of the Ern Malley hoax have we had such an entertaining personality in the literary world here,' he declared.[77]

Other reviews, as they came trickling in, were uniformly positive. All the major literary magazines published something, though most included her book as part of a 'job lot' with other volumes published in the past twelve months, coupling her most often with Chris Wallace-Crabbe and John Blight. In *Quadrant*, the poet and critic T.H. Jones declared her 'almost the best poet writing in Australia nowadays'. In *The Bulletin*, Harry Heseltine singled out her *Poems* as 'the most substantial and intense' of the three books he was reviewing, saying he was 'struck' again and again by 'the originality and power with which her language renders feeling and thought'. In *Southerly*, S.E. Lee wrote that it was 'hard to realize that this is Gwen Harwood's first collection' and spoke of her 'astonishing versatility', 'complexity of theme and variety of statement'. In *Australian Book Review*, Flexmore Hudson praised her book's 'verbal felicity, its range of experience and its depth of thought' and found in the poems 'a sinewy toughness and a power that are rare in a woman's poetry'. In *Westerly*, Peter Jeffery was equally laudatory: 'Highly intelligent, she responds with equal brilliance to themes on art, music, children, love', and maintains 'the human touch' even in her 'most abstract moments', seeing 'poetry and art as liberators in "the dark chasm of the heart"'.

Gwen read the reviews eagerly, devouring the 'lavish hand-out of praise' with satisfaction.[78] The only piece that disappointed her was a 'snotty' review by Evan Jones in *Prospect*.[79] Gwen had met Evan when Jim McAuley invited him to Hobart as a guest of the English department, and they had started up a lively correspondence. She considered him a friend, which made his 'patronising tone' in this review all the more offensive. But though she liked Evan, she had never admired his poems, telling Eddie Tanner a year earlier that 'Evan is (I think) not a poet and hardly ever takes off in spite of long runs & spread pinions'.[80] His review played her off against his friend Chris Wallace-Crabbe, concluding that while Gwen offered 'a greater brilliancy of phrase', she was less technically competent than the younger poet, who had 'a surer craftsmanship' and showed a 'formal sophistication pretty well without precedent in Australian poetry'. Retailing her resentment to Tom Shapcott, she quoted a couple of lines from one of Jones' own poems to make her point that someone who wrote so badly himself should not 'presume to criticise Lady Gwendoline's rhythms'.[81]

Yet the criticism did not sting in the way it would have a couple of years earlier. She felt that she had proved herself with this book and now had no need to do more than swat mildly at impercipient critics. Besides, she was too busy to stew. As well as working, she had decided to learn to drive. Her eldest son had recently gained his driver's licence and on weekends chauffeured the family to beaches and picnic spots in his second-hand VW.[82] For the first time, it dawned on Gwen that if she could drive, she would be able to escape suburbia.[83] Not only that, but she would be free of buses and taxis and kind friends' offers of transport. She began driving lessons in September and passed her test in November, but to her chagrin, Bill and her eldest son barred her from the car for fear she would damage 'their rotten gear box'.[84] It would be another year before the family bought a car specifically for her use, another VW, a 1958 model 'of a deep blue colour'. By this time, she had lost her confidence and had to take more driving lessons. Even after she got behind the wheel, her confidence faltered when she drove with Bill, who had a tendency to lecture her on her faults as a driver. 'I guess husbands & wives should never drive in the same car,' she told the Hoddinotts resignedly.[85] She found driving hugely liberating. Not only did her car give her a new independence but it was also a space of her own; she would come to think of it as 'a kind of turtle-shell or snail's house into which I can withdraw.' By May 1966, she was referring to herself as 'a Hardened Motorist (O the expense!)' who 'burn[s] around just like everyone else'.[86]

◆ ◆ ◆

By August, Gwen was forced to concede that she could not maintain her punishing schedule of paid and unpaid work. Too often she found herself 'down in the cold sloppy laundry at 9 pm'.[87] After some negotiation, she was able to reduce her hours so that she could finish at 3 p.m. each day, and have Thursday afternoons off.[88] Though she was sorry to sacrifice her full-time salary, the new hours suited her better; she was excited that she'd have time to play the piano, and the children were excited that she would have time to make puddings.[89]

The change turned out to be fortuitous. For several months, Bill had been increasingly tired and run-down, and he was losing weight. In early October, at Gwen's insistence, he went to a GP. There followed 'several hellish days with doctors and pathologists' before he was diagnosed with diabetes.[90] He would need daily insulin injections for the rest of his life. Gwen was deeply shocked. Bill was not yet fifty and had always been indefatigable, whether building boats, working in the garden or hiking up Mount Wellington. Much as she often resented him, she had taken for granted that he would always be there. Now they both had to come to terms with the idea that he had 'an incurable disease'.[91] Gwen immediately assumed responsibility for Bill's diet. She learned all she could about insulin and glucose and their complicated dance, and by early November, was writing proudly to Tony that she was 'now a wizard at diabetic cookery & can get you a diabetic meal so delicious you wouldn't notice the difference'.[92] It was a big source of anxiety, however.[93] Those 'terrifying moments of insulin shock' could strike out of the blue – or in unpredictable response to a cold or overexertion, and she felt she needed to be ever-vigilant. But by December Bill was feeling better, and getting back to his usual tasks – 'marking his papers & tending his garden, and eating heartily of meat, veg, salads & saccharine desserts'.[94]

For the first time since they were married, they decided to take a family holiday. With the extra income from Gwen's job, they could afford to hire a cottage at the beach for a fortnight. They boated and fished, and Gwen revelled in days spent walking on the shore, reading, and playing cards and Scrabble with the children. It was mostly too cold to swim, but just being by the sea was restorative: 'I love wandering at the edge of the surf in a kind of elemental balance with myself & the world.'[95] She and Bill were 'never happier than by the sea', she told Tony.[96] By the time they returned to Augusta Road for Christmas, Bill's diabetes had stabilised.

After a year of grief and illness, Gwen was still not writing. She was in what she described as an 'empty tin-can period', rattling 'like a tin in a windy gutter', hardly able even to imagine writing again.[97] Vin assured her that it was natural to feel this way after the 'personal watershed' of her book. 'You are right not to want to write at the moment, I think,' he told her with gentle paternalism. 'When the reviews are all in, forget them, then (gradually) forget the book itself, and you'll find yourself writing again, better than ever.'[98] Gwen was not so sure. 'I've never been so empty of poetry,' she told Tony.[99] But in September, she was offered an artistic collaboration she could not turn down. Larry Sitsky, whose music had so impressed her at the composers' conference the previous year, wanted her to write the libretto for his new one-act opera. It was an opportunity to write without the pressure of forging a new poetic path for herself. It was also, in a way, a harking back to her first literary efforts, in her late teens and early twenties, as a playwright, and she was eager to try her hand at something more dramatic than poetry. Besides, how could she pass up the chance to work with musicians again?

Sitsky's project was an operatic version of Edgar Allan Poe's short story 'The Fall of the House of Usher'.[100] Rex Hobcroft had commissioned it, along with two others, for a second national conference, which was to be held in Hobart in 1965. Gwen had reservations: she could not see, she told Tony, how to write an opera with only three characters, one of whom was 'dead until the last minute'.[101] She warned Larry that she feared the story was 'quite inoperable' but assured him she would 'love to have a go at it'.[102] As Larry was based in Brisbane, the collaboration would be conducted entirely by letter.

Gwen had heard many an opera, and felt that her experiences as a chorister and, even more so, as an accompanist, would stand her in good stead as a librettist – they had given her an ear for what was 'singable'.[103] But she had 'no practical experience with the theatre at all', so putting together a draft was a challenge.[104] Larry told her that for half an hour of music he needed the equivalent of ten minutes of spoken text, but gave her no other guidance. He told her only to 'feel [her] way into the story and then send me a text'. This is what she did. She 'lived with the text' until she had a sense of how it could work on stage, and then wrote a draft, set out like a playscript, with characters, scenes and actions, very much as though she were doing a stage adaptation of Poe's story. Most of the lines she gave her three characters were not poems: they did not have a formal stanzaic structure, and they did not always rhyme. But they were poetic in the sense that they were metaphorical and allusive, dark and mysterious.

She sent the draft off to Larry, who promptly wrote back telling her what he liked and what he didn't. Some of her words, he told her, he could not 'set'. She tried again, and he fed back his responses. This process continued for several months. Gwen saw herself as the 'servant' of the composer and willingly sacrificed anything he did not like. 'Yes of course I'll rewrite the ballad section,' she told him on a postcard in January 1965. 'Please do whatever you like with the text . . . Anytheeng.'[105] Gradually, through trial and error, she was able to work out what Larry wanted. Once she had 'found the kind of cadence that excited his musical ear', she was able to write him 'a text that he set straight through; he was happy with it'.[106] Even then, she had doubts. 'I wish I felt happy about the libretto, but I know it's bad,' she told Tony in April 1965, when Larry's part of the opera was 'really underway'. 'I just couldn't see the story as theatre.'[107]

Her first look at Larry's score did not reassure her. It was 'utterly incomprehensible to me as music', she told Tony. She could not imagine how the tenor would 'sing the vocal line, let alone memorise it'.[108] In addition, Larry was experimenting with tape recorders (then cutting-edge technology) to add layers of sound, including soprano and alto voices played at double speed. Gwen was not sure how this was going to work, and told Eddie that Sitsky was 'either a genius or a crackpot'.[109] She worried that he would once again be 'hissed' by his audience. The other two operas commissioned for the conference, one by James Penberthy and the other by Margaret Sutherland, seemed to have 'reasonable scores – I fear all the fury will fall on Sitsky'. But once Larry arrived in early August and rehearsals began, she was swept up in all the excitement. She took a sick day from work to attend the first rehearsal, and went to as many others as she could fit in around her working day. 'I felt tremendous joy to be back among musicians with their crankiness and their crazy jokes and their brilliant responses.'[110] As she came to know the score, hearing it six or seven times during rehearsal week, she began to appreciate it. Her final judgement was that it was 'a masterpiece';[111] Sitsky was most definitely not a crackpot.

The opera was 'triumphantly successful' in performance: 'everything went right for the occasion, and it was wonderfully effective'.[112] The singers were 'splendid', especially Norman Yemm as Usher, 'who grappled with the difficult music & acted superbly'. Far from hissing the composer, the audience responded enthusiastically. 'We had such applause that I nearly wept

with joy – I had to take calls (stood up in my place & beamed all round).'
She and Bill were invited to have drinks with the governor and his wife:
'We shook the viceregal hands and had whisky and gin, and I was showered
with congratulations by all present; lovely!'

The performance was recorded by the ABC and later shown on television, to her renewed delight. She was particularly happy with the duet
'between Rod and Mad (as the orchestral players called them)', which
'everybody liked'. The scene was played 'molto incestuoso', as Gwen put it:
'Usher is practically on top of her while they sing.'[113] Gleefully, she reported
to Vivian and Sybille a witty complaint about Sitsky's 'way-out music' made
by 'ribald ABC musicians': 'There's not a common chord in the whole piece;
in fact Usher and his sister are the only things in root position in this work.'

The experience was so positive she was eager to repeat it. She and Larry
began to make plans for a new opera, this time a comic one.[114] A year later,
James Penberthy expressed interest in working with her on an operatic
version of the bushranger novel *Robbery Under Arms*. A whole new career
direction was opening up.

Generation of '68

When there's nothing but Cumulus under your feet
and after the journey nobody to greet
and the crazy old engine is missing a beat
*   and ocean is crawling beneath her*
and you know your life jacket's not under your seat
*   then trust Father Aether.*

Gwen Harwood, Letter to Norman Talbot, 3 November 1974
(to the tune of 'The Times They Are a-Changin'')

IN OCTOBER 1966, AFTER TWENTY-ONE YEARS OF EXILE, GWEN returned at last to her beloved Brisbane – though only for a flying visit. She had heard through friends of her mother's that all was not well with Joe and Agnes.[1] Her father, who was losing his sight, was increasingly 'morose and difficult to get on with', and Agnes was struggling to care for him. Gwen was worried about them. She felt sure Agnes would 'crack up if she is forced to stay looking after Dad, who by all accounts is depressed and unwilling to try and make a new life for himself'.[2] Flights to Brisbane were expensive, but Gwen now had money of her own to draw on. She booked the trip. She felt guilty about 'going off on [her] own', but the children were all getting older – the twins, her youngest, were teenagers, while John had just turned twenty – and she knew they could manage without her for a week.

The city to which she returned was very different from the one she had left in 1945. Over the years of her absence, Brisbane had become in her mind a lost paradise, a wondrous place of warmth and light and joie de vivre. Almost unconsciously, she had come to feel that if she could just get back there, she would be happy again, able to 'recapture something (I don't know what it was) that would stand between me & death'. Now she discovered that the city she so loved was nowhere to be found. Brisbane looked 'ugly, dry, downright nasty after Tasmania'. The suburbs sprawled 'mile after mile, many of them like settings for a Tennessee Williams play, with the real deep South look'. The pristine beaches of memory were 'utterly changed, spoilt & suburban or run to mangroves'.[3]

She and Agnes drove around the city to visit all her mother's old friends and this, too, Gwen found depressing. The women were 'gay old devils in their 60s carousing on hot scones & pavlova & arranging "functions" – the odd husband appeared like a pet animal'. Gwen tried to lift Joe out of his misery, encouraging him to learn Braille and embrace what was left of his life. She also met some of the young poets with whom she had been corresponding: Tom Shapcott, Rodney Hall and David Rowbotham. As she told Tom afterwards, 'My visit would have been terribly sad without you & Rodney'. She was relieved when she finally boarded the plane back to Hobart. As she returned to dark, chilly, chronically uptight Tasmania, she felt, for the first time, that 'my home is really here'.[4]

A side benefit of her trip was the chance to see Tony Riddell again. She flew home via Melbourne, and though she had only an hour at the airport, he drove out to see her. They were both 'rather nervous' about meeting again in the flesh, after so much ink had been spilled between them. In their letters, they painted a glowing picture of their friendship, and there was a danger the reality would not live up to the narrative. But in one another's company, their fears fell away: 'We were (we agreed) exactly the same, and rejoiced to find that time has no power over our friendship.'[5]

The trip to her home town also loosened Gwen's poetic tongue. Over the past year or so, she had had lots of ideas, but struggled to turn them into poetry: they came out 'lumpish & dead'. She was lacking the lightning strike – what she once described as the 'mysterious' moment when 'the mind suddenly begins to fuse together the odd scraps and pieces one has laboriously kept' and turns them into a whole.[6] She relived this transformation in dreams but could not reach it in the waking world.[7] But now she found herself writing a new poem in her old 'formal' style.[8] 'In Brisbane' explored her sense of the infinitesimal yet unbridgeable distance between past and present. On the banks of the Brisbane River, she had encountered the girl she had been – 'my ghost, . . . most intimate stranger' – on the other side of the 'glass of time' through which she now looked. That bright girl's future had become her own difficult past, filled with 'unlooked-for love, undreamed-of pain'.

◆ ◆ ◆

Instead of her own poetry, she had been working that year on *Robbery Under Arms* with James Penberthy. Three years older than Gwen, Jim was known among his fellow composers as 'the wild man from WA'.[9] He was eager to see Australia develop a musical tradition distinctively its own, and was desperately impatient with the public's preference for European classical music. In Western Australia, where he co-founded the West Australian Ballet with Kira Bousloff, he wrote and produced many ballets drawing on Aboriginal legends, and his 1958 opera, *Dalgerie*, with a libretto by Mary Durack, was described as 'the first Australian opera on an Aboriginal theme'.[10] He thought it likely he had Aboriginal heritage himself – he believed that his grandmother, Mary, was an Aboriginal woman, though it was never spoken of in his family.[11] Having seen Sitsky's *Fall of the House of Usher*, he wrote to Gwen in mid-1966 to ask if she would collaborate with him on a new Australian opera.

Gwen suggested adapting Rolf Boldrewood's nineteenth-century bushranger novel, featuring the villainous Captain Starlight. Jim approved, and Gwen immediately began to rough out a plan. Within a couple of days she had written the first act, setting it out like a play, as she had with *Usher*, in a series of scenes with briefly delineated settings and characters. Boldrewood's story was much more dramatic than Poe's Gothic tale, with scenes of cattle rustling and highway robbery, and with three acts, she had more room to move.[12] The biggest problem, she reported to Larry, was working out how to keep 'the horses & horse-manure offstage': how to tell the story in a dramatic way that would not be impossible to stage.[13] Her text was spare, more prose than poetry, though it had its lyric moments. She did not agonise over the draft, having learned from Larry that the most important thing was to get something down on paper for the composer to work with. Sending Jim her first attempt at the first act, she urged him to tell her 'if it is the sort of text you want; style is no problem to me – the real work is reducing the massive sprawling narrative to workable proportions'. By the end of September, she was typing up a complete draft for Jim to submit to the Elizabethan Theatre Trust Opera Company for funding.[14] Then it was just a matter of waiting for a judgement from the trust's producer, Stefan Haag. Early in 1967, she learned that they had not been successful.

This knockback was far less painful than the early rejections of her poetry. She had little at stake, since her libretto was only a minor part (in her estimation) of the project, and neither her career nor her reputation would stand or fall on the opera's success. It was a disappointment, after all the work she had put in, but she had enjoyed working with Jim and was confident they would work together again. She did not consider him a genius like Larry, but she admired his work, and felt that in many ways, they were on the same wavelength. Like her, Jim was angry about Vietnam, worried about pollution, intrigued by the moon landing and excited by the peace-and-love vibe of the rapidly burgeoning hippy movement. He was also – a supreme qualification – enchanted by Gwen's words. He would always consider her 'Australia's premier librettist', declaring towards the end of his life that she had 'written most of the great words set to Australian music'.[15]

Their correspondence was lively, and quickly became affectionate. It was also flirtatious – even before they met. In the early 1970s, when Gwen sent him a joke card purporting to be a photograph of herself, he replied: 'O Divinity, O most beautiful among the muses, Diana Vitrix – I liked your picture on the card – marry me by mail – instantly!'[16] He added that he had just finished setting some words she had sent him: 'You really fire me Mumma so let's go.' To this she replied merrily: 'Thanks, just what I needed to cheer me – a long-distance proposal' – and promised to send him a 'true picture' of herself soon, along with more 'deathless words'.[17] When he sent her a brochure that featured a photograph of him, she took it into work with her and reported that she had been 'happily falling in love with you for the past three hours – by nightfall I should be absolutely besotted!'[18] As for their collaboration, she assured him she was 'entirely at your service: beat me daddy with a groovy beat'.[19]

◆ ◆ ◆

While she was working on *Robbery Under Arms*, she published very little poetry. In 1965, she published no Harwoods at all, only one Geyer and two Stones in Vivian Smith's Tasmanian edition of *Poetry Australia*. The following year, she published another three poems (two, if the two parts of 'Past and Present' are counted as a single poem), all Harwoods, all in the same issue of *Australian Letters*. She did not 'feel like publishing at the moment', she explained to Tony, though she was not giving up on poetry: 'I'm sure that sooner or later I shall find my true voice again & start shaping another world.' In the interim, she took up Scottish dancing with her daughter. 'I am very good at hopping & skipping and always lose my cares when I dance.'[20]

Bill's health was still fluctuating, but he was able to travel to the United States in late 1965 for two months' study leave and, on his return, set off again for a round of academic visits in Canberra, Sydney and Armidale.[21]

Over Christmas that year, the family went to the seaside at Cremorne, and when Gwen had to go back to work, they relocated to Carlton River, closer to Hobart, so that she could drive back and forth each day. She relished returning in the evenings to such a 'remote and peaceful' place. She could sit on the verandah with a glass of wine while the dinner cooked '& watch the fading light. I think this is one of life's great pleasures: to be somewhere at nightfall in absolute stillness'.[22] They returned to Cremorne in May 1966, and Bill's health seemed improved by the downtime. It was a rude shock for everyone when, early in July, he had a hypoglycaemic episode in the middle of the night and had to be rushed, unconscious, to hospital.[23] Gwen feared at first that he had had a stroke. 'John and I thought he was dying – it was terrible,' she lamented to the Hoddinotts.[24] She couldn't help but think about what might have happened if Bill had been alone; he would probably 'have died or been permanently damaged'.[25] From this time on, that fear would always haunt her when they were apart. Even when they were together, she felt she needed to be ever vigilant.[26] Work became an escape from this constant anxiety.[27]

Even as she cared for Bill, Gwen was becoming increasingly critical of the traditional marriage roles she had embraced with fervour twenty years before. 'What [men] *really* want is a dolly to play with AND another to nurse them, that is, when they aren't about their real interests,' she wrote caustically to Ann.[28] While some lamented the gradual changes to women's roles, Gwen was excited by them, seeing 'hopeful signs' in younger men of 'a more liberal outlook'. 'One can only hope,' she wrote in another letter to Ann, 'that the next generation of men will be a bit easier on their wives.'[29] Despite her own struggles, however, and her (partly ironic) admiration for 'the new Woman (glorious, feminine, running smoothly on oral contraceptives)', she still could not quite envisage a world where women might choose, in the natural way of things, not to become wives at all.

In terms of social change more generally, Gwen was mostly on the side of the 'long-hairs', as those forging the flower-power revolution were known. Her eldest son was now of an age to be conscripted, but told her that if he was called up, he would risk jail as a conscientious objector rather than go to war.[30] Gwen was immensely proud of him for this. In June 1966, she added her signature to an anti-war letter signed by many Australian writers that was published in newspapers around the country.[31] She went to anti-war meetings and was more than happy for her children to march in the moratorium protests.[32]

She found it difficult to reconcile her conservative friend Jim McAuley's pro-war stance with the admiration she felt for him as a poet, and spoke derisively of his anti-communist fervour. Yet she could not write him off; as distasteful as his views were, she still loved him. The same was true of Peter Bennie. When she met up with him again in Sydney in 1970, for the first time in twenty-five years, she was dismayed to find him an arch-conservative who discoursed confidently on 'the rightness of the foul war'.[33] Gwen was shaken: she had always had Peter on a pedestal; it was one of the fundamental pillars of her life that he was an exceptional human being, entirely worthy of the passionate love she had lavished upon him. She soon decided that his views, though repugnant, could not change her feelings for him. Listening to Handel before the fire in Peter's sitting room, she thought of how the composer, one of her musical idols, had written 'noble celebratory choruses for the loathsome Hanoverian who massacred the Scots at Culloden'; Handel's repellent politics did not interfere with her enjoyment of his music, and neither would Peter's political views affect her personal response to him.

Gwen, meanwhile, was being drawn into her teenage children's world of pop music and hippy fashion, as well as embracing – though with more irony than she had when she was young – their disenchantment with 'the Establishment'. She did not endorse all aspects of youth culture, objecting to recreational drugs on the grounds that they were dangerous, but she loved its rebellious energy. Several times she borrowed from the rhythms – and even the words – of Bob Dylan's 1964 anthem 'The Times They Are a-Changin'' for impromptu poems. It wasn't only Dylan's music she liked. Several of her children took up the guitar as teenagers, and Gwen loved to sing contemporary folk songs with them. In the late 1970s, she would astonish a young poet at a social gathering by not only recognising his allusion to a Neil Young song but also reciting all the lyrics.[34] To Jim Penberthy, in response to a request for some words he could turn into songs, she asked if he wanted 'a wandering Simon & Garfunkel-type effusion? A Mick Jagger thrust-&-growl? Do tell.'[35] Many years later, she would reflect that living with her children 'through the sixties when they were teenagers broke up all the mental adhesions and rigidities I'd acquired and filled me with confidence'.[36]

◆ ◆ ◆

At the end of 1966, the tight knot of the family configuration loosened when Gwen's eldest child, John, left home to get married. Gwen loved her son's new wife, but she knew it was the beginning of the end of the phase of her life dominated by motherhood. One by one, all her children would leave home, and she dreaded the impending loss, even as she welcomed the freedom it would bring. Towards the end of January 1967, Gwen and Bill and the three younger children went back to their favourite spot at Cremorne for a holiday, spending their time fishing, sailing, eating 'delicious meals cooked on an odd assembly of appliances' and spending hours 'reading hilarious extracts from an old magazine to each other, sand in everything'.[37]

It had been an unusually hot, dry summer after an abnormally wet spring, and when the Harwoods returned to Augusta Road on 5 February, the winds were picking up. Two days later, a number of small fires were burning across south-eastern Tasmania, and as the day grew hotter and the wind fiercer, they began to join up. By the afternoon, they had merged into one massive fire front. Mount Wellington was engulfed and a firestorm raged around Hobart. As the light turned an eerie red, every able-bodied person was coopted to fight the fires. Gwen's second son, Chris, joined the volunteers fighting fires on an adjoining street, and when he did not return for dinner, she and John went out to look for him, the two of them searching 'the blackened streets near the bush', dread in their hearts. It was like the firestorms of World War II that she had read about, she told Tony: 'I saw a whole hillside light up at once and a wall of flame explode a house; the timbers simply flew apart. The wind was so hot nobody could stand in it. Burning branches rained down everywhere.'[38] They found no sign of Chris, but at last, at around nine o'clock that night, he managed to get through on the phone to let them know he was safe.

Several days later, with the fires under control, there were still many unaccounted for. Sixty-four people had died, including four from Lenah Valley, and some nine hundred had been injured on what was soon being called Black Tuesday. Around seven thousand homes had been lost. 'Thank God the children everywhere were in school,' Gwen reflected. 'If they had been wandering about on holidays I'm sure many would have been trapped.'[39]

As well as the human cost, Gwen grieved for the environmental destruction. From her first weeks at Fern Tree, she had loved to walk on Mount Wellington. Now all her beloved wild places were gone. A fortnight after the fires, she drove up to Fern Tree on her lunch break to see the damage.

'From the city to Fern Tree every green leaf is gone,' she wrote to Tony. 'I've never seen utter desolation such as this. The trees used to be alive with birds and the air pure and clear. Everything is gone but a few houses.'[40] Their old house at Fern Tree had burnt to the ground, as had Ann Jennings' childhood home. Gwen stood 'in the ruins of the bush', looking out with a sense of unreality on 'a scene of incredible beauty: the Derwent stretching away to the ocean, the farthest hills of south Bruny Island bluer than the sky. Ruin all round, the distance magnificent.'[41] It seemed impossible that the mountain would ever be able to regenerate. 'I wonder how many of the magnificent myrtle gullies are left . . . Tears were useless; one could only remember the beauty lost for ever.' For perhaps the first time, she felt protective of Hobart. When, a few weeks later, she heard of plans to build 'monstrous blocks of flats in Sandy Bay', she was outraged, fearing that 'what Nature has left of Hobart will be ruined by the Council'. She told Ann that 'the tragedy of the fire has made me realise how truly I belong here'.[42] The feeling was strong, though it would not last.

Gwen Harwood with daughter Mary, Mount Wellington, March 1967

◆ ◆ ◆

In March 1967, Iris Murdoch and her husband, John Bayley, visited Tasmania. Gwen loved Murdoch's novels[43] and was thrilled when the ABC asked if she would conduct a radio interview with the couple. She spent a 'blissful' half-hour with 'La Grande Murdoch'. 'I'm quite drunk with delight at having met her – wonderful woman, someone like Sappho I'm sure,' she told Ann.[44] To Tony, she reported excitedly on Murdoch's bizarre style of dress and 'knotty hair', insisting that she was 'beautiful, and not at all formidable, as I feared she would be'. She and Bayley 'glittered intellectually & their "Dialogue on the Novel" was one of the best things I have ever heard; I generally hate talk about literature, but theirs was excellent'.[45]

The invitation to interview these literary heavyweights was evidence of Gwen's growing stature in Hobart. Immediately after the *Bulletin* hoax, there had been talk of her being blacklisted by the ABC; now, she was working for them. As she had hoped, the publication of her book had cemented her reputation, and she felt it was time to follow up with a second volume. Early in 1967, she began to put together a manuscript, made up of poems that had mostly been written before 1964, when her first book was published. She had decided to gather in her pseudonymous poems, including nineteen Francis Geyers (of which nine were Kröte poems) and seven Miriam Stones. Among the Geyers were several she had originally written as hoax poems – the very ones she had derided editors such as the hapless Clem Christesen and the arrogant Jim McAuley for being foolish enough to publish. She told Tony with grand insouciance that the poems had improved with time: 'On re-reading them after some years I found they had gathered power, not lost it; I writ better than I knew at the time.'[46] Also among the Geyers were a handful of poems that had sprung from her affair with Tom Pick, including the heavily disguised break-up poem 'Ebb-tide'. The poems in the last third of the book, published under her own name, included some of those she had written for Rex Hobcroft in 1962 and 1963, as well as those based on her dreams of Vera Cottew. She told Tony that she knew the new manuscript was 'not as good as the first book – that was written as I cannot write again; but I hope to gather myself together for the third book and produce something different and better'.[47]

Despite the critical success of her first volume, she was not confident that Angus & Robertson would accept her second. She admitted to Tony that if they rejected it, she would probably 'have a period of complete self-doubt'. Was she merely deluding herself that she was a real poet, like the Victorian blockbuster versifiers Ella Wheeler Wilcox and Felicia Hemans she loved to mock? 'I bet they wrapped themselves in the bardic mantle, and concluded that the fit was excellent.' This time, at least, she did not have to wait long. Angus & Robertson let her know almost at once that they would publish the book, as long as they could get a subsidy from the Commonwealth Literary Fund to do so. She was somewhat chagrined by this conditional acceptance, and asked both Jim McAuley and Alec Hope to use their influence on her behalf.[48] Both said they would do what they could, though she was pretty sure that Alec, at least, promptly forgot his promise.

In July, she had a call from Vincent Buckley telling her that he was concerned about Hope. When he had seen him recently, he had seemed 'pretty bad', and Vin proposed that he and Gwen cheer the older poet up by writing poems expressing their 'love & admiration' for him. Gwen accordingly set to work on a poem 'of about 60 lines in iambic quatrains rather in Hope's own mode'.[49] After working on the poem 'like fury' for 'a couple of weeks',[50] she sent it off to Vin for his comment. To her perplexity, Vin did not reply, and nor did he send his own poem. She began to wonder just what Vin was up to; had he invented the whole story about Alec's fragile mental health for his own obscure political purposes?[51] Eventually, she decided to send her poem straight to Alec. Vin's own version of the story was that the arrival of Gwen's 'sparkling poem' in the mail some thirty-six hours after their phone call knocked his own fledgling poem, 'then seven lines long and peaky . . . out of the growth business'.[52] But whether Gwen wrote her poem overnight, as Vin claimed, or over several weeks, as she did, she was happy with it and sent it not only to Alec but also to *Meanjin*, where it appeared in December 1967. Alec was somewhat bemused by her tribute, but also grateful. Her poem 'was a noble one', he told her, 'more so than its subject in spite of what you say. It is odd that I should appear so definite a figure to anyone – and touching. But to myself I seem a composite of hesitations, uncertainties and ignorances and you the assured and definite one. Curious isn't it? But thank you for the best thing in my 1967.'[53]

There was still time for Gwen to include the poem in her new book. She learned in November that, having received the requisite grant, Angus & Robertson were planning to bring out *Poems: Volume II* sometime in 1968. She added a handful of other poems to the manuscript and was delighted (if somewhat sceptical) to learn in January 1968 that the book was actually 'at the press'.[54] Even so, it was mid-May before the first copies were in her hands. She was not enthusiastic about the book's design, as she had been with her first volume. She disliked the paper jacket, which featured a 'crazy psychedelic' pattern in purple, pink and blue: the English designer engaged by her publisher 'must have been On a Trip', she told the Hoddinotts.[55] She didn't much like the typeface, either.[56] But she was happy that the book's gestation period had been so much shorter than the last one and pleased to find that the literary world was inclined to make a bit of a fuss of her. When the ACT Arts Council invited her to come to Canberra to give a reading in July, all expenses paid, she agreed.

Gwen Harwood with her poetry notebook, Hobart, 1968

Up until then, she had avoided reading her work in public. As a girl, she had dreamed of appearing on stage as a concert pianist in fabulous gowns, and when she began to achieve some success as a poet, she longed to be invited to read at public events. But when the invitations did finally arrive, she demurred. She worried about her voice, which she felt was too high-pitched ('people think I am a *child* on the telephone)', and about her lack of skill as a reader. Listening to herself on the radio in the mid-1960s, she was horrified: 'I sounded like Minnie Bannister in the Goon Show.'[57] Besides, reading her own poems in public made her more vulnerable than she liked.

It was just too easy for her audience to equate the woman standing before them with the 'I' of the poems – that mysteriously passionate person who had suffered so much from ill-fated love affairs. Gwen preferred to stay out of sight, the enigmatic magician with her mask of 'flashing eyes and floating hair'.[58] But around the time her second book came out, Jim McAuley took her to task for her attitude. He told her that far from being modest by refusing to read, she was being conceited: 'People bought my books and they were interested in them and he felt that I should respond to this.' She thought he had a point, so after some coaching from him on her presentation skills, she decided to do some public readings.[59] Her Canberra gig was her first. She had a fit of nerves before she left, but the flights were booked, and it was too late to back out.[60]

In Canberra, she stayed with Rodney Hall – now the poetry editor of *The Australian* – and his family, who had recently moved from Brisbane. The day of her reading started well, with lunch at Alec Hope's house as a joint celebration of Gwen's book and Alec's sixty-first birthday. Gwen reported to the Hoddinotts that Alec was 'as radiant as ever; I came away with that *Einmal lebt' ich wie Götter* [Once I lived like the gods] feeling, especially as he said that Vol II was his current bedside book [and] "the only book for years that has made me cry"'.[61] Alec also came to her reading, and she read 'To A.D. Hope', the last poem in her book, directly to him, '*con amore*'. She cautiously judged the event to have been a success: it was always difficult, she told the Hoddinotts, to know how such things really went, since 'everyone is so madly polite', but she had enjoyed herself. It was a turning point for her: from now on, she would begin to accept invitations she had previously turned down, and more and more would come her way.

While in Canberra, she also spent a 'glorious day' with Larry Sitsky and his family, who had settled there in 1966 when Larry joined the School of Music at the Australian National University. Under the influence of Hope and the Sitskys, she began to fantasise about moving to Canberra. 'O the galahs and the winter sunshine & the Cotter Dam and the lovely trees in their little gravel beds.'[62] In 1969, when the chair of linguistics at ANU became vacant, she begged Bill to put in for it, but he had no desire to move to the national capital. 'I have put on quite a turn, but without moving him from his decision,' Gwen told Tony gloomily.[63]

Meanwhile, her new book was receiving high praise. *The Canberra Times* published 'a fabulous review' by Maurice Dunlevy, who called her 'the most original "new" poet writing in Australia today'.[64] He compared her favourably with poets who 'write the traditional kind of Australian lyric, a poem about a bird, a flower or animal, from which they draw some generalisation about life', and was impressed with her 'sardonic' approach to life's regrets. 'About to leave her lover for "the dry bread of heartache", she consoles herself with a cigarette and a grunt: "Well, we're in Eden still."' In *The Advertiser*, Katharine England described Gwen as 'the most outstanding talent' among the newer poets. Rodney Hall declared her 'a fine artist' in *The Australian*. Bruce Beaver in *The Sydney Morning Herald* averred that 'Harwood's reputation as a leading Australian poet' would only be fortified by her new book, while in *The Bulletin* (where she was reviewed alongside Sylvia Plath's *Ariel*), Geoffrey Lehmann pronounced her 'an original and gifted poet'. She had emerged, he declared, as 'the doyenne of the post-Hope wave of Australian poets'.

Some reviewers preferred Eisenbart, in her first book, to Kröte, in her second; some felt her strength lay in lyric poetry, others in her satires; some felt her work was distinguished by its extraordinary range, others that her range was narrow. But there was general agreement that she was one of the most significant of Australia's contemporary poets. The one negative review appeared in *Australian Book Review*, from Geoffrey Dutton.[65] But while Gwen was incensed when she read it, ultimately she was unconcerned about being savaged by someone that Sydney poet and Macquarie University lecturer Alexander Craig had described the year before as 'the worst famous poet in Australia'.[66]

Around this time, Tom Shapcott and Rodney Hall published an anthology they claimed was revolutionary. *New Impulses in Australian Poetry* asserted that Australian poetry had definitively changed in the 1960s, when a new generation of poets surged forward, overtaking those bastions of the 1950s, McAuley, Hope and Wright. To Gwen's delight, the editors considered her to be at the forefront of this exciting new movement, and her poetry was generously represented in the book. They even chose a quotation from her poem 'New Music' as their epigraph. Among the so-called 'new impulse' poets were many of the young Turks who were coming increasingly into Gwen's orbit: Bruce Beaver, Bruce Dawe, Craig Powell and Chris Wallace-Crabbe. The more established in their ranks were Francis Webb, Vincent Buckley, Randolph Stow and Vivian Smith, in addition to Gwen herself. Of the twenty-two poets included, there were only two women besides Gwen – Judith Green (later Rodriguez) and Kath Walker (aka Oodgeroo Noonuccal) – and each had only a single poem. Australian poetry was still very much a man's world. Even so, Gwen was happy to be in this company. 'It's a remarkable anthology, quite the liveliest I've seen,' she told Tony, adding disarmingly that she was, of course, 'charmed by the attention I receive therein.'[67]

In strictly generational terms, Gwen did not belong with this cohort of 'new impulse' poets, as more than one reviewer pointed out. The poets championed by Tom and Rod were in their twenties and thirties, closer to Gwen's eldest son's age than her own. But she felt herself to be aligned with them in terms of her poetic concerns. On the whole, she was not greatly impressed with the quality of their work, though they mostly did not suspect this (she had a gift for making younger poets feel warmly appreciated while avoiding being drawn into judgement on their work). She did love their energy, however. Theirs was the poetry being published, read and talked about in newspapers, on radio and in student bars, and she wanted her work to rub shoulders with theirs, not languish in classrooms and libraries with the old guard.

In 1967, she was equally delighted to feature prominently in an anthology put together by Alexander Craig called *Twelve Poets: 1950–1970*. His intention was to create a collection he could use in his teaching, since so much recent Australian poetry was already out of print. Gwen was once again in the company of Webb, Buckley, Wallace-Crabbe, Stow, Dawe and Hall. She was also the only woman.

◆ ◆ ◆

In the late 1960s, Gwen set out to show that it was not such a great feat, after all, to be young and male: even a middle-aged poetess could do it. In July 1968, three poems by the hitherto unknown Timothy Kline appeared in *Westerly*'s Young Writers issue. The first, 'Soldier, Soldier', was a beautifully economical attack on the Vietnam War, couched in the call-and-response form of the children's nursery rhyme 'Soldier, Soldier, Won't You Marry Me?' The 'soldier' of the title exemplifies the attitudes of a new, anti-war generation: for him, there is nothing glorious about going to war, and a soldier's kills only unman him. This poem would be reprinted in a 1971 anti-war anthology, *We Took Their Orders and Are Dead*, and in *Overland*'s 1973 issue devoted to the Vietnam War.

In the other two poems, 'From a Young Writer's Diary' and 'Poet to Peasant', a young writer struggles with his exalted vocation. In the first, he is boarding with a German family and reading the journal of Kafka (his 'patron saint') while lamenting his inability to write. As he reads the paper, drinks wine, stares at the flowers in his room and prays for 'the honesty / of evil thoughts, of torture, nightmare, fear', his pregnant landlady, Frau Schmidt, brings in the washing, prepares the dinner, practices her English, works in the garden. 'Women have an easier life,' the writer concludes. 'How like a gentle animal she is!'

The irony is more muted in 'Poet to Peasant', in which the impassioned poet declares that he lives in the realm of madness and elemental hungers, welling visions and point-blank revelations, and as such cannot be expected to have any truck with 'respectable love'. He frames his poem as a warning to the 'dear, singleminded girl' who seeks from him the tame 'suburban sweetness' of marriage. He was not made, he tells her, for 'a nice house' and 'a tribe of pretty children': 'I know a thousand ways of loving, / But none is yours. Woman, be wise.'

Both poems have a strange power in their plea for a life lived with intensity, and their passionate scorn for the banality of suburbia – represented remorselessly by women. As the work of a single twenty-one-year-old Tasmanian clerk pursuing an interest in 'boat building and canoeing' while 'working on a novel' (as 'Timothy Kline' is described in *Westerly*'s contributor notes), these poems could probably be read literally. But as the work of a forty-eight-year-old married mother of four, a successful poet who was currently reading Kafka's journals with great interest, they must be read as ironic. Yet there was a part of Gwen that had always identified with the brooding male poet. While reading Byron, she told Roger McDonald, she always felt, 'Yes, that is what I am really like, even if I am the one who puts the porridge on.'[68]

Gwen kept very quiet about her Timothy Kline alter ego. (The name was derived from 'klein', the German word for 'little', making him an iteration of Tiny Tim, both a 1930s comic-book character and the saintly child in Dickens' *A Christmas Carol*.) She did not even tell Tony or Alison of his existence at first. His name appeared in print twice more that year: once in *Overland*, with a poem entitled 'Samuel Greenberg' that alluded to the horrors of the Holocaust, and once in *Southerly*, with 'Pensioner'.[69] The following year, 'Space Poem' was published in *The Bulletin*. This work is an extraordinary piece of science fiction in which a group of intergalactic cowboys stops off at a 'large asteroid', where they kill, maim and harass the local aliens, before taking one captive. The poem ends with the narrator calling the 'medic-bank' for help: 'The crew are sickening one by one' from a mysterious illness, while the caged alien watches: 'My God, I'd swear the thing was smiling / if I thought things like that could smile.'

The imaginative storytelling might have suggested that Timothy Kline's novel in progress was a work of science fiction. Gwen herself was fascinated by the genre, which she knew, glancingly, through TV and comics rather than through books. She loved the sci-fi terms 'the kids bandy about'[70] and, in the early 1970s, would write an original libretto set partly on a space station. But for now, it was 'Timothy Kline', not Gwen Harwood, who was experimenting with the sci-fi genre in poetry.

Kline did not confine his poetry to the hot topics of aliens, war, sexual frustration and the hypocrisy of marriage. A number of poems published under his name were thoughtful observations of life in Hobart that could easily have been written by a woman twice his age. As with her earlier pseudonyms, Gwen was using Timothy Kline (and possibly other nom de plumes; she hinted as much)[71] to provide a safe shelter for her own experiments. As she told Tony in October 1968, she was not sure if she was writing well or not. Generally, Timothy Kline, who operated out of a postbox at the Hobart GPO, was very well received, though *Meanjin* rejected a new poem submitted under his name, 'Requiem', as 'slack' and 'conventional'. 'Lucky I'm not a weak-willed beginner,' Gwen remarked to Tony.[72] This poem has not survived; at least, there is no poem of that name in Gwen's *Collected Poems*.

Gwen was bemused when Kline was invited to join the Society of Authors 'as a full member on the strength of ONE poem in the Bully. Whacko! Nobody feels like that about ME'.[73] Kline also received a letter of praise from a young poet and academic at the University of Newcastle, Norman Talbot, who encouraged him to publish a book. When the University of Queensland Press invited Kline to submit a manuscript for its new poetry series, Paperback Poets, Gwen began to feel a little miffed. It was nice that Kline, who had by then published around ten poems, was getting the recognition, but why had she herself not been asked by UQP to submit a manuscript?

She had met the press's new poetry editor, Roger McDonald, the year before, when he was working for the ABC. He and his wife, Rhyll McMaster, had just moved to Hobart, and at Tom Shapcott's behest, Gwen had taken the young couple under her wing, helping them find a flat and introducing them around. Roger went on to produce a short film about Gwen for the ABC's educational arm, and she was delighted with the result. The film featured her in some of her favourite places – walking on the beach at Cremorne, by the waterfront in Hobart, in her own garden – as well as playing her piano and engaged in a chess game with a pipe-smoking Bill. On the soundtrack, several of her poems were read by Tony Riddell, always Gwen's favourite reader. Working on this film cemented Gwen's friendship with Roger, so she could not understand why, when he went to UQP, he approached Kline but not her for the new book series. 'It is interesting to masquerade among those who profess admiration for GH,' she commented drily to Tony. 'Whatever Roger *says* to me, he has solicited Kline & not Harwood.'[74]

Roger was not merely pretending to an admiration for Harwood. In his mind, she was one of the heavyweights of Australian poetry, and Paperback Poets was conceived as a platform for new poets.[75] The whole idea of the series, as he explained to Gwen, was that they would be cheap – they would 'sell for under $1!!'[76] The poets he had his eye on were all 'Generation of '68', including David Malouf (who had helped him pitch the idea to UQP), Michael Dransfield, J.S. Harry and Judith Rodriguez. Still, Gwen felt that he might have made an exception for her as he had done for Rodney Hall, 'a well-established poet with about 5 volumes' who was also, coincidentally, one of Roger's close friends.[77]

Part of her annoyance was the sense that she was, once again, being excluded from the boys' club. When she was struggling to establish herself as a poet in the 1950s, no one had invited her to join an authors' society or publish a manuscript, or even to submit work to an anthology. By the time her first manuscript was accepted, she had published some fifty poems in literary journals and won the *Meanjin* poetry prize twice – yet she had had to solicit a publisher, which then held up publication for more than two years. It was hard to resist the conclusion that Timothy Kline's quick success was due not so much to his talent as to his youth and gender.

Tiny Tim did not last long, however. Late in 1969, he was 'smoked out' by Tom Shapcott (who was making a habit of uncovering Gwen's aliases) and Roger himself. Tom sent Gwen a cautiously worded letter asking her to contact Timothy Kline on his behalf, as he wanted to include him in an anthology of young poets he was putting together. Gwen took the hint, telling Tony resignedly that she had 'emerged from my box, coughing up the Shapcott tear gas, and Admitted All'.[78] She sent Tom a ditty ('Tune: St James Infirmary Blues') to the memory of Timothy Kline:

It was down by the old brick building,
The North Hobárt pee-oh,
That Tom the Bomb and Roger
were waiting & lying low.

Along came Lady Olga,
She walked with stealthy tread,
And peered into her post box,
and these were the words she said:

"I went down to the old Infirmary
To see if my sweetie was there,
And he was laid out on the marble
with laurels in his hair.

"I saw Walter, Frank & Miriam
'He's pretty low, they said.
And as I bent to kiss him,
Good God, he's a-lying there dead.
(Spoken: He's dead!)

Let Tom the Bomb wear mourning
and Roger shed a tear
For the boy who died of tear gas
At the height of his career."[79]

Tom and Roger were delighted with their own perspicacity. (Roger could not forbear to point out that he had asked Gwen a year earlier, when he was still in Hobart, whether she was Timothy Kline and she had denied it.)[80] The two had gone through 'all available Kline poems & "listened" for your voice – O how it came through,' Roger told her gleefully.[81] Even then, 'T.F. Kline, the name at the foot of the poems, still made us doubt a little: "Well, if he's not Gwen he's certainly taken an overdose of her style, interests etc."'

Both men were more than willing to keep the secret. Tom still wanted to publish some Klines in his *Australian Poetry Now* anthology, and Roger begged for 'a MS for Paperback Poets'. Gwen decided against giving Kline his own volume, but she submitted a handful of poems on his behalf for

Australian Poetry Now, along with a biographical statement in verse. She gave Kline a birthday in 1946 (the same year as John's) and listed his 'hobbies' as 'boat-building, sail-making, bush-walking, cake-baking, gliding and soaring, drinking and whoring, cursing and praying, flogging and beating, mutton-bird eating, waving the flag and wearing drag, converting agnostics, writing acrostics, catching and chucking, kissing and collecting pictures of the Royal Family'.

Gwen's appearance in the anthology, even 'in drag', as she put it, was quite a statement. Published in 1970 by Sun Books, *Australian Poetry Now* proclaimed the arrival of 'a new generation of poets', 'inheritors of post-war affluence and admass Techniculture', who were asserting themselves 'with a zeal and recklessness missing from their immediate predecessors'.[82] It was also Timothy Kline's undoing. In a review of the anthology in *The Australian* in December 1970, the critic Sylvia Lawson declared that she had it 'on good authority that Timothy Kline is in fact Gwen Harwood, sending up the whole youthquake with typical expertise. I haven't proof positive, but the internal evidence from the poems is virtually conclusive; they're among her best.' 'How embarrassing to be de-trousered by Sylvia in front of my public,' Gwen remarked sardonically.[83] She decided to abandon Tiny Tim – though he did have one last outing in a 1975 anthology edited by Rodney Hall, *Australians Aware: Poems and Paintings of Today*.

Unlike her earlier pseudonyms, she never brought Timothy Kline into the fold by including his poems in her own collections. Perhaps she felt that his 'youthquake' voice was too far removed from her own. His work would not be republished until after her death. In the meantime, a new generation of editors and anthologists had become hypervigilant, carefully inspecting every new poet for telltale signs of Gwen's fingerprints. 'Jim McAuley & Roger have both accused me of being a new poetaster (the new ones are *all the same!*),' Gwen complained to Tom, even as she responded with injured innocence to his accusation that she was behind a female poet who had recently appeared. 'Meanwhile Honest Gwen struggles on.'[84]

Gwen continued to excel at the sport of editor baiting. She told Roger that she had other pseudonyms 'in the nursery' but had been 'more careful about style' this time.[85] To Tony, she declared herself ready to 'start up again', this time using a Sydney address (courtesy of Ann Jennings), since Hobart addresses were 'useless'.[86] She went so far as to ask Ann whether she could use her address for a 'poetical infant in a wicker basket',[87] though who this particular infant grew up to become has never been identified. Harwood scholar Greg Kratzmann identified one pseudonym from this period, Alan Carvosso, whom Harwood never claimed. It seems probable there were others, but either Gwen was so 'careful' with style that nobody wanted to publish them, or they simply failed to make the kind of splash that Timothy Kline achieved. In any case, she had increasingly less need for masks. Her fame as a poet was growing, and she would soon be in a position to publish almost anything she wrote.

Part III:
1970–1995

18

Restless and Quite Wild

I am in a ferment at present, restless and quite wild, spending a week
alone (alone thank God) in the surgery while Dr & Sr are on holiday.
My need for solitude is so great that I can hardly bear to go home in the
evenings, and set foot in a human habitation.

Gwen Harwood, Letter to Ann Jennings, 11 January 1968

IN LATE MAY 1969, GWEN AND TONY MADE A PILGRIMAGE TO
the Mornington Cemetery at Mount Martha, Victoria, to visit his
parents' grave. It is a small, neat, rather bare graveyard, with none of
the grand funerary edifices and dramatic topography of Gwen's beloved
Toowong Cemetery. But here, strolling with Tony among the pale eucalypts
and concrete slabs, she felt finally 'reconciled . . . with the idea of death'.
It was 'one of the most profoundly reassuring experiences of my life'.[1]

She needed reassurance. In early October the previous year, her father
had died after a mild stroke put him in hospital. He was seventy-nine and
not in good health, and Gwen's first thought was that his death was a blessing. He had 'been spared a good deal of pain – he could only have lived to
suffer'.[2] Yet beneath her calm, adult acceptance of the inevitable, some deep
part of her felt abandoned, 'as helpless as a small child'.[3] Her father, like her
grandmother, was someone who seemed to keep her safe simply by existing. 'He always made me feel loved & secure,' she told Tony; he had given
her the unquestioning confidence that – in a phrase she often used – 'the
waters will bear me'.[4] Now that he was gone, that confidence was disinte-
grating. She found herself suffering 'terrible nightmares almost every night'.
Her thoughts began to turn, with a strange longing, towards her own death.
'Quite elaborate plans for committing suicide so it looks accidental occur to
me at odd times,' she told Tony grimly. She woke every morning 'wishing to
die'.[5] Her suicidal thoughts were 'always accompanied by plans about what's
for dinner and breakfast, so don't worry', she assured Tony. She couldn't be
too serious about ending her own life if she was making dinner plans – so,
at least, she assumed.

Even before her father's death, she had been struggling. Much as she
enjoyed going to work – it was still a joy for her to get out of the house each

day and enter the professional world – she was increasingly tired, and with three teenagers in the house, it was as difficult as ever to find sustained periods of time to write. She was '*desperate* for time, solitude, freedom from domestic tasks', she told Tony in September 1968. 'Sometimes I feel I shall never write a word again.' The idea terrified her. Writing was her hold on life, her identity beyond the domestic world, the thing that gave purpose to her pain.

She should have been moving into a period of greater freedom, yet she felt as trapped as ever. She and Bill were, once again, on very different trajectories. She increasingly wanted to turn outwards, while Bill was becoming progressively withdrawn. For a time, he had shown signs of 'being more reasonable with the world', but by late 1967, he was once more 'retreating'.[6] The Hoddinotts had visited at the end of that year, hoping for their usual holiday-time hikes, picnics and jaunts with the Harwoods, but Bill had declined every invitation. Alison – always one of his favourite people – had told him directly that he was 'getting bad again'.[7]

Gwen could not retreat with him. For all her yearning for solitude, she needed to feel she was part of the fabric of the social world. Yet to insist on seeing her friends and maintaining her social activities in the face of his disapproval still took resolution. She felt that as a wife, she had been a disappointment to him, and this weighed on her, even as she vehemently rejected his right to determine the shape of her life. 'Sometimes I try to imagine the world of F.W.H. if he had bitten me down to his desired shape: one child (he did want one), an immured wife of dowdy aspect who spoke and wrote to nobody without his permission, all surrounded by a wall of giant cactus,' she fumed to Ann. 'Sometimes I feel like a creature slowly regaining its natural shape. Bill should be thankful that I resisted him.'[8] But Bill was not thankful – and she was as reluctant as ever to confront him openly.

Her best antidote to misery was to get away, as her trip to Canberra in mid-1968 had shown her, so when she was invited to read at the Universities Arts Festival in Melbourne in May 1969, she eagerly accepted. She made arrangements to stay with Eddie and Shirley Tanner at Glen Iris for the week, and scheduled a free day to spend with Tony. He took her to the Mornington Peninsula, an hour south of Melbourne, to see the house he and his siblings had inherited – where he lived when he was not in the city for work – and the other 'beautiful places' he cherished. Gwen was charmed by it all: the house and garden, the beautiful beaches, the peaceful cemetery where his parents lay. It was, she told him, 'one of the great happy days of my life'.[9] She felt her life 'resolved and blessed', 'all losses . . . restored'.[10]

'At Mornington', which she wrote soon after, brought together childhood memories of her father with the revelation she experienced, as she stood with Tony beside his parents' grave at Mount Martha, that death was nothing to fear. It wove in, too, the paradox of her own identity, earthbound by nature, yet striving upwards, like the trellised pumpkins she had seen that morning in Tony's garden. The ungainly vegetables trying to climb into the sky were 'a parable of myself', she wrote in an early draft: 'solid, domestic, useful, / but incurably romantic'.[11] As for Tony himself, her love for him had never seemed more complete. She loved him 'more than anyone I have ever loved, anytime, anywhere' – not even excluding, she insisted, her children.[12]

This was just the beginning of a happy week in which Tony shared as much as his schedule would allow. The festival itself was 'fab fab FAB, dreamy, groovy, utterly ravishing'.[13] Hosted by the University of Melbourne, it was the second to be organised by the National Union of Students, and featured not only writers but rock music, art exhibitions and theatre performances. Within four years, it would morph into the Aquarius Festival at Nimbin, sometimes known as Australia's Woodstock and the birth of the Australian hippie movement. But in 1969, it was an exploration and a celebration of all that was new in the arts, and Gwen loved it. She loved hanging out with the poets, eating and drinking at happening restaurants, going to parties and readings – and above all, perhaps, having 'no peace to keep, no frowns to fear, nothing to wash or cook'.[14]

She was among friends. Jim McAuley and Vin Buckley were both on the program, along with Evan Jones, her old Brisbane friend Frank Kellaway and a host of the younger poets who had recently swung into her orbit, including Chris Wallace-Crabbe and Bruce Dawe. Tony went with her to hear Jim McAuley read and was 'deeply moved'; over the course of the week, he also met other of her poet friends. As the dedicatee of both volumes of her poems, he attracted some attention; the 'repellent Melbourne poets' watched them avidly for signs of a secret passion.[15] Gwen took this in her stride, amused rather than offended, and wrote it into 'Winter Quarters', a love poem about 'two captains' who have been 'friends long enough to show/ the heart's true gentleness', and who can say with a look: 'I know // as I am known'. When the poem appeared a year later in *The Age*, she was delighted that 'Tom Shapcott correctly identified Tony as the subject of the poem, even without a dedication.[16]

Her own reading, on the Wednesday night, was shared with Vincent Buckley and younger poet Andrew Taylor. She had her doubts about how Vin would perform, as he was drinking heavily, but on the night he was 'superb'. The next day he took her to lunch, then 'back to his room to meet his Irish mates, who sat drinking whisky and cursing the Queen'. That night, they went to a party at Evan Jones' house. Most of the University of Melbourne's English department were there, as well as a goodly crowd of young poets, and Gwen was impressed by the 'marvellous food & oceans of drink' and by the beauty of the young women, who 'looked like film stars in their boots and miniskirts'. Frank Kellaway's grown-up children were there, and played the guitar while everyone sang. 'Jesus! it was beaut.'[17]

The Beatles were on the hi-fi when Gwen got a drunken Vin up to dance with her. They whirled around the crowded room to 'Lucy in the Sky with Diamonds', 'dismembering in affectionate whispers practically every poet in Australia', until Vin lost his footing and sent them both tumbling into the fireplace. They were not hurt, though their dignity suffered.[18] (Gwen told Tony a week later that she still had 'a great bruise where I fell on to Evan's fireplace'.)[19] Even so, the whole evening was magical in her memory. She was moved by Vin in a way she couldn't quite explain. 'I learned more about him by dancing with him than by talking to him, but he is always masked,' she wrote to Tony. 'He reminds me of a picture (Watteau? Fragonard? I can't remember) of a jester holding up a small image of himself; Vin is simpler & more generous than the effigy he so drunkenly displays.'

When she got home to the Tanners each evening, she and Eddie stayed up late, talking and talking. She had been shocked when she first saw him; a year earlier, he had suffered a stroke which had left him in severe pain, and more recently, he had undergone neurosurgery. She thought he had recovered, but now found that 'he plainly hasn't'. 'He used to be like quick-silver – I could never talk fast enough to keep up with him or stay beside him without running; now he is essentially slow and shuffling.'[20] Nevertheless, the affinity between them was unchanged. In their late evening chats, Eddie told her stories of his life – 'if only I had a tape recorder or a short-hand book!' – and she made her own confidences. 'Remember that our midnight talks are PRIVATE PRIVATE PRIVATE,' she warned him afterwards, 'and if you ever tell a word of them I will close my mouth like that character who said "From this time forth I never will speak word."'[21]

But on Sunday night, on the plane home to Hobart, it was of Vin that she found herself thinking. She was happy after her 'wonderful week', conscious of being 'absolutely restored', and, travelling through the darkness, she felt a sense of exaltation as she looked out at 'Melbourne glittering for miles under a full moon, then tundras of icy cloud, then clear over Tasmania which was awash'.[22] This exaltation would translate into 'Night Flight', a restless meditation on the unrelenting forces of love and desire, in which she would memorialise her drunken dance with Vin, this 'one whom I love'.

◆　◆　◆

Gwen's re-entry into everyday life was difficult. Compared with the freedom of Melbourne, Hobart seemed intolerably confined. It was something she would experience again and again over the next couple of years. Whenever she went to the mainland, she would come back seething with restlessness and dissatisfaction. Her daughter, Mary, told her that she was 'like a diver with the bends' and proposed that she 'return by stages to domestic life'.[23]

This was easier said than done. On the positive side, she had 'numerous poems in a ferment' – including 'one dazzling love poem in strict metre (the greater the emotion, the stricter the formal pattern in my case)' that she felt she could not publish, 'for obvious reasons'.[24] This might have been 'Night Flight' (which she did publish in 1971 in *Poetry Australia*) or 'Winter Quarters' (which appeared in *The Age* in May 1970) or something else entirely. On the negative side, she felt she could not bear to remain in Tasmania. 'I *need* the mainland', she wailed to Tony.[25] 'I feel I have reached a time in my life when I must use all my remaining powers; my vital energy is less than it was . . . and I want to change things before it is too late.'

In one of her favourite Rilke sonnets, 'Archaic Torso of Apollo', the poet muses on a headless statue of the Roman god, reflecting that even in its despoiled state, its beauty and perfection challenge all that is less than perfect in one's own life. The poem ends '*Du Musst dein Leben ändern*' (You must change your life). These words haunted Gwen. Around the time she went to Melbourne, she dreamed she was in a boat off the coast of Sydney, looking back at the cliffs outside the Harbour. On the cliff top was a cemetery, and directly below it, the cliff face was 'glittering' with what looked like mother-of-pearl. As the boat drew nearer, she realised that the glittering fragments were human skulls, spelling out a message: '*Du musst dein Leben ändern*'.[26] The dream struck Gwen with the force of revelation. For the next five years, she would brood over, plan, dream and invent ways to do exactly that. As Bill was unwilling to even consider a move, she was beginning to realise that if she were to leave Tasmania, she would have to do it alone.

In the meantime, she had become a grandmother. John and his wife had had their first child, a red-headed girl named Rachel, in early 1969, and Gwen was besotted. She has 'the most beautiful hair I've ever seen,' she told Tony, 'an intense pure red-gold; dark eyes, rose-white skin, dark lashes'.[27] She had been looking forward to the birth, telling Tony, when she learned of the pregnancy, that she felt 'a great joy at the thought of being Granny to someone'.[28] But John had recently won a scholarship to Cambridge and was soon to take his family to England for several years, so she was to be deprived of 'Rachel's most enchanting time' – those early years of 'discovering the world'. John's departure weighed on her; it would be 'the first real parting of the family',[29] presaging those that were to come.

As well as her job at the surgery and playing grandmother, Gwen had been working on a libretto for Larry Sitsky based on Kafka's *The Trial*. She had thrown herself into the research, reading Kafka's diaries as well as his novels. She felt a strong connection to the brooding, paranoid writer, telling Larry that she had 'dreams just like the ones Kafka records in his diary'. *The Trial* was strikingly relevant to the late 1960s. 'Don't you think K is pitting his existence itself against the insanity of the world, the otherness of it?' she wrote eagerly to Larry. 'Sometimes I feel I live in corridors too.'[30] But soon after she returned from Melbourne, she received a telegram from Larry telling her the work could not proceed. Kafka's estate had decided not to grant them copyright clearance. Gwen was well into the second draft by this time. 'All that work!' she groaned to Tony. 'Not that I mind – Kafka is so rewarding I have no regrets at all about the time spent reading & thinking about him.'[31]

Larry still had his commission for a one-acter from the Australian Opera (then the Elizabethan Theatre Trust, later Opera Australia), so they began to cast around for a new theme. He suggested Strindberg's 'The Father', but Gwen disliked the play.[32] Her suggestion was to produce something based on the life of one of her favourite saints, Thérèse of Lisieux, 'a character who has always fascinated me'.[33] The opera would be 'mostly female characters', she told Larry, 'but her father could have a part; we could have a riotous portrayal of homosexual passions in the Carmel of Lisieux'. But Larry was not interested in French nuns. Finally, in early July, he suggested they try German writer Georg Buchner's novella *Lenz*. Gwen immediately agreed.

Jakob Lenz was a late-eighteenth-century German poet and playwright, at one time a good friend of Goethe's, who famously fell in love with one of Goethe's discarded lovers and suffered a debilitating mental breakdown. Summarising the story for Tony, Gwen described it as 'based on the time when the German poet Lenz went mad in the mountains. I'm sure it will be as sinister as *Usher*.'[34] If she had identified with K in *The Trial*, she connected even more strongly with the mad poet, telling Larry that 'Lenz is my blood-brother'.[35]

She had a first draft within a fortnight. Larry went through it page by page, noting what he liked and what he didn't, what he thought worth developing and what would be 'too hard to set'. Gwen was delighted with his feedback. She was developing a much stronger sense of the kinds of words, rhythms and cadences that would stimulate Larry's compositional juices, as well as what would work on a stage. For her, the crux of the piece was Lenz's repudiation of God following the death of a villager's child. Seized with a kind of ecstatic faith, Lenz stands over the girl and exhorts God to resurrect her: 'The spirit of healing pours into my hands. My time is at hand. The child shall live!' Turning to the child, he declares in biblical tones: 'Rise up and walk!' But the child does not rise up, and Lenz turns on God in fury and despair: 'Monster, monster, you live in the filth of sores, / in scabs, in holes, in the slime of black ravines.'[36] In an extraordinary inversion of the liturgical words of praise to Father, Son and Holy Spirit that Gwen knew so well from her time as one of the Anglican faithful, he curses God. The opera ends with Lenz being taken away in a straitjacket.

The second draft was complete by the end of August, and Larry considered it 'a beauty! And just about the final thing.'[37] He finished the score about eighteen months later, but it would be another three years before it was performed. When it was finally programmed in March 1974 as part of the first season of the brand new Sydney Opera House, Gwen flew over to see it. She found it 'heart-rending and truly a masterpiece'.[38] 'The raising of the dead child was so intensely built up in Larry's music that one could almost feel the rejection of God in Lenz's mind,' she told Tony. The singer who played Lenz 'was as close to the conception as we could ever hope for; the end was almost unbearable'.[39] The good reviews bolstered them both. Arts critic and soprano Maria Prerauer dubbed it 'a musically rich, atmospheric and horribly gripping one-act opera', declaring that in her opinion, it was 'the best operatic work so far to come out of this country'. Kevon Kemp in the *National Times* described it as 'an unmistakable masterwork'.[40]

Though Gwen would never consent to have her libretti published separately – they belonged to the music, she would say – she would always feel that among her works, *Lenz* was exceptional.

◆ ◆ ◆

In May 1970, a year after her joyous trip to Melbourne, she went to Sydney for a reading at the Cell Block Theatre, part of a program jointly organised by the ABC and Sydney University. In the weeks before the trip, she recorded herself reading several of her poems on a cassette tape, which she sent to Tony for his critique. He sent back comments and suggestions to help her improve her delivery.

She was considering reading the two poems that made up 'Father and Child', as a tribute to Joe.[41] The first of these, 'Barn Owl', was based on an incident from her own childhood. The first-person narrator (generally assumed to be female, simply because of the poet's gender) sneaks out to the barn very early one morning, armed with her father's gun. She plans to shoot the resident owl, which comes home from hunting at this time – retribution for its nightly killing spree. She fires, but though her bullet strikes the owl, it does not kill him and she watches in horror as the creature stumbles through the straw, an obscene 'bundle of stuff . . . tangling in bowels'. All at once her father is there, picking up the fallen gun, handing it back to her, telling her to 'End what you have begun'. She fires again, and this time, the owl dies. The poem ends with the child weeping into her father's arm 'for what I had begun'.

When Gwen was asked directly – as she repeatedly was over many years – whether the child in this poem was herself, she would equivocate: she would say that the child was obviously a boy (a 'horny fiend') and therefore could not be her, or that she would 'NEVER be so cruel' as to shoot a bird.[42] But though she refused to affirm that the story was true, she also refused to say that it was not. Certainly in Mitchelton there was a barn, an owl and a gun, and she once told Tony that she had considered herself the 'protector' of the doves which made their nests in the barn.[43] In her seventies, she told Greg Kratzmann that it was her friend Noel Coar, grandson of family friends George Coar and his wife, who shot the owl.[44] Then again, in a late poem, she refers teasingly to the unlucky owl, 'poor witless fowl', who was 'shot with my father's gun':

But fiction glitters on fiction
and truth was clerical grey.
I really was not a remarkable shot
and the real bird got away.[45]

Gwen flew into Sydney on a Thursday evening after work. On the plane, her thoughts turned to Ann Jennings who was now living in the city, an independent woman with a career as a teacher, a new lover (she and Tas Bull had parted ways) and an enviable life. It was such a change – a happy one – from the shadowed existence they had shared as young mothers at Fern Tree. Gwen's life, too, had taken a new course since then. They had feared the constraints of domesticity would defeat them, yet here they both were with flourishing careers, grown children and a freedom they could only dream of in those dark days on the mountainside. By the time her plane arrived, she had written the draft of 'An Impromptu for Ann Jennings', a celebration of their rebirth. 'Time has given again / a hundredfold those lives that we surrendered,' she wrote, 'the love, the fruitfulness; but not the pain.' When she saw Ann that weekend, she gave her the draft, signed and dated.[46]

The reading was an unmitigated disaster – but a great story. The six poets (including the already legendary Michael Dransfield: '21, genius, drug-taker, nomadic')[47] arrived at the venue half an hour early, as requested, but found the theatre locked. The ABC radio team came to set up and could not get in either. Only once the audience was milling around outside did one of the organisers arrive with the key. Alex Craig had decided to project his poems onto a screen, and while wrestling with the overhead projector he cut his finger. It bled 'copiously' until the wound was staunched by a wad of pink tissues supplied by a solicitous audience member. Once the readings began, the poets realised that the two microphones – one to amplify, one to record – could not be reached simultaneously, 'but by this time nobody cared much'.[48]

The poets each read twice, and during Gwen's first reading, she noticed a large white Alsatian at the back of the theatre, sniffing at a couple of drops of Alex Craig's blood on the floor. Leaving its master (the poet Roland Robinson), it made its way through the hall, nose to the ground, emitting 'hair-raising noises of delight', until finally coming up on the stage and snuffling around the poets, 'completely distracting the audience from my master-work'. This exciting interlude was followed by Alex's laborious explanation of his projected poems – 'it was like a dreadful slide evening' – and a reading by Dransfield that was 'so gentle and diffident that nobody could hear it'. Then, as the last reader of the night, Tom Shapcott decided to read 'his poem about an orgasm, which until now has circulated in ms. only' ('I think the dead weight of the audience was getting him down'). The poem contained various unmentionable words – 'and not acrostically either'. From the back of the theatre, 'Roland Robinson shouted angrily, "What do you have to use filthy words for?"'[49]

Afterwards, the poets gathered at Geoff Lehmann's to let off steam, and the party continued the following evening when much the same group assembled at the home of Vivian and Sybille Smith.[50] At this party, Gwen met Craig Powell, a poet and practising psychiatrist with whom she had exchanged a handful of letters. She was delighted to learn that he was an amateur pianist and used to accompany his father in Schubert lieder. Gwen was particularly impressed by his translation of one of her favourite German poems, Hölderlin's 'An die Parzen', and he charmed her by confessing that he had once memorised a Rilke poem in German to impress a girl. He began to recite it – 'Lösch mir die Augen aus' (Put out my eyes) – and Gwen joined in, 'having also committed it to memory'.[51] She had met a kindred spirit.

It was a big weekend. As well as catching up with Ann, she spent an evening with Peter Bennie at St Paul's College at the University of Sydney, where he was the warden.[52] At a festive college dinner, they got very drunk together and ended up 'standing on the warden's table holding hands & singing *Land of Hope & Glory*!' Gwen soon realised that the old flame of her passion for him burned as brightly as ever; she told Tony that she had 'not expected to be so shaken by my meeting with him'.[53] Peter, too, found himself ruminating fruitlessly on old choices, missed paths.[54] After she had gone, he sent her a poem, 'Proust and the Poet', in which he churns through the emotion of the visit in carefully guarded terms. The poem ends with an expression of his own regret: 'One dares not tear apart / All the decisions which one can't undo.' Gwen responded swiftly and in kind. Her poem preaches not regret but calm acceptance. 'The world's what is the case,' she wrote, drawing on one of her favourite lines from Wittgenstein. He had rejected her all those years ago, and so they had built their own separate lives. Yet she was more than willing to affirm that 'time has changed nothing'; all these years later, 'You are still my love.'[55]

♦ ♦ ♦

Gwen and Bill Harwood aboard their yacht Sappho, *1973*

That summer, right through until early autumn, Gwen spent much of her free time sailing. Bill had finally finished building their small ocean-going yacht, *Iris*, in late 1968 – with much assistance from Gwen and the children. Once it was seaworthy, he and Gwen spent holidays and weekends on the water around southern Tasmania. 'Imagine gliding gently along in a soft breeze, with no sound but the lapping water and the cries of the sea-birds,' she told Tony rapturously. 'Imagine, too, a picnic meal packed in a Christmas biscuit tin: egg & lettuce sandwiches, fruit cake, apples and fresh plums.' She loved being out on the water, matching her 'skill at the helm with wind & wave', and found that her differences with Bill faded into the background when they were sailing. 'Bill is at his best on the water as Master of IRIS,' she wrote in April 1971. 'She is his creature in every sense, with no rebellious nonsense in her spirit.' Gwen, of course, was full of 'rebellious nonsense' – but it was in abeyance when they were sailing. They had some 'enchanting days in North-West Bay', in the company of fairy penguins, herons, terns and 'one magnificent sea-eagle'.[56] Around this time, she wrote a poem in which *Iris* became a metaphor for her marriage, an 'ark' they had 'faithfully built' that would bear them both, no matter how seductive the glimmering depths below.

'Iris' addressed Bill directly, beginning: 'Three years with our three sons you worked to build her'. In Gwen's mind, it was a tribute to the life they had made together – 'husband and wife so long we have forgotten / all singularity' – and it had not occurred to her that Bill might object. But when it appeared in *The Australian*, he reacted angrily. To him, it was an intolerable violation of his privacy and further evidence of her indifference to his wishes.[57] Gwen was deeply hurt by his 'scaly coldness' towards her that day. She saw his anger as yet another manifestation of his general dislike of her writing. 'He hates my poetry almost as much as he hated my musical activities,' she told Eddie gloomily.[58] Two years later, she was still smarting, telling Tony that 'nothing I wrote, even a celebration of our marriage, could please him'.[59]

As always, she found it difficult to motivate herself in the face of Bill's displeasure. Yet her reputation as a poet continued to grow. Invitations were flowing in, including one to award the Harri Jones Memorial Prize for Poetry at the University of Newcastle in July. As an established poet, she was to select the person she considered 'the Most Promising Young Poet under 25' and give a lecture on their work. The previous year, Tom Shapcott had awarded the prize to Michael Dransfield. Gwen's choice was Rhyll McMaster. She admired McMaster's poems, which were 'full of sharp & detailed observation and unusual images and dazzling vocabulary'.[60] In late July, she flew to Sydney, then took the train north to Newcastle.

As soon as she was on the 'glorious MAINLAND', Gwen's spirits began to rise. The sudden warmth – relative to Hobart in midwinter – was revivifying.[61] 'As darkness fell, the train [to Newcastle] bore me through the incredible factory area, the endless poor houses, then the rich houses, the country, Gosford . . .'[62] Professor Tony Gibbs, who 'proved to be a delightful man', took her to dinner with the staff of the English department, where she supped on seafood, drank 'splendid wines' and was 'asked whether the Hegelian influence in the Kröte poems was implicit or unconscious (true!)'.[63] One of the lecturers was Norman Talbot, a thirty-five-year-old poet from Suffolk who had moved to Australia with his young family in 1963. Gwen had been struck by a poem of his that had appeared in *Westerly* in 1964,[64] and when she was introduced to him that evening, she seized his hand – the left, which happened to be closest – and breathed: 'let me kiss the hand that wrote "Lonely Girl Gathering Jellyfish"'. Norman turned to her in amazement: 'How did you know I was left-handed?'[65]

They spent much of that evening talking. Gwen told Tony, without malice, that Norman was 'one of the great egocentrics; he simply takes over any conversation in the room'.[66] As a result, she 'didn't get a chance to talk to many people apart from him', though she did warm to 'a quieter young poet, Paul Kavanagh, who impressed me with his quiet remarks'.[67] The next morning, Gwen was up early and went for a long ramble 'on the magnificent beaches and through the town, a strange mixture of old and new, beauty & industrial squalor'.[68] The place reminded her irresistibly of Eddie's paintings, with their 'delicate towers against luminous smoky backgrounds'.[69] This was the countryside he had grown up in.

After her lecture, which 'seemed to go off all right', she had a final drink with the English department before getting back on the train to Sydney.[70] Heading south, 'with the glory fading, the cold increasing, night's vast shadow approaching', she began to have 'thoughts of disappearing'.[71] Why should she return to her cold, narrow existence when the world was so full of sunshine and possibilities? She could get off the train in Sydney and begin a new life. But somehow, she found herself heading obediently back to Hobart. 'We are creatures of conditioning,' she sighed to Ann.[72]

Yet the idea was beginning to take root. Why should she live in exile? Why not just leave? One reason was purely practical: she had no money. Around this time, Gwen set out her financial situation for Eddie, explaining that she worked twenty-four hours a week for $24.00 after tax. 'Out of this I have to buy everything but my food.'[73] Bill, always reluctant to spend money, 'pays all the bills but he wouldn't give me a cent to spend'.[74] Eddie was puzzled. 'There is something patently wrong in your financial set up,' he told Gwen. 'Hasn't Bill heard of a joint bank account?' To him, it made no sense for Gwen to spend her time working in an office instead of on her poetry, and he could not understand why Gwen did not insist on shared finances. 'You have made a rod for your own back within the family,' he told her sternly. 'Please, please preserve your genius as a poet.'[75]

Gwen would have liked to reduce her hours and spend more time on her writing, but she dreaded a return to her old state of economic dependence and was terrified of finding herself confined to the house once more. If she had to choose between home and work, she would choose work. Perhaps she could work her way around Australia, she mused to Tony – though she would not leave until she was sure the children would be able to manage without her.[76] As the 1970s rocked on, traditional ways of life were coming under challenge, and new possibilities were opening up. Even for a married woman in her fifties, a different kind of life seemed possible.

Gwen was very much attuned to the '70s vibe, which she was exploring at that time in a song cycle for Jim Penberthy based on the *Commentaries on Living* by Indian philosopher Jiddu Krishnamurti. Jim's instructions were to write 'six short poems, absolutely hilarious and shocking with a cynical nature but not too much so they won't be censored by the ABC'.[77] Gwen obliged with a libretto that encapsulated the flower-power sentiments of the time: cynicism about consumerism, despair at the persistence of war and a final affirmation that all you need is love.[78] Jim was overjoyed by the work which – as he declared at the premiere – 'prophecies the end of the world by pollution and through the greed, stupidity of us human beings'. In his opinion, it was 'the most important poem ever written in this country – and one of the greatest'.

Gwen was buoyed by Jim's enthusiasm. He was one of the few people who could match her in delight; indeed, she sometimes found herself telling him to 'cool it, baby'.[79] She could not attend the premiere of their 'Commentaries on Living' at the Festival of Perth in February 1972 – she could not get the time off work[80] – but Jim sent her an ecstatic telegram on the night: 'Success people weeping applauding you may have written masterpiece unbearable love . . . JP'[81] She was thrilled and 'deeply moved' – but also warned him not to 'idolise (or idealise)' her: 'I am human and ridiculous like everyone else.'[82]

Far from reducing her work hours, she increased them at the end of 1971, taking on a second job for three hours a day at an anaesthetists' office on Macquarie Street. She was keen to earn more money in the hope of buying her daughter a good second-hand oboe. Mary had taken up the instrument in high school and quickly excelled, but to continue to progress she needed an oboe of her own. Useless, Gwen told Tony, to apply to Bill, who 'would hand out his last cent for anything he thought a necessity' but would 'contribute nothing to musical activities'. There was nothing else for it: 'The ladies must labour for themselves.'[83]

She enjoyed her new job at first. She liked the doctors, including the principal, the handsome and charming Scot, Dr Tom Thomson, and she enjoyed the change of scene. After the office Christmas party, she reported gleefully to Tony that it was a huge improvement on the last office Christmas party she had attended, at the War Damage Commission in 1944: 'Handsome surgeons, gin, brandy, smoked salmon, mince pies, beautiful nurses & secretaries, beer, cheese, luxe, calme and as much voluptè as could be managed with a couple of stern doctors' wives (i.e. the stern wives of doctors) within range.'[84] After the party, she stayed behind to wash up, and was joined by Thomson. They shared a bottle of beer, and he told her that she gave 'no hint of age'. 'I should hope not,' the fifty-one-year-old Gwen answered tartly. 'I am the same age as you are.' But he insisted that there was 'some timeless quality' about her: 'You did not seem out of place with the young girls.' She was touched, and felt her spirits rise. 'As we said good-night he said without reserve "I *love* life, don't you?"' For the first time in a while, she felt she could agree.[85]

◆ ◆ ◆

In early February 1972, Gwen set off with Jim McAuley to give a series of readings for the Festival of Tasmania. Her relationship with Jim had become more intimate since he had been diagnosed with bowel cancer in 1970. After extensive surgery (he was reportedly responsible for the witticism 'better a semi-colon than a full-stop'),[86] he had recovered, but his brush with death had left its mark. Gwen was awed by his new works, which she considered 'the most beautiful poems I have ever read – in the Blake and Donne class'. 'They are lucid & simple and at the same time profoundly moving – like the great themes of Beethoven's last period,' she told Eddie. 'They have all the power of Jim's early lyrics but now there is a grace and weight of experience that lifts them far above anything being written now in Australia.'[87] These poems had the same effect on her that the torso of Apollo had had on Rilke, making her feel once more that 'you must change your life'. She felt that she was very far from such a breakthrough in her own writing, and to reach it she would have 'to experiment and face perhaps years of silence'.[88] But while Jim could count on lots of affirmation 'to reassure him' of the value of his new poetic direction, she felt she was very much alone in her quest for her own 'late style'.

Jim did affirm her, in his own way. She would later say that at their joint readings, he gave her 'total support, utter commitment'.[89] They had developed a program combining poetry with live music, with each of them reading several times over the course of an evening. They began their tour in Hobart, where the venue was 'packed out'. To Gwen's delight, her twins, Peter and Mary, came along. Gwen, who had long ago reconciled herself to Bill's lack of interest in her poetry, was 'very moved' to see her children in the audience, 'sitting listening to the old deathless verse'. Afterwards, they were 'generous enough to say it was good'.[90]

The next day, she and Jim drove to Launceston in a university car, Jim driving very fast, as was his wont, where they repeated the program with local musicians. The following day, it was on to Devonport. From the Sunrise Motel, she reported to Tony that she and Jim had had 'a marvellous dinner' – 'rock oysters and a very good steak, with a bottle of Penfolds vintage claret that Jim discovered by fossicking through a cellar' – and went to their event 'more than relaxed'.[91] The readings were a success, and they would repeat the experience in July, travelling to Launceston to give 'a kind of informal seminar' for the English Teachers Association. They would be invited to do another tour a couple of years later. From these jaunts would spring the vignettes in poems such as 'Infant Spurwing' and 'In Plato's Cave'. McAuley sent Gwen a poem entitled 'Motel, Burnie' from this period, which also seems to have originated in one of these trips.[92]

Over the next couple of months, Gwen made rushed weekend visits to Melbourne and Canberra, to see Eddie and Tony and to read at ANU. Then, at the end of July, she travelled to Brisbane to spend two weeks of her annual leave with Agnes. She had been anxious about her mother now that she was on her own, and wanted to reassure herself that Agnes was well and happy. Together, they made pilgrimages to the beaches of Gwen's childhood, 'from Noosa to Tweed Heads & sat eating coral trout & chips & gazing out to sea with anguish remembering my father'.[93] Agnes swept her daughter off to the Lord Mayor's Ball, a charity function for which she was on the organising committee, and to 'a terrifying morning party in town, with pumpkin scones, asparagus sandwiches and cream sponges'.[94] The guests were Agnes's friends, not Gwen's; during her visit Gwen saw 'nobody at all who remembered me as a young woman, though many who had dandled me on their now bony knees as an infant'. They seemed to her to be relics of her childhood, still 'living in the time when the outer suburbs were the scene of bush picnics and the town hall was a waste block in the city'.

On her way home, she stopped off in Melbourne to deliver a paper at La Trobe University, staying at Brighton with Beverley Dunn, an actor who specialised in reading poetry. She had met Beverly a couple of years before in Hobart at a performance of works by Tasmanian women from the era of European settlement through to the present. Gwen was impressed not only that Beverley had chosen to read two of her poems, 'At the Bistro' and 'In the Park', but also that she read them so well, delivering them with 'real bite'.[95] From then on, Beverley was her preferred reader for radio and television programs featuring her poetry.[96]

Gwen Harwood with Rodney Hall, Melbourne, 1972

After an unprecedented three weeks away from Hobart, Gwen again found re-entry to ordinary life difficult. She had a lot to distract her. Her eldest son and his family had just returned from England, which was cause for great rejoicing, but they would soon be moving to South Australia, which was not. Her second son needed her to type up his honours thesis, which took up her own precious writing time but was a task she enjoyed. She would not have been writing in any case: unlike her 1969 trip to Melbourne, her latest excursion had not stimulated her poetic nerves. 'At present I just can't face poetry (particularly not "poetry"),' she told Tony. 'I should be getting my selection together for A&R, but can't bear the sight of it. Perhaps, like Rilke, I'll have to take 20 years off to recover & write the last works.'[97]

For the first time, her publisher had solicited her for a new volume. They were getting requests for reprintings of her second book from teachers and lecturers who wanted to set her work for their students, and rather than reprint *Poems: Volume II*, they proposed to publish a selected works, incorporating her recent verse as well as poems from her first two books.[98] In theory, Gwen was in favour of the idea; she might even make some money from a paperback edition. But in practice, she found it depressing to go back through her old work. 'I can't stand any of it,' she told Eddie. 'I am quite prepared to let it all die off, and start again with nothing. I don't mean to stop writing, but I feel utterly dissatisfied with my past work. I would keep only six poems, and that's not enough for a selection.'[99]

She was reading *The Dream Songs* of American poet John Berryman, who had killed himself in January of that year, and she found them 'perversely great: fractured syntax, crazy jumps of thought, but marvellous'.[100] She wanted to write with that kind of 'power and vitality', but with an overlay of Jim McAuley's newly discovered 'simplicity & perfection of form'.[101] She was fascinated by Berryman's creation, in the dream songs, of 'two selves, Henry & Mr Bones', who often held 'a sort of dialogue'.[102] It was something she would try in a sequence she was planning featuring two of her own 'selves', Baby and Demon.[103]

She was troubled by Berryman's suicide. 'I wish I could find a way out of my present maze,' she told Tony, apropos of the poet's death.[104] To Eddie she said that it was 'no wonder' Berryman had jumped off the Brooklyn Bridge: 'If you couldn't go on at that level' – if you went backwards as a poet, declining from the high standards you had set for yourself – 'you might as well jump for it'.[105] She herself was once again clouded by 'intense middle-aged depression', as 'empty as a jagged old condensed milk tin on an antheap'.[106] She was in desperate need of an influx of 'irresponsible joy' to fill her creative well – and she would not have long to wait.

19

The Owl and the Pussycat

You longed for the night and the night is coming,
the rays of the daystar fade and die,
the nightwind rises, the tide is waiting,
and the years that are gone lean down from the sky.
Gwen Harwood, 'The Owl and the Pussycat Baudelaire Rock'

A FEW MONTHS INTO 1972, GWEN'S NEW EMPLOYERS ASKED her to come and work for them full time. Things had been growing steadily quieter at Dr Waterworth's, where she had now worked for eight years, so she agreed. But the anaesthetists' office was a less stimulating workplace: there were no patients to interact with, and the anaesthetists themselves – 'faceless technicians' in Gwen's view – were rarely there. As the months went on, she found herself increasingly in conflict with the twenty-one-year-old receptionist, Jenny, whom she found appallingly banal: 'so conventional that you realise Barry Humphries was underdoing it all'.[1] She was a model 1950s kind of wife, 'very pretty in a peachy sort of way'. 'Bill adores her and is always chatting her up,' she sniffed to Ann. 'I do think she is what he wanted, a dolly to play with.' Gwen felt that Jenny had resented her presence in the office, where she had previously presided as 'Queen', and her resentment had grown into powerful dislike; indeed, she believed Jenny had come to 'loathe' the interloper 'from the bottom of her suburban heart'.[2] The office became a battleground, with covert strikes and counterstrikes making them both tense and miserable.

Sometime during this year, Gwen embarked on an affair. It was in no way a repeat of her grand passion of 1957; she was not in love, just trying her wings. When she confided in Ann, she did not name her lover, saying only that he was 'a nice, clean doctor of my own age',[3] but this echo of a phrase she had earlier used about Tom Thomson – whom she considered a 'lovely man' – suggests he was a likely candidate. Many years later, when Greg Kratzmann asked her about this affair, she said only that she couldn't remember – 'and laughed and laughed'.[4]

To Gwen's chagrin, the affair was a let-down. Her lover, she told Ann, was always trying to make her take showers, and 'his bathroom cupboard looked like a fairy's deodorant banquet'.[5] 'I like to be as clean as the next person, but there are times when I like to *sleep*, not get up & take a shower,' she grumbled. The sex was awful, and she very soon realised that she had made 'a terrible mistake'. By the end of the year, she had decided to remove herself from the anaesthetists' rooms altogether – though only after 'a few really nasty & satisfying scenes' with Jenny. When she announced that she was leaving, Tom – her 'delightful Scottish doctor' – offered her a pay rise, and when she declined, three months' holiday on full pay. But even this blandishment left her unmoved.[6] She had applied for and been offered a job with a cardiac specialist and though it was a 'considerable drop in salary', had decided to accept. She was to be 'secretary & receptionist' and trained in 'electrocardiograms and urine testing (fun! fun!)'.[7] It would be another new start.

Changing jobs in early 1973 eased some of the pressure on Gwen. She was working fewer hours, and the new job was less stressful. She liked her employer, Dr Millingen, though he was obsessive about dust and treated her, in the kindliest fashion, like a child. In letters that vividly recall the untamed Gwen of WDC days, she made merciless fun of his idiosyncrasies, but she did not hold them against him, regarding him as 'a brilliant diagnostician'.[8] Yet the new, more peaceful work environment could not entirely mitigate her sense of angst. Her younger children were now finishing their studies and making plans to leave home. 'I don't know what I shall do without my twins,' she told Tony sadly.[9] The time had surely come to change her life, but still she hesitated, unsure what steps to take.

She was desperate to get to Europe and see for herself the places – and artworks – her friends had been talking about for years. 'ONE DAY I WILL SEE THE TURNERS IN THE TATE AND MY BRAIN WILL EXPLODE,' she told Eddie.[10] For years she had been hoping that once the children were grown, Bill would take another period of study leave and they would travel overseas together, but she had now accepted that this was not going to happen. Bill had 'said NO finally and utterly', she reported to Eddie. He would not stop her from going by herself – 'he says if I want to go I can take his savings & go alone' – but she did not consider this a serious offer. 'You can imagine the spirit in which this is said,' she told Eddie gloomily.[11] She would not use his money to go overseas, and she did not yet have enough of her own to pay for herself.[12]

But if overseas travel was out of the question for now, leaving Tasmania was not. 'I am planning to move out of this frozen island next year,' she told Jim Penberthy in May 1973. 'I'll probably set up independently in NSW.'[13]

Around the same time she confided to Ann that once Mary had graduated next year, there would be 'little reason for me to lurk around'.[14] She did not mention divorce, yet she was certainly talking about leaving Bill. He would not care, she told Ann, as he was not 'seriously concerned about what I do'. She added that she wished she had 'a Stephen of my own' – that is, a young poet as a lover, as Ann had – 'but "the times are waxing late"'.

Her old friend Rex Hobcroft had been urging her to make poetry her priority, and his words carried weight. Rex had left Tasmania in 1972 to become the director of the Sydney Conservatorium, but had returned on a brief visit in early 1973. He had pointed out 'that I am wasting my life working endlessly to provide for children who are well provided for anyway with their qualifications,' she told Tony. 'I can see how right he is. I should be using up the last of my talents while I have the energy.'[15] A similar sentiment had earlier made its way into *Lenz,* in which the poet's friends tell him he is 'wasting [his] life': 'You live like a fool, your talents bleed away.' The individual's responsibility to their own gifts was once again on her mind. 'At present I am passing through a time of great sadness, a realisation of how little I have made of the gifts I was born with,' she told Eddie in April.[16] A few months later, she declared again that she was 'only now (aged 53!) beginning to understand how I have wasted my life'.

Her eldest son had recently introduced her to the work of Scottish psychiatrist R.D. Laing,[17] and his ideas about enculturation resonated strongly with her own experience. Laing believed that 'most mental illness is caused by family life', she explained to Tony. 'To be accepted by the group you have to deform yourself to fit in with what is expected of you'.[18] It seemed evident to Gwen that she had for many years actively worked to deform herself to fit others' expectations.[19] The question she would struggle with over the next several years was whether, even armed with this new self-knowledge, she would be able to stop doing so. She was tired, she told Eddie in June, 'right into the marrow of my half-century-old bones'. Ten years of 'getting up before anyone else, feeding them & getting them off to school & university, providing endless meals and clothes & all the money I earned' had left her depleted.[20] She did not blame her family: the fault was hers. She had known, she admitted, from the moment she arrived in Tasmania that it was not the right place for her, but she had never had 'the nerve to desert and set myself up as an independent person of talent'. Instead she had allowed herself to be warped by family life, and now she feared she had been 'destroyed'. A handful of close friends had kept her alive: Tony, Eddie, Rex and Ann.

Eddie was going through a crisis of his own; still in terrible pain, he was fantasising about suicide and questioning everything in his life, including his long and happy marriage. Gwen responded passionately to his outpourings, drawing out that same agonised part of herself to meet his despair. 'In my long and bloody fight I have often been suicidal, not with depression (I am not a depressive) but with sheer *exhaustion*,' she told him. 'THEY HAVE EATEN ME ALIVE. But now you & I are old enough to be mad & responsible only to ourselves & the wits we were born with. Let the rest go.'[21] They were both artists, she assured him, both geniuses – or, at least, she had been before her marriage – and it was time to acknowledge that their chief obligations were to their gifts. When Eddie announced that he had fallen in love with one of his nurses, Gwen urged him to throw himself into this new passion: 'For the celestial heaven's sake, see her, soak yourself in her, eat her, drink her before it's too late.'[22] If Eddie felt he needed to leave his wife, she told him, he should leave her.

For herself, she was less certain. She felt that to reach her full potential as a poet, she would have to leave Bill. She knew he had no interest in her poetry; he would be happy, she believed, if she never wrote another poem. But, more than that, she felt he did not really care about her needs and goals, only about ensuring she helped him meet his. 'If I ceased to write, saw nobody, received no letters, devoted myself to him entirely, mastered current linguistic theory & talked of nothing else, gave up all ideas of seeing the other side of the world before I die – I'd only be a cardboard replica of the doll he wanted to play with.'[23]

Yet summoning up the 'nerve to desert' was as difficult as it had ever been. She felt bound to Bill, just as she had back in 1957. He was still the person she most liked to argue with, her closest intellectual peer, and the pole against which she measured her own trajectory. In some profound way, he was her ballast. On a practical level, too, little had changed – she still did not have the funds to set up on her own. Casting around for sources of income, she decided to apply for one of the writers' grants offered by the Commonwealth Literary Fund under the new Whitlam government. For established writers, they paid six thousand dollars a year for three years – not a large amount (about a third of what Bill earned), but still more than she could earn as a medical secretary.[24] The grants were highly competitive, though, and as she had no confidence she would get one,[25] she began to consider other options as well.

One was to do a TAFE course in hotel management and catering.[26] The idea of running a hotel was something she had quietly contemplated for years. Her grandmother had managed first a café and then a residential college; Gwen felt she could probably do something similar. With skills in hospitality, she could work her way around Australia 'in hotel kitchens' – an idea she mentioned to Tony in 1969 and again to Jim Penberthy in 1971.[27] She would wait until 'the last of the children is through university' and then she would 'stop all this nonsensical pretence of being crisp and competent' and strike out on her own.

Another idea, if she decided to stay with Bill, was to turn the family home into a boarding house for music students.[28] Once the children had all left, it would be much too big for her and Bill, and offering rooms to students would achieve the dual purpose of 'making money & getting company at the same time'. The vision of a house full of earnest young souls practising their instruments, as in one of her favourite novels, *Maurice Guest*, was delightful. 'I have fantasies of Augusta Road filled with young musicians eating nourishing meals and practising far into the night. Pleasure and profit!'[29] But this was never more than a fantasy. If Bill could not tolerate her piano practice, he would never countenance a house full of noisy musicians-in-training. 'The Great Hermit of course can't bear much of the human race', Gwen growled to Rex.[30]

She still had not made any decisions when, halfway through 1973, her boss, Dr Millingen, announced he was closing his practice to take an academic position.[31] Rather than start looking for a new job, Gwen asked Bill for a share of his salary so that she would not need to return to the workforce immediately. He agreed to give her a monthly allowance of $125. Her plan was to do the hotel management course in 1974, but late in July, just before her job ended, she learned that she had been awarded a grant by the Commonwealth Literature Fund. She was to have a guaranteed income for three years, and for the first time in her life, would be able to write full time. At last she would have the means to change her life.

◆ ◆ ◆

The grant payments did not begin at once, and to Gwen's fury, Bill cut off her allowance the moment the grant was announced. 'I am living on my savings at present', she told Ann.[32] 'Scrooge is now quite incredible about money.' But the shortage of funds would only temporarily cramp her plans.

'When the money starts coming (I guess it will take a month or so) I'll assemble some & decide what to do.' She had agreed to write a science-fiction opera with Jim Penberthy, and wanted to complete that 'before I take off'. She was also finally tackling the manuscript for her new book, having signed another contract with Angus & Robertson. Going back over her early poems was as depressing as she had expected – 'They all give me the horrors,' she told Tony[33] – but she was keen to get the manuscript in. Apart from these commitments, she considered herself free. One possibility was to join Ann in London. 'Are you coming back here (in which case I'll stay, or join you for the homeward journey), or staying in England?' she asked eagerly. 'How about Greece?'

Towards the end of August, she went to Sydney for a week as a guest of the North Side Arts Festival Write-In. The idea was that established poets would hold workshops for aspiring poets involving writing exercises and group critiques. Hot on the heels of her invitation to the festival, she received a letter from Norman Talbot, the young poet-academic she had met in Newcastle in 1971, urging her to come. He assured her that the evening performances were 'often fun, the parties & other moral collisions alone worth the journey'. The workshop participants, though 'rarely excellent poets', were interesting.[34] Among the other invited poets were David Campbell, Les Murray, David Malouf, Tom Shapcott, Rodney Hall, Bruce Dawe, Bruce Beaver and Alexander Craig – a litany of emerging male poetry deities (Norman seemed unconscious of any gender imbalance in retailing this list). Gwen was more than happy to participate, now that she was no longer working. She was a little daunted, however, when she checked in at the highly functional Dunmore Lang College at Macquarie University where she was staying. It was 'brand-new' and 'induced immediate and lasting depression and a desire for debauchery and drink'.[35] Luckily, fellow guests Bruce and Brenda Beaver 'produced drink within 5 mins of my arrival'.

Norman was staying off campus at El Rancho, 'an incredible motel right out of Lolita (it appeared to be a pick-up station)'. When he saw Gwen, he swept her into a great bear hug, lifting her off the ground.[36] Gwen was delighted. From that moment, the poetic energy that had flickered between them in their occasional letters ignited. Somewhere between the anodyne corridors of Dunmore Lang and the wood-panelled rooms of El Rancho, they began an affair.

Gwen was fifty-three, Norman not quite thirty-seven. She was tiny and mischievous, he large and ebullient, but they were both poetry mad, both flaming with enthusiasms of all kinds, both keen admirers of each other's writing. They sat side-by-side in the dining room at their 'first supper' like 'two comets with their blazing tails / under the table'.[37] Later, in Norman's room at El Rancho, they drank wine, made love and 'frolicked' in the shower.[38]

Norman Talbot, early 1970s

The motel's 'desert-booted palms', 'saffron' light and 'smoky scarlet' wine would become the secret signifiers of their affair.[39] He was Northman and she Southlady, modes of address which later morphed into Norseman (when Norman began to study Norse poetry), and Dame (or Lady) Gwendolina. He was the heroic knight Tristan and she was his forbidden Irish love, Isolde. She was Goldenwine – a favoured anagram of her name, which quickly evolved into Goldenchild – while he was Father Aether, Hölderlin's sky god. Everything was a pun or an allusion or a secret play on words. He was 'leg-biting' Norman, yet it was 'she alone' who could 'bite / with absolute delight'.[40]

They gave their daily workshops, went to their nightly readings, and ate and drank in happy conviviality with the other poets, and if anyone noticed that their spirits were suspiciously high, no one thought enough of it to say anything. Gwen greatly enjoyed the workshops, and was flattered that the students who chose her as their poetry mentor included 'the brilliant Keith Russell (this year's winner of the farmer's Poetry Prize) and Nicky Hasluck, the GG's son'. Some of the other invited poets also made their way to her workshops from time to time, including Bruce Beaver and Barry Breen. It was nothing but 'lovely talk, shop shop shop for a week', and Gwen was in her element. She did not like the Write-In's organiser, however. Dr Grace Perry twice crashed her workshop, and Gwen found her unpleasantly imperious, even downright rude. Gwen did not scruple to cut Grace's 'tea-and-bikkies farewell' and was amused when a rumour went around that she had disappeared with Rodney Hall.[41]

In fact, she had gone to Central Station with Norman to see him onto the Newcastle Flyer – the very train she had caught two years earlier on her visit to Newcastle. They were in an electric state; everything around them seemed to be imbued with secret significance, and Gwen noted down the text of every sign and the gist of every snatch of conversation. They said goodbye 'somewhat flamboyantly among trolleys labelled NOT TO BE TAKEN FROM SYDNEY STATION – I know that as long as I live a bit of me will not be removed from Sydney Station,' she told Ann joyfully.[42]

Gwen had arranged to spend the weekend with Rex Hobcroft's wife, Lory, who wanted to take the opportunity to begin an oil portrait of Gwen. Posing for Lory was a relief: it meant she did not have to don her usual sociable persona but could 'sit still while nations melted.' In her last days in Sydney, she also managed to catch up with Larry Sitsky, who was visiting the Sydney Conservatorium, and still made it home in time to hear Mary as first oboist in a performance of Schubert's *Unfinished Symphony* at Hobart City Hall.[43]

On the plane, she wrote Norman a brief poem in one continuous spiral on the back of a circular postcard featuring a kangaroo and the legend 'Greetings from Sydney':

> This is a circular to say
> Nothing they do can damage me
> For if my tongue were torn away
> It would reform itself, and be
> Your lamp, your sanctuary flame,
> calling the dark of absence to
> the pure assertion of your name.
> Though I am posted on from you

Unénveloped, & stamped with loss,
flying at 30,000 feet
towards glacial drifts, I'll keep my gloss,
and [?]cry round curves until we meet.[44]

At almost the same time, Norman was scrawling what he called a 'first draught' of an untitled poem about their time together:

I haven't yet been brave enough
to take a very deep breath . . .
Breathing out is less trouble
but leaves me dazed & a little lost . . .[45]

He had begun working on another poem, 'Eyedrops from Ireland', while they were still in Sydney. Sending it to her in late August, he told her it was now in its sixth draft, and that 'the landscape has been changed to protect the totally innocent . . .'.[46] 'It was strange & new,' this poem begins:

You   glancing sideupward
from my poem   from your glass
reflecting you'll put me soon
          into your arms.

He depicts her eyes as 'amber' – a recurring trope in their poems and letters – and describes the 'smallwren vigilant wit' of her 'brilliant glancing' body. 'When a lady goes to a gent's / cabin alone at night', he goes on, playfully, it means 'only one thing / at a time'.

Gwen responded warmly, telling him the poem was 'a heart-breaker (and mender) as direct as your hand laid on me & yet held in its own peaceful space: I am in it and out of it'.[47] She also responded as a poet, with technical advice, telling him, for example, that his choice of one particular word 'grate[d]' – 'but then your work is more chromatic than mine & you may want that note there'.

Immediately after her return from Sydney, she sent him a poem entitled simply 'Morning', which began with a quotation from the sixteenth-century English poet Thomas Wyatt: 'Forget not yet, forget not this', a new version of her eternal cry to her lovers, 'Remember me'. The poem begins:

> We are what darkness has become:
> two bodies bathed in saffron light,
> disarmed by sudden distances,
> pitched on the singing heights of time,
> our skin aflame with eastern airs;
> changed beyond reason, but not rhyme.[48]

She had also written some love poems while they were still together in Sydney, though hers were entirely playful. These poems, the 'Yoken Marker Songs', were inspired by an absurd English translation of the instructions included with the Japanese-made marker pens they had used in the Write-In workshops. Among the phrases on which her poems riffed were 'abstain them from holding the items in their mouth', 'please keep our bodies level after use', and 'plain and slipperly'.[49] The 'Plain and Slipperly' poem begins:

> When I am plain and slipperly
> like Ruskin's Mum (but crazier)
> say to your current Iseult "She
> was great, I was in love with her ..."

It ends with a kind of declaration:

> If I choose to speak
> I'll conjure up the desert-booted
> trees of El Rancho round the week,
> or pentacle of days uprooted
>
> From Time itself . . . .

She was adding her days with Norman to her small hoard of moments outside of time in which her true self shone free of its mortal trappings.

In the weeks and months after her return to Hobart, the poems continued to pour out. On 17 September, just a little over a fortnight after she got back from Sydney, she sent Norman a poem entitled 'Collocational Shift', which began: 'Here and everywhere I meet your lovely bulk / except in dreams – you are too near to dream –' Soon after, she revised this poem a little and submitted it for the 1974 *Poet's Choice* anthology. Some of her revisions were made, she told Norman, 'to protect, as you say, the innocent – though from *what*?'[50] The phrase 'lovely bulk' in the first line became 'crazy scent', while a line in the second stanza that had originally read 'the sign of the Talbots was a running hound' became 'Whose is the emblem of a running hound?' She was delighted when the anthology's editor, Philip Roberts, wrote to tell her the poem was 'a knockout'. It was published in the anthology as 'Meditation on Wyatt I', and was eventually joined, in *Selected Poems* in 1975, by her 'Morning' poem, retitled 'Meditation on Wyatt II'.

The poetic dialogue between the pair continued with Norman's 'Wild Haloes', to which she riposted with 'Thought Is Surrounded by a Halo'.[51] The Tristan poems on which Norman would work for several years also explored his relationship with Gwen, among other things. She responded with 'Isolde's Song', and was delighted when Roberts placed it alongside Norman's 'Father Aether' in the 1975 issue of *Poet's Choice*. 'My dear!' she wrote to him in great glee. 'Does he KNOW?'[52]

◆ ◆ ◆

After the joy and freedom of her week of poetry and illicit passion, the return to domestic life in Hobart was even harder than usual. 'Things are fairly bad for me at the moment, terrible even,' she told Tony, the week she got back.[53] 'My usual state of Angst has reached apocalyptic proportions.' The pleasure of having her days free to read and write was considerable: she was 'reading, really reading after 10 years of gutting books in a tired state', and hoping to write 'better than I have done in the past'.[54] But far from solving her domestic problems, the gifts of time and financial independence only magnified them. 'My decision about leaving work seems a trivial concern compared with trying to keep a marriage together, & wondering if I should try,' she confessed to Tony. 'The grant and the independence it confers have brought to light all the old conflicts that were pushed below the surface when we had children to bring up. Nothing is changed . . . [Bill] makes it clear that in spite of the great physical bond between us, which is as strong as ever, I have been a total disappointment to him.'[55] For her part, she found Bill's 'contempt for the human race less and less bearable'.

Gwen made a point of telling Tony that there was no one else in the picture for either of them. She was not lying. She loved Norman – 'beyond reason, thank goodness' – but did not want to marry him. She saw the affair simply as an injection of joy and excitement into her life, a restorative after the growing darkness of the past couple of years. To Ann, she described it as 'a happy 5-day session in Sydney with a young poet who adores women & delighted me by saying that when I was old he would still count me as the dearest of women – enough to sustain me for a long time'.[56] She felt that his love had changed her for the better: it had 'melted away many of my old sorrows and failures and healed some old wounds I had almost got used to,' as she told Norman himself, almost a year later.[57] But she had definitively moved on from the belief that love – romantic or sexual love, at least – was the answer to her life's question.

Norman was less certain about the status of the affair. He did not want to leave his wife and children, but he was besotted with Gwen. The wild profusion of poetry, the puns and jokes, the Sappho cards and letters flying between them were heady, and Norman was not immune to a sense of gratification that a poet of Gwen's stature would be interested in him. He was a little insecure about the poems he was sending her and tried to pre-empt her possible criticisms by pointing out a weak word or a bad rhyme, and sending revised versions of jeux d'esprit. He knew that he was outclassed: 'I would I had your felicity (what a feline word) in impromptus!' he moaned in one letter.[58] Gwen herself never expressed unease about her love poems. She had been whipping off impromptus of all kinds for most of her life and had no illusions about the genre: it was all to do with the timing, and the odd infelicity was immaterial. Then again, her extemporaneous effusions were dazzlingly proficient. Even poets of the calibre of Vin Buckley and A.D. Hope had fallen by the wayside in epistolary attempts to keep up with the extraordinary flow of her invention.

But if Gwen had no intention of running away with Norman, there is no doubt that the affair was a catalyst for her discontent with her marriage, which came pouring out in letters to Tony, Ann and Eddie. Even so, she could not make up her mind to take any drastic steps. A week after she told Tony her marriage might not be worth saving, she wrote to assure him that she was 'sailing more evenly again'.[59] She added that the news that John and his wife were expecting their second child had damped her 'fiery self-assertion': 'I certainly would not cloud their happiness with any disruptive behaviour'.[60] She was not willing to face the opprobrium, both public and private, that would follow were she to leave Bill. But this meant she was thrown back into her old despair. Two months later, she told Tony that she didn't feel like 'seeing people (except you) – I'm in a hopeless everything-comes-too-late I-see-not-feel-how-beautiful etc. I feel my life has been a succession of wrong choices. If I were a real depressive I'd probably take to drink, but I know I'm not.' Experience told her that she would 'recover', but she was profoundly disheartened by her own seeming inability to change her life. 'I am like the slave who, freed from his chains, kept right on doing the same things,' she told Tony. 'My loneliness is intense.'[61]

Norman, meanwhile, was making plans to see his lover again. The University of Newcastle ran annual poetry workshops at Morpeth, a historical town on the edge of the Hunter Valley, and he made sure she was invited to attend the 1974 workshops as a group leader, alongside Roland Robinson, Dorothy Hewett, Louis Johnson and Norman himself.[62] He was also hoping to wangle her an invitation to be a writer-in-residence at the university in 1975 – which would mean coming to Newcastle for nine weeks. She accepted the invitation to Morpeth in September with alacrity; in the meantime, she had work to do. She was settling into the life of a full-time writer, turning one of the empty bedrooms left by her children's departure into 'a space of my own': 'already it has the untidy look the arts generate'.[63] She was working on an opera with Jim Penberthy, as well as a short libretto for Ian Cugley for a children's opera, *Sea Changes,* which would tell the story of a shipload of boys sent as convicts to the Point Puer prison at Port Arthur.[64] The libretti gave her a focus at those times when 'the Muse has flapped off behind the mountain for a while'.[65]

Her project with Jim was to be a full-length 'space opera' based on an original idea of her own – the first time she had not been tasked with adapting existing material. 'I must start reading the comics again (haven't been taking them since my kids grew up),' she told Jim, 'and see what's going on out there behind Orion.'[66] When she was farewelling Norman at Sydney Station, it struck her that it would be the perfect setting for her opera. She wrote immediately to Jim with an outline of *Station* – a reference both to a railway station (the setting of the first act) and a space station (the second).[67] Jim loved it. 'Let's make something that excites and satisfies everybody to ecstasy – the people, the philosophers, the artists,' he urged. 'Let's satisfy ourselves to ecstasy. Come on honey, hit me!!!!!'[68]

Gwen let her imagination roam not only over science fiction but also over 1970s youth culture. Among her characters were an arrogant scientist (shades of Eisenbart), representing Traditional Values, and a set of gender-fluid twins, representing the New Age of peace and love.[69] Needless to say, the twins triumph, creating a new world with crowds of way-out druggies and hippies. Phrases that sprang from Gwen's poems for Norman found their way into the mouths of the opera's lovers. 'Lullaby, O lullaby,' the hippies sing in the finale, 'you shall be our golden child.'

The opera was never performed – Jim completed the music the following year but could not interest anyone in staging it – but it gave Gwen a priceless opportunity to try out some radical poetic ideas that would later make their way into her poetry. For her hippies' chorus, she wrote a free translation of Baudelaire's 'Recueillement' that would later appear in several poems:

> You wished for the night, and the night is coming,
> the sounds of the city fade and die,
> hunger and shame will sleep until morning,
> the years that are gone lean down from the sky.[70]

The words sung by the hippies when they morph into junkies would also make their way into one of Gwen's poems:

> Baby, baby, short-circuit your brain,
> ground it out for as long as you can,
> Baby, baby, straight to the main
> I'm a fucked-up sinner out of my mind.
>
> You longed for night & the night is coming,
> Your head's burned out and your dreams are gone,
> Baby lie down in stony darkness
> Baby my baby the night comes on.[71]

The violence of this imagery, not to mention the driving power of the rhythms, were new in the Harwood oeuvre. They seemed to presage a darker conception of love than she had yet brought to her work.

Meanwhile, Gwen's professional calendar was becoming increasingly crowded. She was a guest at the Adelaide Writers' Week in March 1974 ('boring boring boring'),[72] and in May spent a week at Monash University in Melbourne with Bruce Dawe, giving 'two readings and many hours of tutorials on our work (we are both "set")'.[73] She also gave a reading at the Melbourne Maydaze Arts Festival with Vin Buckley, Bruce Beaver, Ron Simpson and David Rowbotham, where she was delighted and somewhat abashed to find herself described as a 'Major Poet'.

Her plans to leave Bill and/or Tasmania were beginning to feel less urgent. Ann Jennings had returned to Hobart to live, which made the city much more 'tolerable' for Gwen;[74] having Ann within reach meant she was not so lonely. It also seemed that she might finally make it to Europe. Lory Hobcroft was planning a trip to Greece the following year and asked Gwen to come too, along with a handful of other women. With Gwen's grant money behind her, it seemed possible. Perhaps she would make it to Europe after all, she told Tony excitedly.[75]

For the time being, she was happy to escape to Brisbane for a few weeks in July 1974. She stayed with Agnes – still fit and energetic, though her house looked like 'an abandoned antique shop'[76] – and revelled in being a 'Visiting Person' in her old home town. She addressed the students at her alma mater, the Brisbane Girls Grammar School, recorded poems for the University of Queensland Press, gave a 'talk' about her childhood on ABC radio and did readings for the Speech Teachers' Association, the Conservatorium and the Mount Gravatt Teachers' College.[77] Though she and Agnes drove each other 'crazy', Gwen found northern life 'endlessly pleasant'. The controversial painting *Blue Poles*, which was touring the country, had arrived in Brisbane, and since Agnes was 'on the door' at City Hall for the exhibition, Gwen 'looked at that marvellous work for hours AND had a plate of fine crab sandwiches'.[78]

Her talk on the ABC – she had called it 'A Time beyond Reason', but it was broadcast, to her annoyance, as 'How I Became Gwen Harwood' – was such a success that Roger McDonald, who was still at UQP, invited her to write a book about her life for the press. She was tempted, but hesitated 'because of my family'.[79] If poems were a violation of her husband's privacy, prose would surely not be tolerated. Nevertheless, it was an idea she would return to.

◆ ◆ ◆

The Morpeth poetry workshop in early September was pure delight. The conference centre was on the site of a historical house, Closebourne, which had been the Anglican bishop's residence in the early nineteenth century and had since served as a boys' home and a grammar school. Neighbouring Morpeth House was for many years an Anglican theological college. The gracious sandstone buildings were set on a verdant hillside, removed from the newer, less picturesque constructions, and there was a delightfully monastic walled garden and an austere stone chapel with wood panelling and stained-glass windows. It was an irresistible setting for both poetry and love.

Norman had broken his leg and was on crutches, wearing an extravagant, multi-coloured caftan his wife had made for him. His lack of mobility and their somewhat spartan accommodation caused the lovers much hilarity. On her return to Hobart, Gwen sent Norman a postcard with an acrostic poem spelling out 'The Anglican Bed'. The poem's speaker questions Tristan and Isolde on 'where [they] lay', 'what wide couch, till the break of day'. Tristan refuses to say, but Isolde replies:

> Canter or carioca we could not.
> A piece of furniture designed for dumb
> Novices of pious habits bound us.
> Believe me, sir, although our fragile cot
> Endured, I feared nightlong that all would come
> Down like the walls of Jericho around us.[80]

Around the same time, Norman sent his Isolde a poem beginning:

> Golden child there was something
>   I meant to have told
>   you golden child.[81]

In reply, Gwen sent him a brief poem entitled 'Lullaby' – an echo of a song from 'Stations' – which finished:

> Let me be your golden child,
> settle me inside your arm,
> rock me to the sleep of Always
> hold me in your dream of now.[82]

At Morpeth, the personas of the Owl and the Pussycat sprang into full life. Gwen had already dubbed Norman 'eule', German for 'owl'. A few months after their Morpeth tryst, she would tell him that she had seen an owl looking 'across the dustbrush through the abrupt spears of the rushes, as you looked that wordless morning in the roofless chapel'.[83] From there, it was a small step to cast herself as Edward Lear's pussycat. It seems to have been one of the workshop participants, Vikki, who introduced Lear's poem into proceedings – Gwen described her in a letter as 'the Owl and the Pussycat girl'[84] – but it was Gwen who seized on the nonsense poem's connections with one of her favourite works of Baudelaire, 'L'invitation au voyage'. It was from this poem that Gwen had drawn, many years ago, one of her characteristic refrains: 'Luxe, calme et volupté' (Luxury, peace and pleasure). (A recurrent joke was to label newspaper photographs of trios of dignified churchmen or politicians 'Luxe, Calme et Volupté'.) In Baudelaire's poem, the speaker dreams of travelling to a far land with his beloved ('my child, my sister') where there will be no sorrow or hardship but only 'order and beauty, / Luxury, calm and pleasure'. The owl and the pussycat in Lear's poem similarly plan to 'sail away, for a year and a day' to a mythical land where they can be married and live happily ever after. The two poems even have a similar rhythmical structure: two two-stress lines followed by a three-stress line.

It's easy to see why this fantasy of an unlikely pair of lovers on a voyage to a land of pure happiness would have appealed to Gwen. Soon after Morpeth, she sent Norman a Sappho card featuring a beautiful, contemporary pen-and-ink drawing of the Owl and the Pussycat in their sea-green boat.[85] On the back of the card was a poem, 'The Owl & Pussycat Baudelaire-Type Rock'.[86] The poem begins not with 'L'invitation' but with 'Recuillement' – 'You longed for the night & the night is coming' – but quickly segues to a lovers' voyage to a land 'where all is harmony & delight', picking up images from 'L'invitation' in its depiction of that land, with its 'Fragrance of amber, fathomless mirrors, reflecting the gold and hyacinth light'. Interspersed with the lovers' dream of flight, however, is a version of the druggies' song from 'Stations':

> Baby my baby I'll love you forever,
>> When your head's burned out & your light's all gone
> My eyes will find you in stony darkness.
>> Baby my baby the night comes on.

There is ambivalence here, as well as Gwen's characteristic exuberance and inventiveness.

Two days later, she sent Norman another poem on a card featuring a sinuous owl strumming a guitar. This poem was much lighter – a ballad, to be sung to the tune of 'On the Road to Mandalay'. It began:

> On the lookout at new Lambton
>   gazing eastwards to the sea
> There's a hornèd owl a-singing
>   & I know he thinks of me.
> O the cold spring stars are shining
>   & I read the words they spell:
> come you back to Newcastèl
>   Come you back to Newcastèl . . . . . .[87]

Two further cards in the series would appear a month later, one featuring an elegant pussycat dancing on her hind legs and a poem entitled: 'Pussycat's Address to the German-Speaking Dustbrush Deity' (to be sung to the tune of 'Deutschlandlied'):

> Lean to earth, Immortal Dustbrush!
>   God, whose bristles formed my coat,
> hear the tenebristic cadence
>   from my true love's mournful throat.[88]

For the rest of their lives, Norman and Gwen would address each other in letters by various iterations of these creaturely identities.

◆ ◆ ◆

Soon after her return from Morpeth, Gwen set off on a reading tour of northern Tasmania with Jim McAuley. Organised by the Adult Education department, the tour took in some remote locations, including King Island. Gwen was anxious about flying in a small plane – 'one of Father Aether's shoeboxes' – and jokingly begged Norman to 'Pray for us!'[89] All went well, however, and Gwen would later say that they gave their 'best reading on King Island with the wind howling outside'.[90] She was preoccupied with Norman, thinking longingly of him while she and Jim dined at the motel, 'looking out over the raging waters of the Bass Strait'. 'I needed to say your name, and held my tongue,' she wrote to him. She was delighted when Jim himself brought Norman up, telling her that a critic had sent him an article on Norman's poetry for *Quadrant*.

In a postcard to Norman, she summarised the trip in a poem that revisited Dylan's 'The Times They Are a-Changin'':

I've been on the circuit with Catholic James,
with beautiful posters announcing our names,
and the audience loved all our metrical games
    and gave us a wonderful supper,
and we weren't declared vermin or shot down in flames
    off Pegasus' crupper.

I thought of your tenderness, light of my life,
while James sat and thought of his Catholic wife,
or the Pope – that old voyeur with Abraham's knife –
    as the bottle sank down to its ending
and I had to keep silent to keep out of strife:
    he's so condescending.[91]

Though she seems here to be somewhat dismissive of her old Communist-hating friend-and-foe, in letters to other friends her tone is quite tender. She had been feeling depressed over the news that her son's marriage was ending, and she told Tony gratefully that Jim had been very kind to her. He 'listened when I wanted to talk about my troubles' and 'did his best to cheer me up – he took me to see King Solomon's Cave (a most splendid cave with glorious coloured formations)'.[92] This visit to one of the Mole Creek Caves in central Tasmania was the origin of Gwen's poem 'In Plato's Cave' (she later told Norman it could have been called 'Down the Mine with Catholic James'),[93] which she sent to Jim soon afterwards, telling him it was '*not* for publication'.[94] In the poem, she speaks of the moisture in the dark cave, 'like sweatshine glossing / bodies in nakedness', and draws attention to the 'Columns on all sides / and nature's genial clefts'. She depicts herself as Eurydice, trailing in the wake of Jim's Orpheus, who, unlike the original, has utter confidence that she will 'follow in [his] track'.

Though he was so gracious to her, she got the impression that Jim was not happy. 'One evening he hinted that life was a torture to him: perhaps his health is precarious; I don't know,' she told Tony.[95] Some ten years later, she would tell Alison that on their way back to Hobart after this tour, as they 'sped (Jim driving my car v. fast as usual) on the run from Oatlands', Jim pulled on to a side road and they sat in the car 'kissing one another gently': 'I was in tears because I knew he was going to die, & he said "The only thing that can be said for growing old is that you know: whatever happens I can bear it."'[96] To another friend, she would say that, knowing he was dying,

Jim said they should 'say goodbye now': 'So we kissed one another for the last time.'[97] After a while, they began to wonder where they were:

> We found we were at the Brighton refuse disposal site. I said to Jim:
> > The sweetest kiss, from lip to lip
> > was stolen at the Brighton tip.
> We drove on light of heart for a moment; it was a kind of farewell,
> accepted though not yet endured.[98]

Gwen provided no context for this story in her letter to Alison, and Alison never asked her about it.[99] Did Gwen assume that Alison would understand that this was simply an isolated moment of tenderness? Or was it the opposite: did she assume that Alison would know that she and Jim had had an affair? It does not seem beyond the bounds of possibility that Jim and Gwen had a sexual relationship; their trips to Davenport and Launceston in 1972, and around northern Tasmania in 1974, would certainly have given them an opportunity. Gwen would probably have relished it. Despite her sometimes acerbic comments about him, she was passionately drawn to Jim. 'He is one of the people I love absolutely,' she told Craig Powell, 'so that when he dies part of me will die, too.'[100] But Gwen's sense that their 1974 kisses were a farewell was probably retrospective. He had recovered well from his brush with bowel cancer, as far as anyone knew; it would be more than a year before he was diagnosed with liver cancer, and another ten months before his death in October 1976 at the age of fifty-nine.

◆ ◆ ◆

Long before Jim's death, Gwen's life took an unexpected turn. At the end of 1974, Bill was diagnosed with advanced atherosclerosis, a complication of his diabetes. They had been aware for some months that his health was deteriorating, but all at once he was having trouble with his memory and balance. They saw a number of doctors who all told them the same story: Bill's condition was progressive, irreversible and incurable. He would develop dementia, forgetting 'at intervals who he is and where he's supposed to be'.[101] He was also at increased risk of stroke and heart disease. In all likelihood, he had only a few more years to live. They counselled him to retire at once, drawing on the invalid provisions of his superannuation scheme.

It seemed the only sensible course, though Bill wanted to work until the end of 1975, with reduced teaching commitments. He cancelled his honours course for the year, feeling that he could 'no longer follow the complicated trains of thought needed for advanced linguistics'[102] – though, as Gwen could not help but note with pride, 'he's still ahead of anyone else!' He also stepped down from the position of acting departmental head, which he had been occupying while Jim McAuley was overseas on study leave.

He and Gwen sold their yacht, *Sappho* (which had replaced *Iris*), since it was now too big for him to manage easily, and set about designing a smaller, more practical vessel. And they began to look for a property by the water to which they could retire. Gwen cancelled her trip to Greece with Lory Hobcroft and her friends. She told Norman that this was 'partly for the quite selfish reason that *I* would feel terrible for a long time if anything happened to Bill while I was embracing some antique column (or more likely some antique Apollo)'.[103] Nor could she contemplate accepting the invitation of the University of Newcastle to be its poet in residence in 1975. Norman was devastated; he was going to England on study leave at the end of that year and wanted to see her before he left. 'Please, as you love me, take this 9-week relativistic glory on you if you may,' he begged.[104] But Bill's 'precarious' health meant that she 'couldn't possibly take off for so long'.[105]

She made up her mind to sacrifice her own plans and ambitions in order to be there for Bill in his final years. 'I reckon I have 50 years left (well, 49),' she wrote to Rex Hobcroft, 'and as he has but few it's up to me to make concessions.'[106] Literary invitations continued to pour in, but she said no to them all. 'Alas, I am no longer able to flip off in all directions,' she told Norman. 'People will have to come to me.'[107] Her brief flirtation with freedom was over. Nevertheless, Gwen was far from despairing. To Jim Penberthy, announcing Bill's declining health and their retirement plans, she declared that though she had no choice but to stay put, it did not mean the end of her growth as an artist. 'I'll turn not to escape but to discovery.'[108]

20

Baby and Demon

Rock-a-bye Baby
   in the motel
Baby will kiss
   and Demon will tell.

Gwen Harwood, 'Night Thoughts: Baby and Demon'

I N FEBRUARY 1975, GWEN AND BILL BOUGHT FIVE ACRES OF LAND ON a hillside overlooking the D'Entrecasteaux Channel at Oyster Cove. It was Bill's dream to retire to a 'remote weedy waterfront';[1] Gwen was very much afraid she would be lonely. But now that she had made up her mind to stay – in Tasmania, and in her marriage – she threw herself into preparations for her new life. 'Bill will probably get madder and more withdrawn as the years go on,' she told Tony resignedly, 'but our joint tenancy of the five acres is a guarantee that we'll stay together.'[2]

The place they had chosen, on an undeveloped part of the coast about half-an-hour's drive south of Hobart, was 'breathtakingly lovely and unspoilt', with wonderful views across the channel to Bruny Island. They would be three minutes on foot from the water and could moor their dinghy at Oyster Cove.[3] Gwen was excited by the possibilities of their new acreage. They could have poultry, as in the glory days of Mitchelton, and perhaps even a cow. When their water tank went in, she wrote rapturously of the 'joy' of having a tank stand: 'I hope frogs will come and live under it as they used to do at Mitchelton among the long pale stems of the violets.'[4] She was looking forward to growing fruit and vegetables in abundance, farming geese and catching fish. She could even imagine herself living on alone there, 'if the worst happens', in the company of 'the view & the wildflowers'.[5]

In early 1975, 'the worst' seemed far off. Bill was still working, and their block did not yet have a driveway, let alone a house. They planned to hire a local builder to construct their new home – a 'nice light clean airy NEW dwelling'[6] – but would do most of the preparation themselves: clearing a site for the house, putting in a driveway, organising the power and water supply, building a shed and preparing the scrubby soil for cultivation. For most of that year, they spent their weekends travelling up and down from

Augusta Road with carloads of tools. 'I am terribly thin and fit and strong from all the heavy manual labour,' she told Eddie in October. Bill was in his element. 'We spend our spare time in builders' yards and hardware shops.'

With so much to do, Gwen struggled to get to her own work. 'Any kind of solitude or concentration seems an impossible ideal,' she told Tony despairingly.[7] She was anxious to 'get on with my work for Larry Sitsky and to finish off poems I've got in a half-realised state'. In 1974, she had begun work on a three-act opera for Larry based on the medieval Jewish legend of the Golem of Prague, but early in 1975, he asked her to put that on hold to write a one-act comic opera, *Fiery Tales*, for the Adelaide Arts Festival. It was based on Geoffrey Chaucer's 'The Miller's Tale' and a similar story from Giovanni Boccaccio's *The Decameron*, both featuring a jealous husband and an unfaithful wife, and both proceeding by way of fairly ludicrous bedhopping scenes. Gwen enjoyed the bawdy material and completed the commission quickly before sinking into her research for *The Golem*. The theme was Larry's; the child of Russian Jews, he had long been fascinated by Jewish mysticism and had already composed a work based on the Kabbalah.[8] At Larry's urging, Gwen read Abraham Rothberg's novel *The Sword of the Golem* – 'it's super' – and then John Senior's *The Way Down and Out*, 'a study of the Occult in Symbolist literature'. This in turn led her to 'Jewish legends, and Messiahs': 'I feel a bit bemused by all the mysteries and numbers,' she confessed.[9] From there, she went off into Jewish folklore, histories of medieval Europe, and the history and theology of Judaism.

The scholar Alison Wood has pointed out the extraordinary range and depth of research that underlies Gwen's libretto. Her final text included 'references to ancient and biblical texts, sixteenth-century anti-Semitism and cycles of Jewish prayer', and made use of 'Hebrew, Greek, Latin and Yiddish terms', including 'references to magic and alchemy (the divine incantations around the seven words); Jewish folklore and rituals (Lilith); Sabbath prayers; Latin hymns ("Ave Maria"; the "Hymn to the Virgin"); the presence of the Tetragrammaton (the name of God that is not pronounced); the Kabbalah; and Solomonic Magic'.[10] There were also 'allusions to saints and prominent political figures of the late sixteenth century (the period of the opera setting)' and, at Larry's behest, directions 'for film images of refugees, gas chambers or characters portrayed in SS uniforms to be projected onto a backdrop at certain points'.

In 1975, however, she was still groping her way towards a story. With little guidance from Larry, she needed to come up with a workable cast of characters and a plot with enough drama to keep audiences rivetted for several hours.[11] It was a much bigger project than any they had done before.

At the same time, she was working on new poems. Some of these she included in her *Selected Poems* collection, which appeared at the end of April 1975 as part of Angus & Robertson's Poetry Classics series. It was a small paperback – the first of her books to come out in this format – with a photograph of a central Tasmanian river, the Jordan, on the cover. The photo had been taken by her friend John Brodie from the Harwoods' yacht, *Iris*,[12] and Gwen thought it a vast improvement on the 'psychedelic' cover of her second volume. But she was disappointed with the compressed format ('I asked for a new page for each new poem but they were too mean for that') and inadequate binding ('The book won't even stay open').[13] She was annoyed, too, by the praise quote on the back cover from Vincent Buckley, which seemed to put her in the position of Buckley's junior. But these were mere niggles. Ultimately, she was glad the book was out and that her work would once more be available to poetry enthusiasts and the growing number of schools and universities wanting to set it. With any luck, the new volume would consolidate her reputation.

The book was divided into three parts, beginning with her own selection of poems from her first two volumes and ending with twenty-seven new poems. She did not include either 'Burning Sappho' or 'Chance Meeting' from her second book – the latter, perhaps, because she did not wish to further antagonise Lotte Wilmot. She did, however, slip into the selection from her first volume a work that did not belong there, 'Carpe Diem', which contains a reference – as she pointed out to Norman – to 'the tongue that can never lee'.[14] She included all the Eisenbart poems, and all but one of the Kröte poems. Among the new poems were a further three Krötes, one of which, 'The Flight of the Bumble Bee', was probably written by Vincent Buckley.[15] She also rebadged one of her Timothy Kline poems, 'The Music Breather', as a Harwood, now entitled 'The Carnival of Venice'.

Also among the new poems were those she had written for Tony and Vin after her 1969 trip to Melbourne, 'Winter Quarters', 'At Mornington' and 'Night Flight', as well as her 'Impromptu for Ann Jennings', written during her Sydney trip the following year. She also brought in several of the love poems that had sprung from her affair with Norman: both of the 'Meditation on Wyatt' poems, and 'Thought Is Surrounded by a Halo'. The two 'Carnal Knowledge' poems, which might seem to belong with them, were both written before the affair began. These playful, ecstatic, openly erotic works were from 1972, and Gwen never identified them as belonging to any specific love affair. In fact, in letters to Tony and Eddie she made a point of saying that they were generic, part of a series of love poems she was working on. This series, to be entitled 'Carnal Knowledge', was 'not about actual lovers, though real memories are incorporated in the text, but about the incarnation of physical love in the landscape & substance of nature', she told Eddie.[16] Among these 'real memories', presumably, is one of 'Nestling my cheek against / the hollow of your thigh . . . cockeyed with love / in the most literal sense'.

She hinted to Beverley Dunn that one of the 'Carnal Knowledge' poems, at least, had a very specific setting: the Sandy Bay flat that Beverly had rented when she was in Hobart for the theatre season in 1972.[17] Gwen spent a weekend there, and it provided the inspiration – as she told Tony some years later – for 'Night Thoughts: Baby and Demon'. She had 'sat up late watching the drunks and lovers come out [of the Beach Hotel, across the road from Beverley's flat] into the harsh glare of the street lights, and, when all was silent except for the sea, thinking of the past'.[18] The flat may also have been the scene of the 'Carnal Knowledge' poems. Gwen told Beverly that she would 'recognise Droughty's hills' from the first poem – an allusion to the hills on Droughty Point, visible across the water from her friend's place. This might suggest that despite Gwen's denials, these poems do refer to a specific tryst that took place during that weekend's stay in Sandy Bay: Gwen's unsatisfactory affair with 'a doctor' occurred around this time; this was also the period when she first travelled to northern Tasmania with Jim McAuley. But it is also possible that she was, as she told Tony, thinking only of the past in these poems – longing, perhaps, for the 'drunkenness' of her idyll with Tom Pick, and for a song powerful enough to 'lift these hills / from the shadow of what was' so that she could return to 'naked ignorance / in the hollow of your thigh'. Whether she was speaking of new loves or old, the poems stake a claim for the body's knowledge over the mind's: for the spiritual wisdom that comes from sexual experience. As she once told Norman, for her, all knowledge was carnal knowledge.[19]

The term 'carnal knowledge' was contentious at the time: in legal contexts, it referred to illicit sex with a minor. When Jim Penberthy set one of these poems to music for a performance by the ABC, the broadcaster insisted he change the title to 'Love Song'. Gwen always preferred her own title.

◆ ◆ ◆

Gwen's *Selected Poems* also included one of her so-called 'philosophical' poems, 'Fido's Paw Is Bleeding'. This, too, was going to be one of a series; Gwen planned to write a sequence of poems riffing on Wittgenstein's concept of the 'language-game', which was central to his later, posthumously published work, *Philosophical Investigations*.[20] For her, *Philosophical Investigations* was much more accessible than the *Tractatus*. In the earlier work, Wittgenstein focuses on the precision with which language represents the world, but in the later one he shifts his attention to the ways in which language is used, the multiplicitous 'language-games' we all engage in when we speak, write and think. Wittgenstein's argument is that the meanings of words depend on the different language-games in which they are used.[21] Gwen was fascinated by Wittgenstein's attempt to distinguish 'descriptive language, "reports about the world" in the scientific sense, from metaphor, fantasy, the sphere of what can only be shown in the way poetry shows us the sense of life'.[22] He reminds us that 'a poem, even though it is composed in the language of information, is not used in the language-game of giving information'.[23] For Gwen, the purpose of poetry was the transcendence of all language-games.

For Bill, however, there was nothing 'beyond' the language-game. Poetry was just one language-game among many, with its own rules and conventions that functioned by mutual agreement. It did not refer to some reality beyond or outside of language. Thus the concept of language-games became a new battleground in the old war between Bill's mechanistic view of the world and Gwen's spiritual one. Traces of this conflict appear when Gwen says impatiently in a letter to Eddie: 'Bill keeps telling me that poetry is just a language-game but also that it is a violation of our privacy for me to write poetry – how can a "language-game" be that?'[24] It erupts again in an address on language that she gave to a group of drama teachers in 1987: 'Those who try to discount the imaginative use of language do so because they fear its power,' she declared. 'Whether or not we are programmed for universal grammar, we are all able to be enchanted, to have our visual, auditory and bodily sensations extended, to break out of our self-enclosure and reach other minds, to learn how to shape our experience.'[25] This was her creed. True communication was possible, and it was possible through poetry – 'truth beyond the language game', as she put it in 'The Wasps'.

Her 'philosophical' poem 'Fido's Paw Is Bleeding' puts a sharp edge on this ongoing argument. The poem features three characters: Master, a poet who is alienated from others and from true feeling; Fido, his dog; and

Polly, his talking parrot. Master can understand the pain his dog experiences when he injures his paw, even though the dog cannot speak, but he is oblivious to the silent pain of his 'mistress'. When she leaves him, he is bewildered: 'Did she find his house oppressive? / Who can tell – she would not speak.'

When this poem was published in *The Age* in mid-1974, Gwen told Tony that it 'puzzles the other poets – they feel uneasy about it and keep hunting for acrostics (there are none) and hidden philosophical meanings (there are a few)'.[26] She had earlier told Tony that she feared no one would like this new series about Master, Polly and Fido. The poems were intended as 'commentaries on language, emotion, art etc.'[27] No more poems featuring this particular trio of characters appeared.

Reviewers of her *Selected Poems* noted with approval the more personal voice in her new work. Writing in *The Australian*, academic Jim Tulip observed that 'the person of the poet is being brought continuously into the poetry more and more' – an antidote to her use elsewhere of an excessively 'detached and philosophical' poetic voice. Most reviewers concluded that Gwen's *Selected Poems* had confirmed her standing as a major poet. The poet Suzanne Edgar, writing in *The Canberra Times*, declared that her new poems were 'all touched by the fire of passion and the genius of the true poet'. Literary scholar John Beston opined in *The Sydney Morning Herald* that the book increased her 'stature among the leading Australian poets', putting her alongside 'figures such as Wright, Hope, Beaver, and Stow'. The poet Diane Fahey (writing as Diane Dodwell), in an extended review in *Westerly* in 1977, urged Gwen's readers to 'hear and recognise the essential pulse of her poetic genius'.[28] Gwen was uneasy with the word 'genius' – 'When people tell me I'm a genius I reach for the All-Bran. Sauce is fine but you need bulk'[29] – but she must surely have felt some satisfaction at the way readers and critics alike were deploying this word almost routinely to describe her.

To further elevate her standing, towards the end of 1976 the book was awarded the Grace Leven Prize for 1975, a prestigious annual award for the year's best volume of Australian poetry. Gwen used the two hundred dollars in prize money to buy white goods. For several years, the Grace Leven Freezer would be the repository of the fish she caught, the vegetables she grew and the chop tails she used to lure the flathead to her line.

◆ ◆ ◆

Bill formally retired at the end of 1975, and they had had a last, happy Christmas in the old family home with all but one of their children present. The new house in Oyster Cove was going up, a two-bedroom dwelling made of 'warm pinkish-brown' besser block (for its fire-resistant properties), and they would soon have to vacate their Lenah Valley home for good.

Their last months at Augusta Road were difficult for Gwen. Sorting through almost twenty-five years' worth of life's detritus was 'hideous',[30] but they were finally left with only the things they 'absolutely needed'. 'Spartan simplicity is beaut!'[31] Their books were a particular problem. 'We tried to get people to borrow them and not bring them back, to accept them as tokens of intellectual esteem, to take them away . . . no use.' They gave some to charity, and tried (mostly unsuccessfully) to sell some to second-hand shops.[32] The 'vigorous survivors' they transported via hired truck to the shed they had erected on their new property, the back wall of which sported floor-to-ceiling bookshelves. There they would stay, even after the house was finished. They weren't to be 'allowed into the house', Gwen declared, where experience had shown that they would breed.

The clearing and sorting was emotionally as well as physically taxing. Just before the move, Gwen had a succession of dreams in which vicious animals smashed up her belongings. In one dream, malevolent goats came to 'destroy everything I owned', and in another, 'a horrible pinkish-grey mangy animal' told her: 'No matter what you own, I will smash it. Even if you feed me I will break your things.'[33] But at last they were ready to go. As their new house was not quite finished, they put their furniture into storage and moved into rented accommodation for a couple of weeks, hiring a cottage first at Coningham and then on Bruny Island. Late in February 1976, just before they left Augusta Road, Gwen drove up to Coningham alone to set up the rental cottage for their stay. To her delight, she found herself accompanied on her journey by a 'pure white dove'. Flying 'level with the driver's window', it stayed with her for 'a quarter of a mile'. 'I took it as a sign,' she told Tony. 'From that moment the sadness of leaving 89 left me and thoughts of the new life took possession.'[34]

Bill's health was getting worse, and they were both feeling the strain. 'I haven't been very happy since I last wrote,' she told Larry, early in 1976.[35] 'Bill's illness is making him, and things generally, very deefeecult. He cannot stand the human race any longer, and I cannot live without it.' Though she had made up her mind to stay with him, she did not intend to give up her own pursuits entirely. But as ever, her attempts to create space for her literary activities caused friction in the marriage. 'Sometimes I feel a kind of cosmic exhaustion,' she confessed. 'If I pursue my own paths I'm brought up sharply with cries of Selfish, Unjust – I hope it will all settle down in Oyster Cove.' To Tony she confided that Bill had 'had some alarmingly bad days this month; sometimes he is quite confused and can't finish sentences, and simply sits smoking his pipe and sighing . . . Obviously something is very wrong with his cerebral circulation.' It seemed possible that he would not live out the year. 'I shall certainly look after him myself,' she assured Tony. 'I'd never let him be hospitalized or institutionalized (ugly word) if I could care for him.'[36]

But caring for Bill was not a simple matter, even now, when he was relatively well. In addition to his failing memory, he had times when he was 'furious with me and plays Russian roulette with his diabetic control and his brain cells'.[37] With his health in a precarious state, she could not help but feel some trepidation about moving to an isolated spot in the country, some distance from both medical and social support. Bill could no longer drive, and there were no deliveries to the new house and no public transport, so they were entirely dependent on their car, and on Gwen as their driver. She was only too aware that 'the whole outfit depends on my being well and active' – and present.[38] She would not be able to leave Bill on his own overnight; apart from the practical difficulties if anything should go wrong, her 'absence itself would be a huge strain and might affect his health'.[39] It was a big thing to take on. And, of course, the issues that had always plagued the marriage were still very much present. 'Having Bill round all the time is like having another child under foot – the endless preparation of meals, transport, company, amusements,' she grumbled to Ann from their cottage on Bruny Island. 'I've got that old stir-crazy feeling.' She worried that she was once again being forced into a mould she simply could not fit. 'Sometimes I think I've got into a Black Hole & am being compressed beyond recognition.'[40]

While they were on Bruny, they travelled over to Kettering on the ferry almost every day to put the finishing touches on the house, building cupboards, painting the ceilings, planting a hedge of cotoneasters as a windbreak.[41] Finally, at the end of March, they were able to move in, camping out in the bare rooms for a few days while they cleared up after the builders and waited for their furniture to arrive. From the built-in desk in the spare bedroom, Gwen wrote excitedly to Tony of the block's many beauties. She loved the native bush, and the birds were 'a continual delight'. She had even gone 'walking over the pasture in the moonlight (I'd have liked to run, but feared putting my foot down a rabbit hole) rejoicing in the beauty of the night'.[42] They had cleared the area around the house, but 'kept a strip of native bush with tea tree, gum, coral fern and wildflowers between us and the road'.[43] Gwen made a study of the birds: 'Robins and wrens abound, and spurwing plover, white-faced herons, honey-eaters, pallid cuckoos, tree-martins, fly-catchers and black cockatoos – we've given up calling "Come and look at the . . ." because you just have to look at any part of the hillside and something's there.' She had decided to call the place 'Halcyon', the name of the kingfisher, and a symbol, she told Tony, of 'winter peace'.[44] When she was a child, her father had told her the legend of Halcyon, daughter of the winds, who married a mortal king and loved him so much that when he was drowned at sea, she threw herself into the waves to join him. Touched by her actions, the king and queen of the immortals turned both Halcyon and her husband into kingfishers. Every year in midwinter, when Halcyon sat on her eggs on the seashore, her father held back the winds for a fortnight so that she could hatch them safely: a time of halcyon peace. And so Halcyon and her mate 'lived happily and faithfully for ever on the water'.[45] It was a cheerful way to frame their retreat to what Gwen then believed would be the final nest she and Bill would share.

Gwen planned to walk the two miles into Kettering each day to pick up the mail so that she could enjoy the superb views, first over the channel and then over the bay at Kettering, 'with moored yachts, fishing boats, and the ferry terminal', passing through farms and 'stretches of bush' on the way.[46] She couldn't wait to get their first chooks and ducks and geese, and was already dreaming of the 'meditative days I shall spend drifting and fishing'.[47] But instead of quiet days of rural peace, she found herself plunged into yet more manual labour in the weeks and months after their move. Their first tasks were to level and resurface the terrace around the house, dig a dam, sink a well and clear a stand of radiata pines that posed a fire risk.[48] They were keen to get their garden started, but the soil was not rich enough for vegetables and needed to be built up with loads of blood and bone, and manure. When they did plough a field and plant out 'corn, tomatoes, potatoes, onions, beans, peas and lettuce', they lost their whole crop to 'the bandicoots and possums'. Putting up fences was added to their list of urgent tasks.

Despite their progress, their labours seemed only to grow. Gwen noted proudly that one of her sons had taught her how to use a pick, doubling her productivity: 'I can work all day with a pick, but only half a day with a shovel.'[49] She and Bill built a barn, a garage, a glasshouse, a shadehouse and a fence for the dam, as well as putting up poultry sheds and digging a duck pond. It was a great day when their 'four beautiful geese' arrived. 'The ganders are snow white, one with a crest, and the geese are grey,' Gwen told Tony delightedly, reporting that she had named one of the pairs Polly and Fido. She and Bill also bought six pullets ('the hysterical white kind'), followed by four bantams and a couple of pairs of ducks. The geese were her joy – though they were far from restful creatures. 'They . . . follow me round the paddock and scream at night. I had no idea geese and ganders were so noisy.'[50] They were 'just as individual as humans'[51] – and as they began to multiply, she delighted in observing and naming them. At first she would kill and dress them for the table, just as she would the ducks and hens, but she soon grew 'too fond' of them. They had become her pets, and she simply 'couldn't bear to kill [them] for food'.[52]

There was some trial and error in their first years as smallhold farmers, and some heartbreak, too, when their bantams were killed by feral cats, their newly hatched ducklings eaten by crows, their goslings abandoned by their parents or picked off by hawks. As they grew more adept at gardening in the bush, and as the soil grew richer, their crops began to multiply, and they were soon able to trade their excess veggies and fruit with their neighbours. Gwen spent much time turning berries into jam and jelly, making sauce and chutney from tomatoes, freezing corn, peas and beans. She made her own bread and froze that too. She was also able to harvest oysters straight from the shore, slicing them from the rocks with a knife – a somewhat perilous undertaking that several times led to bloody injuries. The fishing was all she had hoped it would be; taking the boat out was another of her great joys, especially at night, when she could 'lie back in the dinghy and watch the stars rocking'.[53] Her use of the phrase 'rock on' in so many of her poems in the 1970s reflects not just the new idiom of rock music but also the whole-body experience of rocking gently on the waves in her dinghy.

She did sometimes feel uneasy on the water. She was aware of the dark history of this part of Tasmania, and felt sure that the place was haunted by the afterlife of the evil done there by white marauders. Years before she ever thought of moving to the area, she wrote a poem entitled 'Oyster Cove', which reflects on the government's use of the cove in the nineteenth century as a so-called reserve for displaced First Nations peoples. Having been murdered, banished and/or imprisoned by the first wave of white colonialists, the original inhabitants of southern Tasmania were quartered at the

Oyster Cove 'station' in the mid-nineteenth century, where it was hoped they would die out. Gwen's poem depicts a sense of brooding disquiet in this place where 'Dreams drip to stone' and a 'lost / race breathes out cold'. She told an interviewer that from her boat, she 'seem[ed] to see the shadows gathering there, Flora Neptune, Truganini, Queen Caroline, the sad names they gave them when their own beautiful liquid language was gradually being forgotten'.[54] One of the poems she wrote from her new home recorded this sense of a secret, suffering presence:

> This elbow of the shallow bay
>   crooked an unchilded dying race
> whose liquid language ebbed away.
>   Shadows forgather in this place:
>
> Jackey, Patty, Queen Caroline,
>   Lalla Rookh – white contemptuous names
> cloaked the heartsickness of decline.[55]

She was only too aware that while the local Indigenous peoples had suffered 'death after hopeless death' in that place, she herself lived a pleasant life there, heading home from a tranquil evening's fishing to the comfort of 'books, fire and chilled white wine'. Her only recourse was to shape a prayer for forgiveness.

The presence of the dead was, for her, a part of the 'melancholy light' of the sea. The sight of the ferry passing backwards and forwards between Kettering and Bruny Island brought to mind the story of Truganini, kidnapped by 'two white sawyers' on Bruny and bundled into a rowboat to be ferried to the mainland. When her two companions tried to save her, they were thrown from the boat, their clutching hands severed with hatchets. The mutilation, Gwen would write in a later poem, was a 'fourfold wound' for Truganini, who alone survived: 'Four bodiless hands surrender / the snapping derision of bones / to the solid mercy of water.'

Now, in the present, the descendants of those sawyers travelled to Bruny on the ferry for their beach holidays, while beneath them, 'in secret currents black fingers open and close'.[56]

21

The Goose Girl

How will you know me, barefoot in the pasture,
   Dressed as a goose-girl?

Gwen Harwood, 'Goose-girl'
(poem II of 'A Quartet for Dorothy Hewett')

IN 1977, GWEN BEGAN TO JOT DOWN SOME OF HER DAILY ACTIVIties in a small, illustrated desk diary from the National Trust. It quickly became a habit she would keep for the rest of her life. The entries were spare: 'to town with Chris, buy mattock handle', 'Polly has 2 eggs. Sharon sitting', 'To Clifton, v. warm'. Occasionally, something more personal would appear, as on 26 February, when she wrote: 'Drive to Coningham, argue about view of O.C. from hill.' Over the years, she would never use more than the allotted five centimetres of space for each day, but this tiny space was increasingly crowded with her neat, miniscule handwriting. She became a master of this compressed genre, able to convey the tone of her day without a wasted word.

In the 1990s, when she read back through the Oyster Cove diaries, she would be amazed – and depressed – by the sheer volume of physical labour she had recorded. Also among the entries were records of visits to and from her near neighbours, with whom she had quickly made friends. She noted many an 'arvo tea' with Henry and Jean, Ivo and Hilary, Judy and Mick, Albert and Hedwig. Old friends came to visit too: Ann and Stephen; Bill's sailing mate, John Brodie; Bill's former colleagues, and now close friends, Ted and Margaret Stokes and Thea Goodwin. They also had visitors from interstate, particularly over the summer: Alison and Bill Hoddinott, Vivian and Sybille Smith, Richard Zatorski, Craig Powell, Rex Hobcroft and Larry Sitsky, often travelling with their partners and children. Bill's sister came to stay, and their own children were often there. In January 1977, even Tony came for a visit during a brief trip to Australia.

Among their regular visitors were Sally and Edgar Sleinis, a young university couple. Bill had met Edgar in 1973, when he was appointed to the university as a lecturer in philosophy. They had complementary interests: Edgar was the 'logic man', Bill the 'linguistics man'.[1] Gwen liked Edgar too, as impressed by his capacity to hold his own in arguments with Bill as by his knowledge of Wittgenstein. She considered him 'a crack-hot logician (you'll note Mary's influence on my vocabulary) and a splendid handyman'.[2] She also liked Edgar's American wife, Sally, whom Edgar had met during his PhD studies at Johns Hopkins in Baltimore. Sally had a degree in philosophy and was studying for an honours degree in zoology. Like Gwen, she was fascinated by marine animals, and the two women spent many happy hours together on the seashore, inspecting and identifying crustaceans and other sea creatures.[3]

Despite the lively company, Gwen was working – researching and writing both libretti and poems. Early in 1976, Larry again asked her to interrupt her work on *The Golem* to write another libretto, this time for an experimental opera for radio. He was excited by the technological possibilities of audio production, seeing an opportunity to plunge into realms of human experience that were impossible to dramatise on the stage: the occult, the extrasensory, the mystical. He asked Gwen to develop a script featuring mysterious spirit voices in another dimension – a script that would also have action and drama.[4]

Over the following weeks and months, Gwen sent him a barrage of ideas for his 'voices': they could be unborn children in utero, the spirits of the dead, angels or demons, the prophetic voices of mystics or saints. But nothing she proposed was quite right. 'I wish I knew what you *wanted* for voices, instead of what you didn't want,' she grumbled in September 1976. 'Perhaps you have some more definite ideas by now; I'm as nutty as a fruit-cake after so much crazy reading.'[5]

After Larry jettisoned her first two drafts, they finally settled on the story of a woman and a man who fall asleep after making love and wake to find themselves 'in another dimension' – a new iteration of Gwen's long-held belief that sex unlooses the spirit to wander abroad.[6] They put together a cast of voices that included angels and demons – 'angels from the right-hand speaker, demons from the left' – as well as 'ghosts', 'spirit guides' and dead children from across the ages. The final script, which Gwen sent off in April 1977, included a narrator to help the audience navigate through the 'karmic visions' and 'tunnels between parallel worlds' to the final 'serenity and space of an impersonal but beneficent universe'.[7]

Larry got straight to work on the score, and it was finished by September 1977. It would be more than three years, however, before *Voices in Limbo* was finally recorded and broadcast. They had set a high bar for the ABC's producers: the score was, in Gwen's estimation, 'devilishly difficult' and called for technological innovation in producing electronic sounds.[8] But the final product was 'superb, stunning'.[9] 'What a glorious range of sounds you've achieved,' Gwen wrote to Larry, after hearing the broadcast. 'I'm sure this is as great a masterpiece as *Lenz* and feel more shaken by it, in some ways, because it's part of things that can't be said in words.'[10]

◆ ◆ ◆

Some six months before Gwen finished the text of *Voices*, Jim McAuley died. He had attended Bill's much-deferred farewell lunch with the English department in June 1976, looking 'very frail compared with his old self'. 'Nobody knows how long he has to live,' Gwen wrote sadly.[11] 'Bill, to cheer me, said, "He's probably looking forward to his first administrative interview with God."'[12]

But though she knew it was coming, Jim's death in mid-October shook her. When she heard the news, she did not know what to do with herself. She thought of 'taking the dinghy out after flathead; then reflected that if I caught them I'd have to kill them, and decided to add no more to death's tally for the week'. She decided instead to walk on the hillside, where she 'found many of the flowers Jim loved; their names pierced me: scorpion everlasting, waxflower, musk'. During this walk, she began composing an elegy for her friend, which would later be published as 'Springtime, Oyster Cove'.[13]

Her world took on a tinge of darkness. 'My new vinyl tiles, laid on an innocent concrete slab, are full of devils since Jim died,' she wrote a few days later.[14] His death had 'left a pretty big black hole in [her] heart',[15] and it would be a long time before she would begin to recover. When she began to dream of him, almost a year later, she saw it as a sign of healing.[16] Many of these dreams would become poems. She could not share her grief with Bill, feeling that her tears at the funeral had displeased him, but she wrote of the loss to Norman, confiding both her misery and the various mildly scurrilous stories about Jim's last years that were circulating.[17]

Gwen had not seen Norman since the Morpeth poetry school in 1974, but they had kept up their amorous correspondence. They made no claims on one another; in fact, when they parted at Morpeth, Gwen told Norman she did not expect to see him again. Nevertheless, there were implicit expectations. When Gwen did not hear from Norman for several weeks in early 1975, she sent him an angry postcard in verse. She did not care, she asserted, 'who his line has caught / or what or when he screws, / but silence is a thing one ought / not offer to one's Muse'. Lady Gwendoline, she wrote with mock haughtiness, was not one to endure 'indifference'.[18]

Norman replied to this furious missive immediately, addressing her as 'Goldenwrath' instead of his accustomed 'Goldenchild', and demanding: 'Whaddya mean? Silence? I sent thee a letter even 10 days back & was answered by deepsouthern silences.'[19] His letter had gone astray. In response to her probing, he assured her that 'Neither new women nor old wine have crossed my lips for a while, though the latter much more recently'. He was having trouble finishing some poems, he told her, probably because he was 'overworked, sleepy & unlikely to succeed. Melancholia & torpor & hard work don't suit me at the moment – I need a bit of surprise, of daft exuberance. I need you, to put it another way.'

Gwen was mollified. 'Christ knows but probably will not reveal where your missing letter is,' she replied. 'I need you, too.'[20] She went on to catalogue her recent activities for him: working on libretti, reading a life of Mozart, writing a poem on Wittgenstein and Engelmann, preparing a lecture for teachers ('terrifying'), reading criticism of the *Tractatus*, 'comforting' her new grandson and entertaining poets Robert FitzGerald and Nancy Cato, who were visiting Tasmania.

Back in the 1950s, Gwen had written a 'malicious parody' of Nancy's work, which she foolishly showed to Evan Jones, 'who of course flashed it at' Nancy: 'Never tell anyone anything (anythink) in Australia,' she complained. But for this act of malice, Nancy had long ago forgiven her. The two women had met in the 1960s, when Nancy was briefly visiting Tasmania, and had become 'friends at once'.[21]

Despite – or perhaps because of – their friendship, Nancy did not scruple to criticise Gwen's poetry, and she was an astute reader. After making her way through Gwen's second volume, Nancy asked Gwen whether she had chosen her Francis Geyer pseudonym in order 'to make some of the love poems sound more "respectable"?'[22] Of all of Gwen's alter egos, she liked Miriam the best, 'because she expresses what every woman stifled by suburbia & being a housewife and mother has felt; particularly that savage hatred of one's "nearest & dearest" for getting in the way of creative work'. She did not much like Gwen's Kröte poems, suggesting that the drunken musician was really 'a character from a novel you have not written'. A novelist herself, she felt that Gwen had the makings of a fiction writer. She also lightly mocked Gwen's veneration of male poetry luminaries such as Vin Buckley and Alec Hope, which she did not share.

Meanwhile, Norman had begun to write critical essays on Gwen's work, which he happily sent for her opinion. He did admit that for an academic to publish supposedly objective criticism of the work of a poet he was having an affair with had its tricky moments, particularly when he wanted to talk about poems such as the 'Meditation on Wyatt' sequence 'that involve me very directly': 'I tend to make incoherent purring noises about these – but not only these – poems rather than cast a cold academic line into their ripples & snags.'[23] Nevertheless, he felt that he had real insight into her work. Sending her one of his articles, he declared that whether or not she agreed with his conclusions, it was 'undoubtedly different from anything written about you before'.[24] Gwen replied sweetly that his article 'enchanted' her: 'How can I thank you? By loving you, which I do; by doing better, which I shall. I'll write a few comments but they are minor glosses. You have French-polished me and made me valuable.'

To others, she was not quite so laudatory of his critical efforts. Forwarding another of his 'dense commentaries' on her poems to Alison in 1981, she noted, with sardonic admiration, that 'Norman really can write like that on anything; he does diagrams, too. It always astonishes me to read the criticism and then look at the text.'[25] Another article of his she described as 'surprisingly lucid and of course besotted', before going on to condemn his interpretation of one of her poems as 'ingenious but wrong'.[26] In general, though, she was more than willing to encourage Norman's academic labours.

Though there was much playfulness in their interactions, Gwen also gave Norman the odd smack. Late in 1975, he sent her a letter that contained a detailed account of metre in traditional Icelandic poetry.[27] She was unimpressed. 'What is it in my nature that makes those I love want to lecture me?' she complained. 'Some look of stereoscopic innocence? A touch of invincible ignorance? A grand receptiveness? All my life I've been treated to dissertations on The Incidence of Boronia Caerulescens in Australian Heathlands, The Correct Way to Turn a Cuff, Picturesque Hungary, Statistical Methods Applied to Shrew-dissection, The Life of St Ambrose, Fingering of Double Thirds, Inorganic Analysis – but thank you anyway for your piece on dr(o)ttkvaett.' She went on to tell Norman of her various escapades on the water, and to narrate a dream of Tony Riddell's in which she drowned in a swimming pool. For good measure, she threw in an account of her mother's recent 'premonition' that her daughter would die by drowning.

On study leave in East Anglia, Norman was troubled by Gwen's breezy stories of her boating misadventures. He was missing her, painfully aware of the extra miles between them. When Gwen did not write for a few weeks, he became distressed. 'Please write to me, if only the most oblique of Sappho-cartomancies,' he begged from Norwich. 'These doomladen premonitions & seagirt suspicions are depressing . . . It's midmarch, dammit! Are things so very bad with you? . . . Don't the seas get wide.'[28]

Gwen wrote back at once from the cottage on Bruny Island where she and Bill had temporarily parked themselves:

> Du meine Seele, du mein Herz [You, my soul, my heart] –
> My silence was beyond reason
> O north-Professorial
> multi-sartorial
> witty industrious
> loving illustrious
> troubled-obscurely man,
> don't you know surely, man,
> time cannot shake us
> or distance unmake us.

She went on to explain that she had been weighed down by 'Heavy manual labour, homelessness, booklessness' and asked for his forgiveness: 'my spirit was asleep on its feet.'[29]

She also told him of an 'unbearable' dream – full of doubt and anxiety about her place in his life – in which she met him 'in a field of William Morris flowers surrounded by women'. She would later turn this dream into a poem, entitled simply 'A Dream', which would become the fifth of her 'Seven Philosophical Poems'.

Norman responded to her letter with buoyant relief. 'Your dreams are alarming, but not nearly as alarming as your silences,' he wrote.[30] He was amused by her depiction of him as sought-after by multiplicities of women. 'I suppose to figure as an Homme Fatale or Luciferian seducer is terrible because it's so flattering?' In his own dreams, she was a colossus tumbled on the ocean floor, and he a labouring pygmy trying to encompass her.[31]

By September, he was back in Australia, just in time to attend the 1976 Morpeth poetry workshops. Gwen was invited but declined. Now that she and Bill were settled at Oyster Cove, she was turning down all invitations that involved leaving Tasmania. Still, she was happy that Norman was back in the country and wrote longingly of seeing him. Norman set his mind to contriving a meeting and, in early 1977, secured a university grant to go to Tasmania to interview her for a planned paper on sex in her poetry.[32] Gwen was delighted. 'Bring some warm clothes, preferably old, so we can roll in the flora,' she told him joyfully in early February. 'Ah, to see you again after more than three years! To sit beside you while you read me your card about spiders which I haven't deciphered! To fry flathead for you! To rock on the waters in total joy with or without exclamation marks . . .'[33] She and Bill had just bought a ute, a one-tonne Datsun of an 'ochreous-yellow'.[34] In this, she promised, she would collect Norman from the airport, and they would 'ride in fantastic triumph' across the island.

It was a happy, if brief, reunion. Gwen showed Norman around Halcyon, and they went to Bruny Island together on the ferry, 'gathered mushrooms, and read to one another from Leviticus'.[35] Ever afterwards, 'mushrooms' would be a slightly lascivious codeword for their love affair. 'Nature, having provided us with a splendid crop of field mushrooms, has suddenly sent into the field an army of phallic ones,' she wrote to him a couple of months later. 'My dear! Positively indecent! These foolish things remind me of you.'[36] Now that he had visited some of her beloved places, she could indulge in the pleasant fantasy that he was with her in spirit even when he was absent in flesh. She had, she told him, 'a great many moments when you are close, most often on the water'.[37]

After his visit, she wrote 'This Artifice of Air', a playful depiction of the two of them frolicking in the waters off Bruny Island. It featured her spin on a line from a 'Nashville-style' ballad she had shared with Norman: 'Your soul belongs to Jesus, Jacob, / but your body belongs to me.' 'I reckon my wits belong to Wittgenstein, and my body belongs to thee,' she told him.[38]

The final part of the poem is a merry, lyrical and increasingly rapturous pastiche of Lewis Carroll's 'The Walrus and the Carpenter', which tells of how

> Father Aether and Goldenchild
> were floating side by side,
> far from the land whose heavy law
> they could not long abide.

She sent it to him in June, inscribed: 'To dearest Northman, with love, Gwen.'[39]

'This Artifice of Air' was in part a response to Norman's 'Falling Asleep over Queensland', which gave her the phrase she used as her title. In his poem, which sprang from a visit to Queensland in the first half of 1977, he depicts himself looking down from the plane as it flies over her natal state, breathing the 'artifice of air' within the cabin and dreaming of her. He imagines her looking up from the ground to see him passing over, and longs for her to reach up and pluck him from the sky. As he drifts, 'half-asleep in this bright/ insignia of morning', he dreams of 'the tilt of Your smile, content / horizon-long stretch of Your pale body, / the fatal sea beyond, yet You beyond . . .'[40]

◆ ◆ ◆

Gwen did not mention Norman's quick, amorous visit to Tony, nor, apparently, to anyone else. But at least one person knew of it: Western Australian poet and playwright Dorothy Hewett. Dorothy had been one of the poetry tutors at Morpeth in 1974 and seems to have been taken into the lovers' confidence then. Gwen greatly admired Dorothy, both as a poet and as a free-spirited bohemian who cared little for the 'heavy law' that kept so many would-be lovers apart.

In October 1977, Dorothy came to Hobart as part of that year's Book Week festivities, at which she was to read alongside Gwen and a handful of other visiting poets. Gwen collected her from her Hobart billet in the yellow ute and took her to the beach, where the two women talked freely of their love affairs. Dorothy, who was married to writer Merv Lilley, revealed that she was in love with poet Bob Adamson. As Bob was also reading in Hobart that week, along with his estranged wife, Cheryl, the situation was tense. Seeing that Dorothy was 'desperately unhappy', Gwen took her home to Halcyon for the night. When she drove her into the State Library the next day for the first of their readings (Dorothy gloriously dressed 'like Undine in flowing blue'), Gwen found herself the unwitting, though far from unwilling, observer of a passionate drama. Dorothy and Bob staged a 'grand operatic scene' in the library foyer, with a drunken Bob shouting at Dorothy, and Cheryl 'laying into [her]'.[41] Bob and Dorothy then reconciled 'molto appassionato in the Library doorway', under the fascinated gaze of 'the borrowers' (who 'obviously thought it was one of the library's Book Week free displays'), before the trio was whisked away to be photographed.

Tensions continued to simmer at the reading that evening, which was held at the university. 'The Sydney mob were pretty disorderly', Gwen reported to Alison, 'passing bottles of Southern Comfort and Remy Martin as they sprawled on the floor not listening to the musical interludes and making loud comments on the readings. I'd have liked to join in, but with Sandy and John Winter and many other University worthies all round I sat upright in a chair and looked soulful.'[42]

On the second night, the performances were more subdued, as the event was held in the library, where alcohol was not allowed, but the readings were even better: 'very sober and sublime'. 'Michael Wilding was stoned on pot but it added to the quality of his reading – his style was really improved,' she reported.[43] Dorothy again looked 'gorgeous' in 'a scarlet dress embroidered with beads – Hobart has never seen such a woman', and she and Bob 'read crazy poems to one another'.[44] In a poem of her own written around this time, 'Before a Window', Gwen would write of two poets reading in public, 'glowing' like a stained-glass window of Tristan and Isolde, but 'more resembling / the wild originals whose laughter / salted the woods, held the court spellbound'.

During Dorothy's reading, Gwen found herself saddled with Bob, who 'began crying & buried his Marty Feldman head in my bosom': 'He said he was sorry because he'd agreed with Michael Wilding that my work was out of date, irrelevant etc etc. "I'm so *weak*," he said.' Gwen assured him, probably through gritted teeth, that 'there was no worry, mate, what I really liked was going after the flathead, lit crit was trivial': 'He said "But I *do* like your poetry especially Carnal Knowledge" – Fine, fine, I said. I don't think he has the faintest idea of who or what he is. God help Dorothy if she's really in love with him, as she seems to be.'[45]

Though Dorothy was very much caught up in her own drama at the time – she saw the saga as a modern-day equivalent of the goings-on at the court of Camelot, with Bob as Merlin and Cheryl as Morgan le Fay[46] – she had seen a side of Gwen that few saw. Superficially, the two poets were very different, Dorothy wearing her heart on her crimson sleeve and Gwen sitting decorously upright in the regulation chair. Yet beneath the surface they were akin, and Dorothy felt that Gwen understood and empathised with her.

Some four months after her visit, she sent Gwen some poems, including 'one for you especially'. This poem, 'For Sappho', recreated their intimate conversation by the sea during her visit: 'Last landstop on the searoad to Antarctica, / Sappho and I once walked there gathering shells / talking of love, our faltering bodies, burning senses . . .' The poem depicts them as 'two gallant boys', driving in Sappho's 'yellow pick-up truck' past the beach motels in which 'Baby and Demon [were] copulating' and 'telling fragments

/ of cantos in the autumnal air'. It was Dorothy who, in this poem, dubbed Gwen 'a goosegirl in her denims': 'suitably luminous   in Oyster Cove / calling the geese   pulling the mullet in / reading   to each other   the wild and secret / messages we send to be decoded . . .' In another of Dorothy's poems, 'The Inheritors', Sappho herself speaks, calling for 'the singing head' of the dismembered Orpheus: 'A lonely woman dressed in white / Sappho sings beside the sea . . .'

A year later, after another brief visit to Hobart to read, she would send Gwen a further poem, 'For the Glory of God and of Gwendoline', which she described as 'a new light poem for the New Year to cheer me up and maybe you too. It has no pretensions towards anything but gaiety.'[47] The poem was a tribute to Adam Lindsay Gordon's rollicking ballad 'The Romance of Britomart', and made little effort to disguise the true identities of its characters: 'O Gwen so long the mute the burning Sappho / Lancelot's lady & King Arthur's consort / invite me in for we can have such sport . . .' The poem laments that Camelot has fallen on 'evil days', and asserts that it is up to them, as 'ladies fashioned for delight', to set things right in the most incendiary fashion: 'maybe it's not too late to bring the news / that you & I intend to light a fuse / in Camelot.' Perhaps, against all the odds, the women will outstrip 'all the dazzling men' to claim the Holy Grail for themselves. The poem ends with a rousing call to action: 'I say let's ride we've nothing left to lose.' Gwen was somewhat bemused when this 'extraordinary' poem appeared in *New Poetry*'s last issue for 1978. 'Dorothy sent it to me in a letter a while ago saying it was just for holiday fun!' she told Norman.[48]

Dorothy's vigorous feminism delighted her, but it also made her wary. Though her own perspectives on women's suppression – and compression – in the home were strikingly similar to those now being propounded by the emerging women's movement, she was cautious. She did not want to find herself fenced into some kind of female-only enclave as a poet, or dismissed by literary powerbrokers (all male) as a man hater. But neither did she want to be excluded from the exciting new world that female poets were creating. When the groundbreaking poetry anthology *Mother I'm Rooted* appeared in 1975, she was hurt not to be included: 'Nobody asked me to contribute (are they unsure of my sex?).'[49] When she saw the volume, however, she was not entirely sorry to have been left out: it 'was really so unpalatable poetically that I couldn't respond to the excellent and necessary ferocity of the writers'. Brilliant insights and turns of phrase could not make up for a lack of 'formal excellence'.

Dorothy's visits had stimulated poems for Gwen, too. Four of these would be published as 'A Quartet for Dorothy Hewett' in mid-1979 in the first issue of the brand-new literary magazine *The Tasmanian Review* (soon to become *Island*). 'Goose-girl', the second poem of the quartet, gives Gwen's own version of their Hobart meeting. While Dorothy had compared them to the gallant 'prisoners of Zenda', Gwen depicted them as 'princes choosing their disguises', who met 'in joyful recognition / laughing unmasked at life, the royal game, / whose rules are all fatal'. The implication was that with Dorothy, she could take off her mask.

Another of the poems, 'A Simple Story', tells of Gwen's teenage meeting with the conductor Percy Code, and her disappointment that he was interested only in her sexual availability, and not in her musical compositions. It is the kind of story Dorothy would probably have related to; her own autobiography, written many years later, would abound in accounts of older, well-established men trying to solicit, extort or simply loot sexual favours from her teenage self.[50] It seems possible that Gwen shared this story with Dorothy when they walked and talked on the beach, or, if not, that Dorothy's earthy, cynical perspective on sexual politics may have prompted her to frame her youthful experience in this way.

The last poem of the quartet, 'Dorothy, Reading in Hobart', was Gwen's oblique response to 'For the Glory of God and of Gwendoline'.[51] Its opening line – 'Lustrous angel, who, if I cried, would hear me' – evokes the first of Rilke's *Duino Elegies*, but while Rilke is afraid to cry out lest he receive no answer from among the angelic hierarchies, Gwen is confident that Dorothy will hear her cry and come out of Tartarus 'singing / the worst of truth in your voice of shadow'. A litany of darkness, this poem nevertheless celebrates the artist's role as truth teller. Neither Baby nor Demon, Dorothy-as-poet takes the place of the absent gods, filling the 'void' with 'a woman's voice'. Just as Dorothy adopted Gwen's self-mythologising in calling her Sappho, so Gwen uses Dorothy's own preferred mythology to position her as Tennyson's Lady of Shalott.

Dorothy was delighted by the poems. 'A treasure trove!' she wrote from Woollahra. 'A whole set of poems for myself . . . I've never had such an experience before . . . very humbling I assure you.'[52] She saw Gwen very much as the senior poet and was flattered by her friendship. But she also felt that they were allies, standing shoulder to shoulder as women who took 'pleasure' in 'the company of men' and, in a patriarchal world, were made to suffer for it. The two women would stay in touch sporadically, with Dorothy unfolding the latest episode in her private Arthurian drama in letters and phone calls, and urging Gwen to 'keep writing'.

Gwen was happy to gossip with Norman (also a friend of Dorothy's) in their letters about the 'Dorothy-Bob-Cheryl' show.[53] Neither Norman nor Dorothy was particularly concerned about discretion. During a 'long vinous afternoon' at the University of Newcastle's staff club, Norman and Dorothy hatched a plan for a book featuring the four poets – Norman and Gwen, Dorothy and Bob – and the poems that had sprung from their illicit relationships. They thought of calling it '*Four Lovers*, or sommut like that', Norman told Gwen. Would Gwen be interested? She responded cautiously, asking who he had in mind to publish it, and whether they would be 'in sections or all in together? (I mean all mixed up)?'[54] Nothing ever came of this project, but in 1982, Gwen did appear in a chapbook called *Journeys* along with Dorothy and two other poets, Judith Wright and Rosemary Dobson. This little book, which was edited by the emerging poet Fay Zwicky and published by Sisters Publishing, aimed at presenting 'the poetry of the older woman', which, Zwicky asserted in her introduction, was 'very important to the directions to be taken by the next generation of poets'. Each of the poets appeared in her own section.

◆ ◆ ◆

Norman visited Halcyon again in February 1978 for two days, ostensibly to interview Gwen for an American magazine called *Creative Moment*.[55] He stayed with Gwen and Bill, and greatly impressed them by hefting a heavy bag of poultry feed from the ute to his shoulder, asking: 'Where do you want it?'[56] Unsurprisingly, Bill did not like Norman 'at all', but he was 'polite'.[57] Once again, Gwen and Norman went to Bruny Island on the ferry, a trip Gwen would immortalise in 'Bruny's Song', in which the island itself celebrates the coming together of 'Northman' and 'Southlady'.[58] Apart from that, they drank a lot of white wine and 'spent the whole time laughing at one another's jokes or drunkenly reading the dietary rules from Leviticus'.[59] Gwen spent the two days 'in a state of hopelessly irrational joy'.[60] 'Such abundance of love!' she marvelled. 'It was a mysterious time too: I couldn't sleep (for sheer happiness) (and for longing) yet I was profoundly at rest.' On the way to the airport on Saturday, she and Norman stopped in for lunch with Ann Jennings, sitting 'in the glorious sun on her lawn with bread and cheese and retsina and some fresh raspberries'. 'Norman got on very well with Ann's young man, who is going to do an honours degree in classics this year,' she reported to Tony. 'He and Norman had a lively argument on the merits of Theocritus or Petronius as a topic.'[61] Ann's partner, Stephen Edgar, had no idea that Gwen and Norman were involved, though in retrospect, he did think that their high spirits were a telltale sign.[62]

This visit, like Norman's previous one, led to an outpouring of creativity. Gwen's poems were mostly lighthearted: 'Bruny's Song' was followed by the breezy 'Long after Heine'[63] and, in April, a rather ambivalent ditty about the 'bevy' of women pursuing her lover, which finished with an exhortation to him to 'Jump in their taxis, / pursue them with passion – / I know you'll be faithful / to me in my fashion.'[64]

Then, early in May, she sent him 'A Valediction', one of her most dazzling works.[65] In this poem, whose title invokes Donne's 'A Valediction: Forbidding Mourning', she roves over her old loves and many partings, but instead of the pain and heartbreak such thoughts would ordinarily bring, she feels only joy. Her lovers are not truly gone, since they can leap 'into [her] flesh' in an instant when she reads an old love poem, or walks 'at peaceful sunset in the pasture / feeding [her] geese'. She had recently been reading a biography of Lou Andreas-Salomé, a writer and psychoanalyst whose past lovers had included Rilke. Gwen was struck by her unconventional approach to love. 'In her old age Lou said "Whether I kissed Nietzsche on Monte Sacro I cannot now remember,"' she told Tony. 'What an incredible thing not to remember! I've been trying in vain to find a suitable non-memory for my old age.'[66] In her poem, she deploys both Lou and another of her heroines, St Thérèse of Lisieux, as wayfinders for her own course. The meeting with Norman had helped to lay some of her old ghosts to rest, leaving her 'joyful'. What's more, she knew that 'when the afterglow is gone / Lou's ravishing forgetfulness / will rock my soul with saving laughter, / and the single-hearted saint will braid / all loves into one everlasting'.

'A Valediction', with its references to Donne and 'aches from adolescence', seems to allude both to her former piano teacher Robert Dalley-Scarlett (the lover who is 'literally dead'), and that other great love of her youth, Peter Bennie. Peter was about to come back into her orbit for the first time since her 1970 trip to Sydney. In May 1978, he wrote to ask whether he could come to Halcyon for a visit. He had had a difficult year professionally, with his wardenship at St Paul under attack, and was 'low in spirits' and in need of sanctuary. Gwen, enormously touched that he had turned to her in his need, invited him to stay for a week. She had not been sure how she would feel when she saw him again, but when he stepped off the plane, all the old feelings came rushing back. 'The heart melted in my breast as it always does when I see him,' she reported to Tony. 'Forty years, and I'm still in love with him – that's really something to set against time and change.'[67] To Frank Kellaway, she gave a similar account, saying that she was 'shaken to the bones when this man in his 60s got off the plane streaming with the original radiance': 'I suppose you know the story of Baroness Metternich, who, when a young girl asked her when the torments of the flesh ceased, said "Why ask me? I am only 65."'[68] Gwen was only fifty-seven.

They spent the week 'talking, walking, drinking, playing chess, driving round the channel, arguing endlessly'. Peter was a 'superb chess player; he and Bill had some grand games (and some grand arguments on philosophy and linguistics)'.[69] She and Peter talked of poetry – largely, his own: 'he brought me a folder of splendid poems he'd written. I hope he goes on writing, though his formal style is out of favour with the trendies.' Gwen drove him round to see the sights, including the convict prison, Port Arthur, where they took the ferry to the prison cemetery, the infamous Isle of the Dead. 'Fancy sitting on the ferry . . . with the man you were in love with forty years ago!' she told Alison. 'Thank God the ferry has a licence. Brandy and Burning Glances!'[70] On this day, she and Peter found a private spot somewhere to make love.[71] Some twelve years later, Gwen would tell Ann that her two poems 'A Morning Air' and 'A Little Night Music' were 'closer to that day than I can get in prose. (Prose as you rightly say can be guarded.)'[72] In 'A Morning Air', two lovers quiet the seagulls by feeding them a crust of bread and then quiet their own hungering souls with a kiss. In the aftermath, they lie by the ocean amid sighing grasses, 'roofed with silver', while 'Wingbeats rise / from the sea's pure and ardent pulse'. It is an ecstatic, yet somehow muted, song of fulfilment, of perfectly realised passion.

Gwen would always treasure her memories of that day, not only because of the sexual idyll but also because Peter told her on their trip to Port Arthur that he felt they were two sides of the same person. At the same time, he found her 'completely enigmatic'.[73] He would say something similar in a letter a couple of years later: 'Sometimes I think you speak and think exactly as I do – I thought this, as you know, in Tasmania – almost like some Jungian anima; sometimes I feel there are vast stretches of you I do not touch at all, or really know.'[74] Nobody, he told her, had ever loved him as she had. 'I never knew what to do with you.'[75]

Despite her immutable devotion, Gwen was capable of a touch of objectivity. When she introduced him to her other great love, Ann Jennings, she realised that neither could see the other with her eyes. Peter saw Ann as 'a cuddly old lady', while Ann saw Pete as 'endearingly batrachian'.[76] Gwen herself had double vision: she could see both versions of her friends at the same time. She did note, as she had when she saw him in Sydney, that Peter's religious faith was no longer the same. 'Pete has no standard Anglican views now – his enemies say he's an atheist (though he isn't),' she told Tony. 'All the old arrogant certainty is gone. Like me he finds consolation in art and has no way of preventing the horrors of the insomniac hours when one faces "the bottomless black silence". But we spent the time in fits of laughter (his belly-laugh is unchanged: he ROARS) which did us both enormous good.' His visit, like Norman's, left her tranquil. 'It will probably be many years before I see him again, but nothing can outweigh the joy of having been able to offer him the blessings of Halcyon.'

◆ ◆ ◆

Over the course of that year, Agnes's health began to deteriorate. She was suffering from mild dementia, and Gwen had been uneasy about her for a couple of years. In August 1976, one of Agnes's friends rang to tell Gwen that her mother had broken her arm and was refusing to seek medical treatment. Leaving Bill with Mary, Gwen flew at once to Brisbane and found Agnes with her arm in plaster, happily watching TV. 'Nobody can make me do anything I don't want to,' she told Gwen proudly. 'She's right, too,' Gwen sighed.[77] It was obvious that Agnes was no longer coping very well on her own: the house was in chaos, and Agnes was highly resistant to any attempts to reduce it to order. Gwen invited her to move to Tasmania to live with them – a big sacrifice on her part, as Agnes had some years ago developed a 'pathological hatred of Bill'[78] – but Agnes would not hear of it. Gwen then tried, by turns, to convince her mother to 'sell the house, enter a nursing home, buy a unit, retire to the seaside, let the trustees take over her affairs, take in a boarder . . . "Nobody can make me," she said.'[79] So Gwen did what she could, organising as much community-based care for Agnes as possible, and left her to her independence, reflecting sadly that she would 'never again have a lucid conversation with her'.

Soon afterwards, Gwen's daughter, Mary, moved to Brisbane, which made it possible for Agnes to remain at home a little longer. But by October

1978, her situation had become dire, and Gwen knew she had no choice but to put Agnes into nursing care. She flew up to Brisbane for a couple of weeks to make the arrangements, wracked with guilt about 'putting Agnes away'.[80] It was a difficult time. Agnes suspected her daughter of plotting against her and unleashed all her venom on the interloper. The house was a disaster, and Gwen and Mary took a week to set it to rights. 'Sometimes we sat with packets of weevil-infested cereals and bowed our heads in fatigue; sometimes we got at the Beenleigh Rum (she had stocks of it as a medicinal sedative) and . . . shed tears of the purest sorrow for our own flesh and blood.'[81] Agnes settled into the nursing home well, however, and soon 'regained some of her old gaiety',[82] and Gwen no longer lay awake at night 'wondering if [Agnes had] set herself on fire'.

Soon after she returned from this sad trip, Gwen was amazed to learn that she had won the 1978 Patrick White Award. She was only the fifth winner of the ten-thousand-dollar prize, which White had established after his Nobel Prize win to recognise underappreciated Australian writers of outstanding ability. The inaugural winner was Christina Stead; Gwen was the second woman, and the third poet, to win. The award was a very big deal, partly because of its prestige and partly because of the fabulous prize money. Journalists and photographers appeared at her door, congratulations poured in from wellwishers, and she even received a 'fan letter' from the Minister for Post and Telecommunications which, as an avid user and devoted critic of the postal service, filled her with delight.[83] In an interview with Helen Frizell for *The Sydney Morning Herald*, Gwen confessed that not only had she never met Patrick White but she had never heard of his award.[84] She would spend the money, she told Frizell, 'only half-facetiously', on a Bechstein grand piano.

It was her second prize for the year. In February, she had learned she was the recipient of the Fellowship of Australian Writers' annual award, then known as the Robert Frost Medallion, for what she airily called 'good work in the service of the muse'.[85] Gwen was enchanted by the heavy bronze medallion, engraved with her name and a portrait of Frost in high relief. When it arrived in the mail, she took it to Ann's to show it off, and she and Stephen ended up playing bowls with it.[86] It was precisely the kind of award she liked: one she could hurl, with skill and finesse, at any obstacle that might present itself.

22

The Lion's Bride

I have become a complete insomniac, wandering companionless [in] the
dry paddocks . . . I feel like a goblin inhabiting the ruins of my old life.
Gwen Harwood, Letter to Norman Talbot, 12 March 1984

A COUPLE OF YEARS AFTER THEIR MOVE TO OYSTER COVE, Gwen began to dream that she had had another baby, 'an enormous ferocious infant with a crown of red hair'.[1] This baby was always wailing, always needy, but because of the demands of Gwen's farm work she could never manage to tend to it: 'The eggs in the incubator needed turning, the oats needed reaping, the peas needed picking, the ducks had to be done and put in the freezer, the geese needed watering and feeding, the lawn needed mowing, the pump needed to be switched off – all at once, while the baby . . . howled.' Mostly, in these dreams, the baby was 'huge' and 'fierce' and was 'going to wear me out'.[2] Sometimes, however, it was so 'angelically good and quiet' that she forgot all about it, which was even worse. She would go to its cot 'overcome with guilt and dread; it was terribly thin, but still beautiful, and was going to die, but *forgave* me'.[3] The baby's red hair makes it difficult to resist the conclusion that the importunate infant was Gwen herself – her inner artist, perhaps – whose needs were being dangerously neglected in the new life she and Bill had made.

Certainly, it was not the life she had envisaged when they first planned their rural idyll. 'I imagined living quietly in the bush reading and writing and chatting up the pardalotes and bronzewing pigeons,' she wrote. Instead, she was 'always on the road buying hardware or doing heavy manual labour or taking the ride-on mower to remote specialists to be restored to life, or carting the pump to and from Howrah . . .'[4] The list went on and on. 'The corn is ripe, the country is BORing BORing,' she told Norman.[5]

Since the move, Bill had been amazingly well; the cognitive deterioration the doctors had predicted had failed to appear,[6] and it had gradually become evident that he was not going to die from diabetes-related dementia. But in 1979, his blood glucose once again became unstable. A number of times he lapsed into a stupor during the night, groaning loudly but proving difficult or impossible to wake. In the worst cases, Gwen had to administer insulin 'to restore him to consciousness, not one of my favourite operations'.[7] He came to confused and often hostile, and would sometimes refuse the honey or barley sugar that would have helped to stabilise his blood sugar. More than once, he had a seizure during the day. He was losing weight and suffered increasingly from painful joints, to the point where he 'could hardly dress himself, could walk only with great pain, could not use the power tools' and could only sit 'gloomily by the fire'.[8] They both knew that with Bill out of action, they would not be able to manage at Oyster Cove.

They began on a new round of doctors' appointments and specialist visits, and over the course of several months, Bill's diabetes stabilised once more. New arthritis drugs dramatically improved his joint pain and mobility. He still needed to monitor his blood sugar closely, which meant, for Gwen, carefully planning and timing his meals. But he was much happier now that he could get back to his various construction projects. By late 1979, he was once again working on the yacht they had begun building in mid-1978, the successor to *Sappho*, which they would call *Halcyon*.

But now it was Gwen who was struggling. After an ant bite left her breathless and faint, she began a course of weekly anti-allergen injections, which went on throughout the second half of 1979 and for most of 1980. Her diaries record frequent sinus infections, headaches and nosebleeds, painful arthritis in her left knee, and a 'sore bum' – perhaps a complication of the anal surgery she had had some fifteen years earlier. Increasingly, she was having trouble sleeping, and when she did drop off, her dreams were terrifying. She found herself ruminating miserably on past decisions, past mistakes. In her diary, the shorthand symbol for 'depressed' or 'extremely depressed' appears with increasing frequency.

She was writing less often to Norman. Towards the end of 1979, she apologised for her silence, explaining that 'life has been hitting me with bicycle chains'.[9] This colourful phrase she had borrowed from Frank Kellaway, who used it to describe the experience of being in love.[10] But if Gwen was unhappily in love, she kept this to herself. Her letters contained a litany of other laments, however: an old friend with breast cancer, her young friend Sally Sleinis in hospital, the ongoing reverberations of Jim McAuley's death, the death of Alec Hope's only daughter from breast cancer, the death of Ann Jennings' mother (Gwen was making this particular list on the day of her funeral) and the unhappiness of one of her children. She had changed, she told Norman, from Goldenchild to Schwarzkind: child of darkness. She was particularly disturbed by the hospitalisation of Sally, her lively, Scrabble-playing biologist friend, who had schizophrenia. To witness this disease up close was a profound shock for Gwen. 'I curse myself for ever listening to the clever trendies echoing Cooper's "Madness has in our age become some sort of lost truth", she wrote. 'I have never seen such pain and despair.'[11] On the day of Sally's breakdown, Gwen had been scheduled to give a seminar, but she cancelled it to help Sally and her husband Edgar deal with the crisis.[12] Though she did what she could for her friend, she was profoundly upset by the bitter reminder of her own powerlessness in the face of others' tragedies. 'I lapsed into a dream-like state of sorrow over deaths, cancers, madness, the pain others had to bear,' she told Norman. '"The insignificance of the sayable" weighed on me so heavily that I wrote nothing, have written nothing for months. Maybe when the flathead start biting again I'll believe it's the only possible world and learn to live in it.'[13] In her diary on 2 October 1979, a shorthand entry reads simply: 'Dear God, how will I bear this pain?' There is no context, just the usual notations of her daily chores, the hatching of ten goslings, a fishing trip with Tony.

Going fishing with Tony would normally have been a cause for rejoicing. In mid-1979, to Gwen's mingled astonishment and joy, Tony had moved to Tasmania. He bought a house at Woodbridge, just a little further down the Channel Highway than Gwen and Bill's block, and settled down to tend his garden, keep bees and cultivate bucolic pleasures. He had talked about retiring to Tasmania before, but the pull of Europe had always been too strong, and when he sold both his Mornington house and his Melbourne flat at the end of 1975 and moved to England, Gwen believed he was gone for good. But though he felt profoundly at home with English culture, his living expenses were greater than he had anticipated, and his visit to Halcyon in early 1977 convinced him that he would enjoy rural life in Tasmania. In July 1979, he came to the island state to look for a property. He soon found what he wanted: 'a newish, pleasant weatherboard house, very sunny and sheltered from the gales', overlooking the D'Entrecasteaux Channel, with 'the best views in the district – quite breathtaking'.[14] Gwen could hardly believe that 'after a lifetime of air-letters we shall be country neighbours'.

Once he had made the move, he and Gwen saw a lot of each other, going for walks in the bush or on the beach, visiting for lunch and attending concerts in Hobart. Tony bought a subscription to Musica Viva, and every month or so over the summer, he and Gwen would have dinner at

Halcyon, then drive into Hobart together to attend a chamber music performance, leaving Bill happily ensconced at home by the fire. Tony was also a companion at poetry readings and other literary events. (He was amazed to find that Gwen still got nervous when she read: 'She's had such a lot of experience of this in the past; but I guess it's the same nervous tension that all the good performing artists must endure.')[15] Tony's presence meant she got out more. 'Bill hates concerts, lectures and indeed any cultural event, and is happy to stay away, so I'd got into the habit of simply not bothering to make the trip up to town in the bumpy ute,' Gwen explained to Frank. With Tony's company, it was worth the trouble.

Yet not even Tony could chase away Gwen's demons. Somewhat to her dismay, she missed the steady flow of their letters. Writing had long been the central modality of their friendship, and it was just not the same in person. But in any case, no one – no friend, no lover, no matter how cherished – could take away the bitter facts of inevitable decline and death that Gwen was grappling with. Tony was also prone to depression, and when he settled at Woodbridge, he saw himself as in some ways defeated, his life dominated by a 'ruinous sense of failure'.[16] His potential as a singer, actor and writer had not been realised – or so he believed. Only in Gwen's eyes had he retained the patina that had made him shine so brightly in his youth. His only honourable course, as he saw it, was to acknowledge and even embrace his humbled state. This he did so thoroughly that it drained the ordinary cheerfulness out of him, making him a somewhat dangerous companion for Gwen at a time when she was fighting her own black dog.

◆ ◆ ◆

Unlike Tony, Gwen had achieved her writing ambitions, but she increasingly felt that her work counted for little. What were even the finest poems beside the daily suffering of others and the relentlessness of death? She decided to write a prose memoir of her early life, in an attempt, among other things, to capture the 'stories of [her] childhood' before they were lost to history, along with 'the kind of life we lived then'.[17] But this meant returning to scenes now vanished and revisiting old selves she now judged harshly. She quickly realised she did not want to tell the whole truth of her life in stark prose. In fact, she found the process of writing prose much more difficult than she had anticipated, struggling to make headway without the structure of poetic form.[18] Unable to progress beyond early childhood, she abandoned the book and published instead four beautifully wrought first-person stories of her early life, two in *Overland* (1977 and 1982), one in *Westerly* (1981) and one in *The Bulletin* (1982). She also wrote two personal essays, one about her early experiences of music, 'Memoirs of a Dutiful Librettist', and the other a charming, bird's-eye sketch of her adolescent years, 'Time beyond Reason'.[19] This was the end of her attempts to write conventional autobiography; she did, however, continue to write about her childhood in a growing number of poems.

Her work as a librettist also continued. In late 1979, a Tasmanian composer, Don Kay, wrote to ask if she would be interested in working with him on an opera for children. She responded warmly. The opera was to be based on a Japanese fairy story, and she had a source to work from: a beautifully illustrated children's book entitled *The Golden Crane: A Japanese Folktale* by Tohr Yamaguchi. She immediately set herself to find out all she could about Japanese folklore, plunging into an exploration of Japanese art and culture. Don was amazed and delighted by her combination of efficiency and artistry. 'Her words, specially written for music setting, were so right for me. She claimed she could hear my music, in advance, dictating the words for her. I found that quite astonishing.'[20] When the opera was staged in Hobart some five years later, Gwen went to all five performances. Sitting beside her on one such occasion, Don was moved to see tears streaming down her face.

Gwen found Don much easier to work with than Larry. Throughout 1978 and 1979, she and Larry had continued to collaborate on *The Golem*, a much bigger and more demanding work than *The Golden Crane*, and she sometimes felt as though she was groping in the dark. As the libretto took form, she began to incorporate ideas that she had often debated with Bill about the role of language in the formation of the self. In researching Jewish sacred texts, she had discovered that when the first man, Adam, was created by God from the mud of Earth, he was called 'golem, meaning body without soul'.[21] He did not become human until some twelve hours after creation. The Golem in her script, similarly created out of mud by Rabbi Loew, becomes human 'through language', which teaches him 'what it is to be a man'. The idea that we learn to become human by learning language troubled Gwen: it suggested that there was no innate or essential self, that the biological 'raw material' of personhood was infinitely malleable, infinitely vulnerable to social and cultural forces. Bill had always believed that it would one day be possible to build a machine that could think and talk, hypothesising that it would be human in all essential respects; now Gwen was engaged in telling the story of 'a living automaton' who would not only speak, learn and fight but also fall in love.[22]

Her libretto was deeply suffused with the language of the Old Testament. Almost every line quoted or alluded to a phrase or verse from the Psalms, the Song of Songs, the Book of Job or the works of the prophets. The story is a dark one, dramatising the unrelenting efforts of Christians in medieval Prague to rob, murder and destroy the Jews who also called the city home. The Golem, with his supernatural strength, gives the Jews a fighting chance until Rachel, the woman he loves, is murdered. At this point, he loses his faith in humanity and goes on the rampage, attacking Christians and Jews alike. Rabbi Loew, who created him, is mesmerised to see, in the Golem, his own rage given terrifying form:

> Is it my own ghost who walks there?
> Is it my unredeemed self who strikes the enemy down?
> Is it my own violence that rages there, my double,
> my phantom who does what I dare not do?

The Rabbi's horror eerily echoes Gwen's meditations on the destructive impulses of her own alter ego in poems like 'Night Thoughts: Baby and Demon' and 'I Am the Captain of My Soul'. The distraught creator of the golem had sought to bring justice, but was left only with 'ashes, sorrow, death'.

◆ ◆ ◆

This dark view of the world was increasingly Gwen's own as she grappled with the deaths of beloved people. Agnes died in mid-1980, soon after her eighty-second birthday. Though Gwen had known when she moved Agnes into care two years earlier that her mother would not live much longer, her death was still a blow. She was haunted by the sense that she had let her mother down, telling Norman that she wished she had been 'a better girl, married a chartered accountant, pleased old Moth somehow. Too late, cry the Furies.'[23] Many years later, she would tell another friend: 'I did not love my mother enough. She was stylish and beautiful and I regarded her as a dreaded rival for my father's love.'[24] 'Forgive me the wisdom / I would not learn from you,' she begged in the elegy she wrote for Agnes towards the end of the year. Retitled 'Mother Who Gave Me Life' (its original title was 'Lamplight', followed by the inscription: 'i.m. Agnes Foster, 1898–1980'),[25] this poem would end her next book. Surviving drafts show that in her first version of the poem, she thought of 'women teaching / women', rather than 'bearing' them, as in the published version. She regretted her unwillingness to learn what Agnes had to teach.

Agnes's death renewed her old fear of her own mortality. She told Tony she had 'the feeling of being next in line for the Grim Reaper; nightmare after nightmare, often the worse for being comic'.[26] In the past she had clung to her belief that the joy of her happiest moments would counter-balance the misery of the rest. 'What matter if griefs return,' she had written in 'Past and Present': 'I know that joy will come / as a voice in a fugue returns / to enter and alter the texture / of accumulating seasons.' Now, she was not so sure. Instead, as she would write in 'Mid-Channel', she knew only that 'A day will come, / matter-of-fact as knife and plate, / with death's hook in my jaw . . .'. Against the certainty of death she had no bulwark.

Agnes's passing was followed by the death of Edwin Tanner. Over the last couple of years, Eddie's behaviour had become increasingly erratic, which Gwen had put down to the medications he was taking to manage his intractable pain. He had sent her some 'really horrible' letters, which she had quietly burnt, refusing to believe that they represented anything other than the influence of the drugs he had been prescribed.[27] She continued to write to him and, when she had the chance, to see him, but she no longer turned to him as her most trusted fellow labourer in the vineyards of art. By the time his doctors discovered that he had a brain tumour, it was too late to save him.[28] Gwen saw him briefly in November 1979, during an overnight trip to Melbourne to attend a dinner in her honour hosted by *Overland*. She later recalled that they had 'a fierce but affectionate quarrel about a poem of mine he didn't like (he was right; I have disposed of it) and about his cutting down three large gums with a chainsaw because they interfered with light from the east'. Then he went off to buy his lunch and she went off to catch her plane: 'We said goodbye in the street.'[29]

'As for the demons, they bite,' she told Jim Penberthy, retailing her losses.[30] She had recently lost another friend: Dick Fitzgerald, a Hobart dentist, who had committed suicide. Gwen's grief was mingled with bewilderment. He was 'a lovely, graceful, apparently successful man with children and grandchildren; younger than we are, too; he seemed to have everything.

How can you tell?' She simply could not reconcile herself to 'the disappearance of irreplaceable human beings; they die, and demons jump into the empty spaces'. King David's words of grief over his dead son, which she had first heard as a child sitting rapt beside her grandmother in a Brisbane church pew, came to haunt her: 'Can I bring him back again? I shall go to him, but he shall not return to me' (2 Samuel 12:23). She was struggling to find the strength to rouse herself 'to the effort of true vision' – the only way, she told Jim, for the artist to 'break out of the narrow world of his own misery'.[31] She felt she had tumbled into 'a crevasse', and for once, she had lost her confidence that she would be able to climb out again.[32]

◆ ◆ ◆

Despite her encroaching depression, in October 1980 Gwen pulled together a manuscript for a new book and submitted it to Angus & Robertson. The poetry editor at A&R was Les Murray, and Gwen was pleased to hear, a little more than a month later, that 'Old Uncle Les approve[d]' of her manuscript.[33] This book would be the first of her volumes to have a title other than *Poems*: she called it *The Lion's Bride*, after the poem she placed first in the collection. The story of the lion's bride was one she had long known from a Schumann song, but more recently, she had come across the supposedly factual origins of the tale in a book about eighteenth-century Vienna.[34] As the story ran, the daughter of a Viennese zookeeper had made something of a pet of the zoo's lion, going into its cage freely to feed and care for it. On the day of her wedding, she went into the cage one last time to say goodbye, and the lion attacked and killed her. According to the 'sentimental Viennese', it was jealous of her husband-to-be.[35]

'The Lion's Bride haunts me,' Gwen told Tony in November 1975, enclosing her poem. At the time, she thought she 'might write a series of sonnets on the theme', but it seems she wrote only this one, which tells the story from the lion's perspective. He loved his attendant, who brought him every day 'our special bowl', 'our love feast'. But one day, a stranger appeared in her place, 'an icy spectre sheathed / in silk' and wrapped in a scented veil. He made a meal of her and settled down to await the arrival of his 'love', his 'bride', to share his feast. Gwen found the story both tragic and irresistibly comic. Some years later, she would write her projected sonnet sequence as a jeu d'esprit to amuse students at Monash University, ending with a 'minimal version':

Keeper's Brat!
Jeeper's Cat!
Tarry?
Marry!
Dress.
Dummy?
 – Meat!
Eat.
Yummy!
Bride
Inside.[36]

The comic dimensions of the story she associated, happily, with Jim McAuley, who had always been 'leonine' to her. Another poem in *The Lion's Bride*, 'Memento', makes this connection explicit, telling of an occasion in which Jim sat at her piano with a book of Schumann songs and attempted to perform 'The Lion's Bride':

At the moment when the lovecrazed lion
begins to crunch the keeper's daughter
in her bridegroom's presence, the translator
makes the youth, calling for a weapon,
ineptly cry, 'Give me an arm!'
Jim roars and chokes and waves his wineglass,
leonine, overwhelmed by laughter.

Jim features in several poems in this volume. 'Space of a Dream', which records a dream of him and a mutual friend – the poet and academic Graeme Hetherington – refers to his 'lion's body'. In his personal power and magnetism, and perhaps in his carelessness, he is like the lion of the story, inadvertently feasting on the one he loves.

The lion had other meanings for Gwen. In a letter to Alison, she told the story of the dream she had had in her long-ago Brisbane days about Bill as a lion who threatened to bite off her hands. She had entirely forgotten this dream, she told Alison, until she re-read 'Fever', a Kröte poem in *Selected Poems* that contained a 'lion's mane reference'.[37] The reference is actually to the 'wild mane' of Kröte's hair, which is tenderly touched by the young girl, his student, who is in love with him. To love a lion – a Robert Dalley-Scarlet, a Jim McAuley, a Bill Harwood – is dangerous. The moment in which you are most confident that you have tamed the beast is the moment in which you are most at risk. The lion will savage you, not out of malice but simply because it is his nature.

The poems in *The Lion's Bride* are overwhelmingly about love and death. The volume includes a generous scattering of her love poems for Norman ('You'll find yourself there my darling,' she wrote in a note enclosed with his copy), as well as her two recent poems for Peter Bennie, helpfully arranged in sequence. There is even a late poem for her old love, Tom Pick, 'Dreaming's an Art', based on another agonising dream.[38] But the other love poems – in the broadest sense of that term – are all for the dead: Jim McAuley, Edwin Tanner and Agnes. The poems of carnal love seek to set love against death, as in the final section of 'The Sharpness of Death' – which Gwen told Norman should have been called 'In the Roofless Chapel at Morpeth'.[39] Yet in the elegies and pastorals, and creeping into the poems of everyday, is a bitter sense of death's ultimate triumph. 'Even here, in Arcady, are graves,' she writes in the last of the three 'Oyster Cove Pastorals': 'My body wears / the light and substance of the dead'. In 'Sparrows', 'Why does he let them fall / if he loves the world at all?' is an agonised cry. In 'Diotima', it becomes clear that there is nothing that is 'too dear for death's possessing': 'To have the taste / in your mouth and know the wine gone: / that is the anguish of thirst.'

In the face of death, she had come to feel, even desire bleeds away.

◆ ◆ ◆

The Lion's Bride appeared at the end of 1981, with a cover design of autumn leaves and emerald-green endpapers. Gwen had long made a joke of her bibliophilic desire for coloured endpapers, and she was delighted to finally achieve them. 'Isn't the book pretty?' she asked Norman, in a note addressed to 'Northern Lion!' But neither the book's beauty nor the glowing responses to her new work from friends could do much to lighten her increasingly morose state of mind. She was grappling with the growing fear that love was not, in fact – as the Bible promised, and as she had believed for most of her life – stronger than death. Early in 1981, she told Norman that she had taken to reading the Bible every day. 'Every morning after I have cleaned my cell and polished my tins I read a little of the O.T.,' she wrote. If she was seeking comfort, the Bible did not always oblige. 'Today we are up to II Sam. 16, with Absalom going in unto his father's concubines in the sight of all Israel,' she sighed. 'Sometimes the scripture is no help at all.'[40] For two decades, Gwen had been not merely sceptical about Christianity but actively derisive. As recently as 1978, she had told Helen Frizell, in a *Sydney Morning Herald* interview, that she had 'no firm religious belief'.[41] But now she was turning to the Old Testament, whose Elizabethan diction and thunderously vengeful God had been part of the texture of her childhood, for some kind of solace.

Her depression was so unrelenting that she began to contemplate seeking medical treatment.[42] She had always been opposed to antidepressants, telling friends that such medications had dangerous side effects and were best avoided. Her drugs of choice, she liked to say, were music and a little alcohol. But now they were failing her. 'I have the most terrible dreams in which I am cracking up on stage,' she told Alison. 'The audience leaves, not wanting to know, then my mother (young) advances towards me with a glowing white pill saying, "I am the only one who can help you." But before she can reach up to the stage she vanishes. Is this A SIGN that I should get myself on to the trankies before it's too late?'[43] Soon after, she dreamed that she went to see a doctor and told him she was 'cracking up'. He handed her a prescription, 'smiling and saying "Nearly everyone cracks up sooner or later."' Then, when she looked at his account, she realised he was not a real doctor, and the prescription was for liver pills. 'Well, advice from the Gates of Horn: don't commit yourself to the medical profession.'[44]

The onset of winter was always particularly difficult for her. In 1982, as the world grew darker and the days shorter, life became more intolerable.[45] She lost another friend, Henry Oakes, who had recently retired to his holiday house at Oyster Cove. Gwen's diaries record many afternoon teas, drinks and walks with Henry. His sudden death from a heart attack left her feeling even more isolated. 'It was rotten of him to die,' she told Alison.[46] 'I used to go down and talk to him about the troubles of a diabetic spouse, music and art (he was a good amateur painter), rural problems etc. I really miss him.'[47] After the funeral, his family buried his ashes under a banksia tree on their property, and Gwen took to sitting by the tree to talk with him when she was lonely. Sometimes, she confessed to Vin Buckley, she would 'tell him he's lucky'.[48] Death was at least an escape.

She was not sleeping well, lying awake for hours, unable to drift off, or waking in the early hours to 'wrestle with total Angst in the huge spaces between what I've done and what I ought to have done; death coming closer,

God knows what horrors'.[49] She worried about her children, fretted about the breakdown of friends' marriages, quailed before the seemingly unassuageable unhappiness all around her. In the pre-dawn hours, she could not escape the realisation that 'the desolation is NOW, not something possible in the future'.[50] 'As I have to drive I can't take sleepers or tranquillizers,' she told Frank. 'The only remedy seems to be to sneak into the spare room and listen to the wireless through the early hours. It's generally too cold to walk round though on mild nights I join the nocturnal creatures.'[51] Not surprisingly, she felt 'mortally tired'. 'Really I think I need a holiday (ridiculous as it may sound from one living in a rural paradise),' she told Tony.[52] Caring for Bill, whose diabetes still needed careful management, took a toll. She longed to have someone take care of her in the way she took care of him. 'Absolutely buggered,' she noted in her diary for 28 April 1982. 'Need a wife to look after me.'

◆ ◆ ◆

In the late 1970s, after her grant ran out, Gwen took on work for the Adult Education department, writing guides for literary texts and tutoring in writing at the College of Advanced Education in Rosny. Her diaries of that period record the enormous amount of reading and writing she did for the role. Tony observed in a letter to Frank that 'much of that work is intellectually demanding, for some of the books discussed in the classes are quite extreme'. His examples were Patrick White's *The Cockatoos* and Joyce's *Ulysses* – 'though neither of those fills her with enthusiasm'.[53]

Tony could be a touch dismissive of the 'classes of suburban housewives etc.' who would read and discuss Gwen's guides, but Gwen never was. As a 'housewife' herself, she was very attuned to the specificities of such women's lives, and keen to speak to them. In 1979, she told Dorothy Hewett that she had spent 'a couple of hours at one of the Colleges with a class of housewives doing their HSC English after years away from school': 'Absolutely delightful – I was deeply moved by their response when they found out I was a late starter. God knows what they've been through to get to that two-hour class once a week.'[54] A couple of years later, she spoke in similar terms to Jim Penberthy of going to Rosny 'to talk to some mature students eager to get back to the stream of life after years in the kitchen': 'Their enthusiasm is heartening. To them I seem remote and glorious because I've published books. I have to convince them I've been in there chopping up cucumbers, unpublished and unencouraged.'[55]

As ever, she liked to be working: she enjoyed both the income and the social interaction. For the first time in her life, she also took on reviewing gigs, writing on both fiction and non-fiction for *The Sydney Morning Herald* in 1982 and 1983. 'I HATE doing reviews,' she told Alison, 'but they pay $100 for 700 words (and some of them are words like "and" and "but").'[56] Her own experiences of being reviewed had done little to change her mind on the value of criticism. 'It seems insulting to praise or dismiss in a few pages work that has taken years to write,' she commented in 1983.[57] She was careful in her reviews. No matter how tetchy she could be in private about the work of other writers, publicly she was more inclined to praise than to dismiss. Even her poetry reviews – of which she did a handful for a newish literary magazine, *Luna*, run by a women's collective – were unfailingly generous.

Though she barely left Tasmania, her reputation continued to grow. In 1979, the American Academy of Poets invited her to visit the United States with Les Murray and David Malouf as part of a reading tour. 'Of course I can't accept,' she told Norman, 'but I'm loved and wanted.'[58] A couple of years later, the Literature Board invited her to read in Canada, all fares paid.[59] Again, she declined; she missed being on the literary circuit, but she simply could not contemplate leaving Bill alone. Her fear was that he might fall into a diabetic coma in her absence. 'WHAT IF? I ask myself, would I spend the whole of the rest of my life saying . . . IF ONLY . . . I had been there.'[60]

But though she did not travel, she was not isolated from other writers. She accepted invitations to speak at schools and community gatherings in Tasmania, to launch books, give readings, hand out prizes and attend literary lunches. She often met writers from interstate at such events – some, such as Tom Shapcott and Judith Rodriguez, were old friends, others, such as Rosemary Dobson and Kathy Lette, new acquaintances. Kathy she pronounced 'a lovely lively girl and great fun', noting with satisfaction that when she read from *Puberty Blues*, 'Some of the devoted followers of the arts were rigid with distaste'.[61] Now and then, young writers from the mainland would make a pilgrimage to Oyster Cove to meet her. She was happy to welcome 'three young poets', Kevin Hart, Philip Mead and Alan Gould, to Halcyon one afternoon. They 'sat round the fire eating tea and fruit cake and talking non-stop for a couple of hours', she reported to Tony. 'I was very touched that these young folk wanted to meet me.'[62]

She also knew many Tasmanian writers. Early in 1979, she agreed to take on the role of consulting editor for *The Tasmanian Review* (later *Island*), and officially launched the magazine at a party in Hobart in June.

She did not keep her editorial position long, however, resigning in protest after the *Review* published a 'vicious attack' on some local artists, including her friends Max Angus and Patricia Giles. (She was 'pleased to hear' that her resignation 'upset' the publication's editors.)[63] She was ambivalent about 'the boys on the *Review*', suspecting that they found her 'hopelessly old-fashioned and formal': 'but who cares? I don't even bother to read the ratshit stuff these days.'[64] Nevertheless, she still sent the *Review* poems from time to time.[65]

Launching The Tasmanian Review *in 1979. Left to right: Michael Denholm, Gwen Harwood, Stuart Heather and Andrew Sant*

A less palatable aspect of her growing reputation was the importuning letters she received from aspiring writers. Manuscripts arrived with daunting frequency from would-be poets seeking 'a word' from an established poet to set them on the path. Gwen could not bring herself to ignore this unsought correspondence. To Tony and Alison, she often complained about the deluge, vowing again and again to be ruthless and simply ignore the piles of unsolicited work mounting up – but she never did. Some sense of obligation or responsibility, of fellow feeling, compelled her to read and respond, even though it meant taking time away from her own creative work.

By the early 1980s, she was writing again. Larry had commissioned her to write a concert piece based on Oscar Wilde's *De Profundis*, and she spent several weeks immersed in the text while she was recovering from leg injuries she had suffered from walking into a glass door.[66] It seemed fitting that she was 'virtually imprisoned' while she was working on Wilde's prison letter.[67] She used only Wilde's words, selecting and arranging them for best effect, and produced a text that would be described by one listener as 'sixty minutes of baritone anguish'.[68] When Gwen saw Larry's score, she was dazzled, as ever: 'It looks marvellous, you old genius'.[69]

At the same time, new poems were 'pouring out, metre fairly strict but just enough rhyme to hold it together like the little gadgets on a glasshouse'.[70] (The simile was deeply felt: she and Bill had recently built 'fiendishly difficult' glasshouses for themselves and Tony.) She was working on a series of poems about a talking crab who had begun to visit her dreams. Her crab was the ghost of one her father had caught when she was a child and brought home for dinner. The family had gone to the pictures, she explained to Tony, leaving the crab, still alive, in a box, but while they were out it escaped, 'leaving a trail of chewed objects (rulers, pencils, toys)'. Joe had to catch it again before they could boil it for their supper. In Gwen's dream, the murdered crab appeared 'with a seaweed cloak (like [O]ndine's father in [Ashton and Henze's] ballet) and said, "I come to you in a dream of ages past."'[71] In waking life, Gwen had been searching for a theme for a couple of poems she had agreed to write for a friend, and in her dream, she asked the crab what she should write. 'He instructed me to write THE DIRE BELLY VARIATIONS, writing it down in case I missed the pun on The Diabelli Variations. What a rocker!'[72] This was only the crab's first appearance. For some months, he came to her in dreams that were 'recurrent, terrible, sometimes funny'.[73] They stimulated her interest in crabs, and she read up on them, learning their Latin names and studying their behaviour at the seashore. The result was the four poems of 'Night and Dreams'.

Though her dream crab was 'a joker',[74] he brought her back to 'the great questions', 'such as: what am I doing here / in gumboots and a summer nightdress / in a moonlit garden chasing sheep?' Minus the sheep (which belonged to a neighbour and had knocked down the fence), it was a question she would increasingly return to. 'Sweet old whistling Jesus what am I doing here after 36 years?' she wrote in her diary in September 1981, a week or so after her thirty-sixth wedding anniversary.[75] She was once again questioning her marriage and her decision to stay with Bill. It was only her feelings of guilt, she told Alison, that kept her 'immured here'.[76] One day, having cut her thumb while cooking, she complained to Alison (quoting Sylvia Plath's 'Cut') that it was one of those 'my-thumb-instead-of-an-onion days': 'Bloody and bandaged, raging, wondering how Sylvia Plath stuck it as long as she did.' Bill's constant presence drove her crazy. 'I never have the house to myself and am rapidly exhausting the crabs and limpets as sources of entertainment,' she complained.[77]

In 1981, they bought an electronic chess set, 'an all-but-human computer that plays chess at eight levels'. 'Bill adores it,' she told Alison dryly, 'because it's an automaton.'[78] A year or so later, they bought a home computer, an early model IBM that was even more effective at keeping Bill entertained. Bill liked to program it to solve 'Problems in Boolean algebra', which would tie up the hard drive for hours.[79] He was 'utterly besotted', she declared, and was soon planning to buy 'a better one with more capacity (a young, lovely and brilliant new computer – oh, well, I think he'll keep *me*)'.[80]

To keep her sanity, she made herself 'a basic camp down in the last bit of bush near the road' where she could read and write in solitude. It was 'just a fireplace of convict bricks with some big stones for visitors to sit on (haven't had any yet) and an old tin trunk (my grandfather's wedding trunk, rusty but watertight) with billy tea materials', but it was away from Bill.[81] 'He'll come upon it sooner or later and try to "improve" it, no doubt,' she told Alison sardonically.[82]

Gwen at her bush camp at Oyster Cove, 1984

She was increasingly convinced that rural retirement was not for her. Now that Bill was not dying, she could not see why she should continue to suffer being 'lonely but never alone'. She had begun to 'think with longing of the days when I was at work with a stream of people to talk to, or whizzing round Oz to littry events,' she told Rex Hobcroft and his new wife, Perpetua, in October 1983.[83] Bill was not averse to returning to the city, where he would have more independence – provided he could find a house that would give him the privacy he craved. They were both disappointed with the rapid development at Oyster Cove. When they first arrived, theirs was 'the only house on 40 acres', but by early 1984, there were houses all around them. Gwen could no longer roam freely over the hillside: it was 'all fenced off and defended by noble dogs'.[84] It was time to move.

Gwen tried to talk Bill into relocating to Brisbane; she had inherited Agnes's house at Camp Hill and thought they could renovate it, sell it, then 'settle somewhere nice in lovely Queensland'.[85] But Bill's feelings about Queensland were the opposite of Gwen's: his dislike of the climate, the lifestyle and the people matched in intensity Gwen's passion for them. Hobart was the best compromise they could reach.

After many months of looking at house after house, towards the end of 1984 they saw a cottage in Pine Street in West Hobart that they both felt would suit them. On an inner block, reached by a long driveway, the house could not even be seen from the road. Gwen was charmed by the 'delightful old garden', once part of an orchard, just like the old house at Mitchelton.[86] Though it was small, there was a room 'where the computer can go and flicker away by itself thank Christ'.[87] Visitors could sleep in the parlour. They made an offer at once.

By early December, they had sold Halcyon and were busy organising a sale of all the tools and equipment they had accumulated over their years of heavy labour. Then they had only to 'sort through [their] battered worldlies' and they would be on their way back to the city.

23

Night and Dreams

*I feel as if I'd returned from Elfland – the nine years in pleasant exile
have compressed to a day, and my tongue is my own again.*

Gwen Harwood, Letter to Rex and Perpetua Hobcroft,

10 February 1985

GWEN'S SPIRITS SOARED ON HER RETURN TO HOBART. THE house on Pine Street, though quiet and private, was in walking distance of the CBD for someone as energetic as Gwen. The Knocklofty Reserve, at the foot of Mount Wellington, was also only a vigorous walk away, for those times when she needed to 'go deep into the bush'.[1] There was an excellent grocery shop on the corner of their street, run by a Greek family with whom she quickly made friends. Even the suburbia of West Hobart delighted her; when Mary came to visit, mother and daughter 'walked endlessly peering through knotholes in high fences and sneaking up shadowy lanes'.[2] The old houses were charming, with 'oddly designed additions or renovations or "features"',[3] and she was pleased to discover that there were bantam hens on her street, and that the new house was 'cat-attended'.[4] (Her beloved Siamese, Mr Gabriel Fur, had died at Oyster Cove, though he still put in appearances in her poems – notably in the lovely elegy 'Twilight'.)[5] Local friends dropped in: Sally and Edgar, Ann and Stephen, and Gwen and Bill's old friend from the University English Department, Thea Goodwin. Interstate friends visited: Sybille and Vivian Smith and their family, Alison Hoddinott, Beverley Dunn. Gwen could slip down to the library whenever she wanted, or go to the movies with Thea. 'The ice has really melted after my years in Elfland or whatever it was down among the mushrooms,' she wrote to Norman in January.[6] Like Tom the Rhymer, the lonely years of exile had elapsed, and she was now back in the human world, alive, awake, 'with my tongue still my own'.[7]

One of the things about the neighbourhood that especially delighted her was the sound of church bells on Sunday mornings.[8] Soon after they had settled in at Pine Street, she went with Thea to Sunday mass at the Anglican Cathedral. 'It was (you might say) heavenly to go off to Mass,' she declared.[9] A month or so later, she went with Sally to the Sunday service at

318

Thea's local parish, the small Anglican community of All Saints in South Hobart. Like its namesake in Brisbane, All Saints in Hobart was High Anglican, with all the trappings of Catholicism that Gwen loved.[10] She had initially attended simply to support Sally, who was exploring the possibility of joining the church,[11] but she found herself 'quite at home with the stained glass & gorgeous vestments'. The little church community was to her 'uncannily like its Brisbane counterpart' where she had worshipped all those years ago. 'Anglo-Catholic churches are all the same; you can go in and find the people you knew 50 years ago in another human frame,' she told Alison.[12] The services had changed somewhat – she 'loathe[d] the new rite', which used modern English – but this in itself did not disrupt the welcome sense of homecoming. Besides, 'the vestments are good & the music tolerable', she reported. There was also the eternal allure of the church organ. 'Maybe one day the organist will drop dead & my time will come: "Excuse me, but I have played for mass many times . . ." or "Is there a musician in the audience?"'[13] Soon, she and Sally were attending mass every Sunday.

Late in March, she noticed a raw, inflamed spot on her calf. Assuming she'd been bitten by a spider, she dressed it and thought no more of it until a fortnight or so later, when she realised it was getting worse. When she finally took herself to the doctor, he told her that it was a skin cancer. He then checked her thoroughly for other lesions, and found a suspicious lump in her right breast. 'Naturally I don't believe it's anything fatal,' she told Alison on 4 June. 'I am in excellent health.'[14] Still, she could not help but wonder 'what made me write those crab poems with jokes about cancer'. Her visit to the breast-cancer surgeon, Desmond Cooper, was not as reassuring as she had hoped. 'He examined the aging bosom delicately and said he could take the lump out next Tuesday,' she reported.[15] The plan was to do a biopsy, but he did ask Gwen if he could make his own judgement, during the surgery, as to what action to take if he found the lump was 'something serious'. Gwen understood this to mean that there was a chance she would wake from surgery to find her right breast gone.

In the days between this appointment and her admission to hospital, she did her best to resign herself to the potential loss of her breast. Even so, she did not really believe it would happen. As she told the surgeon, 'my mother and her mother and hers lived on into their 80s with perfect health', so it seemed to her 'unlikely' it would actually turn out to be cancer.[16] Her sixty-fifth birthday fell two days before the surgery, and to celebrate, Tony took her and Bill to the Oyster Cove Inn for lunch. As a birthday gift, he made a recording of himself reading his favourites among her poems, as well as a handful of classic poems they both loved. Gwen found the recordings 'beautiful': 'so resonant & intelligent it made you forget there was a mediator between you & the poem'.[17]

After spending several days cooking casseroles, soups and cakes to keep Bill going while she was away, she took herself off to St Helen's hospital by cab the night before her surgery. When she was settled in, she wrote to Alison from her hospital room of the 'cityscape' she could see from her window, including the Savings Bank of Tasmania: 'Its bright red revolving SBT sign is the only moving object until the moon gets up – though I can flatten myself against the wardrobe and see the cars going up Davey St when I get tired of the SBT sign.' The next day, she added that the sign had gone off 'at midnight so I had to depend on the moon (a crescent) until morning. Venus was glorious over the Lands Dept building'.[18] The view would make it into her hospital poem 'The Night Watch' – but that would be some time later.

That afternoon, she woke from surgery to find she still had her breast, and added a postscript to her letter to tell Alison that she felt 'OK and cheerful and glad to be in the world even with drainage lines & an intravenous drip'. The surgeon came to tell her that the pathology results were promising: no sign of cancer. That day, she wrote cheerfully to Norman that she had even said 'I told you so' when the surgeon came 'with the good news'.[19] Bill, Tony, Sally and Thea visited, and all seemed well. But the following day, the surgeon brought a very different report. Further test results had shown that she did have cancer after all. She was asked to choose between a radical mastectomy and chemotherapy; the surgeon recommended the mastectomy as quicker and 'probably less painful'. 'For me the year's deep midnight indeed,' she wrote to Norman.[20]

She went home for three days, cleaned the house, stocked up the fridge and freezer once again with home-cooked meals, and went back to St Helen's for the next, much more gruelling operation. She was shaken: much as she had felt death stalking her over the past few years, she had not seriously believed it would come so close. But she told Alison she was resigned to whatever was to come: she had 'abandoned [her]self to fate'. Alison wanted to come down from Armidale, but Gwen asked her not to, telling her to visit later, when she was on her feet again. This time, her optimism was warranted. The surgery was 'devastating, appalling', but she survived. 'It's over and I am alive & will be well,' she told Larry: 'What more could I want?'[21] Of course, her demonic alter ego immediately supplied the answer:

Voice of tempter: 1 Porsche
                      1 ruby necklace
                      1 round the world trip
                      1 early Picasso
                      and my bosom back.
Voice from On High: Yer can't.

Her surgeon reported that there were no secondary cancers, a welcome piece of good news. 'If it hadn't been for the chance visit to my GP last week I might have been in the TOO LATE group,' she told Alison. 'Somebody, something, loves me enough to keep me here.'[22] She was determined to bounce back. On the second day after her surgery, her surgeon came in 'and said "Give me your hand" – extending his. I used all my strength to show him that the muscles were intact and that I *would not* give up.'[23]

She would think of this moment six weeks later, when she was out of hospital and slipping back into her normal routines. Reading a novel by Elaine Feinstein, she came across the line: 'Give me your hand, my love.' She thought of the surgeon, and then she thought of the day in 1974 when she and Jim McAuley drove back to Hobart from their reading tour in the north and pulled off the road to canoodle. She had been singing '"La ci darem" (Give me your hand, from Don Giovanni)' when Jim decided to make the unscheduled stop. It all seemed mysteriously, miraculously connected as 'a great many things suddenly [fell] into place.'[24]

Gwen was in hospital for about ten days after the surgery, a respite from household chores for which she was thankful. Friends and family rallied round to make sure she and Bill were taken care of. Sally was her most stalwart support, making sure Bill was fed, going on errands for Gwen, visiting her daily. Gwen was touched and grateful. 'She's been marvellous,' she told Alison. 'At her worst I never thought she'd function again & here she is looking after *me*.'[25] Once she was out of hospital, things returned to normal with almost alarming speed. Her plans to do less cooking came to naught when Bill refused to eat supermarket food, insisting on her home-prepared meals. She was so eager to prove to others how quickly she had recovered, how entirely well she was – in order, mainly, to spare them worry – that she found herself rushing around as though nothing had happened. She was tired, though, and sore – particularly her right arm, which, as she told Alison rather resentfully, was her 'cooking arm'.[26]

She also had to try to come to terms with the loss of her breast. 'The first time I saw the scar a tear rolled down,' she confessed to Norman.[27] She knew she would need to 'go deep into the bush on Knocklofty . . . and weep and rage and accept my wound'.[28] She told Alison, only half-jokingly, that her 'secret plan' to go to North Queensland for her final years had been ruined, since she could no longer 'wear a sleeveless dress or swim suit'.[29] Her characteristic nostalgia for Queensland intensified in the months after her surgery, but she was aware that 'what I'm grieving for is my own wholeness'.[30] She felt that she needed 'the rage of poetry' to enable her to get through the trauma, but she was struggling to 'transform the loss; I've written some new poems but they stop short of saying anything really funny enough to show how serious I am'.

The poems would come. In the meantime, Norman flew down to Hobart to cheer her in April 1986. He was ostensibly there to give some lectures at the University of Tasmania and to visit his daughter and granddaughter, who were now living in Hobart, but he was most eager to see Gwen. She was eager to see him too. Before his visit, she told him she had been fitted for a prosthesis soon after the surgery and was impressed by how 'lifelike' it was 'when tucked in the bra'.[31] 'My artificial bosom is firmly balanced,' she assured him. 'You can clasp me hard and not dislodge it. There should be a phrase equivalent to "cockeyed muse" to suit my present frame of body, but I haven't thought of it yet.'[32]

In their brief time together, Norman was able to make her feel that she was still beloved. 'It was good to breathe an atmosphere of crazy love,' she told Ann after his visit. 'Even the bit of me reconstructed from silicon seemed to respond.'[33] It had been six years since they had seen one another, and Gwen found it a 'joy' to be with him again, doing nothing in particular but simply 'wandering & talking'.[34] On the day he left, she sent him one of her old ditties: 'Come you back to West Hobart / to the groves of love and art / You can hear the plane trees whisper: / Norman Talbot has my heart.'[35]

◆ ◆ ◆

Despite her avowed intention to take things easier, Gwen's days were soon alarmingly full once more. Once she was out of hospital, she went straight to the library to find out as much as she could about breast cancer. 'I keep feeling what-if,' she told Alison. 'What if I'd rested more, drunk less, ate more alfalfa sprouts (FAIL! eaten), insisted on a holiday etc etc etc.'[36] Her research into '*what* could have spared me' shed little light: 'Nothing, it seems. One factor: prolonged and unremitting stress.'[37] Now that the stress was 'gone', as a result of her fortnight in hospital ('the cure was terrible'), she was determined not to allow it to return. 'I am going to avoid henceforth anything I don't want to do,' she declared. 'No, I am too weak to read your sonnet sequence; too sore to open your exhibition; too frail, alas, to judge the Upper Moonah literary competition; too shattered to attend your reading of your recent epic . . . see, my arm cannot scrape those barnacles and lift that flat iron.'[38] Yet she did not keep her resolution.

Soon after she returned home, Sally, who had risen so magnificently to the occasion of Gwen's illness, had a breakdown and was admitted to the detox ward of a Hobart hospital. Gwen was appalled by conditions on the ward and promptly took Sally home with her, undertaking to help care for her for six weeks, until she could fly home to her parents in America. She was only a month out of hospital herself, and caring for Sally was 'Exhausting!': 'She seems to need total activity seven days a week & never just lies on the couch reading a book or potters in the garden or goes for a purposeless walk looking at the world.'[39] Once Sally had gone, Gwen was quickly drawn into the old whirlwind of social activity. 'The phone rings incessantly,' she complained to Tony. 'Speak here, attend there, review this or that, read this deathless manuscript, say a few words to our little creative group – all lovely people, but there are too many of them.'[40]

By mid-1987, she was wondering whether she should rent a room nearby to work in, just to be free of the 'knockers & ringers'.[41] Despite her determination to be 'fierce', she found it almost impossible to say no to those who importuned her, especially when the event or activity was for a good cause. She spoke to schoolchildren and to senior citizens at the University of the Third Age. She judged writing competitions for organisations ranging from the Women's International League for Peace and Freedom to the National Book Council. She wrote testimonials for grant seekers, launched books for friends, gave workshops and attended luncheons. She read countless manuscripts from aspiring writers (the volume of manuscripts she received had reached such proportions that Bill had to build a special letterbox for them).

Though she complained, she enjoyed being part of the community again. Much as she lamented having to wade through endless piles of marginally literate short stories, or smile sweetly at tin-eared poets while uttering those infamous words, 'That's lovely, dear', she did take delight in the bustle and buzz of the literary world. She had felt so isolated at Oyster Cove that it was all too easy to overcompensate now. Besides, she was determined to show her wellwishers how completely she had recovered.[42]

She had little desire to turn down invitations to travel interstate. Now that she and Bill were back in town, with shops, medical care and reliable friends close by, she felt she did not need to worry about leaving him for a few days. Travelling to Queensland on literary business was especially sweet. 'Brisbane was magical, beyond all memories,' she told Rex in 1987, after a week at the Warana Literary Festival. She had been 'shaken to bits by the flowering trees, the warmth, the light at sunset (at one stride comes the dark), the warmth, the little salty fresh bay prawns'. She revisited her 'old haunts' and felt 'serenely happy and free of angst'.[43] Breathing the air of her home town once more, soaking up the congenial atmosphere of the festival, she had 'one of the great revelations': '*Of course* joy is possible, in spite of age and mutilation and lost loves and life's inevitable miscalculations.'

It was a turning point; she put behind her once and for all the dragging misery of her last years at Oyster Cove and the pain and fear of her brush with cancer. There was still joy in the world for her, and she was ready to grasp it.

◆ ◆ ◆

Simply spending time with like-minded literary folk was rejuvenating. In her mind, every such gathering was a riposte to Bill in their ongoing argument about the value of the arts. 'Really I am *not* abnormal in my love for art, music, friendly company,' she told herself in her diary, after yet another argument with Bill. 'I must remind myself of this.'[44] As well as attending national festivals and conferences, she also began to go to events held by the local branch of the Fellowship of Australian Writers and, in 1987, joined Hobart's Hamilton Literary Society, a long-established women-only group known affectionately as 'the Hammos'.[45] Gwen found the society satisfyingly anachronistic: it was patronised by the wife of the current governor and Lady Mayoress Doone Kennedy, whom Gwen – in this regard her mother's daughter – was delighted to consider a friend. She enjoyed the discussion and the cucumber sandwiches in equal degrees.

She was writing, too. The draft of 'The Night Watch' was written 'when I was in hospital, wired up. I was able to compose the poem in my head in one long sleepless night.' 'Bone Scan' was written around the end of 1986, after a series of follow-up tests. Suffering from 'appalling' headaches and 'exhaustion', she had been sent for scans of her brain and bones, as well as the usual diagnostic blood tests. 'It was weird to see my own skeleton on the monitor screen glittering with radioactive isotopes,' she told Alison.[46] The test results were all clear: whatever was causing her to feel so unwell, it was not yet – as she had self-mockingly prophesied in her diary – 'The End'.[47]

She also wrote a series of nine pastorals at the request of her cancer surgeon, Desmond Cooper. At the end of 1985, when she was leaving his office after her final check-up for the year, he suggested that she 'write him some poems on his place at Kettering', a seaside holiday home not far from Halcyon. She was more than willing, and drove down early in 1986. As the gate was open, she didn't go in, not wanting to disturb the family. Instead, she simply stood outside and 'absorbed the peaceful air'. From this she wrote 'in the next two days a poem which I took with me to the [March] consultation. The dear man was delighted.'[48] She joked to Alison that if she was able to get one good poem simply by standing at the gate, she would probably be able to get an entire book by actually going onto the property. Her subsequent visits to the Coopers' place, charting the course of autumn, winter and spring, gave rise to poems that were, like the sea wind in 'Threshold', prayers of 'peace and healing'.

At the same time, she was working on two new musical works, one with Don Kay and one with Larry Sitsky. Both had been commissioned as part of the Australian Bicentennial celebrations in 1988, for which specifically Australian works were being created.

She and Larry had been talking about the possibility of a work for the Bicentennial since 1984, tossing ideas back and forth for a full-length opera based on the life of Truganini, Henry Handel Richardson's novel *Maurice Guest* or the story of Bennelong, an Aboriginal man who had been captured by the first European settlers and became a mediator between them and other Indigenous people.[49] They still had no clear idea of what they might do when Larry learned, early in 1986, that his vague proposal for a Bicentennial work had been approved. They had to put something together, and he suggested they use Henry Lawson's short story 'The Drover's Wife' as a centrepiece.[50] Gwen sent him some sketches, but they didn't inspire Larry and the project stalled. In early 1987, Gwen suggested they combine episodes from 'The Drover's Wife' with episodes from the life of an officer of the first fleet, Lieutenant Ralph Clark, whose journals and letters she had been reading. This did not inspire Larry either. In February, she told him disgustedly that she hated 'the fucking Bicentennial' and wished they could do '(say) Philoctetes or somethink [*sic*] similar'.[51] Nevertheless, she pushed on, writing the text for a series of episodes drawn from the stories of various figures in Australian colonial history.

In July, she interrupted these labours to write some poems for the seventieth birthday of Jan Sedivka, a brilliant Czechoslovakian-born violinist who taught at the Tasmanian Conservatorium of Music. He and his wife, the equally brilliant pianist Beryl Sedivka, along with cellist Sela Trau, who was also part of their household, made up a 'legendary' string trio. Gwen had first met the Sedivkas in 1966 through Rex and was dazzled by them. 'How warm & REAL they are after the desiccated academics – & the enchanting Sela!' she had written to Larry.[52] She attended the performances of all three artists whenever she could. For Jan's retirement festschrift at the end of 1982, Gwen had written four poems, all with a musical theme, which she collected under the title 'Divertimento' in her next book. For his seventieth birthday, she wrote another four poems, this time conceived as companions to Larry's composition for Jan, 'Tetragrammaton: Four Pieces for Violin and Piano'. In Jewish sacred lore, the Tetragrammaton is the name of God, made up of four Hebrew letters (sometimes translated into English as YHWH or Yahweh), which must not be pronounced. The four movements of Larry's work were intended to represent those four letters, while the four poems that made up Gwen's own 'Tetragrammaton' were named for the letters Yod, He, Vau and He. Larry's piece was performed by Jan and Beryl at a concert at the university on 31 October 1987, with both Gwen and Larry in attendance.

Things were a bit tense between composer and librettist. Larry had recently become embroiled in a stoush with the Australian Opera over *The Golem*, and Gwen had been dragged into it when they asked for changes to the libretto. Unbeknown to her, the Australian Opera had submitted her text to some 'experts' for review. Larry sent their report on to Gwen, telling her that he had agreed to rework some of the text, since it seemed to be the only way the opera would ever reach the stage. The report made 'some fairly shitty remarks about the libretto', and Gwen was furious, both with the unknown report writers and with Larry for having handed her work over to them without consulting her. She fired off a letter to Larry asking 'how *he* would behave if I gave his music over to some anonymous person and then sent him a report. The report I got was not only misspelt, but had grammatical mistakes. Who is this person . . . what are his/her qualifications?'[53] She told Larry that under no circumstances was he to change her text or allow anyone else to tamper with it. If he was not happy with it, he could employ someone else to write a new libretto, though she stressed that she would not allow this new librettist to read her text. She even gave him the names of several poets he could approach. The composer's handmaiden had her limits.

After Jan's birthday concert, Gwen and Larry went out to dinner with staff from the conservatorium, and Gwen was 'enraged' when Larry told the table a version of the story that was designed, she felt, to make her look bad. 'He said "Madam here blew her top when she saw the criticism" and got a big laugh.' Good manners required her not to 'make an issue of it' at the dinner table, but she was deeply offended. She felt that he was 'determined to show himself in the best possible light', at her expense.[54] This incident, combined with the difficulties they were having reaching agreement on the Bicentennial commission, led to a pronounced cooling of their relations. Gwen blamed Larry when the Bicentennial commission fell through, telling Rex that he had 'given [her] the run-around': 'I finished my text but he didn't get on with it . . . Next thing I get a letter from the Bicentennial Authority saying they won't pay the other half of the fee – I have done *all* my work & am not going to get the $1500. Larry hasn't even *written* to me about it.'[55]

By contrast, as she told Rex with energy, it was a 'pleasure' to work with 'the gentle & lovable Don Kay!'[56] The Bicentennial piece they did together early in 1987 had been commissioned by the Mersey Valley Festival of Music. A twenty-five-minute choral suite, it was conceived as a celebration of Tasmania's north-west, where Don had grown up. Gwen did her own research into the region, going to the library and fossicking through second-hand book shops and boxes of old postcards, and asked Don to write out some memories of his childhood. Don was delighted with the words she came up with, which 'seemed to immediately conjure up the spirit of the place in my imagination'.[57] In 'Petroglyphs', the second of the four movements, two choruses are interwoven, one of local Indigenous people singing of how their women and their land were stolen from them, and the other of European settlers intoning biblical injunctions to go forth and take over the earth. The movement ends with a plea by the settlers for forgiveness. The final movement, 'In the Cave', has echoes of

Gwen's earlier poem 'In Plato's Cave'; both poems report the guide's 'brief joke' as he plunges the cave into darkness: 'A dollar to get out.' 'Light, light,' the choir sings, 'let there be light!'

◆ ◆ ◆

In 1986, Gwen was also engaged in a quite different project. For some years, her old friend Alison Hoddinott had been working on a book about Gwen's poetry, and Gwen had given her permission to consult the various papers of hers that had been entrusted to the Fryer Library at the University of Queensland. Alison's life, like Gwen's, was changing as her children grew up and left home. She was able to devote more time to her academic work and had written an article explicating Gwen's use of Wittgenstein in her poems, which she situated in the context of Gwen's ongoing battle with Bill over positivist and materialist approaches to language. She was aiming to follow this with a full-length critical study.

Gwen had been derisive of much of the critical work that had so far appeared on her poems, beginning with Alec Hope's long-postponed article, which was 'a raging disappointment' when it finally appeared in 1972. Instead of saying 'something illuminating about my work', he had spent most of the article attacking a fellow critic, Dennis Douglas – someone 'of no importance' as far as Gwen was concerned.[58] Subsequent studies were little better. It seemed to her that most critics did not read her texts attentively, focusing instead on proving their own pre-formulated theories. Alison, however, was different. To Gwen, her supreme qualification was that 'she loves the work as art, not as an object of academic study', and as a result, 'nothing can equal Alison's interpretation'.[59]

In the early 1980s, while Alison was working on her book, the two women spent time together establishing the biographical facts of Gwen's life, and Gwen wrote Alison a series of long and detailed letters in answer to specific questions. In these letters, she wrote without reserve about the contexts from which her poems had grown, even telling her friend of the affair that had led to the 'tearful poem' 'Tom the Rhymer', and identifying the other poems associated with that relationship.[60] She spoke freely about her childhood and her Brisbane days, about Vera Cottew, Peter Bennie and Tony Riddell, and about her relationship with Bill. These letters, and the conversations around them, established a new intimacy between them, and Gwen's everyday letters to Alison increasingly bore the stamp of this. Alison became the chief confidante of her growing sense of depression at Oyster Cove and her discontent with Bill. Their intimacy only intensified when Bill Hoddinott died suddenly in late 1984. Gwen was deeply saddened by this loss: the two couples had been close friends since the late 1950s, social-ising together when the Hoddinotts were in Hobart, holidaying together after they left and sharing their intellectual interests as well as their personal lives. Acutely aware of what this blow must mean for Alison, she was increasingly tender, even protective, towards her friend.

Alison had completed her book in 1984, but could not find a publisher: Gwen was not well-known enough, they told her, and in any case, books about poetry did not sell. She did not give up on her manuscript, but in the meantime a new idea had fired her imagination. While she was going through Gwen's papers in the Fryer Library, she had come across the letters Gwen had written to Tony in the early 1940s, which he had lovingly pre-served through many years of travel before entrusting them to the Fryer for safekeeping. She found them fascinating and hilarious, a dazzling portrait not only of the youthfully anarchic Gwen but also of Brisbane in wartime. It seemed to her that they would make a wonderful book. Gwen liked the idea. Tony had always said that their letters from that period should be published;[61] now, at last, it seemed like the right time.[62] She gave Alison her blessing to prepare an edition, and Alison began the painstaking detective work needed to sequence the undated letters.

Towards the end of 1986, with the first draft of the manuscript complete, Alison came to Hobart for three weeks to work through it with Gwen. They met at the home of a mutual friend in order to keep the project out of Bill's way. Gwen was only too aware that Bill's ongoing disapproval of her letter-writing dated to this very period, while Alison was conscious that there was potentially sensitive material in the last letters. Tony thoroughly approved of the project, but he was also wary of Bill's possible reaction. Having heard Bill express 'scorn for the whole field of personal letters in print', he sus-pected that 'it would be distasteful to him to see *any* of G's letters in print, let alone any referring to himself'.[63]

As Gwen made her way through the manuscript, she was mostly pleased by what she read. She was amazed to discover how uncompro-mising, how thoroughly fierce, her younger self had been. She did want to make cuts, though – many more than Alison had proposed. One target was the red-bearded dwarfs, who had originally sprung from the Beach-comber columns. She felt that without their context, they simply would not make sense to contemporary readers, but Alison insisted on keeping at least some of their adventures. Gwen also sought to smooth over some episodes that she thought cast her in a bad light, but Alison stood firm, insisting that Gwen not 'edit' her younger self in any way.[64] It was not until the very end of Alison's visit that Gwen read the last dozen letters in the collection. Until then, she had had no clear recollection of what was in them. Now, it all came rushing back: Bill's interdiction on her correspondence with Tony, his insistence that she cut Tony out of her life and her flouting of his will with a few scattered letters begging Tony to resume their correspondence secretly. She knew at once that none of these letters could be published. If they were, she told Alison, it would be the end of her marriage.

Before they could reach a resolution, Alison had to go back to Armidale. A few days later, Gwen reported that she had had it out with Bill. 'B is *utterly appalled* at the prospect of publishing *any* of the letters,' she wrote. 'He really worked me over – his knowledge of what is in them is minimal but he is furious with me (1) for ever giving *anything* to the Fryer (2) for letting the material out of Dracula's vault (3) for *ever* having written *anything*.'[65] The argument was devastating for Gwen, escalating from Bill's dislike of her letter-writing to his disapproval of her character and activities more generally. Because of her, he said, his life had been miserable: he had been forced to work in a job he loathed 'only to earn money', had had to pay out 'endlessly for the children who got through the contraceptive barriers of the time' and had had to endure her 'literary connections'. 'I feel RATSHIT,' Gwen wailed. She had tried to argue with him, pointing out that he had given every indication that he enjoyed his research in linguistics, giving far more time to it than he was obliged to do simply to keep his job.[66] But Bill stood his ground, insisting that he 'was *always* unhappy at the university'.

Gwen felt 'pretty far down with the weight of his lifelong unhappiness', and determined to do nothing more to exacerbate it. The only solution was to cut the offending letters. 'We must leave out the grim bits at the end, story or no story,' she told Alison. 'I no longer have the fighting strength to beat off his emotional blows. It's absurd that we ever got married.'[67] Alison felt that from a scholarly perspective, it would be wrong to omit any of the letters; the only reason to do so would be 'to distort & therefore to falsify what happened'.[68] But after hearing from Gwen and going through the letters again, she realised that if they ended the collection in September 1943, before Bill and Gwen met, they would not be doing violence to the truth. It did mean they would be publishing a 'comedy' instead of a 'tragedy', but that was all to the good.[69] So she went ahead with producing a truncated version of the letters, consulting Gwen and Tony regularly as she did so.

Bill seemed content when Gwen explained that they were publishing only letters written 'before I'd met him, none after'.[70] But the contretemps left its mark on her. She and Bill were not 'getting on at all well,' she told Alison, and she was 'so lonely I could die'.

These kinds of flare-ups were not uncommon between them. Early in 1986, even before the letters became an issue, Gwen made a brief, enigmatic note in her diary that began with the German phrase 'Und er hat mich auch nie geliebt' (And he has never loved me), adding 'not since I published my first book anyway. What about Coleridge!' The reference to Coleridge is, presumably, a reference to the man she thought she was marrying back in 1945: the Coleridge scholar with a passion for Romanticism. This man had never really existed – or so Bill claimed; he had always 'hated literature', which was why he had 'got out of that into linguistics' as soon as he could.[71] Gwen was once again forced to the conclusion that they were simply ill matched. It wasn't just that he disliked art and music, while she lived for them; it was their profound differences of temperament. He needed to feel that his home was a sanctuary, while Gwen felt suffocated whenever the drawbridge was up; he wanted single-hearted fidelity, while Gwen's nature was polyamorous.

Though she had long ago decided to pursue her own path regardless of Bill's disapproval, his criticism did take a toll. Even after forty years of marriage, forty years of the same dynamic playing out between them in which she sought his approval and he withheld it, she was still distraught when he withdrew from her. Her diaries from Pine Street record many occasions when Bill lectured her on her 'defects of character' or delivered 'intolerable criticism' of her.[72] Her response was almost always furious despair and self-loathing, and/or a renewed determination to leave him. She often thought of how different her life might have been if he had been her champion. 'It did me good to be among accepting equals at the [Salamanca] Writers' weekend,' she wrote to Alison in late December 1986. 'A lot of my time is wasted cheering myself up.'

By the late 1980s, she was again fantasising about, and even plotting, her departure – from Bill, and from Hobart. '*Utterly* sure I should leave,' she scribbled in her diary one day. 'I just *annoy* B.'[73] Another day, she wrote: 'O God. Half a century in Tartarus.'[74]

◆ ◆ ◆

Early in 1986, Gwen's second son, Chris, and his wife bought a beach shack, 'Herongate', at Marion Bay, a tiny, undeveloped community less than an hour's drive north of Hobart. As Chris and Lucy did not live in Tasmania, Gwen and Bill became the shack's unofficial caretakers, and Gwen threw herself into the role with relish. She loved the place at once, loved the birds and the ocean and the solitude and the quirky, shabby little property. Along the estuary there were black swans, pelicans, oystercatchers and white egrets, while the wild ocean beach was a 'grand Beethovenish walk'.[75] Flocks of herons haunted the marshes, and she loved to 'lean over the bridge on the causeway and watch them', mesmerised by 'their wonderful stillness as they brood over the water'.

In the first few months of her caretakership, she travelled up whenever she could, sometimes alone, sometimes with Bill, bringing furniture and tools, and doing various chores: clearing bracken, mowing the lawn, making and hanging curtains, even digging a bore. She built a little outdoor fireplace 'to cook my chops on'.[76] Then she began to take up favourite books with her, leaving them in the bookcase Bill had built, along with notebooks and papers, so that she could spend quiet hours there reading and working. She even bought a desk diary especially for Herongate. She put up things that gladdened her eye: a 'Chateaux of France' tea towel that had been a gift from Thea, a poster of the wildfowl of Great Britain, some ducks given to her by Tony. It was 'a nest that I shaped to myself'.[77] 'Marion Bay seems to have taken the place of Queensland in my dream-of-paradise longings,' she told Alison. 'I hardly ever think of Brisbane these days, but long to be at Marion Bay with the lovely light and space.'[78] Above all, it was a place she could be alone.[79] She told several friends it was the only 'room of my own' she had ever had,[80] a more comfortable and certainly more weatherproof version of her bush camp at Oyster Cove. She even fantasised about moving there permanently, writing in her diary early in 1989 that she had resolved 'to live at Marion Bay'.[81]

This resolution was never put to the test. In May, about six weeks after she made this note, Gwen got a phone call from the police to tell her the shack had burned to the ground. Someone had broken in and set the place on fire. Gwen was distraught, and her feelings only intensified when she saw the ruins. The destruction seemed somehow apocalyptic. Lines from Isaiah hammered at her: 'It shall never be inhabited, neither shall it be dwelt in from generation to generation . . . And the wild beasts of the islands shall cry in their desolate houses, and dragons in their pleasant palaces: and her time is near to come, and her days shall not be prolonged' (Isaiah 13: 20–22).

To Alison, she confessed that she was 'utterly desolated at losing my retreat'.[82] To compound her grief, she had lost 'irreplaceable papers and beloved books'.[83] 'I keep forgetting that Herongate is gone,' she wrote to Tony a couple of weeks later, 'and then remembering with anguish that I'll never again open the door and get out mower, mattock, rake, shears . . . make coffee and read in peace, look round with delight . . .'[84] Almost at once she began to have 'terrible dreams of going to Marion Bay and finding the shack restored. As I open the door I see my hand is the hand of a skeleton – the shack is as it was but *I* have died.'[85] Somehow, the devastation of her beloved private place seemed a prophecy, or even a mirror, of her own devastation. 'Inside I'm all charcoal like Herongate,' she told Ann.[86]

Despite all the good things that were happening in her life – the acceptance she had found at All Saints and in Hobart's literary community, the new friends she had made – she felt panic-stricken. She lived, she told Alison, in a 'perpetual state of total anxiety', though 'outwardly I look fine and carry on briskly at innumerable meetings'.[87] 'It isn't mental, it's quite physical: the sort of panic you have when the plane begins to drop from the sky or you feel the impact of another car and wonder if you're going to be crushed badly.' Herongate had helped her keep this panic at bay. Now, she had nothing to help. She worried that she had finally snapped: 'Perhaps the long strain of diabetic spousehood has finally worn something out.' Or perhaps she was ill, and the Herongate blaze was a portent of her own doom. She felt distressingly helpless.

Soon after the fire, her poet friend Graeme Hetherington sent her a poem about Herongate that drew on her dream. It began: 'You dream you are opening the door / Of Herongate lost in the fire.' His verses spurred Gwen to write her own 'Herongate' poem, beginning with his opening lines.[88] She would finish her poem with an invisible presence, 'like a satyr straight out of Isaiah', who is awaiting her return with the dark news that her 'days will not be prolonged'.

24

A Smiling Public Woman

Now at three-score and ten, I seem to live
Most of the time in existential terror.

Gwen Harwood, 'Midwinter'

BY THE LATE 1980S, GWEN'S STANDING WAS HIGH – HIGHER than she had ever imagined it could be in the days of Burning Sappho, when she was propping up poetry books over the sink to read while she washed the dishes. Invitations to speak, read, lecture, launch and confer were pouring in. She was working on a one-act opera with Jim Penberthy – a mischievous, proto-feminist update of the Adam and Eve story[1] – and, having made up with Larry Sitsky, began work on a new operatic version of *Faust*.[2] She was also writing some of the best poems of her life. When her fifth collection, *Bone Scan*, appeared at the end of 1988, she was widely acclaimed as 'one of the most outstanding poets of her generation'.[3]

For once, Gwen had not been anxious about her new book's reception. She was happy with this volume, telling Rex it was her best yet.[4] Her readers agreed. Praise poured in from her poet friends, and reviewers were unreservedly positive. Rosemary Dobson launched the book – which once again featured a photograph by John Brodie on the cover, and a dedication 'To Thomas Riddell' – and the thirty-five advance copies supplied by Angus & Robertson were 'quickly snapped up', with orders taken for 'a whole bunch more'.[5] Three months later, it had sold out: Gwen herself could not get copies to give to friends.[6] In fact, the failure of A&R to keep up with demand was Gwen's only real gripe. When the book was awarded the Victorian Premier's Prize for Poetry, she was thrilled to attend the 'Glittering Dinner' in Melbourne, but disgusted by her publisher's failure to capitalise on the publicity. 'They could have sold thousands of Bone Scans on the strength of the Premier's Prize if they'd had enough energy to print and distribute it before Christmas,' she grumbled.[7] When it went on to win the Adelaide Festival's poetry prize, she was delighted to be flown over for the opening-night presentation, but deeply chagrined to find that the book would not be reprinted in time for copies to be sold at the festival.

She had a wonderful time at both events. It was one of her gifts to be able to simply accept and enjoy honours when they came her way – usually while gently lampooning them. In her pleasure in grand occasions, she was her mother's daughter. She was always excited to join throngs of people in their best clothes with nothing to do but enjoy themselves – especially when the food and wine were good and the conversation high-spirited. To her, parties were joyous events, and when they were given in her honour, it was simply an opportunity to share the happiness around.[8]

By this time, she was becoming almost accustomed to the glitter. In mid-1989, she learned she had been awarded an Order of Australia, which led to a flurry of media attention – a front-page story in the *Mercury*, appearances on both radio and TV – as well as a deluge of congratulatory letters and phone calls. 'Donald Horne wrote me a letter of congratulation ("Dear Gwen") in his Chairman of the Australia Council role ("Donald"),' she chortled to Tony. 'I thought he'd never forgive me for Fuck All Editors but here we are, all AOs together.'[9] She was thrilled and fascinated by the investiture ceremony at Government House, with 'Sir and Lady' doing the honours and an array of local dignitaries in attendance.[10] Bill was present, though he had to wait outside while the honourees were taken through their paces. He did not want to attend the evening celebrations, so Gwen did not go either. She did not mind. 'It was utterly lovely to have a morning of glory.'[11]

Now, everyone wanted her to speak at their function or bless their literary enterprise with a few inspired words. To enliven the dull business of speech-making, she would often compose her addresses in verse, setting herself the challenge of using particularly tricky metres that would sound, at first, like prose. She did not rate these performances highly as poems: they were not art but entertainment. 'I give them to the official body or the person for whom they're written, and say, "this is your poem, this was for your occasion," she explained. 'It's like a birthday gift.'[12] She did not preserve them (though the recipients often did) and did not seek to publish them, though she allowed them to be published in works commemorating the occasion.

Several of these occasional poems were substantial essays in verse. The address she gave in early 1988 to the Retired Teachers' Association in Hobart, for instance, was a sustained meditation on ageing composed of thirty-one Pushkin stanzas – sixteen pages in manuscript. This extraordinary technical feat may have been inspired by the recently published verse novel *The Golden Gate* by Vikram Seth, which also made use of this form. Gwen had heard Vikram read at the Warana Writers' Festival in Brisbane in 1987 and been 'enchanted' by his rhythms. 'I made my way to him afterwards and said, "I've been working in that metre, and I can't tell you what joy your mastery of it gives me." Remembering A.D. Hope I continued, "I feel like a lonely traveller in a great desert who hears camel bells and then sees a gorgeous caravan approaching."' Vikram was somewhat bemused: 'His literary minder told me afterwards that Vikram said, "Who on earth is that old dear?"' But the following day he came to her session, at which she read a new poem of her childhood, 'Slate', which was also in Pushkin stanzas. The day after, he gave her a copy of his book with the inscription: 'To Gwen, the long-sought-for camel in the other direction – with affection & delight.'[13]

The Pushkin stanza was one of her favourites for speeches. She liked the challenge of such a strict form and the way it 'almost forces you to break up old chains of thought'.[14] Nevertheless, she was under no illusions about how these feats of poetic ingenuity were received by her audience. 'Some slept, some smiled vaguely as if they weren't sure of what they were listening to, most spent some of the time coughing,' she reported after one event.[15] Sometimes she chose her form in subtle tribute to a poet she loved. Her lecture for the Tasmanian Peace Trust in 1993, a serious and thoughtful work of more than two hundred lines, paid homage to the Homeric epics of war, *The Iliad* and *The Odyssey*, by adopting their poetic form, unrhymed hexameter. The lecture was a playful exploration of the literature of war, which interwove Virgil, Homer, Milton and Blake with the Old Testament, Gwen's own childhood and the disastrous conflicts of the twentieth century to arrive finally at Wittgenstein, Bertrand Russell and the power of language ('a complex of skills we learn, whereby we learn to think') to bring about peace. She had a swipe at Bill's beloved behaviourists along the way, and noted that however despised the arts may be, 'it wasn't the Poets' Union that gave us atomic weapons'. She ended with a declaration of her own philosophy: that real communication is possible between human beings through language, and that through such communication, through 'think[ing] with others', we are able to 'resolve our human problems without violence or hatred'. By 'communication', she did not mean poetry. It was neither in literature nor in scripture that we 'share our daily lives' but 'in ordinary speech / through intonation, gesture, tone', and through such sharing, we arrive at peaceful solutions to our differences.[16]

Despite her increasing number of speaking engagements, Gwen was never entirely comfortable on a podium. She always insisted that she was not an academic. She was well read in both literature and philosophy, and well versed in academic thought and argument, but she did not like to deal in abstractions or to talk about 'beliefs uncoloured by the prism / of personal experience'. She felt that the role of lecturer did not really suit her. Heading off to Launceston one day to give yet another speech, she told Ann that she felt 'like a dog I saw on Saturday in the rain on the back of a truck wearing a child's yellow rain-coat with its front paws through the sleeves'.[17] Nevertheless, if people wanted her, she believed she should not disappoint them – especially once she had been honoured with an AO. She had been given so much that she felt it was her civic duty – in Agnes's terms – to give back. But making up speeches took up time she would rather have spent working on her own poems, or just relaxing with *Days of Our Lives* – which she watched most days when she was home ('it keeps me sane').[18]

Receiving an Honorary Doctorate of Letters
at the University of Queensland, 1993

Nevertheless, the academic community embraced her. In 1988, the University of Tasmania awarded her an Honorary Doctorate of Letters – 'a late glory for me'[19] – and the University of Queensland and La Trobe University followed suit in 1993 and 1994. Bill's explanation – 'They run out of people to give them to' – kept Gwen 'humble'.[20] Still, having spent her adult life as the wife of an academic and seen all four of her children through university, she was delighted to be invited to join the academy 'in an absolute sense, not as a kind of in-law'.[21] She felt, she told Ann, like 'an elderly cat who has always lived in the yard being given my very own basket by the fire'.[22]

◆ ◆ ◆

Around the time *Bone Scan* was published in 1988, Gwen's 'old love' Vincent Buckley died. She had been half-expecting it: Vin was five years younger than she was, but he had not been in good health. She had last seen him only a few months earlier when she was in Melbourne for the Spoleto Arts Festival. They had spent a 'calm happy day' together, both aware that it might be their last meeting.[23] They talked over their 'long time on earth as friends (nearly 30 years), the spiky times as well as the calm and loving times', and 'there was a feeling of resolution'.[24] With his wife and daughters, they drove to a nearby park and went for a long walk, and on their return, Gwen, 'in a state of calm happiness', decided to walk back to Vin's house instead of going in the car with the family: 'As I came round the corner into Elm Street I saw an old man sitting on a low fence and as I approached he smiled at me. I smiled too and when I drew level he stood up, and it was Vin. "O fool and slow of heart . . ." How could I have seen him and not known him?'[25]

The quotation is from the biblical story of the Road to Emmaus, in the Gospel of Luke. In the story, after Jesus' death and resurrection, two of his disciples were walking to Emmaus when they were joined by Jesus himself, 'but their eyes were holden that they should not know him'. The incident at Elm Street seemed mysterious and significant to Gwen; after his death, she would dream of 'a lovely poem for Vin with the central image of the Road to Emmaus (and the strange non-recognition) and another theme: one person becoming a gathering of people – himself and the figures he had become in writers' works'.[26] Though the poem evaporated when she woke, she incorporated this episode into one of her elegies for Vin, 'The Present Tense'.[27]

As so often when groping for a poetic analogue for her feelings, she reached for Wittgenstein in this poem. The second part begins: 'Pain's your continuing absence from the world' and cites a handful of aphorisms by 'Saint Ludwig of Vienna'.[28] But her meditation on 'old Witters' – as she sometimes referred to him in letters – is far less reverential than of old. 'A difficult man,' she muses, 'one much in need of friendship. / A genius. Didn't like women, but.' After decades of idolising the author of the *Tractatus*, she was beginning to find him 'pompous' and lacking in human kindness. Around this time, she read Ray Monk's biography of the philosopher and was disconcerted to find that the Wittgenstein he portrayed was very different from her image of him – 'much stranger than I thought'.[29] Disconcertingly, she saw 'a likeness' between the great philosopher and the less palatable aspects of Bill's character: the two men had 'the same gaunt contempt for most of the human race'.[30] Both needed, she felt, to 'learn to praise'.

Now when she saw Wittgenstein in her dreams, he was no longer the transcendent being whose gaze could transfigure her life. In a dream recounted in 'Wittgenstein's Shoebox', she comes across an old shoebox of his in a market, 'crammed with paper slips: // mixed-up observations, thoughts / on the origins of human language'. No longer is his work a source of mystical truth; instead, it is a collection of random phrases that leaves her, 'as always, with my problems / unsolved'. Her poem 'On Uncertainty', which she read at the University of Tasmania in Launceston late in 1991, is even less ambiguous. Wittgenstein, she declares, was not just 'silly like us', as Auden famously said of Yeats, but 'sillier'. Pondering an epigraph from Wittgenstein in which he wonders why we can't teach cats 'to retrieve', she muses on all the qualities of cats to which Wittgenstein was oblivious. 'If only he'd kept a cat,' she concludes, 'and held it in his lap, and brushed it, / and really listened to its purring, / he might have been a happier man.' It seems possible she was thinking not only of Wittgenstein, here, but of her husband.

◆ ◆ ◆

In the year that *Bone Scan* was published, Gwen joined the executive of the Hobart branch of the Fellowship of Australian Writers. She was soon judging its poetry competitions and tutoring at its annual Writers' Weekend. The high regard in which she was held by her fellow FAW members rather amused her: they saw her, she told Alison, 'as some kind of saviour/cargo cult leader'.[31]

In February 1989, she was elected president. She took her duties seriously; as one FAW member noted, 'She was able on one hand to receive the Governor or the Lord Mayor at the beginning of a meeting and afterwards to wield a broom to help clean the hall.'[32] This was probably the time in her life when she most resembled Agnes, with her unrelenting activity on behalf of public-spirited committees and agencies. As president, Gwen was bombarded not only with 'endless paperwork' but also with 'trivial worries about who will bring the biscuits'.[33] Her diaries record a wide range of FAW activities, from preparing meeting agendas and typing up minutes to canvassing local arts funding bodies, writing applications to the Literature Board and organising the Writers' Weekend.

During her first year in the presidency, the FAW secretary became seriously ill, and Gwen coopted long-time member Robyn Mathison onto the executive. By 1991, Robyn had become secretary in her own right, and Gwen's mainstay in all FAW matters. She lived near Pine Street, and the two women often walked around to each other's houses to drop off correspondence, confer on FAW business or just chat over a cup of tea.[34] Gwen loved Robyn's cats and hens. 'Yoo-hoo,' she'd call and walk into the kitchen. 'I'm just out for a walk and I've come to Mary Street to see the chookies.' Gwen took the younger woman under her wing, calling her 'my kitten' and promising to train her in all the necessary skills – including, Robyn remembered, how to stay awake during boring meetings.[35]

With the paperwork mounting, Gwen took the unprecedented step of buying herself a desk and a new electric typewriter and setting herself up in a corner of the parlour – 'about 5' x 5' in the corner between the door and the piano'.[36] Though she had never, throughout the course of her married life, made claims on the household space as a writer, she was willing to do so on behalf of her role at FAW. With a space (if not a room) of her own, she could 'SHUT THE PARLOUR DOOR and leave work in the typewriter while we have meals' – luxury to someone used to working on the kitchen table.

The highlight of the FAW year was the annual Writers' Weekend, which, under Gwen's leadership, became legendary in Tasmanian FAW circles. The weekends were usually held in a remote location, in camp-style accommodation, with a handful of established writers acting as tutors. One participant spoke of how the sight of Gwen in an enormous striped woollen cardigan at the centre of a sociable gathering by the fire was a 'picture of absolute happiness'.[37] The two days would almost always include bushwalks and evening singalongs around the piano. Gwen's own workshops were full of laughter.[38] By the time she got home on the Sunday night, however, she would be dropping with fatigue. One year, she told Alison she felt 'like Jesus after a day of exhausting preaching and healing'.[39] It was good work, and lovingly done, but she needed rest and solitude to recharge.

Yet the demands of her community work continued to grow. FAW members remembered her as 'always – *always* – helpful and encouraging to new writers'.[40] This led to a new deluge of manuscripts proffered for her expert opinion. 'O the poems and prose poems and poem-like objects that people harbour!' she lamented to Alison.[41] When she shared her frustration with Fay Zwicky, who was visiting Hobart as writer-in-residence, Fay could not understand her attitude. 'Why not *tell* them they're no good?' she demanded. Gwen's response was: 'I've got to *live* here.' It was a difficult dance. Her approach was always to find something to praise in the work: if not a stanza, then a line; if not a line, then a phrase or even a word. This would then become the place from which the writer could start to improve.

In 1991, her duties became more onerous still when she took on the FAW federal presidency. This role was rotated through the various states, and as Gwen was in the chair when it was Tasmania's turn, she became federal president ex officio. 'The FAW at Federal level drives me crackers,' she moaned to Alison. 'I quite enjoy the local body but the federal one would make Jesus weep.'[42] The administrative load was soul destroying. 'Can *I* be the Gwendoline of *Blessed City*?' she wailed, reporting on the pile of correspondence she was working her way through. 'What's happened to me?'[43]

◆ ◆ ◆

Blessed City, Alison's edition of Gwen's 1940s letters to Tony, appeared late in 1990 to a storm of praise. Literary and non-literary readers alike were charmed by this 'exquisitely humorous collection', with its tales of Little Gwendoline, her eccentric family and her running battles with the public service.[44] Gwen did TV appearances and newspaper interviews, taking it all in her stride.[45] Nobody seemed to think there was anything odd about the volume ending where it did, with Lieutenant Riddell heading back to Brisbane on leave and bringing with him his friend Lieutenant Harwood – who, evidently, would go on to sweep Gwen off her feet. Many readers did feel, though, that they were reading a love story and wondered why Gwen had not gone on to marry Tony. Gwen told Alison somewhat scornfully that an *Age* reporter 'tried to make a Mills & Boon style romance out of it all: God knows what she will write'.[46] Even her friend Craig Powell, fellow poet and psychiatrist, felt that her letters to Tony were 'suffused with a young girl's tender eroticism'. It seemed to him that Gwendoline Foster was 'truly in love with her "Tony"', and he could not help wondering 'if this has anything to do with a poem like "Dust to Dust" which seems to be about the anguish of thwarted love in Brisbane'.[47]

Gwen was delighted by the idea of her youthful self's 'tender eroticism' and wrote back teasingly that she had indeed been so suffused. 'I was always deeply in love with Peter Bennie but I was attracted to a great many people (and still am – there are people I can hardly keep my hands off)', she told him. But 'Dust to Dust' was about her dear friend Vera Cottew. She explained that Tony had loved her 'as a friend but was not interested in young women' – and that she had not really understood this at the time. 'Peter and Tony seemed to me incredibly brilliant and destined for glory', she went on, 'but it didn't happen quite like that.' Though she did not say it, both of her 'brilliant' friends were grappling now with a sense of failure, while she herself, a mere lovestruck girl to them, had had 'everything from life – children, success in my field, wonderful friends'.[48]

Craig was not the only person to write to her about *Blessed City*. People she had not been in touch with since her Brisbane days made contact to exclaim and reminisce. Her brother, Joe, was amused to find himself immortalised as 'Hippo' (though he made a point of telling anyone who would listen that Gwen had exaggerated her stories of him to the point of untruth).[49] Her children were 'delighted to see how different I was before I became Mother'.[50] She did not send a copy of the book to Peter Bennie – 'he doesn't really have the sense of humour'[51] – but he bought a copy for himself and wrote her a long letter full of praise. 'You give a desperate portrait of what Kierkegaard called the fate of genius in a provincial society, that of "slowly being trampled to death by geese"', he wrote.[52]

The approval she most wanted was Bill's, but he remained stubbornly, determinedly silent. She did not know whether he had even looked at the book, she told Alison shortly after its release, though she suspected he might have snuck a peek while she was out. His silence weighed on her. 'He's like a Victorian father who won't acknowledge a servant's bastard – doesn't want to lose the servant but won't acknowledge the child.'[53] Finally, several months after the book's launch, when a friend made a facetious remark about the 'peanut-stealer' (as Bill is referred to, fleetingly, in the book), Bill remarked: 'I read a couple of pages but it was so UTTERLY BORING I gave up.'[54] Gwen could not help but feel wounded. 'The equivalent in a drunken wife basher would be a blow in the face I suppose', she told Alison.

Bill seemed a minority of one. In November 1990, Gwen and Alison learned that *Blessed City* had been chosen as *The Age*'s Book of the Year. They both went to Melbourne for the prize-giving, a glamorous lunch at the Hyatt, where they were presented with three thousand dollars and a leather-bound copy of the book. Gwen had planned to give her acceptance speech in verse, as was her wont, but had been unexpectedly rushed that morning before the flight and had not finished it. When she arrived for the ceremony, she asked Alison to go to the bathroom with her and quickly wrote out her speech there. She had been working on it in her head on the plane, she explained to her astonished friend. They went back to the dining room, and Gwen delivered the speech, with utter sangfroid, to a roomful of devoted admirers.[55]

Soon after *Blessed City*, Angus & Robertson published Alison's book on Gwen's poetry, *The Real and the Imagined World*. Gwen declared her friend's book 'a delight' and noted that Bill actually read the whole thing – a sign of his respect not for his wife's poetry but for Alison's scholarly mind.[56] He declared the book 'old-fashioned', which Gwen, at least, considered high praise, and told Alison he thought she had got him 'mostly right'.[57] Gwen was bemused by the rise of postmodern theory in literary criticism ('I'm preparing for another day of the dialogic construction of subjectivity and problematising of thematic closure,' she wrote gloomily to Ann from an academic conference in Ballarat in 1992),[58] and longed for critique that paid close attention to the poems themselves. Most contemporary criticism, she felt, obscured rather than enhanced interpretation, but Alison had managed to avoid the pitfalls of postmodernism. 'The book is beautiful, death-defying, luminous, fascinating, affectionate, reassuring, funny,' Gwen told Alison. 'I feel more consoled and comforted than you can imagine.'[59]

Peter Bennie read it, and wrote to say that he now understood how important Bill's 'abrasive positivism' had been to her poetry. 'The whole thing reminded me of Baron von Hügel's observation that science was the purgatory of religion,' he told her. 'If you are concerned with ultimates it is so easy to slip over into nonsense, and Alison H., who obviously likes and admires Bill tremendously, makes it plain how salutary the necessity for constant defence of your own insights has been.'[60] In other words, Bill's opposition to Gwen's Romantic view of poetry had saved her from falling into airy generalities about universal goods; her marriage had given her work 'rigour'. In this, Peter probably underestimated Gwen's own capacity for rigorous thinking. But his analysis homes in on one of Alison's key insights: that Gwen's writing was overwhelmingly dialectical.

Three further books of criticism were soon in the pipeline, all by women Gwen had recently come to know. She was a little anxious about these prospective works: 'I feel like peaches being put in a tin & the lid soldered on. I'll never get back on the tree as an innocent blossom.'[61] Interest was growing in the details of Gwen's life. As literary scholar Stephanie Trigg noted in the introduction to her 1994 book on Harwood, discussion of the poet often degenerated into 'prurient speculation' about her life. 'Who, after all, has not been tempted to read the repressed narrative of a wartime romance behind the letters in *Blessed City*? To whom were all those later, burning love poems addressed? Or in a question that has actually been put to the poet on the strength of what I call her suburban satires, such as "In the Park", did she really love her children?'[62] These were questions Gwen considered either stupid or impertinent, or both. She had no intention of feeding the gossips, and had her own ways of evading or freezing out unwelcome questioners. Besides, it was her deep conviction that her poems could stand alone: it was not necessary for her readers to understand anything about her personal life to understand the poems. All they needed to do was read attentively.

For some years, she had been deflecting requests that she either write the story of her life or allow someone else to do it. Norman had proposed that he should write it back in 1982, but, as she told Alison, 'I don't plan to let him. Apart from not wanting to tell what happened in them faroff days I simply haven't the energy to deal with his prose.'[63] Besides, she was sure Bill would not tolerate it: Norman's 'rapturous variations on my shaky reminiscences, though hilariously entertaining, would probably be the final breach between the literary and non-literary members of a Certain Household'. To Norman, she insisted that there was nothing to tell. 'A life, forsooth!' she wrote. 'Who wants my extempore reminiscences?' She felt she could sum up her life in two sentences: 'Since coming to Tasmania I've been in a state of neurotic angst. This is relieved only by getting away to the north or having visitors from faraway Oz.'[64] A couple of years later, Carmen Callil of London publisher Chatto & Windus wrote to ask if she would be interested in writing her autobiography for them, telling her as an inducement that they were soon to publish Dorothy Hewett's.[65] Gwen was derisive. 'Whacko!' she wrote merrily to Alison. 'What would it be – a cook book? Hints for cleaning the bath? How not to go crackers? 256,000 diabetic meals? My life as a cement-mixer?'[66]

Early in 1991, she was approached by a young medievalist from La Trobe, Gregory Kratzmann, about the possibility of writing her biography.

Her response was characteristic. There was 'little to tell': 'I've never climbed higher than 1270 metres or been out of Australia or divorced or psychoanalysed or pursued by a bear.' She was 'one flake of paint in an impressionist painting – the rest of the picture is what defines me'. Nevertheless, she acknowledged that if a biography were to be written, it would be better if the author didn't know her. She directed him to the 'hundreds and thousands of letters' she had written, 'some of which are libellous', and to Peter Bennie, the person 'who knows me best': 'If you really want to write a biography you should talk to him before he dies.'[67]

Greg took her advice. He went to the Fryer Library to read her correspondence, then to see Peter Bennie, whom he found 'rather intimidating'.[68] He then proposed to come to Hobart in November to see her, and though she continued to express reservations about a biography, she also assured him he would be welcome in Hobart, promised to take him round to the various places she had lived, and suggested he contact her brother, Joe.[69]

At the same time, she was talking to Alison about the possibility of her writing a biography. Soon after she told Greg that he was welcome to come and see her, she assured Alison that she was actively discouraging him. 'I don't think we'll have much trouble stalling him,' she wrote. 'My line with him will be: I am the very model of a modern mother-general. Boring, boring.'[70]

A week later, she wrote again to Greg to say that she felt 'more and more that the time is not right' for a biography, and that she was 'not going to allow any more letters to be quoted'.[71] She had been looking forward to 'a year or two of quiet time to read and play the piano and SPEND A LOT OF TIME WITH OLD FRIENDS instead of always being at meetings and looking at unsolicited manuscripts or organizing anything'. What she really wanted was 'just to be left alone for a while'. She did not forbid him to come to Hobart, however, and he made his visit in mid-November as planned.

As soon as they met, Gwen's fears and reservations vanished. She felt that Greg was a kindred spirit to whom she could speak openly about her life.[72] She would tell him anything he wanted to know, she promised, provided he respect her stipulation that he write nothing that would 'cause pain'.[73] During this first visit, they talked and talked. They went through her photo albums together, and she took him to Oyster Cove and Fern Tree, gave him lunch and dinner, and revelled in his company. She did, however, baulk at his request to record their conversations. He was free to turn on the tape recorder, she told him, with her most mischievous smile, but if he did, 'I'll lie'.[74]

Kratzmann went ahead and signed a publishing contract with Oxford University Press, arranging to take study leave in the second half of 1992 to get the project off the ground. Meanwhile, Gwen assured Alison that she was 'my authorised biographer'.[75] When Greg discovered that Alison was approaching the same people he was for biographical interviews, he delicately sought clarification from Gwen, who admitted that she had made Alison her 'official biographer', since she 'badly wanted to be'.[76] She also confirmed that she had decided to make Alison her literary executor – which would give her the power to deny him access to materials after Gwen's death. Greg responded with a 'rather worried letter',[77] and Gwen hurriedly assured him he could have 'access to read anything in the libraries', and that she herself would decide 'what he can *quote*'. She then had to write to Alison to explain this revision of the situation. 'Just so you know,' she told Greg, 'I feel like the child held up before Solomon' – condemned to be torn in two so that each biographer could have a piece.[78] She was still hoping to be able to accommodate them both.

At this point, Alison decided to withdraw – to the relief of all parties.[79] Greg became the 'official biographer', and over the next four years, spent much time with Gwen, visiting her in Hobart, accompanying her to occasional conferences and literary festivals, meeting her family and friends (including Alison, Tony, Norman Talbot, Rex Hobcroft and Frank Kellaway), and becoming a cherished confidante. Gwen was keen to see what he would write, but with a full-time job and other commitments, Greg's progress was slow. 'Will he ever write a word?' she asked Alison, rhetorically, towards the end of 1992. 'I don't reckon.'[80] In this, she wronged him.[81] But by this time, it did not much matter. The 'ever-faithful Greg' was part of her life, and his friendship was worth much more to her than any biography.

25

Dear Boy

The desert seems to be the place where I feel serenely confident – a creature with both wings and fangs.
Gwen Harwood, Letter to Alan Farrell, 11 October 1994

GWEN'S STAR CONTINUED TO RISE. IN 1991, OXFORD UNIVERsity Press brought out a *Collected Poems* in the United Kingdom, the first time her work had been published internationally. The publishers invited her to come to London for the launch, and an old friend, Maria Clark, offered to lend Gwen and Bill her flat. Bill did not want to go, of course, and Gwen did not think it feasible to go alone, so the book was launched without her. It received a glowing review from British poet D.J. Enright in the *Times*, who rejoiced that her work was at last available to UK readers: 'Strange,' he commented, 'that it should take so long for a solid reputation to cross the Commonwealth.'

At the end of 1991, Enright would choose her collection as his 'best international book of the year',[1] and a couple of years later, the UK Society of Authors would select Gwen as one of the winners of the Cholmondeley Award (pronounced 'chumly', to Gwen's delight), a prize of two thousand pounds given to four 'distinguished poets' each year. She was in excellent company: one of the first winners of the award was Stevie Smith, a favourite of Gwen's, and Gwen's fellow honourees in 1994 included Ruth Fainlight and Elizabeth Jennings.

The UK edition of *Collected Poems* was also distributed in the United States, where, Gwen was to learn, it garnered her 'a following'.[2] In the mid-1990s, she would be invited to the United States to read and lecture at Johns Hopkins University and Mount Holyoke College, among other places.[3] Without ever travelling outside of Australia, she was at last becoming known beyond her own shores.

At home, she was greatly in demand for literary festivals, poetry competitions and even arts administration (she sat on the Literature Board in 1993). She agreed to as many things as she could. This was partly due to her old sense of 'Public Duty'; after her honorary doctorates, she told Alison, she felt obliged to 'put in my time as a literary public servant to show

I earned it'.[4] But she also enjoyed being a senior figure in the Australian literary world, and was amused to find herself being treated 'like the Queen Mother' at festivals.[5]

Though she was quite aware that she looked like 'a sweet little old lady',[6] she had no intention of being relegated to that role. She more than held her own with the new breed of performance poets, winning the Poetry Ashes at the Circular Head Arts Festival in 1989[7] and the Launceston Poetry Cup – from 'a strong field of 26 belligerent bards including Tim Thorne, Allan Lake, Komninos, John Ashton and Dorothy Porter' – in 1991.[8] The cup was awarded 'to the person who elicits the loudest audience response to the reading or recitation of an original poem within a strictly enforced time limit of one minute', and in her performance, Gwen called down 'divine retribution on Launceston if she should fail to win – and eternal blessings were she to succeed'. At the Association for the Study of Australian Literature conference in Ballarat in 1992, she easily outshone the competition to win the Parody Prize with 'The Sick Philosopher', a brilliant spoof of postmodern jargon which reworked Adam Lindsay Gordon's 'The Sick Stockrider'. The following night, at the conference dinner, she and her old friend Cassandra Pybus won the jive section of the ballroom dancing competition. Wherever she went, she brought with her that 'intense and special power of delight'.[9]

In February 1992, she stepped down as president of the Tasmanian chapter of the Fellowship of Australian Writers. It had simply taken over too much of her life. Her resignation meant she was free of the 'grocery boxes of shitty correspondence' that fell to the president's lot,[10] but she was still very involved in the organisation (she would be vice-president for another year) as well as with the Tasmanian Writers' Union and the Hamilton Literary Society.

Gwen was also increasingly involved with the tiny Anglican community of All Saints. Early in 1986, her friend Sally, now restored to good health, had decided to join the Anglican church and asked Gwen to be her sponsor. Gwen agreed, and they went through the prescribed course of instruction together. At Sally's baptism on 20 June, Gwen became her friend's godmother. She and Sally had got into the habit of attending early mass on Friday mornings as well as high mass on Sundays, and Gwen would sometimes also attend Evensong on Sunday evenings. Increasingly, she stopped in for early mass on weekdays too. After mass, she would join the rector, Father Bill Paton, and the other parishioners (when there were any – sometimes she was the only worshipper) for morning coffee or break-fast in the vestry.[11] It was quite a progression for someone who had feared being 'struck by lightning' when she first went through the church doors (it didn't happen, though she was 'worried by a raging high wind one morn-ing – I thought the roof would lift & Lucifer & his mob come for me').[12]

Soon, she was taking on official roles within All Saints, from secretary of both the Mothers' Union and the local cell of the Society of Our Lady of Walsingham to pastoral visitor at St John's Hospital and St Ann's aged-care facility. She enjoyed these roles, telling Tony that she loved the old people at St Ann's, where she sometimes played the piano for services.[13] She also made hot cross buns to share at Easter, arranged flowers for the altar and took her turn cleaning the rectory. In 1989, she even helped set up a liter-ary magazine, the *All Saints Occasional Magazine*. It ran to only two issues, the first edited by Sally, who had begun writing short stories and poems in hopes of a literary career. Gwen had a poem in both issues: 'Midwinter' in the first and 'Night Thoughts' in the second, darkly religious poems full of pained, restless questions.

Despite her commitment to All Saints, Gwen remained ambivalent about Christianity. She liked the trappings of the Christian faith, finding 'peace and refreshment' in the early mass, in particular.[14] She also liked being part of the church community, which she saw as 'a pleasant sort of social club'.[15] But she maintained a certain ironic distance from Christian beliefs. Sally observed that Gwen's Christianity was 'unorthodox': 'She read the Bible assiduously, but there were things in it with which she did not agree,' she wrote. 'She didn't think that crucifixion represented the ulti-mate torture. She also eschewed any belief in an afterlife.' What made her a Christian, Sally believed, 'was her sense of Christian morality, which she valued supremely'.[16] Yet Gwen's morality often did not align with traditional Christian morality, particularly in the area of sexual ethics. Nor did she value conformity to Church teachings, the basis of Christian morality. She baulked at the idea that the sin by which humanity first fell from grace in the Garden of Eden was disobedience. 'Suppose the original sin had been not disobedience / but cruelty,' she would ask in one of her verse-lectures. 'What then?'[17]

Gwen wanted to believe in an afterlife and rehearsed the arguments for and against the idea in poems like 'Infant Spurwing' and 'Resurrection'. But she could not find this kind of faith. 'Where in / this universe could hell be?' she asked in 'Night Thoughts'. The only eternity she could bring herself to believe in was that of the present moment, 'Space of a crow-call, enclosing / the self and all it remembers'.[18] Yet her world view was far from secular. Her life, like her poems, was full of invisible presences: her beloved dead, the angels and demons of her dreams, her memories of the past. The God of the Old Testament, introduced to her in childhood, had become a kind of mental reflex, embedded in the very roots of language. Besides, regardless of disparities of belief, she felt a strong sense of kinship with Christians; the world of the church was one in which she felt at home.[19]

She did not feel the need to explain herself to her fellow parishioners, who tended to assume she was as devout as she appeared to be. She happily used the language of piety, promising to pray for people, sharing devotions and even speaking to one devout friend of 'singular favours' she had received 'from the B[lessed] V[irgin] M[ary]' at the Shrine of Our Lady of Walsingham.[20] But there was an element of performance to all this. 'There was always a little hint of a smile or even a touch of wry humour attaching to her participation in the church's activities,' wrote one of her fellow parishioners. 'This is not to say that she was at all frivolous or insincere, but she did sometimes give the impression that she was observing herself carrying out the church's observances. She was at once a participant and an appraising onlooker with a little twinkle in her eye.'[21]

Another parishioner, the poet Stuart Barnes, who was about ten years old when he met Gwen at All Saints, also noted this sense of her 'doing the fly-on-the-wall thing': leaning against the wall with her arms crossed, just watching, taking it all in.[22] At the same time, he remembered her 'holding court' after mass, surrounded by a circle of laughing, joking, good-humoured people enjoying themselves. Among the other parishioners, she was a central figure, not because she was famous – many of her fellow churchgoers did not even know she was a poet – but because she was so warm and engaged. She noticed things others did not and was especially kind to anyone who seemed vulnerable in some way. She was particularly fond of Stuart, singling him out and telling him with oracular power that he would be a poet. He remembered her pressing volumes of poetry from the church's op shop into his pocket after mass.

According to Sally, Gwen often sat in church writing furiously. 'I never knew what to make of all the pages of shorthand,' she confessed. It's tempting to speculate that these carefully encrypted sheets expressed Gwen's dissent; it's easy to imagine jokes, sardonic remarks and the shorthand equivalent of eye-rolling going into these pages. But it's also possible that she was simply taking notes on the sermon, or on passages of scripture, or even that, as Sally suggested, she was working on her own 'creative writing'. Did she write her meditations on Job ('Midwinter') or on Jacob wrestling with the angel ('Night Thoughts') while she sat in the little church listening to the day's Bible readings?

She had always had a soft spot for members of religious orders, and lately she had befriended a handful of poetry-writing nuns and brothers. She liked Father Bill Paton, too, and they became friends and correspondents after he retired.[23] The new rector, Alan Farrell, a former musician and broadcaster, was installed in 1992. It was 'friendship at first sight', Gwen would later say, adapting a phrase from Robert Frost.[24] She described the new clergyman, delightedly, as 'a 42-year-old choirboy, compactly chubby and curly-haired, wonderfully articulate and great on the ritual'.[25] Like Gwen, Father Farrell preferred the traditional forms of worship, introducing what was 'essentially the Latin mass in English' and 'reviving the music, arranging plainsong classes and choral evensongs'. He seemed to be a priest 'with vision who wanted to go beyond the respectable façade'.[26]

The quality that most endeared him to Gwen was his similarity to Peter Bennie. Reporting to Alison that he was 'mad keen on lace, Latin, and Francis Thompson', she added that he took her back to her youth: 'I see again the young Peter Bennie quoting "Turn but a stone & start a wing" – when that resounded from the pulpit last Sunday my life was like an evening gone. I remembered myself.'[27] She had always felt that All Saints in South Hobart was a version of All Saints on Wickham Terrace, miraculously transported fifty years forward in time. Now she had found a version of her first love too. It was almost too good to be true: through Father Farrell, she would be able to recover her lost self, that satin-lipped idealist, 'young and merry', who had sat at Father Bennie's feet, 'discoursing on life and art'.[28] Alan seemed to her to have all of Peter's virtues, and she embraced this new friendship with fervour.

◆ ◆ ◆

In August 1992, Father Farrell asked Gwen to sit on the parish council. She was then elected parish secretary and, in the middle of the following year, became a church warden, one of three parishioners responsible for the day-to-day management of the church. She even began to fill in from time to time on the organ. Her role on the council meant she was back to attending

long meetings, typing up minutes and taking care of dull official correspondence, but she didn't mind. All Saints made her happy in the same
way that being among literary friends did. On the final day of the Salamanca Writers' Festival in late 1992, she went to the morning sessions, bid
farewell to some visiting writers, had lunch with Ann and Stephen at Pine
Street, went to St Ann's retirement home to run a service for the residents
and brought Alan home to Pine Street for dinner, later dropping him back
at the rectory. 'Mild day, sunny,' she wrote in her diary. 'So happy! What a
delight to live in such an atmosphere. O how I long to travel back – and
take life easy.'

Vikram Seth and Gwen Harwood, Hobart, 1992

References to being 'happy ++' began to contend seriously with the
more consistent references to being 'depressed ++'. It had been a good year,
beginning with a boost to her general happiness quotient when Vikram Seth
came to visit in late 1991. Gwen had felt a strong affinity with Vikram when
they met at Warana in 1987, and they had been corresponding since. She
picked him up from the airport on 28 December 1991, and while they waited
for his luggage, 'he drew from his pocket a miniature score of *Winterreise*
and sang'.[29] This was pure enchantment for Gwen, and ushered in a week of
'utter bliss'.

Vikram was 'a fine lieder singer & we've been rehearsing Schubert, or just talking shop, or drinking in the bar of the Marquis of Hastings & playing the juke box . . . It's nice to know I haven't forgotten what happiness can be like: it's like being back in the Blessed City'.[30] They wandered the streets of West Hobart, calling in on Gwen's friends, shared meals with Gwen's literary colleagues and spent 'heavenly' evenings of 'champagne, music, talk'.[31] One evening, Vikram finished off her daily diary entry for her. Gwen had written: 'V. returns for dinner. Cold evening, heaters on. V writes in parlour.' Vikram added a comma and the line: 'sending amicable vibrations towards dining room, where Gwen laughs at TV program'.[32] On another day, he wrote the whole entry himself, beginning with the opening line of the Beatles' 'A Day in the Life': 'Woke up, got out of bed, dragged a comb across my head.'

By the time she took him to the airport on 4 January, Gwen had 'lost [her] Angst'. It was one of those times to which only her favourite Hölderlin quote could do justice: 'I've had a few days of absolute delight and that suffices. *Einmal lebt' ich wie Götter*'.[33] Vikram was equally delighted. 'What a lovely time I had in Hobart!' he wrote after his departure. 'Just thinking of that week makes me smile – from "*Ich hört ein Bächlein rauschen . . .*" [I hear the sound of a stream] at the luggage carousel to the last glimpse of you through double glass at dawn. One of the *best* in my life.'[34]

For Gwen, the year would also be distinguished by several trips to the Blessed City. In May, her brother, Joe, got married again and Gwen went to Brisbane for the wedding. The moment she stepped off the plane, her mood soared: 'Joe & I stood in the sub-tropic night and agreed we'd never been happy away from the Blessed City'.[35] On the Sunday after the wedding, she went to mass at All Saints on Wickham Terrace, then had lunch with some friends from her WDC days, 'three old ladies' who were 'girls to each other, unchanged in affection though ruined by time'.[36] To her amusement, 'they were still quoting malicious rhymes from Blessed City days – these weren't written down, but somehow preserved'.[37] The following day, she caught the bus to Taringa to see an even older friend: Joyce Dalley-Scarlett, Bob's widow, who was ninety-one, 'frail but whole-witted' and determined to 'live to see the new century'. Gwen referred to her as 'Moth's oldest surviving friend', but Joyce was also a last link to Bob, and thus to a treasured, though secret, part of Gwen's own past.

The bus trip to Joyce's retirement home took Gwen through her old stamping ground of Toowong, and she was enraptured by the sight of 'the leafy green flaking suburb'. She spoke to the driver about Brisbane, and he whistled 'Memories' on the way home: 'Little did he know. I blessed the filthy river and the Regatta Hotel and Sylvan Road and the Albatross fell off.'[38] Away from Hobart, everything was suddenly simple. 'Free of Angst I understand how . . . I should have my fair share of things instead of trying to play a hopeless let-others-win game,' she told Alison. 'It's not too late to be gifted and happy.' Yet again, she vowed, with Rilke, to change her life: 'I've outsoared a few shadows in these wonderful days.'[39]

A couple of months later, she was off to Brisbane again, this time as guest of honour for the 130th anniversary celebrations of All Saints on Wickham Terrace. Peter Bennie was to be there, too.

Gwen had not seen Peter since his visit to Oyster Cove in 1978. His life had been tumultuous after that, with the death of his wife from cancer in 1981 throwing him into darkness. He had poured out his anguish in passionate letters to Gwen, and sometimes in drunken phone calls. The letters were quite amorous, beginning 'Dearest Gwen', calling her 'darling', and telling her again that their relationship was 'Animus & anima . . . and always was, and . . . quite incestuous'.[40] He made rather ponderous attempts at salacious humour, and characterised himself (wrongly) as the secret lover of Brisbane poems such as 'Dust to Dust'. Telling her that he had 'the ambivalent task of tutoring in you (I can think of a number of more pleasant things to do in that position)', he explained that his students had picked up on the presence of 'the dark gentleman of the sonnets' in her work, and were full of curiosity about the true identity of her lost love. They assumed, he went on, that 'he must have been some unscrupulous Archbishop. They so revere you they could not think that you would have truck with a mere assistant curate.'

Gwen found this amusing, but also slightly annoying. Sending one of his letters on to Alison, she dismissed his 'strange' account of 'Dust to Dust', and noted, 'How can Peter not see that the one addressed in Dust to Dust is *dead*?'[41] Nevertheless, she responded to him, as always, with calm love. When she confessed her own sense of angst in her rural isolation, he replied eagerly. 'I know all about the horror,' he wrote. 'When the dinner & the dialogue is done, there are these 17 cavernous echoing rooms. Life is so fucking arid.'[42]

If ever there was a time to 'undo' the decisions of their youth, which both Gwen and Peter had lamented could never be undone, it was then. But Gwen seems not to have considered leaving Bill for Peter, despite her unhappiness. Even so, a year or so later, when Peter told her that he was soon to marry again, she was a little jealous. He sent her a cycle of poems mythologising his attraction to his new wife, which he said was the easiest way for him to explain what had been going on with him. The poems expressed 'the fear that my life has been pointless, wasted and useless', but also the hope that it could be redeemed by a new love. When he was back at All Saints in Brisbane in the 1950s, there was a 'beautiful child' who used to 'play there with my own children'. This child, Jan, now an adult, had recently been in touch, and told him 'that she felt she owed her hold on reality and her sanity itself to me'. She had first fallen in love with him, she averred, 'at the age of 8 when her parents took her to All Saints' in 1940, when I was Asst Curate and you, my dear Asst organist'. They were now to marry on the advice of their psychiatrist.[43] Jan was fifty-three to Peter's seventy. 'I've been mad about him for 20 years longer than she has,' Gwen scrawled on the bottom of Peter's letter announcing the wedding.[44]

The All Saints' anniversary celebrations in Brisbane were her first chance to see Peter again. But Jan was in tow. Gwen noticed that Jan seemed 'very wary of me', and others also registered that Jan was 'insanely jealous' of Gwen, who wore openly her prior claim on Peter.[45] Peter himself continued to delight the besotted Gwen. 'I love him as much now as I ever did,' she told Greg, who came across them one morning in Gwen's hotel room, sitting side by side on the couch, holding hands.[46] It was 'lovely to be with him', she told Alison. Though she saw him so rarely, it mattered that he was 'in the world'.[47] As long as he was alive, she felt that she could carry on.

◆ ◆ ◆

Back at All Saints in Hobart, there were increasing divisions among the churchgoers about Father Alan Farrell. Gwen was his loyal champion, but some were uneasy about his heavy drinking and what they saw as erratic behaviour. Now and then, he would show up late for early mass, evidently 'the worse for wear', as Gwen put it, and sometimes did not appear at all. One parishioner remembered him toppling over during mass, dead drunk.[48] Gwen was not at all disturbed: as she told Alan, she came from a family of 'heroic drinkers' and regarded his boozing as endearing. But disquiet was growing in the congregation, particularly after Alan was picked up for drink driving twice within a short space of time.

Many of the parishioners were also uneasy with Alan's rumoured homosexuality. Gwen was no more concerned about this than she was about his drinking. Some in the church still saw homosexuality as a perversion, but Gwen – as she declared to Alan – did not believe that 'there *are* in fact sexual perversions'. The only perversion she acknowledged was 'cruelty to living things'. Apart from that, she was 'on the side of Keats – negative capability and all that – ambiguous, ambidextrous or just amphibian'.[49] In any case, it was one of the fundamental tenets of her philosophy of friendship that one should never judge those one loved but simply embrace them – and rely on them to do the same for you. Much of the All Saints community, however, was decidedly ruffled.

In mid-October 1993, Gwen flew to Sydney to attend the premiere of *The Golem*. Almost ten years after it was written, the 'unstageable' opera had finally made it to the Sydney Opera House in an extraordinary production by Barrie Kosky in which the set became 'one big mud pit'. The performance featured nine tenors, a large orchestra with grand piano and more than twenty choruses, and it was spectacular.[50] Gwen was thrilled to see the work on the stage; she had begun to doubt that it would ever be mounted. She told Jim Penberthy that the performance was 'very moving though I thought Barrie Kosky put too much unmusical "business" on stage'. 'Larry had a couple of good choruses which cheered up the voters. It lasts 3½ hours and no laughs.'[51] At the end of the performance, she was called to the stage to take a bow with Larry and the cast. It was a joyous moment, one of her 'once I lived like the gods' occasions. She would later say that whatever else happened in her life, it was 'enough for me to have stood on stage holding the Golem's muddy hand and [Larry's] creative hand on that glorious night'.[52]

She returned from her rapturous weekend in Sydney to the news that Alan had been assaulted at his home and was in hospital recovering from his injuries. She went at once to see him and was horrified by his state. He had been 'bashed, bound, gagged and locked inside a linen cupboard', where he had been found an hour later when he failed to appear for morning mass.[53] Swinging immediately into 'rescuer' mode, Gwen took care of whatever practical matters she could while assuring him of her undying love and support.

The All Saints community was shocked that such violence could have been perpetrated in their wholesome little community. The official story was that Alan had stumbled upon a robbery. There were whisperings, however, that he had been drinking with his assailants and had solicited them for sex, and that this had led to the assault.[54] Gwen was outraged by these rumours and by what she saw as the general lack of support for Alan in his trouble from the parish community. She stood up for him at every opportunity and poured out her love and sympathy in a rain of postcards, letters and home-cooked meals. She even asked him, in December 1993, to accept the dedication of her next book.[55] The book was entirely hypothetical at this stage; she had no immediate plans to bring out a new volume. But she wanted to make a public display of her support and this was the most unequivocal way she could think of to do it.

The church was dividing into pro- and anti-Alan camps, and things began to get tense on the parish council. Recording in her diary a 'bloody fight' at a council meeting in February 1994, she finished angrily: 'Why do I keep on with these religious cranks?'[56] A week later, Alan was arrested and charged with abducting and raping a young man he had brought home to his flat.[57] For Gwen, it was a huge shock. Writing to Greg to tell him the news, she declared at once that she simply did not 'believe evil of Alan. God knows what has really happened – perhaps the thugs who beat him up have something to do with it'.[58] The following day, the story was on the front page of the *Mercury*. Phone calls flew back and forth as parishioners tried to find out what had happened. 'Mortally distressed', Gwen wrote in her diary that she wished she had 'died long ago'.[59] She attended court with Alan, along with other supporters from the church; after several adjournments, he was committed for trial in October. Meanwhile, he was convicted on two separate drink-driving offences, fined a thousand dollars and deprived of his licence for four years.

At All Saints, the 'vultures' were gathering, as Gwen recorded grimly in her diary.[60] Many felt the parish should immediately stop supporting Alan; he had been suspended pending trial but was still living in accommodation provided by the church and collecting his stipend. Outraged, Gwen again went into battle for him on the parish council. All Saints was no longer the haven it had been. 'To All Ss v depressing,' she wrote in her diary on 1 May 1994. The community was fracturing, with battlelines drawn and the debate becoming increasingly hostile. Gwen called on all of Agnes's committee skills to try to best the anti-Alan faction on the council, but could not seem to win any outright victories.

Meanwhile, Yvonne Withington, one of Alan's most stalwart supporters, left the Anglican church in disgust and became a Roman Catholic. 'Some members of this congregation love and care selectively,' she wrote in her resignation letter.[61] Other allies left All Saints but not the Anglican church, or turned their backs on Christianity entirely. Alan was pushing Gwen to leave, too, as a protest against his treatment, but Gwen told him she would stay for a bit longer to keep an eye on his 'enemies'.[62] She assured him that she was planning an eventual exit that would be 'nasty and spectacular'.[63] In one card, she apologised to him for participating in the Easter services, confessing that she had wanted to 'perform the Pachelbel' on the organ but realised this was wrong of her: he was 'right to rebuke' her, she told him humbly.[64]

Since his arrest, she had seen more of Alan than ever before. As he no longer had a driver's licence, she and Yvonne, among others, took him to the police station for his weekly sign-in, to shopping centres and appointments, and to their own houses for meals, as well as coming to his rescue when he found himself stranded. For a time, he moved into a flat at Yvonne's house. Gwen found the whole thing disastrously stressful. 'This is the worst summer of my life,' she wrote in her diary on 9 April 1994. 'Worse than 1979. Worse than anything.' She was having trouble sleeping again and, for the first time, asked her doctor for tranquillisers. She was prescribed Normison, a benzodiazepine used to treat insomnia and anxiety, but found it 'useless'.

Meanwhile, Bill was not happy about Gwen's absorption in Alan's affairs. He was not alone in this; a number of Gwen's friends were dubious about Alan and concerned about her passionate involvement with him.[65] But Bill's dislike of Alan went back to the beginning of the friendship, long before Alan was charged with anything. As ever, he did not trouble to disguise his antipathy, which meant Gwen was tense and anxious when Alan visited her at home. The previous year, Gwen had invited Alan and Greg Kratzmann, then visiting Hobart, to lunch at Pine Street. During the meal, Bill made a dismissive remark about Alan's work as a clergyman, and Alan responded sharply. According to Greg, the two men began to 'bicker' like schoolboys until Gwen leapt up from the table and ran out into the garden. He found her sobbing, vowing to leave Bill and go back to Brisbane.[66]

It was a threat she made increasingly often. More and more, Gwen slept in the fold-out bed in the parlour – unless they had visitors or it was too cold, as it usually was in the dead of winter. Conflict could flare up over almost anything, but there were a couple of reliable triggers: Bill's tree-trimming and the management of his diabetes. Their fights over the trees were a bizarre replay of the battles Gwen had had fifty years earlier with Agnes at Grimes Street. Bill would 'hack' the trees in their yard (healthy pruning, in his view) and Gwen would rail in fury and weep in distress at the violence done to her beloved friends. 'B hacks star jasmine. V. depressed ++++', she wrote in her diary on 12 September 1990. 'Bill has hacked daisy!' appeared in December, and in January 1991: 'B extirpates shrubs in corner near porch.' In April, she noted grimly that 'B has butchered viburnum. Displayed to passers by.'[67]

As for Bill's diabetes, Gwen was convinced he used his illness as a means to control her. He did not like to have a snack before dinner, which meant that if she was running late with the evening meal, he would be at risk of hypoglycaemia. She would then have to scramble to prepare dinner with the threat of his imminent collapse hanging over her. 'Crisis [diabetic] for the 5th time this week at dinner – hasty carbohydrate,' she wrote in her diary on 19 February 1994. 'A biscuit at afternoon tea would solve this but no – dinner rushed, evening spoilt.' 'Another rush for carbohydrate,' she wrote the next day. 'What *control* diabetes gives over the spouse. O God.' Similar entries appear throughout the year. 'B needs quick carbohydrate. Get lunch quickly,' she wrote on 23 December. 'O God, continual stress.' She would make the same complaint to Alison the following year: 'After *four* consecutive diabetic crises at mealtimes I wonder why he doesn't do what Dr Kelly told him to in 1964: eat a biscuit at morning & afternoon tea. But I fear the pleasure of making me jump to attention is too great.'[68]

Bill knew Gwen was ready to leave him; though he himself would not take any steps to end the marriage, he told her that if she wanted to go, she could go.[69] Gwen suspected that he was calling her bluff. 'He seems on the whole indifferent to my planned departure,' she wrote to Greg in May. 'No doubt he doesn't believe it will happen.'[70] She was worried about supporting herself if she did leave. She still felt that she could take nothing from Bill and would need 'to get enough money together to keep me in any style however humble in Queensland'. This was not easy; book royalties and speaker's fees did not amount to much, and she was generous to a fault with friends, giving money away freely. The small nest egg she had built up she had already promised to Alan for his legal fees, if he should need it.

Even in his current parlous state, Alan's company made her happy. As a priest he reminded her of Peter, but as a man, he reminded her of her father, whom he was 'very like . . . in appearance': 'the curly hair and bright eyes, . . . the lovely voice.'[71] In her diary, she often recorded the simple word 'Happy!' after she had been with Alan – taking him to the beach for a walk with his dog, Max, perhaps, or having a meal at a café.[72] Going to his flat for lunch was pure delight, especially if her church friends Rosemary and

Greta were there too. With Yvonne, she referred to Alan as 'the boy',[73] and some of her letters to him began 'Dear Boy' or simply 'Dear One'. For his birthday that year, he hosted a luncheon party at Greta's home for all his supporters. The food was sumptuous, 'as at an Elizabethan feast'. 'We wandered and talked and ate and Robert played the piano in a nearby room . . . Alan was relaxed and happy and sober.' For Gwen, it was 'like stepping back to the great days of Crimes Lodge'.[74]

She knew that Alan could be 'Very Trying', as she put it, particularly to poor Yvonne, who bore the brunt of it while he was living at her house. 'He is mostly pissed and has twice lost Max in town (tied him up and forgot where he left him),' she told Greg in August. 'He spent his birthday drinking, and lost Max so efficiently that they couldn't find him . . . The poor dog must wonder where his next tin of Pal is coming from.'[75] She herself was sometimes called upon to 'rescue' the rector. Once, he called her when he found himself 'stranded' in a café without the means to pay his bill. When she arrived, having left a dinner party to come to his aid, she found him 'sitting weeping into a cappuccino with two small children keeping him company in an interested sort of way'.[76] But though she saw the state he was in, she did not love him any less. She believed absolutely in his innocence and went to every court hearing expecting the case to be thrown out. Those of her friends who felt that Alan was unworthy of her fierce loyalty learned to avoid the subject.

Given the multiplying tensions in Hobart, it was a relief to fly to Darwin in mid-September, where she was to spend a week as writer-in-residence at Northern Territory University. She had never been to Darwin before, though Bill and Tony had both spent time there during the war.[77] She loved it at once. 'O the blissful heat & the frangipani & the bougainvillea & the palm groves,' she wrote to a friend. 'O the easy friendliness and the feeling that happiness will last forever.' At once, 'Tasmania and its troubles' seemed 'faint and far away'. She spent the week attending readings and seminars at the university, as well as making a side trip to Darwin High and going to lunches and dinners with friendly university staff. Returning to Tasmania was, as usual, a painful dislocation. Arriving home after a long day of travel just in time to make Bill's dinner, she felt '*utterly* depressed'.[78]

Her mood did not improve when she went to All Saints the following day to get the mail and discovered that someone had changed the locks on the parish mailbox: her key no longer worked. It was a covert strike from the anti-Farrell members of the parish council. Gwen was furious. At the next parish council meeting, she made her feelings known, and when she failed to sway the chair, she resigned in protest. Several other councillors walked out with her, including her friend Rosemary. The following day, she sent a letter to the bishop announcing her resignation and explaining in detail the reasons for it, copying her missive to every church dignitary she could think of.

The counterstrike was swift: the chair of the parish council expunged Gwen's name from the pew sheet, affecting to believe she had resigned not just from her role as parish secretary but from her role as churchwarden as well. Gwen and a number of her supporters wrote letters of protest, again copying their letters to the church higher-ups, and demanded reinstatement. Politely worded missives of vindictive outrage flew back and forth for some days before Gwen was reinstated as churchwarden. She had won her point, but the bitterness of this exchange would linger. She had very little desire now to go to All Saints, even for the pleasure of confounding her enemies. The time of finding 'peace and refreshment' at early mass beneath the dusky vault of the little church was over.

26

My Sister, My Spouse

Thou hast ravished my heart, my sister, my spouse; thou hast ravished
my heart with one of thine eyes, with one chain of thy neck.
How fair is thy love, my sister, my spouse! How much better is thy love
than wine! And the smell of thine ointments than all spices!

Song of Songs 4: 9-10

AT THE MELBOURNE WRITERS FESTIVAL IN OCTOBER 1994, Gwen looked out from the stage and saw a familiar face looking back at her, a 'gentle and beautiful' visage whose presence filled her with joy. Rosemary Cohen was a librarian in her mid-forties who since 1992 had been attending All Saints regularly. She and Gwen had met at daily mass, and gradually a friendship had developed. Discovering that Rosemary had once thought of doing some writing, Gwen had taken the younger woman under her wing and encouraged her to join the Fellowship of Australian Writers and attend writers' festivals. She had not known, however, that Rosemary would be at this session. She read one of her older poems, 'The Owl and the Pussycat Baudelaire Rock', carrying the audience with her from phrase to phrase with the skill of the consummate performer. From her place in the crowd, Rosemary was captivated. The reading itself was utterly magical, but it was not only that: Edward Lear's poem was one she had a passion for. Unbeknown to Gwen, she had been collecting illustrated editions of the tale for years, and had even written her own 'Owl and the Pussycat' parody.

When Gwen finished her reading, the audience leapt up and swarmed around her. Seeing that Gwen was in her element, Rosemary left her to her public. But when Gwen returned to her room at the Park Royal late that afternoon, she found 'a great vase of daisies' from Rosemary.[1] It was 'the best moment of the Festival'.[2] 'What a darling,' she wrote happily to Alan that night.[3]

She and Rosemary had been growing closer for some time. Rosemary was a fellow member of the parish council, and Gwen found her presence at 'those poisonous vestry/PC meetings' revivifying: 'I look at you to gain strength,' she told her.[4] Outside of church functions, she simply loved

Rosemary's company, drawn to her calm intelligence and beauty. Rosemary was 'a pard-like spirit beautiful and swift',[5] and Gwen wanted to spend as much time with her as possible. She took to dropping in on her, often with Alan in tow, and drew her into her own literary activities as much as possible. The younger woman's pleasure in her company and eager interest in literature, art and music were balm to Gwen's spirit. Bill lectured her on the 'defects of [her] character';[6] Rosemary thought her perfect. As their relationship deepened, Gwen's dream of forging a solitary life in Brisbane began to fade. They had 'entered a space of pure happiness', she told Alan in early 1994.[7]

Rosemary Cohen and Gwen Harwood, Pine Street, 1995

Gwen had been attracted to women before: Vera Cottew, Ann Jennings, Lotte Wilmot. In each of these relationships, she had recognised her feelings as intensely passionate and romantic, and not significantly different to those she had for the men she had fallen in love with. Mostly, she was happy not to assign any particular label to this attraction to women, and was content with affectionate but limited physical contact with them. In the late 1970s, her demeanour with Ann had raised questions, if not eyebrows, among younger acquaintances. She had gone to Bruny Island to spend the day with her friend, who was holidaying there, and they had attended 'a charming house-party under great trees overlooking the sea'. As they ate fresh oysters and drank white wine, 'one beautiful girl (early 20s) said "O but everyone is bisexual now." "Not us," I said to Ann. "Not us," said Ann. "We were born too early in the century." We were sitting with our arms round one another. One child added "Consciously or not."'[8]

By the early 1990s, homosexuality had become much more visible in Australian society, and Gwen had many poet and writer friends who were openly gay. In 1992, she attended a session on gay writing at the Salamanca Writers' Weekend and went to lunch with the author Robert Dessaix. Robert included her poem 'Ganymede' in his 1993 anthology *Australian Gay and Lesbian Writing*, along with works by Gwen's old friend Hal Porter and new friends David Malouf, Peter Rose and Dorothy Porter.

Gwen was particularly intrigued by Dorothy. In the mid-1970s, Norman Talbot had shown her a photograph of the young poet, and she had been drawn to her beauty. 'Such a mysterious face – I hope I shall meet her,' she told Norman. 'She reminds me very much of Vera Cottew, long dead, who had the same sort of beauty.'[9] The two women did not meet for almost twenty years, however, by which time Dorothy had published not only a series of well-regarded volumes of poetry but also a novel in verse, *Akhenaten*. In August 1993, they were both writers-in-residence at Charles Sturt University in Wagga Wagga, where they gave readings and workshops and Gwen attended a 'long seminar' on Dorothy's novel. They met again at a literary festival in Hawthorn early the following year, and in mid-August, Dorothy came to Hobart as writer-in-residence at the Salamanca Arts Centre. During this visit, they saw each other often, and Gwen agreed to launch Dorothy's new verse novel, *The Monkey's Mask*, first in Hobart and then in Sydney. Gwen was both delighted by and wary of Dorothy's frank sexuality. She loved her 'obscene book', and gave a copy to Alan Farrell. But she was also a little daunted by her unrelenting anarchy, telling Alan that Dorothy was 'so feral it's exhausting'.[10]

It seems likely that the increasing acceptance of homosexuality in Gwen's own circles enabled her to explore her attraction to Rosemary more freely. Theirs was never an avowed relationship – both women were married, and neither wanted to force their friendship into some predetermined mould – but it was a powerful, loving connection with romantic and erotic dimensions. Alan was Gwen's chief confidante, and his flat, where the three of them sometimes had lunch or dinner, was a safe place for them to meet. Rosemary and Gwen would also visit each other's homes (Bill liked Rosemary) and spend time together at a beach cottage where Rosemary sometimes stayed alone. Gwen's letters refer blissfully to 'superb' meals (Rosemary was an excellent cook, a skill Gwen, who loved food, greatly prized), long walks in the bush or on the beach and afternoons spent paddling in the water and gazing into rock pools.

After one particularly 'wonderful day', she sent Rosemary a fragment of a Theodore Roethke poem that she always reached for when some experience of hers verged on perfection:

> I cherish what I have
> had of the temporal:
> I am no longer young
> but the winds and waters are;
> What falls away will fall;
> all things bring me to love.[11]

That day, Rosemary had dressed up to perform her parody of 'The Owl and the Pussycat' for Gwen. When Gwen got home, she sent her friend a signed copy of 'The Owl and the Pussycat Baudelaire Rock'.

On another occasion, early in January 1995, Rosemary prepared lunch for Gwen, Alan and another friend at Alan's flat, dressing up as a French waitress to serve them at a table she had set up under the walnut tree. The following day, Gwen sent her a postcard with a quote from Petronius which she translated as: 'I have lived: never shall an unkinder fate take from us what was given in an earlier hour.' The card featured a Van Gogh painting, *Bank of the Seine near the Pont de Clichy, 1887*: 'the pea-green boat is invisible among the foliage,' Gwen assured her.[12]

Her joy and pleasure in this burgeoning relationship contrast sharply in her 1994 diary with her misery over the ongoing proceedings against Alan, her stoushes with Bill and her increasingly crippling headaches. Early in the year she had been so deeply weary, so plagued with headaches, nosebleeds, aching bones and general malaise, that she had felt convinced she must have cancer again.[13] She underwent the standard tests and her doctor assured her there was nothing seriously wrong. For a while, she felt better, but the headaches continued, along with the insomnia and anxiety.

Early in October, she recorded in her diary that she had been bleeding in the night, adding ironically: 'O God is this The End?'[14] Although she knew bleeding was not a good sign for a woman in her seventies, she told herself it was probably 'just a minor cystitis': 'Decide not to worry.' Little more than a month later, however, she was again recording 'Trouble with bleeding in night'.[15] The bleeding continued for several days, but she got on with her life, recording on 23 November: 'Bleeding. O God' but also 'Happy day', after having Rosemary to lunch.

It was early January before she finally went to the doctor. Her old GP had retired and she found herself consulting a 'lovely young brightly dressed informal intelligent woman', who impressed her very favourably.[16] Her new doctor discovered that her blood pressure was 'alarmingly high' and sent her for 'various tests for "invasive cells"' – her great fear. 'I do hope nothing is going to take over and occupy any Sibylline spaces.' A couple of days later, she made an appointment for an X-ray, then packed a picnic lunch and went off to spend the day with Rosemary.[17]

The two women had a blissful time at a remote beach on the South Arm Peninsula, walking, wading, reading and reciting poetry, and exploring rock pools. Later, Gwen would playfully link South Arm with the biblical Song of Songs, the long erotic poem attributed to King Solomon. This poem she had once asked Rosemary to read to her in the beautiful King James version. 'Thou hast ravished my heart, my sister, my spouse,' she wrote on a card in March. 'His left hand is under my head, and his right hand doth embrace me,' became, on Gwen's lips, 'her South arm is under my head . . .'[18]

A day or two later, Rosemary left Hobart to attend the Sydney Writers' Festival, and a couple of days after that, Gwen went for her scans. She wrote to *die ferne Geliebte* – the distant beloved – on 17 January with the results of her initial tests, which were mixed: it seemed her left kidney had stopped working, but her other kidney was functioning well, and there were no 'invasive cells'.[19] Rosemary need not hurry back, she insisted. 'It will soon be fixed up, whatever it is. I'm making plum chutney & thinking how lucky we are: "Then changing hearts, to join them, so we shall / Be one, and one another's All" (Donne).'

The language of Donne was the language of Gwen's earliest love affairs from her Brisbane days. It was also the language she had used to evoke her relationship with Vera Cottew in poems like 'Dust to Dust'. Those old, intensely spiritual and romantic feelings were rushing back in this new affair. The following day she sent Rosemary a postcard featuring an erotic image of a semi-naked woman beginning 'Geliebte', a greeting she glossed as follows: 'German word: it means "I wish we were sitting in a rock pool stroking the sea anemones.'"[20] She included in her card – which she had enclosed, contrary to her lifelong practice, in an envelope – a warning to 'keep away from the Pope', who 'has never sat in a rock pool in his life and knows nothing except a bit of Latin'. She signed off with: 'Keep safe, my beautiful one. You are present with me always.' The following day, she went to the urologist to get the results of her scans and learned that, far from having no invasive cells, she had a large malignant tumour in her left kidney and required immediate surgery.

◆ ◆ ◆

Much as she had dreaded such news, she had not truly expected it. As a child, she had been promised a long life by a fortune teller who lived at the end of her street, and though she had no faith in divination, at some level she had believed her.[21] She had thought to live into her eighties, at least, like her mother and grandmother. Certainly, she had assumed she would outlive Bill, whose longevity had surprised everyone. Now she was forced to realise that she might well go first – and soon.

When she left the specialist's rooms, she went straight to Alan's flat. She wanted his comfort, and she also wanted, as she told Rosemary the next day, to be where she and Rosemary had been together only a few days before, 'with the great [walnut tree] . . . and the beautiful leafy light enclosing us'.[22] Only after she had spoken to Alan did she have 'the strength to tell the family, calmly'.[23] Then she swung into action, going to St Helen's hospital herself to organise her admission. That night, she called Tony and Rosemary, and the following day, she wrote to her 'geliebte' to assure her that after her brief hospital stay, they would 'go to the Gardens & the rock pools & I'll sing thee songs of Araby'.[24] In her diary, she was less sanguine, noting on 21 January that she was 'V. ill & tired': 'Lie down (except getting meals). Terrible night. Moonlight – so we'll go no more a roving.' A week later, after a series of extremely brief entries recording her hospital visit ('Terrible day "on tubes"!', 'Terrible day', 'Catheter out – relief. V. sick but upright'), she stopped making diary entries altogether.

The news following the surgery was not good. The surgeon had removed the tumour from the left kidney, but it had already 'invaded the bladder' and was 'heading for the other kidney': 'I can't remember the medical terminology but it was basically Good Night Sweetheart.'[25] She could expect to have about six months.

Rosemary hastily returned from Sydney,[26] and she and Yvonne came over and 'brightened the day with roses, cabbages, rabbit casserole and (from Yvonne) a medal of St Peregrine'. Bill was, Gwen noted, 'very worried', his anxiety quickly sliding into despondency. '[He] keeps saying "there is no solution" as if there *should* be a solution.'[27] Tony was desolate. He and Gwen had not seen as much of each other of late, in part because Tony, increasingly reclusive, was losing his hearing, which made conversation difficult. But they were as close as ever, exchanging regular letters and cards, and meeting for festive meals. Tony had always assumed Gwen would outlive him; he had even bequeathed precious objects to her in his will. It was a terrible blow for Greg too. In a vicious coincidence, his wife, Chasely, had also recently been diagnosed with terminal cancer. Though he continued with his efforts towards a biography, Gwen saw with aching sympathy that he was 'numb with grief'.[28]

In the weeks after the diagnosis, Gwen's doctors told her that surgery on her functioning kidney, combined with chemotherapy or radiotherapy, could extend her life by another six months, but would not save her. For Gwen, it was an easy decision: as she explained to Craig Powell, 'I really would rather die than have more ghastly operations.' She knew there was a good chance that further treatment would lead to more pain down the track, as the cancer spread beyond the kidneys and began to attack nerves.[29] Death from kidney failure seemed preferable: it would at least be 'fairly quick & not painful'. In any case, she could not see the point in postponing the inevitable. As she had once told Tony, she hated 'illusions': 'All that matters is the truth about oneself, however painful.'[30] She would not seek comforting illusions now. Her children supported her decision. '"Go for it, Moth!" was the cry – "don't have nasty invasive things done to you! Drink champagne! We'll come when you call."'[31]

Over the following weeks and months, Gwen veered between calm acceptance and resentful fury. When she first came out of hospital, she felt better than she had for some time, due to a lengthy blood transfusion. Though she was very tired, she was well enough to continue with her daily round: preparing meals, cleaning the house, doing the grocery shopping, ferrying Alan around and, once his rape trial began, attending court with him.

When she was at home, she was deluged with 'relentless ringers and knockers': friends, acquaintances, wellwishers and literary groupies, all wanting to see her and all laying siege to her strongholds with dogged determination.[32] Following the patterns of a lifetime, she made the visitors tea and coffee, and offered them home-baked goodies and even lunch or dinner if they dropped in at meal times. As she got sicker, however, she became increasingly exasperated by the utter lack of consideration of those who called – especially when they shyly produced a manuscript from a back pocket for her to cast an eye over from her sickbed, or delicately reminded her that she had promised to write in support of their grant application. All her life, she had been able to meet the demands of miscellaneous others without entirely neglecting her own needs by being almost supernaturally quick and efficient. Now, she simply did not have the energy. On days she felt well enough, she wanted to spend time with Rosemary and Alan and a select group of close friends. Instead, she found herself 'holding a kind of endless teaparty for the get-well-sooners and get-on-with-your-lifers'.[33] Every kindly visitor told her she should rest, but their unrelenting presence made it impossible for her to take their advice. 'What is it they want?? Are they writing memoirs??' she snapped to Alison. 'I am going to KILL the next well-wisher who says to me "Now remember, you have nothing to do but look after yourself now." I am going to KILL AND MUTILATE the next person who says "Now remember, you have to KEEP WRITING, that's all that matters."'[34]

To her intense irritation, Bill was no use in keeping the importunate from the door. She fumed at his inability to do for her what she had done for him for so long. 'I remember when Bill had high blood pressure and retired,' she told Alison. 'I answered all calls, all knocks-at-the-door, all invitations and suggestions. I made excuses for what he didn't want to do, took him where he wanted to go, acted as nurse, carpenter's mate, everything.'[35] Bill had been oblivious to the care she provided then, she felt, and was oblivious to her need for care now. In fact, far from looking after her, he was adding to her stress. 'Now & again I have a brief access of energy but not enough to whip up the old succession of supper foods,' she told Alison in early March. 'B looks desolated as he examines the cake tin, finding "bought cakes."'[36] When friends brought over a stew or a pot of soup to save Gwen cooking, Bill would complain about the quality of the food and sometimes refuse to eat it.[37] To add to Gwen's worry, he was not controlling his diabetes well, and had numerous 'hypoglycaemic crises'.[38]

She still found joy with Rosemary. They spent time together whenever they could – 'I've just had a blissful afternoon with Rosemary,' she wrote to Alan in early February[39] – and throughout February, March and April, Gwen sent off a stream of postcards (enveloped) to her beloved, featuring erotic images of women and quotations from love poems. On one she copied out a poem by John Clare:

> I loved thee, though I told thee not,
> Right earlily and long,
> Thou wert my joy in every spot,
> My theme in every song... .[40]

She had been reading back through her 1993 diary, seeking traces of the love that was emerging between them, but was then unspoken. Declaring that 1993 was a terrible year, she added: 'How utterly lovely this year is!' It is an extraordinary statement, given her terminal diagnosis. But in terms of her relationship with Rosemary, it was true.

She was even penning a few lines of her own for her 'radiant one', just to amuse them both. One day in early April, she was writing some 'light-hearted, quite improper verses to cheer Rosemary' when the Anglican Bishop called to see her.[41] Luckily, she told Alan, she had been checking a reference from the Song of Songs when he appeared, and he assumed she had been piously reading her Bible. The verses she had been working on – to be sung to the tune of 'Home on the Range' – set love beside death, and avowed that love was stronger:

> O what shall I do
> when my skin is slate-blue
> and my kidney is set to expire?
> When the time is not long
> I'll read Solomon's Song
> in the arms of my love by the fire.
>
> On the skin of the bear
> (or the panther) we'll share
> the warmth that eclipses all ills.
> I'll be safe from all harm
> As a seal on thine arm
> when the leopards* come down from the hills.

We'll be safe in our house
my sister, my spouse,
with the treasures of music and art.
Though black or dull blue
I'll be comely to you
as I breathe 'Thou has ravished my heart'.

* Revised version: social workers[42]

Rosemary was struggling. She loved Gwen deeply and had cherished their ever-growing relationship. Now, her beloved was dying. She wanted to take care of her, but she was stuck in a strange limbo; because her relationship with Gwen was unacknowledged, she had no more access to Gwen than any other of her friends. Several of the flats next door to Gwen's house were vacant at that time, and Rosemary suggested to Gwen that she rent one so she could be close by. Gwen was touched, but would not allow it: 'I don't want a broom-wielder or assistant laundress,' she explained to Alan. 'I want a crazy selfish bright-tongued lover.'[43] She wanted Rosemary to be her secret source of joy and comfort for as long as possible, but she did not have the energy to fight for more. She understood Rosemary's plight – as she told Alan, it was 'always harder for the one who's left'[44] – but she was increasingly preoccupied with her own misery.

◆ ◆ ◆

As the months went by and Gwen became ever sicker, her equanimity 'vanished'. She suspected that it had never been more than 'chemistry': 'no doubt the body was protecting itself in some way'.[45] At the end of March, she began to make arrangements for palliative care, and the reality of what she was facing became inescapable. 'I had thought of being on earth until the end of the century and hadn't ever reckoned with what has happened to me,' she told Alison. 'I wish I did not have to live through what's coming.'[46] She was still making the effort to function normally when she had visitors, but it was 'a strain'.[47] She did not want people – particularly those she loved – to see her sick, miserable, disfigured by illness and drugs. Above all, she was determined not to 'let the children see me cast down'.[48] As late as April, she still felt able to '*act* the usual part', telling Alison she had 'been offstage only for a few hours here & there'. But as the cancer progressed, it became all but impossible for her to play her old roles.

One way she dealt with this was by asking people not to come and see her. All her old friends interstate and many new ones made plans to visit while she was still well enough to see them; she refused them all. Norman, terribly upset by the news of her terminal prognosis, insisted on flying down to Tasmania for a quick visit in May. Gwen saw him, but made it clear he was not to come again. 'Having had so brief a time with you, I came back last night somewhat tense and tearful,' he wrote on his return to Newcastle. 'Still, I am glad I came to Hobart, if only to be given my congé and pushed out into the universe . . .'[49] This was her attitude to old friends and lovers alike: if she was to see them at all, it was to let them go. When Peter Bennie rang to say he was coming to visit, and would take her, Bill and Tony out to lunch, she was horrified. 'O God, I can imagine the whole show: Peter drunk & telling filthy jokes, Tony deaf & frowning & Bill in a state of scaly coldness.' She managed to put him off by saying she would probably have to go back into hospital and would let him know 'when the time was suitable'.[50] She was happiest with those friends who could simply accept that she was dying and commiserate with her on her bad luck. When Vikram Seth rang 'to say goodbye', she was relieved 'to hear the calm acceptance in his beguiling voice – no get-well-soon non-sense, just rejoicing in a happy friendship. I was delighted that we had a few Last Words.'[51]

Towards the end of May, she went for a period of respite care to the Whittle Ward at the Repat hospital, where she had chosen to go for pallia-tive care when the time came. She hated it. It was busy and noisy, and she had none of the privacy she so craved. 'Everyone had total access – clergy, beautician, Sister Pat . . . , professional do-good visitors, social workers, care-advisers, professional supporters, Red Cross, counsellors . . .', she told Ann. 'I have never had a less peaceful week.'[52] 'Of course they were all kind caring courteous loving encouraging and quick to tell me I could have some more jelly and ice cream. But for me it was the worst kind of prison.'[53] She did not have to stay this time. After an eight-hour blood transfusion, she recovered dramatically and was discharged feeling 'well and human again'.[54] She was even 'able to carry on with cooking etc', though from now on, she would get help with the cleaning and lawn mowing.

The burst of good health raised her spirits for a while, but as the days grew shorter and the weather colder, she found herself falling once more into 'the pit'.[55] The prospect of another winter in the Island of Despair filled her with alternating rage and depression. 'It's an awful day,' she told Alison in late June: 'a great Bridgewater Jerry, total bleak greyness, mortal cold and overwhelming horror that I've somehow allowed myself to live in this place after 50 winters.'[56] She was consumed with bitter regret that she had not left Tasmania after her first child was born, with or without Bill. 'Almost all my life here has been spent longing for the *other life*: warmth, praise when things were worth praising, friends made welcome, music, holidays (it was 18 years before I had a holiday – that was when I went back to work), fruit bats in the subtropical sunset, swimming in warm salt water, simple affection,' she wrote to Ann.[57] 'If I could only have persuaded B to go for the Queensland Chair in 1952,' she lamented to Alison. 'Night after night I dream of Brisbane.'[58]

She thought often of suicide, making plans to stockpile her sleeping tablets or convince a doctor to prescribe something that would carry her off.[59] One of her favourite fantasies was to go back to Brisbane alone, find a retreat of some kind – a 'grotty room', a cave on the riverbank – and take an overdose of barbiturates. She had always had a horror of dying in Tasmania. Yet when her children tried to make plans to take her to Queensland for a holiday, she refused to go. 'What would be the point of that?' she asked Greg. 'I can't sleep, taste, sit still, walk far, concentrate.'[60] To Alison, she said that she would return to the Blessed City only 'as ashes blowing in the wind'.[61]

◆ ◆ ◆

Early in July, Alan Farrell was convicted of rape, aggravated sexual assault and assault, and sentenced to eight years in prison. Gwen had not been in court to hear the verdict; she was no longer well enough for anything 'strenuous'.[62] She was 'stunned' by the news. '[I] cannot really believe it. It passes the limits of the sayable.'[63] Quite apart from her faith in Alan, the case itself, as she had watched it unfold, had seemed weak;[64] none of his supporters had thought a guilty verdict likely. But Gwen did not waste energy bemoaning the fact. Alan had been taken straight to Risdon Prison, and she immediately began to think about what could be done to ensure he was as comfortable as possible there until he was freed on appeal, as she was sure he would be.[65] She had already promised him whatever financial help she could give. Now she assured him of her unchanging love, and of her certainty that he would one day be exonerated, though she herself would not 'live long enough to see the end of it'.[66] She also encouraged him to begin writing the memoir he had often spoken of, plotting to send him a dictionary and a style manual as invaluable aids.[67] Other friends would take over the practical side of things: packing up his flat, visiting him in prison, lobbying on his behalf. She could only send him cards and letters, and exhort friends such as Greg to do the same.

She was no longer well enough to drive, and the loss of this final bit of independence weighed heavily on her. 'I feel imprisoned,' she told Alison.[68] Rosemary took her to her medical appointments, and as she grew sicker, doctors and nurses came to her at Pine Street. She was doing no writing, beyond the letters she continued to send faithfully to Tony, Alison, Ann, Alan and other friends with whom she felt she did not have to wear a mask of saintly forbearance.

From the beginning of her illness, she declared that she no longer had any interest in literature.[69] She was too tired, and perhaps too disgruntled, to contemplate the effort involved in writing a serious poem. Soon after her diagnosis, she also abandoned her preparatory work for an opera with Larry based on *Maurice Guest*. This was a project she had wanted to do for years; Richardson's novel had always been one of her favourite works, a 'musician's book' that she felt had wonderful dramatic potential. It had recently come out of copyright and the time seemed right. But the discovery that she had terminal cancer made her labours seem pointless, and she wrote to Larry to suggest he approach another poet-librettist, Peter Goldsworthy.

Larry, dismayed by her diagnosis, was indignant. 'Dammit, this is OUR piece. You'll have to tell me, in so many words, that you can't or won't do it. Otherwise, I would say, let's get on with it.' Despite her 'bombshell', he was inclined to be optimistic. She was pretty tough, he wrote, and 'as you say, you could go on for years, confounding the confounded doctors'.[70] But Gwen could not be persuaded. She did not want to get well launched on the project only to have to leave it unfinished, she told Larry, nor would she contemplate handing over an incomplete draft to another librettist to work on.[71]

As she grew sicker, she was reading less, finding it too difficult to concentrate. To Rosemary, she confided her sense that words were no longer her medium. 'I feel ravaged by this winter (which I didn't expect or wish to live through). Language itself is leaving me – like the animals I'm immured in primary representation. If only one could *disappear*.'[72]

She was still publishing, though. When Alison asked, in April, whether Gwen would like to bring out a final volume before she died, she agreed, with the proviso that Alison do all the work of pulling the book together and seeing it through to press. After more than thirty years with Angus & Robertson, Gwen had a new publisher, Tom Thompson, who had left A&R in 1994 to set up on his own. She asked Alison to negotiate the contract with the ebullient Tom, as she did not have the energy.[73] Alison then set about tracking down the poems Gwen had published in various journals and magazines in the years since *Bone Scan*. Much of the work she found had a decidedly elegiac tone. Poems such as 'Night Thoughts', 'Herongate' and 'In Worse Armes', which open the volume that would become *The Present Tense*, seem to refer directly to Gwen's impending death. In fact, they had grown out of her 1985 brush with cancer and had first appeared in 1990 and 1991. The four mystical poems of 'Tetragrammaton', which might suggest a spiritual state of mind as she approached her death, had actually been written in 1987. The series of elegies for Vincent Buckley, 'Autumn', 'Midwinter Rainbow' and 'The Present Tense', moving meditations not only on her friendship with Vin but on death itself, were all in print by 1990.

The sense in *The Present Tense* of a summing-up, of an ending consciously welcomed, even embraced, was further reinforced by the inclusion of six of Gwen's verse addresses, under the title 'Six Odes for Public Occasions', and her four autobiographical stories. The prose pieces looked back with tender nostalgia to her childhood, while the addresses seemed to provide an overview of her philosophy of life. The love poems that make up 'This Artifice of Air' were resurrected from old letters to Norman uncovered by Greg. 'The Owl and the Pussycat Baudelaire Rock' was another piece from the 1970s that Gwen did not publish until 1994. Its inclusion at the end of the book seemed to encompass both Norman and Rosemary, as well as her own deep longing for a peaceful death, akin to putting out to sea in a gently rocking boat.

Though she was 'heavily doped', Gwen was able to go through various drafts of the collection and answer Alison's editorial questions. She checked the proofs in mid-July, and told Alison that she wanted to dedicate the book to Alan Farrell, as a public testimonial of her faith in him. Alison, like most of Gwen's friends, was ambivalent about this, but told Gwen it was up to her. When Gwen sent back the final proofs, she had added the simple dedication: 'To my children'. It was the only one of her poetry books she did not dedicate to Tony. She told Alison a few weeks later that she had been 'reflecting that the *family* is the great thing; all the children are calmly affectionate and although the three boys have had five divorces among them (true!) they still love *us*! Mary, happily unmarried, leads a dazzling life.'[74] She had been deeply touched by the care and tenderness her children had shown for both her and Bill over the past year. Though she did not want them to feel they had to disrupt their lives by coming to see her, and often felt that she simply did not have the strength to see them, she was always soothed by their presence. They looked after her in ways no one else could, taking over the cooking, anticipating her needs, giving 'affectionate atten-tion to things that might make things easier'.[75] 'It was nice to have fresh flowers in the house and small attentions and affectionate pattings,' she noted, after a visit from Mary.[76] Just as important to Gwen, the children took care of Bill so that she did not have to, even taking him out occasion-ally so that she could have some precious time to herself.

Increasingly, though, even 'small attentions and affectionate pattings' could not do much to make her life more bearable. The medication she was on had caused her to swell up, and she felt physically repulsive. She could no longer get her feet into shoes and was reduced to wearing socks and tracksuit pants. 'My legs & feet are monstrous, elephantine,' she told Ali-son. At the same time, her muscles were wasting and she could 'hardly lift a big book'.[77] She felt unrecognisable, as if 'aliens' were 'changing my appear-ance and character (how did I get so lachrymose?) before they move me to be a slave on Alpha Centauri'.[78] In mid-August, she told Alison that she was 'longing for release': 'The world has dwindled to getting up off a chair – can I do it this time?' 'There is nothing to help that I can think of – except music,' she added.[79] Her children had given her a CD player, and she had had many gifts of favourite pieces, composers, singers. At last she could lis-ten, uninterrupted, to *Israel in Egypt* or Dietrich Fischer-Dieskau singing *Winterreise*. 'Music fills up the fearful spaces.'[80]

As she lay in bed resting and drifting, Gwen found herself experiencing 'long total-recall stretches of half-waking half-dreaming memories'.[81] Her mistakes seemed so obvious now. 'Fifty years ago I was looking forward to getting married,' she told Ann. 'I thought I should have a household like my hospitable mother's. How could I know?' She and Bill had reached their golden wedding anniversary, but neither was in a celebratory mood. Gwen brooded on how little they were suited. The previous year, she had read a volume of Patrick White's 'astringent letters', and it occurred to her now that there were some similarities between the famous writer and her own misanthropic husband: 'the same gaunt contempt for most of the human race, the same scathing comments on others' work'.[82] 'B can't understand how charmed I am by simple warmhearted affection in people,' she mused to Alison. 'If only he'd learned to *praise* – he said to me once there was very little he could praise.'[83]

Her reflections were not all dismal, however. 'I lie half waking with pictures of the summer in my head,' she wrote to Rosemary. 'The walnut tree, the balcony, the beach at South Arm, the luncheon party at your place, the walk in Greta's garden.'[84] Though Gwen had been determined to retain a lover-like relationship with Rosemary, the younger woman had inevitably slipped into the carer role. She did what she could for Gwen, taking her to medical appointments, cooking for her and refreshing her with a 'wonderful procession of cards'.[85] But sitting in rock pools was impossible.

Tony was a steadfast friend, coming to see her now and then, and sending a continuing stream of letters and cards. He thought of her 'constantly', he told her. Gwen told Alison proudly that they were once again writing to one another 'as in 1943', quoting their favourite poets, sharing the minutiae of their daily lives.[86]

Ann also visited when she could, and with her, Gwen felt she did not need to pretend. But Ann was grappling with her own health problems. She had been diagnosed with diabetes some years earlier and was now very much afraid she was developing dementia. Gwen had promised her that she would help her to die if it came to that; but now she could not give that kind of help even to her beloved Ann. They kept up their old correspondence, shifting from cards to letters when Gwen complained she was 'overwhelmed' by cards. She did not want to see another card, she told her friend – unless Ann could find her a three-dimensional one featuring a pop-out death's head with the message: 'YOU'RE NEXT.'[87]

◆ ◆ ◆

When *The Present Tense* appeared early in October, Gwen was too sick and miserable to take much interest. 'I hope people like it but don't really care,' she told Alison.[88] She had been ambivalent about the book since the beginning, telling Greg that there really weren't 'many poems in the collection – more public occasion odes'.[89] She was uneasy about the inclusion of her short stories – she felt there was no room for prose in a poetry book – and about the publication of the occasional pieces, which she had never intended to preserve. But more than that, the book represented a part of her life, a dimension of herself, that was irretrievably gone. 'I no longer think of myself as the person who wrote all that stuff: it seems to be someone else in a distant time & I'd burn all the books for one day of good health.'[90] Nevertheless, she was pleased when a positive review appeared in *The Age*, and touched by the enthusiastic letters she received. 'I'm glad I've lived long enough to see *TPT* out and about,' she told Alison in late October.[91]

She had wanted to stay at home as long as possible, and had surprised everyone with her longevity. But in mid-November, when she could no longer stand or eat solid food, she had no choice but to return to hospital. She was determined not to go back to the Whittle Ward, so she went to St John's instead, where she was given a pleasant private room that was blessedly quiet. She could not concentrate well enough to read, but spent her days watching TV and drifting 'in and out of sleep'. 'It is utter bliss to be protected from pests (they know where I am but can't get me) and to tear up letters and impertinent requests,' she told Tony.[92] 'There's a cork bulletin board where I can have my postcards pinned, so I've got a little art gallery.' The morphine ensured she slept well. 'For a moment after waking I forget I am ill.'

All her fears of death had been replaced by a longing for release. 'Baby I'm sick to death / but I can't die,' she groaned to Greg, citing her own 'Night Thoughts: Baby and Demon'.[93] 'The dreadful thing is that I'm not dying but just getting weaker,' she told Alison, just before she went into hospital.[94] Her biggest fear was that she would wake up on life support: that the hospital would not let her die. There seemed to be nothing left of her Christian beliefs, if she had, indeed, had a resurgence of faith during her time at All Saints. She had told Rosemary back in June, 'If there is another life I'll say pussycat—'.[95] As for the church she had attended faithfully for almost ten years, she wanted nothing to do with it. When she specified her funeral arrangements, she was adamant that 'the Church [was] to play no part'. She told family and friends that she did not want any kind of religious service and was to be 'cremated *before* the death notice appears'. The only people to be in attendance were immediate family and those who had been like family: Tony; Ann and her partner, Stephen; and Ted and Margaret Stokes, who were Bill's closest friends from his years at the university.[96] Her ashes were to be taken to Queensland: 'Not one ash is to remain in this melancholy island.'[97]

Bill came to visit every day, ferried by friends, and sat by her bedside holding her hand while they watched TV together. Rosemary also came daily, bringing a red rose from her garden; if Gwen was asleep, she would leave the rose.

Gwen had not lost her spark. One friend remembered how, as she was leaving one day, Gwen smiled at her with the old mischief in her eyes and said: 'Get well soon.'[98] To Ann, she wrote with her old stinging humour of having undergone 'what the nurse politely called "Manual evacuation of stools" and it wasn't moving little pieces of furniture about – up your bum with a rubber glove': 'I am hideously marked with magenta blotches and can only sit on my sore fundament and cry alas.'[99]

Late on the evening of 4 December, after Bill had left for the night, she woke and asked for him. The hospital called him, and he came back by taxi at about 1 a.m. He told Rosemary later that she had tried to talk to him but couldn't make herself understood. She had said Rosemary's name. He sat by her, holding her hand, and they both drifted off. When he woke at 3 a.m., she was gone.[100]

Epilogue

Wrap me in rags of time.
You are gone to the treasures
of darkness. I remain.

Gwen Harwood, 'Midwinter Rainbow'

IN AUGUST 1996, A SMALL GROUP GATHERED AT THE CITY Botanic Gardens in Brisbane to scatter Gwen Harwood's ashes. Two of Gwen's children – Mary and John, with his wife, Robin Haines – and her first grandchild, Rachel, joined Greg Kratzmann in the early morning on a brief pilgrimage to the water's edge.[1] On a small jetty over the Brisbane River, just past the mangroves, John read 'At Mornington', and Mary strewed her mother's ashes over the water. Gwen's mortal remains were at home in the Blessed City at last.

Some two years later, another group gathered at All Saints' Anglican Church on Wickham Terrace in Brisbane for the dedication of a statue of St Cecilia in Gwen's honour. Greg had commissioned the small wooden figure ('Queensland beech, appropriately') from sculptor Leopoldine Mimovich and invited Gwen's friends and supporters – including the universities that had awarded her honorary doctorates – to contribute to the cost. The patron saint of music, St Cecilia is depicted as a slender young woman with organ, book and quill. Gwen's brother, Joe, who attended the dedication, noted that the saint's expression was 'rather pensive': 'Gwen had that look when she was "cooking up something".'[2] Tony Riddell, now eighty-four, was there, as were both Alison Hoddinott and Greg. Bill, still living alone in West Hobart, did not make the trip up.

By this time, Alison and Greg – now firm friends – were at work on Gwen's *Collected Poems*, trawling through letters and archives in search of unpublished material and tracking down poems she had published but never gathered into one of the six volumes that appeared during her lifetime. The finished book, which appeared in 2003, was surprisingly substantial, running to some six hundred pages. As the poet Stephen Edgar noted in his launch speech, Harwood had not seemed to be so prolific. She had written 'a lot' of poems that were never intended for publication: they were 'private – to friends, on the back of postcards'.[3] Many, though not all, of those poems have now taken their place in her public body of work. Those she discarded or destroyed, either because she felt they were not good enough to publish or because in the conservative world of Hobart she considered them too 'fierce', are lost forever.

Reviewers of her *Collected Poems* were overwhelmingly delighted and sometimes astonished by her sheer virtuosity. Writing in *The Times Literary Supplement*, Peter Porter declared that Harwood, 'undoubtedly Australia's most loved poet' at the time of her death, had now been revealed as 'the most accomplished poet the country produced in the twentieth century'.[4] Alberto Manguel, writing in *The Spectator*, went further, claiming her as 'one of the finest poets of the twentieth century' – without qualification.[5]

Gwen's international profile would undoubtedly have been higher if she had travelled overseas, as she was often invited to do in her later years; even so, she had her supporters in both the United Kingdom and the United States, and with her inclusion in major anthologies of poetry in English, her standing only continues to rise. Within Australia, her work is studied in high schools and universities, and a handful of her poems – including 'In the Park' and 'Barn Owl' – have been anthologised so often they have garnered 'classic' status. She might have been bemused by the solidity of her reputation, but she would not have been surprised. She always believed that if her work was worth anything, it would last.

She never wanted her poems to be corralled in the school curriculum, however. 'What I like to think is that there are a few people who have my poems and are alone with them and like them, and that the poems mean something to them,' she once told an interviewer.[6] Her hope was that her poetry would one day be to others what the work of long-dead poets had so often been to her: a source of connection, solace, joy. Poetry, for her, was communication, 'a unique way of reaching from one mind to another', whether she was speaking to beloved friends, chance acquaintances or anonymous readers.[7] Whenever she was asked whether she would go on writing even if she was never published, she was always unequivocal: she did not write for the bottom drawer. Her poems were 'meant for others.' 'I would write for one,' she told an interviewer, 'but not for none.'[8] For her, poems were 'an entrance gate to regions of being both poet and reader can share'. In these regions of the mind, she would find her immortality.[9]

Acknowledgements

WHEN I FIRST BEGAN TO WRITE ABOUT GWEN HARWOOD, I contacted Dr Gregory Kratzmann to fill in some gaps for me. I had heard he was writing Harwood's biography, but he quickly set me straight: he had incorporated all of his biographical research into his extensive selection of her letters, *A Steady Storm of Correspondence*, and did not intend to write anything else. A couple of years later, when I had begun to think I might quite like to write her biography myself, I approached Greg again. His advice was unequivocal: 'Don't.'

Given the challenges he had encountered, he wanted to save me years of fruitless labour. But then he decided to help me instead, and his help changed everything. He told me about his friendship with Gwen and his experiences as her biographer. He told me the secrets she had confided in him. He told me about the people he had interviewed who had known Gwen well, and who had since died. When I went to the Fryer Library at the University of Queensland – the chief repository of Harwood's papers – to begin working my way through her unpublished letters, he was always there, at the other end of the phone, to answer my proliferating questions. Over the following years, he was always interested in where I had got to with my research, what I was doing, what I was writing. One day, he rang to say he had been having a bit of a clean-up and had discovered some old notes and papers relating to Harwood that I might want. A few weeks later, I visited his home in Carlton and, after a joyful afternoon, left with a suitcase full of priceless biographical material.

When I finished the first draft, he read every word (there were many more then), corrected a few errors and told me he was satisfied. It was a huge relief to me to have his approval. Even so, it never occurred to me that he might not be around when the book was published. His death in early 2021 was a shock I'm still feeling. I am very grateful for all he did to help bring this book into the world.

Alison Hoddinott has been equally helpful. I first met her in 2015 when I travelled to Armidale from Brisbane, where I was temporarily living while I worked at the Fryer. Like Greg, she was initially dubious about my biographical venture. In the early 1990s, when she was planning her own Harwood biography, she went to the National Library in Canberra to work with their Harwood manuscripts. When the Chief Librarian learned what she was doing, he said: 'I feel sorry for you.' These were pretty much Alison's sentiments about me. She knew too well what I was soon to learn – that Harwood delighted in leading earnest scholars on a merry chase.

Nevertheless, she was unfailingly generous to me. She shared with me her unparalleled knowledge of Gwen, garnered over a friendship of more than forty years, as well as the riches of her scholarly insight into her friend's poetry. She gave me the run of her filing cabinets and bookshelves, and let me rootle among papers and photographs. She also gave me a sense, in her own brisk, lively self, of both Gwen's and Bill's conversation – the lilt of their voices, their characteristic expressions. I am deeply grateful for her willingness to entertain my questions and tolerate my presence over a number of years.

I would also like to thank John Harwood, Gwen Harwood's eldest son and literary executor, for reading the manuscript and offering his insights with such warmth and generosity. I am most grateful to him, too, for granting me permission to quote from Harwood's unpublished writings.

The Fryer Library at the University of Queensland has been central to this project. To get my research off the ground, I spent six months there in 2015, making my way through thousands of pages of letters, diaries and manuscripts, under the kindly eye of a procession of knowledgeable, efficient and helpful librarians, for whom nothing was ever too much trouble. Joan Keating and Cassie Doyle, in particular, were invaluable. I am also very grateful to the Fryer Librarian, Simon Farley, who went in to bat for this project at a time when the challenges seemed insuperable. His feeling for and commitment to Australian literature are great assets to the scholarly community.

Throughout my research, the AustLit database, hosted by the University of Queensland, has been invaluable. It enabled me to easily access information about when and where Harwood's poems were first published, which works were published alongside them, the provenance of the journals themselves, and much more. Its contribution to scholarship in Australian literature is enormous.

I must also acknowledge the support of Central Queensland University in granting me a period of study leave so that I could spend a six-month period at the Fryer Library. In particular, I extend my thanks to the head of the School of Access Education, Karen Seary, for her ongoing support for this project.

In 2017, I was awarded the Hazel Rowley Literature Fellowship, which enabled me to spend several months in Tasmania, getting to know some of Harwood's places and devoting some undisturbed time to writing. The cheerful interest of Della Rowley and the other trustees, and their unfailing belief in the project, has been sustaining.

In Tasmania, I came to know Karen Darby, eldest daughter of Ann Jennings, who showed me the places Gwen shared with Ann on Bruny Island and Fern Tree, took me walking on kunanyi/Mt Wellington, invited me to stay in her beautiful Bruny hideaway and proved a cornucopia of endless riches: photographs, letters and manuscripts. I am especially grateful to her for letting me read Ann's unpublished diaries, fascinating personal and historical documents in themselves and invaluable for the light they shed on Harwood's earliest years in Tasmania.

I also want to thank Claire Blichfeldt, daughter of Charlotte Wilmot, for telling me about her early childhood and her extraordinary mother, and for trusting me with precious letters and photographs.

Above all, I want to thank Rosemary Cohen for telling me her story, allowing me to read her correspondence with Gwen and letting me handle *Little Buttercup's Picture Book*. I am so grateful to her for allowing me to add a beautiful, hidden dimension of Harwood's life to the public record.

Many other people have given me permission to read their Harwood correspondence and/or shared with me their memories of Harwood, and I thank them all for their time and generosity. Special thanks to Stuart Barnes, Robert Cox, Berenice Eastman, Stephen Edgar, Father John Flader, Laurie Hergenhan, Kevin Hart, Robyn Mathison, Roger McDonald, Desmond O'Grady, Craig Powell, Cassandra Pybus, Judith Rodriguez, Peter Rose, Andrew Sant, Thomas Shapcott, Larry Sitsky, Edgar Sleinis, Vivian Smith, Janet Upcher, Chris Wallace-Crabbe and Yvonne Withington.

On a personal level, I want to thank Jane Moore, Alice Priest and Suellen Choudhary, who took the journey with me – literally, on several memorable occasions, on several memorable beaches, headlands and hillsides. Special thanks to Alice, who went with me to mass at All Saints in Brisbane (and told me when it was okay to sneak out), waited patiently while I took endless photographs, and insisted I read 'The Sea Anemones' aloud when we found those 'gouts of blood' beneath the water at South Arm. All three were indefatigable in the matter of pep talks, cups of tea, listening ears and blind faith, and I'm so grateful for them all. My dad, too, has been there for me throughout the biography's gestation, while going through his own fairly harrowing journey. I owe him so much.

Thanks also to Gemma Mann, colleague extraordinaire, who never failed to ask me how the book was going – and to listen to the answer. Gemma also read draft chapters, as did John Fitzsimmons and Jane ('snippety-snip') Moore, for which they have my heartfelt thanks.

I owe a big debt of gratitude to my editors at Black Inc. / La Trobe University Press, Julia Carlomagno and Kate Hatch, for their great patience, extraordinary attention to detail, and for taking the inchoate mass of my manuscript and shaping it into something resembling a story.

I also want to thank Sally Bird, my agent, who has been so patient, so unfailingly interested, and so much fun to talk to over the many years of this project – as well as being a wonderful advocate for this book.

Finally, most importantly, I thank my husband, John, who has traipsed with me through churches in Hobart, cemeteries in Mornington, fields at Morpeth and second-hand book shops in Uralla, who has been endlessly interested, amused and responsive, and who has learned more about Gwen Harwood than anyone not writing a biography should ever have to know. I'm more grateful for him than I can say.

Sources

ABBREVIATIONS

In notes citing Gwen Harwood's correspondence, initials have been used for
Harwood and her most common correspondents:

A.&B.H.	Alison and Bill Hoddinott
A.F.	Alan Farrell
A.H.	Alison Hoddinott
A.J.	Ann Jennings
E.T.	Edwin Tanner
F.K.	Frank Kellaway
G.H.	Gwen Harwood
G.K.	Gregory Kratzmann
J.P.	James Penberthy
L.S.	Larry Sitsky
N.T.	Norman Talbot
R.C.	Rosemary Cohen
R.H.	Rex Hobcroft
T.R.	Tony Riddell
V.B.	Vincent Buckley
V.S.	Vivian Smith

MANUSCRIPT COLLECTIONS

Unpublished letters and manuscripts frequently cited in the notes are held in
the following collections at the Fryer Library, University of Queensland (FL);
National Library of Australia (NLA); and Special Collections, UNSW Canberra:

Vincent Buckley, letters to G.H.: FL, UQFL45, Box 1, Folder 6, and Box 28,
Folder 2; letters from G.H., NLA, Papers of Vincent Buckley 1952–1986
[manuscript], MS 7289, Series 1, Folders 1–3.

Alan Farrell, letters from G.H.: FL, UQFL340 Father Alan Farrell Collection,
Boxes 1–2.

Kevin Hart, letters from G.H.: NLA, Papers of Kevin Hart, 1968–2006
[manuscript], MS8016, Series 6, File 2.

Rex Hobcroft, letters from G.H.: NLA, Papers of Rex Hobcroft, 1907–2005
[manuscript], MS8019 & MSAcc06.015, Box 78, Folders 560–66.

Alison Hoddinott, letters from G.H.: FL, UQFL332, Box 1, 1960/1-1973; Box 2,
1973–1983; Box 3, 1984–1991; Accession 050824, 1990–1995.

A.D. Hope, letters to G.H.: FL, UQFL45, Box 2, Folder 6 (1959–1974), and Box 28, Folder 7.

Ann Jennings, letters from G.H.: FL, F3144 Letters to Ann Jennings 1956–1995; UQFL45, Box 14; UNSW Canberra, MSS311 Papers of Gwen Harwood and Ann Jennings Box 1, Folders 1–3.

Frank Kellaway, letters from G.H.: NLA, Papers of Frank Kellaway, 1942–2009 [manuscript], MS7071, Box 1, Folders 1–2.

Roger McDonald, letters to G.H.: FL, UQFL45, Box 2, Folder 16; letters from G.H.: FL, UQFL45, Box 7, Folder 3.

James Penberthy, letters from G.H.: NLA, Papers of James Penberthy 1935–2003 [manuscript], MS9748, Series 2, Folder 7.

Hal Porter, letters from G.H.: FL, UQFL45, Box 2, Folder 26; Box 7, Folder 1; Box 28, Folder 14.

Tony Riddell, letters from G.H.: FL, UQFL45, Box 7, Folders 4–18 (1942–1965); Box 8, Folders 1–11 (1966–1976), Box 11, Folder 5 (1975–1989).

Thomas Shapcott, letters from G.H.: NLA, Papers of Thomas Shapcott, 1946–1997 [manuscript], MS 5577, Folder 1.

Larry Sitsky, letters to and from G.H.: NLA, Papers of Larry Sitsky [manuscript], MS5630, Box 1, Folders 2–4; Box 16, Folders 141–42; Box 17, Folder 143; Box 34, Folders 260–61; Box 48, Folders 346–47; Box 65, Folder 449.

Vivian Smith, letters from G.H.: NLA, Papers of Dr Vivian Smith, MS 4853, Series 2, Folders 41–43.

Norman Talbot, letters to G.H.: FL, UQFL45 Box 5, Folder 1, Box 25, Folder 10; letters from G.H. in private collection, G.K.

G.H. Diaries: FL, UQFL45, Box 22, Diaries 1979–1991; Box 30, Diaries 1977–1978, 1992–1994.

PRIVATE COLLECTIONS

Private collections of correspondence with Gwen Harwood and other materials are held by:

Claire Blichfeldt (correspondence of Lotte Wilmot)

Rosemary Cohen

Karen Darby (correspondence of Ann Jennings, unpublished diaries of Ann Jennings, 1940–1961)

Alison Hoddinott

Gregory Kratzmann (letters from Gwen Harwood to Norman Talbot)

Craig Powell

Notes

INTRODUCTION

1   G.H, Letter to Stephen Edgar, 22 June 1992, FL, F3162 Letters and poems sent to Stephen Edgar 195[-]–1993, Series A/1-60.

2   Alison Hoddinott, pers. comm., 20 February 2015.

3   Alison Hoddinott and Greg Kratzmann, 'Celebrating Gwen Harwood', *Island*, no. 67, 1996, p. 26.

4   Gwen Harwood, *Blessed City: The Letters of Gwen Harwood to Thomas Riddell, January to September 1943*, ed. Alison Hoddinott, Angus & Robertson, North Ryde, 1990, p. 124.

5   G.H., Letter to A.H., 11 January 1962.

6   Andrew Taylor, 'Gwen Harwood: The Golden Child Aloft on Discourse', in Robert Sellick (ed.), *Gwen Harwood*, Centre for Research in the New Literatures in English, Adelaide, 1987, p. 73.

7   See, for example, G.H., Postcard to F.K., 22 August 1956. The 'stately flower' is from Tennyson's poem 'Isabel', depicting the perfect wife, while 'Burning Sappho' is from Byron's *Don Juan*.

8   Harwood, *A Steady Storm of Correspondence: Selected Letters of Gwen Harwood, 1943–1995*, ed. Gregory Kratzmann, University of Queensland Press, St Lucia, p. 66.

9   Chris Wallace-Crabbe, pers. comm., 26 October 2015. See also Chris Wallace-Crabbe (ed.), *Author! Author! Tales of Australian Literary Life*, Oxford University Press, Melbourne, 1998, p. 199.

10 G.H., Letter to L.S., 7 March 1977.

11 G.H., Letter to E.T., 26 September 1973: 'Jesus, Eddie, I have deformed myself to please others who were indifferent'; cf. G.H., Letter to A.J., 3 October 1972, referring to R.D. Laing's concept 'that family life causes most mental illness: to belong to the group you have to deform yourself by becoming what others require of you'.

12 Harwood, 'Chance Meeting', *Collected Poems, 1943–1995*, eds Alison Hoddinott and Gregory Kratzmann, University of Queensland Press, St Lucia, 2003, p. 160.

13 G.H., Letter to E.T., 24 September 1973.

14 Diane Dodwell, 'Worlds beyond Words: Gwen Harwood's *Selected Poems*', *Westerly*, no. 2, 1977, pp. 73–79, p. 78.

15 Peter Porter, 'Satires in C Major', *The Times Literary Supplement*, 9 May 2003.

16 G.H., Letter to J.P., 7 July 1974.

17 'Thomas the Rhymer', in Arthur Quiller Couch (ed.), *Oxford Book of English Verse 1250–1900*, Oxford University Press, Oxford, 1919.

CHAPTER 1

1   G.H., Postcard to N.T., 27 June 1975.

2   Harwood, 'The Richness of the Commonplace', in J.D. Gryse & A. Sant (eds), *Our Common Ground: A Celebration of Art, Place & Environment*, University of Tasmania, Hobart, 1994, p. 32.

3   This line from Goethe's *Mignon* was one of Harwood's preferred ways of referring to Brisbane: see e.g., the poem '1945' and her letter to V.S., 14 June 1959.

4   Harwood, 'The Richness of the Commonplace', p. 32.

5   Harwood, 'Goddess of the Crossroads', in *The Present Tense*, HarperCollins, Pymble, 1995, p. 42; see also Gwen Harwood, 'Freely They Stood Who Stood', in *Collected Poems*, p. 494.

6   Harwood, 'Goddess of the Crossroads'.

7   G.H., Letter to E.T., 3 April 1961; Gwen Harwood, 'Four Impromptus', in *Collected Poems*, p. 166.

8   G.H., Letter to E.T., 18 May 1973. See also G.H., Letter to Craig Powell, 16 December 1982; Stephen Edgar, 'An Interview with Gwen Harwood', *Island Magazine*, no. 25–26, Summer–Autumn, 1986, pp. 74–76.

9   Alison Hoddinott, pers. comm.

10   G.H., Letter to A.H., 12 March 1984; Edgar, 'An Interview with Gwen Harwood'.

11   There are several contenders for the honour of being Harwood's 'earliest memory'. She told Rex Hobcroft (n.d. [1963?]) and Ann Jennings (22 June 1960) that her earliest memories were of her grandmother adjuring her to remember (see also 'Estuary', in *Collected Poems*, p. 173), but she told Vivian Smith that her 'earliest memories are of being dandled on knees at functions' (20 December 1958) and A.D. Hope that the story of 'The Glass Jar' was her earliest memory (14 March 1961).

12   Edgar, 'An Interview with Gwen Harwood'; see also Harwood, 'Richness of the Commonplace', p. 31.

13   G.H., Letter to A.J., 22 June 1960. The eclipse is documented in 'The Solar Eclipse', *The Worker* (Brisbane), 28 September 1922, p. 6.

14   Harwood, 'Richness of the Commonplace', p. 31.

15   Stephen Edgar, 'In Memory of Gwen Harwood: 1920–1995', Stephen Edgar website, 14–15 December 1996, http://www.stephenedgar.com.au/newsite/selected-prose/18-in-memory-of-gwen-harwood.

16   Harwood, 'The Double Image', in *Collected Poems*, p. 106.

17   G.H., Letter to A.J., 9 March 1960; Letter to A.H., January 1992.

18   Harwood, 'In Zurich by the Tideless Lake', in *Collected Poems*, p. 39.

19   Harwood, 'Lamplit Presences', *Southerly*, vol. 40, no. 3, 1980, p. 248; see also Gwen Harwood, Interview with Alison Hoddinott (transcript), National Library of Australia, Canberra, 1988, pp. 10–11.

20   Harwood, Interview with Hoddinott, p. 79.

21   G.H., Letter to A.F., 7 April 1994.

22   See Harwood, 'Among the Roses', 'Goddess of the Crossroads', 'Gemini' and 'The Glass Boy', in *The Present Tense*, pp. 33–65. On her attempt to write an

autobiography, see Peter Ward, 'The Poet As a Prize Winner', *The Australian*, 17 November 1978.

23 G.H., Letter to T.R., 6 January 1964.

24 G.H., Letter to V.S., 7 January 1964.

25 Harwood, 'Words and Music', *Southerly*, vol. 46, no. 4, 1986, pp. 357–76, especially p. 369; Harwood, 'Lamplit Presences', p. 247.

26 Harwood, 'Little Buttercup's Picture Book', in *Collected Poems*, p. 445.

27 *The Townsville Daily Bulletin*, 15 December 1915; *The Western Champion and General Advertiser*, 13 July 1897, p. 6.

28 The Rockhampton newspaper, *The Morning Bulletin*, contains many laudatory accounts of Maud's community work during World War I; Harwood noted that Maud was 'highly skilled in all the domestic arts': 'Lamplit Presences', p. 247.

29 G.H., Letter to T.R., 25 February 1960. The letters pages of Rockhampton's *The Morning Bulletin* in 1919 show that she did not hesitate to take the mayor to task.

30 G.H., Letter to A.F., 30 August 1994; cf. G.H., Letter to Fr John Flader, 29 January 1995, private collection: Maud 'was afraid of nothing'.

31 She passed the crocodile skin – supposed proof of this feat – on to Gwen's daughter, Mary: G.H., Letter to Craig Powell, 5 September 1981, private collection.

32 *The Tie that Binds: A History of the Brisbane Branch of the Old Girls' Association of the Rockhampton Girls' Grammar School, 1933–1993*, Brisbane Branch of the Old Girls' Association of the Rockhampton Girls' Grammar School, Brisbane, 1993.

33 Joseph Richard Foster, Statement of Service, National Archives of Australia.

34 At the end of the war, Joe Foster made a speech warmly extolling the 'excellent bond of sympathy existing between Mrs Jaggard and the returned soldiers': *Capricornian*, 28 December 1918, p. 15.

35 Harwood, Interview with Hoddinott, p. 6.

36 Ibid.

37 *The Morning Bulletin*, 21 October 1918, p. 6.

38 G.H., Letter to Craig Powell, 16 December 1982.

39 Harwood, 'Time beyond Reason', in Sellick, *Gwen Harwood*, pp. 15–16.

40 Harwood, The Richness of the Commonplace', p. 31.

41 Harwood, Interview with Hoddinott, p. 69; Harwood, 'Lamplit Presences', p. 248.

42 G.H., Letter to A.J., 11 May 1960.

43 Harwood, 'Lamplit Presences', p. 248.

44 Gwen Harwood, Interview with Diana Ritch, recording, 1990, National Library of Australia.

45 'Lamplit Presences', p. 248.

46 G.H., Letter to V.S., 20 December 1958.

47 Harwood, Interview with Hoddinott, p. 67.

48 'Coin Evening', *The Telegraph* (Brisbane), 29 October 1928.

49 Gwen Harwood, *Blessed City*, p. 143.

50 Ibid.

51 Harwood, Interview with Hoddinott, p. 7.

52 His 'vigorous recruiting address[es]' stretched the truth to breaking point: see e.g. *Maryborough Chronicle, Wide Bay and Burnett Advertiser*, 6 May 1918, p. 3.

53 Harwood, Interview with Hoddinott, p. 25.

54 Ibid., p. 24.

55 Harwood, *Blessed City*, p. 70.

56 Harwood, Interview with Hoddinott, p. 23.

57 Harwood, 'Words and Music', p. 369.

58 G.H., Letter to E.T., 12 February 1968.

59 *The Telegraph* (Brisbane), 25 September 1926, p. 14.

60 G.H., Letter to E.T., 19 March 1968, 18 May 1973.

61 Harwood, Interview with Hoddinott, p. 8; Harwood, 'Religious Instruction', in *Collected Poems*, p. 370.

62 Harwood, Interview with Hoddinott, p. 23.

63 G.H., Letter to E.T., 18 May 1973; see also Ibid., p. 8.

64 Gwen Harwood, 'Gemini', in *The Present Tense*, p. 51.

65 Harwood, Interview with Hoddinott, p. 20.

66 G.H., Letter to E.T., 18 May 1973; 24 September 1973.

67 Harwood, 'A Piece of Ivory', in *Collected Poems*, p. 507.

68 Edgar, 'An Interview with Gwen Harwood', n.p.

69 Harwood, *A Steady Storm of Correspondence*, pp. 160–61. John Berryman describes a similar revelation in his poem 'Homage to Mistress Bradstreet', published in 1956 (cf. Eileen Simpson, *Poets in Their Youth: A Memoir*, new ed., Farrar, Straus and Giroux, New York, 1990, pp. 225–26).

70 Harwood, *A Steady Storm of Correspondence*, pp. 160–61.

71 'the child is myself, the dream real': G.H., Letter to A.D. Hope, 14 March 1961, in Ibid., p. 119.

72 G.H., Letter to E.T., 3 April 1961.

73 Harwood, 'Words and Music', p. 368.

74 Harwood, 'Freely They Stood Who Stood', p. 493.

75 Harwood, 'Time beyond Reason', pp. 13–14; see also Gwen Harwood, 'Syntax of the Mind', in *Collected Poems*, p. 432.

76 Harwood, 'Goddess of the Crossroads', p. 45.

77 G.H., Letter to E.T., 19 March 1968 (see also Harwood's poems 'Religious Instruction' and 'Syntax of the Mind' and her story 'Goddess of the Crossroads').

78 G.H., Letter to Craig Powell, 21 January 1991.

79 G.H., Letter to E.T., 24 September 1973.

80 G.H., Letter to E.T., 2 July 1961; see also Letter to E.T., 24 September 1973.

81 See e.g. 'Religious Instruction'.

82 Greg Kratzmann, pers. comm.

83 Harwood, Interview with Hoddinott, p. 94.

84 Quoted in Giles Hugo, 'Gwen's Wild Passion and Strict Structures', *The Saturday Mercury*, 7 October 1989, p. 19; see also Harwood, Interview with Hoddinott, p. 27.

CHAPTER 2

1 Harwood, Interview with Hoddinott, p. 24.

2 Harwood, 'A Scattering of Ashes', in *Collected Poems*, p. 352.

3 John Hale (int.), 'Beyond the Black Stump', Radio program, tape recording (no date or source given), FL, UQFL332, Acc 050824, Box 1.

4 Harwood, 'Words and Music', p. 367.

5 See Harwood, 'Affetuoso' and 'The Magic Land of Music', in *Collected Poems*, pp. 380 & 405.

6 Hale, 'Beyond the Black Stump'.

7 'Bandsman 40 Years', *The Courier Mail*, n.d., FL, UQFL45, Box 23.

8 Harwood, Interview with Hoddinott, p. 28.

9 Ibid.

10 Harwood, 'Memoirs of a Dutiful Librettist', in Sellick, *Gwen Harwood*, p. 2.

11 Harwood, Interview with Hoddinott, p. 29.

12 Harwood, 'Words and Music', p. 371.

13 Harwood, Interview with Hoddinott, p. 3.

14 Ibid., p. 8; G.H., Letter to E.T., 18 May 1973.

15 *The Courier Mail*, 11 May 1937.

16 Harwood, Interview with Hoddinott, p. 13.

17 Harwood, Interview with Ritch.

18 Harwood, 'Time beyond Reason', p. 370; see also Gwen Harwood, 'Night and Dreams' II, in *Collected Poems*, p. 399.

19 Harwood, *Blessed City*, p. 43; Harwood, Interview with Ritch; cf. G.H., Letter to Lucinda Foster, 18 January 1991; and Joe Foster, Letter to G.H., 5 September 1991, FL, UQFL45, Box 18, Folder 5.

20 G.H., Letter to V.S., 7 January 1964.

21 John Beston, 'An Interview with Gwen Harwood', *Quadrant*, vol. 19, no. 7, 1975, pp. 84–88; Harwood, 'Words and Music', p. 370; G.H., Letter to E.T., 2 February 1968, in *A Steady Storm of Correspondence*, p. 214.

22 John Pearn, *Auchenflower: The Suburb and the Name*, Amphion Press, Brisbane, 1997, p. 149; see also Harwood, *Blessed City*, pp. 50–51.

23 Pearn, p. 143.

24 Harwood, 'Time beyond Reason', pp. 14–15.

25 Ibid., p. 15; cf. G.H., Letter to N.T., 27 April 1976.

26 Margaret Deeth, Robert Spiers and June Packman, *Toowong State School Centenary 1880–1980*, Toowong State School, Toowong, 1980, n.p. The authors

note that in the late 1920s, the school was dangerously overcrowded.

27 Harwood, Interview with Ritch.

28 G.H., Letter to V.S., 4 February 1959, in *A Steady Storm of Correspondence*, p. 68. This incident would form the basis of the 'Religious Instruction' poem of 'Seven Philosophical Poems', in *Collected Poems*, p. 287.

29 See e.g., her ironic apostrophe in her letter to T.R. of 29 October 1959: 'Ah, the tender lambs of Jesus. How lovely to be a parent. Who can express the rewards of parenthood?'

30 G.H., Letter to T.R., 23 February 1968, in *A Steady Storm of Correspondence*, p. 217. According to Joe Foster Jr., the local police had a standing invitation to join the party: Letter to G.K., 1995, FL, UQFL45, Box 21, Folder 2.

31 Harwood, 'Time beyond Reason', p. 15.

32 G.H., Letter to T.R., 23 February 1968, in *A Steady Storm of Correspondence*, pp. 216–17.

33 Ibid.

34 Harwood, 'Words and Music', p. 370.

35 Ibid.; see also Harwood, Interview with Hoddinott, p. 29.

36 G.H., Letter to V.B., 20 November 1962.

37 *The Courier Mail*, 7 December 1936, p. 20.

38 *The Courier Mail*, 8 May 1940.

39 Harwood, Interview with James Murdoch (videorecording), The Writers: Archival Film Series, P. Campbell (producer), Australia Council, Sydney, 1987.

40 Harwood, Interview with Hoddinott, pp. 29–30.

41 G.H., Letter to V.S., 27 December 1958.

42 G.H., Letter to N.T., 20 August 1980, referring to Harwood's 'Words and Music'.

43 Harwood, 'Time beyond Reason', p. 16. See also, e.g., references to her 'wretched adolescent muddles' (Letter to E.T., 26 May 1958), her 'stormy adolescent troubles' (Letter to T.R., 21 June 1957), and her 'troublesome adolescence' (Letter to A.J., 24 December 1969).

44 G.H., Letter to N.T., 20 August 1980.

45 Harwood, 'Past and Present', in *Collected Poems*, p. 176.

46 Harwood, Interview with Ritch.

47 G.H., Letter to T.R., 25 February 1960, in *A Steady Storm of Correspondence*, p. 91.

48 G.H., Letter to E.T., 2 February 1968; see also Harwood, *A Steady Storm of Correspondence*, p. 214.

49 G.H., Letter to T.R., 6 August 1962.

50 G.H., Letter to A.J., 12 April 1967.

51 G.H., Letter to E.T., 2 February 1968, in *A Steady Storm of Correspondence*, p. 214; G.H., Letter to T.R., 5 November 1959, in *A Steady Storm of Correspondence*, p. 84.

52 Gwen Harwood, 'An All-Purpose Festival Poem', in *Collected Poems*, p. 566.

53 G.H., Letter to A.J., 17 April 1961.

54 Harwood, Interview with Hoddinott, p. 21.

55 Amanda Bell, 'Our Unending Heritage: A Critical Biography Based on the Life of Ella Osborn Fry', PhD Thesis, University of Technology Sydney, 2008, pp. 35–36.

56 Joyce Dempsey (nee Chandler), 'Old School Ties', blog post, Brisbane Girls Grammar School website, 29 August 2012, www.bggs.qld.edu.au/2012/08/old-school-ties.

57 G.H., Letter to E.T., 3 April 1961.

58 Harwood, *A Steady Storm of Correspondence*, p. 6.

59 G.H., Letter to V.S., [2 April 1959?].

60 G.H., Letter to T.R., 7 July 1958.

61 *The Central Queensland Herald*, 25 August 1938, p. 52.

62 G.H., Letter to A.J., 30 July 1974; 'Seasons: To the Memory of Lexie MacMillan', BGGS school magazine, 1975.

63 Hugo, 'Gwen's Wild Passion', p. 19.

64 Jenny Digby (ed.), *A Woman's Voice: Conversations with Australian Poets*, University of Queensland Press, St Lucia, 1996, p. 62; see also Ann-Marie Priest, '"Colour and Crazy Love": Gwen Harwood and Vera Cottew', *Southerly*, vol. 73, no. 3, pp. 26–41.

65 'Birdlike': G.H., Letter to Craig Powell, 5 September 1981.

66 G.H., Letter to R.H., [8 June 1970?].

67 G.H., Letter to Craig Powell, 5 September 1981.

68 Harwood, 'Past and Present' I; see Harwood, Interview with Ritch for the origins of this poem.

69 G.H., Letter to A.H., 27 July 1983; Digby, *A Woman's Voice*, p. 63.

70 Harwood, 'Nasturtiums', part III of 'The Sharpness of Death', in *Collected Poems*, p. 296.

71 'Personal Paragraphs', *The Morning Bulletin*, 15 July 1940; Harwood, 'Memoirs of a Dutiful Librettist', p. 3.

72 'My letters to [Vera] (from 1935 to 1950) were returned to me in her will; but since old Moth was the one who got the packet she treated them as of equal status with mountains of other old stuff and had a bonfire': G.H., Letter to A.H., 27 July 1983.

73 The artist Ella Fry noted that Vera 'became a very close friend after I left school': cited in Bell, 'Our Unending Heritage', p. 48.

74 Harwood, Interview with Ritch.

75 Queensland State Archives.

76 Harwood, Interview with Hoddinott, p. 64.

CHAPTER 3

1 G.H., Letter to V.B., 20 November 1962.

2 Harwood, Interview with Murdoch.

3 Harwood, 'Suburban Sonnet', in *Collected Poems*, p. 159.

4 *The Courier Mail*, 23 October 1937, p. 17.

5   Harwood, 'Gainful Employment', in Andrew Sant (ed.), *Toads : Australian Writers: Other Work, Other Lives*, Allen & Unwin, North Sydney, pp. 48–49.

6   Samantha Owens, 'Robert Dalley-Scarlett (1887–1959) and Handel Reception in Australia between the World Wars', *Musicology Australia*, vol. 34, no. 2, 2012, pp. 165–83.

7   Ibid., p. 177.

8   Franz Holford, 'Robert Dalley-Scarlett: Obituary', *Canon*, August, 1959; see also A.W., 'Robert Dalley-Scarlett', *The Bulletin*, 12 August 1959.

9   Quotations in this paragraph are from *People*, 23 April 1952, cited in E.J. Lea-Scarlett, 'Robert Dalley-Scarlett Part II', *Descent*, vol. 2, no. 1, 1963, pp. 3–19, pp. 15–16; and Ernest Briggs, 'The Unappeasable Mind: Memorial Lecture on Robert Dalley-Scarlett', FAW (Qld), 1961, unpublished, FL, UQFL38, Box 2, Folder 5. 'Mr Magoo': Greg Kratzmann, pers. comm., 24 August 2014.

10 G.H., Letter to V.S., 13 October 1960.

11 G.H., Letter to G.K., 1 March 1994.

12 Peter Roennfeldt, pers. comm., 9 May 2016.

13 In her seventies, Harwood would say that a man she worked with in the 1940s was 'a feeler-upper': 'We used to warn the new girls about his improper hands. If you bent over his desk with some papers he'd slide his hand gently up your stocking and snap your suspender' (G.H., Letter to A.H., 28 February 1990). She insisted, however, that this did not make him 'offensive': 'he was just a suspender-snapper and everyone knew it' (G.H., Letter to A.H., 11 March 1993).

14 *Western Argus*, 22 March 1921, p. 12.

15 Harwood, Interview with Hoddinott, p. 104.

16 Newspaper accounts record Gwen attending, for instance, the last Brisbane performance of French organist Marcel Dupré with Bob and Joyce, and going alone with Joyce to the Princess Theatre for the opening night of a University Dramatic Society production of *Tilly of Bloomsbury*.

17 Letter to Joyce Dalley-Scarlett from 'Knox', 4 August 1959, FL, UQFL38, Box 2, Folder 1.

18 Eileen Simpson, *Poets in Their Youth: A Memoir*, new ed., Farrar, Straus and Giroux, New York, 1990, pp. 5–6.

19 Kathleen Spivack writes of the women who married the 'genius' American poets of the 1960s: 'Wives of that era seemed to have a heroic tolerance'. Kathleen Spivack, *With Robert Lowell and His Circle: Sylvia Plath, Anne Sexton, Elizabeth Bishop, Stanley Kunitz, and Others*, Northeastern University Press, Boston, 2012, p. 147. See also Drusilla Modjeska's discussion of the implications of Stravinsky's domestic requirements in *Stravinsky's Lunch*, Pan Macmillan Australia, Sydney, 1999.

20 She expresses this view in letters in relation to the affairs of married friends such as Frank Kellaway, Ann Jennings and Graeme Hetherington, as well as enacting it in her own marriage.

21 See e.g., G.H., Letter to V.B., 20 November 1961, NLA, MS 7289/1/1-3.

22 See e.g., G.H., Letter to V.S., 20 December 1958.

23 The poems 'A Simple Story' and 'David's Harp' are both based on real-life incidents from Harwood's youth.

24 Gregory Kratzmann, pers. comm., 24 August 2014.

25 G.H., Letters to G.K., 13 February 1994; 14 February 1994.

26 Gregory Kratzmann, pers. comm., 24 August 2014.

27 G.H., Letter to G.K., 14 February 1994.

28 *Western Argus*, 22 March 1921, p. 12.

29 Note by Gwen Harwood attached to book of Dalley-Scarlett compositions, FL, UQFL45, Box 25.

30 G.H., Letter to G.K., 13 February 1994.

31 *Collected Poems*, p. 356; 'The Silver Swan' 'refers back' to another Kröte poem, 'Fever': 'the child [in 'Fever'] is now the woman who finds him old' (G.H., Letter to A.H., 12 July 1981).

32 In a 1958 letter, Harwood mentions that she is working on an Eisenbart poem, evidently 'Prize-Giving', in which 'he meets his mistress at a girls' school speech night': G.H., Letter to V.S., 1 December 1958. 'Prize-Giving' was not the first Eisenbart poem she wrote, however; that was 'Early Light'.

33 As Jennifer Strauss argues, 'all the Eisenbart poems show the man of intellect struggling with the fact that he is not exempt from the two aspects of common fortune, love and death': *Boundary Conditions: The Poetry of Gwen Harwood*, University of Queensland Press, St Lucia, 1992, p. 68.

34 Harwood, 'Time beyond Reason', p. 16; see also Harwood, Interview with Murdoch: Harwood explains that she 'hadn't at that time really understood how a good pianist should be out and clear by the time they're about fifteen'.

35 Contributors' Notes, *Meanjin Papers*, vol. 3, no. 3, 1944.

36 Eric Cassidy wrote 'mystical poems' she set to music: G.H., Letter to A.H., 28 February 1990; 'Will' asked her to write a song for him: *A Steady Storm of Correspondence*, pp. 73–74.

37 G.H., Letter to G.K., in *A Steady Storm of Correspondence*, p. 7; G.H., Letter to N.T. (referred to in a letter to G.H., 12 February 1979, FL, UQFL45, Box 16, Folder 29). The prose version she gives in a letter to V.B. (20 November 1961) differs in some respects from the poem: e.g. the attempted 'seduction' happens outside, rather than in a hotel room.

38 Harwood, 'Gainful Employment', p. 48; see also Harwood, 'Time beyond Reason', p. 16.

39 G.H., Letter to V.S., 20 January 1959.

40 G.H., Letter to A.H., 2 May 1985.

41 Harwood, 'Words and Music', p. 371; Owens, 'Robert Dalley-Scarlett (1887–1959)', p. 172.

42 G.H., Letter to T.R., 19 October 1956; 4 December 1958.

43 G.H., Letter to V.B., 26 September 1961. The 'Scottish tenor' is the subject of the poem 'David's Harp': G.H., Letter to V.S., 25 June 1959, in *A Steady Storm of Correspondence*, pp. 73–4.

44 G.H., Letters to T.R., 26 August 1958; 19 October 1956. Cf. versions of these stories in Harwood, 'Words and Music', p. 372.

45 *The Telegraph* (Brisbane), 1 May 1940, p. 14.

46 'Promising Pianist', *The Courier Mail*, 8 May 1940.

47 'Fine Music, Elocution At Prize-giving', *The Courier Mail*, 18 May 1940.

48 Harwood, *A Steady Storm of Correspondence*, pp. 53–54.

49 Harwood, 'Time beyond Reason', p. 16.

CHAPTER 4

1 D.L. Kissick, *All Saints Church Brisbane 1862–1937*, All Saints Parish, Brisbane, 1937, p. 11.

2 G.H., Letter to E.T., 26 May 1958; Harwood, 'Words and Music', p. 372.

3 G.H., Letter to E.T., 19 March 1968.

4 G.H., Letter to Roger MacDonald, 7 December 1969, in *A Steady Storm of Correspondence*, p. 239.

5 G.H., Letter to T.R., 28 May 1970, in Ibid., p. 248.

6 G.H., Letter to F.K., 11 March 1980.

7 G.H., Letter to G.K., 12 September 1991.

8 Harwood, 'Time beyond Reason', p. 17.

9 Harwood, *Blessed City*, pp. 17, 49.

10 G.H., Letter to A.F., 5 June 1994.

11 G.H., Letter to G.K., 13 February 1994.

12 G.H., Letter to A.J., 23 October 1992: all of her contemporaries 'had been in love with him long ago. He told us individually he'd loved us all "But you best", the old demon'. Elsewhere, she wrote that he 'had a way of making each of us seem gifted and special': Harwood, 'Words and Music', p. 372.

13 Trinity College magazines 1935–1938, University of Melbourne.

14 Harwood, 'Words and Music', p. 372; G.H., Letter to T.R., 17 November 1958.

15 G.H., Letter to A.H., 15 March 1983.

16 G.H., Letter to A.H., 13 September 1990.

17 Gwen Harwood, Interview with Mark Davies, *Northern Perspective*, vol. 18, no. 1, 1995, pp. 55–62.

18 G.H., Letter to A.H., 27 June 1995; see also Edgar, 'An Interview'.

19 Harwood, 'Gainful Employment', p. 50. Years later, she would change her mind about *Ulysses*, telling Alison Hoddinott that she found it 'so depressing that I can't enjoy it' (G.H., Letter to A.H., 21 August 1991).

20 Harwood, 'Words and Music', p. 372; Edgar, 'An Interview'; Harwood, Interview with Murdoch.

21 Kissick, *All Saints Church Brisbane*.

22 Harwood, *Blessed City*, p. 178.

23 G.H., Letter to E.T., 28 May 1958.

24 Quotations from Harwood, 'Time beyond Reason' (p. 17) and 'Words and Music' (p. 372).

25 Ross Fitzgerald, *From 1915 to the Early 1980's: A History of Queensland*, University of Queensland Press, St. Lucia, 1984.

26 Harwood, 'Time beyond Reason', p. 19.

27 Harwood, *Blessed City*, pp. 121, 122.

28 Ibid., excised passage from Letter 58, FL, UQFL45, Box 7, Folder 4.

29 Ibid, p. 124.

30 Harwood, Interview with Davies, p. 61.

31 Harwood, 'Words and Music', p. 374.

32 Ibid., pp. 374–75. This couple, whom Harwood identifies as a 'married couple, both doctors', may have been Dr Gertrude Langer, an art historian, and her husband, Dr Karl Langer: see Michele Elizabeth Anderson, 'Barjai, Miya Studio and Young Brisbane Artists of the 1940's: Towards a Radical Practice', BA (Hons) thesis, University of Queensland, 1987, pp. 68–69.

33 G.H., Letter to G.K., 13 February 1994 (private collection).

34 Harwood, *Blessed City*, p. 18.

35 Ibid., p. 21.

36 Peter Bennie, Letter to G.H., 24 April 1993, FL, UQFL45, Box 18, Folder 2.

37 Peter Roennfeldt, 'Dalley-Scarlett, Robert (1887–1959)', *Australian Dictionary of Biography*, National Centre of Biography, Australian National University, http://adb.anu.edu.au/biography/dalley-scarlett-robert-5870/text9985.

38 Harwood, Interview with Ritch.

CHAPTER 5

1 G.H., Letter to E.T., 26 May 1958; see also, e.g., references to the Sisters of Mercy in Harwood, 'The Glass Boy', in *The Present Tense*, HarperCollins, Pymble, 1995, p. 58.

2 Harwood, *Blessed City*, p. 186.

3 Ibid., p. 32.

4 Ibid., p. 186.

5 Ibid., p. 32.

6 'Another Country', unpublished, FL, UQFL45, Box 9, Folder 3.

7 See Harwood, *Blessed City*, p. 186.

8 Kissick, *All Saints Church Brisbane*, p. 64.

9 In a 1942 letter, she tells of three friends from All Saints who have either joined or intend to join convents: Harwood, *Blessed City*, excised passage from Letter 3, FL, UQFL45, Box 7, Folder 4.

10 G.H., Letter to T.R., 21 June 1957.

11 In 'The Feast of Gwendoline' (in *Collected Poems*, p. 556), she writes of being 'changed from sex kitten into wife'.

12 'Rule of the Handmaids of St Clare', Records & Archives Centre, Diocese of Brisbane, Anglican Church of Australia, SSFRS 165-5.

13 Harwood, *Blessed City*, pp. 39, 40, 43.

14 Harwood, 'Time beyond Reason', p. 19.

15 Ibid., pp. 19–20; Hoddinott and Kratzmann, 'Celebrating Gwen Harwood', pp. 18–27.

16 Harwood, 'Words and Music', p. 374.

17 Sr Clare Elisabeth, 'Notes on the Community of the Daughters of St Clare', Records & Archives Centre, Diocese of Brisbane, Anglican Church of Australia, SSFRS165-3 Miscellaneous, Folder SSF BI4 B3.

18 G.H., Letter to A.H., 28 February 1990.

19 Harwood, 'Words and Music', p. 374.

20 Harwood, *Blessed City*, p. 35.

21 Ibid., p. 195.

22 Ibid., p. 126.

23 Ibid., pp. 204–05.

24 Ibid., p. 204.

25 Ibid., pp. 108; Harwood, *A Steady Storm of Correspondence*, p. 14.

26 G.H., Letter to A.H., 28 February 1990; see also Ibid., p. 426: her friend was Dorothy Foreman.

27 Harwood, *Blessed City*, p. 186.

28 Harwood, *A Steady Storm of Correspondence*, p. 426.

29 Harwood, *Blessed City*, p. 20.

30 Gregory Kratzmann, pers. comm., 24 August 2014.

31 Harwood, *A Steady Storm of Correspondence*, p. 239; Jan Bennie, 'Memoir on the Life of Joyce Lillian Bennie', unpublished ms., All Saints Church archives, Brisbane.

32 G.H., Letter to F.K., 11 March 1980; cf. Ibid., p. 239.

33 Harwood, *A Steady Storm of Correspondence*, p. 65; G.H., Letter to E.T., 26 May 1958.

34 John A. Moses, 'Peter Bennie at All Saints, Wickham Terrace, and as Editor of *The Australian Church Quarterly*, 1952–1963', Project Canterbury website, accessed 25 January 2022, http://anglicanhistory.org/aus/moses_bennie.pdf, p. 2.

CHAPTER 6

1 Fitzgerald, *From 1915 to the Early 1980s*.

2 Harwood, 'Time beyond Reason', p. 18.

3 The venture was extremely successful, raising more than ten thousand pounds: 'Opportunity Shop Very Popular', *The Telegraph* (Brisbane), 25 March 1944, p. 2.

4 'School That Is Real Home', *Courier-Mail*, 30 May 1940, pp. 13–14; Lee Butterworth, *St Christopher's Lodge (1934–1959)*, Find & Connect website, 2014, www.findandconnect.gov.au/guide/qld/QE00439.

5 Harwood, *A Steady Storm of Correspondence*, pp. 165–67.

6 Ibid, pp. 165–67.

7 Ibid., p. 174; Harwood, *Blessed City*, excised part of Letter 37, 11 May 1943, FL, UQFL45, Box 7, Folder 4.

8 Harwood, *A Steady Storm of Correspondence* p. 167.

9 Ibid., pp. 165–67.

10 Harwood, *Blessed City*, p. 108.

11 Ibid., pp. 212–13.

12 Ibid., excised section of Letter 37, FL, UQFL45, Box 7, Folder 4.

13 Ibid., p. 49.

14 Ibid., pp. 58–59; see also p. 48.

15 Ibid., pp. 48–49

16 Ibid., p. 63; see also pp. 48–49.

17 G.H., Letter to T.R., 22 June 1959.

18 See e.g., Harwood, *Blessed City*, p. 129. The unexpurgated letter contains a more extensive discussion of English mysticism.

19 Fitzgerald, *From 1915 to the Early 1980s*, pp. 106, 107.

20 Judith Wright, 'Brisbane in Wartime', *Overland*, no. 100, September 1985, p. 65.

21 Fitzgerald, *From 1915 to the Early 1980s*, pp. 106, 107.

22 Raymond Evans and Jacqui Donegan, 'The Battle of Brisbane', *Politics and Culture*, no. 4, 2004.

23 Wright, 'Brisbane in Wartime', pp. 64–68.

24 Harwood, 'Gainful Employment', p. 49.

25 The American Postal Exchange was destroyed during the riot known as the 'Battle of Brisbane': John Hammond Moore, *Over-Sexed, Over-Paid & Over Here: Americans in Australia 1941–1945*, University of Queensland Press, St Lucia, 1981, p. 218.

26 Harwood, 'Gainful Employment', p. 51.

27 G.H., Letter to A.H., 28 February 1990.

28 Harwood, *Blessed City*, pp. 85–86.

29 Ibid., p. 146.

30 Ibid., p. 167.

31 Ibid., p. 53.

32 G.H., Letter to T.R., 25 September 1958.

33 'Obituaries', *Great Scot*, September 2004, https://www.scotch.vic.edu.au/greatscot/2004sepgs/obit.htm; *The Argus*, 22 November 1937.

34 *Blessed City* ms., Letter 116, early May 1944, FL, UQFL45, Box 7, Folder 4.

35 William Hartston, 'Beachcomber: The World's Oldest Newspaper Columnist Is 100 Years Old Today', *Daily Express*, 2 August 2017.

36 Harwood, *Blessed City*, pp. 101, 83.

37 See e.g., ibid., p. 101.

38 Ibid., pp. 101, 218, 219.

39 Ibid., p. 145.

40 A selection of Gwen's letters from this time was published in 1990 as *Blessed City*. Tony's letters to Gwen have not survived.

41 *Blessed City* ms., excised section, 1943, FL, UQFL45, Box 7, Folder 4.

42 *Blessed City* ms., Letter 116, [11 or 18 May 1944?], FL, UQFL45, Box 7, Folder 4.

43 G.H., Letter to A.H., 28 February 1990.

44 G.H, *Blessed City*, p. 112.

45 Ibid., p. 220: quoted material includes excised section from Letter 65, FL, UQFL45, Box 7, Folder 4.

46 Ibid., p. 212.

47 Ibid., p. 136.

48 Ibid., p. 134.

49 *Blessed City* ms., [1944?], FL, UQFL45, Box 7, Folder 4.

50 Harwood, *Blessed City*, pp. 289–90.

51 Ibid., p. 112.

52 Ibid., p. 128.

53 On the devastating inner conflict this created for Harwood's slightly younger American contemporaries, Anne Sexton and Sylvia Plath, see Spivack, *With Robert Lowell and His Circle*, ch. 25.

54 Harwood, *Blessed City*, p. 242.

55 Gwen Harwood, Diary, 23 July 1992.

56 *Blessed City* ms., Letter 93, FL, UQFL45, Box 7, Folder 4.

57 Ibid., Letter 96 (19/20 January 1944), FL, UQFL45, Box 7, Folder 4.

58 Karen Lamb, *Thea Astley: Inventing Her Own Weather*, University of Queensland Press, St Lucia, 2015, pp. 51-55; Wright, 'Brisbane in Wartime', p. 64.

59 Harwood, *Blessed City*, p. 221; quotation includes excised sentence from Letter 65, FL, UQFL45, Box 7, Folder 4.

60 Ibid., p. 222.

61 Ibid., p. 224.

62 Her copy of the 1939 edition of Mark Van Doren's *An Anthology of World Poetry*, heavily annotated, has her maiden name, Gwendoline Foster, on the flyleaf.

63 Excised part of Letter 37, *Blessed City* ms., 11 May 1943, FL, UQFL45, Box 7, Folder 4.

64 G.H., Letter to A.J., 27 August 1963.

65 *Blessed City* ms. Letter 108, 21 March, FL, UQFL45, Box 7, Folder 4.

66 Ibid., Letter 91, [December 1943?], FL, UQFL45, Box 7, Folder 4.

67 Ibid., Letter 93, 8 January 1944, FL, UQFL45, Box 7, Folder 4.

68 Harwood, Interview with Ritch.

69 G.H., Letter to Craig Powell, 21 January 1991: 'I'd probably have married [Manfred] at the end of the war if I hadn't met Bill (physically the same type as Manfred).'

70 Harwood, *Blessed City*, p. 109 (ellipsis in original).

71 Ibid., p. 135.

72 See e.g., ibid., pp. 175, 17.

73 Ibid., p. 84.

74 Ibid., p. 291.

75 G.H., Letter to Craig Powell, 21 January 1991.

76 G.H., Letter to A.H., 21 February 1990.

77 Harwood, *A Steady Storm of Correspondence*, p. 29.

CHAPTER 7

1   Harwood, Interview with Ritch.

2   G.H. to A.H., note 90 on *Blessed City* manuscript, letter of 21 December 1943 (Alison Hoddinott private collection).

3   G.H., Letter to A.H., 10 December 1986.

4   Peter Bennie to G.H., 4 June 1991, FL, UQFL45, Box 18, Folder 2.

5   Harwood, *Blessed City* ms., Letter 108, FL, UQFL45, Box 7, Folder 4.

6   G.H., Letter to John Beston, 26 October 1973, FL, UQFL45, Box 6, Folder 15.

7   *Blessed City* ms., Letter 92, FL, UQFL45, Box 7, Folder 4.

8   *Blessed City* ms., Letter 108, FL, UQFL45, Box 7, Folder 4.

9   F.K., Letter to G.H., 28 March 1956.

10   Frank William Harwood Naval Record, National Archives of Australia; Brisbane Military Telephone Directories, October 1943 and May 1944, Ozatwar.com, accessed 25 January 2022, www.ozatwar.com/sigint/aib.htm; Eric Feldt, *The Coastwatchers*, Oxford University Press, Oxford, 1946, p. 332.

11   Allison Ind and Daniel MacArthur, *Allied Intelligence Bureau: The Secret Weapon in the War Against Japan*, rev. ed., Bibliopoesy, n.p., 2014, p. 291.

12   Joan Hazell, Interview with Australians at War Film Archive, archive no. 883, Australians at War Film Archive, UNSW, Canberra, accessed 25 January 2022, http://australiansatwarfilmarchive.unsw.edu.au/archive/883-joan-hazell, p. 46.

13   1935/1150 Harold Robert Harwood: Inquest, Inquest Deposition Files (VPRS24), Public Record Office Victoria.

14   Alison Hoddinott, pers. comm.

15   Hazell, Interview with Australians at War Film Archive, pp. 27–28.

16   *Blessed City* ms., Letter 93, FL, UQFL45, Box 7, Folder 4.

17   *Blessed City* ms., Letter 90, FL, UQFL45, Box 7, Folder 4.

18   *Blessed City* ms., Letter 101, FL, UQFL45, Box 7, Folder 4.

19   G.H., Letter to A.H., 21 August 1991.

20   *Blessed City* ms., Letter 97, FL, UQFL45, Box 7, Folder 4.

21   *Blessed City* ms., 8 January 1944, FL, UQFL45, Box 7, Folder 4.

22   *Blessed City* ms., 11 April 1944, FL, UQFL45, Box 7, Folder 4.

23   *Blessed City* ms., Letter 102, FL, UQFL45, Box 7, Folder 4.

24   *Blessed City* ms., Letter 120, FL, UQFL45, Box 7, Folder 4.

25   *Blessed City* ms., Letter 101, FL, UQFL45, Box 7, Folder 4.

26   *Blessed City* ms., Letter 101, FL, UQFL45, Box 7, Folder 4.

27   *Blessed City* ms., Letter 94, FL, UQFL45, Box 7, Folder 4.

28   From Donne's 'The Dissolution': *Blessed City* ms., Letter 123, FL, UQFL45, Box 7, Folder 4.

29   *Blessed City* ms., Letter 108, March 21 1944, FL, UQFL45, Box 7, Folder 4.

30   *Blessed City* ms., Letter 106, FL, UQFL45, Box 7, Folder 4. She would make use of this language in a later poem, speaking of the kind of love in which 'all is given and nothing kept' in 'O Could One Write as One Makes Love' (*Collected Poems*, p. 72).

31 *Blessed City* ms., Letter 123, FL, UQFL45, Box 7, Folder 4.

32 *Blessed City* ms., Letter 114, FL, UQFL45, Box 7, Folder 4.

33 *Blessed City* ms., Letter 101, FL, UQFL45, Box 7, Folder 4.

34 *Blessed City* ms., Letter 103, FL, UQFL45, Box 7, Folder 4.

35 *Blessed City* ms., Letter 106, FL, UQFL45, Box 7, Folder 4.

36 *Blessed City* ms., Letter 102, FL, UQFL45, Box 7, Folder 4 (*A Steady Storm of Correspondence*, p. 32).

37 G.H., Letter to A.H., 14 July 1981.

38 *Blessed City* ms., Letters 110 & 111, FL, UQFL45, Box 7, Folder 4.

39 G.H., Letter to T.R., 4 June 1959.

40 *Blessed City* ms., Letter 116, FL, UQFL45, Box 7, Folder 4.

41 *Blessed City* ms., Letter 118, FL, UQFL45, Box 7, Folder 4.

42 *Blessed City* ms., Letter 116, FL, UQFL45, Box 7, Folder 4.

43 T.R., Letter to F.K., 18 October 1943, NLA, MS7071, Box 1, Folder 4.

44 *Blessed City* ms., Letter 119, FL, UQFL45, Box 7, Folder 4.

45 *Blessed City* ms., Letter 118, FL, UQFL45, Box 7, Folder 4.

46 *Blessed City* ms., Letter 119, FL, UQFL45, Box 7, Folder 4.

47 *Blessed City* ms., Letter 121, FL, UQFL45, Box 7, Folder 4.

48 *Blessed City* ms., Letter 123, FL, UQFL45, Box 7, Folder 4.

49 Ibid.

50 *Blessed City* ms., Letter 108, FL, UQFL45, Box 7, Folder 4.

51 G.H. to A.H., Note 92 on *Blessed City* ms. (AH private collection).

52 Bill 'talked her out of' her 'firm anglo-catholic view': G.H., Letter to E.T., 26 May 1958.

53 G.H., Letter to A.H., [1 August 1982?].

54 Harwood, *A Steady Storm of Correspondence*, p. 44.

55 G.H., Letter to T.R., 26 November 1957.

56 G.H., Letter to A.H., 27 July 1983.

57 G.H., Letter to T.R., 26 November 1957.

CHAPTER 8

1 G.H., Letter to A.J., 15 August 1995.

2 Harwood, '1945' & 'Syntax of the Mind', *Collected Poems*, pp. 407 & 456.

3 G.H., Letter to E.T., 20 May 1973; see also Harwood, '1945'; 'Memoirs of a Dutiful Librettist', p. 20.

4 Harwood, 'Syntax of the Mind'.

5 Hugo, 'Gwen's Wild Passion', p. 19.

6 G.H., Letter to T.R., 3 August 1950.

7 Brisbane's population in 1947 was 402,030, while Hobart's was 76,534: Australian Bureau of Statistics 3105.0.65.001 Australian Historical Population Statistics, 2008.

8 Vivian Smith, 'Growing up in Hobart', in Carol Patterson and Edith Speers (eds), *A Writer's Tasmania*, Vol. 1, Esperance Press, Dover, 2000, p. 6.

9   G.H., Letter to V.S., 4 May 1959.

10   Hal Porter, *The Paper Chase*, University of Queensland Press, St. Lucia, 1980.

11   G.H., Letter to V.S., 11 March 1959.

12   G.H., Letter to T.R., 15 November 1953.

13   G.H., Letter to A.F., 27 October 1994.

14   G.H., Letter to A.H., 25 June 1991.

15   G.H., Letter to V.S., undated, postmarked 15 September 1959.

16   Alison Hoddinott, pers. comm. John Stuart Mill's *Autobiography* describes how he began reading Greek and Latin classics from the age of three.

17   G.H., Letter to A.F., 27 October 1994.

18   Harwood, *A Steady Storm of Correspondence*, p. 431.

19   Barbara Williams, 'Interview with Gwen Harwood', *Westerly*, vol. 33, no. 4, 1988, p. 56.

20   G.H., Letter to T.R., 26 April 1957.

21   Betty Pybus, *I Shall Be Good as New*, Betty Vivian Pybus, Lower Snug, 1997, ch. 4. The 'Fern Tree ladies' would remain friends throughout their lives, meeting once a year throughout the 1980s and 1990s for a reunion lunch.

22   Ann Jennings diaries, ms., 6 December 1946.

23   Ibid., 24 August 1947.

24   Ibid., 22 May 1949.

25   In 1953, she would say that Peter Bennie had changed her from 'a neurotic child' to 'a reasonable woman': G.H., Letter to T.R., 4 September 1953, in *A Steady Storm of Correspondence*, p. 46.

26   G.H., Letter to T.R., 18 August 1950.

27   G.H., Letter to A.J., 15 August 1995.

28   Ibid.

29   G.H., Letter to A.H., 7 September 1995. See also Harwood, 'Gainful Employment', p. 52.

30   G.H., Letter to A.J., 15 August 1995.

31   G.H., Letter to A.J., 11 May 1960.

32   T.R., Letter to G.H., 29 May 1959; cf. G.H., Letter to T.R., 13 November 1954, about the tension between Bill and Agnes: 'we don't have scenes but we *do* have "atmospheres"'.

33   G.H., Letter to T.R., 26 March 1958: she spoke of her 'old fear of his threat, spoken or implied, with which he always whipped me to heel: if you so & so, perhaps I shan't love you'.

34   G.H., Letter to A.J., 11 January 1968.

35   *Blessed City* ms., Letter 93, early 1944, FL, UQFL45, Box 7, Folder 4.

36   Harwood, 'Memoirs of a Dutiful Librettist', p. 4.

37   G.H., Letter to T.R., 12 April 1959 (origin of quote unknown).

38   G.H., Letter to T.R., 3 December 1954, 2 May 1957, 30 April 1956.

39   G.H., Letter to T.R., 9 May 1962, in *A Steady Storm of Correspondence*, p. 159.

40   Digby, *A Woman's Voice*, p. 53.

41 Vivian Smith, 'Notes on Gwen Harwood', ms., written for A.P.,
    22 November 2015.

42 G.H., Letter to T.R., 13 July 1957.

43 G.H., Letter to T.R., 29 April 1960; Beston, 'An Interview with Gwen
    Harwood', p. 88.

44 Ann Jennings diaries, ms., [3 June 1946?].

45 Alison Hoddinott, pers. comm.

46 Ann Jennings diaries, ms., 6 December 1946.

47 Ibid., 24 August 1947.

48 Ibid., 22 May 1949.

49 G.H., Letter to A.J., 4 November 1959 & 24 August 1960.

50 Ann Jennings diaries, ms., 4 April 1948.

51 Ibid., 4 September 1944.

52 Ibid., 27 July 1949.

53 Ibid., 22 May 1949 & 14 June 1949.

54 Rodney Hall, 'The Poetry of Gwen Harwood', Audio recording, ABC
    Radio, Sydney, 4 September 1977; see also Harwood, *A Steady Storm of
    Correspondence*, p. 39.

55 G.H., Letter to Mary Lord, cited in Mary Lord, *Hal Porter: Man of Many
    Parts*, Random House, Milsons Point, 1993, p. 57.

56 G.H., Letter to A.J., 3 November 1993.

57 Gwen Harwood, Interview with Anne Lear, *SPAN*, vol. 26, 1988, pp. 1–11, p. 1.

58 Ann Jennings diaries, ms., 10 December 1946.

59 Harwood told Greg Kratzmann that she destroyed most of her poems from
    this period: *A Steady Storm of Correspondence,* p. 40.

60 G.H., Letter to *Meanjin*, 1 April 1949, Baillieu Library, University of
    Melbourne, 2005.0004 *Meanjin* Editorial Records of CB Christesen, Box
    No. 340, Part 1, Elizabeth Vassilieff Folder.

61 Clement Christesen, Letter to G.H., 13 May 1949, Baillieu Library, University
    of Melbourne, 2005.0004 *Meanjin* Editorial Records of CB Christesen,
    Box No. 164, Part 1, Gwen Harwood file.

62 Gwen Harwood, *Idle Talk: Letters 1960–1964*, ed. Alison Hoddinott, Brandl &
    Schlesinger, Blackheath, 2015, p. 9.

63 Ann Jennings diaries, ms., 4 April 1948; 5 April 1948.

64 Ibid., 20 August 1946, 21 August 1946.

65 Peter Bennie, Letter to G.H., [6 July 1948?], A.H. transcription.

66 *Collected Poems*, p. 597, n. 1.

67 Harwood, Interview with Hoddinott, p. 17.

68 Ibid., p.16.

69 Ibid., p. 82.

70 Ibid., p. 84.

71 Harwood, *Blessed City*, p. 125; Harwood, Interview with Hoddinott, p. 85.

72 G.H., Letter to T.R., [23 April 1956?].

73 G.H., Letter to V.S., 2 January 1959.

74 G.H., Letter to T.R., 9 April 1958.

75 See e.g., Gwen Harwood, 'Nightfall: To the Memory of Vera Cottew', *Collected Poems*, p. 164.

CHAPTER 9

1 Harwood copied Gervase Markham's quotation into a notebook she gave to Tony Riddell, with her comment below it: FL, UQFL292, Box 2, undated, c. 1970.

2 See e.g., G.H., Undated letter to R.H.: 'I woke with a feeling of her presence. I suppose it's built into my brain cells.' Poems include 'Dreaming, Waking', 'Past and Present II' and 'The Visitor'.

3 Peter Bennie, Letter to G.H., 11 November 1951; 11 July 1950; 20 January 1951; 24 January 1952 (A.H. transcription).

4 Harwood, *Idle Talk*, p. 8; Alison Hoddinott, pers. comm.

5 Alison Hoddinott, pers. comm., 21 February 2015.

6 Harwood, *Idle Talk,* p. 9; Hoddinott and Kratzmann, 'Celebrating Gwen Harwood', p. 21; Alison Hoddinott, pers. comm., 21 February 2015.

7 G.H., Letter to T.R., 23 November 1952, in *A Steady Storm of Correspondence*, p. 44.

8 G.H., Letter to V.S., 27 December 1958.

9 Harwood, Interview with Ritch, tape 1, 23:00.

10 Peter Bennie, Letter to G.H., 6 November 1952.

11 G.H., Letter to T.R., 23 November 1952.

12 G.H., Letter to A.J., 8 March 1960.

13 G.H., Letter to T.R., 16 April 1958.

14 A colleague of Bill's who first met her in the 1950s felt that she was 'imprisoned in the Augusta Rd house': Laurie Hergenhan, pers. comm., 6 September 2018; Harwood, 'An Impromptu for Ann Jennings', *Collected Poems*, p. 231.

15 Williams, 'Interview with Gwen Harwood', p. 56; Harwood, Interview with Hoddinott, p. 36.

16 'I would rather have been happy': G.H., Letter to V.B., 30 August 1961, and 6 February 1963, in *A Steady Storm of Correspondence,* pp. 136, 173; 'savage, nasty': Beston, 'An Interview with Gwen Harwood', p. 88; 'I need to have silence': G.H., Letter to E.T., 20 February 1961. For further discussion of this inner conflict, see Ann-Marie Priest, 'Baby and Demon: Woman and the Artist in the Poetry of Gwen Harwood', *Hecate*, vol. 40, no. 2, 2015, pp. 67–83.

17 The following discussion is heavily indebted to Chapter 6 of Alison Hoddinott's *Gwen Harwood: The Real and the Imagined World* (Angus & Robertson, North Ryde, 1991, pp. 142–64) and to my conversations with Hoddinott about her studies with Bill Harwood.

18 He would go on to write *An Introduction to English Syntax* (1957) with B.G. Mitchell, a local headmaster, as well as publishing a number of scholarly articles on linguistics. An undated newspaper article (c. 1956) in Gwen's scrap book (FL, UQFL332, Box 2, Folder 8) says: 'Mr Harwood, of the

English department, has been working for some years on a new grammatical system based on mathematical symbols'.

19   Hoddinott, *The Real and the Imagined World*, p. 143.

20   Harwood, Interview with Lear, p. 5.

21   Harwood, 'The Creative Poet', in Warren R. Lett (ed.), *The Creative Artist at Work*, McGraw-Hill, Sydney, 1975, p. 23.

22   G.H., Letter to E.T., 13 April 1973; G.H., Letters to T.R., 11 September 1959, 24 November 1964.

23   Graeme Marshall, 'Wittgenstein in the Antipodes', in Graham Oppy, N. N. Trakakis, Lynda Burns, Steven Gardner and Fiona Leigh (eds), *A Companion to Philosophy in Australia & New Zealand*, Monash University Publishing, Clayton, 2010.

24   Harwood, 'Imagination and Meaning', unpublished keynote address presented at the 7th National Association of Drama in Education (NADIE) Conference, 1987, p. 26.

25   Ibid., p. 27, citing Engelmann.

26   G.H., Letter to J.P., 8 July 1974.

27   G.H., Letter to V.B., 4 October 1961.

28   G.H., Letter to E.T., 8 May 1964. Many years later, another Australian poet, Clive James, would echo this view, drawing attention to Wittgenstein's 'poetic quality' and 'sensitivity to language': *Cultural Amnesia: Notes in the Margin of my Time*, Picador, London, 2007, p. 806.

29   G.H., Letter to E.T., 19 February 1962, in *A Steady Storm of Correspondence*, p. 159: 'I wish I had seen Wittgenstein, if only once crossing a street.'

30   Beston, 'An Interview with Gwen Harwood', p. 87.

31   Cyril Connolly's *The Unquiet Grave: A Word Cycle by Palinurus* (Hamish Hamilton, London, 1945) begins: 'the true function of a writer is to produce a masterpiece and . . . no other task is of any consequence.' Harwood herself, who read the book in Brisbane in 1945 and later said that it 'formed her style', would always hold that 'The only point of writing is to produce a masterpiece': G.H., Letter to A.F., 14 March 1994.

32   See Hoddinott, *The Real and the Imagined World*, pp. 147–48.

33   Harwood, *Idle Talk*, p. 10.

34   Hoddinott and Kratzmann, 'Celebrating Gwen Harwood', p. 21.

35   Alison Hoddinott, pers. comm., 20 February 2015.

36   Vivian Smith, pers. comm., 22 November 2015.

37   Hoddinott and Kratzmann, 'Celebrating Gwen Harwood', p. 21.

38   Harwood, *Idle Talk*, p. 10.

39   G.H., Letter to T.R., 11 September 1961.

40   G.H., Letter to A.J., 11 January 1968.

41   G.H., Letter to T.R., 7 October 1953.

42   G.H., Letter to V.S., 17 December 1958.

43   G.H., Letter to Mary Lord, cited in Lord, *Hal Porter*, p. 57; G.H., Letter to Tom Shapcott, 11 May 1966.

44 Harwood, Interview with Hoddinott, p. 74.

45 Lord, *Hal Porter*, p. 57.

46 Hal Porter, Letter to V.S. (cited in Smith, 'Notes on Gwen Harwood').

47 Hal Porter, Letter to G.H., Easter Sunday, 1956, FL, UQFL45, Box 28, Folder 14.

48 Hal Porter, Letter to G.H., 31 July 1960, FL, UQFL45, Box 2, Folder 26.

49 G.H., Letter to T.S., 12 May 1966; G.H., Letter to V.S., 17 December 1958 ('Bill loathes him & won't have him here'); see also GH's 'How delightful to meet Mr Porter!', a spoof of Eliot's 'Lines to Ralph Hodgson Esqre', which refers to 'husbands' who 'abhor and hate' Mr Porter, 'and order him out of their homes': Letter to A.J., 17 October 1954, in the possession of Karen Darby.

50 G.H., Letter to Tom Shapcott, 12 May 1966.

51 See G.H., Letters to V.S., 11 March 1959 and T.R., 10 March 1959.

52 G.H., Letter to V.S., 11 March 1959.

53 G.H., Letter to T.R., 22 February 1959; the 'mutual friend' referred to is Frank Kellaway, who also met Hal Porter in the 1950s.

54 On 1 September 1953, Harwood wrote to Riddell as though in medias res to tell him she was 'not greatly disturbed' by his 'scepticism' about the ludicrous notices she had told him about, as he would be able to see them for himself 'when next you visit Hobart'.

55 G.H., Letter to T.R., 4 September 1953.

56 G.H., Letter to T.R., 6 September 1953.

57 G.H., Letter to T.R., 14 September 1953.

58 Peter Bennie described her youthful self as a 'zany, gamin girl': quoted in G.H., Letter to A.H., 13 September 1990. Frank Kellaway spoke of her 'extraordinary vital brown eyes': undated letter to G.H., early 1990s, FL, UQFL45, Box 19, Folder 1.

59 G.H., Letter to T.R., 16 September 1953.

60 G.H., Letter to T.R., 23 November 1965.

61 G.H., Letter to T.R., 7 October 1953.

62 G.H., Letter to T.R., 19 March 1955.

63 G.H., Letter to T.R., 18 April 1956.

64 Ibid.

65 G.H., Letter to A.J., 16 February 1960.

66 G.H., Letter to T.R., 19 March 1954.

67 Claire Blichfeldt, pers. comm., 1 and 3 January 2019.

68 G.H., Letter to T.R., 18 April 1956.

69 In a letter to A.H. of 11 December 1986, Riddell wrote that he and Bill had 'never discussed the old breach & never will now' (A.H. private collection); 'uneasy trio' cited by G.H. in letter to T.R., 11 September 1961.

70 G.H., Letter to T.R., 21 June 1957.

71 G.H., Letter to F.K., 2 June 1956.

72 G.H., Letter to F.K., 22 August 1956.

73 Harwood copied this quotation into a notebook she gave to Tony Riddell: FL, UQFL292, Box 2, undated, c. 1970.

74 'I am "fighting love's long war with trivial cares," as the Sappho of Lenah Valley, my sinister ego, has it': G.H., Letter to T.R., 18 April 1956, citing her own poem 'The Old Wife's Tale'.

75 Aka Keats and Shelley (following W.H. Auden): G.H., Letter to A.H., 27 September 1963.

76 Mark Van Doren (ed.), *An Anthology of World Poetry*, Reynal & Hitchcock, New York, 1936, p. 257.

77 G.H., Letter to T.R., 13 November 1954, in *A Steady Storm of Correspondence*, p. 46.

78 G.H., Letter to T.R., 27 April 1956.

79 I am indebted to Vivian Smith for this insight.

CHAPTER 10

1 G.H., Letter to T.R., 8 September 1958.

2 T.R., Letter to G.H., 8 January 1958, Claire Blichfeldt, private collection.

3 See e.g. G.H., Letter to T.R., 11 September 1959.

4 G.H., Letter to T.R., 1 November 1956.

5 Ibid.

6 G.H., Letter to T.R., 10 January 1958.

7 See Michael Heyward, *The Ern Malley Affair*, Faber & Faber, London, 1993, pp. 101–48.

8 G.H., Letter to John Beston, 19 January 1974, FL, UQFL45, Box 6, Folder 15.

9 G.H., Letter to John Beston, 26 October 1973, FL, UQFL45, Box 6, Folder 15.

10 G.H., Letter to V.S., 24 February 1959.

11 Peter Bennie to G.H., 8 May 1963, FL, UQFL45, Box 1, Folder 3.

12 G.H., Letter to T.R., [3 or 9 October 1959?].

13 Harwood, *A Steady Storm of Correspondence*, p. 57.

14 G.H., Letter to T.R., 3 October 1959.

15 G.H., Letter to E.T., 5 September 1961.

16 G.H., Letter to T.R., 26 April 1957.

17 G.H., Letter to E.T., 10 February 1965.

18 G.H., Letter to T.R., 8 September 1958.

19 G.H., Letter to T.R., 26 April 1957.

20 Ibid.

21 G.H., Letter to T.R., 5 August 1957.

22 G.H., Letter to V.B., 1962.

23 Cited in Mary Lord, *Hal Porter*, p. 57.

24 Ibid., p. 57.

25 James McAuley, 'A Precious Collection', *The Observer*, 8 March 1958.

26 G.H., Letter to T.R., n.d. [November 1963?].

27 G.H., Letter to N.T., 11 October 1975.

28 Vincent Buckley, 'Australian Poetry 1957', *The Age Literary Supplement,* 7 December 1957, p. 19.

29 Digby, *A Woman's Voice*, p. 49.

30 Hal Porter, Letter to G.H., Easter Sunday 1958, FL, UQFL45, Box 28, Folder 14.

31 G.H., Letter to T.R., 22 June 1958.

32 Smith, 'Notes on Gwen Harwood'.

33 G.H., Letter to V.S., 1 December 1958.

34 Gwen Harwood, 'The Alphabet of Truth', *Art and Australia*, n.d., pp. 396–97.

35 Ibid., p. 396.

36 E.T., Letter to G.H., 10 August 1964.

37 E.T., Letter to G.H., 'abt October 1961'.

38 G.H., Letter to E.T., 10 September 1957.

39 Harwood, 'Memories of Edwin Tanner', *Art Bulletin of Tasmania*, 1986, p. 6.

40 E.T., Letter to G.H., 12 June 1963.

41 G.H., Letter to E.T., 29 September 1960. She was greatly impressed when one of his Eisenbart paintings later sold in New York for $20,000: G.H., Letter to John Beston, 30 October 1975.

42 G.H., Letter to E.T., 26 September 1973.

43 E.T., Letter to Margaret Carnegie, 19 September 1966, FL, UQFL45, Box 17, Envelope 4.

44 G.H., Letter to T.R., 26 April 1957.

45 E.T., Letter to Margaret Carnegie, 19 September 1966, FL, UQFL45, Box 17, Envelope 4; see also Cassandra Pybus, *Gross Moral Turpitude: The Orr Case Reconsidered*, William Heinemann, Port Melbourne, 1993.

46 Pybus, *Gross Moral Turpitude*, p. 21.

47 G.H., Letter to E.T., 20 May 1973.

48 G.H., Letter to T.R., 19 December 1956.

49 G.H., Letter to T.R., 13 November 1954. The surgery was in July 1953.

50 G.H., Letter to A.J., 20 October 1956.

51 Ibid. 'The Poem' referred to here is the 'one great work' of Hölderlin's, 'An die Parzen'.

52 G.H., Letter to T.R., 18 March 1957.

53 Ibid.

54 G.H., Letter to T.R., 19 December 1956.

55 G.H., Letter to T.R., 5 August 1957.

56 G.H., Letter to V.S., 25 June 1959. It was a popular painting for ekphrastic poems: Walter de la Mare, William Carlos Williams and John Berryman all wrote on it. When Gwen encountered Berryman's 'Winter Landscape' in his 1948 volume *The Dispossessed*, she told Vivian she would 'never have attempted "A Postcard"' if she'd known of it (3 November 1960).

57 T.R., Letter to G.H., 28 July 1957.

CHAPTER 11

1   G.H., Letter to T.R., 27 April 1956.

2   G.H., Letter to T.R., 2 May 1957.

3   G.H., Letter to T.R., 25 February 1958.

4   'Thomas M. Pick, Ph.D.', accessed 8 August 2015, http://users.atw.hu/drpick/en/myself.html.

5   Commonwealth of Australia Incoming Passenger Card 644 (Thomas Pick) & 655 (Louisli Pick), 1 March 1950, National Archive of Australia.

6   G.H., Letter to T.R., 13 July 1957.

7   *The Argus* (Melbourne), 16 October 1952, p. 2.

8   G.H., Letter to T.R., 2 May 1957.

9   Ibid.

10   Ibid.

11   G.H., Letter to T.R., 5 August 1957. Though Harwood confided in Tony, she did not reveal the name of her lover in her letters. In the early 1990s, she told G.K. that he was Tom Pick (pers. comm.). She did write to Alison Hoddinott of 'the real Tom' in the early 1980s (G.H., Letter to A.H., 10 April 1983) but did not give his full name, saying only that his native tongue was German.

12   G.H., Letter to A.H., 10 April 1983.

13   Harwood, 'Sonnet'. Harwood identifies this as a Tom Pick poem in a letter to A.H., 10 April 1983.

14   G.H., Letter to T.R., 26 November 1957. Quote from Russell's *Portraits from Memory and Other Essays*, Simon & Schuster, n.p., 1956, p. 89.

15   Harwood gave a list of poems associated with the affair in a letter to A.H., 10 April 1983. She identifies others in passing in letters to Tony or Ann.

16   A.H., pers. comm. This poem is written from the point of view of the man who has left his lover behind in Tasmania ('that freezing island') and longs for a word from her.

17   'Tom the Rhymer': in this poem, Gwen casts herself as the (male) poet Tom, and the real-life Tom as the (female) Elf Queen.

18   Iterations of this can be seen in 'In Zurich by the Tideless Lake' (*Collected Poems*, p. 39), 'Caro Autem Infirma' (*Collected Poems*, p. 47) and 'Triste, Triste' (*Collected Poems*, p. 60), among others.

19   G.H., Letter to T.R., 9 September 1957.

20   'Daphne Restored' (*Collected Poems*, p. 37) depicts her pain and bewilderment. In Gwen's telling, the traditional Greek myth is inverted: Daphne is turned from tree to woman, snatched from the joyous heights of 'myriad-green significance' and forced into the 'rhymed anatomy of man'. She longs to discover the magic form of words that will change her back into her true arboreal shape, but 'cannot find / one word to call the lightning down'.

21   *NSW Government Gazette*, 11 April 1958. He would subsequently settle, with his family, in America.

22   G.K., pers. comm, 2015. Gwen first mentions the affair to T.R. on 25 June 1957, and tells him they have 'parted forever' on 5 August 1957.

23 G.H., Letter to T.R., 10 January 1958.

24 G.H., Letter to T.R., 26 November 1957.

25 G.H., Letter to T.R., 12 December 1957.

26 G.H., Letter to A.H., 10 April 1983.

27 G.H., Letter to T.R., 9 September 1957.

28 G.H., Letter to T.R., 27 November 1959.

29 G.H., Letter to T.R., 12 July 1960.

30 G.H., Letter to T.R., 9 September 1957.

31 Ibid.

32 A.H., pers. comm.

33 G.H., Letter to T.R., 30 October 1957.

34 G.H., Letter to T.R., 10 January 1958.

35 G.H., Letter to T.R., 10 January 1958; G.H., Letter to E.T., 2 April 1958, in *A Steady Storm of Correspondence*, p. 60.

36 G.H., Letter to T.R., 10 January 1958.

37 G.H., Letter to V.S., 7 August 1958.

38 G.H., Letter to A.J., [1958?], FL, UQFL45, Box 14.

39 G.H., Letter to T.R., 26 March 1958.

40 Ibid.

41 On 8 July 1971, she told Eddie Tanner that for twelve years she had 'tried to bend [her]self into [Bill's] frames', and had 'ended up with cracks everywhere'. Twelve years since her marriage in 1945 brought her to 1957.

42 G.H., Letter to T.R., 26 March 1958.

43 G.H., Letter to T.R., 21 July 1958.

44 G.H., Letter to T.R., 8 September 1958, re 'Group from Tartarus'.

45 Harwood, 'Lamplit Presences', p. 250. The poems she is specifically referring to here are 'I Am the Captain of my Soul', 'Alter Ego', 'The Wine Is Drunk' and 'Triste, Triste'. The image of the mother duck appears in Saul Steinberg's comment about Sidney Nolan, quoted in Cynthia Nolan's *Open Negative* (1967): 'Every word that Sidney says is camouflage. Everything he says goes off on a trail away from what he really believes, thinks, intends to do, has done in the past. He is like the bird dragging a wing, leading the hunter away from its nest and young.'

46 G.H., Letter to T.R., 8 September 1958.

47 G.H., Letter to E.T., 5 December 1958.

48 G.H., Letter to A.H., 10 April 1983; see also G.H., Letter to T.R., 18 February 1964.

49 G.H., Letter to T.R., 28 August 1960.

50 Letter to G.H. from *Meanjin*, 1 March 1959 (Baillieu Library, University of Melbourne, 2005.0004 *Meanjin* Editorial Records of CB Christesen, Part 1, Box No. 164, File: Gwen Harwood).

51 G.H., Letter to T.R., 1 March 1959.

52 A.H., pers. comm., 21 February 2015.

53   G.H., Letter to T.R., 25 May 1961, in *A Steady Storm of Correspondence*, p. 122.

54   G.H., Letter to T.R., 6 June 1958. Cf. G.H., Letter to T.R., 15 June 1960, in which she quotes 'Anniversary': winter 'drags on as usual here, with terrible memories for me – "I learn the weight of light and stone"'.

55   G.H., Letter to T.R., 5 November 1959.

56   G.H., Letter to T.R., 21 July 1958.

57   See, for example, 'Caro Autem Infirma', 'Triste, Triste', 'In Zurich by the Tideless Lake', 'The Wine Is Drunk'.

58   Harwood was influenced here by John Berryman's 'Sonnet 25' (published in October 1952 in *Poetry*), which she told Vivian Smith was 'on the same theme as "I am the Captain" – "Lockt in and humming, the Captain's nailing/ a false log to the lurching table"': G.H., Letter to V.S., 3 November 1960.

59   Clem Christesen, Letter to G.H., 11 December 1958, Baillieu Library, University of Melbourne, 2005.0004 *Meanjin* Editorial Records of CB Christesen, Part 1, Box No. 164, File: Gwen Harwood.

60   G.H., Letter to T.R., 29 April 1959.

61   G.H., Letter to V.S., 25 November 1959.

62   G.H., Letter to T.R., 27 November 1959.

63   Ibid.

64   G.H., Letter to A.J., 6 October 1959.

65   G.H., Letter to A.J., 3 January 1960.

66   G.H., Letter to A.J., 18 January 1960; 3 January 1960.

67   G.H., Letter to A.J., 4 November 1959.

68   G.H., Letter to A.J., 5 August 1959.

69   G.H., Letter to A.J., 4 November 1959.

70   G.H., Letter to A.J., 18 January 1960.

71   G.H., Letter to T.R., 31 March 1959; 20 June 1958. Hoddinott remembered Harwood telling her that she and Lotte had fallen out when Gwen smacked Lotte's daughter, Claire (pers. comm., April 2020).

72   Michael Roe, Charlotte Wilmot and Canon John May, interviewed for the University of Tasmania Oral History Project 1978–1983 [Audio], http:// eprints.utas.edu.au/17805.

73   G.H., Letter to T.R., 13 December 1958.

74   G.H., Letter to V.S., 21 June 1959.

75   G.H., Letter to T.R., 18 July 1959.

76   G.H., Letter to T.R., 22 June 1959.

77   G.H., Letter to T.R., 7 July 1958.

78   G.H., Letter to T.R., 29 May 1959.

79   G.H., Letter to V.S., 21 June 1959.

80   From Rilke's 'Book of Hours'; G.H., Letter to T.R., 29 May 1959.

81   G.H., Letter to T.R., 4 June 1959.

82   G.H., Letter to T.R., 16 July 1959.

83   G.H., Letter to T.R., 18 July 1859.

84 G.H., Letter to A.J., 13 February 1965.

85 G.H., Letter to T.R., 14 August 1959.

86 G.H., Letter to T.R., 23 October 1959.

87 G.H., Letter to T.R., 28 November 1960. Harwood told the Hoddinotts that the 'bluestocking' in this poem was based on Lotte: A.H., pers. comm., 21 February 2015. It is a companion piece to her 1963 poem 'Critic's Nightwatch', which memorably describes critics as 'mean, solitary masturbators' (*Collected Poems*, p. 42).

88 Harwood knew Loewe's setting of a German translation of 'Archibald Douglas' and was deeply moved by its opening lines: 'Seven years have passed, and I cannot bear more' (see e.g., G.H., Letter to A.H., 10 April 1983).

89 Claire Blichfeldt, pers. comm, 1 and 3 January 2019.

90 G.H., Letter to T.R., 23 June 1971, in *A Steady Storm of Correspondence*, p. 259.

91 G.H., Letter to T.R., 3 July 1971.

CHAPTER 12

1 G.H., Letter to T.R., 2 November 1958.

2 G.H., Letter to V.S., undated, December 1958.

3 G.H., Letter to V.S., 1 December 1960.

4 G.H., Letter to T.R., 23 October 1959.

5 G.H., Letter to T.R., 25 February 1960.

6 G.H., Letter to T.R., 5 November 1959.

7 G.H., Letter to T.R., 5 February 1960.

8 Enclosed in G.H., Letter to T.R., 29 February 1960.

9 G.H., Letter to A.J., 18 November 1959.

10 G.H., Letter to T.R., 9 November 1959.

11 G.H., Letter to V.S., 13 November 1959.

12 G.H., Letter to Clem Christesen, 9 November 1959, in *A Steady Storm of Correspondence*, p. 86.

13 David Moody, Letter to G.H., 18 November 1959, Baillieu Library, University of Melbourne, 2005.0004 *Meanjin* Editorial Records of CB Christesen, Part 1, Box No. 164, File: Gwen Harwood.

14 G.H., Letter to T.R., 27 November 1959.

15 G.H., Letter to T.R., 9 November 1959.

16 G.H., Letter to T.R., 29 February 1960, in *A Steady Storm of Correspondence*, p. 92.

17 G.H., Letter to T.R., 5 November 1959. NB: In the published version of this letter (in *A Steady Storm of Correspondence*, p. 84), 'texture' has been changed to 'note'.

18 G.H., Letter to T.R., 16 December 1959.

19 G.H., Letter to T.R., 8 March 1960.

20 G.H., Letter to T.R., 12 November 1959.

21 G.H., Letter to T.R., 8 March 1960.

22 G.H., Letter to T.R., 14 February 1961.

23 G.H., Letter to T.R., 1 September 1960.

24 The single exception was 'that silly little piece "To my children"': G.H., Letter to T.R., 21 December 1959.

25 G.H., Letter to E.T., undated, 1958.

26 G.H., Letter to T.R., 31 March 1960.

27 Harwood, *A Steady Storm of Correspondence*, p. 119.

28 G.H., Letter to T.R., 21 December 1959.

29 A.D. Hope, Letter to V.B., 4 March 1955, in Penelope Buckley, 'A.D. Hope and Vincent Buckley: A Correspondence (1952–1955)', *Southerly*, vol. 61, no. 1, 2001, pp. 140–45.

30 G.H., Letter to E.T., [1963?].

31 Chris Wallace-Crabbe, 'Buckley, Vincent Thomas (1925–1988)', *Australian Dictionary of Biography*, National Centre of Biography, Australian National University, 2007, http://adb.anu.edu.au/biography/ buckley-vincent-thomas-12261/text22003.

32 G.H., Letter to T.R., 21 December 1959.

33 G.H., Letter to T.R., 21 March 1960; 29 October 1959.

34 G.H., Letter to T.R., 31 March 1960.

35 Harwood, Interview with Hoddinott, p. 68.

36 G.H., Letter to T.R., 2 May 1960. Tony wrote three times, in the persona of Lehmann and, in the third letter, called Christesen's failure to return the poems 'gross discourtesy' and made a vague threat to 'take further steps': 'Walter Lehmann', Letter to Clem Christesen, 2 June 1960, Baillieu Library, University of Melbourne, 2005.0004 *Meanjin* Editorial Records of CB Christesen, Part 1, Box No. 164, File: Gwen Harwood.

37 G.H., Letter to T.R., 29 June 1960.

38 G.H., Letter to T.R., 2 May 1960.

39 G.H., Letter to T.R., 4 July 1960, in *A Steady Storm of Correspondence*, p. 101.

40 G.H., Letter to T.R., 20 July 1960, in *A Steady Storm of Correspondence*, p. 102.

41 Ibid.

42 G.H., Letter to E.T., 4 May 1958.

43 G.H., Letter to E.T., c. March 1960.

44 G.H., Letter to T.R., 15 August 1960.

45 G.H., Letter to V.S., 20 August 1960.

46 G.H., Letter to T.R., [26 August 1960?].

47 G.H., Letter to T.R., 28 August 1960, in *A Steady Storm of Correspondence*, p. 106.

48 G.H., Letter to A.J., 17 August 1960.

49 G.H., Letter to T.R., 7 September 1960, in *A Steady Storm of Correspondence*, p. 107.

50 G.H., Letter to E.T., 17 February 1961.

51 G.H., Letter to T.R., 1 September 1960.

52 G.H., Letter to T.R., 28 November 1960, in *A Steady Storm of Correspondence*, p. 112.

53 Quoted in a letter to T.R., 1 November 1960.

54 Harwood, 'A Magyar Air', 'October', 'Refugee', in *Collected Poems*, pp. 144, 119 and 151.

55 G.H., Letter to R.H., 7 September 1963.

56 *Collected Poems* notes, p. 584.

57 The poem 'Last Meeting', which has a similar theme, was written before Harwood's affair with Tom Pick, 'as an academic exercise (if poetry ever is that!)': G.H., Letter to T.R., 25 February 1958.

58 Harwood, 'Professor Kröte', in *Collected Poems*, p. 118.

59 G.H., Letter to T.R., 9 August 1959.

60 G.H., Letter to T.R., 11 August 1960.

61 G.H., Letter to T.R., 15 August 1960.

62 G.H., Letter to T.R., 14 February 1961.

CHAPTER 13

1 Two further poems appeared under the names 'Gwen Harwood' ('The Sentry') and 'Francis Geyer' ('Dead Guitars') that Harwood did not write, as discussed below.

2 G.H., Letter to T.R., 22 September 1960.

3 Lehmann 'sent *everything* back': G.H., Letter to T.R., 26 August 1958. 'My 8 best poems have been rejected by *The London Magazine*': G.H., Letter to T.R., 28 August 1960. In a letter to Ann Jennings of 8 January 1961, she says that she is trying to 'break into the English anthologies' with Geyer, but again, she had no luck. She didn't try the American journals, as her research showed they never published Australian poets.

4 G.H., Letter to T.R., 16 April 1958.

5 G.H., Letter to V.S., 20 April 1959.

6 G.H., Letter to A.J., 22 June 1960.

7 G.H., Letter to T.R., [late August 1961?].

8 G.H., Letter to T.R., 2 November 1959.

9 G.H., Letter to A.J., 20 October 1956.

10 G.H., Letter to T.R., 2 November 1959.

11 G.H., Letter to T.R., 21 March 1960.

12 G.H., Letter to T.R., 20 April 1960.

13 G.H., Letter to T.R., 25 February 1960.

14 G.H., Letter to A.F., 7 April 1994. See also: G.H., Letter to V.S., Regatta Day 1959; G.H., Letter to T.R., 25 February 1958.

15 G.H., Letter to T.R., 25 February 1958.

16 G.H., Letter to A.J., 11 May 1960.

17 Ibid.

18 G.H., Letter to A.J., 9 March 1960.

19 G.H., Letter to A.J., 27 May 1960.

20 G.H., Letter to T.R., 30 May 1960.

21 G.H., Letter to A.J., 27 May 1960.

22 G.H., Letter to A.J., 2 February 1961.

23 Ibid.

24 G.H., Letter to V.S., 2 January 1959.

25 G.H., Letter to V.B., 3–4 December 1961.

26 G.H., Letter to T.R., 29 February 1960. Princess Marie of Thurn and Taxis, nee Princess of Hohenlohe, was Rilke's patron.

27 G.H., Letter to T.R., 29 June 1960.

28 G.H., Letter to T.R., 10 May 1960.

29 G.H., Letter to T.R., 11 May 1960.

30 G.H., Letter to A.J., 11 May 1960.

31 G.H., Letter to T.R., 11 May 1960.

32 G.H., Letter to T.R., 12 May 1960.

33 G.H., Letter to T.R., 15 May 1960.

34 Harwood, *Idle Talk*, p. 28.

35 G.H., Letter to V.S., 6 August 1959.

36 G.H., Letter to T.R., 2 November 1958.

37 G.H., Letter to T.R., 9 August 1959, in *A Steady Storm of Correspondence*, p. 77.

38 Ibid., p. 78.

39 A.D. Hope to G.H., 15 September 1959, FL, UQFL45 Box 2, Folder 6.

40 G.H., Letter to T.R., 18 September 1959, in *A Steady Storm of Correspondence*, p. 80.

41 Ibid., p. 81.

42 G.H., Letter to T.R., 5 November 1959, in *A Steady Storm of Correspondence*, p. 82.

43 G.H., Letter to T.R., 25 February 1960; 20 June 1960.

44 G.H., Letter to T.R., 17 January 1961, in *A Steady Storm of Correspondence*, p. 114; cf. G.H., Letter to A.J., 23 January 1961.

45 A.D. Hope to G.H., 13 March 1961, FL, UQFL45 Box 2, Folder 6.

46 G.H., Letter to A.D. Hope, 14 March 1961, in *A Steady Storm of Correspondence*, p. 119.

47 A.D. Hope to G.H., undated, postmarked 26 June 1961, FL, UQFL45 Box 2, Folder 6.

48 G.H., Letter to A.H., 25 June 1961, in *A Steady Storm of Correspondence*, p. 128.

49 G.H., Letters to A.J., 23 January 1961; 18 July 1961. Harwood, *Idle Talk*, p. 57.

50 Harwood, *Idle Talk*, p. 31.

51 G.H., Letter to A.J., 18 July 1961.

52 Harwood, *Idle Talk*, p. 41.

53 G.H., Letter to A.J., 22 November 1962.

54 Ibid.

55 See e.g., G.H., Letter to A.H., 26 May 1983.

56 G.H., Letter to L.S., 7 March 1977.

57 G.H., Letter to N.T., 11 December 1976, in *A Steady Storm of Correspondence*, p. 319.

58 G.H., Letter to T.R., 9 September 1959.

59 James McAuley, *The End of Modernity*, Angus & Robertson, Sydney, 1959, pp. 128–29.

60 Harwood, *A Steady Storm of Correspondence*, p. 136.

61 Vincent Buckley, *Cutting Green Hay: Friendships, Movements and Cultural Conflicts in Australia's Great Decades*, Penguin, Ringwood, 1983, p. 172. Cf. Laurie Hergenhan, pers. comm., 6 September 2018. Hergenhan, who joined the English Department at the University of Tasmania in 1960, at the same time as James McAuley, said that McAuley did not rate Harwood as a poet at first.

62 G.H., Letter to T.R., [November 1963?].

CHAPTER 14

1 V.B., Letter to G.H., 3 May 1961.

2 G.H., Letter to V.B., 5 May 1961, in *A Steady Storm of Correspondence*, p. 121.

3 G.H., Letter to A.&B.H., 25 May 1961, in *A Steady Storm of Correspondence*, p. 125.

4 G.H., Letter to T.R., 23 June 1961.

5 G.H., Letter to A.&B.H., 25 May 1961, in *A Steady Storm of Correspondence*, p. 125.

6 Leonie Kramer, 'An Approach to the Muse', *The Bulletin*, vol. 82, no. 4234, 5 April 1961, pp. 31–32.

7 G.H., Letter to E.T., 18 August 1961.

8 Harwood, *A Steady Storm of Correspondence*, p. 126.

9 Ibid., p. 126.

10 Ibid., p. 127.

11 Harwood refers to this evening in 'Autumn: To the Memory of Vincent Buckley', in *Collected Poems*, p. 462.

12 G.H., Letter to T.R., 23 June 1961, in *A Steady Storm of Correspondence*, p. 123.

13 Harwood, *Idle Talk*, p. 34.

14 G.H., Letter to T.R., 23 June 1961, in *A Steady Storm of Correspondence*, p. 124; see also Ibid., p. 35.

15 Harwood, *Idle Talk*, p. 36.

16 Ibid.

17 G.H., Letter to A.&B.H., 6 August 1961.

18 G.H., Letter to T.R., [? August 1961].

19 G.H., Letter to T.R., 17 August 1961 (letter 1 of 2).

20 Gwen believed she was speaking to Desmond O'Grady, but O'Grady had no recollection of the phone call (pers. comm., 13 July 2018), so it is possible it was someone else, perhaps even the editor-in-chief, Donald Horne.

21 Harwood, *Idle Talk*, p. 45.

22 Peter Coleman, '*The Bulletin*, the Editor and *The Cherry Orchard*: A Tale of

the 1960s', *Voices: The Quarterly Journal of the National Library of Australia*, vol. 7, no. 1, 1997, pp. 88–95.

23 Desmond O'Grady, pers. comm.

24 G.H., Letter to T.R., 17 August 1961.

25 Ibid.; see also Harwood, *Idle Talk*, p. 45.

26 Harwood, *Idle Talk*, p. 45.

27 G.H., Letter to E.T., 18 August 1961.

28 Thomas Shapcott, *Biting the Bullet: A Literary Memoir*, Simon & Schuster Australia, Brookvale, 1990, pp. 110–11.

29 'Sad Jest', *The Bulletin*, 19 August 1961, p. 3.

30 G.H., Letter to E.T., 5 September 1961.

31 Harwood, *Idle Talk*, pp. 55–56.

32 G.H., Letter to T.R., 5 September 1961.

33 Ibid.; Harwood, *Idle Talk*, p. 59.

34 G.H., Letter to T.R., 17 August 1961.

35 G.H., Letter to A.J., 16 August 1961.

36 G.H., Letter to A.J., 25 August 1961.

37 G.H., Letter to T.R., 3 September 1961.

38 F.K., Letter to G.H., undated, FL, UQFL45 Box 9, Folder 9.

39 G.H., Letter to T.R., 6 September 1961.

40 G.H., Letter to A.H., 21 August 1961; 'The Hoax That Misfired', *The Bulletin*, 19 August 1961, p. 8.

41 G.H., Letter to V.B., 30 August 1961, NLA MS 7289, Series 1, Folders 1–3.

42 G.H., Letter to T.R., 24 August 1961.

43 G.H., Letter to A.&B.H., 21 August 1961; see also G.H., Letter to T.R., 18 August 1961.

44 'Tas. Housewife in Hoax of the Year', *Truth* (Tas.), 23 August 1961, p. 1.

45 See Ann-Marie Priest, '"The Hoax That Misfired": Gwen Harwood's Cultural Dissent', *Southerly*, vol. 77, no. 1, 2017, pp. 115–36.

46 Harwood, *A Steady Storm of Correspondence*, p. 133.

47 G.H., Letter to T.R., 17 August 1961.

48 G.H., Letter to V.B., 3 October 1961.

49 A.D. Hope, Letter to G.H., undated [late August or early September 1961?], FL, UQFL45 Box 2, Folder 6.

50 G.H., Letter to T.R., 3 September 1961.

51 G.H., Letters to T.R., 17 August 1961; 3 September 1961. See also G.H., Letter to A.H., 3 September 1961.

52 Desmond O'Grady, pers. comm.

53 Harwood, *Idle Talk*, p. 49.

54 G.H., Letter to T.R., 15 August 1961.

55 G.H., Letter to A.&B.H., 3 September 1961.

56 Donald Horne, *Into the Open: Memoirs 1958–1999*, HarperCollins, Sydney, 2000, pp. 56–57.

57 A.D. Hope, Letter to G.H., 15 September 1961, FL, UQFL45 Box 2, Folder 6.

58 Ibid.

59 Harwood, *A Steady Storm of Correspondence*, p. 141.

60 G.H., Letter to T.R., 11 September 1961.

61 G.H., Letter to T.R., 25 January 1962.

62 Harwood, *A Steady Storm of Correspondence*, p. 135; G.H., Letter to E.T., 18 August 1961.

63 Harwood, *A Steady Storm of Correspondence*, p. 123.

64 V.B., Letter to G.H., 26 August 1961.

65 V.B., Letter to G.H., 30 August 1961.

66 G.H., Letter to V.B., 3 September 1961.

67 G.H., Letter to E.T., 5 September 1961.

68 G.H., Letter to A.&B.H., 2 October 1961.

69 G.H., Letter to T.R., 6 September 1961.

70 G.H., Letter to T.R., 11 September 1961, in *A Steady Storm of Correspondence*, p. 138.

71 G.H., Letter to T.R., 23 October 1961.

72 G.H., Letter to V.B., 28 October 1961.

73 G.H., Letter to V.B., 20 July 1961.

74 G.H., Letter to V.B., 21 July 1961, in *A Steady Storm of Correspondence*, p. 129.

75 G.H., Letter to T.R., 11 September 1961, in *A Steady Storm of Correspondence*, p. 138.

76 G.H., Letter to T.R., 27 July 1960.

77 G.H., Letter to V.B., 4 October 1961.

78 G.H., Letter to T.R., 14 October 1960, in *A Steady Storm of Correspondence*, p. 109.

79 G.H., Letter to A.J., 9 December 1960.

80 G.H., Letter to A.&B.H., 8 August 1961.

81 G.H., Letter to T.R., 6 September 1961.

82 G.H., Letter to A.&B.H., 2 October 1961.

83 V.B., Letter to G.H., undated [mid-October 1961].

84 John McLaren, *Journey Without Arrival: The Life and Writing of Vincent Buckley*, Australian Scholarly Publishing, North Melbourne, 2009, pp. 151–60.

85 G.H., Letter to V.B., 5 October 1961.

86 G.H., Letter to V.B., 25 September 1961.

87 Donald Horne to Francis Geyer, 27 November 1961, FL, UQFL45, Box 1, Folder 6.

88 G.H., Letter to V.B., 3 October 1961.

89 Quoted in G.H., Letter to T.R., 20 November 1961, in *A Steady Storm of Correspondence*, p. 144.

90 G.H., Letter to V.B., 4 October 1961.

91 See G.H., Letter to V.B., 26 December 1962.

92 G.H., Letter to T.R., 5 December 1961.

93 G.H., Letter to A.&B.H., 11 January 1962, in *Idle Talk*, p. 95.

94 G.H., Letter to T.R., 5 December 1961.

95 Ibid.; G.H., Letter to A.&B.H., 11 January 1962, in *Idle Talk*, p. 95.

96 Shapcott, *Biting the Bullet*, p. 111.

97 This is Harwood's account in a letter to V.B., 27 December 1962; in *Biting the Bullet*, Shapcott says that they wanted to invite Geyer to contribute to *New Impulses*, which did not appear until 1968.

98 Thomas Shapcott, Letter to Chris Wallace-Crabbe, undated, Wallace-Crabbe, Christopher Keith Collection, 1976.0011 Correspondence 1956–1975, Unit 2 of 2, University of Melbourne Archives.

99 G.H., Letter to V.B., 27 December 1962.

100 G.H., Letter to V.B., 8 December 1961.

101 G.H., Letters to T.R., 29 June 1960; 11 July 1961.

102 G.H., Letter to Chris Wallace-Crabbe, 19 February 1963, Wallace-Crabbe, Christopher Keith Collection, 1976.0011 Correspondence 1956–1975, Unit 2 of 2, University of Melbourne Archives.

103 G.H., Letter to T.R., 28 April 1963.

104 G.H., Letter to T.R., 9 May 1963.

105 G.H., Letter to V.B., 30 August 1961, in *A Steady Storm of Correspondence*, 136.

106 G.H., Letter to A.&B.H., 2 October 1961.

107 G.H., Letter to V.B., 2 November 1961; see also to T.R., 14 November 1961.

108 G.H., Letters to T.R., 4 November 1961; 30 November 1961.

CHAPTER 15

1 G.H., Letter to A.&B.H., 6 January 1962.

2 G.H., Letter to V.B., 30 August 1961, in *A Steady Storm of Correspondence*, p. 136.

3 Harwood's idea of her vocation as the 'gift that is death to hide' is discussed in Ann-Marie Priest, *A Free Flame: Australian Women Writers and Vocation in the Twentieth Century*, UWA Publishing, Crawley, 2018, pp. 18–24.

4 See e.g., G.H., Letter to E.T., 5 September 1961.

5 Harwood cites 'Alter Ego', 'Group from Tartarus' and 'I am the Captain of my Soul' in a letter to E.T. (5 September 1961) explaining the compulsion she felt she was under to write.

6 V.B., Letter to Miriam Stone [Gwen Harwood], 28 March 1962.

7 G.H., Letter to V.S., 16 August 1962.

8 G.H., Letter to E.T., undated [late 1962 or early 1963].

9 G.H., Letter to E.T., 21 August 1962.

10 Wilson Blackman, 'Four Poets in One: Gwen Harwood', *The Creative Arts*, Radio Australia, 5–7 April 1964.

11 Harwood, 'In Hospital' and 'The Wound', in *Westerly*, November 1962.

12 V.B., Letter to G.H., 23 July 1962.

13 G.H., Letter to A.&B.H., 10 September 1962.

14 G.H., Letter to T.R., 16 February 1962.

15 G.H., Letter to A.H., undated (Fryer Library, UQFL45, Box 1). See also G.H., Letter to A.&B.H., 30 November 1962, in *Idle Talk*, p. 136: 'Yes Porter did take a Stone story, but I took it straight out again to the annoyance of A & R who had it all set up for the printer; they wrote me a letter of flattering praise but I decided not to write prose after all – everyone seems to know who wrote Burning Sappho etc etc so Zorro will have to find another mask'.

16 G.H., Letter to T.R., 17 April 1962: 'I thought of those evenings at the piano "so manche nacht in alter Zeit" [many a night in the old days]'.

17 'astonishingly': G.H., Letter to V.S., 4 May 1962; 'disturb me': G.H., Letter to T.R., 17 April 1962.

18 Penny Thow, 'Kudos for a Life of Sound', *Sunday Tasmanian*, 9 January 2005.

19 Harwood, Dream diary, FL, UQFL332, Box 2, Folder 8.

20 Ibid.; some evident slippage between Beethoven and Bill here.

21 Ibid., 26 October 1953.

22 Harwood, 'Beethoven in a shabby room', in *Collected Poems*, p. 102.

23 'The Waldstein', in *Collected Poems*, p. 44.

24 G.H., Letter to R.H., 15 November 1962: 'Suns through a lofty bleakness fall', in *Collected Poems*, p. 107. She told Rex Hobcroft this poem was 'an attempt to express the feeling of *renewal*'.

25 G.H., Letter to T.R., 2 February 1963.

26 Poem II of 'Four Impromptus', in *Collected Poems*, p. 166.

27 G.H., Letter to R.H., 17 October 1962.

28 Ibid.

29 G.H., Letter to R.H., 25 November 1962.

30 The published version of this poem begins 'Those who are lucky' (*Collected Poems*, p. 167).

31 G.K., pers. comm., 5 January 2017. When Kratzmann first spoke to Rex Hobcroft about Harwood, they were about ten minutes into the conversation when Rex interrupted to say: don't you want to ask me if Gwen and I had an affair? He then explained that they hadn't; while there was certainly sexual attraction there, they were both married and felt it would have been stupid.

32 G.H., Letter to R.H., 2 February 1963.

33 G.H., Letter to R.H., 7 September 1963; see also 3 September 1963.

34 G.H., Letter to R.H., undated note on poem [mid-1963?].

35 G.H., Letter to T.R., 8 November 1962.

36 G.H., Letter to T.R., 17 April 1962.

37 G.H., Letter to T.R., 20 June 1962.

38 G.H., Letter to T.R., 13 July 1962.

39 G.H., Letter to T.R., 3 September 1963.

40 G.H., Letter to T.R., 24 January 1964.

41 G.H., Letter to T.R., 17 July 1964.

42 G.H., Letter to T.R., 9 November 1965.

43 For example, 'Nightfall: To the Memory of Vera Cottew', sent to Hobcroft on 12 July 1963 (*Collected Poems*, p. 164); 'Dreaming, Waking' (*Collected Poems*, p. 175); 'Person to Person' (*Collected Poems*, p. 184).

44 G.H., Letter to T.R., 9 December 1965.

CHAPTER 16

1 G.H., Letter to T.R., 12 April 1962.

2 G.H., Letter to T.R., 28 November 1962.

3 G.H., Letters to T.R., 10 February 1963; 10 March 1963.

4 G.H., Letter to T.R., 28 November 1962.

5 G.H., Letter to V.B., 14 May 1963, in *A Steady Storm of Correspondence*, p. 177.

6 Shapcott, *Biting the Bullet*, p. 112.

7 G.H., Letter to A.&B.H., undated, mid-1963.

8 G.H., Letter to V.B., 19 June 1963.

9 G.H., Letter to T.R., 1 October 1963. The reference is to Yeats' 'Among School Children'.

10 G.H., Letter to T.R., 14 November 1963.

11 G.H., Letter to T.R., 24 March 1963.

12 G.H., Letter to T.R., 19 March 1963.

13 Ibid.

14 G.H., Letter to T.R., 28 April 1963.

15 Harwood, *A Steady Storm of Correspondence*, p. 177.

16 G.H., Letter to T.R., 9 May 1963.

17 G.H., Letter to T.R., 23 September 1964.

18 David Reid, 'James Penberthy – Music and Memories', Tablo website, accessed 25 January 2022, https://tablo.io/david-reid-1/192e51523e4a; G.H., Letter to T.R., 12 May 1965.

19 G.H., Letter to T.R., 9 May 1963.

20 G.H., Letter to T.R., 12 July 1965; 6 August 1962.

21 G.H., Letter to T.R., 12 July 1965.

22 Ibid.

23 G.H., Letter to T.R., undated [November 1963?].

24 G.H., Letter to T.R., 20 April 1962.

25 Ibid.

26 G.H., Letter to T.R., 9 May 1962.

27 G.H., Letter to T.R., 6 August 1962.

28 G.H., Letter to A.J., 27 August 1963.

29 G.H., Letter to T.R., 9 May 1962.

30 G.H., Letter to V.B., 5 September 1961.

31 G.H., Letter to T.R., 9 May 1963.

32 G.H., Letter to T.R., 10 March 1963.

33 G.H., Letter to E.T., 20 December 1962.

34 G.H., Letter to E.T., 17 July 1963; see also G.H., Letter to V.B., 22 July 1963, in *A Steady Storm of Correspondence*, p. 180.

35 G.H., Letter to E.T., 17 July 1963.

36 G.H., Letter to T.R., 18 July 1963.

37 G.H., Letter to T.R., 26 July 1963.

38 G.H., Letter to A.&B.H., 28 July 1963, in *Idle Talk*, p. 161.

39 G.H., Letter to T.R., [28 July 1963?].

40 G.H., Letter to T.R., 5 August 1963.

41 G.H., Letter to T.R., 9 December 1963.

42 David Moody, 'Books in Review: The Poems of Gwen Harwood', *Meanjin Quarterly*, December 1963, pp. 418–21.

43 G.H., Letter to T.R., 18 December 1963.

44 G.H., Letters to A.&B.H., 16 December 1963; 8 January 1964.

45 G.H., Letter to A.&B.H., undated [late October 1963].

46 G.H., Letter to T.R., 18 December 1963.

47 G.H., Letter to A.&B.H., 2 January 1964; see also G.H., Letter to V.S., 7 January 1964.

48 G.H., Letter to T.R., 6 January 1964.

49 G.H., Letter to E.T., 8 May 1964.

50 G.H., Letter to T.R., 27 January 1964.

51 G.H., Letter to T.R., 8 January 1964.

52 G.H., Letter to A.&B.H., 8 January 1964.

53 G.H., Letter to T.R., 27 January 1964.

54 G.H., Letter to V.B., 26 January 1964, in *A Steady Storm of Correspondence*, p. 188.

55 G.H., Letter to E.T., 27 February 1964.

56 G.H., Letter to T.R., 10 January 1964.

57 G.H., Letter to V.S., 14 February 1964.

58 G.H., Letter to T.R., 1 March 1964.

59 The publication date on the copyright page was 1963, so the book is usually regarded as having been published in that year.

60 G.H., Letter to A.&B.H., 11 March 1964.

61 G.H., Letter to T.R., 22 March 1964.

62 G.H., Letter to T.R., 1 September 1964.

63 G.H., Letter to T.R., 18 February 1964.

64 G.H., Letter to T.R., 24 April 1964; see also G.H., Letter to A.J., 9 August 1965.

65 Margaret Scott, *Changing Countries: On Moving from One Island to Another*, ABC Books, Sydney, 2000, p. 160.

66 For instance, she told Eddie that her *Bulletin* hoax struck a blow at 'bourgeois affectation': G.H., Letter to E.T., 5 September 1961.

67 G.H., Letter to T.R., 1 March 1964.

68 G.H., Letter to V.S., 14 February 1964, in *A Steady Storm of Correspondence*, p. 189.

69 G.H., Letter to T.R., 21 September 1965.

70 G.H., Letter to T.R., 18 February 1964.

71 G.H., Letter to T.R., 1 March 1964.

72 G.H., Letter to A.J., 9 August 1965.

73 G.H., Letter to T.R., 18 February 1964.

74 G.H., Letter to T.R., 4 February 1964.

75 G.H., Letter to A.&B.H., 19 March 1964.

76 G.H., Letter to T.R., 22 March 1964.

77 Blackman, 'Four Poets in One'.

78 G.H., Letter to T.R., 10 June 1964, referring specifically to the *ABR* review.

79 G.H., Letter to T.R., 27 June 1964; G.H., Letter to Thomas Shapcott, 7 July 1964, in *A Steady Storm of Correspondence*, p. 193.

80 G.H., Letter to E.T., 17 July 1963.

81 G.H., Letter to Thomas Shapcott, 7 July 1964, in *A Steady Storm of Correspondence*, p. 193.

82 G.H., Letter to A.&B.H., 11 November 1964.

83 G.H., Letter to T.R., 1 December 1965.

84 G.H., Letter to T.R., 11 November 1964.

85 G.H., Letter to A.&B.H., 16 February 1966.

86 G.H., Letter to A.&B.H., 10 May 1966.

87 G.H., Letter to A.&B.H., 11 September 1964.

88 G.H., Letter to T.R., 19 August 1964; G.H., Letter to A.&B.H., 11 September 1964.

89 G.H., Letter to T.R., 19 August 1964.

90 Ibid.

91 G.H., Letter to Thomas Shapcott, 27 October 1964.

92 G.H., Letter to T.R., 11 November 1964.

93 G.H., Letter to A.&B.H., 26 November 1964.

94 Ibid.

95 G.H., Letter to T.R., 23 September 1964.

96 G.H., Letter to T.R., 24 May 1966.

97 G.H., Letter to E.T., 7 April 1960.

98 V.B., Letter to G.H., 12 March 1964.

99 G.H., Letter to T.R., 1 June 1964; see also G.H., Letter to E.T., 8 May 1964, in *A Steady Storm of Correspondence*, p. 191.

100 Judith Crispin, 'The Nuctemeron of Sitsky', *Current Issues in Music*, vol. 2, 2008, pp. 7–38, p. 29, n. 78; p. 32, n. 118.

101 G.H., Letter to T.R., 23 September 1964.

102 G.H., Letter to L.S., 30 September 1964.

103 Gwen Harwood, 'By Way of Music', *OzMuZe*, vol. 1, no. 3, December 1990, n.p.

104 G.H., Letter to T.R., 12 May 1965.

105 G.H., Letter to L.S., 22 January 1965.

106 Hale, *Beyond the Black Stump*.

107 G.H., Letter to T.R., 22 June 1965.

108 Ibid.

109 G.H., Letter to E.T., 20 June 1965.

110 Harwood, 'By Way of Music'.

111 G.H., Letter to T.R., 20 August 1965.

112 Ibid.

113 G.H., Letter to V.S. and Sybille Smith, 18 August 1965, in *A Steady Storm of Correspondence*, p. 201.

114 G.H., Letter to T.R., 23 November 1965.

CHAPTER 17

1 G.H., Letter to T.R., 23 November 1966; G.H., Letter to A.J., 17 October 1966.

2 G.H., Letter to T.R., 26 September 1966.

3 G.H., Letter to A.J., 9 November 1966.

4 Ibid.

5 Ibid.

6 See e.g., G.H., Letter to T.R., 11 September 1959.

7 G.H., Letter to T.R., 24 November 1964.

8 G.H., Letter to T.R., 23 November 1966.

9 Larry Sitsky, 'James Penberthy', Obituary, *The Sydney Morning Herald*, 9 April 1999.

10 Ffion Murphy, 'Madame Ballet', *Brolga*, 1 June 2002, p. 16.

11 Reid, 'James Penberthy'.

12 G.H., Letter to J.P., 23 July 1966.

13 G.H., Letter to L.S., 10 June 1968.

14 G.H., Letter to T.R., 27 September 1966.

15 J.P., Letter to G.H., undated [late 1971].

16 J.P., Letter to G.H., 29 September 1971.

17 G.H., Letter to J.P., 6 October 1971.

18 G.H., Letter to J.P., 30 December 1971.

19 G.H., Letter to J.P., 24 September 1971.

20 G.H., Letter to T.R., 9 November 1965.

21 Ibid.

22 G.H., Letter to T.R., 21 January 1966.

23 G.H., Letter to T.R., 3 July 1966.

24 G.H., Letter to A.&B.H., 4 July 1966.

25 G.H., Letter to A.J., 25 July 1966.

26 G.H., Letter to T.R., 2 November 1967.

27 G.H., Letter to A.J., 25 July 1966.

28 Ibid.

29 G.H., Letter to A.J., 23 February 1965.

30 G.H., Letter to T.R., 19 July 1966; to A.J., 25 July 1966.

31 G.H., Letter to A.J., 17 October 1966; to T.R., 20 June 1966.

32 G.H., Letter to A.J., 17 October 1966.

33 G.H., Letter to T.R., 28 May 1970.

34 The poet was Andrew Sant: Stephen Edgar, 'The Golden Wine of Rest,' in *Behind the Masks,* eds Robyn Mathison & Robert Cox, Ginninderra Press, Port Adelaide, 2015, p. 38.

35 G.H., Letter to J.P., 14 April 1972.

36 G.H., Letter to A.F., 28 March 1994.

37 G.H., Letter to T.R., 29 January 1967.

38 G.H., Letter to T.R., 10 February 1967.

39 G.H., Letter to A.J., 20 February 1967.

40 G.H., Letter to T.R., 23 February 1967.

41 Ibid.

42 G.H., Letter to A.J., 3 April 1967.

43 See e.g., to A.&B.H., 27 September 1963.

44 G.H., Letter to T.R., 31 March 1967; G.H., Letter to A.J., 22 March 1967.

45 G.H., Letter to T.R., 31 March 1967.

46 G.H., Letter to T.R., 20 April 1967.

47 G.H., Letter to T.R., 19 April 1967.

48 G.H., Letter to T.R., 3 July 1967; G.H., Letter to R.H., 27 October 1967.

49 G.H., Letter to T.R., 16 October 1967.

50 G.H., Letter to T.R., 22 May 1968.

51 G.H., Letter to T.R., 16 October 1967.

52 Buckley, *Cutting Green Hay,* pp. 169–70.

53 A.D. Hope, Letter to G.H., 22 December 1967.

54 G.H., Letter to T.R., 8 January 1968.

55 G.H., Letter to A.&B.H., 30 July 1968.

56 G.H., Letter to T.R., 21 May 1968.

57 G.H., Letter to T.R., 11 March 1965.

58 Hall, 'The Poetry of Gwen Harwood'.

59 Harwood, Interview with Ritch; see also G.H., Letter to Thomas Shapcott, 10 April 1970; Vivian Smith, pers. comm., re tips from James McAuley.

60 G.H., Letter to T.R., 15 July 1968.

61 G.H., Letter to A.&B.H., 30 July 1968.

62 Ibid.

63 G.H., Letter to T.R., 5 June 1969.

64 Maurice Dunlevy, 'Poet of Man's Regrets', *The Canberra Times*, 29 June 1968; 'fabulous review': G.H., Letter to A.&B.H., 30 July 1968.

65 Geoffrey Dutton, 'Three Conservatives,' *Australian Book Review*, vol. 7, no. 9, 1968, p. 162.

66 Alexander Craig, 'Australian Poetry – Nobody's Rocking the Boat', *The Bulletin*, vol. 89, no. 4567, 16 September 1967, pp. 31–32.

67 G.H., Letter to T.R., 31 July 1968.

68 G.H., Letter to Roger McDonald, 2 March 1970, in *A Steady Storm of Correspondence*, p. 240.

69 See Alison Hoddinott, 'Timothy Kline: A Trans-Gendered Trans-Generational Impersonation', *New England Review*, no. 12, Winter, 2000.

70 G.H., Letter to T.R., 6 March 1968.

71 Kratzmann has shown that at least one of Timothy Kline's poems, 'The Carnival of Venice', was also sent out under the name 'William Berry': Gregory Kratzmann, 'Who Was Alan Carvosso?', *Meanjin*, vol. 63, no. 1, 2004, p. 180.

72 G.H., Letter to T.R., 25 October 1968.

73 G.H., Letter to T.R., 29 September 1969.

74 G.H., Letter to T.R., 15 October 1969.

75 Roger McDonald, pers. comm., 3 May 2017.

76 Roger McDonald, Letter to G.H., 5 September 1969, FL, UQFL45, Box 2, Folder 16.

77 G.H., Letter to T.R., 29 September 1969.

78 G.H., Letter to T.R., 22 October 1969.

79 G.H., Letter to TS, 24 October 1969.

80 Roger McDonald, Letter to G.H., 20 October 1969, FL, UQFL45, Box 2, Folder 16.

81 Ibid.

82 Thomas Shapcott, 'Preface', in *Australian Poetry Now*, ed. Thomas Shapcott, Sun Books, South Melbourne, 1970, p. ix.

83 G.H., Letter to Roger McDonald, 8 January 1971, FL, UQFL45 Box 7, Folder 3.

84 G.H., Letter to TS, 8 June 1969.

85 G.H., Letter to Roger McDonald, 20 October 1969, FL, UQFL45 Box 7, Folder 3.

86 G.H., Letter to T.R., 22 October 1969.

87 'wicker basket': G.H., Letter to T.R., 22 October 1969; G.H., request to A.J., 24 December 1969.

CHAPTER 18

1 G.H., Letter to E.T., 22 July 1969.

2 G.H., Letter to T.R., 2 October 1968.

3 G.H., Letter to T.R., 21 October 1968.

4 G.H., Letter to T.R., 9 October 1968.

5 G.H., Letter to T.R., 25 October 1968.

6 G.H., Letter to A.J., 11 January 1968; see also G.H., Letter to T.R., 2 November 1967.

7 G.H., Letter to A.J., 11 January 1968.

8 Ibid.

9 G.H., Letter to T.R., 3 June 1969.

10 G.H., Letter to T.R., 19 August 1969, citing Shakespeare's Sonnet 30.

11 Handwritten draft of 'At Mornington' enclosed in a letter to T.R., September 1969. These two lines are the only substantial excision in the published version.

12 G.H., Letter to Thomas Shapcott, 17 June 1969, in *A Steady Storm of Correspondence*, p. 229.

13 Ibid.

14 Ibid.

15 T.R., Letter to A.H., 28 January 1987 (AH private collection).

16 G.H., Letter to T.R., 6 May 1970. Harwood said the poem, which begins with a paraphrase of the opening of the ballad of *Sir Patrick Spens*, was suggested by one of Horace's Odes, "O saepe mecum tempus in ultimum" (A Friend Returned), No. 7 of Book II.

17 G.H., Letter to Thomas Shapcott, 17 June 1969, in *A Steady Storm of Correspondence*, p. 230.

18 Chris Wallace-Crabbe, pers. comm., 26 October 2015.

19 G.H., Letter to T.R., 3 June 1969.

20 G.H., Letter to Thomas Shapcott, 17 June 1969.

21 G.H., Letter to E.T., 2 June 1969. The character is Iago from Shakespeare's *Othello*.

22 Ibid.

23 G.H., Letter to T.R., 2 September 1973.

24 G.H., Letter to L.S., undated, 1969.

25 G.H., Letter to T.R., 12 June 1969.

26 G.H., Letter to L.S., 21 May 1969; see also G.H., Letter to J.P., 9 May 1973.

27 G.H., Letter to T.R., 2 September 1969.

28 G.H., Letter to T.R., 10 July 1968.

29 G.H., Letter to T.R., 29 April 1969.

30 G.H., Letter to L.S., 10 March 1969.

31 G.H., Letter to T.R., date obscured [late 1969].

32 G.H., Letter to T.R., 12 June 1969.

33 G.H., Letter to L.S., 12 June 1969.

34 G.H., Letter to T.R., 11 August 1970.

35 G.H., Letter to L.S., 23 July 1969.

36 *Lenz*, Scene VI, transcription from the score, FL, UQFL45, Box 37, Parcel 1.

37 L.S., Letter to G.H., [31 August 1969?].

38 G.H., Letter to A.J., 2 April 1974.

39 G.H., Letter to T.R., 19 August 1975.

40 Reviews of *Lenz* from unsourced clippings in Gwen's scrapbooks, FL, UQFL45, Box 23. Ken Healey wrote that the performance was greeted with 'unanimous critical acclaim' (Healey, 'A Spirit Making Music', p. 8); see also W.L. Hoffman, 'Sitsky Writing Another Work', *The Canberra Times*, 19 June 1974, p. 15.

41 G.H., Letter to T.R., 6 May 1970.

42 Harwood reports giving this answer to a questioner in G.H., Letter to E.T., 18 May 1973; see Ann-Marie Priest, 'Sharon Olds, Gwen Harwood, Dorothy Hewett: Truth, Lies, Poetry', *Cordite Poetry Review*, vol. 56, 2016.

43 Harwood, *Blessed City*, p. 51.

44 Gregory Kratzmann, pers. comm.

45 Harwood, 'An All-Purpose Festival Poem', *Collected Poems,* p. 566.

46 G.H., Letter to A.J., 14 May 1970, 'aloft, Hobart–Sydney'.

47 G.H., Letter to L.S., 20 May 1970.

48 Ibid.

49 G.H., Letter to the Sitskys, 20 May 1970, in *A Steady Storm of Correspondence*, p. 246.

50 G.H., Letter to T.R., 29 June 1970; G.H., Letter to N.T., 16 March 1978.

51 G.H., Letter to T.R., 29 June 1970.

52 G.H., Letter to T.R., 28 May 1970, in *A Steady Storm of Correspondence*, p. 248.

53 Ibid., p. 247.

54 Cf. Peter Bennie, 'Proust and the Poet', *Poetry Australia*, no. 38, 1971, p. 49.

55 Poem enclosed in Peter Bennie, Letter to John Harwood, 30 June 2000, FL, UQFL45, Box 30; published in *Collected Poems* as 'Late Autumn, Sydney', p. 515.

56 G.H., Letter to T.R., 21 April 1971.

57 G.H., Letter to E.T., 26 September 1973.

58 G.H., Letter to E.T., 8 July 1971.

59 G.H., Letter to T.R., 1 September 1973.

60 G.H., Letter to T.R., 18 August 1971.

61 Ibid.

62 G.H., Letter to A.J., 25 August 1971.

63 G.H., Letters to T.R., 5 August 1971; 18 August 1971.

64 G.H., Letter to T.R., 22 June 1965.

65 G.H., Letter to N.T., 15 July 1994.

66 G.H., Letter to T.R., 18 August 1971.

67 Ibid.

68 G.H., Letter to A.J., 25 August 1971.

69 G.H., Letter to E.T., 10 August 1971; see also Harwood, 'Memories of Edwin Tanner', pp. 6–11.

70 G.H., Letter to T.R., 18 August 1971.

71 G.H., Letter to A.J., 25 August 1971.

72 Ibid.

73 G.H., Letter to E.T., 29 April 1971.

74 G.H., Letter to E.T., 20 July 1970.

75 E.T., Letter to G.H., 25 April 1973, FL, UQFL45 Box 5, Folders 2–6.

76 G.H., Letter to T.R., 19 February 1969.

77 J.P., Letter to G.H., 7 July 1971.

78 Harwood, 'Commentaries on Living', unpublished, FL, UQFL45, Box 25, Folder 13.

79 G.H., Letter to J.P., 23 April 1974.

80 G.H., Letter to J.P., 30 December 1971.

81 J.P., Letter to G.H., 25 February 1972.

82 G.H., Letter to J.P., 1 March 1972.

83 G.H., Letter to T.R., 18 November 1971.

84 G.H., Letter to T.R., 14 January 1972.

85 Ibid.

86 Peter Pierce, 'Writers' Careers – and James McAuley', University of Tasmania 125-Year Anniversary website, accessed 25 January 2022, http://125timeline. utas.edu.au/timeline/1960/writers-careers-and-james-mcauley.

87 G.H., Letter to E.T., 1 August 1972.

88 G.H., Letter to T.R., 24 October 1972.

89 Harwood, Diary, 9 October 1982.

90 G.H., Letter to E.T., 16 February 1972.

91 G.H., Letter to T.R., 17 February 1972.

92 James McAuley, 'Motel, Burnie', FL, UQFL45, Box 23. 'In Northern Tasmania', in McAuley's last collection, *Time Given*, may also refer to one of these trips.

93 G.H., Letter to E.T., 26 December 1972.

94 G.H., Letter to A.J., 6 September 1972.

95 G.H., Letter to TS, 10 April 1970, in *A Steady Storm of Correspondence*, p. 244.

96 Brian Rogers, explanatory notes on correspondence, FL, UQFL45, Box 19, Folder 6.

97 G.H., Letter to T.R., 4 October 1972.

98 John Abernathy, Letter to G.H., enclosed in G.H., Letter to T.R., 18 August 1971.

99 G.H., Letter to E.T., 1 August 1972.

100 G.H., Letter to A.J., 13 February 1973; see also G.H., Letter to T.R., 23 October 1972: 'Berryman is perverse & odd and often unintelligible, but enough comes through to convince me of his power and skill'.

101 G.H., Letter to E.T., 26 December 1972.

102 G.H., Letter to T.R., 24 October 1972.

103 Harwood mentioned working on several poems in the 'Baby and Demon' sequence in letters to T.R. on 27 June 1973 and 15 November 1973, and possibly also 22 May 1973, as well as in a letter to E.T., 15 September 1973. Only one of these poems has survived: 'Night Thoughts: Baby and Demon', in *Collected Poems*, p. 267.

104 G.H., Letter to T.R., 24 October 1972.

105 G.H., Letter to E.T., 26 December 1972.

106 Ibid.

CHAPTER 19

1 G.H., Letter to A.J., 6 September 1972.

2 G.H., Letter to E.T., 13 April 1973.

3 G.H., Letter to A.J., 11 September 1973.

4   Gregory Kratzmann, pers. comm.

5   G.H., Letter to A.J., 13 February 1973.

6   G.H., Letter to T.R., 3 December 1972.

7   Ibid.

8   G.H., Letter to E.T., 18 May 1973.

9   G.H., Letter to T.R., 11 May 1973.

10 G.H., Letter to E.T., 15 September 1973 (*A Steady Storm of Correspondence*, p. 284).

11 G.H., Letter to E.T., date unclear [12 December 1971?]; see also G.H., Letter to A.J., 18 May 1973.

12 G.H., Letter to A.J., 18 May 1973.

13 G.H., Letter to J.P., 7 May 1973.

14 G.H., Letter to A.J., 18 May 1973.

15 G.H., Letter to T.R., 10 May 1973, in *A Steady Storm of Correspondence*, p. 277.

16 G.H., Letter to E.T., 15 April 1973.

17 G.H., Letter to A.J., 3 October 1972.

18 G.H., Letter to T.R., 4 October 1972.

19 G.H., Letter to E.T., 26 September 1973.

20 G.H., Letter to E.T., 18 June 1973.

21 G.H., Letter to E.T., 26 September 1973.

22 G.H., Letter to E.T., 15 September 1973.

23 G.H., Letter to E.T., 8 July 1971.

24 G.H., Letter to A.J., 11 September 1973.

25 See e.g., G.H., Letter to E.T., 16 July 1973.

26 G.H., Letter to A.J., 11 September 1973.

27 G.H., Letter to J.P., 30 December 1971.

28 G.H., Letter to R.H., 14 March 1975.

29 G.H., Letter to A.H., 15 July 1981.

30 G.H., Letter to R.H., 14 March 1975.

31 Harwood, *A Steady Storm of Correspondence*, p. 280.

32 G.H., Letter to A.J., 11 September 1973.

33 G.H., Letter to T.R., 15 November 1973.

34 G.H., Letter to A.J., 15 June 1973.

35 Harwood, *A Steady Storm of Correspondence*, pp. 281–82.

36 G.H., Letter to N.T., 15 July 1994.

37 G.H., Letter to N.T., 9 September 1973, Yoken Marker Poems, 'Plain and Slipperly'.

38 G.H., Letter to N.T., 29 November 1974: 'remember/ how we frolicked in the shower/ at El Rancho'.

39 G.H., Letter to N.T., 8 October 1974.

40 G.H., Sappho card to N.T., 30 September 1974.

41 Harwood, *A Steady Storm of Correspondence*, pp. 281–82.

42 G.H., Letter to A.J., 11 September 1973.

43 Harwood, *A Steady Storm of Correspondence*, p. 282.

44 G.H., Letter to N.T., undated, postmarked August 1973.

45 N.T., Letter to G.H., 28 August 1973. He published a slightly revised version in his book *Find the Lady* (South Head Press, Five Dock, 1977) as 'Early Draught of a Hoarse Epistle' (p. 84).

46 N.T., Letter to G.H., 28 August 1973. This poem was also published in *Find the Lady* (p. 61).

47 G.H., Letter to N.T., 7 September 1973.

48 G.H., Letter to N.T., 31 August 1973. This poem would become 'Meditation on Wyatt II' (*Collected Poems*, p. 271).

49 Two Yoken Marker Songs are in a letter to N.T. dated 7 September 1973 (these appear in *Collected Poems*, p. 520); another, 'You can easily wipe the writings out', is in a letter dated 9 September 1973.

50 G.H., Letter to N.T., 3 October 1973.

51 Ibid.; Norman Talbot's notes on Harwood's letters, made for Gregory Kratzmann, say that 'Thought' is a response to 'Wild Haloes'.

52 G.H., Letter to N.T., 18 November 1975.

53 G.H., Letter to T.R., 1 September 1973.

54 G.H., Letter to A.J., 11 September 1973.

55 G.H., Letter to T.R., 1 September 1973.

56 G.H., Letter to A.J., 11 September 1973.

57 G.H., Letter to N.T., 4 May 1974.

58 N.T., Letter to G.H., undated, beginning 'O Gwendolina!'

59 G.H., Letter to T.R., 7 September 1973.

60 Ibid.

61 Ibid.; G.H., Letter to T.R., 15 November 1973.

62 G.H., Letter to T.R., 17 July 1974.

63 G.H., Letter to T.R., 2 September 1973.

64 'Sea Changes', libretto ms., FL, UQFL45, Box 35, Folder 6.

65 Williams, 'Interview with Gwen Harwood', p. 57.

66 G.H., Letter to J.P., 6 June 1973.

67 G.H., Letter to J.P., 28 August 1973.

68 J.P., Letter to G.H., undated, 1973.

69 See draft libretto, FL, UQFL45, Box 35, Folder 2.

70 See 'The Owl and the Pussycat Baudelaire Rock' and 'Later Texts II'.

71 In a later version, the obscenity has been edited out. Cf. 'The Owl and the Pussycat Baudelaire Rock' and 'Night Thoughts: Baby and Demon'.

72 G.H., Letter to A.J., 2 April 1974.

73 G.H., Letter to T.R., 21 May 1974.

74 G.H., Letter to A.J., 18 May 1973.

75 G.H., Letter to T.R., 23 June 1974.

76 G.H., Letter to T.R., 10 July 1974.

77 G.H., Letter to T.R., 31 July 1974.

78 G.H., Letter to A.J., 30 July 1974.

79 G.H., Letter to T.R., 12 August 1974.

80 G.H., Letter to N.T., undated [September 1974].

81 'How Gold Sinks Like a Stone', published as the third of three poems 'For Sylvia Plath' in *Find the Lady*.

82 G.H., Letter to N.T., undated [September 1974].

83 G.H., Letter to N.T., 13 November 1974. In a note to N.T. dated 17 September 1979, Harwood writes that 'Death I will tell you now' could be retitled 'In the roofless chapel at Morpeth'.

84 G.H., Letter to N.T., 22 October 1974.

85 The drawing was by Monique-Alika Watteau, from Francis Steegmuller's *Le Hibou et la Poussiquette*, Rupert Hart-Davis, London, 1961.

86 G.H., Letter to N.T., 8 October 1974.

87 G.H., Letter to N.T., 10 October 1974.

88 G.H., Letters to N.T., 19 November 1974; 25 November 1974.

89 G.H., Letter to N.T., 1 October 1974.

90 G.H., Letter to R.C., 27 June 1994.

91 G.H., Letter to N.T., 31 October 1974.

92 G.H., Letter to T.R., 23 October 1974.

93 G.H., Letter to N.T., 25 March 1975.

94 G.H., Letter to James McAuley, 11 November 1974, Mitchell Library, MLMSS 7920, Series 2, Box 6.

95 G.H., Letter to T.R., 23 October 1974.

96 G.H., Letter to A.H., 17 August 1985.

97 G.H., Letter to A.F., 20 April 1994.

98 G.H., Letter to A.H., 17 August 1985.

99 Alison Hoddinott, pers. comm.

100 G.H., Letter to Craig Powell, 2 August 1976.

101 G.H., Letter to E.T., 21 October 1975.

102 G.H., Letter to E.T., 5 May 1975; see also G.H., Letter to N.T., 8 April 1975.

103 G.H., Letter to N.T., 11 December 1974.

104 N.T., Letter to G.H., undated, late 1974.

105 G.H., Letter to N.T., 8 April 1975.

106 G.H., Letter to R.H., 14 March 1975.

107 G.H., Letter to N.T., 30 April 1975.

108 G.H., Letter to J.P., 1 February 1975.

CHAPTER 20

1 G.H., Christmas card to A.J., undated [c. 1973].

2 G.H., Letter to T.R., 11 April 1975.

3 G.H., Letter to L.S., 4 March 1975; G.H., Letter to TR, 14 March 1975; G.H., Letter to ET, 21 October 1975.

4   G.H., Letter to N.T., 24 November 1975.

5   G.H., Letter to T.R., 23 October 1974.

6   G.H., Letter to R.H., 14 March 1975.

7   G.H., Letter to T.R., 18 December 1975.

8   Alison J.E. Wood, 'The Poetics of Libretti: Reading the Opera Works of Gwen Harwood and Larry Sitsky', MA thesis, University of Adelaide, 2007, p. 37.

9   G.H., Letter to L.S., 2 October 1974.

10 Wood, 'The Poetics of Libretti', pp. 35–36.

11 G.H., Letter to L.S., 7 March 1977.

12 G.H., Letter to T.R., 30 May 1975, in *A Steady Storm of Correspondence*, p. 300.

13 Ibid.

14 G.H., Letter to N.T., 16 March 1978.

15 In 1969, Harwood sent the first stanza of this poem to Thomas Shapcott, Roger McDonald and Vincent Buckley and asked them to complete it to win the inaugural Harwood Memorial Fruitcake Award. All three poets entered, and Harwood awarded the prize to Buckley. The version of the poem that Harwood published in her *Selected Poems* is included among Shapcott's papers with Buckley's signature. See Ann-Marie Priest, 'The Harwood Memorial Fruitcake Award', *Australian Book Review*, no. 432, June 2021, pp. 49–52.

16 G.H., Letter to E.T., 15 April 1973.

17 G.H., Letter to Beverley Dunn, 11 April 1972, in *A Steady Storm of Correspondence*, p. 265.

18 G.H., Letter to T.R., 30 May 1975, in *A Steady Storm of Correspondence*, p. 299. Cf. Priest, 'Baby and Demon'.

19 G.H., Letter to N.T., 22 October 1974. Cf. Diane Dodwell, 'Worlds beyond Words', on a recurrent theme in GH's poetry: 'a vision of the "darkness" (incomplete understanding) at the heart of human knowing redeemed in sexual love' (p. 76).

20 G.H., Letter to E.T., 15 September 1973.

21 Clive James, *Cultural Amnesia*, pp. 802, 805.

22 Gwen Harwood, 'A Note on Noel Stock's Note on Wittgenstein's *Tractatus*', *Poetry Australia*, no. 67, 1978, p. 79.

23 Ibid., citing Wittgenstein's *Zettel*, p. 160.

24 G.H., Letter to E.T., 26 September 1973.

25 Harwood, 'Imagination and Meaning', p. 29.

26 G.H., Letter to T.R., 5 June 1974 [misdated 5 August 1974].

27 G.H., Letter to T.R., 15 November 1973.

28 Suzanne Edgar, 'Poems', *The Canberra Times*, 5 September 1975, p. 12; John Beston, *The Sydney Morning Herald*, 18 October 1975, p. 21; Dodwell, 'Worlds Beyond Words'.

29 G.H., Letter to E.T., 18 May 1973, in *A Steady Storm of Correspondence*, p. 280.

30 G.H., Letter to Brian Rogers, 26 October 1976, FL, UQFL45, Box 19, Folder 6.

31 Ibid.

32 G.H., Letter to E.T., 5 April 1976.

33 G.H., Letter to E.T., 23 February 1976.

34 G.H., Letter to T.R., 19 February 1976.

35 G.H., Letter to L.S., 12 January 1976.

36 G.H., Letter to T.R., 25 January 1976.

37 G.H., Letter to R.H., 2 February 1976.

38 G.H., Letter to F.K., 9 November 1977.

39 G.H., Letter to F.K., 8 November 1978.

40 G.H., Letter to A.J., 15 March 1976.

41 G.H., Letters to T.R., 24 February 1976; undated [late March 1976] (from Bruny).

42 G.H., Letter to T.R., 30 March 1976; 4 May 1976; 12 April 1976.

43 G.H., Letter to Brian Rogers, 26 October 1976, FL, UQFL45, Box 19, Folder 6.

44 G.H., Letter to T.R., 5 January 1976.

45 Helen Frizell, '10,000 Accolades for Poet', *The Sydney Morning Herald*, 17 November 1978, p. 7.

46 G.H., Letter to T.R., 12 April 1976.

47 G.H., Letter to T.R., 16 January 1976.

48 G.H., Letters to T.R., 21 May 1976; 23 May 1976.

49 G.H., Letter to N.T., 2 April 1976.

50 G.H., Letter to N.T., 21 July 1976.

51 G.H., Letter to F.K., 9 October 1981.

52 G.H., Letters to F.K., 1 December 1979; 15 July 1981; see also G.H., Letter to F.K., 15 May 1981.

53 G.H., Letter to N.T., 18 March 1976.

54 Hale, *Beyond the Black Stump.*

55 Gwen Harwood, 'Evening, Oyster Cove', in *Collected Poems*, p. 302.

56 Gwen Harwood, 'Looking towards Bruny'; see also 'Shellgrit', which refers to 'old oyster middens' in 'a place where history's evil/ grows luminous in distance,/ haunted and beautiful' (*Collected Poems*, p. 304).

CHAPTER 21

1 Edgar Sleinis, pers. comm., 3 November 2015.

2 G.H., Letter to T.R., 21 August 1976.

3 G.H., Letter to N.T., 27 April 1977.

4 Wood, 'The Poetics of Libretti', pp. 40–42.

5 G.H., Letter to L.S., 20 September 1976.

6 Harwood, 'Memoirs of a Dutiful Librettist', p. 8.

7 Harwood, 'Memoirs of a Dutiful Librettist', pp. 8–9.

8 G.H., Letter to L.S., 21 September 1977.

9 G.H., Letter to L.S., 4 May 1981.

10 G.H., Letter to L.S., 13 August 1981.

11 G.H., Letter to Craig Powell, 2 August 1976.

12 G.H., Letter to N.T., 15 September 1976.

13 G.H., Letter to A.J., 26 November 1976.

14 G.H., Letter to N.T., 17 October 1976.

15 G.H., Letter to R.H., 25 June 1977.

16 G.H., Letter to Craig Powell, 3 September 1977.

17 Harwood, *A Steady Storm of Correspondence*, p. 320; on an obituary she enclosed in a letter to N.T. (17 October 1976), Harwood annotated the line 'He had a penetrating understanding of beauty' with: 'the right word as many beauties can testify'.

18 G.H., Letter to N.T., 19 March 1975.

19 N.T., Letter to G.H., 21 March 1975.

20 G.H., Letter to N.T., 25 March 1975.

21 Harwood, *A Steady Storm of Correspondence*, p. 213.

22 Nancy Cato, Letter to G.H., 5 April 1969, FL, UQFL45, Box 1, Folder 8.

23 N.T., Letter to G.H., 24 January 1975.

24 N.T., Letter to G.H., 12 June 1975.

25 G.H., Letter to A.H., 10 August 1981.

26 G.H., Letter to A.H., 10 April 1983.

27 N.T., Letter to G.H., 18 November 1975.

28 N.T., Letter to G.H., 12 March 1976.

29 G.H., Letter to N.T., 18 March 1976.

30 N.T., Letter to G.H., 22 March 1976.

31 N.T., Letter to G.H., 15 July 1976.

32 N.T., Letter to G.H., 23 January 1977.

33 G.H., Letter to N.T., 8 February 1977.

34 G.H., Letter to T.R., 14 February 1977.

35 G.H., Letter to N.T., 16 February 1978.

36 G.H., Letter to N.T., 27 April 1977.

37 G.H., Letter to N.T., 15 June 1977 (edited version in Harwood, *A Steady Storm of Correspondence*, p. 330).

38 Ibid.

39 It appeared in the short-lived literary journal *riverrun* in 1978, but she did not include it in her next volume, nor in later editions of her *Selected Poems*.

40 N.T., Letter to G.H., undated, FL, UQFL45, Box 25, Folder 10.

41 G.H., Letter to N.T., 17 October 1977.

42 G.H., Letter to A.&B.H., 31 October 1977.

43 Ibid.

44 G.H., Letter to Craig Powell, 27 October 1977.

45 Ibid.

46 Hewett to G.H., 6 November 1977, FL, UQFL45, Box 28, Folder 7.

47 Hewett to G.H., 28 December 1978, FL, UQFL45, Box 28, Folder 7.

48 G.H., Letter to N.T., 25 January 1979.

49 G.H., Letter to Craig Powell, 30 September 1975.

50 Dorothy Hewett, *Wild Card*, Penguin, Ringwood, 1990.

51 Harwood refers to writing this poem in a letter to N.T. on 25 January 1979.

52 Dorothy Hewett, Letter to G.H., 26 February 1979, FL, UQFL45, Box 28, Folder 7.

53 N.T., Letter to G.H., 23 January 1978 [misdated 1977].

54 G.H., Letter to N.T., 27 January 1978.

55 G.H., Letter to T.R., 14 February 1978.

56 G.H., Letter to T.R., 24 February 1978.

57 G.H., Letter to A.&B.H., 18 September 1978.

58 G.H., Letter to N.T., 20 February 1978.

59 G.H., Letter to A.H., 18 September 1978.

60 G.H., Letter to N.T., 28 February 1978.

61 G.H., Letter to T.R., 24 February 1978.

62 Stephen Edgar, pers. comm., 21 October 2015.

63 G.H., Letter to N.T., 8 March 1978.

64 G.H., Letter to N.T., 26 April 1978.

65 G.H., Letter to N.T., 2 May 1978 (note from G.K. indicates that 'A Valediction' was enclosed with this letter).

66 G.H., Letter to T.R., 22 March 1978.

67 G.H., Letter to T.R., 1 June 1978.

68 G.H., Letter to F.K., 18 September 1978.

69 G.H., Letter to T.R., 1 June 1978.

70 G.H., Letter to A.H., 18 September 1978, quoted in Hoddinott, *Gwen Harwood: The Real and Imagined World*, p. 37.

71 Harwood told Gregory Kratzmann (pers. comm.) that she and Peter Bennie had sex during this time, and her comments in a later letter to Ann Jennings indicate that it was on this particular day.

72 G.H., Letter to A.J., 12 September 1990.

73 From GH's handwritten notes for Hoddinott on the *Blessed City* ms. (A.H. private collection); see also G.H., Letter to A.J., 12 September 1990.

74 Peter Bennie to G.H., 3 March 1982 (FL, UQFL45, Box 16).

75 From GH's handwritten notes for Hoddinott on the *Blessed City* ms. (A.H. private collection).

76 G.H., Letter to T.R., 1 June 1978.

77 G.H., Letter to N.T., 15 September 1976.

78 G.H., Letter to Roger McDonald, 8 January 1971, FL, UQFL45 Box 7, Folder 3.

79 G.H., Letter to N.T., 15 September 1976.

80 G.H., Letter to T.R., 29 October 1978.

81 G.H., Letter to F.K., 15 December 1978.

82 G.H., Letter to N.T., 28 November 1978.

83 G.H., Letter to A.H., 27 November 1978.

84 Frizell, '10,000 Accolades for Poet'.

85 G.H., Letter to L.S., 2 April 1978.

86 G.H., Letter to N.T., 4 April 1978.

CHAPTER 22

1 G.H., Letter to F.K., 20 December 1977.

2 G.H., Letter to A.H., 24 March 1983.

3 Ibid.; cf. Harwood, Diary, 5 December 1982: dream of 'Les Murray & forgotten giant baby'.

4 G.H., Letter to A.H., 25 June 1991.

5 G.H., Letter to N.T., 27 March 1979.

6 G.H., Letter to Craig Powell, 2 August 1976; G.H., Letter to L.S., 23 April 1979.

7 G.H., Letter to Rex and Perpetua Hobcroft, 20 October 1983.

8 G.H., Letter to N.T., 16 May 1979.

9 G.H., Letter to N.T., 17 September 1979.

10 F.K., Letter to G.H., 1957 (A.H. transcription): 'why oh why do you regard the state of being "in love" as blessed? In my experience it is like being bashed round the ears with a bicycle chain.'

11 G.H., Letter to N.T., 17 September 1979.

12 Harwood, Note on diary-entry for 31 July 1979: 'This is the day Sally went mad – I was booked to give seminar at university but cancelled it & collected Sally. Edgar stayed at night.'

13 G.H., Letter to N.T., 18 September 1979.

14 G.H., Letter to F.K., 28 June 1979.

15 T.R., Letter to F.K., 15 October 1981.

16 G.H., Letter to F.K., 14 March 1981.

17 Peter Ward, 'The Poet as a Prize Winner', *The Australian*, 17 November 1978.

18 G.H., Letter to F.K., 9 October 1981: 'I've been trying my hand at prose (isn't it *hard*!)'. She told Hoddinott that poetry was much easier than prose because 'you already had the structure' (pers. comm.).

19 She mentions working on 'Among the Roses' and 'Gemini' in her diary in 1980, and 'The Glass Boy' in 1981. 'Memoirs of a Dutiful Librettist' and 'Time beyond Reason' were published in 1987 in Sellick, *Gwen Harwood*.

20 Don Kay, 'The Sweet Singer of Pine Street', in Robyn Mathison and Robert Cox (eds), *Behind the Masks: Gwen Harwood Remembered by Her Friends*, Ginninderra Press, Port Adelaide, 2015, pp. 21–26.

21 Harwood, 'Memoirs of a Dutiful Librettist', p. 11.

22 G.H., Letter to T.R., 28 July 1982; cf. G.H., Letter to L.S., 26 November 1974.

23 G.H., Letter to N.T., 20 August 1980.

24 G.H., Letter to A.F., 24 October 1994.

25 G.H., Letter to F.K., 26 November 1980.

26 G.H., Letter to T.R., 1 July 1980.

27 G.H., Letter to A.H., 27 May 1991.

28 G.H., Letter to A.H., 15 July 1981.

29 Harwood, 'Memories of Edwin Tanner', p. 11.

30 G.H., Letter to J.P., 26 November 1980.

31 Ibid.

32 G.H., Letter to N.T., 7 December 1980.

33 G.H., Christmas card to A.H., 1980.

34 G.H., Letter to T.R., 14 October 1975.

35 G.H., Letter to A.H., 14 July 1981.

36 *The Monash Reporter*, 6 July 1988, reprinted in Strauss, *Boundary Conditions*, p. 179.

37 G.H., Letter to A.H., 14 July 1981.

38 G.H., Letter to A.H., 10 April 1983.

39 G.H., Letter to N.T., 17 September 1979.

40 G.H., Letter to N.T., 1 March 1981.

41 Frizell, '10,000 Accolades for Poet'; see also Elizabeth Riddell, 'Making Good Books after a Late Start', *The Australian*, 24 January 1970, in which Gwen responds to the question 'Are you religious?' with: 'Not in the Christian sense. But all poets are religious.'

42 Harwood, Diary, 11 September 1982; G.H., Letter to A.H., 25 March 1985.

43 G.H., Letter to A.H., 19 May 1982.

44 G.H., Letter to A.H., 21 June 1982.

45 See e.g., G.H., Letter to T.R., 20 July 1981.

46 G.H., Letter to A.H., 11 November 1982.

47 G.H., Letter to Craig Powell, 16 December 1982.

48 Harwood, *A Steady Storm of Correspondence*, p. 362.

49 G.H., Letter to J.P., 17 June 1982.

50 Harwood, *A Steady Storm of Correspondence*, p. 362.

51 G.H., Letter to F.K., 15 November 1983.

52 G.H., Letter to T.R., 20 July 1981.

53 T.R., Letter to F.K., [2 May 1980?].

54 G.H., Letter to Dorothy Hewett, 1 July 1979, NLA MS6184, Series 1, Box 1, Folder 7.

55 G.H., Letter to J.P., 10 November 1982.

56 G.H., Letter to A.H., 24 March 1983.

57 Gwen Harwood, Review of *Trillium* by Susan McGowan, Kathryn Purnell and Audrey Longbottom, *Luna*, no. 17, 1983, pp. 23–29.

58 G.H., Letter to N.T., 17 September 1979.

59 G.H., Letter to T.R., 15 July 1982.

60 G.H., Letter to A.H., 17 February 1983.

61 G.H., Letter to A.H., 8 December 1982.

62 G.H., Letter to T.R., 23 August 1980.

63 G.H., Letter to F.K., 31 July 1980; cf. G.H., Letter to F.K., 4 March 1980.

64 G.H., Letter to F.K., 31 July 1980.

65 Andrew Sant, pers. comm., 3 January 2017.

66 G.H., Letter to L.S., 5 February 1982.

67 Harwood, 'Memoirs of a Dutiful Librettist', p. 10.

68 Wood, 'The Poetics of Libretti', p. 53.

69 G.H., Letter to L.S., 27 July 1982.

70 G.H., Letter to A.H., 11 October 1982.

71 G.H., Letter to T.R., 4 August 1982, in *A Steady Storm of Correspondence*, p. 359.

72 G.H., Letter to A.H., 17 September 1982.

73 G.H., Letter to N.T., 2 April 1983.

74 Ibid.

75 Harwood, Diary, 16 September 1981.

76 G.H., Letter to A.H., 17 February 1983.

77 G.H., Letter to A.H., 12 March 1984.

78 G.H., Letter to A.H., 14 July 1981.

79 G.H., Letter to R.H., 9 August 1983.

80 G.H., Letter to N.T., 12 March 1984; see also G.H., Letter to R.H., 9 August 1983.

81 G.H., Letter to N.T., 9 July 1984; G.H., Letter to T.R., 12 June 1984.

82 G.H., Letter to A.H., 17 June 1984.

83 G.H., Letter to Rex and Perpetua Hobcroft, 20 October 1983.

84 G.H., Letter to Magda Sitsky, 6 June 1984.

85 G.H., Letter to Rex and Perpetua Hobcroft, 9 August 1983.

86 G.H., Letter to L.S., 3 December 1984; see also G.H., Letter to Kevin Hart, 2 October 1985.

87 G.H., Letter to L.S., 3 December 1984.

CHAPTER 23

1 Harwood, *A Steady Storm of Correspondence*, p. 380.

2 Ibid., p. 372.

3 Ibid.

4 G.H., Letter to N.T., 23 January 1985.

5 Poem I of 'A Quartet for Dorothy Hewett'; see also 'Evening: "Et in Arcadia ego"', Poem III of the Oyster Cove Pastorals, 'The Secret Life of Frogs', and 'Sheba'.

6 G.H., Letter to N.T., 23 January 1985.

7 G.H., Letter to N.T., 20 February 1985.

8 G.H., Letter to A.F., 23 March 1994.

9 Ibid.

10 John Chilcott, 'Observer in the Chaucer Mould', in Mathison and Cox, *Behind the Masks*, p. 53.

11 G.H., Letter to A.H., 13 July 1985.

12 G.H., Letter to A.H., 27 May 1991.

13 G.H., Letter to A.H. 4 June 1985.

14 Ibid.

15 G.H., Letter to A.H., 5 June 1985.

16 G.H., Letter to N.T., 12 June 1985.

17 G.H., Letter to A.H., 10 June 1985.

18 G.H., Letter to A.H., 11 June 1985.

19 G.H., Letter to N.T., 12 June 1985.

20 G.H., Letter to N.T., 21 June 1985.

21 Ibid.

22 G.H., Letter to A.H., [12 June 1985?].

23 G.H., Letter to A.H., 17 August 1985.

24 Ibid.

25 G.H., Letter to A.H., 23 June 1985.

26 G.H., Letter to A.H., 13 July 1985.

27 G.H., Letter to N.T., 15 July 1985.

28 Harwood, *A Steady Storm of Correspondence*, p. 380.

29 G.H., Letter to A.H., 13 July 1985.

30 G.H., Letter to N.T., 29 October 1985.

31 G.H., Letter to A.H., 13 July 1985.

32 G.H., Letter to N.T., 24 August 1985.

33 G.H., Letter to A.J., 13 May 1986; see also G.H., Letter to A.H., 3 May 1986.

34 G.H., Letter to A.H., 3 May 1986.

35 G.H., Letter to N.T., 4 May 1986.

36 G.H., Letter to A.H., 23 June 1985.

37 G.H., Letter to A.H., 17 August 1985.

38 G.H., Letter to A.H., 23 June 1985.

39 G.H., Letter to A.H., 24 July 1985.

40 G.H., Letter to T.R., 16 July 1987.

41 Ibid.; 'knockers & ringers' in G.H., Letter to A.H., 5 June 1995.

42 G.H., Letter to A.H., 13 July 1985.

43 G.H., Letter to R.H., 10 November 1987.

44 Harwood, Diary, 12 November 1992.

45 Berenice Eastman, pers. comm., 16 November 2017.

46 G.H., Letter to A.H., 17 November 1986.

47 Harwood, Diary, 13 October 1986.

48 G.H., Letter to A.H., 8 March 1986.

49 G.H., Letter to L.S., 7 June 1984; 19 September 1984. See also L.S., Letter to G.H., 28 September 1984.

50 L.S., Letter to G.H., 11 April 1986.

51 G.H., Letter to L.S., 12 February 1987.

52 G.H., Letter to L.S., 15 December 1966.

53 G.H., Letter to J.P., 2 November 1987.

54 Ibid.

55 G.H., Letter to R.H., 4 November 1988.

56 Ibid.

57 Kay, 'The Sweet Singer of Pine Street'.

58 G.H., Letter to T.R., 21 June 1972.

59 G.H., Letter to T.R., 23 May 1991.

60 G.H., Letter to A.H., 10 April 1983.

61 Letter 116, *Blessed City* ms., [11 or 18 May 1944?], FL, UQFL45, Box 7, Folder 4.

62 G.H., Letter to A.H., 2 February 1985 (postmarked 1986).

63 T.R., Letter to A.H., 11 December 1986.

64 Alison Hoddinott, 'Editing Gwen Harwood', *Island*, no. 111, 1987, pp. 29–45.

65 G.H., Letter to A.H., 10 December 1986.

66 G.H., Letter to A.H., 8 December 1986.

67 G.H., Letter to A.H., 10 December 1986.

68 A.H., Letter to T.R., 4 December 1986 (A.H. private collection).

69 Hoddinott, 'Editing Gwen Harwood'.

70 G.H., Letter to A.H., 28 February 1990.

71 G.H., Letter to A.H., 8 December 1986.

72 For example, Harwood, Diary, 4 and 10 December 1991, 14 July 1993, 17 October 1993, 26 December 1993.

73 Harwood, Diary, 17 April 1993.

74 Harwood, Diary, 24 June 1994.

75 G.H., Letter to A.H., 19 March 1986; G.H., Letter to William Paton, 14 January 1991, in *A Steady Storm of Correspondence*, pp. 421–22.

76 G.H., Letter to A.H., 12 May 1989.

77 Gwen Harwood, 'Herongate', in *Collected Poems*, p. 481.

78 G.H., Letter to A.H., 19 March 1986.

79 G.H., Letter to R.H., 16 July 1986.

80 Harwood, *A Steady Storm of Correspondence*, p. 422; G.H., Letter to Craig Powell, 13 August 1989.

81 Harwood, Diary, 24 March 1989.

82 G.H., Letter to A.H., 26 May 1989.

83 G.H., Letter to Craig Powell, 13 August 1989.

84 G.H., Letter to T.R., 1 July 1989, her ellipsis.

85 G.H., Letter to Craig Powell, 13 August 1989.

86 G.H., Letter to A.J., 17 February 1990.

87 G.H., Letter to A.H., 2 September 1989.

88 Harwood, *A Steady Storm of Correspondence*, p. 422.

CHAPTER 24

1 Reid, 'James Penberthy'. Harwood's 'Songs of Eve II' were originally written for this work, which was entitled 'The Creation of the World, or Eight Songs of Eve'. The opera was never performed.

2 They were unable to get a grant for this project, so it was never completed: G.H., Letter to L.S., 4 August 1993.

3 Geoff Page, 'Persistent Unpredictability', *The Canberra Times*, 9 June 1990, p. 28.

4   G.H., Letter to R.H., 4 November 1988.

5   Unidentified newspaper clipping in Harwood's 1989 Diary.

6   G.H., Letter to A.H., 6 March 1989.

7   G.H., Letter to A.H., 16 February 1990.

8   Some people saw Harwood's delighted demeanour on such occasions as unbecoming. On one occasion, Harwood told Hoddinott that she was in the midst of saying 'how much I enjoyed the ceremony and how everyone else seemed to' when she remembered the sour remarks of one of her 'enemies' on a previous occasion: 'but it was too late to be humble!' G.H., Letter to A.H., 21 May 1988.

9   G.H., Letter to T.R., 22 June 1989.

10   G.H., Letter to A.J., 14 September 1989.

11   Ibid.

12   Harwood, Interview with Hoddinott, p. 56.

13   Harwood, *A Steady Storm of Correspondence*, p. 418; see also G.H., Letter to Stephen Edgar, 20 September 1987, FL, F3162 Series A/1-60.

14   G.H., Letter to A.J., 14 March 1988.

15   G.H., Letter to Kevin Hart, 15 March 1988.

16   Cf. Harwood, 'Imagination and Meaning', in which she concludes that language enables us to 'break out' of our own 'self-enclosure' and 'reach other minds' (p. 29).

17   G.H., Letter to A.J., 16 March 1988.

18   G.H., Letter to A.H., 26 July 1991. Hoddinott remembered both Bill and Gwen watching the show when she was visiting; Bill explained the plot to her: 'They both seemed to enjoy it' (pers. comm.).

19   Harwood, Interview with Hoddinott, p. 56.

20   G.H., Letter to A.F., 10 February 1994.

21   Harwood, Interview with Hoddinott, p. 66.

22   G.H., Letter to A.J., 3 May 1988.

23   G.H., Letter to Craig Powell, 14 February 1989; G.H., Letter to A.H., 14 November 1988.

24   G.H., Letter to A.H., 14 November 1988.

25   G.H., Letter to Kevin Hart, 3 February 1989.

26   Ibid.

27   The other two elegies are 'Midwinter Rainbow' and 'Autumn'.

28   This section of 'The Present Tense' was first published as a separate poem entitled 'Absence: In Memoriam Vincent Buckley' in her 1992 chapbook: Gwen Harwood, *Night Thoughts*, National Library of Australia, Canberra, 1992.

29   G.H., Letter to A.H., 7 May 1991; G.H., Letter to Kevin Hart, 31 July 1991.

30   G.H., Letter to A.H., 24 August 1995. Harwood makes this point in relation to Bill and Patrick White, then extends it to Wittgenstein. See also Harwood's 'On Uncertainty (*Collected Poems*, p. 483).

31   G.H., Letter to A.H., late March 1989, in *A Steady Storm of Correspondence*, p. 410.

32 Wal Eastman and Berenice Eastman, 'Madam President', in *Behind the Masks*, pp. 35–36.

33 G.H., Letter to A.H., 22 March 1989.

34 Robyn Mathison, pers. comm.; Robyn Mathison, 'Of Pseudonyms and Serendipity', in *Behind the Masks*, p. 45.

35 Robyn Mathison, pers. comm., 3 November 2015.

36 G.H., Letter to A.H., 29 February 1990.

37 Berenice Eastman, pers. comm.; see also Eastman and Eastman, 'Madam President'.

38 Berenice Eastman, pers. comm.

39 G.H., Letter to A.H., 29 October 1990.

40 Eastman and Eastman, 'Madam President'.

41 G.H., Letter to A.H., 22 March 1989.

42 G.H., Letter to A.H., 7 May 1991; 11 March 1991.

43 G.H., Letter to A.H., 6 May 1991.

44 Sian Powell, 'There's Nothing Quite Like Little Gwen', *The Sydney Morning Herald*, 18 August 1990, p. 74.

45 G.H., Letter to A.H., 21 September 1990.

46 G.H., Letter to A.H., 22 November 1990.

47 Craig Powell, Letter to G.H., 14 January 1991, FL, UQFL45, Box 16, Folder 20.

48 G.H., Letter to Craig Powell, 21 January 1991.

49 Alison Hoddinott, pers. comm., 20 February 2015.

50 G.H., Letter to J.P., 6 November 1990.

51 G.H., Letter to A.H., 13 September 1990.

52 Quoted in ibid.

53 G.H., Letter to A.H., 13 September 1991.

54 G.H., Letter to A.H., 8 October 1990.

55 Alison Hoddinott, pers. comm., 21 February 2015.

56 G.H., Letter to T.R., 23 May 1991.

57 G.H., Letter to T.R. 23 May 1991; A.H., pers. comm.

58 G.H., Letter to A.J., 7 July 1992.

59 G.H., Letter to A.H., 27 May 1991.

60 Peter Bennie, Letter to G.H., undated [attached to G.H., Letter to A.H., 21 September 1991].

61 G.H., Letter to Stephen Edgar, 22 June 1992, FL, F3162 Series A/1-60.

62 Stephanie Trigg, *Gwen Harwood*, Oxford University Press, Melbourne, 1994, p. 2.

63 G.H., Letter to A.H., 21 June 1982.

64 G.H., Letter to N.T., 6 September 1982.

65 Carmen Callil, Letter to G.H., 17 February 1984 (enclosed in Harwood, Diary, 1984).

66 G.H., Letter to A.H., 12 March 1984.

67 G.H., Letter to G.K., 28 February 1991, in *A Steady Storm of Correspondence*, p. 422.

68 G.K., Letter to G.H., enclosed in G.K., Letter to A.H., 12 September 1991.

69 Harwood, *A Steady Storm of Correspondence*, p. 433.

70 G.H., Letter to A.H., 21 September 1991.

71 G.H., Letter to G.K., 26 September 1991, in *A Steady Storm of Correspondence*, p. 436.

72 G.H., Letter to A.J., 6 May 1992.

73 G.K., Letter to G.H., 7 July 1991.

74 Gregory Kratzmann, pers. comm.

75 G.H., Letter to A.H., 8 January 1992.

76 G.H., Letter to G.K., 25 February 1992.

77 G.H., Letter to A.H., 12 March 1992; G.K., Letter to G.H., 9 March 1992.

78 G.H., Letter to G.K., 3 April 1992.

79 G.K., Letter to G.H., 20 March 1992; G.K., Letter to G.H., 24 March 1992; Alison Hoddinott, pers. comm.

80 G.H., Letter to A.H., 15 December 1992.

81 Kratzmann did not write a biography, but his extensive selection of her letters (published after Harwood's death) was supported by a detailed biographical summary of each decade of her life as well as meticulous annotations.

CHAPTER 25

1 'International Books of the Year', *The Times Literary Supplement*, 6 December 1991.

2 G.H., Letter to A.H., 3 September 1995, reporting on a letter from US poet Mark Strand.

3 Ibid.; Craig Powell, 'Gwen Harwood (1920–1995): Craig Powell Recalls a Friend and a Poet', *Five Bells*, vol. 3, no. 4, 1996, pp. 6–7.

4 G.H., Letter to A.H., 21 September 1991.

5 G.H., Letter to R.H., 14 August 1988.

6 Greg Kratzmann, pers. comm. Kratzmann tells of attending a conference with Harwood, where Hoddinott's book was on display, with its cover photo of Gwen in her demure Peter Pan collar. 'What a sweet little old lady!' Gwen said, when she caught sight of it. 'I wish I knew someone like that.'

7 Tim Thorne, 'First Sight of the Famous Poet', in *Behind the Masks*.

8 Tim Thorne, 'High Noonin' Gwen Grabs Cup', *Mercury* (Tas.), 12 October 1991.

9 T.R., Letter to G.H., 28 July 1957.

10 G.H., Letter to A.H., 26 July 1991.

11 Harwood, Diary, 28 June 1987.

12 G.H., Letter to A.H., 26 August 1985.

13 G.H., Letter to T.R., 6 June 1994.

14 G.H., Letter to A.F., 27 January 1994.

15 G.H., Letter to R.C., 14 April 1994.

16 Sally Sleinis, 'To My Godmother', *Famous Reporter*, June 1996, p. 52.

17 '"Freely they stood, who stood, and fell who fell": The Tasmanian Peace Trust 1993 Lecture', in *Collected Poems*, p. 499.

18 Gwen Harwood, 'Crow-Call', in *Collected Poems*, p. 388.

19 Harwood, *A Steady Storm of Correspondence*, p. 430.

20 G.H., Letter to Barry Hassell Keane, 22 January 1992, FL, UQFL45, Box 21, Folder 2.

21 John Chilcott, 'Observer in the Chaucer Mould', in *Behind the Masks*, pp. 53–54.

22 Stuart Barnes, pers. comm., 8 February 2017.

23 G.H., Letter to A.F., 20 July 1994.

24 G.H., Letter to A.F., 28 May 1995.

25 G.H., Letter to G.K., 10 March 1992, in *A Steady Storm of Correspondence*, p. 440.

26 G.H., Letter to R.C., 14 April 1994.

27 G.H., Letter to A.H., 7 August 1992.

28 See Gwen Harwood, 'A Valentine', 'Forty Years On' and 'In Brisbane' (*Collected Poems*, pp. 335, 408 & 169).

29 G.H., Letter to Craig Powell, 4 July 1995.

30 G.H., Letter to A.H., undated, c. January 1992.

31 Harwood, Diary, 31 December 1991; Robyn Mathison, 'Of Pseudonyms and Serendipity', in *Behind the Masks*; Sarah Day, 'Demolition Dust and Doulton Cups', in *Behind the Masks*.

32 Harwood, Diary, 1 January 1992.

33 G.H., Letter to A.H., undated, c. January 1992.

34 Vikram Seth, Letter to G.H., 7 February 1992, FL, UQFL45, Box 20, Folder 1.

35 G.H., Letter to A.J., 16 May 1992.

36 G.H., Letter to A.H., 17 May 1992.

37 G.H., Letter to A.H., 19 May 1992.

38 G.H., Letter to A.H., 20 May 1992.

39 G.H., Letter to A.H., 19 May 1992.

40 Peter Bennie, Letter to G.H., 19 March 1982, FL, UQFL45, Box 16, Folder 2.

41 G.H., Letter to A.H., 19 October 1983.

42 Peter Bennie, Letter to G.H., 19 March 1982, FL, UQFL45, Box 16, Folder 2.

43 Peter Bennie, Letter to G.H., 13 May 1984, FL, UQFL45, Box 16, Folder 2.

44 Bennie, Letter to G.H., 8 July 1984. Harwood's comment was for Hoddinott, to whom she forwarded the letter.

45 Gregory Kratzmann, pers. comm., 24 August 2014.

46 Ibid.; Kratzmann (pers. comm.) said that Harwood 'beamed' and said: 'I love him still.'

47 G.H., Letter to A.H., 7 September 1992.

48 Stuart Barnes, pers. comm., 8 February 2017.

49 G.H., Letter to A.F., 1 June 1995.

50 Ralph Lane, Interview with Larry Sitsky, CD liner notes, *The Golem: A Grand Opera in Three Acts*, Larry Sitsky, Libretto by Gwen Harwood, ABC Classics and Opera Australia, 2003.

51 G.H., Letter to J.P., 1 November 1993.

52 G.H., Letter to L.S., 12 February 1995.

53 'Anglican Priest Bashed, Robbed in Home', *Mercury* (Tas.), 16 October 1993.

54 See Harwood, Diary, January 1994; G.H., Letter to A.F., 25 June 1994.

55 Harwood, Diary, 16 December 1993.

56 Harwood, Diary, 22 February 1994.

57 'Anglican Priest Facing Charges of Raping Man', *The Canberra Times*, 3 March 1994, p. 10.

58 G.H., Letter to G.K., 1 March 1994.

59 Harwood, Diary, 3 March 1994.

60 Harwood, Diary, 13 March 1994.

61 Yvonne Withington, Letter to Parish Council, 1 July 1994, FL, UQFL45 Box 21, Folder 1.

62 G.H., Letter to A.F., 4 April 1994.

63 G.H., Letter to A.F., 7 April 1994.

64 Ibid.

65 Alison Hoddinott, pers. comm., Janet Upcher, pers. comm., Berenice Eastman, pers. comm.

66 Greg Kratzmann, pers. comm., 15 February 2015. Cf. Harwood, Diary, 10 December 1994, referring to a dinner with Alan and Greg at Pine Street: 'B distressingly bloody minded through dinner . . . V. distressed.'

67 Harwood, Diary, 7 April 1992; Robyn Mathison, pers. comm.

68 G.H., Letter to A.H., 10 June 1995.

69 Alison Hoddinott, pers. comm.

70 G.H., Letter to G.K., 23 May 1994.

71 G.H., Letter to G.K., 12 June 1994.

72 See e.g., Harwood, Diary, 12 April 1994; 21 September 1994.

73 Yvonne Withington, pers. comm., 8 January 2019.

74 G.H., Letter to G.K., 8 August 1994.

75 G.H., Letter to G.K., 5 August 1994.

76 G.H., Letter to G.K., 23 August 1994.

77 G.H., Letter to R.C., 13 September 1994.

78 Harwood, Diary, 17 September 1994.

CHAPTER 26

1 G.H., Letter to A.F., 17 October 1994.

2 G.H., Letter to R.C., 18 October 1994.

3 G.H., Letter to A.F., 17 October 1994.

4 G.H., Letter to R.C., 14 April 1994.

5 G.H., Letter to A.F., 22 March 1995, quoting Shelley's 'Adonais'.

6 Harwood, Diary, 14 July 1993. See also Harwood, Diary, 17 October 1993; 26 December 1993.

7 G.H., Letter to A.F., 4 January 1994.

8 G.H., Letter to N.T., 27 January 1978.

9 G.H., Letter to N.T., 8 April 1975.

10 G.H., Letter to A.F., 21 December 1994.

11 G.H., Letter to R.C., 30 November 1994.

12 G.H., Letter to R.C., 4 January 1995.

13 G.H., Letter to Helen Mills, 14 July 1994 (private collection).

14 Harwood, Diary, 6 October 1994.

15 Harwood, Diary, 21 November 1994.

16 G.H., Letter to A.F., 9 January 1995.

17 Harwood, Diary, 12 January 1995.

18 G.H., Letter to R.C., 23 March 1995; 29 March 1995.

19 G.H., Letter to R.C., 17 January 1995.

20 G.H., Letter to R.C., 18 January 1995.

21 See Harwood, 'Goddess of the Crossroads', *The Present Tense*, p. 45.

22 G.H., Letter to R.C., 20 January 1995.

23 G.H., Card to A.F., undated, January 1995.

24 G.H., Letter to R.C., 20 January 1995.

25 G.H., Letter to Craig Powell, 29 January 1995.

26 G.H., Letter to A.F., 30 January 1995.

27 G.H., Letter to A.H., 8 March 1995; 27 June 1995.

28 G.H., Letter to A.H., 20 March 1995.

29 G.H., Letter to A.H., 8 March 1995.

30 G.H., Letter to T.R., 10 February 1963.

31 G.H., Card to A.F., undated [late January or early February 1995].

32 G.H., Letter to R.C., 27 July 1995.

33 Ibid.

34 G.H., Letter to A.H., 19 March 1995.

35 G.H., Letter to A.H., 26 March 1995.

36 G.H., Letter to A.H., 8 March 1995.

37 G.H., Letters to A.H., 10 June 1995; 27 June 1995.

38 G.H., Letter to A.H., 27 June 1995.

39 G.H., Letter to A.F., 7 February 1995.

40 G.H., Letter to R.C., 2 March 1995.

41 G.H., Letter to A.F., 2 April 1995.

42 G.H., Letter to R.C., 2 April 1995.

43 G.H., Letter to A.F., 22 March 1995, quoting Shelley's 'Adonais'.

44 G.H., Letter to A.F. 30 March 1995.

45 G.H., Letter to A.H., 12 April 1995.

46 G.H., Letter to A.H., 31 March 1995.

47 G.H., Letter to A.H., 8 March 1995.

48 G.H., Letter to A.H., 12 April 1995.

49 G.H., Letter to N.T., 18 May 1995.

50 G.H., Letter to G.K., 4 March 1995.

51 G.H., Letter to A.H., 1 August 1995.

52 G.H., Letter to A.J., 29 May 1995; G.H., Letter to A.H., 31 May 1995.

53 G.H., Letter to A.H., 26 May 1995.

54 Ibid.

55 G.H., Letter to A.H., 27 June 1995.

56 Ibid.

57 G.H., Letter to A.J., 20 July 1995.

58 G.H., Letter to A.H., 12 April 1995.

59 See e.g., G.H., Letter to A.J., 29 May 1995.

60 G.H., Letter to G.K., 19 July 1995.

61 G.H., Letter to A.H., 11 July 1995.

62 G.H., Letter to G.K., 8 July 1995.

63 G.H., Letter to R.C., 8 July 1995.

64 G.H., Letter to G.K., 8 July 1995.

65 Alan Farrell was freed in 1998 after an appeal to the High Court, which quashed his conviction and ordered a retrial. In 1999, the crown prosecutor decided not to proceed with a second trial. Catherine Anderson, 'Rape Accused Walked Free', *Mercury* (Tas.), 20 July 1999, p. 1; Melanie Alcock, 'Cleared Priest's Witch-Hunt Fears', *The Examiner*, 21 July 1999.

66 G.H., Letter to A.H., 11 July 1995.

67 G.H., Letter to G.K., 8 July 1995.

68 G.H., Letter to A.H., 20 July 1995.

69 'The anaesthetics and drugs have erased any interest in literature': G.H., Letter to N.T., 29 January 1995.

70 L.S., Letter to G.H., 6 February 1995.

71 G.H., Letter to L.S., 12 February 1995.

72 G.H., Letter to R.C., 3 July 1995.

73 G.H., Letter to A.H., 26 April 1995.

74 G.H., Letter to A.H., 9 August 1995.

75 G.H., Letter to R.C., 28 August 1995.

76 G.H., Letter to A.H., 28 August 1995.

77 G.H., Letter to A.H. 7 September 1995.

78 G.H., Letter to A.J., 3 August 1995 (misdated 1985).

79 G.H., Letter to A.H., 16 August 1995.

80 G.H., Letter to A.H., 28 August 1995.

81 G.H., Letter to A.H., 7 September 1995; see also AJ, 15 August 1995.

82 astringent: G.H., Letter to A.F., 21 December 1994; 'gaunt contempt': G.H., Letter to A.H., 24 August 1995.

83 G.H., Letter to A.H., 24 August 1995.

84 G.H., Letter to R.C., 28 August 1995.

85 G.H., Letter to R.C., 14 August 1995.

86 T.R., Letter to G.H., 24 August 1995 (G.K. private collection); G.H., Letter to A.H., 20 September 1995.

87 G.H., Letter to A.J., 5 November 1995.

88 G.H., Letter to A.H., 2 October 1995.

89 G.H., Letter to G.K., 17 July 1995.

90 G.H., Letter to A.H., 6 August 1995.

91 G.H., Letter to A.H., 23 October 1995.

92 G.H., Letter to T.R., 29 November 1995, in *A Steady Storm of Correspondence*, p. 479.

93 G.H., Letter to G.K., 20 September 1995.

94 G.H., Letter to A.H., 3 November 1995.

95 G.H., Letter to R.C., 27 June 1995; Harwood's comment alludes to John Berryman's 'Dream Song 90: Op. Posth. No. 13', one of her favourites of the *Dream Songs*: John Harwood, pers. comm., 19 January 2022.

96 G.H., Letter to A.J., 20 July 1995, and elsewhere.

97 G.H., Letter to A.H., 5 June 1995.

98 Janet Upcher, pers. comm.

99 G.H., Letter to A.J., [20 November 1995?].

100 Alison Hoddinott, Rosemary Cohen, Janet Upcher, pers. comm. See also Craig Powell, 'Gwen Harwood: 1920–1995'.

EPILOGUE

1 Greg Kratzmann, pers. comm., 17 September 2020; John Harwood, pers. comm., 1 January 2022.

2 Joe Foster, Letter to A.H., 16 May 1998 (private collection).

3 Riddell, 'Making Good Books'.

4 Porter, 'Satires in C Major'.

5 Alberto Manguel, 'Books of the Year', *The Spectator*, 22 November 2003.

6 Beston, 'An Interview with Gwen Harwood', pp. 84–88.

7 Harwood, 'The Creative Poet', p. 24; Harwood, Interview with Lear, pp. 1–11.

8 Riddell, 'Making Good Books'.

9 Harwood, 'The Creative Poet', p. 24.

Image Credits

'Gwen Foster with grandmother Maud Jaggard (left) and glamorous "aunts", her namesake Gwendoline Stenlake (right) and Clarice Stenlake, Mitchelton, 1921' (p. 11): Fryer Library, University of Queensland, UQFL45, Box 15.

'Agnes Jaggard and Joseph Foster, Rockhampton, 1918' (p. 14): National Library of Australia, http://nla.gov.au/nla.obj-136766047.

'Mock wedding party, with Gwen and her brother, Joey, in drag, c. 1928' (p. 17): Fryer Library, University of Queensland, UQFL45, Box 21, Folder 3.

'Brisbane *Telegraph*, 27 March 1934' (p. 24): National Library of Australia.

'Brisbane Girls Grammar School prefects, 1937 (Gwen Foster 2nd row, 1st left)' (p. 30): courtesy of Brisbane Girls Grammar School.

'Vera Cottew in 1943' (p. 33): courtesy of Brisbane Girls Grammar School.

'Gwen Foster, 1940' (p. 44): Fryer Library, University of Queensland, UQFL45, Box 15.

'Lieutenant F.W. (Bill) Harwood, c. 1945' (p. 73): Photographer unknown, from *Blessed City: The Letters of Gwen Harwood to Thomas Riddell*, ed. Alison Hoddinott, Angus & Robertson, North Ryde, 1990.

'Gwen and baby John at Fern Tree, c. 1947' (p. 89): Fryer Library, University of Queensland, UQFL45, Box 17, Env. 5.

'Fern Tree friends' (p. 94): courtesy of Karen Darby.

'Lotte Wilmot and Gwen Harwood with their children at Augusta Road, c. 1955' (p. 112): courtesy of Claire Blichfeldt.

'Thomas (Tony) Riddell, Hobart, 1955' (p. 113): Fryer Library, University of Queensland, UQFL477, PIC410a.

'Dr Thomas Pick, 1950' (p. 127): National Archives of Australia, 1643667.

'A Gwen Harwood Sappho card, sent to Vivian Smith, 1 December 1960' (p. 143): National Library of Australia, Vivian Smith collection: MS 4853, Series 2, Folder 41.

'Gwen Harwood, Augusta Road, 1963' (p. 201): Fryer Library, University of Queensland, UQFL45, Box 15.

'Gwen Harwood with daughter Mary, Mt Wellington, March 1967' (p. 219): Fryer Library, University of Queensland, UQFL45, Box 15.

'Gwen Harwood with her poetry notebook, Hobart, 1968' (p. 222): Fryer Library, University of Queensland, UQFL45, Box 15.

'Gwen and Bill Harwood aboard their yacht *Sappho*, 1973' (p. 245): photo by Alison Hoddinott, Fryer Library, University of Queensland, UQFL45, Box 21, Folder 3.

'Gwen Harwood with Rodney Hall, Melbourne, 1972' (p. 251): Fryer Library, University of Queensland, UQFL45, Box 21, Folder 3.

'Norman Talbot, early 1970s' (p. 259): Fryer Library, University of Queensland, UQFL45, Box 15.

'Launching *The Tasmanian Review*, 1979' (p. 314): Stuart Heather, courtesy of *Island* magazine.

'Gwen at her bush camp at Oyster Cove, 1984' (p. 316): Fryer Library, University of Queensland, UQFL45, Box 17, Envelope 5.

'Receiving an Honorary Doctorate of Letters at the University of Queensland, 1993' (p. 337): Fryer Library, The University of Queensland Library, UQFL466, AH/P/74.

'Vikram Seth and Gwen Harwood, Hobart, 1992' (p. 352): photo by Giles Hugo, Fryer Library, University of Queensland, UQFL45, Box 21, Folder 3.

'Rosemary Cohen and Gwen Harwood, Pine Street, 1995' (p. 363): courtesy of Rosemary Cohen, UQFL45, Box 17, envelope 5.

Index

Gwen Harwood and Bill Harwood are referred to as G.H. and B.H respectively.